[redacted]

FROM SABBATH TO LORD'S DAY: A Biblical, Historical, and Theological Investigation

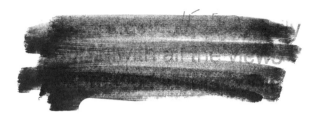

FROM SABBATH TO LORD'S DAY: A Biblical, Historical, and Theological Investigation

edited by

D. A. Carson

Academie Books
Grand Rapids, Michigan
Zondervan Publishing House

FROM SABBATH TO LORD'S DAY: A BIBLICAL, HISTORICAL, AND THEOLOGICAL INVESTIGATION

ACADEMIE BOOKS are published by Zondervan Publishing House,
1415 Lake Drive, S.E., Grand Rapids, Michigan 49506

Library of Congress Cataloging in Publication Data

Main entry under title:
From Sabbath to Lord's Day.

Includes bibliographical references and indexes.
1. Sunday. 2. Sabbath. I. Carson, D. A.

BV111.F76 263 81-16343
ISBN 0-310-44531-0 AACR2

Printed in the United States of America

84 85 86 87 88 — 10 9 8 7 6 5 4 3

CONTENTS

ABBREVIATIONS

Abbreviations for biblical books, intertestamental apocryphal, pseudepigraphic and other literature (including Qumran, Philo, and Josephus) are self-explanatory, as are the abbreviations for the writings of the Fathers. In any case they may be checked against the indexes, where the full name of each work is provided. The abbreviations for the rabbinic literature are largely obvious; but it should be noted that tractates from the Mishnah receive no prefatory designation: e.g., Macc. 1:6, not *M.Macc.* 1:6 or the like. By contrast, tractates from the Babylonian Talmud are prefaced by *B.* (e.g., *B.Bes.* 16*a*), as those from the Jerusalem Talmud are prefaced by *j.* Abbreviations for other things, primarily journals and standard works of reference, are listed below. Wherever possible we have conformed to the system adopted by *The Expositor's Bible Commentary*. The names of journals not listed below have been written out in full in the text and notes.

AJSL	American Journal of Semitic Languages and Literature
ASTI	Annual of the Swedish Theological Institute
AUSS	Andrews University Seminary Studies
BAG	A *Greek-English Lexicon of the New Testament and Early Christian Literature*, W. Bauer, tr. and revised by W. F. Arndt and F. W. Gingrich
BAR	Biblical Archaeology Review
BC	*The Beginnings of Christianity*, ed. F. J. Foakes-Jackson and Kirsopp Lake
BDB	*Hebrew and English Lexicon of the Old Testament*, F. Brown, S. R. Driver, and G. A. Briggs
BFBS	The British and Foreign Bible Society
Bib	Biblica
BiLe	Bibel und Liturgie
BJRL	Bulletin of the John Rylands Library
BR	Biblical Research
BRR	Baptist Reformation Review
BZ	Biblische Zeitschrift
BZAW	Beihefte zum ZAW
BZNW	Beihefte zum ZNW
CCL	*Corpus christianorum. Series latina.*
CBQ	Catholic Biblical Quarterly
C.D.	*Church Dogmatics*, Karl Barth
ELC	Encyclopedia of the Lutheran Church
EphTheolLov	Ephemerides Theologicae Lovaniensis
ET	English translation
ExpT	The Expository Times
FRLANT	Forschungen zum Religion und Literatur des Alten und Neuen Testaments
HAT	Handbuch zum Alten Testament
HE	*Historica Ecclesiastica*, Eusebius

Hennecke-Wilson	New Testament Apocrypha, ed. E. Hennecke and W. Schneemelcher; tr. R. McL. Wilson
HeyJ	Heythorp Journal
HTR	Harvard Theological Review
HUCA	Hebrew Union College Annual
ICC	International Critical Commentaries
IDB	*Interpreter's Dictionary of the Bible*
Inst.	Calvin's *Institutes of the Christian Religion*
Int	Interpretation
JAOS	Journal of the American Oriental Society
JBL	Journal of Biblical Literature
JETS	Journal of the Evangelical Theological Society
JJS	Journal of Jewish Studies
JQR	Jewish Quarterly Review
JSNT	Journal for the Study of the New Testament
JTS	Journal of Theological Studies
KB	*Lexicon in Veteris Testamenti Libros*, ed. L. Koehler and W. Baumgarten
KerDog	Kerygma und Dogma
LDOS	Lord's Day Observance Society
LSJ	A *Greek-English Lexicon*, H. G. Liddell and R. Scott, Jones
LW	Luther's Works
LXX	*Septuagint*
MelSciRel	Mélanges de Sciences Religieuses
M.1 (2, etc.)	J. H. Moulton's *Grammar*, vol. 1 (vol. 2, etc.)
MS(S)	manuscript(s)
MT	Masoretic text
NBD	*New Bible Dictionary*
NEB	New English Bible
NIDNTT	*New International Dictionary of New Testament Theology*
NIV	New International Version
NovTest	Novum Testamentum
NTS	New Testament Studies
PG	*Patrologia Graeca*
PL	*Patrologia Latina*
RB	Revue Biblique
RevTheolLouv	Revue Theologique de Louvain
RHPR	Revue d'Histoire et de Philosophie Religieuses
RQ	Restoration Quarterly
RSV	Revised Standard Version
SBK	*Kommentar zum Neuen Testament aus Talmud und Midrasch*, H. L. Strack and P. Billerbeck
SDATS	Seventh Day Adventist Theological Seminary
SE	Studia Evangelica
SJT	Scottish Journal of Theology
SLA	*Studies in Luke-Acts*, ed. L. E. Keck and J. L. Martyn
ST	Aquinas' *Summa Theologica*
ST	Studia Theologica

SuppNovTest	Supplements to *NovTest*
SwJT	Southwest Journal of Theology
TB	Tyndale Bulletin
TDNT	*Theological Dictionary of the New Testament*
ThR	Theologische Rundschau
TZ	Theologische Zeitschrift
VetTest	Vetus Testamentum
ZAW	Zeitschrift für die alttestamentliche Wissenschaft
ZKG	Zeitschrift für Katholische Theologie
ZNW	Zeitschrift für neutestamentliche Wissenschaft
ZThK	Zeitschrift für Theologie und Kirche
ZWT	Zeitschrift für die wissenschaftliche Theologie

PREFACE

This book began as a research project on "Sunday" sponsored by the Tyndale Fellowship for Biblical Research in Cambridge, England, in 1973. We are indebted to the members of that larger group for stimulating discussion and for mutual critique. The contributors to the present volume were at that time doctoral or post-doctoral research students enjoying the rich facilities and heritage of Cambridge University.

Our successive drafts were originally criticized within the study group, and when we moved apart, the task of coordinating and editing the project fell to me. We have continued our research and circulated our findings among the contributors for the benefit of the work as a whole.

The introductory chapter explains how this book was written and points out that it is not merely a symposium but a unified, cooperative effort. The explanation will be given later, but the subtitle of the work is important: it reads, *A Biblical, Historical, and Theological Investigation*, rather than *Biblical, Historical, and Theological Investigations*. We have moved to various parts of the world since 1975. Richard J. Bauckham now lectures in the Department of Theology at the University of Manchester. Harold H. P. Dressler teaches at Northwest Baptist Theological College in Vancouver. Douglas R. de Lacey teaches at London Bible College, but he has just been appointed to a post at Ridley College, Cambridge. Andrew T. Lincoln taught for five years in the New Testament department at Gordon-Conwell Theological Seminary and is now at St. John's College in Nottingham. M. M. B. Turner is the Librarian at London Bible College, and also lectures in New Testament. Chris Rowland has taught at the University of Newcastle-upon-Tyne and is now Dean of Jesus College, Cambridge University. I am now teaching New Testament at Trinity Evangelical Divinity School in Deerfield, Illinois.

So many people have helped us in this project that I am reluctant to begin a list, lest someone be omitted by mistake. Nevertheless, I must gratefully acknowledge the help of several people without whom this work would have been less comprehensive. John Hughes, though never a member of the study group, spent many hours providing thoughtful, written critiques of some of the early papers. Gerhard F. Hasel and Samuele Bacchiocchi have been most helpful in providing Seventh Day Adventist bibliographies and even in lending books otherwise difficult to procure. Considering the technical complexity of several of the chapters, Patty Light and Karen Sich cheerfully prepared the final typescript with remarkable speed and skill. My graduate assistant Linda Belleville spent scores of hours on technical details and made my task much lighter. To all of them I owe an enormous debt of gratitude. All the contributors worked valiantly to meet deadlines, but I must mention with special gratitude the industry of Richard Bauckham and Andrew Lincoln in particular, not only because the largest assignments fell on their shoulders, but because their written criticisms of the repeatedly circulated papers were the most detailed and painstaking, making my task as editor much easier than it would otherwise have been. Dr. Stan Gundry and his colleagues at Zondervan have handled this long and technical manuscript with extraordinary efficiency. Mr. Tony Plews assisted with the indexes.

Finally, profound thanks go to my wife, Joy, who not only patiently endured but cheerfully supported her husband as he wrestled during long hours with assorted manuscripts.

Soli Deo gloria.

D. A. Carson

1

INTRODUCTION

D.A. CARSON

D. A. Carson is Professor of New Testament at Trinity Evangelical Divinity School in Deerfield, Illinois.

The Need for This Investigation

The number of books on this subject might prompt the casual observer to think that yet another volume would be superfluous. A brief survey will show that there is a place for our work as well.

Perhaps this spate of books was touched off by the work of Willy Rordorf, who argues that Sabbath in the Old Testament began as a day of rest and ended as a day of rest and worship, and that Sunday in the New Testament was a day of worship that has become in the history of the church a day of worship and rest parallel to the Old Testament Sabbath.[1] Apart from hundreds of articles that have been written since the publication of Rordorf's thesis, a substantial number of books, representing most of the major European languages, have appeared. J. Francke defends the view that has dominated Protestant theology in the last three centuries.[2] He is joined by R. T. Beckwith and W. Stott.[3] This interpretation holds that the principle of one day in seven for rest and worship was established at creation, incorporated into the Mosaic code, and formally presented as moral law. This view states that for people of the Old Testament the appropriate day for the Sabbath was the seventh day, and that the Lord's resurrection on the first day of the week effected a legitimate shift to Sunday. Sabbath or Sunday observance is viewed as symbolic of the special "rest" that God's people enjoy now and will enjoy in fullness after the Parousia.

Paul K. Jewett adopts a similar structure.[4] But because he acknowledges that the evidence in the New Testament for a transfer from Saturday to Sunday is meager, he bases Sunday observance partly on his estimate of the *practice* of the early church, and much more on the observation that although the "rest" of God was introduced by Christ, its culmination awaits Christ's return; therefore it is still appropriate to select a day to symbolize the rest yet to come. The first Christians, having been set free from slavish observance of the *seventh* day by Christ's claim to lordship over the Sabbath, found it increasingly difficult to join in worship with Jews on the Sabbath and opted instead for Sunday, the day of their Lord's resurrection. In other words, Jewett ultimately comes very close to the position of Francke, Beckwith and Stott, and others, but he gets there by a more circuitous route.

In the same tradition is the work by F. N. Lee, which is approved by the Lord's Day Observance Society (LDOS).[5] Lee's work, however, besides being quite heated and polemical, is often eccentric. It has some valuable insights, but it is difficult to take seriously a book that bases important conclusions on the identification of the precise hour of the Fall!

We do not lack more specialized volumes. C. S. Mosna traces Sunday observance to the fifth century.[6] Niels-Erik A. Andreasen attempts to uncover the roots of the Sabbath in the Old Testament and earlier, while tracing development through the Old Testament itself.[7] N. Negretti provides a theology of the Sabbath in the Old Testament based on a critical reconstruction of Sabbath traditions.[8]

Without doubt, the work that has stirred up most interest in the subject, at least in the English-speaking world, is that of Samuele Bacchiocchi.[9] Remarkably, Bacchiocchi wrote his book as a doctoral dissertation for the Pontifical Gregorian University even though he himself is a Seventh Day Adventist. He argues that Sunday observance, as opposed to seventh day observance, did not arise in the Jerusalem church, which practiced seventh day Sabbath observance until the second destruction of the city in A.D. 135. Sunday observance, he suggests, arose in Rome during the reign of Hadrian (A.D. 117–135) when Roman repression of the Jews prompted the church to adopt policies of deliberate differentiation. Sunday was chosen, as opposed to some other day, because Christians could easily adopt the symbolism of the powerful pagan Sun cults and Christianize them.

Bacchiocchi's book has exerted vast influence due to several factors. In the first place, it is well written and easy to follow, even though it is extensively documented. On the whole it has received very positive reviews. Moreover, because the work has been marketed well (inexpensive price and extensive advertising among clergy), it had sold, by June 1979, in the vicinity of 42,000 copies.[10] Bacchiocchi has also popularized his findings in several places, most recently in *Biblical Archaeology Review*, where his article sparked voluminous correspondence.[11] Most important of all, he has established links with the LDOS. As a Seventh Day Adventist, Bacchiocchi obviously cannot agree with the LDOS people on every point, but he did give the ninetieth-anniversary address to the LDOS (14 February 1979), outlining possible areas of cooperation. He insisted, among other things, that "a proper observance of God's holy day reflects a healthy relationship with God, while disregard for it bespeaks of spiritual decline or even death."[12]

Interest in these matters, then, is not restricted to academic circles. Two of the contributors to this book have been involved with dialogues between Christians and Jews, and in each instance the Sabbath/Sunday question quickly arose. Moreover, even within Christendom, the diversity of perspectives is a deeply divisive thing. We shall do well to continue probing as honestly and industriously as possible all areas of dispute, in the hope of narrowing some differences of opinion or at least of establishing the reasons for those differences.

Fairly early in our study we came to several conclusions that were reinforced as time went by, and that set our direction apart from much recent investigation. This confirmed that another book was needed. This introduction is not the place to set out our conclusions, nor to detail the contributions that we hope this volume will make; but it may be worth listing some of the arguments and conclusions of previous study with which we have come to disagree.

First, we are not persuaded that the New Testament unambiguously develops a "transfer theology," according to which the Sabbath moves from the seventh day to the first day of the week. We are not persuaded that Sabbath keeping is presented in the Old Testament as the norm from the time of creation onward. Nor are we persuaded that the New Testament develops patterns of continuity and discontinuity on the basis of moral/civil/ceremonial distinctions. However useful and accurate such categories may be, it is anachronistic to think that any New Testament writer adopted them as the basis for his distinctions between the Old Testament and the gospel of Christ. We are also not persuaded that Sunday observance arose only in the second century A.D. We think, however, that although Sunday worship arose in New Testament times, it was not perceived as a Christian *Sabbath*. We disagree profoundly with historical reconstructions of the patristic period that read out from isolated and ambiguous expressions massive theological schemes that in reality developed only much later.

Yet to say so many negative things is to run the risk of giving a false impression. We have not written in order to demolish the theories of others. Indeed, as a matter of policy we have focused attention on primary sources; we refute opposing positions only when it is necessary to do so in order to establish our own position. Our final chapter takes considerable pains to be as positive and synthetic as possible. We want to provide a comprehensive guide to the interpretation of the sources for Christian readers.

The Scope of This Investigation

One of the reasons why the Sabbath/Sunday question continues to arouse such interest is that it impinges on so many areas of study. The same fact means that any competent discussion must be painfully broad if it is to prove satisfying.

In the first place, the Sabbath/Sunday question demands close study of numerous passages in both Testaments of the canon—so numerous, in fact, that broad knowledge of biblical theology is indispensable. Inevitably, exegetical discussion of these passages brings up questions of authenticity, dependence, text, and the like. Moreover, broad areas of history outside the canon must also be explored, including both the intertestamental period and the history of the church. The study of church history dissipates false notions, exposes anachronisms, and adds depth by revealing that the church has always wrestled with these questions. Our modern options are so often the same as those of earlier but forgotten periods. Although it is not on the same level as Scripture, church history has the salutary effect of promoting humility.

The Sabbath/Sunday question also touches many areas of theological study. I have already mentioned creation ordinance and moral law. Other areas include the relationship between the Old Testament and the New, the relationship among the covenants, the proper understanding of salvation history, the nature of prophecy and fulfillment, biblical patterns of eschatology, and the normativeness of any particular biblical law.

Implicitly, of course, because the Sabbath/Sunday question touches the relationship between the Testaments, it also involves ethics. In that sense, the Sabbath/Sunday question is a test case, an important paradigm for broader theological and ethical reflection. One cannot consider these things in depth without asking such questions as these: On what basis should Christians adopt or reject Old Testament laws concerning slavery? On what basis should one applaud the insistence on justice in Deuteronomy and Amos, but declare invalid the racial segregation of Nehemiah and Malachi?

Small wonder, then, that the Sabbath/Sunday question continues to attract attention. It is one of the most difficult areas in the study of the relationship between the Testaments, and in the history of the development of doctrine. If it is handled rightly, however, our further study of this question ought to provide a synthesis that will at least offer a basic model for theological and ethical reflections.

We are under no illusions that our study will convince everyone, but in addition to the specific reconstruction we propose in these pages, we would like to convince as many as possible that the view of Joseph Hart (1712–1768), expressed in quaint poetry, is to be applauded for its forbearance and catholicity:

> Some Christians to the Lord regard a day,
> And others to the Lord regard it not;
> Now, though these seem to choose a diff'rent way,
> Yet both, at last, to one same point are brought.
>
> He that regards the day will reason thus—
> "This glorious day our Saviour and our King
> Perform'd some mighty act of love for us;
> Observe the time in mem'ry of the thing."
>
> Thus he to Jesus points his kind intent,
> And offers prayers and praises in his name;
> As to the Lord above his love is meant,
> The Lord accepts it; and who dare to blame?

For, though the shell indeed is not the meat,
'Tis not rejected when the meat's within;
Though superstition is a vain conceit,
Commemoration surely is no sin.

He also, that to days has no regard,
The shadows only for the substance quits;
Towards the Saviour's presence presses hard,
And outward things through eagerness omits.

For warmly to himself he thus reflects—
"My Lord alone I count my chiefest good;
All empty forms my craving soul rejects,
And seeks the solid riches of his blood.

"All days and times I place my sole delight
In him, the only object of my care;
External shows for his dear sake I slight,
Lest ought but Jesus my respect should share."

Let not th' observer, therefore, entertain
Against his brother any secret grudge;
Nor let the non-observer call him vain;
But use his freedom, and forbear to judge.

Thus both may bring their motives to the test;
Our condescending Lord will both approve.
Let each pursue the way that likes him best;
He cannot walk amiss, that walks in love.

The Method of This Investigation

It is important at the outset to insist that this work is not a symposium in the ordinary sense of that word; it is a unified, cooperative investigation. The contributing scholars have written in areas of their special competence and submitted their work to the scrutiny of their colleagues. Most of the essays have been rewritten three times; all have been edited to ensure proper integration. Chapters 4 and 5 necessarily overlap a little, and the final chapter, a synthesis, necessarily reviews earlier findings. The argument is progressive and sustained despite the plurality of authors. In the earliest stages, the papers were circulated and there were sessions in which the contributors discussed and criticized each other's work by the hour. The synthesis forged on the anvil of those discussions is well tempered.

This is not to say that each contributor agrees with every other contributor in all details; close reading will reveal minor differences of opinion. Each writer is responsible only for his own work. Nevertheless, the argument is based on close study of the manuscripts, topics, and periods indicated by the chapter headings, and the results of this study converge in a single reconstruction.

Some may wish we had focused more attention on a particular subject; for example, the intertestamental period or the rise of seventh-day groups in the Christian era. We have had to make decisions about what to include and what to exclude; these decisions reflect partly our own interests, but also our judgment concerning where proper emphasis should be laid. Similarly, regarding bibliography and interaction with secondary literature, we have tried to be broadly (but not exhaustively) comprehensive; we have then chosen to interact in detail with representative works and positions. Any other approach would have unnecessarily lengthened the book.

The result of these methodological priorities and strictures lies in the next eleven chapters.

Notes

[1]W. Rordorf, *Sunday: The History of the Day of Rest and Worship in the Earliest Centuries of the Christian Church* (London: SCM, 1968), first published in German in 1962.

[2]J. Francke, *Van Sabbat naar Zondag* (Amsterdam: Uitgeverij Ton Bolland, 1973).

[3]R. T. Beckwith and W. Stott, *This Is the Day: The Biblical Doctrine of the Christian Sunday in Its Jewish and Early Christian Setting* (London: Marshall, Morgan and Scott, 1978).

[4]Paul K. Jewett, *The Lord's Day: A Theological Guide to the Christian Day of Worship* (Grand Rapids: Eerdmans, 1971).

[5]F. N. Lee, *The Convenantal Sabbath* (London: LDOS, 1969).

[6]C. S. Mosna, *Storia della domenica dalle origini fino agli inizi del V Secolo* (Rome: Libreria editrice dell' Università gregoriana, 1969).

[7]N.-E. A. Andreasen, *The Old Testament Sabbath* (Missoula: Scholars Press, 1972).

[8]N. Negretti, *Il Settimo Giorno: Indagina critico-teologica delle tradizioni presacertodali e sacerdotali circa il sabato biblico* (Rome: Biblical Institute Press, 1972).

[9]S. Bacchiocchi, *From Sabbath to Sunday: A Historical Investigation of the Rise of Sunday Observance in Early Christianity* (Rome: Pontifical Gregorian University, 1977). Dr. Bacchiocchi is about to publish a companion volume on the theology of the Sabbath.

[10]Dr. Bacchiocchi told me this in a private telephone conversation.

[11]S. Bacchiocchi, "How It Came About: From Saturday to Sunday," *BAR* 4/3 (1978): 32–40.

[12]Dr. Bacchiocchi graciously provided me with a copy of his paper, which was subsequently published in "The Sabbath Sentinel," April, 1979.

2

THE SABBATH IN THE OLD TESTAMENT

Harold H. P. Dressler

Harold H. P. Dressler teaches Old Testament as Associate Professor of Biblical Studies at Northwest Baptist Theological College in Vancouver, B.C.

Introduction

By decree, precept, and exhortation the Sabbath was set before the people of Israel as one of the most important parts of the law. The violation of this law carried the death penalty, and its neglect was one of the reasons for Israel's national catastrophe. Although initially the commandment to keep the Sabbath had no promise attached to it, eventually promises were given to those who observed it. It hardly needs to be mentioned that for the Christian formulation of a Sunday theology the Old Testament material regarding the Sabbath is of great importance, especially when it comes to the questions of transference and "creation ordinance."

This chapter will be limited to the material found in the Old Testament, with special emphasis on the Pentateuch. Detailed exegeses cannot be offered in view of the scope of this chapter.

The Origin of the Sabbath

One of the more recent investigations of the Sabbath comes to the conclusion that "the origin and early history of the Sabbath . . . continue to lie in the dark."[1] With this warning in mind we may briefly summarize five common theories before turning to the biblical view:

Babylonian Origin

According to this theory, the Hebrews found the seven-day week in Canaan, and subsequently transformed the Sabbath into an institution.[2] The Canaanites in turn, had received the seven-day week and the Sabbath (as a taboo day) from the Babylonians.[3] "The *ūmu šabattu* was *um nuḫ libbi (a day of rest for the heart)*."[4]

Lunar Origin

Another theory is that the Babylonian *ūmu šabattu (Sabbath day)* is the day of the full moon.[5] The planetary movements have been decisive for the Sabbath as well as for the other festivals.[6] The word *šabbat* may mean "completed moon"; that is, full moon.[7] The last stage in the development of moon celebrations was the celebration of the seventh day, receiving the name "Sabbath."[8]

Kenite Origin

Starting with Exodus 35:3 (the prohibition against lighting a fire), this theory assumes that the law had at its core a fire taboo.[9] The Sabbath, then, was an ancient taboo day for the Kenites, the forgers (smiths) of the desert, with whom Moses came into contact by marriage.[10]

Socioeconomic Origin

In this view, the Sabbath is a "social institution equalizing all creatures"[11] or a "period of taboo."[12] It was an economic and social institution similar to the Roman market-day *(nundinae)*.[13] The Sabbath, then, would have derived from an "almost universal custom of keeping days of rest, or feast days, or market days, at regular intervals."[14]

Calendar Origin

Two conflicting theories are proposed with great erudition: There is the fifty-day scheme that is based on the seven winds of the world and develops into the seven day week,[15] and there is also the fifth-month scheme, i. e., the Akkadian *hamuštu*, which was the six-day week of ancient West Asia, to which an additional day as a day of rest was appended in view of God's cessation of work after his six days of creation.[16]

To refute each one of these five theories is beyond the scope of this chapter; besides, it would do an injustice to their proponents to treat them too briefly. It must be left to the reader to do further research in accordance with personal interests. The author, however, is convinced that the origin of the Sabbath has not been discovered in extrabiblical sources.

The Biblical View

The biblical view is unequivocal: the Sabbath originated in Israel as God's special institution for His people.[17] That such a momentous creative achievement should have been the product of the people of Israel[18] is usually regarded with extreme scepticism if not complete rejection.[19] Even Martin Buber maintains that the Sabbath was "not created *ex nihilo*" but "the material used . . . was adopted by a mighty force of faith."[20] Thus, it is assumed that the Sabbath was already an institution with Israel's nomadic ancestors[21] or simply an ancient institution of probable Babylonian origin.[22] But to refuse to credit Israel with any cultural achievements of consequence, which some time ago was very fashionable, is certainly unreasonable. Even if no theological reasons that necessitate an Israelite origin could be advanced, is it too daring and provocative to suggest that Israel herself might have been responsible for the creation of the seven-day week and a Sabbath?[23] Or, must we exclude Israel a priori, and state that she "certainly could not have invented it"?[24] On this question, the evidence is unequivocal; only the ancient Hebrew literature speaks definitely about a seven-day week and a Sabbath.

A question that must be discussed in connection with the origin of the Sabbath is the etymology and meaning of the word שַׁבָּת. Lexicographers group it with the verb שָׁבַת *(to cease, stop; to stop working, celebrate; to rest)*.[25]

Hehn emphasizes that the meaning "to rest" is foreign to this verb; the nature of *šbṯ* is "to cease, to be finished."[26] Schmidt sees no original interdependence between the verb שָׁבַת and the noun "Sabbath"; there is only a very early connection.[27] From the etymology, Beer and Mahler understand the action of "being complete."[28] De Vaux points out that the noun formation from the verb שָׁבַת is irregular; "the regular form would be *shebeth.*" In its grammatical form it "ought to have an active meaning, signifying 'the day which stops something, which marks a limit or division. . . .' "[29] The Sabbath would thus be a day that marks the end of the week or the ceasing of the week's work.[30]

Summary

Since all available sources have failed to produce conclusive evidence for an alternative origin of the Sabbath, we suggest that the Sabbath originated with Israel and that with the Sabbath came the seven-day week.[31]

The Sabbath Commandments

This section deals with the commandments concerning the observance of the Sabbath found in the Pentateuch.[32] These commandments will be treated in the order of the biblical text without considering the reconstructions of Source Criticism, since the result is nearly the same.[33]

The Texts

Exodus 16:22–30. The first occurrence of the word and concept of Sabbath is found here; the passage allows the view that the institution of the Sabbath was unknown to the people of Israel at this time.[34] Their sojourn in Egypt had taught them the ten-day "week."[35] Hence, this first Sabbath is explained in its full form, שַׁבָּתוֹן שַׁבַּת־קֹדֶשׁ, "a sabbatical celebration, a holy sabbath."[36] Moreover, even as the daily gathering of manna, so the gathering on the sixth day in preparation for the Sabbath became a touchstone of obedience (vv. 27–29).[37] Thus, viewed within the chronological scheme of the narrative, a few months before the actual commandment of the Sabbath (i.e., in the Decalogue), the people of Israel were trained in the keeping of the Sabbath as a day in which there was no need to do the daily chore since the Lord had provided for them a rest.[38] Verse 30 ("so the people ceased [to gather] on the seventh day") does not give the impression of a Sabbath celebration indicated in verse 23 by the phrase "to Yahweh," so that one is led to the conclusion that at this stage the emphasis is not on the cultic aspect but on the humanitarian side by way of preparation.[39]

Exodus 20:8–11. The Decalogue[40] contains the next reference in the form of an explicit command: "Remember the sabbath day, to keep it holy."[41] Consistent with the previous introduction of the Sabbath, Israel is now commanded "to *remember* the sabbath," to keep it as a very special day separate from every other day and dedicated "to God" (thus "holy"). In its specifications the commandment is proleptic as it reflects work conditions of the settlement: Israel is told to refrain from all work, and an enumeration of possible workers is given.[42] As in the commandment against idolatry, the Sabbath injunction contains a reason for the giving of this law, an analogy to God's work at creation and His rest on the seventh day.[43]

Exodus 23:12. Within the first session of the giving of the law, a short reminder of the Sabbath commandment is given that includes a social concern as reason. Thus it fits into the context of regulations governing Israel's social behavior (v. 9: sympathy for strangers; v. 10: support of the poor). It also supplies a logical transition to the celebration of feasts and the offering of sacrifices (vv. 14–19) since the Sabbath incorporated celebration as well as offering.

Exodus 31:12–17. God concludes His instructions to Moses about the building of the tabernacle, its furniture, etc., by appointing the artisans and by reiterating the Sabbath law. Now the Sabbath is called a sign (אוֹת) of God's sanctifying Israel.[44] It must be kept on threat of death, it is called a perpetual covenant, and finally, it is a sign that God ceased to work after six days of creation work. This, then, is the most forceful and explicit statement of the Sabbath law. It explains the Sabbath in terms of a sign, a covenant between God and His people, and commands the cessation of work by everyone on threat of the death penalty.

Exodus 34:21. Another short reminder is issued in connection with God's giving of the second set of tablets, with the added explanation: "in plowing time and in harvest you shall cease to work." For a people who were about to possess a land and cultivate it as farmers such an addition is not only relevant, but it is also an affirmation of God's promise that they would indeed possess the land given to them.

Exodus 35:2–3. Before Moses asks the people for a contribution to the building of the tabernacle, the Sabbath commandment is repeated in its most solemn form, "You shall have a holy sabbath, a sabbatical celebration unto Yahweh." The people are reminded that a death penalty has been imposed on all transgressors, and that no fire should be kindled in the homes. Thus, housework on the part of the wife (with cooking and baking) would be prohibited, although this could have been understood from Exodus 16:23.

Leviticus 19:3, 30. The commandment occurs here in its shortest form: "you shall keep my sabbaths." In verse 3 it is in juxtaposition with the commandment to honor one's parents and in verse 30 with the precept to reverence the sanctuary. For the first time God now claims this day as His own, "*my* sabbaths." By implication and appointment this day did not belong to mankind but to God and the ensuing consequences of this fact would have to be worked out by man.

Leviticus 23:3. A list of appointed feasts begins with the Sabbath. The commandment is expressed by the now familiar solemn formula שַׁבָּתוֹן שַׁבַּת (a sabbath of sabbatical celebration) to which מִקְרָא־קֹדֶשׁ (a holy convocation) is added. No work must be done since this day is "a sabbath to the LORD in all your dwellings." It is noteworthy that the expression "in all your dwellings" occurs here exactly as it does in Exodus 35:3 in the prohibition against building a fire on the Sabbath.

Leviticus 26:2. This is an exact repetition of Leviticus 19:30.

Deuteronomy 5:12–15. In Moses' repetition of the Decalogue, the Sabbath commandment opens with "observe" rather than "remember."[45] It adds "ox and ass" to the list of workers and the clause "that your manservant and your maidservant may rest as well as you." Another reason is given for the commandment; it is a reminder of Israel's redemption from slavery in Egypt.

Conclusion. The Sabbath concept was introduced some time before the Sinai event. The first formulation of the commandment is found in Exodus 20 within the Decalogue.[46] There were various elaborations and emphases. We note the following particulars with regard to the Sabbath law within the Pentateuch:[47] (1) All daily work must cease by everyone (Exod. 20:10); (2) those who profane the Sabbath must die (Exod. 31:14); (3) plowing and harvesting must cease (Exod. 34:21); (4) no fire may be kindled in the homes (Exod. 35:3).

REASONS FOR THE COMMANDMENT

The Sabbath law is clearly motivated by religious and social concerns. First of all, the Sabbath was introduced to remind the people of Israel of a divine timetable.[48] This timetable, the seven-day week, is to be followed on earth. This is followed by a social concern, workers need a period of regular rest, which is provided for everybody—animals, servants, and aliens. But the Sabbath is more than an imitation of a divine pattern or an expression of social concern; it is a *sign*, a "perpetual covenant" between God and His people.[49] This sign tells of God's grace (sanctifying His people), God's holiness (for the people and Yahweh), and God's authority (a covenant that must be obeyed). Within the context of this theological significance one is not surprised to find the death penalty attached to this commandment.[50]

Moses' final address (and recapitulation of the Ten Words) picks up the theological reasons[51] and, within the context of his emphasis that God's covenant was perpetual (not just "made with our fathers . . . but with us"), ties the Sabbath law as a covenant together with the supreme covenant of God manifested by the Exodus and sealed by the giving of the law at Sinai.

In short, the reasons for the Sabbath law are twofold: vertical and horizontal, theological and social.[52]

Prohibitions

From the first giving of the Sabbath law within the context of the wilderness journey to the last recapitulation of it before the possession of Canaan, only *one* prohibition is mentioned: "you shall not do any work." This prohibition is expressed at first in the form of "staying at home" in opposition to going out of the camp as on any other day to gather manna. And as God prepared sufficient manna for His people on the day before the Sabbath, so the people should continue to prepare enough for the Sabbath day.

That regular, occupational activity is meant by the word for "work" is made clear by the command "not to profane" (חָלַל) the Sabbath. A holy day is profaned when it is considered like any other day, lacking any special significance. Such profaning can be done if one continues to work on the Sabbath as one does on any other day. If we ascribe the term "nomad" to the people of Israel during their sojourn in the wilderness, then "staying at home" in their tents is a sufficient prohibition. In terms of a sedentary people the command not to plow or to harvest again clearly encompasses all typical routine farm work. It remains for the housewife to receive directions with regard to her daily chores of preparing food for the family, since these also would be interrupted for the sake of celebrating a day unto Yahweh. The instruction is not to kindle a fire on the Sabbath. As Israel developed into a commercial nation, an additional prohibition would forbid carrying wares and goods into the community to sell (Jer. 17:21–22; cf. Neh. 13:15–22).

Briefly, then, more specific prohibitions beyond the general one of not doing any work point to the intention of this law, namely to relieve the people of Israel of their daily occupational work[53] for one day in seven in which they could worship God and refresh their bodies.[54]

The Inauguration of the Sabbath

Does the Sabbath belong to those universal institutions referred to as "creation ordinances" so that it implies a one-in-seven scheme decreed by the Creator for the well-being of mankind, or is it rather an Israelite institution based on the heavenly pattern and eschatological in its ultimate purpose and goal? This question is extremely problematic and interpreters have taken opposite sides. We shall attempt to make clear our own position.

It needs to be stated from the onset that the term "creation ordinance" is not a particularly helpful term. Lutheran theologians of the nineteenth century, for example, argued that such social institutions as family, state, economy, civilization (and later, political order and race) were included by the Creator and hence were "bound to make [their] appearance, because from his very beginning man was endowed with the disposition and the organs for a rational order of life."[55]

The criterion for the identification of a creation ordinance, in this view, was that the "function, basic value and goal of a specific institution remain in principle the same throughout human history."[56] These "creation ordinances" are said to "originate with an inescapable necessity and thus must be considered as implied in the divine plan of creation."[57] Against this view, Helmut Thielicke takes sharp issue. He distinguishes precisely between the state of creation before the Fall and after the Fall, concluding:

> This world (including man who inhabits it) has not thus, namely as it is, come forth from the hand of God, but it is alienated from these hands. Hence, it is not, in the strict sense, "creation." Consequently, it does not possess the character of finality but it will pass away. (The term "creation ordinance," with the exception of marriage, is therefore for the same reasons inadequate, indeed erroneous.)[58]

Perhaps it is with this kind of caveat in mind that von Rad reminds us with regard to Genesis 2 that "the divine rest is not . . . made normative for the rhythm of human life . . . nothing is said here of the Sabbath law, and Israel learns of it only at Mt. Sinai."[59] But other scholars detect in Genesis 2 a creation ordinance with universal implications.[60] What about the text itself? Does Genesis 2 indicate such an ordinance?

Genesis 2 does not mention the word "Sabbath." It speaks about the "seventh day." Unless the reader equates "seventh day" and "Sabbath," there is no reference to the Sabbath here. Genesis 2 does not speak about a religious, cultic feast day or any institution at all. There is no direct command that the seventh day should be kept in any way. What we are told is that God finished His creation activities on the sixth day and that He ceased from such activities on the seventh day.[61] In retrospect we are told that God "rested" (וַיָּנַח, Exod. 20:11) and was "refreshed" (וַיִּנָּפַשׁ, Exod. 31:17). Both anthropomorphic terms are employed not to tell us about God's activities but to inform us what man is to do.[62]

However, Genesis 2 does inform us that God "blessed the seventh day and hallowed it." Can we recognize here the inauguration of the Sabbath, perhaps in the sense that God blessed and sanctified the observance of the one-in-seven cycle, so that the keeping of the seventh day as a day of rest would come under the special blessing of God?

Again, interpreters are divided on this point. Some authors have attempted to separate both concepts, i.e., blessing and sanctifying, so that בָּרַךְ (bless) means that "God takes this day and impresses upon it some special importance. He puts into this day the powers of life . . ."[63] and קָדַשׁ (sanctify) signifies the process of separation.[64] But it has been argued convincingly that the terms are synonymous in this passage so that the blessing of the seventh day is to be understood "in the sense of 'sanctification,' i.e., separation and election."[65] According to this interpretation, the blessing of the seventh day is explained in terms of "sanctifying," i.e., separation and election. God separated the seventh day; we interpret this in terms of an eschatological, proleptic sign indicating some future rest.[66] Thus, the statement in Genesis 2:3 is to be understood not in terms of blessing the Sabbath (according to our understanding of Exod. 20:11 such a blessing accompanied the inauguration of the Sabbath at Sinai) but in terms of the ultimate rest for the people of God.[67]

If the blessing and sanctifying of the seventh day of creation is understood in an eschatological sense, this does not imply that Genesis 2:2–3 has no reference to the order of creation. In fact, an essential statement is made by these verses, namely, that Genesis 1:1–2:4 does *not* speak primarily about man or recognize the climax of creation in the creation of man.[68] Genesis 2:2–3 is a fitting capstone in the magnificent structure of Genesis 1–2:3. The awe-inspiring grandeur of God's creation impressing the reader with its ordered structure is concluded by these two verses that internally and externally express the significance of the seventh day. Internally, we discover a dwelling on the number seven (each sentence in vv. 2 and 3*a* consists of seven words) and externally, the term "the seventh day" is repeated three times, indicating the poetic break within each line (pattern 4+3 — 3+4 — 5+2).[69] The concluding words are literally translated, "which God created to make," and remind us of the beginning words, ". . . God created. . . ."[70] The immediate impact, then, is one of ultimate importance; all of creation was finished in six days and had earned God's predicate "very good." On the seventh day God declared his work officially completed[71] and demonstrated that His work is followed by a period of contemplation and rest. As we are told that God ceased from working on the seventh day to "rest" and be "refreshed" (although He needed neither rest nor refreshing), this can only indicate that the goal of creation is not mankind, that the crown of creation is not man, but that all creative activities of God flow into a universal rest period.[72] The mystery of this seventh day cannot be explained away in human terms but finds its goal and solution in the revelation related in the New Testament.

Thus, the creation account of Genesis 1:1–2:3 proclaims *God's* activity, *His* majesty, and *His* power. Man takes his place within creation at his allotted position. God's last[73] creative act is not the making of man but the creation of a period of rest for mankind.[74] This creative act of God does not take the usual form of decree or fashioning but is simply an act of ceasing, resting, and being refreshed.[75]

Genesis 2 does not teach a "creation ordinance" in our opinion; the institution of the Sabbath for the people of Israel, however, was based on the creation account and became a sign of God's redemptive goal for mankind.

The Sabbath as a Sign of the Covenant

The question has been asked about the relationship between the cult and the covenant or the "covenant feast," i.e., "there was surely a ceremony which instituted covenant and repaired or renewed it when it was broken. . . ."[76] Connected with this question is the idea "of a regularly recurring covenant feast."[77] McCarthy states emphatically: "The cult was . . . a medium which handed on knowledge of the covenant as a relationship and a doctrine."[78] It appears that the answer lies in an understanding of the Sabbath as a *sign* of the Mosaic covenant.[79]

Exodus 31:13–17 designates the Sabbath as "a sign between Me and you throughout your generations, that you may know that I, the Lord, sanctify you." This reiteration of the Sabbath commandment concludes the lawgiving event on Sinai. Consequently, this commandment fits not only into the immediate context ("although I have commanded you to make me a sanctuary, *nevertheless . . . my sabbaths*—all the sabbaths that will occur in the period of the Tabernacle's construction—*you shall keep. . . .*"[80]) but also into the wider context of the Mosaic covenant,[81] which God made with the people of Israel, and which was recorded on the two tablets.[82]

As a sign[83] of the covenant the Sabbath can only be meant for Israel, with whom the covenant was made. It has a "perpetual" function, i.e., for the duration of the covenant,[84] and derives its importance and significance from the covenant itself. Every celebration of the Sabbath reminded the believer that God had made a covenant with Him and that the fulfillment of the obligations of this covenant was His responsibility. To break the Sabbath, the sign of the covenant, meant to violate the covenantal relationship, to reject the spiritual renewal of the covenant; and hence the penalty was death.[85]

Since the Abrahamic covenant included the promise of the land of Canaan,[86] it comes as no surprise that the Sinaitic covenant[87] is made with references to the land (Exod. 20:2 "out of the *land* of Egypt," Exod. 20:12 "in the *land* which Yahweh your God gives you") and that the land is included in the legislation for the Sabbath (Lev. 25:2). It is stressed that God has made a covenant with the sons of Israel as a master with his slaves (Lev. 25:55), which the master released from previous bondage (Exod. 20:2; Lev. 25:38, 42, 55) and which have obtained the special status of being God's possession (Exod. 19:5). Since the land is also God's possession (Lev. 25:23), it must be treated with proper respect and care; every seventh year the land must be given a *rest* from its seasonal cultivation, and there must be no sowing of field, pruning of vineyard, harvesting of aftergrowth, nor gathering of grapes.[88]

Clearly, the land is involved in the covenant that God made with Israel. If Israel keeps the covenant, the land with its inhabitants will be blessed (Lev. 26:4); there will be abundant produce (v. 5), peace (v. 6), the elimination of dangerous beasts from the land (v. 6), and God's dwelling place will be among them (vv. 11–12). If, however, the covenant is broken, the land will suffer the consequences with its inhabitants. Enemies will eat the crops (v. 16), no rain will fall in the land (vv. 19–20), destructive wild beasts will return (v. 22), and the land will be devastated (v. 32).[89] As Israel is God's servant, so the land is Israel's servant. As Israel must cease from her daily work and be restored, so the land must cease from its annual work and be restored. Thus there is a horizontal implementation of the vertical covenant relationship; the redemption of Israelites who lost their freedom and property comes in the year of jubilee (Lev. 25:8–12, 28), the fiftieth year.[90]

The Sabbath as a sign of the covenant between God and the people of Israel was not only a weekly cultic celebration, a "covenant feast" that reinforced the knowledge about the covenant God (Exod. 31:13), but was also celebrated as a sabbatical year or year of rest for the land every seventh year (Lev. 25:1–7). The year of jubilee (שְׁנַת הַיּוֹבֵל) was a special sabbatical year. In this year the sign of the covenant emphasized the covenant God as Redeemer, Liberator, and Savior; He restores His people and the land on which they live. The land takes an additional rest in this year, and the people who had become servants were liberated. Land that had been sold in payment of debts reverted to its original owner. Thus every jubilee year was highlighting the Sabbath as a sign of the covenant leading the people to special worship[91] of the God of the covenant as Redeemer and Savior.

In summary, the designation of the Sabbath as a sign of the covenant takes the weekly celebrations of the Sabbath as "covenant feasts," which are then highlighted every seventh year by the sabbatical year and every fiftieth year by the year of jubilee. In the words of McCarthy, this cult of the regularly recurring Sabbath, "was a medium which handed on knowledge of the covenant as a relationship and a doctrine."[92]

The Promise of the Sabbath

The Sabbath commandments in the Pentateuch contain no promises; however, at a later stage there are promises for those who keep the Sabbath. These promises are given in general to every person who keeps the Sabbath, and then specifically to some who keep the Sabbath although they are on the fringe of society, namely, the eunuch and the alien:

> Blessed is the man . . . who keeps the sabbath, from profaning it . . . (Isa. 56:2).
>
> To the eunuchs who keep my sabbaths . . . I will give my house and within my walls a monument and a name better than sons and daughters; I will give them an everlasting name which shall not be cut off (Isa. 56:4–5).
>
> And the foreigners . . . who keep(s) the sabbath, and do not profane it, and hold(s) fast my covenant . . . I will bring to my holy mountain, and make them joyful in my house of prayer; their burnt offerings and their sacrifices will be accepted . . . (Isa. 56:6–7).
>
> If because of the sabbath, you turn your foot from doing your pleasure on my holy day, and call the sabbath a delight . . . and shall honour it . . . then you will take delight in the LORD, and I will make you ride upon the heights of the earth; I will feed you the heritage of Jacob your father . . . (Isa. 58:13–14).

From these passages it is clear that Yahweh promises to reward specifically those who keep this commandment. The eunuch, who longs to be remembered after death, will receive a memorial and an eternal name. The alien, who longs to be accepted into the fellowship of the society, will be received into the inner fellowship of the sanctuary. The Israelite will receive a threefold reward: joy, peace, and prosperity.

The Observance of the Sabbath

It is one thing to receive a command and quite another to obey it. In light of the prophets' predictions of judgment for failing to keep the Sabbath, the question arises whether preexilic Israel kept the Sabbath at all.[93] The Sabbath was, without doubt, kept at least as a *religious institution* until the Babylonian Exile, but the *spirit of the law* was probably soon forgotten. The observance of the Sabbath as an external religious exercise can be traced from the wilderness days to the reign of Hezekiah,[94] and there is no reason to believe that Josiah did not keep the Sabbath, also, but there is no specific reference.[95]

The prophets' complaints that Israel had not kept the Sabbath must be taken seriously. Keeping the Sabbath was not simply an external affair; it was a spiritual attitude as well, since every Sabbath celebration was, in a sense, a renewal of the covenant relationship. Though Israel kept the seventh day as an official day of rest with the prescribed sacrificial offerings, she also profaned the Sabbath by inward iniquity, greed, idolatry, and rebellion. God was not interested in the Sabbath as a national religious holiday but as a sign of His covenant. Only those who celebrated the Sabbath "with all their heart" truly *kept* the Sabbath.[96] God has no interest in empty sacrifices, prayers, liturgies, and assemblies. Observing the Sabbath *unto Yahweh* to keep it holy meant to enter into this day with a thankful spirit, praising God's loving loyalty (חֶסֶד) and faithfulness, proclaiming the omnipotence and righteousness of Yahweh,[97] at the same time keeping justice and doing righteousness as his covenant people.[98] The Sabbath had been inaugurated to be a *spiritual* holy day, a day that would refresh both body *and soul*.

The question of the length of the Sabbath must be mentioned briefly in this context. The length of a day was reckoned from morning until morning in Egypt; from evening until evening in Mesopotamia.[99] The Egyptian system seems to be reflected in such passages as Genesis 1:3–5, Deuteronomy 28:66–67, Judges 19:4–9. On the other hand, the Mesopotamian system apparently is in evidence in Exodus 12:18, 1 Kings 8:29, Nehemiah 13:19, Psalm 55:17, Isaiah 27:3, Jeremiah 14:17. De Vaux proposes a change of reckoning "between the end of the monarchy and the age of Nehemiah."[100] However, this change is not clearly attested, and it is possible that both systems were used simultaneously.

The actual celebration of the Sabbath is not described in detail.[101] As far as sacrifices were concerned, a special burnt offering was prescribed for the Sabbath day, which was to be offered over and above the continual offerings. This special burnt offering consisted of "two male lambs a year old without blemish, and two tenths of an ephah of fine flour for a cereal offering, mixed with oil, and its drink offering" (Num. 28:9–10).

In Psalm 92 we are given a list of activities in which the Israelite could engage on the Sabbath, giving thanks, singing praises, declaring God's loving loyalty and faithfulness, rejoicing with instruments and singing, admiring His works and wisdom, trusting in God's justice, and praising His care, concern and power. Murray rightly points out that ". . . the sabbath . . . is not to be defined in terms of cessation from activity, but cessation from that kind of activity involved in the labour of the other six days."[102]

One is not surprised to learn of other apparently legal activities of the Israelites on the Sabbath. There were military campaigns,[103] marriage feasts (Judges 14:12–18), dedication feasts (1 Kings 8:65; 2 Chron. 7:8), visiting a man of God (2 Kings 4:23), changing the temple guards (2 Kings 11:5–9), preparing the showbread (1 Chron. 9:32), offering sacrifices (1 Chron. 23:31; 2 Chron. 8:13), duties of the priests and Levites (2 Kings 11:5–9; cf. 2 Chron. 23:4, 8) and the opening of the East gate (Ezek. 46:1–3). Beyond these, one may surmise that Israel must have engaged in other activities that either enhanced the enjoyment of this "holiday" or were required by necessity.[104]

After the Exile the people of Israel had learned their lesson.[105] They took the Sabbath seriously again: the showbread was prepared every Sabbath (1 Chron. 9:32), the people covenanted not to buy anything on the Sabbath (Neh. 10:31), and they promised their support of the Sabbath offerings (Neh. 10:32–33). The prophet Ezekiel had made it quite clear that the Exile was partly due to the profaning of the Sabbath (Ezek. 22:8, 26, 31). For the celebration of the Sabbath instructions are given:[106]

The East gate of the inner court shall be opened, the prince shall enter . . . from without and stand beside the post of the gate; then the priests shall offer sacrifices and the prince shall worship at the threshold of the gate; the people shall worship at the entrance of that gate before the LORD; then the prince shall go out, but the gate is to remain open until the evening (Ezek. 46:1–3).

This prescription of Sabbath ceremony is indicative of the prophet's concern not to fall into any fault and consequent judgment of God. Nehemiah also expressed this concern and resorted to drastic measures to prohibit buying and selling on the Sabbath (Neh. 13:15–22).

In brief, Israel kept the Sabbath according to the letter of the law but often profaned it according to the spirit of the law. For the celebration of the Sabbath we are given some indications in Psalm 92, Numbers 28:9–10, and Ezekiel 46:1–3.

CONCLUSION

No convincing evidence has been produced that locates the concept of the Sabbath in extrabiblical sources. The biblical evidence is that the Sabbath was inaugurated for the people of Israel to be celebrated as a weekly sign of the covenant. The Sabbath is not viewed as a universal ordinance for all mankind but as a specific institution for Israel. As a sign of the covenant it was to last as long as that covenant.

The giving of the Sabbath law was not meant to be a burden; in fact the Sabbath was to reflect God's compassion for His people, as well as to emphasize the character of His holiness. But this intention was forgotten in arrogance and rebellion as legalism and traditionalism grew. The true concept of the Sabbath law was proclaimed again and again by God's prophets who stressed the covenant relationship, but people were unwilling to listen. Instead of understanding it to be their privilege to rest on the Sabbath, they viewed it as deprivation; instead of recognizing their opportunity to commune with God, they saw only inconvenience and hardship. Rather than discovering freedom to worship, they felt in bondage to a law, and instead of grasping the idea of renewal of their covenant relationship to God, they experienced the tragedy of legalism.

God instituted the Sabbath for His people as a constant, regular source of blessing for both spiritual and physical renewal; it was to express social concern and compassion. The Sabbath was a reminder that God was in control of man's time. Consequently, the Sabbath should have been celebrated as a day of joyfully assembling before God. He had liberated them from slavery, and their devotions, praises, and thanksgivings were to flow from grateful and appreciative hearts. The death penalty, introduced after their rebellion against this commandment, showed that God intended to secure the observance of the Sabbath even in the midst of an arrogant and rebellious people. For an institution of this magnitude with such far-reaching theological implications austere and drastic measures were appropriate.

For those among the people with spiritual discernment, no threats were necessary. No one had to compel them to enjoy the blessings of this consecrated day. At Sinai, the Sabbath had been instituted for the benefit of man (and not man for the Sabbath). After that encounter with God the glory of the Sabbath permeated Israel's working days and enabled her to see all her labors, anxieties, and shortcomings in the light of His grace. Trained by the regular recurrence of this gracious gift of the Sabbath, Israel was to be able to stand before the Creator in freedom, responsibility, trust, and gratitude; she worshiped Him, the Lord of the Sabbath, and looked forward with joy and anticipation to the coming of the final Rest.

NOTES

[1]Niels-Erik A. Andreasen, *The Old Testament Sabbath* (SBLDS; Missoula: Scholars Press, 1972), p. 8.

[2]H.-J. Kraus, *Worship in Israel* (Richmond: John Knox, 1966), p. 87; W. Eichrodt, *Theology of the Old Testament* (Philadelphia: Westminster, 1961, 1967) 1:120; J. Morgenstern, "Sabbath," *IDB* 4:137: "There can be little question that this institution, the seventh-day sabbath, was strictly observed by the Canaanites and was borrowed from them. . . . As a Canaanite religious institution it was entirely negative in character, an evil day. . . ." Morgenstern's assertion is without foundation. Cf. also Lohse, "*σάββατον*" *TDNT* 7:3: "The idea that they might have taken over the Sabbath from the Canaanites is ruled out by the fact that no trace of the Sabbath has been found among the latter."

[3]E. Mahler, "Der Sabbath" in *Jubilee Volume Bernhard Heller*, ed. S. Scheiber (Budapest: n.p., 1941), p. 239; F. Delitzsch, *Babel und Bibel* (Leipzig: J. C. Hinrichs, 1903), pp. 40–41; Alfred Jeremias, *Das Alte Testament im Lichte des Alten Orients* (Leipzig, J. C. Hinrichs, 1906), p. 186; but *contra*, N. H. Tur-Sinai, "Sabbat und Woche," *Bibliotheca Orientalis* 8 (1951), 1–14; E. Lohse, *σάββατον*, 7:3; G. Fohrer, *Geschichte der israelitischen Religion* (Berlin: Walter de Gruyter, 1969), p. 108; K. Balkan, *Studies in Honor of Benno Landsberger*, ed. H. G. Güterbock and T. Jacobsen (Chicago: University of Chicago Press, 1965), p. 159, note 1, attacks the concept of *Amstag* (official's day) as "completely fictitious" and the distinction between *hamuštu* and *hamištu* as unjustified since the former is a form of the latter.

[4]E. Mahler, "Der Sabbath," p. 139: "ein Tag der Ruhe des Herzens."

[5]Ibid., but cf. Norman H. Snaith, *The Jewish New Year Festival* (London: SPCK, 1947), p. 103, who claims that "the Sabbath was originally the *new-moon day*" (italics mine).

[6]Georg Beer, *Schabbath–der Mischnatractat "Sabbath"* Tübingen: J. C. B. Mohr, 1908), p. 11; also a more recent study by Bruce A. Kimball with an emphasis on the "uniqueness of the Sabbath arising . . . from its grounding in Hebraic religion" ("The Origin of the Sabbath and Its Legacy to the Modern Sabbatical," *The Journal of Higher Education* 49 [1978]:303–12).

[7]Ibid., pp. 12–13: E Mahler, "Der Sabbath," p. 239; J. Meinhold, *Sabbat und Woche im Alten Testament*, FRLANT 5 (Göttingen: Vandenhoeck und Ruprecht, 1905); but Johannes Hehn, "Siebenzahl und Sabbat bei den Babyloniern und im Alten Testament," *Leipziger Semitistische Studien*, Zweiter Band, Heft 5 (Leipzig, J. C. Hinrichs, 1907), p. 92.

[8]E. Mahler, "Der Sabbath," p. 239; Felix Mathys, "Sabbatruhe und Sabbatfest," *TZ* 4 (1972): 248: "It is characteristic of the Israelite 7-day-week to be independent of the moon-phases, even though the significance of the number seven originally dates back to lunar movements" (my translation); but cf. G. Fohrer, *Geschichte der israelitischen Religion*, p. 108; U. Cassuto, *A Commentary on the Book of Exodus* (Jerusalem: Magnes Press, 1967), p. 224. Cf. W. W. Hallo, "New Moons and Sabbaths," HUCA 48 (1977): 1–18.

[9]B. D. Eerdmans, *Der Sabbath*, BZAW 41 (Berlin: Walter de Gruyter, 1925), p. 80; followed by L. Köhler, "Der Dekalog," *ThR* 1 (1929): 181; K. Budde, "The Sabbath and the Week," *JTS* 30 (1929): 1–15; H. H. Rowley, "Moses and the Decalogue," BJRL 34 (1951–52): 114ff.

[10]B. D. Eerdmans, *Der Sabbath*, p. 80; Eduard Nielsen, *The Ten Commandments in New Perspective* (London: SCM, 1968), p. 103; but compare E. G. Kraeling, "The Present Status of the Sabbath Question," *AJSL* 49 (1932–33): 219; G. Fohrer, *Geschichte der israelitischen Religion*, p. 108; J. J. Stamm, M. E. Andrew, *The Ten Commandments in Recent Research*, (London: SCM, 1967), pp. 91–92.

[11]A. Menes, cited in E. G. Kraeling, "The Present Status of the Sabbath Question," p. 225.

[12]Hutton Webster, cited in Kraeling.

[13]Max Weber, cited in Kraeling, p. 226.

[14]Kraeling, "The Present Status of the Sabbath Question," p. 228; Roland de Vaux, *Ancient Israel* (London: Darton, Longman, & Todd, 1961), p. 480; but compare G. Fohrer, *Geschichte der israelitischen Religion*, p. 108.

[15]J. and H. Lewy, "The Origin of the Week and the Oldest West-Asiatic Calendar," *HUCA* 17 (1942): 1ff.

[16]Tur-Sinai, "Sabbat und Woche," p. 24, who views the origin of the Sabbath as indigenous to Israel in "full agreement with Biblical tradition"; R. M. Johnston, "Partiarchs, Rabbis and Sabbath," *AUSS* 12 (1974): 97: "The Sabbath was Israel's own bride and belonged to no other. Exodus 16:29 was interpreted in an exclusive sense: The Lord hath given *you*—Israel—the Sabbath, but hath not given it to the heathen. This, then, was the prevailing conception . . . of what had become normative Rabbinic Judaism. . . ." *Contra:* G. Fohrer, *Geschichte der israelitischen Religion*, p. 118.

[17]Cf. pp. 27–31, below.

[18]R. North, "The Derivation of Sabbath," *Bib* 36 (1955): 201.

[19]G. von Rad, *Old Testament Theology* (London: SCM, 1962), 1:16; Alfred Jeremias, *Das Alte Testament*, p. 182.

[20]Martin Buber, *Biblical Humanism* (New York: Simon and Schuster, 1968), p. 72; cf. also North, "The Derivation of Sabbath," p. 201.

[21]G. von Rad, *Old Testament Theology*, 2:16.

[22]G. Ringgren, *Israelite Religion* (London: SPCK, 1966), p. 202; and all who favor the Babylonian and Lunar Origin theories.

[23]Th. C. Vriezen, *The Religion of Ancient Israel* (Philadelphia: Westminster, 1967), p. 150: ". . . a religious institution peculiar to the people"; W. Zimmerli, 1. *Mose* 1–11 (Zürich: 1943), p. 117: "The Sabbath belongs to Israel" (Der Sabbath ist das Vorrecht Israels).

[24]A. Jeremias, *Das Alte Testament*, p. 182, "The institution of this weekly cycle . . . was a

great intellectual accomplishment. From whom the Israelites got it cannot be determined. *They could not have invented it;* there is no trace left that the Israelites, who were decidedly dependent in cultural matters, occupied themselves with such things" (emphasis mine).

[25]KB, pp. 946–47; BDB, p. 992*a*.

[26]J. Hehn, *Siebenzahl und Sabbat*, p. 101.

[27]W. H. Schmidt, *Die Schöpfungsgeschichte der Priesterschrift* (Neukirchen-Vluyn: Neukirchener Verlag, 1964), p. 156.

[28]G. Beer, *Schabbath–der Mischnatractat "Sabbath,"* p. 13; E. Mahler, "Der Sabbath," p. 239.

[29]R. de Vaux, *Ancient Israel*, p. 476.

[30]R. North, "Derivation," p. 186, especially n.3: "*šbt* has nothing to do with resting in the sense of enjoying repose. . . . It certainly cannot be translated as 'the day of rest.' " This latter statement can be questioned since it is based on the etymology rather than the usage of the word.

[31]This is *not* a denial of the existence of seven day time-periods in the Ancient Near East long before Israel's history. In fact, there are verses in Genesis and Exodus before the Sinai event that demonstrate such periods; Genesis 7:4, 10; 8:10, 12; 29:27, 28; 31:23; 50:10; Exodus 7:25; 12:15, 19; 13:6. The chronological measurement of seven days is a phenomenon to be expected among the peoples of the Ancient Near East as it reflects a simple, observational calculation based on the moon-phases. But there is no evidence of an on-rolling week that disregards the beginning of a new month. Cf. in this connection W. Rordorf, *Sunday* (London: SCM, 1968), pp. 19–20.

[32]Consequently, the one additional mentioning of the Sabbath in Numbers 28:9–10, which is not a commandment but a stipulation regarding the type of sacrifice, is excluded.

[33]Cf. the valuable and comprehensive tradition-historical study by Niels-Erik A. Andreasen, *The Old Testament Sabbath*, notwithstanding earlier divergencies by other scholars.

[34]In verse 22 the leaders told Moses about the extra portion of manna that the people had gathered. Moses explains that the Lord "has given you the sabbath" (v. 29). Cf. also Lohse, TDNT, s.v. *σάββατον*; but against this, cf. M. Buber, *Moses* (Oxford: East and West Library, 1946), p. 80; W. Rordorf, *Sunday*, pp. 12–13.

[35]Richard A. Parker, "The Calendars and Chronology," *Legacy of Egypt* (Oxford: University Press, 1971), p. 17: "The seventh day was called 'part day.' . . ."

[36]BDB: "sabbath observance; sabbatism"; KB: "sabbatical feast" (i.e., Sabbatfeier).

[37]The injunction of verse 29, "let no man go out of his place on the seventh day," is obviously not a prohibition to travel but carries the implied contextual sense ". . . to gather" (cf. v. 27). Also cf. Hehn, *Siebenzahl und Sabbat*, p. 98.

[38]Cf. Vriezen, *The Religion of Ancient Israel*, p. 151. A curious interpretative twist is offered by Karl Elliger, *Leviticus*, HAT 4 (Tübingen: Mohr, 1966), p. 312. "The Sabbath was known to Israel from her beginning in the desert and was originally connected, quite independent from the course of the moon, with the number 7 as a special, one might almost say an uncanny day, in which a person in all events might better leave certain things undone (שָׁבַת "to cease") and stay at home (Exod. 16:29 J ?), a day in which one indeed also 'celebrated,' but in a totally different sense. . . ." Such a game of semantics will always have fatal consequences for exegesis!

[39]The anarthrous construction carries significance (i.e., "The whole idea was new") as pointed out by G. Rawlinson, *Exodus* (London: Kegan, Paul, Trench & Co., 1906), p. 52; A. Dillmann, *Die Bücher Exodus und Leviticus* (Leipzig: S. Hirzel, 1897), p. 175; P. Heinisch, *Das Buch Exodus* (Bonn: Hanstein, 1934), p. 133; G. Henton Davies, *Exodus* (London: SCM, 1967), p. 140. This construction of the word שַׁבָּת occurs only four times in the Pentateuch, Exodus 16:23; 20:10 (followed in v. 11 with an articular construction) and Exodus 35:2 (followed in v. 3 by an articular construction). In the latter three instances this construction occurs within a formula: "six days work may be done, but on the seventh day there is a Sabbath. . . ." The anarthrous construction in Exodus 16:23, 25 is unique and may, therefore, well signify the newness of an idea.

[40]Attributed by source critics to E, though verses 10*b*–11 are attributed to P.

[41]Cf. J. D. W. Watts, "Infinite absolute as Imperative and the Interpretation of Exodus 20:8,"

ZAW 74 (1962): 144, who translates: "Remembering the sabbath day to hallow it, six days you shall labour and do all your work . . ." There is no forceful reason to subscribe to R. J. Meeks's claim that here is another instance of a hanging clause, the *casus pendens* ("Lapses of Old Testament Translators," *JAOS* 58 (1938): 123.

[42]The wife is not mentioned because a man and wife were considered a unity (Gen. 2:24) and also because a wife does not work *under* but *beside* her husband.

[43]We do not agree with the interpretation that treats the latter part of verse 11 ("therefore the LORD blessed the sabbath day and hallowed it") as a revelatory explanation of Genesis 2:3 ("then God blessed the seventh day and hallowed it"). Rather, we interpret the statement in verse 11*b* as an explanation of God's blessing activity in connection with the new institution of the Sabbath on the analogy of God's blessing activity with regard to the seventh day at creation. Our interpretation is guided by two considerations: comparing with Deuteronomy 5:15, the Sabbath commandment is based on a previous historical event and the implication is stated (because God rested then, therefore He has blessed the Sabbath now—because God rescued you out of Egypt then, therefore He commanded you at Sinai to keep the Sabbath; cf. R. Frankena, "Einige Bemerkungen zum Gebrauch des Adverbs *'al-kēn* im Hebräischen," *Studia Biblica et Semitica* [Wageningen: H. Veenman, 1966], p. 95). The other consideration is that the particle עַל־כֵּן, is used in both Exodus 20:11 and Deuteronomy 5:15, and translated "therefore," in a majority of cases is employed in the Pentateuch to connect causally an event in the past with a situation some time later (cf. Gen. 2:24; 25:20; 42:21; 47:22; Exod. 13:15; Num. 21:27, Deut. 24:18); hence, it is better translated "consequently now" (in the sense of *post hoc* ["after this"] and *propter hoc* ["on account of this"]).

[44]See section on "The Sabbath as a Sign of the Covenant," later in this chapter.

[45]A. R. Hulst, "Bemerkungen zum Sabbatgebot," *Studia Biblica et Semitica* (Wageningen: H. Veenman, 1966), p. 159, shows that these words are used synonymously, but although it may not be conclusive, one can make a case for a difference in the context here.

[46]Form-critical studies make the following distinctions: Yahwist Decalogue (Exod. 34:21), Book of the Covenant (Elohist—Exod. 23:12), Holiness Code (Lev. 23:1–3), E-Decalogue (Exod. 20:9, 10*a*), and D-Decalogue (Deut. 5:13–14*a*)—cf. among others W. Rordorf, *Sunday*, G. Fohrer, *Geschichte der israelitischen Religion*.

[47]As to its form cf. E. Gerstenberger, *Wesen und Herkunft des sogenannten "Apodiktischen Rechts" im Alten Testament* (Bonn: Rheinische Friedrich-Wilhelms-Universität, 1965), p. 46; G. Fohrer, *Studien zur Alttestamentlichen Theologie und Geschichte* (Berlin: de Gruyter, 1969), p. 148 (who claims it is a "rule for life and conduct in apodictic formulation").

[48]Exodus 20:11.

[49]See the further section of this chapter, "The Sabbath as a Sign of the Covenant"; Exodus 31:13–17—"perpetual" until fulfillment (cf. priests' office [Exod. 29:9], sacrifices [Lev. 24:9], and statutes [Num. 19:21]).

[50]It is in consequence of this understanding that the man who gathered wood on the Sabbath was executed (Num. 15:32–36). Significantly, this event is reported after verses 30–31, which explain that anyone acting "defiantly," reviling the Lord, despising the word of the Lord, and thus breaking His commandments shall be cut off. This man was not stoned because he took a Sabbath afternoon stroll into the woods and happened to find and collect a few sticks for his hearth. He broke the Sabbath law deliberately. Without this light, Exodus 16:27, where some of the people went out to gather manna on the Sabbath, would be difficult to understand. However, their offense seemed to have been treated as a "first offense," i.e., the people did not realize the full impact of their disobedience. Hence, they were only reprimanded. For a scholarly discussion of this incident in Numbers 15:32–36, cf. J. Weingreen, "The Case of the Woodgatherer," *VT* 16 (1966) p. 362–64, A. Phillips, "The Case of the Woodgatherer Reconsidered," *VT* 19 (1969): p. 125–28, where the question of "fence around the Torah" is debated, and E. Ruprecht, "Erzählung vom Mannawunder (Ex. 16) im Aufbau der Priesterschrift," ZAW 86 (1974): 269–305.

[51]F. Mathys, "Sabbatruhe und Sabbatfest," "In Deuteronomy man does not exist for the Sabbath, but the Sabbath for man" (editor's translation).

[52]Ibid., p. 252: "The historical and theological foundation of the Sabbath is tied up with the socially determined purpose of a day of rest" (editor's translation).

[53]K. Elliger, *Leviticus*, p. 313: "What is in view is the work of one's calling *(Berufsarbeit)* . . . not excluding cooking and baking . . ." (editor's translation).

[54]Cf. F. Mathys's statement, "Sabbatruhe and Sabbatfest," p. 249, that "basically the commandment of sabbath-rest is shown to be an 'empty formula' which time and again had to be filled by Israel."

[55]Otto Piper, *Christian Ethics* (London: Nelson, 1970), p. 228.

[56]Ibid., p. 188.

[57]Ibid., p. 159.

[58]*Der Evangelische Glaube*, 2. Band (Tübingen: Mohr, 1973), p. 362 (translation mine).

[59]Gerhard von Rad, *The Problem of the Hexateuch and other Essays* (New York: 1966, p. 101, n.9. Others of similar opinion are: H. C. Leupold, *Exposition of Genesis*, Vol. 1 (Grand Rapids: Eerdmans, 1953); W. H. Schmidt, *Die Schöpfungsgeschichte der Priesterschrift*; W. *Zimmerli, 1. Mose 1–11*, 1. Teil; J. Calvin, *Commentaries on the First Book of Moses called Genesis*, Vol. 1 (Edinburgh: Calvin Translation Society, 1847); G. von Rad, *Genesis* (London: SCM, 1961); H. H. Rowley, *Worship in Ancient Israel.*

[60]U. Cassuto, *A Commentary on the Book of Genesis* (Jerusalem: Magnus Press, 1961); W. Eichrodt, *Theology of the Old Testament*, Vol. 1; Richard Kraemer, *Die biblische Urgeschichte* (Wernigerode: G. Koezle, 1931); J. Barton Payne, *The Theology of the Older Testament* (Grand Rapids: Zondervan, 1962); C. Westermann, *Genesis* (Neukirchen-Vluyn: Neukirchener Verlag, 1974); John Murray, *Collected Writings*, Vol. 1 (Carlisle, Pa.: Banner of Truth Trust, 1976).

[61]W. Zimmerli, *1. Mose 1–11*, p. 102 emphasizes that the seventh day of creation was not a void or emptiness because "one more work is being done . . . God blessed . . . and hallowed it." However, on the basis of Genesis 2:3 one may argue that God's blessing and sanctifying activity took place on the following day (". . . God blessed the seventh day . . . because in it he *had* ceased . . . :" employing the pluperfect suggests a retrospective action).

[62]Anthropomorphisms do not disturb us but evoke an immediate reaction: these terms must be explained on a different level than the human one. God needs no rest or refreshing as His strength never fails. In fact, the term "refreshed" is used only here of God in the whole Old Testament, and the verb "rest" without a qualifying preposition is used only in this verse to describe an action of God.

[63]Zimmerli, *1. Mose 1–11*, p. 102.

[64]Gerhard Wehmeier, *Der Segen im Alten Testament* (Basel: F. Reinhardt Kommissions Verlag, 1970), p. 134. Wehmeier sees בָּרַךְ standing beside קִדֵּשׁ (and derives his interpretation from this viewpoint) whereas we recognize בָּרַךְ as the main term explained by קִדֵּשׁ (so that, קִדֵּשׁ stands beside בָּרַךְ).

[65]F. J. Helfmeyer, "Segen und Erwählung," *BZ* 18 (1974): 208–23.

[66]G. von Rad, *Problem of Hexateuch*, p. 101 and n.9; H. D. Leupold, *Exposition of Genesis*, 1: p. 103; W. Zimmerli, *1. Mose 1–11*, p. 117.

[67]Cf. Hebrews 4:1–10, and A. T. Lincoln, chapter 7 of this volume; and briefly, later in this paper.

[68]C. Westermann, *Genesis*, p. 235, claims that the concern, intention and emphasis of the creation account is man. E. Sauer, *The King of the Earth* (Grand Rapids: Eerdmans, 1962), sees man as the crown of creation.

[69]Verse 3b contains nine words and can be disregarded for stylistic purposes as it is a relative clause introduced by כִּי.

[70]We assume that the additional לַעֲשׂוֹת (only apparently redundant) serves the style of these verses very well as the first sentences end in עָשָׂה.

[71]For this meaning versus the assumption of MT error cf. U. Cassuto, *Genesis*, p. 62, who compares pertinently with Genesis 17:22; 24:19; 49:33; Exodus 40:33–34.

[72]Significantly, the seventh day does not conclude with the formula "and there was evening and there was morning, the seventh day."

[73]Within the creation account.

[74]The rest pattern for man that derives from his knowledge of God's working pattern is most important in this interpretation.

[75]Thus, God created in a threefold manner: by word (Gen. 1:3, etc.), by fashioning (Gen. 2:7), and by example (Gen. 2:2). Was man's first day of work God's seventh day? The answer is no. Man's first day was the day of his creation, the day before God's rest day. But it is idle to speculate when man's first day of work was (i.e., whether man began to work on the sixth day of creation, the seventh, or eighth, etc.).

[76]D. J. McCarthy, *Old Testament Covenant* (Oxford: Blackwell, 1972), pp. 57–58.

[77]Ibid.

[78]Ibid., p. 88.

[79]R. J. Rushdoony, *The Institutes of Biblical Law* (Nutley: Craig Press, 1973), p. 128. (with reference to M. G. Kline, *Treaty of the Great King* [Grand Rapids: Eerdmans, 1963], pp. 63–64) and pp. 143, 154.

[80]U. Cassuto, A *Commentary on the Book of Exodus*, p. 404.

[81]Exodus 19:5ff.; 24:7–8; 34:10, 27–28.

[82]"Two tables of the testimony" (Exod. 31:18); "the words of the covenant, the ten words" (Exod. 34:28).

[83]Attention is drawn to the other two signs of the previous covenants, viz. the *rainbow* for the world (corresponding to the cosmic nature of the Noahic covenant, Gen. 9:12–17) and *circumcision* for the descendants of Abraham (Gen. 17:7–11). Signs of the covenant and institutions of the covenant (sacrifices, priesthood, temple, and monarchy) ought not to be confused. From the New Testament perspective, all the institutions were fulfilled in Christ: the Sacrifice "once for all," the Priest "after the order of Melchizedek," the Temple/body "which is the church," and the King over the "kingdom of God/heaven." To attempt to transfer the signs and institutions of the old covenant to the new covenant, equating circumcision with baptism, passover with communion, priest with pastor, temple with church, tithing with giving, Sabbath with Sunday, monarchy with ecclesiastical government, etc., is not valid in our opinion. In each case there are essential differences that would negate these equations. New Testament baptism, for example, is explained in terms of Old Testament baptisms (1 Cor. 10:1–2; 1 Peter 3:20–21), circumcision is retained for New Testament believers in a spiritual sense (Col. 2:11; Rom. 2:29), and communion is a bloodless celebration, etc.

[84]It follows that the sign of the new covenant should be the celebration and remembrance of the resurrection of Jesus Christ.

[85]Exodus 31:14–16 (In Hebrew, note the use of "to cut" in v. 14, corresponding to the "cutting" of a covenant, and the use of "to do" the Sabbath in v. 16, in contrast to "do" work in v. 15).

[86]Genesis 17:8.

[87]These terms, viz. Noahic, Abrahamic, Mosaic covenant, are merely terms of convenience rather than theological designations in the tradition of covenant theology.

[88]"Rest," therefore, is relative: the land continues to produce in the Sabbath year (Lev. 25:6) and man continues to harvest its crops (though only to eat and not to store), but it produces not "by force," as it were, but on its own.

[89]However, the desolation of the land in consequence of breach of covenant is viewed as beneficial to the land. The land would have been exploited through disobedience of the Sabbath-for-the-land commandment. Its restoration is seen in terms of "enjoying its sabbaths all the days of the desolation" (Lev. 26:34).

[90]In actual fact, the year of jubilee constitutes a two-year Sabbath for the land since the forty-ninth year is a sabbatical year (cf. R. J. Rushdoony, *The Institutes of Biblical Law*, pp. 137ff.)

[91]That the "principle purpose of the sabbath is not worship but rest" (R. J. Rushdoony, *The*

Institutes of Biblical Law, p. 138) is refuted by Ezekiel 46:1–3 (the prince and the people shall worship before the Lord on the Sabbaths) and by Psalm 92 (a song of worship and praise to Yahweh for His חֶסֶד and אֱמוּנָה).

[92]Cf. above, n. 78.

[93]Isaiah 1:13; Jeremiah 17:27; Ezekiel 20:12–13, 16, 20–21, 24; Hosea 2:11; Amos 8:5; also cf. 2 Chronicles 36:21; Nehemiah 9:14–31.

[94]Exodus 16:30; Numbers 28:9–10; 1 Chronicles 23:31; 2 Chronicles 2:4; 8:13; 2 Kings 4:23; 2 Chron. 23:4; 31:3.

[95]But cf. 2 Kings 22:2: "And he did what was right in the eyes of the LORD, and walked in all the way of David, his father, and he did not turn aside to the right hand or to the left." Note also 23:3!

[96]Indeed, this is the import of Malachi 2:13–3:18 and 3:4!

[98]Isaiah 58:13–14: "If . . . [you] call the sabbath a delight, the holy day of the LORD honorable; if you honor it, not going your own ways, or seeking your own pleasure, and speaking your own word, then you shall take delight in the LORD. . . ." Also Psalm 92.

[98]Isaiah 56:1–2 (cf. also vv. 3–8).

[99]R. de Vaux, *Ancient Israel*, p. 180.

[100]Ibid. p. 182.

[101]Cf. K. Elliger, *Leviticus*, p. 313.

[102]John Murray, *Principles of Conduct* (Grand Rapids: Eerdmans, 1957), p. 33.

[103]Joshua 6:15; 1 Kings 20:29; 2 Kings 3:9 (obviously not by professional soldiers).

[104]E.g., military campaigns.

[105]The concept of an intensification of the Sabbath institution after the Exile (cf. W. Rordorf, *Sunday*, p. 45: "Now the sabbath became an article of faith, the direct concern of theology, integrally associated with the election of Israel"; E. Lohse, TDNT, s.v. σάββατον. "The sabbath-commandment becomes the most important piece of the divine law"; G. Fohrer, *Geschichte*, p. 107) has come under severe criticism by Andreasen, *The Old Testament Sabbath*, pp. 235ff.

[106]Probably an indication of the traditional Sabbath celebrations not mentioned elsewhere.

3

A SUMMARY OF SABBATH OBSERVANCE IN JUDAISM AT THE BEGINNING OF THE CHRISTIAN ERA

C. ROWLAND

Chris Rowland has taught at the University of Newcastle-upon-Tyne and is now Dean of one of the colleges in Cambridge.

In the period after the Exile, the growth of a body of sacred Scriptures meant that the Jews tended to see obedience to God in terms of the application of these Scriptures to particular situations. The need for direction was intensified with the waning of the prophetic movement, and the consequent lack of an authoritative word from God meant that the will of God was not always apparent on the basis of the scriptural text alone (e.g., 1 Macc. 4:46). There was thus a need to interpret and apply the past revelation of God's will to the various situations that confronted the community. The guidelines for ethics, as well as apparently outmoded regulations, were applied by prominent teachers to the ever changing situations that confronted the Jewish nation. This process continued over a long period of time, and the oral decisions of the Jewish teachers of several generations were codified for the first time in the collection of Halakah, which we know as the Mishnah. Although every attempt was made to ground the decisions pertaining to ethics in Scripture itself, some of them had been hallowed by time and were accepted as normative even though they were not grounded in Scripture.[1]

For the Jew, love of God involved obedience to the Torah; but in many instances, obedience to the Torah was easier to state as a principle than to put into practice. In many areas of life the Torah was not explicit and did not give clear-cut guidance. This was especially true in the case of Sabbath observance. Despite the fact that the keeping of the Sabbath was one of the cornerstones of Judaism, especially in the Diaspora, Scripture itself offered very little detailed advice on how this special day was to be kept. Sometimes when explicit advice was given, such as the prohibition in Jeremiah 17:22, it proved to present such practical difficulties in its fulfillment that it was inevitable that further explication became necessary. In the light of such problems, we can understand the variety of regulations that were developed by Jewish teachers, especially those contained in the Halakah. They made explicit for the Jew what the Torah itself left unsaid. Hence, a substantial body of tradition developed that enabled the Jew to ascertain exactly what would be expected of him in a variety of situations even if the Torah was not explicit.

Since the Torah was the most authoritative way to ascertain God's will on a particular matter, it became the focal point of all attempts to explain what was left unsaid or vague. A variety of exegetical techniques was developed to enable the interpreter to extract every ounce of meaning from the sacred text. Even passages that did not appear to relate to the issue under discussion could be made to offer guidance by the use of the appropriate exegetical device.[2] In this way the whole of Scripture became a mine from which various nuggets of information could be dug to help solve those problems that arose from the lack of direct advice.

The Sabbath, together with circumcision and the study of the Torah, occupied an important place in Jewish religion; in the Diaspora it became one of the distinguishing features of Jewish life.[3] Its central significance for Jews only intensified the problem of its proper practice, especially in the face of a world that was scornful of the apparent laziness of the Jews on the seventh day. How were Jews to keep the Sabbath commandment when they lived in an alien culture, or when life, religion and ancestral customs were threatened with destruction at the hands of a foreign power?

An illustration of the typical Jewish dilemma is found in 1 Maccabees 2:31–38. In this incident the enemy took advantage of the Jews' observance of the Sabbath, by destroying a thousand people who had refused to fight on the Sabbath. In light of this tragedy, Mattathias and his friends resolved thereafter to fight on the Sabbath in defense of their lives and their ancestral religion (1 Macc. 2:41). Jews who tried to put into practice the laws of God were often faced with a similar dilemma. What were the situations that permitted one to break the law of God? When surrounded by a pagan environment or the harsh realities of economic necessity, was there no possibility of a relaxation of the harsh demands that were being put upon the Jew by many interpreters?

In what follows, various Jewish attitudes toward the Sabbath will be examined. It will become apparent that the different positions espoused by various Jewish groups reflect the same predicament that faced the Jews at the time of the Maccabean tragedy. At that time there were Jews who put obedience to the law of God above all else, even if it meant losing one's life. But there were also those who considered temporary disobedience justified for the sake of one's life and the perpetuation of one's religion. Radically different approaches confront us in the Jewish literature of the period.

Jubilees and the Damascus Document

These two works represent a rather strict and uncompromising attitude toward the observance of the Sabbath. It is probable that both of these works originated within sects with a similar, if not identical, outlook. The exclusive nature of these sects makes it understandable how such a strict observance could be maintained, for the pressures and problems of life in society would impinge only very slightly upon them.[4] How strict their Halakah was can be seen from Jubilees 50:6–13, where even sexual intercourse was forbidden (v. 8; cf. *B.Baba Kamma* 82*a* and *B. Ketuboth* 62*b*). The only labor that was permitted was the offering of sacrifices to God. (v. 11; cf. CD 11:17f). The writer of Jubilees considered Israel's participation in the Sabbath to be an extension of the rest that was demanded in the heavenly realm. According to Jubilees 2:18, not only the angels, but God Himself had to keep the Sabbath.[5] Jubilees saw the setting apart of the Sabbath at creation as having a very close link with the election of Israel as the people of God; Israel, and no other nation, was set apart to keep the Sabbath (Jub. 2:20). The strictness of the Sabbath observance in Jubilees did not mean less joy than on any other day. In fact, better quality food was to be served, and fasting was considered inappropriate (Jub. 50:10ff.). Nevertheless, the punishment for breaking the Sabbath was severe; Jubilees 50:13 prescribes the death penalty and is entirely consistent with the uncompromising tone of certain scriptural passages (e.g., Exod. 31:15).

There are several similarities between Jubilees and the Damascus Document (CD) with regard to the regulations for the Sabbath. For example, both state that it is not lawful for anyone to eat anything that has not been prepared in advance (CD 10:22–23 and Jub. 2:29). In Jubilees 2:29 (cf. also *Shabb.* 1:1), there is a prohibition against carrying an object out of a private house into a public area, and the Damascus Document prevents a similar act (CD 11:7–8). Although strict legal interpretations are to be found in both documents, the Damascus Document allows the saving of life to take precedence over the observance of the Sabbath (CD 11:16–17). Such transgression was permitted only in the case of an emergency, however,[6] and helping an animal about to give birth or rescuing it from a pit on the Sabbath was not permitted (CD 11:13f.). A journey on the Sabbath was limited to a thousand cubits (CD 10:21), based on Exodus 16:29 and Numbers 35:4. In defining the limit of the Sabbath journey the writer uses the same passage from Numbers to interpret Exodus 16:29 as do some of the early rabbis of the tannaitic period, though he comes to a different conclusion.[7] The Damascus Document allows only a thousand cubits for a journey on the Sabbath, although it permits a man to go two thousand cubits when pasturing an animal (CD 11:5ff.).

If we are correct to link the Damascus Document and the Qumran scrolls with the Essenes, then Josephus's reference to the Sabbath practices of the latter sect is relevant for our discussion.[8] Josephus considers the Essenes far more strict than other Jewish groups (*BJ* ii. 147). He tells us that they prepared their food the day before the Sabbath and so avoided lighting any fires on that day. The Essenes' prohibition of work extends even to defecation. According to Philo, the Essenes marked the Sabbath as a day of teaching and assembly (*Om. Prob. Lib.* 81; cf. *Vit. Contempl.* 30f.).[9] Although nothing is said in the Manual of Discipline (1QS) about the Sabbath practice of the Qumran community, it may be assumed that the communal gatherings described in 1QS 6 typify what happened on the Sabbath. The fact that the breaking of the

Sabbath is not mentioned in the list of misdemeanors in 1QS 7 is probably of little significance; it may suggest a rigid discipline in which the Sabbath was kept so invariably that there was no need to mention it.[10]

In the discussion of Sabbath observance within Judaism, something should be said about the Sadducees; they seem to have obeyed the letter of the law (*Ant.* xviii. 16), although they had their own interpretations of it (e.g., *Macc.* 1:6). There are few specifically Sadducean regulations for the Sabbath, but some indication of their position can be gained from the Tosephta (*Sukk.* 3. 1). Part of the ritual feasts of Succoth involved striking the ground around the altar with branches of willow-trees; the Pharisees performed the rite even when it fell on the Sabbath, but the Boethusians (a sect of the Sadducees) plotted to hide the branches from the people so that the Sabbath would not be profaned. This incident, therefore, demonstrates a very strict attitude toward Sabbath observance when even a ritual of some importance, which formed part of a religious festival, was considered to be an abrogation of the Sabbath.

The Pharisaic-Rabbinic Tradition[11]

More relevant to early Christian Sabbath practice is the teaching of the rabbis on the observance of the Sabbath. The Pharisaic approach is important because it wrestles with the tension between precepts and a humanitarian outlook on life, which arises within normal social circumstances. That is not to suggest that the strict Halakah was a mere repetition of scriptural commandments; that would be far from true. Nevertheless the rabbis were attempting to relate the demands of the Torah to situations that would not have affected the life of a closed community such as the one at Qumran. There seem to be two major questions concerning the Sabbath that are answered in the Halakah. First, there are detailed regulations on exactly what constitutes an offense against the law of God. Precision in legal matters enabled the individual to know exactly where he stood and to be free to do all that was not covered by the regulations. Rabbis admitted that scriptural guidance was inadequate in the case of the Sabbath, and further rules on the matter were necessary (*Hag.* 1:8). Second, it was essential to know exactly what circumstances could release a person from the obligation to fulfill the Sabbath commandments. Guidance on these two questions was necessary in order that the righteous might conduct the private, social, and business concerns of their lives without fear that their actions were transgressing the will of God.

It would be wrong to think of rabbinic Sabbath regulations as a unity; difference of opinion was a hallmark of the rabbinic schools. This is clear from the conflicts between the schools of Hillel and Shammai, which offer different approaches to the obedience of the divine commandments. There was, for example, a dispute between the two houses over the extent to which ordinary activity was to be regarded as religious: "It was likewise taught: Beth Shammai say, 'From the first day of the week, prepare yourself for the sabbath.' Beth Hillel say 'Blessed be the Lord day by day'" (*B. Bes.* 16a).

In the saying of Beth Shammai the importance of the Sabbath is stressed; all else is subordinated to it. For Hillel, ordinary acts have a religious value in their own right, independent of the written commandments. Hillel thus sees the whole of human life as lived under the view of heaven. Consequently, mundane activities take on a significance that might place them on the same level as the regulations of the Torah. The way is open, then, for seeing a religious value in precisely those every day acts that ordinarily would be subordinate to the observance of the commands of the Torah.[12] Thus saving life and making a living to protect one's family from starvation become religious acts that could be regarded as sufficient reason to set aside aspects of the Sabbath laws.

The difference in attitude toward the Sabbath between Beth Shammai and Beth Hillel is further exemplified in a dispute recorded in the *Mekilta de R. Simeon b. Yohai* on Exodus 20:9. The liberal attitude of Beth Hillel is apparent:

> Six days shall you work and do all your labour. This is what Beth Shammai say: they do not soak ink, dyestuffs and vetches except so that they may be (wholly) soaked while it is day. And they do not spread nets for beasts and birds except so that they may be caught while it is day. . . . And they do not lay down olive-press beams or the wine-press rollers unless they flow while it is day. And they do not place meat, onion and egg on the fire while it is still day. . . . And Beth Hillel permit in all of them. Beth Shammai say: Six days you will work and do all your labour, that all your work may be finished by the sabbath-eve. And Beth Hillel say: Six days you shall work. You labour all six days and the rest of your work is done of itself on the sabbath.[13]

Beth Hillel here allows for the needs of ordinary life and gives positive value to what is done in the six days preceding the Sabbath. There can be maximum opportunity for economic activity without breaking the Sabbath.

A major concern of the Halakah was to enable the individual to avoid inadvertent transgression of the commandments. For example, it is stated that "a tailor should not go out with his needle near to nightfall, lest he forget and go out" (*M. Shabb.* 1:3). This is designed to prevent accidental transgression of the command of Jeremiah 17:22. Much space is devoted to this matter at the opening of this tractate in the Mishnah. Exactly what constituted a violation of this law is explained in *Shabbat* 1:1:

> If a poor man stood outside (a house) and the householder inside, and the poor man stretched his hand inside and put anything into the householder's hand, or took

anything from it and brought it out, the poor man is culpable and the householder is not culpable; if the householder stretched his hand outside and put anything into the poor man's hand, or took anything from it and brought it in, the householder is culpable, and the poor man is not culpable. But if the poor man stretched his hand inside and the householder took anything from it, or put anything into it, and (the poor man) brought it out, neither is culpable; and if the householder stretched his hand outside and the poor man took anything from it, or put anything into it and (the householder) brought it in, neither is culpable.

There is a very fine line separating the culpable from the blameless person in this case. The action of the poor man who stretched his hand inside a house and put something into the hands of the householder or took something out broke the law of Jeremiah 17:22. If, on the other hand, the poor man stretched his hand inside and the householder placed something into it, this was permissible, for the poor man is merely a passive recipient and considered innocent of carrying a burden out of the house. This kind of casuistry becomes important when precisely the situation envisaged becomes a reality. How can the individual keep the demands of the law and at the same time take care of his brother who is in need? The example given shows how practical concerns can be met without complete neglect of the demands of Scripture.

The problems presented by the regulation in Jeremiah 17:22 were also alleviated by means of the principle of *'êrub* (a term for various devices that justify certain activities on the Sabbath), which converted a number of homes into a single house for the purpose of the Sabbath obligation. The area within which burdens could be carried without breaking the Sabbath was considerably enlarged in this way. The joining together of several homes (e.g., all those sharing a common court) was achieved in principle by collecting all the food and placing it together to signify that the participants regarded the whole area as a common dwelling (*Erub.* 6–7). Another means of achieving the same effect was by shutting off a court or some other confined space by a beam of wood and a doorpost, thus making the whole area one common dwelling with a common entrance for the duration of the Sabbath (*Erub.* 1–2). The principle of *'êrub* was applied to the question of travel on the Sabbath as well, for this was a problem for the more rigid groups. By means of this principle of interpretation the rabbis made it possible to double the distance that could be traversed on the Sabbath.[14]

There was much discussion over the reasons for activities that superseded the Sabbath regulations. It was noted that the writer of Jubilees excused the activities of the priests who offered sacrifices in the sanctuary, and many rabbis realized that exceptions to Sabbath laws were necessary. One of the most famous passages dealing with this question is related in *Mekilta de*

R. Ishmael Shabb. 1., and concerns several prominent rabbis of the second century A.D.:

> Once R. Ishmael, R. Eleazar b. Azariah and R. Akiba were walking along the road . . . and the following question was discussed by them: Whence do we know that the duty of saving life supersedes the sabbath laws? R. Ishmael answering the question, said: Behold it says, If a thief be found breaking in (Ex. 22, 2), now of what case does the Law speak? Of a case when there is doubt whether the burglar came merely to steal or even to kill. Now by using the method of *kal wahomer*, it is to be reasoned: even shedding of blood which defiles the land and causes the *shekinah* to remove is to supersede the laws of the sabbath. . . . How much more should the duty of saving life supersede the sabbath-laws? R. Eleazar b. Azariah answering the questions said, If in performing the ceremony of circumcision, which only affects one member of the body, one is to disregard the sabbath laws, how much more should one do for the whole body when it is in danger. The sages, however, said to him: From the instance cited by you, it would follow that just as there (in the case of circumcision) the sabbath is to be disregarded only in a case of certainty. R. Akiba says: If punishment for murder sets aside even the Temple-service, which in turn supersedes the sabbath, how much more should the duty of saving life supersede the sabbath-laws. R. Jose the Galilean says, When it says, But my sabbath you shall keep, the but (*'ak*) implies a distinction. There are sabbaths on which you must rest, and there are sabbaths on which you should not rest. . . . R. Nathan says: Behold it says, Wherefore the children of Israel shall keep the sabbath to observe the sabbath throughout their generations. This implies that we should disregard one sabbath for the sake of saving the life of a peson, so that the person may be able to observe many sabbaths.[15]

This attitude, especially the final dictum of R. Nathan, is not dissimilar to that of Mattathias and his companions in 1 Maccabees, which caused them to take up arms on the Sabbath to ensure that they would be free to observe the Sabbath in the future (1 Macc. 2:41). The principles of Sabbath observance in this section are epitomized in the remark of R. Simeon b. Menasiah, which has resemblance to the saying of Jesus in Mark 2:27: "And ye shall keep the sabbath, for it is holy unto you. This means: The sabbath is given to you, but you are not surrendered to the sabbath."[16]

There were many traditions that helped give the Sabbath its distinctive character; on the eve of the Sabbath, for example, a lamp was lit.[17] This act was the responsibility of the woman of the house (*M. Shabb.* 2 and 6f.). The Sabbath itself was a day of festivity, and meals formed an important part of the day (*Mekilta de R. Ishmael Ki-tissa* 1). Fasting was not appropriate to it (Tos *Ta'an.* 4:13 and *B.Shabb.* 12*a*, *B. Ber.* 31*b*). The beginning of the Sabbath day was marked by a prayer of dedication over the wine (*Mekilta Bahodesh* 6; cf. Tos. *Ber.* 3:7 and *Ber.* 8:1), and at the end of the day there was a prayer separating the Sabbath from the coming week (*Ber.* 8:5).[18]

Rabbinic literature gives few details about worship on the Sabbath; more importance is attached to the proper observance of the day itself. E. Lohse has suggested (on the basis of *B. Pes.* 68*b*) that compulsory attendance at the synagogue was regarded as part of the Sabbath observance,[19] but the primary reference of this saying is to the festival days generally and not to the Sabbath. R. Joshua suggests that half the day should be devoted to God and half to oneself (cf. B. Nedarim 37*ab*). Clearly there was a difference in the lectionary for festival and the Sabbath (cf. *Meg.* 4:2), and Moore is probably right to stress that with the rise of the synagogue the Sabbath began to function as a day of religious instruction and edification.[20] In a later midrash (*Shir ha-Shirim R.* 8:13), R. Aha (c. A.D. 450) says: "So although Israel is occupied with its work for six days of the week, on the sabbath they arise early and go to the synagogue and recite the *shema*ʿ and pass in front of the ark and read the Torah and a passage from the prophets."

The centrality of the Sabbath for the rabbis is well illustrated by the penalties they prescribe for willful neglect of the commandments (e.g., *Sanh.* 7:4). Nevertheless, if a person acted in error without premeditation he was not subject to the death penalty; he was to offer a sin offering (*Sanh.* 7:8). The humanitarian approach of the sages can be discerned here. The Mishnah is more lenient than the writer of Jubilees 50:13 where the death penalty is prescribed for Sabbath breaking; the midrash on Numbers 15:32–36 reflects this leniency (*Sifre* on Num.).[21]

> And while the children of Israel were in the wilderness, they found a man gathering sticks on the sabbath. Scripture relates this incident to show up Israel's lack of piety: they kept only one sabbath, the second they profaned. And they who found him gathering sticks brought him to Moses. Why is it repeated? It implies that the man had been warned beforehand concerning works of this kind that are prohibited on the sabbath. Hence the rule concerning all those chief works,[22] which according to the Torah are not to be done on the sabbath, that a warning must be given first.

The fact that the biblical passage repeats that the man was found gathering sticks is taken as an indication that it is necessary to give a warning to an individual before the extreme penalty is exacted. The leniency, therefore, is justified because it is suggested in the detail of the Scripture itself.

Philo

Philo Judaeus represents the position of the Jew in the Diaspora; he lived in Alexandria in the middle of the first century A.D. Philo allows us insights into the life of a Jew who lived in a Gentile environment and had to justify his religion to his neighbors who were often hostile to Judaism. The observance of the Sabbath in particular was open to abuse from pagan writers.[23]

The fact that the Sabbath was the *seventh* day of the week was of great significance to Philo; he devotes much space to a discussion of the properties and symbolic value of the number seven (*Op.* 90ff.; *Spec. Leg.* II, 56ff.; *Leg. Alleg.* I, 8). One of the taunts of non-Jews was that Jews were lazy and the observance of the Sabbath was merely a way of avoiding work (*Spec. Leg.* II, 60). Philo points out, however, that the purpose of the Sabbath is to give men relaxation so as to send them out refreshed to their accustomed activities. Prohibitions against physical labor did not hinder the exercise of the mind; Jews spent some of their time studying ancestral philosophy. Study was related to God's contemplation after creation: "On the seventh day God ceased from his works and began to contemplate what had been so well created, and, therefore, he bade those who would live as citizens under this world-order follow God in this as in other matters" (*Decal.* 97).

The seventh day, therefore, was to be devoted to the "study of wisdom" and as reflection on the activities of the week. People had to determine whether any offense had been committed and exact from themselves,

> in the council chamber of the soul with the laws as their fellow-assessors and fellow-examiners, a strict account of what they had said or done in order to correct what had been neglected and take precaution against repetition of sin.

In working six days and spending the seventh in reflection, Philo saw a proper balance between the practical and contemplative aspects of life. Only with a proper balance between the two can a properly ordered life be lived. Philo had more to say elsewhere about the Sabbath (*Mos.* II, 216). He chided those who occupied their leisure time in sport and entertainment through which the soul is reduced to slavery, and recommended instead the pursuit of wisdom, which involved not the study of secular philosophy but the ancestral wisdom of the Jewish nation. Philo called the Jewish places of prayer in the cities of the hellenistic world "schools of prudence and temperance." It would appear, therefore, that Philo presumed that at least part of the Sabbath was to be spent in the synagogue studying the "ancestral philosophy."

For Philo, the Jewish synagogue was a paradigm for all who wished to lead a sensible life (*Spec. Leg.* II, 60). On the Sabbath the Jews pursued a life of contemplation, and as a result their minds were perfected. In his attempts to justify the Jewish Sabbath, Philo placed less emphasis on rest and more on the study of ancestral philosophy. This emphasis on the activity within the synagogues on the Sabbath must be understood as an apology in the light of the taunts made against the Jews. He was anxious to show the value of what the Jews accomplished week by week, and this would not have been possible if he had placed greater emphasis on the element of rest from work, which is the major preoccupation of the rabbinic material.

Despite the universal significance that Philo attributed to the Sabbath (e.g., in *Op.* 89, where it is called "the festival of the universe"), it would be wrong to suppose that he intended the Sabbath to be universally binding regardless of religious affiliations. It is obvious that the God-fearers (proselytes who attended the synagogue) would have observed the Sabbath (e.g., Acts 13:16), but it is to be doubted that they were encouraged to do so because it was an obligation for all creation and not merely for the Jews.[24] While Philo encouraged all men to keep the Sabbath, it is clear that he did not distinguish the command to keep the Sabbath from the other commandments, as the phrase *καθάπερ ἐν τοῖς ἄλλοις* (*Decal.* 98) shows. Philo regarded the Decalogue as the source of all the legislation in the Torah (*Decal.* 19 and 154),[25] but there does not appear to be evidence that he distinguished the Sabbath law as universal, rather than mere ancestral custom. Jewish Sabbath practice was justified and recommended to non-Jews, all part of the necessary apologetic activity in which Egyptian Judaism was much involved.[26]

Conclusion

Various Jewish approaches to the observance of the Sabbath resulted in a variety of regulations with varying degrees of complexity. The many practical problems that arose in everyday life indicated that the biblical regulations were either too vague or too stringent to be applied under changed social conditions. We saw how the problem was resolved by one group during the Maccabean struggle and how the rabbis sought to make the Torah applicable to every generation. It is tempting to regard some of this rabbinic legislation as circumvention of the Torah. This judgment, however, fails to take into account the factors that necessitated such an approach. The non-Jew may react unfavorably to the concept of *'êrub*, but the device was intended to make the will of God relevant to ordinary people with problems in the fulfilling of biblical regulations. The attempt by the rabbinic schools to meet the needs of such people was based on the conviction that the Torah did in some way speak to every human situation.

The concern of the rabbis was to make God's will a possibility for their own generation; they did not have the same tendencies toward obscurantism or literalism found in the Sabbath regulations of some conservative groups that took an unrealistic approach. The fact that many of these conservative groups were isolated from the Gentiles and even from community life meant that they could espouse a more literal approach to the biblical laws. The living conditions of most ordinary people, however, prevented such literal observance. For them the pressures of earning a living and even mere subsistence demanded a more human approach to Sabbath observance, in which the spirit of the law, if not its letter, was observed. Clearly, the Halakah, however hypothetical some of the examples may have been, recognized the desire of the individual to obey God; at the same time it reckoned with the difficulties in seeing that life of obedience merely as an exact repetition of the biblical laws. The complexities of Jewish Sabbath practices are to be understood as sincere attempts to translate the revealed will of God into the complex social setting of the Hellenistic world.

Notes

[1]On this see L. Finkelstein, *The Pharisees* (Philadelphia: Jewish Publication Society of America, 1962).

[2]For a concise summary see J. W. Doeve, *Jewish Hermeneutics in the Synoptic Gospels and Acts* (Assen: Van Gorcum, 1954), p. 52ff. See also W. Bacher, *Die exegetische Terminologie der jüdischen Traditionsliteratur* (Leipzig: J. C. Hinrichs, 1905).

[3]According to Rabbi the Sabbath commandment is equal to all the commandments of the Torah (*j.Ber.* 3*c*), see further E. E. Urbach; *The Sages; Their Concepts and Beliefs* (Jerusalem: Magnes Press, 1976), p. 348; and G. F. Moore, *Judaism in the First Centuries of the Christian Era* (Cambridge, Mass.: Harvard University Press, 1927), 2:16. See further R. Goldenberg 'The Jewish Sabbath in the Roman World Up to the Time of Constantine the Great,' in ed. W. Haase *Aufstieg und Niedergang der römischen Welt* II.19:1 (Berlin/New York, 1979), pp. 414ff.

[4]On the setting of these works see L. Rost, *Judaism Outside the Hebrew Canon: An Introduction to the Documents* (Nashville: Abingdon, 1976), pp. 129ff., 169ff. On the Sabbath at Qumran see L. H. Schiffman, *The Halakhah at Qumran* (Leiden: E. J. Brill, 1975); S. T. Kimbrough, "The Concept of Sabbath at Qumran" *RQ* 5 (1962): 483ff.; and C. Rabin, *The Zadokite Documents* (Oxford: Clarendon Press, 1954).

[5]The question whether God keeps the Sabbath is discussed in John 5:17 and by Philo. The latter rejects the idea in *Leg. Alleg.* 1, 5ff. as also does *Shem.R.* 30:9 where, by application of the concept of *'êrub* it is stressed that God is permitted to work both in heaven and on earth on the Sabbath.

[6]See Schiffman, *The Halakhah at Qumran*, p. 126f.

[7]Ibid., pp. 91ff.

[8]On the link between the Essenes and the Qumran community see the most recent restatement in G. Vermes, *The Dead Sea Scrolls: Qumran in Perspective* (Cleveland: Collins World, 1977), pp. 116ff.

[9]"Now these laws they are taught at other times, but most especially on the seventh day, for the seventh day is accounted sacred, on which they abstain from all other employments and frequent the sacred places which are called synagogues, and there they sit according to their age in classes, the younger sitting under the elder, and listening with eager attention in seemly order. Then one takes up the (holy) books and reads to them, and another of the men of the greatest experience comes forward and explains what is not very intelligible, for a great many precepts are delivered in enigmatical modes of expression and allegorically as the old fashion was; and thus the people are taught piety and holiness and justice" (*Om. Prob. Lib.* 81).

[10]It should also be noted that in one of the liturgical fragments mention is made of hymns for the Sabbath: see M. Baillet, "Un recueil liturgique de Qumrân, Grotte 4: Les paroles des luminaires." *RB* 68 (1961): 212.

[11]In this essay the word "Pharisee" is used to denote the predecessors of the rabbinic tradition before the fall of Jerusalem in A.D. 70, though it is recognized that the precise relationship between the rabbis and the Pharisees is not completely clear. On this see J. Neusner, *The*

Rabbinic Traditions about the Pharisees before 70 (Leiden: E. J. Brill, 1971), especially volume 3. But compare E. Rikin, *Hidden Revolution* (Nashville: Abingdon, 1978)

[12]On this passage see Urbach, *The Sages: Their Concepts and Beliefs*, pp. 340–41.

[13]The translation is taken from Neusner, *The Rabbinic Traditions about the Pharisees*, 2:10–11.

[14]In Schiffman's opinion the Qumran Sabbath *halāḵāh* probably antedates the evolution of the device of *'êrub: The Halakhah at Qumran*, p. 133. The root ערב is used at CD 11:4–5, but there is no question of any reference to the technical term here (so also Schiffman, *The Halakah at Qumran* p. 109, n. 167).

[15]Translation from J. Z. Lauterbach, *Mekilta de R. Ishmael* (Philadelphia: Jewish Publication Society of America, 1935).

[16]Further exceptions can be found in *Shabb.* 16:1ff. and in H. L. Strack and P. Billerbeck, *Kommentar zum Neuen Testament aus Talmud und Midrasch* (München: C. H. Beck, 1926), 1:618, 623ff.

[17]On the Sabbath light see Finkelstein, *The Pharisees*, and Lauterbach, "The Sabbath," in *Rabbinic Essays* (Cincinnati: Hebrew Union College Press, 1951).

[18]Further details in I. Elbogen, *Der jüdische Gottesdienst in seiner geschichtlichen Entwicklung* (Frankfurt: J. Kauffmann, 1931), p. 107ff.

[19]Article *σάββατον*, *TDNT* 7:15. Also of interest is the brief account of the Sabbath and its worship in Josephus, *Contra Apionem* ii.175, and further A. Schlatter, *Die Theologie des Judentums nach dem Bericht des Josefus* (Gütersloh: C. Bertelsmann, 1932), p. 101f.

[20]*Judaism in the First Centuries*, 2:38–39.

[21]Translation from P. Levertoff, *Midrash Sifre on Numbers* (London: SPCK, 1926).

[22]On the chief works prohibited on the Sabbath see *Shabb.* 7:2, and Moore, *Judaism in the First Centuries*, 2:28. The incident in Numbers 15:32–33 is discussed by Philo in *Spec. Leg.* II, 65ff.

[23]On Gentile attitudes, see Lohse, *σάββατον*, 7:17, nn. 134–35, M. Stein, *Greek and Latin Authors on Jews and Judaism*: Vol. 1: *From Herodotus to Plutarch* (Jerusalem: Israel Academy of Sciences and Humanities, 1976), and Goldberg, *The Jewish Sabbath*, pp. 430ff.

[24]On the God-fearers and Jewish requirements, see SBK 2:719–72 and 3:36ff.

[25]See Urbach, *The Sages: Their Concepts and Beliefs*, pp. 360ff.

[26]Another example of this literature is the Sibylline Oracles: see J. J. Collins, *The Sibylline Oracles of Egyptian Judaism* (Missoula: Scholars Press, 1974). An example of an attempt to justify Sabbath observance to a Gentile is to be found in the legendary confrontation between Tinneus Rufus and R. Akiba in *Ber.R.* 11:5. On this type of story see Urbach, *The Sages: Their Concepts and Beliefs*, p. 107.

4

JESUS AND THE SABBATH IN THE FOUR GOSPELS

D. A. CARSON

D. A. Carson is Associate Professor of New Testament at Trinity Evangelical Divinity School in Deerfield, Illinois.

This chapter comprises exegetical examinations of passages in the synoptic Gospels that indicate Jesus' attitude toward the Sabbath. Although some critics will doubt that we can know anything of Jesus' own views on the Sabbath,[1] I do not share their scepticism. The authenticity of many of the sayings of Jesus is finding new defense,[2] but I shall argue the case only in particularly contested passages where the distinction between Jesus' teaching and that of the evangelist is of special importance.

This is not to overlook the contributions and peculiar emphases of the synoptists, still less to ignore the differences among them. That is why, after examining the relevant pericopes in order to discover what Jesus held concerning the Sabbath, it is necessary to adopt as a second approach a brief examination of the manner in which the synoptic evangelists use such material. Because Luke's material is treated with Acts in chapter 5, I shall restrict myself to comments on Matthew and Mark (Luke-Acts takes up one quarter of the New Testament, and Luke's attitude toward the law has come into dispute in recent years).

Jesus' attitude toward the law in general as reflected in the synoptic Gospels (especially Matthew and Mark) could easily call forth a large volume, but that would take us too far afield. On the other hand, it would be presumptuous to attempt a presentation of Jesus' attitude toward the Sabbath law without offering at least some guidelines as to how our findings fit into Jesus' attitude toward the law in general. At the risk of oversimplification, therefore, I have included a brief section (not prescriptive or detailed) on that broader question.

I shall also examine the Fourth Gospel, first focusing on the Sabbath pericopes, and then attempting to relate those findings to larger themes in John's presentation of Jesus.

Jesus and the Sabbath in the Synoptic Gospels

Mark 1:21–28; Luke 4:31–37[3]

We find Jesus teaching in a synagogue in Capernaum on the Sabbath.[4] The word διδαχή ("teaching") may refer to manner or content of speaking or both; Jesus evoked amazement because of His authoritative teaching. Just then (Mark has εὐθύς) a protest erupted from a man possessed by an unclean spirit. The details of the outburst are not significant for this inquiry except to note that the initial question, τί ἡμῖν καὶ σοί, means "What have we in common?"[5] Here it may bear the force of "Mind your own business!"[6] or "Why do you meddle with us?" The antagonism between the unclean spirit and Jesus sets Jesus apart, exposes His mission, and portrays His authority. The words ἦλθες ἀπολέσαι ἡμᾶς may be taken as a question[7] or as a defiant assertion: "You have come [into the world] to destroy us" (cf. Luke 10:18).[8] In any case, fundamental antagonism between Jesus, the Holy One of God who has come preaching the gospel (Mark 1:14), and the unclean spirits is thus set forth at the very beginning of Mark's Gospel—and that on a Sabbath day.

Because the text contains no hint of Sabbath *conflict* here, some have thought that mention of the day takes its significance from its eschatological relation to the overthrow of darkness and the introduction of messianic authority[9]—authority both in teaching (Mark 1:22) and in respect of demon forces (Mark 1:27).[10] The note of authority, and the uncertainty among the people as to its significance, are no less strong in Luke's account. Indeed, following as it does on the story of Christ's claims made on the Sabbath spent at Nazareth (Luke 4:16–31), there is even more of an excited messianic expectation pulsating through the narrative.[11] But no explicit connection between eschatological, messianic authority and the Sabbath is offered in the text itself, unless Luke 4:16–31 is taken as a reference to the messianic jubilee (cf. further discussion, below). Mention of the day, in Mark at least, is related solely (and somewhat casually) to Jesus' entry into the synagogue[12] to teach.

The fact that Jesus does not suffer public outrage for His exorcism cannot escape notice; perhaps no Pharisees were present, but in any case a synagogue ruler must have been present, and he could have opposed Jesus' Sabbath practices (cf. Luke 13:10–17). In what immediately follows,[13] Jesus performs another miracle, one of healing (Mark 1:29–31, Luke 4:8–39), and again there is no adverse reaction, although it may be argued that the miracle occurred in the privacy of a home.

The absence of opposition may, however, have a more comprehensive explanation. Up to this point Jesus has been scrupulous as far as the Torah is concerned, and has not clashed even with the Sabbath regulations of the Halakah. The Halakah was designed to put a fence around Torah while still leaving the people free to perform necessary tasks and (in the majority view) acts of mercy. It is doubtful that any consideration was given in the early stages to the legitimacy of Sabbath *miracles*, since the regulations dealt with *work* on the Sabbath. If the Halakic comments about healing were intended to govern medical practitioners and the ministrations of relatives and the like, it is hard to see how Jesus committed any offense at all. It appears, then, that Jesus' Sabbath practices were not reviled by anyone at first, until opposition began to mount and *Jesus himself* was reviled. At that point, the Sabbath legislation was used against Him, and attacks against Him were rationalized on the basis of the Halakah.

The next incident (Mark 1:32–34) is related to what precedes it by the words "That evening, at sundown," as well as by the reference to the door in 1:33 (presumably the door of the house of Simon and Andrew, 1:29). Luke 4:40–41 and Matthew 8:16–17 also suggest that what follows occurs at the close of a memorable day, although Matthew does not relate it to a Sabbath. Mark and Luke make it appear that the crowd waited until sundown, the end of the Sabbath, before they came to Jesus for healing, prompting G. B. Caird to remark, "The crowds were more scrupulous than Jesus and waited until sunset when the Sabbath ended before taking advantage of his healing power."[14] Such scrupulosity need not be with respect to healing alone; some would have had to break regulations concerning a Sabbath day's journey (one thousand cubits) to get to Jesus, and some of the patients presumably would have to be carried (φέρω, Mark 1:32, may mean either "bring" or "carry"), which would also violate Sabbath laws (cf. *Shab.* 7:2). The Evangelists themselves make no specific point with these details, but it is possible that they are already implicitly criticizing Pharisaic regulations that keep people from Jesus.

Finally, it is worth observing that the exorcism (Mark 1:23–28) was prompted by spontaneous demonic antagonism, and the initial healing (Mark 1:29–31) by an artless request. In neither case can there be any suggestion that Jesus was deliberately *provoking* a Sabbath confrontation.

Mark 2:23–28; Matthew 12:1–8; Luke 6:1–5. The questions raised by these pericopes are both intricate and far-reaching, and involve important theological, exegetical, and methodological differences of opinion.

Fifty years ago K. L. Schmidt called Mark's account "a capital example of a particular story that is not tied down to a specific time and place."[15] In terms of the specific time and place of the event, that assessment was correct; we are told only that it transpired in a field on a Sabbath.[16] Not a few scholars dismiss the narrative framework as artificially constructed to provide a setting for the saying of Mark 2:27.[17] But Taylor, noting other Sabbath controversies, remarks that because the church worshipped on the first day of the week from the earliest date (a point to be demonstrated in subsequent chapters), it was only natural that stories such as this would be preserved. Such considerations, he affirms, forbid the scepticism of Schmidt and Bultmann; and he adds, "The free use of the story of David corresponds to the manner in which He (Jesus) uses the Old Testament elsewhere, and the broad humanity is characteristic."[18] Some scholars, observing that Jesus is made responsible for an action of the disciples in which He did not participate, affirm that the story is composite.[19] But it must be obvious that a leader is often blamed for the conduct of his followers. Why should Jesus escape such criticism?[20]

The Greek ἤρξαντο ὁδὸν ποιεῖν τίλλοντες ("and as they made their way, [his disciples] began to pluck") could mean that the disciples began to make a road by plucking the ears of corn or perhaps that they began to advance by clearing a way for themselves in this manner. Jewett suggests that the disciples were making a road for Jesus![21] But how could a path be made merely by plucking the *ears*, and why was not the charge of "working on the Sabbath" clearer? The text means rather that the disciples began, as they went, to pluck and eat.[22] Nor should it be assumed that Jesus and the disciples were "really journeying from one place to another on the missionary work of the Kingdom," and along the way began to stave off hunger.[23] Such an approach hopes to invest the offense with kingdom significance. But then why are the disciples, and Jesus not accused of breaking the restrictions concerning a Sabbath day's journey? Why are they not traveling along the roads instead of wandering through grain fields? The scene is more plausibly a Sabbath afternoon stroll than a missionary expedition, and that is why the presence of the Pharisees is not strange.[24] The offense, then, is in the harvesting and preparing of food on the Sabbath and nothing else.[25] Gleaning itself was allowed (Deut. 23:25), but on the Sabbath it might have been considered harvesting, and thus forbidden (Exod. 34:21).

Jesus replied to the allegation by referring to David and the consecrated bread (cf. 1 Sam. 21:1–7). This is not to be construed as a messianic allusion.[26] Nor is our Lord conceding the principles of the Pharisees for the moment, content to point out that such rules admit of exceptions.[27]

> Rather, the drift of the argument is that the fact that scripture does not condemn David for his action shows that the rigidity with which the Pharisees interpreted the ritual law was not in accordance with the scripture, and so was not a proper understanding of the law itself.[28]

Ransack the Torah as you will, it remains difficult to see what law was broken by the disciples. Regulations about harvesting and preparation of food seem to be given within a structure of "six days work and one day rest unto Yahweh." The Sabbath entailed a sweeping rest from regular work.[29] But in this instance the disciples are neither farmers nor housewives who are trying to slip in a little overtime on the sly; they are ex-fishermen and ex-businessmen, itinerant preachers doing nothing amiss (Matthew's account specifically acquits them; see further discussion, below). The Halakah, of course, has been broken, but it is precisely such legalism that Jesus repeatedly combats.[30]

The suggestion of some rabbis that David ate the forbidden bread on the Sabbath[31] (perhaps based on the fact that the consecrated bread was freshly laid out on the Sabbath), is irrelevant; David did not do something forbidden on the Sabbath but simply something forbidden. Besides, D. Daube has observed that a Haggadah (popular homiletic material) cannot properly serve as the basis for a Halakic proof from Scripture.[32]

Rordorf's handling of this passage requires special treatment. After examining how 1 Samuel 21:1–7 is used, he concludes that the lack of logical continuity between the problem and the citation makes it unlikely that the story was invented to provide a setting for the quotation (despite what Bultmann says), "since we should have to admit to some surprise that a more suitable setting had not been selected."[33] On the other hand, he argues that the incident and the quotation have not belonged together from the beginning, because Mark does not mention the word "hungry" (Matt. 12:1), making the connection yet more tenuous. The addition of the word by Matthew is "an attempt to assimilate the story of the plucking of the ears of corn to the quotation from scripture." Hence he states that the quotation and the narrative "illustration" in Mark 2:23–26 (and parallels) "are clearly (!) inappropriate to the account of the sabbath break and its justification,"[34] and "supposes" that Jesus' original answer is preserved in Mark 2:27.

Rordorf's whole argument turns on the word "hungry"; and to this we may reply: (1) For what reason other than hunger would the disciples be picking heads of grain? Is it not obvious that they were hungry? The *most* that can be inferred from Matthew's insertion of the word is that he has made the matter explicit.[35] The word itself bears no theological significance, and Luke confirms this opinion; he says that the disciples were rubbing and *eating* the grain. On the other hand, one must not overplay the hunger. Sabbatarian apologists sometimes see in the disciples' hunger adequate reason to call their plucking a work of "necessity" or "mercy."[36] This is highly dubious. Jesus does not use this recognized and acceptable argument here, even though He does in other circumstances, besides, it is unlikely that their hunger—of a day's duration at most—is to be compared with that of David and his companions. (2) Jesus' reply (Mark 2:25–26) is typical of His other replies. He not infrequently avoids direct answers and gets to the root of the matter or else exposes the hypocrisy or false presuppositions of the questioner (cf. Mark 7:5ff.). Besides, as M. D. Hooker has pointed out, there *is* a coherent relation between the narrative and the scriptural citation in the pericope before us:

> Jesus' words about David relate how regulations which were made to safeguard something which is holy were set aside for David, who enjoyed a special position, and for "those who were with him"; he and they were allowed to eat what was normally permitted only to the priests. So now, in the case of Jesus and his disciples, the regulations which were made to safeguard something which is holy—in this case the Sabbath—are again set aside for one who is in a special position and for those with him. In this case, however, the reason is not any pressing need, but the fact that the Son of man is lord of the Sabbath.[37]

We are thus brought to the final sayings, Mark 2:27–28. Again there is considerable disagreement among scholars.[38] Not a few isolate these sayings from the cornfield episode.[39] Taylor advances four reasons for doing so, but all of them can be faulted: (1) He claims that Mark 2:23–26 reaches a climax with the question about David. But as we have seen, Rordorf questions this. More to the point, if the above analysis is correct, including Hooker's observations, the citation about David builds directly toward Jesus' authority as the Son of man. (2) The words "And he said to them" (καὶ ἔλεγεν αὐτοῖς) may be a formula of citation. So they may; however, they may suggest a small literary pause;[40] or if a formula of citation, they may indicate something Jesus said not infrequently, but in particular on this occasion.[41] (3) Although Taylor admits that 2:27 agrees with the ideas of 2:23–26, and 2:28 presupposes 2:27, Taylor assserts that 2:28 is awkward in its present setting. Unfortunately, he does not explain how or why; we shall shortly discuss ways of linking them. (4) The sayings of 2:27–28, he says, are gnomic as compared with the polemical utterances of 2:25–26. True, verse 27 (but not verse 28) is gnomic in *form*; but even formally gnomic sayings become highly polemical in the appropriate context. And 2:28, a christological claim with many implications, must be reckoned at least as polemical (from the perspective of the Pharisees) as anything that precedes it.

W. Lane argues that 2:27 is an authentic saying from another context, which is evidenced by καὶ ἔλεγεν αὐτοῖς. He takes the next verse (2:28) to be Mark's own conclusion to the entire pericope (2:23–27), not to 2:27 only.[42] However, a great deal depends on his handling of the "Son of man" saying at Mark 2:10, where he ingeniously argues that 2:10*a* is parenthetically inserted to explain the significance of the healing for *Christian* readers. Having thereby established that this one "Son of man" saying does not come from Jesus Himself, he is free to treat 2:28 similarly. This view is plausible, but not convincing; these would be the only instances in the Gospels where the expression was not from Jesus Himself as purported. Moreover, R. N. Longenecker has pointed out[43] that both Matthew and Luke take over Mark 2:10*a* as it is, awkward syntax included, treating it as a genuine self-designation, not a Markan editorial comment, which they would elsewhere drop. Hooker notes similarly, that although many commentators adopt Mark 2:27 as authentic and relegate 2:28 to the category of church-inspired polemic, the hard evidence—that Matthew and Luke preserve 2:28 but not 2:27—if anything argues the other way.[44]

Some have insisted that Mark 2:27 cannot be authentic because no Jewish teacher could have made such a remark, which, it is alleged, "sounds more like Protagoras of Abdera."[45] Rordorf agrees that the statement is in some ways unique, but still judges it to be authentic. He holds that 2:27 is nothing less than an entirely new principle, one that virulently attacks not merely the causistical refinments of the Pharisees but the Sabbath commandment itself.[46] On the other hand, following Käsemann,[47] Rordorf argues that 2:28 is a church-inspired weakening and limitation of what Jesus Himself meant in 2:27:

> The primitive Church obviously (!) found man's fundamental freedom with regard to the sabbath enunciated by Jesus in this passage to be monstrous. It certainly recognized Jesus' own freedom with regard to the sabbath; the primitive Church interpreted this freedom in a messianic sense and did not claim it for itself.[48]

Both of these approaches fail to give enough weight to the well-known rabbinic parallel, "The Sabbath is delivered unto you, but you are not delivered unto the Sabbath."[49] That there is new content and significance in 2:27 is not disputed, but the assertion that no Jew could have said them is simultaneously glib and doctrinaire.

We must inquire what 2:27 and 2:28 teach in their present context, whether or not they are a unity with the pericope.

A number of scholars understand both 2:27 and 2:28 to refer to man. In this view, the expression "the Son of man" is a mistranslation of the Aramaic;[50] however, it is difficult to understand how an answer to the effect that man as man is lord of the Sabbath would convince the Pharisees. The interpretation would have plausibility if 2:27 were originally a detached saying, but in that case Mark chose to express something simple in desperately obscure fashion—with all the difficulties of the "Son of man" concept. On the other hand, T. W. Manson argues that the Aramaic concept "Son of man" was mistranslated in 2:27 but correctly translated in 2:28; i.e., 2:27 should read, "The sabbath was made for the Son of man, not the Son of man for the sabbath."[51] Manson says that the Sabbath was made for the Jews (not for man in general), and that the Aramaic "Son of man" may refer to the nation collectively as well as to Jesus specifically. The view suffers from want of evidence that Jesus taught that the Sabbath was made for the Jews, as well as from the assumption that "Son of man" has corporate significance in the New Testament.[52]

Although Manson thinks the Sabbath was made for the Jews, others see in "man" (ἄνθρωπος) generic significance and conclude that the passage supports the view of the Sabbath as a creation ordinance. Lee's view is extreme. He thinks that 2:27 means, "Man was not made for the sabbath, but the sabbath was *made for* (that is, intended to be kept by) man."[53] This interpretation is, quite simply, contextually impossible, as it completely destroys the antithetic parallelism, and hence any contextual meaning in the verse. This is immediately made clear when the nonsense-question is raised. "How could man be *kept by* (which Lee takes to be the meaning of *made for* in the second line) the Sabbath?"

A milder form of the same argument takes 2:27 to mean that God established the seventh day for man and not man for the day, but then goes on to see secondary support for a creation ordinance.[54] Some continue to insist that ἄνθρωπος is generic in meaning.[55] It has even been argued that, since the rabbis believed that the Sabbath was given to Israel alone, the use of ἄνθρωπος in 2:27 is a rejection of the rabbinic view in favor of a "creation ordinance" for all men. I consider this argument to be precisely the opposite kind of misinterpretation to that of Beare and Gils discussed above. In the view of Beare and Gils, it was argued that no Jew could have uttered Mark 2:27; here, it is argued that 2:27 is a conscious adaptation of a well-known Jewish opinion. That there are rabbinic parallels to 2:27 is undisputed; whether 2:27 is a deliberate correction of such parallels remains to be demonstrated. It appears that the passage is simply not dealing with the extension of rabbinic maxims to the Gentile world, but in any case, to insist that ἄνθρωπος has generic and racial significance is without adequate contextual warrant.[56]

The "creation ordinance" view further argues that the verb ἐγένετο (became) could refer to creation, but could not refer to the giving of the law at Sinai. In other words, Mark 2:27 asserts that the Sabbath was made (ἐγένετο) for man at some particular point in time; linguistically, it is argued, that point in time could not be at the giving of the law.

But this argument is linguistically unsound[57] and fails to observe the context and form of 2:27. The verse is an aphorism. The word "man" is used neither to limit the reference to Jews, nor to extend it to all mankind; that question is not considered. Moreover the verb ἐγένετο is simply a circumlocution for God's action.[58] The meaning of the verse is that, "The absolute obligation of the (Sabbath) commandment is . . . challenged, though its validity is not contested in principle."[59] Jesus is not suggesting that every individual is free to use or abuse the Sabbath as he sees fit, but that Sabbath observance in the Old Testament was a beneficial privilege, not a mere legal point—an end in itself,[60] as the Pharisees seemed to think.

Verse 28 is even more sweeping. If the Sabbath was made for man, it should not be too surprising (ὥστε, so) that the messianic Son of Man, whose authority to forgive sins has just been emphasized (2:10) should also be Lord even (καί) of the Sabbath. Here, as in Matthew and Luke, "lord" (κύριος) receives the emphasis: "The Son of man controls the sabbath, not is controlled by it,"[61] and Jesus is that Son of Man. Is he also "Lord of the Sabbath" in the sense that he is to be worshiped? That is not demonstrably in view; but even so, the claim is momentous, and means much more than the mere authority to tamper with the regulations of the Halakah.[62]

> . . . if the Son of man is lord of the Sabbath—and is therefore entitled to abrogate the regulations concerning it if he wishes—then he possesses an authority at least equal to that of the Mosaic Law, a law which was not of human origin, but was given by God himself. Once again, therefore, the authority of the Son of man goes beyond any merely human authority: his lordship of the Sabbath is another element of the New Age, a part of man's restoration and God's activity ἐπὶ τῆς γῆς [on earth].[63]

At the same time, there is evidence for the fact that the Sabbath itself is associated with the theme of restoration and the messianic age.[64] Within such a framework the fact that Jesus is the Lord of the Sabbath becomes the more significant, for the very concept of Sabbath begins to undergo transformation. That Jesus Christ is Lord of the Sabbath is not only a messianic claim of grand proportions, but it raises the possibility of a future change or reinterpretation of the Sabbath, in precisely the same way that His professed superiority over the Temple raises certain possibilities about ritual law. No details of that nature are spelled out here, but the verse arouses expectations.

The setting of the incident in Mark and Luke is identical: it follows immediately our Lord's comments about new wine in new wineskins; i.e., "the Lord taught that He had brought a complete renewal of the religious forms and their application. And now He shows that this also applies to the keeping of the Sabbath."[65] But Luke has no parallel to Mark 2:27; the passage leaps from the David incident to the affirmation of the lordship of the Son of Man over the Sabbath, so that the pronouncement of the authority of Jesus stands out even more.[66]

Matthew's account is notable in several respects. Whereas neither Mark nor Luke includes a reference to time, Matthew 12:1 begins with the phrase "At that time" (ἐν ἐκείνῳ τῷ καιρῷ), i.e., Matthew links the pericope with what precedes: "it is at the time when Jesus sets his 'light burden' over against that of the Pharisees that the Sabbath conflict arises."[67] Further, although Matthew has no parallel to Mark 2:27, he records two extra arguments, adduced from Scripture, as part of Jesus' defense.[68] Besides the appeal to the historical books (12:3–4 and parallels), there is one to the Torah proper (12:5f.), and another to the prophets (12:7). The appeal to Torah adds a new thought. Formally speaking, the priests break the law every Sabbath because of the work they are required to do as part of the right worship of God (cf. John 7:22–23 for a similar argument). The point is not only that some laws by their very nature formally conflict with other laws, but that the more important law or principle takes precedence. In the Old Testament, this opinion entails a startling result: some men, namely the priests, break the Sabbath repeatedly, and yet are innocent. Indeed, if the Old Testament principle were really "one day in seven for worship and rest" instead of "the seventh day for worship and rest," we might have expected Old Testament legislation to prescribe some other day off for the priests. The lack of such confirms the importance in Old Testament thought of the *seventh* day, as opposed to the mere one-in-seven principle so greatly relied upon by those who wish to see in Sunday the precise New Testament equivalent of the Old Testament Sabbath. More important for the passage at hand, Jesus is saying that just as the Old Testament Scriptures made provision for a certain class of persons with authority to override the Sabbath because of their work, so Jesus Himself has the authority to override the Sabbath becaue of His work. This does not mean that Jesus here actually breaks the Sabbath or overrides it, at least as far as Torah is concerned, but it does mean He claims authority to do so, and in a sense questions the Pharisees' right to question Him.

The argument about the priests would be meaningless unless Jesus could claim at least similar authority; in fact, He insisted that something greater than the temple priests was present (whether the greater thing was the kingdom or Jesus,[69] the point is clear). In the apparent conflict between what Jesus and His disciples did and the Sabbath regulations, Jesus claimed the authority to supersede the Sabbath without guilt. It is not a matter of comparing Jesus' actions with those of the priests, nor is it likely that this is an explicit reference to Jesus as High Priest. Rather, it is a question of contrasting His authority with the authority of the priests.[70] This interpretation is reinforced by Matthew's use of 12:8.

But we must pause at Matthew 12:7. The quotation from Hosea 6:6 (already used at Matt. 9:13) accuses the Pharisees of being unmerciful. The tables are turned; the accusers (12:2) are being accused (12:7). Not only are the disciples quite innocent, but the Pharisees are quite heartless.

Matthew 12:8 has great significance, because of the word γάρ (for). If γάρ refers to 12:6, the thought pattern is very similar to the entire passage up to and including 12:7, which is the more natural way to take it, the idea is that the disciples are innocent *because* Jesus as the Son of Man is Lord of the Sabbath. What is potential in Mark 2:28 now becomes actual because it is spelled out.

> (The disciples) were indeed without any guilt with respect to the charge made against them by the Pharisees, "for" in picking and . . . eating this food they were doing what Jesus allowed and wanted them to do.[71]

Rordorf's understanding of this pericope is unusual. He writes, "Matthew thinks the disciples were guiltless (12:7) because they were hungry."[72] He goes on to insist that, whether the disciples were hungry or not, it is improper for Matthew to argue against the binding force of the commandment: they could have been reproached for not having prepared their meals the day before, or they could have fasted. Hence, following G. D. Kilpatrick,[73] he concludes that "Matthew here marks the beginning of a new Christian casuistry." But this line of approach is susceptible to many attacks. In the first place, although Matthew 12:7 does declare that the disciples were innocent, it does not establish their innocence by referring to their hunger. Such an inference is gratuitous in the light of the γάρ in 12:8; innocence is based on Christ's authority over the Sabbath. But even if this were not so, we may well ask what explicit Torah regulation has been broken (assuming that the laws about harvesting were given with the farmer, not the Sabbath stroller, in mind).

In all three Gospels, Jesus responds to the charge of Sabbath breaking by appealing to David's example, thereby showing that in principle at least the Sabbath law might be set aside by other considerations. In Matthew this point is reinforced by the addition of a further example from Torah itself. Mark alone records the saying about the purpose of Sabbath (2:27), but more or less the same point is made by Matthew where Jesus speaks of His easy yoke and then appends the quotation from Hosea about mercy. Matthew's concern for a liberalizing of pharisaic restrictions for the purpose of doing good is stressed also in the next pericope by all three synoptic Gospels (cf. discussion below) in the arguments for doing good on the Sabbath. Luke, by leaving out any form of Mark 2:27 and Matthew 12:5–7, jumps from the example of David to the lordship of Christ over the Sabbath, and thus may be saying in effect, "A greater than David is here." All three Gospels stress Christ's lordship over the Sabbath; Mark and Luke place the pericope after Jesus' remarks on new wineskins, and hint that in this area too Jesus makes things new. It is remarkable in all this evidence that neither Jesus nor His disciples appear to be guilty of transgressing any injunction of Torah, despite the implicit rejection of the Halakah.

One final observation may help to pave the way for subsequent discussion. In sabbatarian apologetic, it is common to distinguish between moral, ceremonial and civil law. The Sabbath commandment is then thought to be binding on all not only because it is alleged to be a "creation ordinance," but also because it is part of the Decalogue, which is classified as "moral." The distinction between moral, ceremonial, and civil law is apt, especially in terms of functional description, but it is not self-evident that either Old Testament or New Testament writers neatly classify Old Testament law in those categories in such a way as to establish continuity and discontinuity on the basis of such distinctions.[74] Even if such categories are applied, it should be noted that both David's law-breaking and that of the priests (found only in Matthew) come from *ceremonial* law. It is difficult, then, to resist the conclusion that their applicability to the Sabbath case puts Sabbath law in the ceremonial category with them.

Mark 3:1–6; Matthew 12:8–14; Luke 6:6–11[75]

The only word in Mark 3:1–6 that links this pericope with what precedes is "again" (πάλιν), which probably harks back to 1:21, unless, with Bengel, we take it to mean *alio sabbato* (on another Sabbath).[76] The verb παρετήρουν (they watched) (3:2) is not impersonal, representing a passive, nor is it general, meaning that everyone watched; the enemies who watched were the scribes and the Pharisees (cf. 3:6 with Luke 6:7).[77] In all three Gospels the malicious intent of the watchers is stressed, although the details differ. Mark implies that Jesus discerned the thoughts of the Pharisees, and Luke explicitly states that "he knew their thoughts." This increases the impact of Jesus' first command to the man with the withered hand, beckoning him into the glare of attention. "In sharpest contrast to the secretiveness of the spies, Jesus acts perfectly openly so that all may know His attitude in the matter."[78] Matthew is not interested in observing that Jesus read their minds, but brings the conflict into focus by recording the *voiced* objection of the Pharisees (their comment may have been prompted by the man's coming into the inner circle of the crowd). The miracle will provide a clear and decisive answer as to whether Jesus will perform healing miracles on the Sabbath or not. Mark and Luke (but not Matthew) emphasize in addition that Jesus Himself precipitates the conflict by calling the crippled man forward. The operative word is "precipitates," which must not be understood to mean "provokes," since the antagonism was already present as they watched for an excuse to destroy Jesus. Our Lord's action brings the matter into the open.

Jesus' reply (Mark 3:4) has called forth varied interpretations. Several commentators think that Jesus here teaches that failure to do good is itself an evil thing.[79] W. Manson writes:

> Nothing could better illustrate the uncompromising positiveness of Jesus' whole conception of moral obligation than the issue here formulated. Jesus will recognize no alternative to the doing of good except the doing of evil. The refusing to save life is tantamount to the taking of it. Therefore he invalidates at one stroke the do-nothing attitude, which, under cover of the principle of not working on the Sabbath, his contemporaries mistook for obedience to the will of God.[80]

This interpretation, however, is a trifle simplistic. In the first place, it fails to give sufficient weight to two exegetical points: (1) Jesus is talking about what is lawful (ἔξεστιν), not what is required, (2) Jesus' answer concerns what is permitted *on the Sabbath*, not what is demanded throughout all of life. Second, someone must decide what is good and what is evil, and the

Pharisees would surely argue that keeping the Sabbath is good, and breaking it is evil. In other words, even within Manson's framework of interpretation, Jesus' reply makes little sense, and does not really come to grips with the issues. Third, if the refusal to do good is itself evil, then no man ever has the right to any rest whatsoever, and that is patently absurd; Jesus Himself recognized the need for rest both of a physical kind (Mark 6:31) and of a more deeply rooted variety (Matt. 11:28–30).

Jesus' answer does indeed set doing right on the Sabbath over doing wrong, but His statement has a particular reference. It was wrong for the Pharisees to accuse Jesus. Jesus Himself, on the other hand, was about to do good by healing the man.[81] It may be objected that such an interpretation is too subtle, but it is difficult to see the force of the objection, since Jesus by His reply reduced His opponents to guilty silence when they might otherwise have argued that the man could have waited until the next day; his case was not urgent.[82]

Implicitly, of course, there is an attack on the Halakah, or at least on their application of the Halakah to this case. The Torah itself says nothing about healing on the Sabbath, but the rabbis interpreted healing as proscribed work (Exod. 31:14) and then modified this stringent rule to allow exceptions in a case of theatening death (e.g., *Shab.* 18:3; *Yoma* 8:6). But Jesus was not a medical professional or a ministering relative; He does not fit the usual categories. "Even from their own point of view the Pharisees must have found it difficult to call this breaking the Sabbath, for Jesus used no remedy, performed no action, simply spoke a word, and the man merely stretched forth his hand."[83]

Mark records (3:4) that Jesus looked around in anger and was grieved[84] by their insensitivity. It is difficult to be certain precisely what evoked this reaction from our Lord. It may have been the Pharisees' insensitivity to the needs of their fellow-men, or their hypocrisy about scrupulous Sabbath regulations when their avowed intent was to ensnare Jesus, or their failure to grasp the weighty matters of the Torah, or their blindness to the inbreaking of the kingdom and the witness of the Messiah's words and deeds.

And so the man was healed, and the cure itself was both an act of benevolence and a reply to their unbelieving accusation. This pericope, situated where it is in all three of the synoptic Gospels, serves as the climactic demonstration that Jesus is Lord of the Sabbath. Moreover, it is Jesus' attitude toward the Sabbath that fills the Pharisees with rage (Luke 6:11) and brings about the strange alliance with the Herodians,[85] a major factor contributing to the Cross, which begins to loom large on the horizon (Mark 3:6). Later, we must at least ask why, in the light of the fact that Jesus' actions on the Sabbath contributed to opposition against Him, the charge of Sabbath breaking was not levelled against Him at His trial.

The material found in Matthew 12:11–12 will be discussed later in connection with the parallels in Luke 13:15 and 14:5.

Mark 6:1–6a;[86] *Matthew 13:54–58; Luke 4:16–30*[87]

In Mark 6:1, the use of ἐκεῖθεν (from there) suggests that Jesus went from the home of Jairus in Capernaum to His home town of Nazareth. The reference to His disciples probably indicates that this was not a private visit, although Swete's conclusion is probably overstated: "He came as a Rabbi, surrounded by His scholars."[88]

Jesus apparently uses the Sabbath synagogue service as an opportunity to teach.[89] In Mark's account, astonishment and anger (6:2–3) prompt the reader to wonder if the sermon included distinctive messianic claims: such a supposition links Mark and Luke rather neatly. The words αἱ δυνάμεις τοιαῦται (what mighty works) do not demonstrably refer to miracles performed *on that Sabbath.*[90] The antagonism, therefore, has not been evoked by alleged Sabbath breaking by healing, but because the people are offended by Jesus' unique claims and authoritative teaching. The only answer is that home towns and near relatives will not honor local prophets; they are simultaneously so skeptical and so proud that they assume the prophet is putting on airs, especially if there is a suspicion that the prophet is an illegitimate child.[91]

That no opposition is aroused by alleged contravention of Sabbath law seems to be confirmed by Matthew's omission of the fact that it is a Sabbath. Mark's mention of this detail appears to be part of the rationale for Jesus' ministry in the synagogue rather than the cause of any antipathy. The same thing appears to be true of Luke's account, in which the addition of the words "as his custom was" (Luke 4:16) has the same function; it establishes the reason for Jesus' presence and ministry on this occasion.

Luke, however, does tell us more of the circumstances and content of Jesus' preaching. When he rose to read, the scroll of Isaiah was handed to him. Whether or not Isaiah 61:1, 2 was part of the prescribed lection for that Sabbath is impossible to say with certainty.[92] The original Isaiah passage describes Yahweh's ideal Servant; it promises release of the captives, return to Jerusalem, and a liberty like that of a year of jubilee. But the words are fulfilled in a higher sense in Christ, and it "is obvious that both figures, the return from exile and the release of the jubilee, admirably express Christ's work of redemption."[93] Such, at least, was the view of most older commentators;[94] and this interpretation has been revived by R. B. Sloan.[95] Even if Sloan forges too tight a link between Sabbath and jubilee (cf. M. M. B.

Turner, chapter 5 in this volume), nevertheless it is clear that the great eschatological event has arrived, and probably Luke is telling us that Jesus the Messiah brings with Him the climactic rest of the year of jubilee.[96] But the people, far from being intrigued and relieved by promise of rest, are incensed at the audacity of the claim, so much so that they almost commit murder on the Sabbath day. The primary offense does not concern the Sabbath regulations, but the messianic claim itself (Luke 4:18–21), including the reference to the extension of God's mercy in Old Testament times to non-Jews (4:25–27).

Luke 13:10–17

This is the last mention of Jesus' synagogue ministry in Luke. Jesus healed a woman who had been crippled for eighteen years. The duration of the infirmity is evidence that this was not an emergency case, even though it was tragic. Jesus took the initiative; no request from her is recorded. The cure drew sharp rebuke from the ruler of the synagogue, however. "He indirectly censures the act of Jesus by addressing the people as represented by the woman."[97]

Jesus addressed His opponents as hypocrites (*ὑποκριταί*), indicating that others were siding with the ruler of the synagogue, referred to in verse 17 as "his adversaries" (*ἀντικείμενοι*). Their hypocrisy is seen superficially in the fact that they profess zeal for the law when their real motive is resentment directed against the healer. Their own Sabbath behavior is inconsistent, they are prepared to untie an ox or an ass from its stall and lead it to drink on the Sabbath,[98] but they will not allow a fellow Israelite, a daughter of Abraham, to be released from her bondage to Satan.[99] There are two deductions that should be made *a minori ad maius* ("from the lesser to the greater"):[100] if an animal was to be helped, how much more a daughter of Abraham? and if being bound for a few hours and unable to drink should cause pity for an animal, how much more being bound by Satan for eighteen years?

Caird and others have argued on the basis of 13:16 that this pericope teaches that the Sabbath is particularly appropriate for the works of the kingdom.[101] However, under such an interpretation one might also conclude that the Sabbath is particularly appropriate for untying donkeys. It seems better to understand Jesus' argument that kingdom activity, as well as humane treatment of animals, must go on seven days a week.

Again, it is difficult to see how Jesus here breaks any precept in the Torah. Moreover, the initiative taken by Jesus testifies to His concern for getting on with His mission, rather than to any putative desire to rock the boat of legalism, otherwise Jesus might have noticed the woman during the week and then waited until the Sabbath to heal her. Although there is no obvious attempt to overthrow the Sabbath (even if the sensitivities of the synagogue rules are ignored), there is a hint that the real significance of Sabbath is release from bondage.

Luke 14:1–6

This pericope is peculiar to Luke. It was not uncommon to invite guests to dinner after the synagogue service,[102] but the man suffering from dropsy seems out of place.[102] Conceivably, he may have been invited in anticipation of a Sabbath violation, but one might have expected γάρ (for) in verse 2 in that case. Further, both "behold" (ἰδού, 14:2), and "let him go" (ἀπέλυσεν, 14:4), suggest that the man was not an invited guest.[103] The man may have been there seeking Jesus, like the woman in 7:36–38, and the "watching" of the Pharisees may have been broader initially, before it focused on the Sabbath healing question.

Jesus' question, "Is it lawful to heal or not?" is directed toward their critical thoughts, and is typical (cf ". . . to do good or to do harm?" [6:8] and ". . . from heaven or from men?" [20:4]). The alternative is clear, for even if they suggest that the man should wait until the Sabbath is over, they are in effect answering no to the question. The Pharisees can scarcely answer yes without removing their ground of complaint; they cannot answer no without appearing harsh. So they keep silent, thus forfeiting the right to criticize afterward.

Having cured the man, Jesus asked another unanswerable question; Which of them would refuse to rescue a son[104] or (even) an ox from a well, on the Sabbath? The form of the question suggests that Jesus was appealing to the actual practice of his opponents;[105] their guilty consciences render them quite powerless to reply. As in Matthew 12:11–12, the comparison between an animal and a man isolates the double standard to which Sabbath legalism had led. P. K. Jewett misses the bluntness of Jesus' words; he thinks it is difficult to justify the example Jesus gives because the element of emergency has been introduced. Therefore, he concludes that Jesus is really saying that each of His healings was an emergency healing.[106] But Jewett's approach is too subtle; Jesus does not argue that His healings are emergency cases, in order to submit to the framework of the Halakah. Rather, He performs what is good and defends it on the that ground, attacking His critics for their own inconsistency. Thus, He implicitly rejects the framework of the Halakah.

Matthew 24:20

Matthew alone preserves this reference to the Sabbath. It is not to be taken to mean that Jesus taught His disciples that any kind of travel, including escape, on the Sabbath day was wrong. He does not suggest they refrain from fleeing on the Sabbath, but presupposing that they will flee, He exhorts them to pray that their flight may be on another day. Nursing mothers (24:19) and winter rains and cold (24:20*a*) would slow them down and cause loss of life, and so also would the Sabbath regulations, since gates would be shut, shops would be closed, and there would be impediments for any who attempted to exceed the travel distance allowable on the Sabbath day.[107]

It is not legitimate to deduce from this passage that Jesus Himself never envisaged the abandonment of Sabbath. When Jerusalem finally fell, Sabbath keeping Jews (Christian or no) made up most of the population, so the Sabbath restrictions would be everywhere. In any case, to demand too much from this text is to demand that the text be adjudged anachronistic.[108]

Emphases in Mark and Matthew

Mark immediately refers to the beginning of the gospel (1:1) and, at the end of his prologue, outlines its basic content: "The time has come, the kingdom of God is near; repent and believe the gospel" (1:14–15; cf. 8:35; 10:29; 13:10; 14:9).[109] Thus, Mark immediately adopts an eschatological orientation, which proclaims that the long-awaited time *has come:* in Jesus, God is working out His ultimate purpose of victory.

This kingdom is seen in Jesus' works: we are immediately told of an exorcism (1:21–28), which establishes His authority (1:27). The initial drama is repeated many times (1:32–34, et al.). The fact that the first exorcism recorded by Mark takes place on a Sabbath (1:21) sets the stage for the Sabbath works and healings that follow (2:23–3:6). Before these are presented, Mark again stresses Jesus' extraordinary authority—authority even to forgive sins (2:10). When Jesus is questioned about His disciples' carelessness in regard to fasting (2:18–20), He replies that the joy of *His own presence* is more significant. Mark immediately appends the saying about new wineskins (2:21–22); not only are Jesus' person and authority central to the content of the "gospel," but there are new forms as well as new content. It is no accident that two Sabbath controversies immediately follow;[110] both of these pericopes focus on the saying that the Son of man is Lord of the Sabbath (2:28).

Even in the Sabbath controversy in Nazareth (Mark 6:1–6*a*), the central point is that Jesus is not honored as He ought to be. His own villages had no faith, in marked contrast to the faith exhibited at the end of the previous chapter (5:21–43). The different responses, however, reflect Mark's *Messiasgeheimnis* (messianic secret) theme;[111] they do not call in doubt that Jesus should have been better treated that He was.

Matthew does not introduce any Sabbath controversy until almost half way through his Gospel. Two Sabbath pericopes (Matt. 12:1–14), appear immediately after Jesus' invitation to the burdened and weary to find rest in His easy yoke. As if such a juxtaposition were not enough, Matthew then carefully points out that the Sabbath conflicts occurred "at that time" (ἐν ἐκείνῳ τῷ καιρῷ)—presumably at or near the time when Jesus had spoken of His rest. This is as much as to say that the rest He offers surpasses the rest that the Pharisees wanted the people to observe.

Bacchiocchi passes too quickly from similar observations to the conclusion that "Christ made the Sabbath the fitting symbol of His redemptive mission."[112] It is true that the "rest" of Matthew 11:28–30 refers to Jesus' teaching and mission,[113] and that this is linked in some way with the Sabbath, but there is a question about the nature of that link. Elsewhere, for instance, Jesus links His mission with the temple, but the temple is not a *symbol* of His mission but something that *pointed toward* His mission. Jesus, after all, sees Himself as greater than the temple (Matt. 12:6). Neither Stephen (Acts 7) nor the author of the Epistle to the Hebrews falsely construes the thrust of Jesus' thought in this regard. John admits that the relationship between Jesus and the temple was obscure until after the Resurrection (John 2:22), but it is not obvious that John's later understanding is a misrepresentation of what Jesus had in mind. Clearly, Jesus saw Himself as the focal point in redemptive history, for even the temple pointed to Him. In this sense, the temple does not now serve as the symbol of Christ's mission; rather, it lived out its life as a pointer toward Christ's mission.

This interpretation, to be valid must agree with the evangelists' presentation of the relationship between Jesus and the law. This thorny question I shall consider briefly in the next section. Perhaps it is worth noting in passing that at the Transfiguration (Matt. 17:1–8), the whole point of the Matthean account is that Jesus alone and not even Moses or Elijah is to be heard as the voice of God; "Listen to him!"[114]

By an analogous argument, then, it may be premature to conclude, with Bacchiocchi, that the juxtaposition of Matthew 11:28–30 and Matthew 12:1–14 suggests that the Sabbath is presented as the symbol of the messianic rest. Rather, the Sabbath is another of the Old Testament pointers to the messianic rest. Matthew 12:1–14 shows how the Sabbath was misconstrued and abused; the first of these two pericopes concludes by affirming the Son of man's lordship over the Sabbath, and the second pictures Jesus performing a messianic healing on that day. This, then, agrees with Matthew's fulfillment motifs. The gospel rest to which the Sabbath had always pointed was now dawning.

In short, as R. Banks says, Jesus "takes a position above [the Sabbath] so that it is incorporated into an entirely new framework and viewed from a quite different perspective. As a result, what is acceptable or unacceptable in the way of conduct upon it is defined in relation to an altogether new reference point i.e., Christ's estimate of the situation."[115]

JESUS AND THE LAW IN THE SYNOPTIC TRADITION (especially Matthew and Mark)[116]

Limitations of space require brevity; therefore, I treat this subject suggestively, not exhaustively. There is not room even to survey the multiplicity of ideas that have been advanced to express Jesus' view of the law. Even the last few years have witnessed the publication of several lengthy monographs on Matthew's presentation of Jesus and the law.[117] The following paragraphs indicate tentative conclusions; in particular, I am concerned to show how Jesus' attitude toward the Sabbath may be placed within a reasonable and believable description of His attitude toward the law.

Jeremias is correct when he warns us that in order to assess Jesus' attitude to the law, it is mandatory that we separate the Torah from the Halakah and examine them independently.[118] By the end of the second century A.D. the oral Torah (or Halakah) had come to be regarded as no less authoritative than the written Torah. Both, it was believed, were given to Moses on Sinai and transmitted down an unbroken line to the contemporary times. There is no compelling reason to think that such a view prevailed in Jesus' day, but at least the Halakah was widely accepted as authoritative, even if its authority did not equal that of Torah.

In general, Jesus rejects the Halakah in a radical way, without sympathy and without equivocation, especially when it conflicts with His own use of the Old Testament, or with His kingdom teaching.[119] For example, some of His most trenchant remarks deal with the *corban* casuistry (Mark 7:9–13, par.; cf. SBK 1:711–17; see also Matt. 16:5–12; 23:1–39, par.). A possible exception is Matthew 23:3; but the verse is limited by both the immediate context and the more extended one (e.g., Matt. 15:6), and indeed may be irony. It is certainly not meant to express an unqualified approval of the Halakah; rather, the stress lies in the second half of the verse with its sharp condemnation of the attitude of the scribes, an attitude that gives the lie to all their theology.[120]

On the other hand, Jesus' attitude to the written Torah is more positive and more varied. He cites the Old Testament frequently as the Word of God. "Only when this basic attitude of Jesus has been made clear can one assess what it means that Jesus should venture to make more radical, to criticize, indeed to supersede the words of Torah."[121] This includes intensification of Old Testament law (e.g., Exod. 20:13–14; Matt 5:21–22, 27–28) and repeal (e.g. Mark 7:14–23).[122]

The crucial passage is Matthew 5:17–20, and the operative word is πληρῶσαι ("to fulfill," v. 17). The verb has been interpreted in different ways;[123] but the most helpful suggestion has come from Robert Banks.[124] Many have noted that "to fulfill *prophecy*" means to answer to it, to be the realization of it; the problem is how to understand what "to fulfill the *law*" can mean.[125] Resort is commonly made to "inner-outer" distinctions; Jesus has come to show what the law really means.[126] Others say that Jesus "fulfills" the law in that He performs it perfectly. Banks, however, argues that the same thing applies to law as to prophecy;[127] he interprets the verb eschatologically. Matthew elsewhere explicitly insists that both the prophets and the law *prophesy* (11:13).

> The word "fulfill" in 5:17, then, includes not only an element of discontinuity (that which is more than the Law has now been realised) but an element of continuity as well (that which transcends the Law is nevertheless something to which the Law itself pointed forward).[128]

In short, the antithesis of 5:17 is not between abolishing the law and preserving it in the same form, but between abolishing it and fulfilling it. I have elsewhere argued that

> Jesus does not conceive of his life and ministry in terms of *opposition* to the Old Testament, but in terms of *bringing to fruition* that toward which it points, Thus, the Law and the Prophets, far from being abolished, find their valid continuity in terms of their outworking in Jesus. The detailed prescriptions of the Old Testament may well be superseded, because whatever is prophetic must be in some sense provisional. But whatever is prophetic likewise discovers its legitimate continuity in the happy arrival of that toward which it has pointed.[129]

Within this interpretive framework, the next verse, Matthew 5:18, will not require efforts to restrict the extent of its reference (an iota or a dot). Some have said that it is only the moral law that will not pass away (e.g., J. Hänel; M.-J. Lagrange); others say the wholeness of the law without reference to details is intended (e.g., H. Ljungman; K. Benz); another view is that the Decalogue and/or love commandments are permanent (S. Schulz), and some scholars dismiss the saying as barbed irony aimed at the Pharisees (T. W. Manson). The whole law (Old Testament Scripture?—so A. Schlatter) will not pass away, until "heaven and earth pass away," "until all is fulfilled, accomplished." The first qualifying clause may be a rhetorical figure that emphasizes how hard it is for the law to pass away;[130] but objections have been offered against that view.[131] The second, I submit, clarifies the problem; it refers to the fulfillment of Old Testament Scripture in the person and work of Christ.[132] If we understand this fulfillment to take place in the ministry, passion, resurrection, and exaltation of Jesus as well as in His subsequent reign *culminating in the age to come,* then the phrase "until heaven and earth pass away" may be taken literally. Some of the law is fulfilled immediately in the coming of Christ and the dawning of His kingdom; some of the promises must await the return of Christ for their fulfillment. It is in this sense that the second clause clarifies the first.[133]

E. Lohmeyer, J. M. Gibbs, and R. Banks,[134] then go on to argue that the best contextual sense of "one of the least of these commandments" in 5:19 is that Jesus is not referring to Old Testament law, but to his own teaching. Other features, at first glance, appear to support this view. For example, although ἐντολή ("commandment") commonly refers to Old Testament commandments, it can be used of Jesus' commands (cf. 28:20, as a verb); and ἀνομία ("lawlessness") occurs more frequently with respect to Jesus' commands than with respect to the Old Testament. In context, "these commandments" might be thought to contrast with "law." Moreover, those who keep these commandments are ranked within the kingdom, and as a group are set over against the Pharisees and scribes who do not enter it (5:20). All three Synoptists record that Jesus insisted His own words would not pass away (Matt. 24:35; Mark 13:31; Luke 21:33). In other words, Jesus not only "fulfills" the law and the prophets in the sense outlined above, but His own teaching has full divine authority behind it. Nevertheless, a small refinement removes the awkward fact that in Matthew ἐντολή nowhere clearly refers to Jesus' teaching; we ought to understand that in 5:19 it does not refer to Old Testament commandments over against Jesus' teaching, nor to Jesus' teaching over against Old Testament commandments, but rather to Old Testament law in the relation to Jesus' teaching, which has just been described in the previous two verses.[135]

In this interpretive framework, Matthew 5:20 makes admirable sense. Jewish readers would not be likely to take it to mean that the kingdom of heaven can be attained only by a stricter observance of the rules than that practiced by the scribes and Pharisees. What is needed is greater righteousness than theirs, greater than that which can be obtained by keeping rules. How this is obtainable comes out of the corpus of the teaching of *Jesus,* who has come to fulfill the *law and the prophets.* The clear implication of such stupendous authority is that it must be nothing less than divine; for was not the mosaic law divine in origin?

The development of the distinctions "moral law," "ceremonial law," and "civil law," is traced in later chapters of this volume, but it must be insisted that to read such categories back into Matthew 5:17–20 and conclude that only moral law is in view would be anachronistic. This is not to deny that Jesus Himself makes no distinctions whatever in Old Testament law,[136] nor to say that the distinctions are always invalid. Rather, it is to say that the New Testament writers do not in any case appear to establish patterns of continuity or discontinuity on the basis of such distinctions. Certainly the phrase "an iota or a dot" excludes any interpretation of the passage that claims that only "moral" law is in view.

I am aware how uncertain the results of the exegesis of this difficult passage must remain. Nevertheless, it must be vigorously insisted that sabbatarian appeal to the eternal validity of the Old Testament law—including Sabbath law—on the basis of Matthew 5:17–20 bristles with problems. If "abolish" in 5:17 is given absolute force, for example, consistency demands the conclusion that our Lord's abolition of the food laws was a mistake. And if, instead, "fulfillment" is taken to mean something like "show what the true meaning is," that same interpretation must be applied to Old Testament Sabbath law as well—and then we are back to our attempt at surveying just how the New Testament takes up the Sabbath theme. Matthew 5:17–20 is a difficult passage of primary importance in trying to understand Jesus' attitude to the law. But it is not a panacea for any particular hard-pressed interpretation of how the New Testament writers view the Sabbath, despite the impression given by certain Sabbatarian publications.

Part of the problem in grappling with Jesus' view of the law is that although Jesus Himself lived under the old covenant, He was the messenger of the new, and actually introduced the eschatological aeon by His death, resurrection, and exaltation. The Christian community, then, becomes the heir and the validation of God's promises.[137] We have already noticed that Jesus clearly and authoritatively modified, intensified, repealed, or invested with deeper meaning, various parts of the Old Testament, but there is no undisputed example of a specific precept of the written Torah that He Himself actually contravened.[138] Rather, Jesus' authoritative teaching *anticipates* the change, which does not actually come until the Resurrection. As Paul puts it, Jesus was "born under the law" (Gal. 4:4). Hence, Jesus demands that the temple be hallowed (Mark 11:15–18 par.; Matt. 23:16–22); He even extends His comments to sacrificial worship (Matt. 5:23–24). Yet at the same time He predicts that the temple is doomed, on its way to collapse, and then insists that the real temple is His body. Our Lord in such fashion gathers up the law in Himself, recapitulating Israel's history and taking over its institutions in His own being (a theme especially important in Matthew and John).

> Thus it was Jesus himself who shook the foundations of the ancient people of God. His criticism of the *Torah* [I doubt that this phrase is accurate]; coupled with his announcement of the end of the cult; his ejection of the *Halakah* and his claim to announce the final will of God, were the decisive occasion for the action of the

> leaders of the people against him, finally brought into action by the cleansing of the Temple. They took Jesus to be a false prophet. . . . This accusation brought him to the cross.[139]

The general argument may be established from a broader scrutiny of the Gospels. Although I am not entirely satisfied with all of R. Banks's conclusions, his central points are, I think, amply justified by the evidence. Throughout the synoptic tradition, the person and ministry of Christ dominate, and the law as a whole points to, prophesies of, and anticipates Him. But He Himself teaches like a sovereign, not like the teachers of His day (Mark 1:27). If we may adopt the standard dogmatic categories, even the "moral law" within the Torah points prophetically to Jesus' teaching and lives on in His teaching. This in no way denies that there is an eternal moral law bound up with the character of God. What it does rather is to try to approach the Old Testament from Jesus' perspective as that perspective has been preserved for us, so that the bounds of the "moral" content of the law, as those of any other content, are determined finally by reference to Him.

Jesus' view of the law appears to be ambivalent: He emphasizes that it is from God and that Scripture cannot be broken; yet in another sense, "law" continues only until John, and then the kingdom to which it points takes over. Although this is emphasized in Matthew, it is not peculiar to his gospel, for Jesus is the eschatological center of Mark as well,[140] even though Mark does not treat fulfillment themes extensively. And in Luke, the fulfillment motifs again come to the fore, albeit with slightly different emphases (cf. Luke 24:27–44).

Into this matrix of relationships between Jesus and the law, Jesus' attitude toward the Sabbath fits coherently and consistently. And, along with Machen, Longenecker, Jüngel, Ridderbos and others, I submit that the teaching of Jesus in this area is the *presupposition* behind Paul's teaching on the law.[141]

The Fourth Gospel

Because Jesus' attitude to the Sabbath as recorded in John is similar in many respects to what is recorded in the Synoptics, the following remarks are restricted to what is distinctive in John.[142]

John 5:1–18[143]

The invalid whom Jesus heals in this chapter is singularly dull and backward.[144] He is skeptical when Jesus asks him if he wants to get better: the healing is due solely to the initiative of Jesus. Further, he lets his benefactor slip away without discovering so much as His name, and then, when he does find out, promptly informs the religious authorities. This background must be weighed carefully when we consider whether or not John expects his readers to believe that Jesus performed this miracle to *provoke* a confrontation. The man is so slow there is progress only when Jesus does seize the initiative (5:6–8, 14). Verse 6 suggests that Jesus saw the man there, and, as usual, brooked no delay in performing the cure. On the other hand, there was a multitude of sick, blind, lame, and impotent folk gathered at the same place (5:3). Does not the healing of one of them raise questions about the real motivation behind the cure?

Yet all this may be better explained in terms of the strong predestinarian note in this gospel.[145] Even the command to carry the pallet on the Sabbath day contravenes no clear proscription in Torah (although it is implicitly forbidden in *Shab.* 7:2, last item; and 10:5).[146] Moreover, elsewhere Jesus gives the same command to other paralytics when the Sabbath is not involved (Mark 2:9, 11, par.). In short, although it is remotely possible that Jesus is here presented as provoking a clash over rabbinical legalism about the Sabbath, there is no compelling reason to suppose He is precipitating a crisis over the Torah.

As elsewhere (cf. 9:14), John remarks that the day of the cure was a Sabbath only after the description of the healing itself (5:9). Carrying the pallet attracts antagonistic attention, and the healed man, not anxious to be a hero, promptly blames his benefactor. That the Pharisees probe the man about the person who commanded him to carry his pallet, but ask nothing about the healing (5:11–12), is characteristic of John, and is calculated to draw attention to their hypocrisy. It also suggests that the pallet-carrying charge was potentially more serious and less debatable than the charge of breaking the Sabbath by healing.

When Jesus finds the man again, He warns him not to sin any more lest something worse befall him. Although illness is not inevitably the direct result of sin (cf. 9:3), that is the implication in this instance; therefore this Sabbath cure is more directly related to the soteriological work for which the Lamb of God came into the world (1:29).

All this takes on added significance when we examine Jesus' reply to the Pharisees, "My Father is working still, and I am working."[147] The reply not only has eschatological significance,[148] but is also a claim to equality with God (5:18).[149] As such the answer is not far removed from Mark 2:28 and parallels; indeed, if anything it is weightier.[150] Instead of pointing out that He has not really broken the Torah even if He has transgressed Halakah, Jesus replies that He can work on the Sabbath because His work is of a piece with God's work. That work is more fully described in verses 19–29. Jesus' claim takes the discussion out of the realm of Sabbath controversy, which subject cannot properly be assessed until the claim is dealt with, and for this reason the theme of Sabbath drops from view (to be picked up again later, in chap. 7) as the Christological implications override it.

S. Bacchiocchi has rightly protested[151] against those commentators who insist that John intends by 5:17–18 to abolish the Sabbath. But he goes too far when he insists that John is in reality reaffirming the Sabbath, linking it to Jesus' redemptive mission.[152] To reverse a common phrase: Bacchiocchi is right in what he denies but wrong in what he affirms. It would be better to say that John, by taking the discussion into Christological and eschatological realms, does not deal explicitly with the question of whether or not Christians are to observe the weekly Sabbath. That question, however, might find an answer in relating John's treatment of the Sabbath to some larger Johannine themes.

In the light of the entire narrative, it appears that the Pharisees approach Jesus not only about the offense of His healing, but especially about the offense of His command to carry a pallet. If this be so, then Jesus' reply in 5:17 is designed to exonerate not only Himself, with respect to His own actions, but also the paralytic, since the "illegal" activity of the latter sprang from Jesus' work and word. The point to be noticed is that His claim affects not only His own conduct but also that of others.

John 7:19–24

These verses appear to refer to the healing in John 5. Jesus' argument about circumcision accurately reflects rabbinic theory.[153] The point is, once again, that some laws override other laws; and this is evidenced by "the Jews'" own practices, in which circumcision overrides Sabbath. Shall not an act as important as healing likewise take pride of place? What sort of Halakah is it which forbids making a man well on the Sabbath? The form of the argument is *a minori ad maius* ("from the lesser to the greater"); the content is barbed and directed toward the inconsistency of legalism.

John 9:1–41

Technically speaking there are several breaches of Sabbath Halakah here, apart from the healing itself. Mixing is forbidden (*Shab.* 24:3), and kneading is one of the thirty-nine classes of prohibited work (*Shab.* 7:2). Smearing the clay on the eyes of the blind man might well come under prohibited anointings (*Shab.* 14:4). Such rules, of course, are nowhere to be found in the written Torah.

The debate that develops between the tribunal of Pharisees and the once congenitally blind man serves to confirm what we have already learned about Jesus' attitude to the Sabbath.[154] We should notice, however, that it is the result of this conflict that draws from Jesus the condemnation of 9:39–41. The Pharisees think they have sight; they refuse to acknowledge their blindness, and therefore their sin remains. But even in the context of this chapter, it is not so much their unbending attitude regarding the Sabbath that prevents them from seeing who Jesus really is, as their implacable enmity toward Him. They deny the obvious evidence before them and use alleged Sabbath offenses as a basis for rejecting Him (9:13–16, 19). Some of the Pharisees are at first troubled by the apparent healing (9:16*b*), but the problem is resolved as skepticism wins the day (9:19). At issue again is the authority of Jesus; if the authorities admitted to the healing and therefore to the messianic implications that John sees, their own authority, including their interpretation of Sabbath law, would have to bow to Jesus. The Pharisees think they have light, light which includes their own interpretations; but they are blind to Jesus' person and work even while they are certain that they see, and so fall under the condemnation of 9:41. If, on the other hand, a person believes in the Son of man (9:35), he is given light to see, and in that case there is no more effort to resolve the alleged breaches; the authority of the Son of man overrides everything.

LARGER CONSIDERATIONS IN THE FOURTH GOSPEL

Wayne Meeks is correct when he writes:

> In each passage which mentions the Law or Scripture of Moses, the Fourth Gospel indicates a direct relationship between that Law and Jesus. The relationship is emphatically ambivalent. On the one hand, Jesus and his revelation stand over against or at least superior to the Torah (cf. 1:17; 8:17). . . . On the other hand, Jesus is the one of whom "Moses wrote in the Law" (1:45; 5:46), so that a faithful comprehension of "the Scriptures" would discover testimony to Jesus (5:39, 46–47).[155]

Pancaro has clearly shown that for the Christian Jews among John's readers, the Old Testament law was being followed in the teaching and praxis of the church, which enjoyed the *fulfillment* of the law brought about by Christ.[156] In short, the Christian understanding of the Old Testament was the only correct one.

But we may go further: since the publication of W. D. Davies's *The Gospel and the Land*,[157] scholars have been made sensitive to the *replacement* themes in John's Gospel, where various institutions point toward Christ, who in some sense *replaces* them. Some of these themes are explicit; some are merely hinted at. Jesus replaces the temple, various feasts, Israel as the vine, and so on. Against the prevailing view, some have suggested that even ἀντί (John 1:1b, "upon, against") refers to replacement rather than accumulation.[158] It is just possible that, in the Fourth Gospel, Jesus Himself replaces the Sabbath.[159] If so, it is a suggestion that owes most of its potency to its surroundings. If present, such a theme might well be linked with Hebrews 4.

Concluding Observations

We are now in a better position to formulate some of the findings that have emerged from this exegetical study and to tie up a few loose ends. No attempt is made to bring together all the relevant observations stemming from the exegesis; I shall merely try to pick up the most important threads of thought and weave them into a pattern that may be helpful as a background to chapter 12.

1. There is no hard evidence that Jesus Himself ever contravened any written precept of the Torah concerning the Sabbath.[160] Nevertheless, one must not make too much of this observation.[161] One dare not conclude on this basis that Sabbath observance is still mandatory. The same argument would require that we continue to sacrifice in the temple. Jesus' attitude toward the Sabbath cannot rightly be assessed apart from the consideration of His relationship to the law.

2. On the other hand, Jesus did contravene Halakic Sabbath regulations.[162] The rigor of the Halakah is contrary to the will of God as far as Jesus is concerned. "The rules about the Sabbath . . . are as mountains hanging by a hair, for (teaching of) Scripture (thereon) is scanty and the rules many."[163]

3. There is no compelling evidence that Jesus went out of His way to make Sabbath conduct an issue. Indeed, there is some evidence that hatred toward Jesus prompted the Pharisees' use of Sabbath regulations against Him, so that Jesus did not initiate these confrontations.

4. Some of the Sabbath controversies became springboards for messianic claims. This was only natural, since ultimately the question was part and parcel of Jesus' whole relationship to the law (the most important of these controversies are Mark 2:23–28, par., and John 5:1–47). The lordship of Jesus over the Sabbath is ultimate; and the insistence on this fact by all four evangelists moves the argument away from purely legal questions to essentially christological ones.

5. Jesus views the law as essentially prophetic of Himself and His ministry. It is within the framework of this central motif that other emphases are best understood; Jesus' attitude toward the Sabbath is most readily understood as an example of this.

6. Although the Sabbath controversies contributed to the condemnation of

Jesus (Mark 3:6), the absence of any formal charge of Sabbath breaking at Jesus' trial is not surprising. There may have been difficulty in finding consistent witnesses (Mark 14:56–58) or the authority of Halakah may not at that time have been sufficient for the death sentence. Moreover, all but one of the recorded Sabbath conflicts concerned exorcism or healing, and it would not be psychologically advantageous to press such charges when there was so much in the defendant's favor. Blasphemy, temple destruction, and insurrection were perhaps much more promising.

7. It appears that much (but not all; cf. Mark 2:27–28) of Jesus' explicit treatment of the Sabbath is not so much in terms of *positive* formulation as in terms of *negative* formulation, i.e., He shows what is *not* meant by the law rather than what *is* meant by it. Nevertheless, there are suggestions that the Sabbath rest is intrinsically bound up with God's eschatological purpose of salvation. These hints come to clearest expression in John 5. Because the eschatological significance of Sabbath rest in the New Testament is being explored in chapter 7, I have merely touched on these points in passing.

8. There is no hint anywhere in the ministry of Jesus that the first day of the week is to take on the character of the Sabbath and replace it.

9. The first Christians would never have treated the Sabbath as a shadow of the past—as indeed they did—unless they had grasped the significance of Jesus' teaching in this connection.[164] But to enlarge on the Sabbath practice of the early church would be to step beyond the limits of this chapter.

10. In passing, one should also observe that although the mosaic Sabbath met a human need, so also did the law requiring the return of land in the Jubilee year, the prescribed punishment for blasphemy, and many of the food laws, etc. Everyone, including Jesus (Mark 6:31), would agree that human beings need rest; but that observation must not be used to introduce the notion that the mosaic Sabbath was therefore "moral" law, unless one is prepared on similar grounds to draw the same conclusion from all demonstrably useful laws in the Old Testament.

Notes

[1]E.g., R. Bultmann, *Jesus and the Word* (London: C. Scribner's Sons, 1958), p. 14.

[2]Cf. C. Hinz, "Jesus und der Sabbat," *KerDog* 19 (1973) p. 91. "Because of the freedom of the disciples with respect to Sabbath law the Pharisees and orthodox Jews took offense. But behind the controversy of the disciples' community stands the historical kernel of Jesus himself." On the general question of the authenticity of the sayings of Jesus, cf. R. T. France, "The Authenticity of the Sayings of Jesus," *History, Criticism and Faith*, ed. C. Brown (Leicester: Inter-Varsity Press, 1976), pp. 101–143; I. H. Marshall, *The Origins of New Testament Christology* (Downers Grove: InterVarsity Press, 1976), pp. 43–62; and, with respect to the Gospel of John, D. A. Carson, "Historical Tradition in the Fourth Gospel: After Dodd, What?" *Gospel Perspectives*, Vol. 2, ed. R. T. France and David Wenham (Sheffield: JSOT Press, 1981), pp. 83–145.

[3]R. Bultmann, *The History of the Synoptic Tradition* (Oxford: Blackwell, 1963) pp. 208–209, identifies this pericope as a "miracle-story" and considers it irrelevant to Jesus' view of the Sabbath. Because its form does not meet all of M. Dibelius's specifications, he calls it a paradigm "of a less pure type" (*From Tradition to Gospel* [London: Ivor, Nicholson and Watson, 1943], p. 43). But form criticism is being abused when, instead of identifying forms, it begins to legislate what forms ought to be present, as Bultmann then attempts to do. Cf. C. E. B. Cranfield, *The Gospel According to St. Mark* (Cambridge: Cambridge University Press, 1972), p. 71: "To try to force this section into conformity with the specifications of a form-critic's ideal miracle-story by the use of Procrustean methods is doctrinaire. The truth is that we have here a story more primitive than the rounded form of the common miracle-story. . . ." Similarly, V. Taylor, *The Gospel According to St. Mark* (London: Macmillan, 1966), p. 171, concludes that the material is Petrine.

[4]The words *τοῖς σάββασιν* (Sabbaths) are plural only in form; *σάββατον* (Sabbath) is a second declension noun, but in the New Testament it has a third declension ending in the dative plural. "Successive sabbaths are not meant, for the plural is usual when feasts are mentioned" (Taylor, *The Gospel according to St. Mark*, p. 172). Cf. similarly *τὰ ἄζυμα* (Jewish Feast of Unleavened Bread), *τὰ ἐγκαίνια* (Jewish Feast of Dedication), *τὰ γενέσια* (birthday celebration). In Acts 17:2 *σάββατον* occurs as a plural in sense. Cf. R. Pesch, *Das Markusevangelium* (Freiburg: Herder, 1977), 1:120.

[5]For examples, cf. *LSJ*, "*εἰμί* (sum)," C.III.2.

[6]So Cranfield, *The Gospel According to St. Mark*, p. 75. The expression no doubt represents Hebrew idiom (cf. Josh. 22:24; Judg. 11:12; 1 Kings 17:18; etc.).

[7]E.g., H. B. Swete, *The Gospel According to St. Mark* (London: Macmillan, 1902), p. 19; M.-J. Lagrange, *Saint Marc*, (Paris: J. Gabalda, 1947), p. 23; A. Plummer, *The Gospel According to St. Luke* (Edinburgh: T. & T. Clark, 1901), p. 67.

[8]E.g., A. E. J. Rawlinson, *St. Mark* (London: Methuen, 1942), p. 16; E. Klostermann, *Das Markusevangelium* (Tübingen: Mohr, 1936), p. 16.

[9]E.g., H. Riesenfeld, "The Sabbath and the Lord's Day in Judaism, the Preaching of Jesus and Early Christianity," *The Gospel Tradition* (Oxford: Blackwell, 1970), p. 118: "Therefore deeds of healing on Sabbath days must be interpreted as signs that in the person of Jesus was being realized something of what the Sabbath had pointed forward to in the eschatological expectations of the Jewish people."

[10]SBK 4:527, notes that according to Jewish traditions, demonic power would be crushed in the messianic age. There are complicated textual problems in Mark 1:27*b*: cf. Taylor, *The Gospel According to St. Mark*, p. 176 n. 2; B. M. Metzger, *A Textual Commentary on the Greek New Testament* (London: United Bible Society, 1971), p. 75. In addition, commentators are divided as to whether to take *κατ'ἐξουσίαν* (with authority) with the following clause, or with *διδαχὴ καινή* (a new teaching). The former alternative may be an assimilation to Luke 4:36; but the difference is negligible in light of the last clause of Mark 1:27, even if that clause stands alone. For discussion, cf., G. D. Kilpatrick, "Some problems in New Testament Text and Language," *Neotestamentica et Semitica*, ed. E. E. Ellis and M. Wilcox (Edinburgh: T. and T. Clark, 1969), pp. 198–201.

[11]Cf. E. E. Ellis, *The Gospel of Luke* (London: Nelson, 1969), p. 99: "The ultimate meaning of the ministry in Capernaum is not the healings or the edification of the people. It is who and what these actions reveal. The significance is lost on the people."

[12]Luke does not mention the synagogue at the beginning of the pericope (4:31), but it is implied that the teaching took place in the Capernaum synagogue (4:38).

[13]Mark's connection is ambiguous, since *εὐθὺς* could mean "so then," but it is natural to take the word to mean "immediately." This is certainly the force of Luke 4:38. Matthew 8:16–17 records the incident but does not tie it in with a Sabbath.

[14]*The Gospel of St. Luke* (London: A. and C. Black, 1963), p. 89.

[15]*Der Rahmen der Geschichte Jesus* (Berlin: Kösel, 1919), p. 89.

[16]Luke's mysterious *δευτεροπρώτῳ* ("on the second Sabbath after the first") need not detain

us; even if the text were certain, few claim certainty as to what it means. Cf. discussion in Plummer, *The Gospel According to St. Luke*, pp. 165–66; H. S. Schürmann, *Das Lukasevangelium* (Freiburg: Herder, 1969), 1:302; and I. H. Marshall, *Commentary on Luke* (Grand Rapids: Eerdmans, 1978), p. 230. In view of these uncertainties, W. Rordorf, *Sunday* (London: S. Con, 1968), pp. 61–62 is a trifle too certain about the Lukan redaction. Cf. also discussion by J. M. Baumgarten, "The Counting of Sabbath in Ancient Sources," VT 16 (1966): 282ff.; E. Delebecque, "Sur un certain sabbat, en Luc, 6,1," *Revue de Philologie* 48 (1974): 26–29; E. Metzger, "Le sabbat 'second-premier' de Luc," TZ 32 (1976): 138–43.

[17]E.g., Bultmann, *History*, pp. 16–17; F. W. Beare, "The Sabbath Was Made for Man?" JBL, 79 (1906): 130–36.

[18]*The Gospel According to St. Mark*, pp. 214–15.

[19]E.g., Bultmann, *History*, p. 17; Lohse, *σάββατον*, TDNT 7:20 and n. 172; E. Lohmeyer, *Das Evangelium des Markus* (Göttingen: Vandenhoeck und Ruprecht, 1953), pp. 62–63.

[20]W. Lane, *The Gospel According to Mark* (Grand Rapids, Eerdmans, 1974), p. 115, says that among scribes "it was assumed that a teacher was responsible for the behaviour of his disciples." The question the Pharisees raise concerns what is permitted of prohibited; cf. E. Lohse, "Jesu Worte Uber den Sabbat," *Judentum, Urchristentum, Kirche*, ed. W. Eltester (Berlin, Töpelmann, 1960), p. 86 and n. 27. Note that Jesus' answer in verse 26 is also couched in legal language.

[21]P. K. Jewett, *The Lord's Day* (Grand Rapids: Eerdmans, 1971), p. 37. The suggestion goes back at least as far as B. W. Bacon, *The Beginnings of Gospel Story* (New Haven, Conn.: Yale University Press, 1925), pp. 30–31.

[22]So Swete, *The Gospel According to St. Mark*, p. 47; Plummer, *The Gospel According to St. Luke*, p. 94; Lagrange, *Saint Marc*, p. 51; Taylor, *The Gospel According to St. Mark*, p. 215; H. Anderson, *The Gospel of Mark* (London: Oliphants, 1976), p. 109; and most commentators. Matthew has *ἤρξαντο τίλλειν* ("they began to pluck"), and Luke has *ἔτιλλον* ("they were plucking"). M. Zerwick, *Biblical Greek* (Rome: Biblical Institute Press, 1963), par. 376, is no doubt right when he suggests the participle sometimes functions as the main verb.

[23]T. W. Manson, *The Sayings of Jesus* (London: SCM, 1949), p. 190.

[24]Despite F. W. Beare, "The Sabbath Was Made for Man?" p. 133, and Lohmeyer, *Das Evangelium des Markus*, p. 63, who comments, "How the Pharisees come to be there, one is not supposed to ask." The presence of the Pharisees likewise tells against the suggestion of S. Bacchiocchi, *From Sabbath to Sunday* (Rome: Pontifical Gregorian University Press, 1977), p. 50, following R. G. Hirsch, to the effect that the quotation from Hosea 6:6 ("I desire mercy and not sacrifice"), cited in Matthew 12:7, suggests a rebuke from Jesus to the Pharisees for failing to take Jesus and His disciples home for lunch after synagogue service; this alleged discourtesy was the cause of the disciples' hunger. But if the Pharisees had been home having lunch, they would not have been in the field. Such reconstructions are speculative, and far removed from the text.

[25]On the thirty-nine major classes of work forbidden by the rabbis, cf. *Shab.* 7:2; also SBK 1:615–18; 623–29; TDNT 7:11–14. For a summary of the detailed applications (many of them later than Jesus' day), cf. A. Edersheim, *The Life and Times of Jesus the Messiah* (Grand Rapids: Eerdmans, rep. 1967), p. 2, App. 17.

[26]Cf. Rawlinson, *St. Mark*, p. 34; Cranfield, *The Gospel According to St. Mark*, p. 115.

[27]Despite Swete, *The Gospel According to St. Mark*, p. 48.

[28]Cranfield, *The Gospel According to St. Mark*, pp. 11–12; cf., also Lane, *The Gospel According to Mark*, p. 117.

[29]Cf. H. H. P. Dressler, chapter 2 of this volume.

[30]In *j.Shab.*VII.c.9c, the plucking of grain is an act of reaping. C. G. Montefiore, *The Synoptic Gospels* (London: Macmillan, 1927), 1:63–64, rightly points out that, in spite of the many Sabbath regulations, "the Sabbath was upon the whole a joy and a blessing to the immense majority of Jews throughout the Rabbinic period." Similarly, Manson, *The Sayings of Jesus*, pp. 189–190; and many others. No doubt the Jews' custom of eating well on the Sabbath contributed to their festal joy (cf. SBK 1:611ff.), but when all allowances are made for the Pharisees' casuistry

as a sincere effort to lighten the burden of Sabbath law, it should be noted that the burden was largely self-imposed by the Halakah itself, but also by the rigid interpretation of the written Torah presupposed in the Halakic regulations on the Sabbath. Moreover, it must not be assumed that the ethical grandeur of the rabbinic literature can be read back into the attitudes of the Pharisees of Jesus' day. By the time the Mishnah had been compiled, Jerusalem itself had been destroyed, Christianity had experienced great success, and rabbinic Judaism had undergone something of a Counter Reformation.

[31]Cf. SBK 1:618–19; Lohse, TDNT 7:22.

[32]*The New Testament and Rabbinic Judaism* (London: Athlone Press, 1956), pp. 77ff.

[33]*Sunday*, p. 6.

[34]Ibid., p. 61. E Delebecque, "Les épis "égrenés" dans les Synoptiques," *Revue des Etudes Grecques* 88 (1975): 133–42, likewise draws momentous conclusions from these details.

[35]A. Schlatter, *Der Evangelist Matthäus* (Stuttgart: Colmer Verdag, rep. 1959), p. 392, argues for the priority of Matthew, and says that Mark intentionally dropped the word "hungry."

[36]E.g., Bacchiocchi, *From Sabbath to Sunday*, p. 52.

[37]*The Son of Man in Mark* (London: SPCK, 1967), pp. 97–98.

[38]For useful summaries, cf. F. Gils, "Le sabbat a été fait pour l'homme et non l'homme pour le sabbat (Mark 2, 27)," RB 69 (1962): 506–13; Pesch, *Das Markusevangelium* (Freiburg: Herder, 1977), 1:16; F. Neirynck, "Jesus and the Sabbath: Some Observations on Mark II, 27," in *Jésus aux origines de la christologie* (Gembloux: Duculot, 1975), pp. 228–70; and G. Gnilka, *Das Evangelium nach Markus* 1. Teilband (Züruch/Neukirchen-Vluyn: Neukirchener Verlag, 1978), pp. 119ff.

[39]E.g., Bultmann, *History*, pp. 16–17; Schmidt, *Das Rahmen der Geschichte Jesus*, p. 97; V. Taylor, *The Gospel According to St. Mark*, p. 218.

[40]Lagrange, *Saint Marc*, p. 56.

[41]Rordorf has no difficulty with *καὶ ἔλεγεν αὐτοῖς* under his reconstruction, since he is persuaded that 2:25–26 has already been interpolated into Mark.

[42]*The Gospel According to Mark*, pp. 118–20. On page 120, note 103, Lane says that *ὥστε* (2:28) designates the conclusion that Mark draws from the act and word of Jesus. Similarly Anderson, *The Gospel of Mark*, p. 111.

[43]"'Son of Man' Imagery: Some Implications for Theology and Discipleship," *JETS* 18 (1975): 8, n. 12. Cf. also Marshall, *Origins*, pp. 63–82.

[44]*The Son of Man in Mark*, pp. 94–95, 98. Since Mark 2:27 is missing from *D a c e ff² i*, and in addition 2:27b is absent from W syr^sin, a case could be made for the suggestion that 2:27 is a Western non-interpolation, but few commentators accept this. Another reason for rejecting the unity of 2:27 and 2:28 is expressed by W. Thissen, *Erzählung der Befreiung: Eine exegetische Untersuchung zu Mk 2,1–3,6* (Würzburg: Echter, 1976), p. 72, viz. "man" and "son of man" probably do not refer to the same thing in these verses. But cf. further discussion below.

[45]Beare, "The Sabbath Was Made for Man?", p. 32; similarly, Gils, "Le sabbat a été fait," pp. 516–521.

[46]P. 63ff.

[47]E. Käsemann, *Essays on New Testament Themes* (London: SCM, 1964), p. 39.

[48]P. 65.

[49]*Mekilta Shabbata I* to Exod. 31:13–14; SBK 2:5. Cf. B. *Yoma 85b*. where the same saying is attributed to Jonathan ben Joseph, instead of to R. Simeon ben Menasya. See also the statement of Mattathias in 1 Macc. 2:38–41.

[50]E.g., J. Wellhausen, *Das Evangelium Marci* (Berlin: Georg Reimer, 1903), p. 22; Bultmann, *History*, pp. 16–17; A. H. McNeile, *The Gospel According to St. Matthew* (London: Macmillan, 1915), p. 170; O. Cullmann, *The Christology of the New Testament* (London: SCM, 1963), p. 152ff.; Rordorf, *Sunday*, p. 64.

[51]T. W. Manson, "Mark ii.27f.," *Coniectanea Neotestamentica* XI (Lund: Gleerup, 1947), pp. 138–46.

[52]Cf. Hooker, *The Son of Man*; Cranfield, *The Gospel According to St. Mark*, pp. 272–77;

and esp. cf. A. J. B. Higgins, "Son of Man-*Forschung* since 'The Teaching of Jesus,' " *New Testament Essays*, ed. A. J. B. Higgins (Manchester: University of Manchester Press, 1959), pp. 126–27, who summarizes criticism against Manson's idea that "Son of man" can be identified simply with the Christian community.

[53]F. N. Lee, *The Covenantal Sabbath* (London: LDOS, 1969), p. 195.

[54]The number of writers who reason thus is staggering. See, among others, J. A. Schep, "Lord's Day Keeping from the Practical and Pastoral Point of View" in *The Sabbath-Sunday Problem*, ed. G. van Groningen (Geelong: Hilltop Press, 1968), pp. 142–43; Lee, *The Covenantal Sabbath*, p. 195; Swete, *The Gospel According to St. Mark*, p. 49; R. T. Beckwith and W. Stott, *This Is the Day* (London: Marshall, Morgan and Scott, 1978), pp. 7, 11.

[55]E.g., R. A. Zorn, "The New Testament and the Sabbath-Sunday Problem," *The Sabbath-Sunday Problem*, pp. 48–49.

[56]J. A. Bengel, *Gnomon Novi Testamenti* (Tübingen: Mohr, 1860), commenting on this passage, actually says that τὸν ἄνθρωπον ("the man") = Adam! The noun ἄνθρωπος occurs in Mark as follows: (1) in the expression "sons of men," 3:28; (2) in "Son of Man," 2:10, 28; 8:31, 38; 9:9, 12, 31; 10:33, 45; 13:26; 14:21 (twice), 41, 62; (3) with reference to a particular man or men, 1:23; 3:1, 3, 5; 4:26; 5:2, 8; 8:24, 27; 12:1; 13:34; 14:13, 21 (twice), 71; 15:39; (4) as "man" generically, 1:17; 7:7–8, 15 (three times), 18, 20 (twice), 21, 23; 8:33, 36–37; 10:7, 9, 27; 11:2, 30, 32; 12:14. The distinction between (3) and (4) may be artificial, as in 12:1 or the parables. Neither the article nor the number changes the meaning of the noun itself (cf. 7:21 and 7:23). It must be concluded, therefore, that 2:27 cannot refer to "mankind" merely on the basis of the word ἄνθρωπος.

[57]Mark's use of γίνομαι is significant: (1) It is used in a manner analogous to the Hebrew *waw-consecutive*, in particular, it is similar to וַיְהִי in use; although it is not a Greek idiom, the LXX usually translates the Hebrew expression by καὶ ἐγένετο . . . καί (e.g., Genesis 4:8). This idiom becomes rare in the Apocrypha. In the New Testament, it is found in the Synoptics and Acts (not John); Luke especially preserves it (39 times). Matthew has the idiom five times, and Mark four times; they tend to omit καί in the second clause. F. Büchsel, TDNT 1:682, regards the form as a conscious imitation of the style of the LXX. The four instances in Mark are: 1:9; 2:23; 4:4; 9:7. (2) There is one occurrence, at 2:15, of a more Greek-like structure for the same thought: "and it comes about." (3) There are also time references involving this verb; all but one (11:19) are aorist participles. (4) The last category is more difficult. Often the verb means simply "to be," but sometimes it has the meaning, "to become." This distinction may be difficult to detect, but when it has the latter sense, it may require a different verb in English. For example, note Mark 4:37, "a great storm *arose*" (γίνεται). See also Mark 4:39. The meaning of ἐγένετο in Mark 2:27 follows the same pattern: the Sabbath *was* or *became* for man, and so we say in English that it "was made for man." In Greek, γίνομαι often served as the passive of ποιέω, but to understand it here as a technical word for "created" would be tenuous (some of the early copyists made this mistake: W, fl, and syr have "was created"). To quote Büchsel, TDNT 1:681: "Usually the term has no particular religious or theological interest in the NT," although he cites John 8:58 as an exception. But what is to be made of the use of ἐγένετο with reference to creation (e.g., John 1:3)? The construction is not the same as in Mark 2:27, where διά with the accusative shows the *reason for* the Sabbath. By contrast, in John 1:3 the preposition is followed by the genitive to denote the *agent* of creation. In another construction, the same verb has reference to the introduction of law (Gal. 3:14). These observations are meant to show that the verb itself, as used in Mark 2:27, in no way entails a reference to a creation ordinance. Cf. also Jewett, *The Lord's Day*, p. 38: "Some have argued that when Jesus said the Sabbath was made for man, he meant mankind in general, not just the Jews in particular. Thus the obligation to keep the Sabbath, that is, the Lord's Day, is given a universal scope. But this is to discover a meaning quite alien to the context, which has to do not with the universal scope, but with the ultimate purpose of the Sabbath rest."

[58]J. Jeremias, *New Testament Theology* (London: SCM, 1971), 1:10 n. 18.

[59]Lohse, "Jesu Worte über den Sabbat," p. 22.

[60]This is the true significance of Mark's use of this saying, as opposed to the meaning when analogous statements are found on the lips of rabbis. The rabbinic principle "would only mean that where life was at stake, things might be done on the Sabbath which otherwise would be forbidden. If v. 27 is closely connected with vv. 23–6, what Jesus is saying has a much more general application, for there is no indication that the disciples were in danger of starvation" (Cranfield, *The Gospel According to St. Mark*, p. 117). Some have also tried to draw a parallel between this passage and Jesus' attitude toward divorce: note His appeal to the order of things at the creation (Matt. 19:4–9). Was Jesus perhaps appealing to creation here as well? But that begs the question since there is no "from the beginning" expressed here. He is not appealing to a determinate time, but to a determinate purpose.

[61]Plummer, *The Gospel According to St. Luke*, p. 162. This interpretation of the ὥστε, a simple *a minori ad maius* (from the lesser to the greater) argument, is to be preferred above that of Bacchiocchi, *From Sabbath to Sunday*, p. 59, who must postulate an unexpressed jump.

[62]Despite Plummer, *The Gospel According to St. Luke*, p. 168; J. N. Geldenhuys, *Commentary on the Gospel of Luke* (Grand Rapids, Eerdmans, 1951), p. 200; and others.

[63]Hooker, *The Son of Man in Mark*, p. 102.

[64]Ibid. pp. 99–102; F. H. Borsch, *The Son of Man in Myth and History* (London: SCM, 1967), p. 322; cf. notes below on Luke 4:16–30. E. C. Hoskyns, "Jesus the Messiah," *Mysterium Christi*, ed. G. K. A. Bess and A. Deissmann (London: Longmans, Green & Co., 1930), p. 74ff., argues that Jesus attaches primary significance to the Sabbath not as the hallmark of God's people but as a ritual anticipation of the messianic age.

[65]Geldenhuys, *Commentary on the Gospel of Luke*, p. 199.

[66]Cf. Caird, *The Gospel of St. Luke*, p. 99. For the sake of completeness, it should be noted that in Codex Bezae (D), Luke 6:5 is displaced to follow 6:10, and in its stead are inserted the lines (in Greek): "The same day, seeing someone working on the Sabbath, he said to him, 'Fellow, if you know what you are doing, you are blessed; but if not, you are cursed and a transgressor of the law.'" J. Jeremias, *Unknown Sayings of Jesus* (London: SCM, 1958), pp. 49–53, thinks the saying is authentic. Rordorf, *Sunday*, pp.87–88, more convincingly, does not; and few, in any case, would consider it part of Luke.

[67]D. Hill, *The Gospel of Matthew* (London: Oliphants, 1972), pp. 209–10.

[68]M. Cohen, "La controverse de Jésus et des Pharisiens à propos de la cueillette des épis, selon l'Evangile de saint Matthieu," *MélSciRel* 34 (1977): 3–12, argues that Matthew adds these two arguments because only he among the three evangelists perceived that the first argument, concerning David, wasn't very convincing. But if this paper is correct, Cohen has himself misunderstood the significance of that first argument.

[69]G. Gander, *L'Evangile de l'Eglise* (Aix-en-Provence: Faculté libre, 1970), 1:109–10, makes a good case for the latter.

[70]Cf. Jewett, *The Lord's Day*, p. 37. It is the failure to note this stress on Jesus' *authority* that mars the arguments of D. M. Cohn-Sherbok, "An Analysis of Jesus' Arguments Concerning the Plucking of Grain on the Sabbath," *JSNT* 2 (1979): 31–41. To focus on the *hunger* of Jesus' disciples and note (correctly) that their hunger was not extreme, or to observe (again correctly) that the plucking of the grain was not a *religious* activity akin to that of the priests, is rather to miss the point. Equally, despite the arguments of E. Levine, "The Sabbath Controversy According to Matthew," NTS 22 (1975–76): 480–83, it is not at all clear that Matthew has in mind the duty of *reaping* the first sheaves. It is possible that Jesus is implicitly claiming to be a priest, if we accept the arguments for the existence of this class offered by C. E. Armerding, "Were David's Sons Really Priests?" *Current Issues in Biblical and Patristic Interpretation*, ed. G. F. Hawthorne (Grand Rapids: Eerdmans, 1975), pp. 75–86; but Matthew 12:3–4 does not make such a contrast very obvious (it could have by inserting the word "levitical" before the word "priests").

[71]W. Hendriksen, *Exposition of the Gospel According to Matthew* (Grand Rapids: Baker, 1973), p. 515.

[72]*Sunday*, p. 61 n. 3.

[73]*The Origins of the Gospel According to St Matthew* (Oxford: Oxford University Press, 1946), pp. 116–17.

[74]This is not to deny that "moral law" exists, in the sense of unchangeable prescriptions of right and wrong, or that some laws are ceremonial and others civil. But I question the view that this classic three-fold distinction was used by New Testament writers in their presentation of the relationship between law and gospel. I shall say more on this matter later.

[75]Both Bultmann, *History*, p. 12, and Taylor, *The Gospel According to St. Mark*, p. 220, deny that this is a miracle story and prefer to describe it as an apophthegm (Bultmann) or Pronouncement Story (Taylor) because the healing is subordinate to the religious question of the Sabbath. Such alternating concern with form and content reveals the limitations of rigid literary categories. E. Lohse, "Jesu Worte über den Sabbat," pp. 83–85, insists that this account reflects an authentic incident in Jesus' ministry.

[76]Bengel, *Gnomon Novi Testamenti*, 1:173. Matthew has μεταβὰς ἐκεῖθεν (he went on from there), which taken by itself would suggest but not require the same Sabbath as the grain-plucking episode; Luke has ἐν ἑτέρῳ σαββάτῳ (on another Sabbath). Whether Mark 3:1 includes the article before συναγωγήν (synagogue) is not important for this study: cf. J. S. Sibinga, "Text and Literary Art in Mark 3:1–6," *Studies in New Testament Language and Text*, ed. J. K. Elliot (Leiden: Brill, 1976), pp. 357–365.

[77]Cf. Lagrange, *Saint Marc*, p. 57; Taylor, *The Gospel According to St. Mark*, p. 221; C. E. B. Cranfield, *The Gospel According to St. Mark*, p. 119.

[78]Geldenhuys, *Commentary on the Gospel of Luke*, p. 212.

[79]E.g., Klostermann, *Das Markusevangelium*, p. 31; Plummer, *The Gospel According to Luke*, p. 169; Cranfield, *The Gospel According to St. Mark*, p. 120; Geldenhuys, *Commentary on the Gospel of Luke*, pp. 202–204. Cf. the excellent discussion in Gnilka, *Evangelium*, pp. 127–128.

[80]W. Manson, *The Gospel of Luke* (London: Macmillan, 1930), p. 60.

[81]So, for example, Swete, *The Gospel According to St. Mark*, p. 52; Rawlinson, *St. Mark*, p. 36; Lohmeyer, *Das Evangelium des Markus*, p. 69; Taylor, *The Gospel According to St. Mark*, p. 222. Cf. Lane, *The Gospel According to Mark*, p. 125: "Jesus answered the question of what is permitted on the Sabbath by healing the man with the withered hand. Ironically, the guardians of the Sabbath determine to do harm and to kill (cf. 3:6)."

[82]Cf. SBK 1:623ff. D. Flusser, in the foreword to R. L. Lindsay, *A Hebrew Translation of the Gospel of Mark* (Jerusalem: Dugith, 1973), pp. 4–5, is not convincing when he puts Luke against Matthew and Mark, and claims that Luke alone does not present any *plot* among the Pharisees, but only further *discussion* (καί διελάλουν πρὸς ἀλλήλους, "they were discussing among themselves"). But this not only fails to reckon with Luke's insistence that the Pharisees were looking for a reason to accuse Jesus, it also overlooks his witness that the event called forth their fury ("But they were filled with fury" [Luke 6:11]). Cf. the more nuanced discussion by Marshall, *Commentary on Luke*, p. 236.

[83]J. A. Broadus, *Commentary on the Gospel of Matthew* (Valley Forge: American Baptist Publication Society, 1886), p. 262.

[84]The verb συλλυπέω is used only here in the New Testament; the active meaning is "hurt with," and the passive means "to sympathize, share in grief." Neither of these meanings quite suits the context. M. 2:325 suggests the meaning is perfective, i.e., "utterly distressed," and although there is no other example of such usage, it is required by the context. W. L. Knox, *Some Hellenistic Elements in Primitive Christianity* (London: Published for the British Academy by H. Milford, 1944), p. 6 n.4, observing that Latin *contristari* has this meaning as early as Seneca (*Ep.* 85:14), wonders if "we might have here an isolated instance of a Latin influence on the *koine*, the lack of parallels being due to chance" Cf. Taylor, *The Gospel According to St. Mark*, p. 223. G. Stählin, TDNT 5:428, and R. Bultmann, TDNT 4:323–24, who conclude that the verb here means Jesus was grieved.

[85]The Herodians were not a religious sect or an organized party, but friends and supporters of Herod Antipas (cf. Josephus, *Ant.* xiv.450). Lohmeyer, *Das Evangelium des Markus*, p. 67,

objects that Pharisees would never make a league with Herodian pragmatists, but common hostilities, like shared grief, produce strange unions (cf. Luke 23:12). E. A. Russell, "Mk 2^{23} - 3^{6}—A Judean Setting?" SE 6 (1973): 466–72, finds in references to Pharisees and Herodians a prime reason for ascribing a *Judean* setting and a late period in Jesus' ministry to Mark 2:23–26. However, he does not adequately explain the reason for the present setting, and questions so many details of the text as we have it, that he arouses suspicions that the text is being made to fit the theory.

[86]Again, the form critics do not agree. Dibelius, *From Tradition to Gospel*, p. 43, classifies this pericope as a paradigm "of a less pure type"; Bultmann, an apophthegm, indeed a *Musterbeispiel* (a master example) of an ideal scene constructed from an Oxyrhynchus saying. Taylor, *The Gospel According to St. Mark*, p. 298, responds, "This hypothesis is surely a *Musterbeispiel* of subjective criticism," and insists this be called quite simply a story about Jesus.

[87]Most writers agree that the Lukan passage refers to the same incident as do the other two (despite Lane, *The Gospel According to Mark*, p. 201, n.2, who theorizes that *two* visits to Nazareth are recorded by the Synoptists); but it is far more difficult to decide what extra source material was available to Luke. Cf. discussion in Marshall, *Commentary on Luke*, p. 179ff.

[88]Swete, *The Gospel According to St. Mark*, p. 111.

[89]Cf. Philo, *de Sept*. 2.

[90]Cf. 6:5–6; Lane, *The Gospel According to Mark*, p. 201.

[91]Assuming that the reading ὁ υἱὸς τῆς Μαρίας ("the Son of Mary") is correct (cf. Taylor, *The Gospel According to St. Mark*, p. 300; Metzger, *Textual Commentary*, pp. 88f.), it is likely that this description of Jesus implicitly declares Him to be illegitimate for "to call someone the son of his mother in Eastern lands is to cast a slur on his true sonship" (R. P. Martin, *Mark: Evangelist and Theologian* [Exeter: Paternoster, 1972], p. 123, following E. Stauffer, "Jeschu ben Mirjam," *Neotestamentica et Semitica*, ed. E. Earle Ellis and M. Wilcox [Edinburgh: T. & T. Clark, 1969], pp. 119–28).

[92]No one knows whether the Jewish lectionary cycle stretches back that far. Cf. L. Morris, *The New Testament and the Jewish Lectionaries* (London: Tyndale, 1964); W. A. Meeks, *The Prophet-King* (Leiden: Brill, 1967), p. 92, n.2; J. Heinemann, "The Triennial Lectionary Cycle," *JJS* 19 (1968): 42–48.

[93]Plummer, *The Gospel According to St. Luke*, p. 121.

[94]Cf. R B. Sloan, *The Favorable Year of the Lord: A Study of the Jubilary Theology in the Gospel of Luke* (Austin: Schola Press, 1977), p. 19, n.4. The debate over the *length* of the jubilee year is incidental; cf. most recently S. B. Hoenig, "Sabbatical Years and the Year of Jubilee," JQR 59 (1968–69): 222–36.

[95]*The Favorable Year of the Lord*.

[96]Jeremias, *New Testament Theology* 1:206–7, points out that in 4:18–19 Jesus breaks off in mid-sentence, omitting the words "and the day of vengeance of our God"—i.e., the day of vengeance on the Gentiles. The reaction of the crowd to Jesus' preaching is expressed in 4:22 "all spoke well of him and wondered at the gracious words that proceeded out of his mouth." In Greek, both verbs are ambiguous; μαρτυρεῖν with the dative can mean "witness for" or "witness against," and θαυμάζειν can mean "be enthusiastic about" or "be shocked about." Jeremias chooses the negative meaning in both cases: "The continuation of the pericope shows that the word must be interpreted *in malem partem* [in the bad sense]." He thinks the words ἐπὶ τοῖς λόγοις τῆς χάριτος ("at the gracious words") explain that the people of Nazareth are shocked that Jesus quotes only the words of grace from Isaiah 61 and omits the rest. This interpretation has attractive features, and is not unimportant with respect to a later section of this chapter dealing with Jesus' attitude to the law, but its serious weakness is that the text portrays the offense of the synagogue crowd in terms of Jesus' personal claims, rather than in terms of Jesus' authoritative use of Scripture. At best, Jeremias's view is a secondary motif, a merely possible one at that.

[97]Plummer, *The Gospel According to St. Luke*, p. 342.

[98]As far as the Mishnah is concerned, cf. *Shab*. 5:1–4 for rules about watering cattle, 7:2 on tying knots, 15:1–2 on important exceptions. Cf. also *'Érub*. 2:1–4. The Talmud expresses

reservations: water can be drawn for an animal but must not be carried to it in a vessel. Cf. discussion in E. Lohse, TDNT 7:1.

[99]There is no reason to think that the woman's bondage was due to some specific sin.

[100]This was an accepted rabbinical method of arguing, the so-called *qal wahomer* ("light and heavy") principle.

[101]Caird, *The Gospel of St. Luke*, pp. 107–8. Cf. also W. Grundmann, *Das Evangelium nach Lukas* (Berlin: Evangelische Verlagsanstalt, 1961), pp. 278–281; Ellis, *The Gospel of Luke*, p. 185; Bacchiocchi, *From Sabbath to Sunday*, p. 37.

[102]Cf. SBK on this passage. Grundmann, *Das Evangelium nach Lukas*, p. 290, suggests a Jerusalem setting since the host is a "ruler" of the Pharisees. Ellis, *The Gospel of Luke*, p. 192, points out that the contrast between the invited guest and the unfortunate intruder provides the backdrop for the entire episode, i.e., not just the healing, but also the two precepts (14:7–11, 12–14) and the concluding parable (14:15–24).

[103]Despite T. Zahn, *Das Evangelium des Lucas* (Leipzig: A. Deichert, 1913), pp. 544–45, followed by Geldenhuys, *Commentary on the Gospel of Luke*, p. 388, who argues that καὶ ἰδοὺ ("and behold") following παρατηρούμενοι ("they were watching him") suggests that the presence of the ill man was unexpected by Jesus but arranged by the Pharisees as an intentional trap.

[104]This is the most likely reading. Cf. Marshall, *Commentary on Luke*, pp. 579–80.

[105]*Zadokite Fragments* (=CD) 13:22ff., discusses the case of the animal in the well and arrives at the opposite conclusion; but Manson, *The Sayings of Jesus*, p. 188, says that this document does not represent "normative Judaism" (whatever that is). Cf. also CD 11:16–17; plus K. Schubert, in *The Scrolls and the New Testament*, ed. K. Stendahl (New York: Harper, 1958), pp. 127–28.

[106]*The Lord's Day*, pp. 40–41.

[107]See Hill, *The Gospel of Matthew*, p. 321; Gander, 2:426. There is no need to take μηδὲ σαββάτῳ ("or on a Sabbath") as a Matthean redaction reflecting Jewish Christianity (so among others, L. Goppelt, *Apostolic and Post-Apostolic Times* (London: Black, 1970), p. 204.

[108]Cf. R. A. Morey, "Is Sunday the 'Christian Sabbath'?" *BRR* 8/1 (1979): 13–14.

[109]Cf. R. P. Martin, "The Theology of Mark's Gospel," *SwJT* 21 (1978): 33–34.

[110]Cf. also A. B. Kolenkow, "Healing Controversy as a Tie Between Miracle and Passion Material for a Proto-Gospel," *JBL* 95 (1976): 623–38.

[111]Cf. the brief but elegant treatment by G. R. Beasley-Murray, "Eschatology in the Gospel of Mark," *SwJT* 21 (1978): esp. 42–45.

[112]*From Sabbath to Sunday*, p. 62.

[113]Cf. among other works M. Maher, "'Take my yoke upon you' (Matt.xi.29)," *NTS* 22 (1975–76): 97–103.

[114]Cf. J. Zens, "'This is my beloved Son . . . hear him': A Study of the Development of Law in the History of Redemption," *BRR* 7/1 (1978): 15–52, esp. 27.

[115]R. Banks, *Jesus and the Law in the Synoptic Tradition* (Cambridge: Cambridge University Press, 1975), pp. 122–23.

[116]Again, the reader is referred to the next chapter for a consideration of Luke's treatment of the law.

[117]E.g., A. Sand, *Das Gesetz und die Propheten: Untersuchungen zur Theologie des Evangeliums nach Matthäus* (Regensburg: Pustet, 1974); Banks, *Jesus and the Law*; J. P. Meier, *Law and History in Matthew's Gospel: A Redactional Study of Mt. 5:17–48* (Rome: Biblical Institute Press, 1976); K. Berger, *Die Gesetzeauslegung Jesu: Ihr historischer Hintergrund im Judentum und im Alten Testament*, Teil I: *Markus und Parallelen* (Neukirchen-Vluyn: Neukirchener Verlag, 1972). Cf. also the unpublished doctoral dissertation of B. L. Martin, "Matthew and Paul on Christ and the Law: Compatible or Incompatible Theologies?" (McMaster University, 1976). Matthew's Gospel is particularly important: background studies are nicely summarized by J. Rohde, *Rediscovering the Teaching of the Evangelists* (London: SCM, 1968); and by D. J. Harrington, "Matthean Studies since Joachim Rohde," *HeyJ* 16 (1975): 375–88, who rightly notes that one of the emerging trends is a growing recognition of the complexity of Matthew's attitude to the law.

[118]*New Testament Theology*, 1:206.

[119]One might envisage a theoretical situation in which Jesus complied with Halakah for the sake of the Kingdom; there is no unambiguous record of such, whether in the synoptic Gospels or in the fourth Gospel.

[120]M. Hubaut, "Jésus et la Loi de Moïse," *RevTheolLouv* 7 (1976): 401–25, attempts to qualify Banks; but he is not convincing. Moreover, the above interpretation does not at all raise the question whether or not Jesus' own teachings may properly be classified as Halakic as P. Sigal ("The *Halakah* of Jesus of Nazareth according to the Gospel of Matthew," Ph.D. dissertation, University of Pittsburgh, 1979) claims (I have not yet read this work; I am indebted for the reference to Dr. Peter Davids.).

[121]Jeremias, *New Testament Theology*, p. 206; similarly, H. von Campenhausen, *The Formation of the Christian Bible* (London: Black, 1972), p. 5ff.

[122]Despite H. J. Schoeps, "Jésus et la loi juive," *RHPR* 33 (1953): 15–17. For adequate comment, cf. W. D. Davies, "Matthew 5:17–18," *Christian Origins and Judaism* (London: Darton, Longman and Todd, 1962), pp. 37–43; and cf. R. Longenecker, *Paul: Apostle of Liberty* (New York: Harper, 1964), pp. 138–42. Besides the commentaries on Mark 7:1–23, cf. especially J. Lambrecht, "Jesus and the Law: An Investigation of Mark 7:1–23," *EphTheolLov* 53 (1977): 24–82. Berger, *Die Gesetzeauslegung Jesu*, pp. 534–35, may be taken as representative of those who deny the authenticity of Mark 7,15; but cf. H. Hubner, "Mark vii. 1–23 und das 'Judisch-Hellenistische' Gesetzes Verständnis," *NTS* 22 (1975–76): 319–45.

[123]For a survey of the literature, cf. W. D. Davies, "Matthew 5:17, 18," 31ff.; and R. Banks, "Matthew's Understanding of the Law: Authenticity and Interpretation in Matthew 5:17–20," *JBL* 93 (1974): 226–42; and the monographs already cited.

[124]Ibid. Cf. also his book, *Jesus and the Law in the Synoptic Tradition*.

[125]Cf. Jeremias, *New Testament Theology*, pp. 82–85, who on the basis of this difficulty takes the verb to mean "to fill up," "to complete."

[126]E. g., D. Wenham, "Jesus and the Law: An Exegesis on Matthew 5:17–20," *Themelios* 4 (1978–79): 92–96.

[127]Banks, "Matthew's Understanding of the Law."

[128]Ibid., p. 231. On the antithetical structure of 5:17, see R. A. Guelich, "Not to Annul the Law Rather to Fulfil the Law and the Prophets," Hamburg, Diss., 1967, which Banks also cites. The sense of "fulfill" as related to prophecy is richer than mere prediction/fulfillment, but is most akin to C. F. D. Moule's third category: cf. his article, "Fulfilment-Words in the New Testament: Use and Abuse," *NTS* 14 (1967–68): 293–320. Several scholars who do not adopt Banks' entire structure nevertheless concur with his essentially eschatological understanding of "to fulfill." For example, cf. R. E. Nixon, "Fulfilling the Law: The Gospels and Acts," *Law, Morality and the Bible*, ed. B. Kaye and G. Wenham (Downers Grove, InterVarsity, 1978), pp. 55–56; B. L. Martin, "Matthew and Paul," p. 54; and especially, J. P. Meier, pp. 79–80; J. Zens, pp. 23–24.

[129]D. A. Carson, *The Sermon on the Mount: An Evangelical Exposition of Matthew 5–7* (Grand Rapids: Baker, 1978), p. 37.

[130]Cf. W. Trilling, *Das wahre Israel* (München: Kösel, 1964), pp. 167–68.

[131]E.g., Wenham, *Jesus and the Law*; G. Bahnsen, *Theonomy in Christian Ethics* (Nutley: Presbyterian and Reformed, 1977), pp. 76–78.

[132]W. D. Davies, "Matthew 5:17, 18" (cf. also his *The Setting of the Sermon on the Mount* [Cambridge: Cambridge University Press, 1963], on the same subject), suggests that the reference is eschatological. The eschatological age has been inaugurated by Jesus' death and resurrection (A. Feuillet, "Le Discours de Jésus sur la Ruine du Temple," *RB* 56 (1949): 85, prefers the fall of Jerusalem.). Jeremias, *New Testament Theology*, 1:207, argues similarly: "Jesus is claiming to be the *eschatological messenger of God*." Part of the strength of Davies' approach rests on his belief that there was a marked amount of Jewish speculation that the new age would bring significant transformation to Torah: cf. his *Torah in the Messianic Age and/or the Age to Come* (Philadelphia: Society of Biblical Literature, 1952), incorporated into his *Setting*, pp. 109ff. This view has

also been supported by H. M. Teeple and R. Longenecker. An even stronger position—that the new Torah would displace the old, not merely modify it—was held, among others, by G. Dalman and A. Edersheim, and reiterated recently by H. Schoeps and J. Jocz. But E. Bammel, G. Barth, and, most comprehensively, R. Banks, "The Eschatological Role of Law in Pre- and Post-Christian Jewish Thought," *Reconciliation and Hope*, ed. R. Banks, (Exeter: Paternoster, 1974), pp. 173ff., have strenuously and persuasively denied the existence of such speculation in the first century.

[133]I have not found this interpretation of the two clauses elsewhere; and by suggesting it, I am abandoning my support of Trilling (n.130; as found in Carson, *The Sermon on the Mount*). It seems to me that such a fit is consistent with the passage, with linguistic usage, and with Matthean theology; and it is far simpler than the detailed delineation of a mixed crowd among the readers, thought possible by R. G. Hamerton-Kelly, "Attitudes to the Law in Matthew's Gospel: A Discussion of Matthew 5:18" *BR*17 (1972): 19–32; J. Zumstein, *La condition du croyant dans l'Evangile selon Matthieu* (Göttingen: Vandenhoeck und Ruprecht, 1977). It is also much to be preferred above the approach of Bahnsen, *Theonomy in Christian Ethics*, who rightly notes the exhaustive force of *ἰῶτα ἒν ἢ μία κεραία* ("not an iota, not a dot"), but who takes *πληρῶσαι* ("to fulfill") to mean "confirm, ratify," and takes the phrase "until heaven and earth pass away" in the most absolute sense. Bahnsen fails to come to grips with the New Testament's perspective on redemptive history.

[134]E. Lohmeyer, *Das Evangelium des Matthäus* (Göttingen: Vandenhoeck und Ruprecht, 1956), pp. 111–12; J. M. Gibbs, "The Son of God as Torah Incarnate in Matthew," *SE* 4 (1968): 43; R. Banks, "Matthew 5:17–20," pp. 238–40.

[135]For this suggestion I am indebted to Andrew Lincoln. For further discussion cf. chapter 12, esp. n.82.

[136]E.g., Matthew 23:23! Cf. W. C. Kaiser, "The Weightier and Lighter Matters of the Law: Moses, Jesus and Paul," *Current Issues in Biblical and Patristic Interpretation*, ed. G. F. Hawthorne (Grand Rapids: Eerdmans, 1975), pp. 176–192. It is important to note that Jesus never treats the Decalogue as the perfect sum of moral law; cf. the excellent if brief discussion by R. E. Nixon, pp. 64–65. In this Jesus is like the rabbis and unlike Philo; cf. E. E. Urbach, *The Sages: Their Concepts and Beliefs* (Jerusalem: Magnes, 1975), p. 360. For further discussion cf. F. E. Vokes, "The Ten Commandments in the New Testament and in First Century Judaism," *SE* 5 (1968): 146–54.

[137]Cf. H. Frankmölle, *Jahwebund und Kirche Christi: Studien zur Form und Traditionsgeschichte des 'Evangeliums nach Matthäus* (Münster: Aschendorff, 1974).

[138]Cf. Longenecker, *Paul, Apostle of Liberty*, pp. 138–40 (esp. p. 140). C. F. D. Moule, "From Defendant to Judge—and Deliverer," *SNTS* 3 (1952): 52–53, followed by W. D. Davies, "Matthew 5:17–18," pp. 56ff., argue persuasively that if Jesus lived in the consciousness that as the Servant of Yahweh He was destined to die, then until that death occurred there was need for a certain reserve about the claims He might advance concerning Himself. The reticence is caused not so much by the disciples' unpreparedness, as by Jesus' awareness that only through death could He fulfill His mission.

[139]Jeremias, *New Testament Theology*, p. 211.

[140]G. R. Beasley-Murray, "Eschatology."

[141]Respectively, J. G. Machen, *The Origin of Paul's Religion* (Grand Rapids: Eerdmans, reprint 1970); Longenecker, *Paul, Apostle of Liberty*, esp. pp. 128–55; E. Jüngel, *Paulus und Jesus* (Tübingen: Mohr, 1972), pp. 268–73; H. Ridderbos, *Paul and Jesus* (Philadelphia: Presbyterian and Reformed, 1957). I am not arguing that these writers would support my understanding of Jesus and the law.

[142]For detailed study of these passages, besides the commentaries, see especially S. Pancaro, *The Law in the Fourth Gospel* (Leiden: Brill, 1975).

[143]On the unity and coherence of this section, cf. especially J. Bernard, "La guérison de Bethesda: Harmoniques judéo-hellénestiques d'un récit de miracle un jour de sabbat," MélSciRel 33 (1976): 3–34; 34 (1977): 13–44.

[144]Cf. R. E. Brown, *The Gospel According to John* (London: Chapman, 1966), 1:209.

[145]Cf. D. A. Carson, *Divine Sovereignty and Human Responsibility: Some Aspects of Johannine Theology Against Jewish Background* (London: Marshall, Morgan and Scott, 1981).

[146]The prohibition against carrying things in Jeremiah 17:19–22 apparently has commerce in view, not a pallet carried by a miraculously healed man.

[147]The first clause of Jesus' reply is not unrelated to the much debated question in both Hellenistic and rabbinic Judaism as to whether God Himself kept the Sabbath. Both groups decided negatively: there are some areas, e.g., moral government, in which God works all the time (Cf. SBK 2:461–62; Philo, esp. *Leg.All* 1, 6;—Cf. C. H. Dodd, *The Interpretation of the Fourth Gospel* [Cambridge: Cambridge University Press, 1953], pp. 320–28).

[148]By relating John 5:17 to Mark 2:27, R. Maddox, "The Function of the Son of Man According to the Synoptic Gospels," *NTS* 15(1968–69): 67–68, tries to invest Mark 2:27 with eschatological significance. He thus approves the study by H. Riesenfeld, "Sabbat et jour du Seigneur," *New Testament Essays*, ed. A. J. B. Higgins (Manchester: Manchester University Press, 1959), pp. 210–17. But whereas it is difficult to avoid the eschatological overtones of John 5, it seems to me that to discover them in Mark 2:27 would be eisegesis. *Both* passages are richer in christological than eschatological affirmations. On another note, O. Cullman, "*Sabbat und Sonntag nach dem Johannesevangelium*," *Vorträge und Aufsätze* (Tübingen: Mohr, 1966), pp. 187–91, says that ἕως ἄρτι ("until now" 5:17) refers *both* to Jesus' resurrection (on the first day of the week) *and* to the rest of the new creation "at the End" and on this basis he concludes that the text is "an indirect theological reflection" that connects the Old Testament God-ordained *Ruhetag* ("day of rest") with the primitive Christian *Auferstehungstag* ("Resurrection day").

[149]Cf. Lohse, TDNT 7:277: "The story of the breaking of the Sabbath raises the decisive question whether the authority of Jesus as the One whom God has sent is recognized or not." It is exegetically unreasonable to take this statement as a paradigm of human behavior, in the fashion of some older writers: e.g., W. B. Trevelyan *Sunday* (London: Longmans, Green & Co., 1902), p. 134: "The eternal energy of God forbids us to interpret rest as equal to idleness. . . . (Man's) true rest is not a rest *from* earthly labour, but a rest *for* divine heavenly labour." J. Murray, *Principles of Conduct* (Grand Rapids: Eerdmans, 1957), p. 33, makes the same leap from Jesus to the believer, only in a more sophisticated fashion and within a different theological framework: "Jesus is not here obliterating the rest of the sabbath; he is not saying that the sabbath has been abrogated. He is indicating the work he performed as consonant with the rest of the sabbath precisely because the rest the sabbath requires is not the rest of inaction. Sabbath rest is not inactivity; it is not unemployment, but employment of another sort from that of the six days." The leap from Jesus to the believer is a basis for ethical behavior in some places in the New Testament; but there is no evidence for it here. In addition to the leap from Jesus to the believer, there are two other reasons for rejecting the view that John 5 has as secondary motif the idea that God's rest serves as a paradigm for man's weekly rest. First, "inactivity" accurately sums up the way Sabbath prescriptions in the Old Testament are largely formulated. Second, there is no mention in John 5 of the *change* in God's work over the course of a seven day cycle, but only of the *constancy* of God's work. Indeed, elsewhere in the fourth Gospel, we read that the disciples join Jesus in the work (9:4). Jesus' "Sabbath" work is thus the constant eschatological work of the One sent down from heaven. Whether or not this work is in John climaxed by the Cross which introduces the Sabbath of eternal rest (as P. Ricca, *Die Eschatologie des Vierten Evangeliums* [Zürich: Gotthelf-Verlag, 1966], p. 63ff., argues on 19:28–31) cannot be argued here. But the following remarks by A. Corell, *Consumatum Est* (London: SPCK, 1958), p. 63, deserve being weighed: "It is not merely a question of the Jewish Sabbath versus the Christian Sunday; rather is it a question of the old dispensation versus the new. The old Sabbath was but a preparation for, and a pledge of, this new dispensation. Now, however, the time of fulfilment has come while the ancient eschatological promises are being realized in the works of Christ. Indeed, it was by an appeal to the nature of his works that Jesus refuted the Jews when they accused him of breaking the Sabbath—'My Father worketh even until now and I work' (v. 17). Thus he poined out that, while the Law of Moses forbade that man should do their own work on the Sabbath, it could in

no wise forbid or prevent the accomplishment of God's work on that day. He, himself, had come to do the works of God . . . which, being of eschatological significance, belonged to the Sabbath in a very special way. . . . Indeed, his very doing of these things was a sure sign that the real Sabbath of fulfillment had come. Since, moreover, the risen and ascended Christ lives and works within the Church, her life itself is one continuous Sabbath—a pledge and foretaste of the consummation and the great Sabbath of eternity."

[150]Hooker, *The Son of Man in Mark*, pp. 101–2, writes that "the Johannine interpretation is perhaps only a clear expression of the idea that is implicit in Jesus' words (in Mark 2:28)." Note, too, that Mark 2:1–12 deals with Jesus' authority to forgive sin, an idea not unrelated to John 5:8–9, 14.

[151]S. Bacchiocchi, "John 5:17: Negation or Clarification of the Sabbath," a paper presented at the annual meeting of SBL, Nov. 21, 1978. Cf. also W. Stott, NIDNTT 3:409.

[152]The title itself (ibid.) reveals a forced pair of alternatives. John's treatment of the Sabbath may be neither "negation" nor "clarification" but an instance of prophecy/fulfillment or of transcended categories. Moreover, on a point of detail important to Bacchiocchi, ἕως ἄρτι ("until now") does not necessarily mean precisely *usque hoc* ("until now"); it *can* mean "until now" without reference to whether or not there is continuity beyond the "now," as lexical study reveals, and as C. K. Barrett, *The Gospel According to St John* (Philadelphia: Westminster, 1958), pp. 255–56, rightly notes.

[153]E.g., *Shab.* 18:3; 19:6.

[154]For an excellent analysis of the proceedings, cf. C. H. Dodd, *Interpretation*, pp. 79–81. The intricate questions connected with 7:32–33, 35, need not be probed here. In the last few years the work of J. L. Martyn, recently revised (*History and Theology in the Fourth Gospel* [Nashville: Abingdon, 1979]), has focused a great deal of attention on John 9, and he has concluded that everything from verse 8 on refers to the polemics of John's day and not to events in Jesus' day. Although I am inclined to agree with Martyn's thesis that John is concerned with certain church/synagogue polemics of his own day, I am not at all persuaded that any of the verses are on this account inauthentic. Cf. the discussion of parts of Martyn's book in Carson, "Historical Tradition."

[155]W. A. Meeks, *The Prophet-King* (Leiden: Brill, 1954), p. 288.

[156]*The Law in the Fourth Gospel.*

[157](Berkeley: University of California Press, 1974). Cf. also the last few pages of Richard Morgan, "Fulfillment in the Fourth Gospel: The Old Testament Foundation," *Int* 11 (1957): 155–65.

[158]E.g, J. S. King, "The Prologue to the Fourth Gospel: Some Unsolved Problems," *ExpT* 86 (1974–75): 372–75.

[159]Not only the possibility of taking John 5 this way springs to mind, but one also wonders at the irony in John 19:31, for there the Jews want to take Jesus' body down from the cross because of the onset of the Sabbath—indeed, a special Sabbath!

[160]So, rightly, E. J. Young, "Sabbath," *NBD*, pp. 1110–11.

[161]E.g., Beckwith, *This Is the Day*, pp. 22–24.

[162]Since Rordorf, *Sunday*, pp. 65–66, fails to make this distinction, his conclusions are invalid.

[163]Mishnah, *Hag.* 1:8.

[164]Cf. H. Riesenfeld, "Sabbat et Jour du Seigneur," pp. 214–15.

5

THE SABBATH, SUNDAY, AND THE LAW IN LUKE/ACTS

M. Max B. Turner

M. Max B. Turner is Lecturer in New Testament at London Bible College.

More than a quarter of the New Testament comes from the hand of Luke.[1] This writer was, in measure, both a theologian of the early church and a witness concerning its history.[2] This chapter seeks to investigate what light his writings throw on the use of the Sabbath and the first day of the week in the apostolic church.

The Σabbaton References in Luke's Gospel

The word σάββατον appears 21[3] times in Luke (4:16, 31; 6:1, 2, 5 (*twice*), 6, 7, 9; 13:10, 14 (*twice*), 15, 16; 14:1, 3, 5; 18:12; 23:54, 56; 24:1[4]). The first nine of these references, and the last three are all found in Markan contexts. Those in chapter 13 belong to Luke's special material, as does 18:12. There is some evidence that the Sabbath incident in Luke 14 is derived from Q. We shall examine the material in accordance with this source analysis.

The Σάββατον References in Markan Contexts

Luke has taken much of his material on the Sabbath from Mark without making significant changes. Luke retains the whole of Mark 1:14–3:18 as a unit; thus demonstrating his sensitivity to the structure and purpose of this block in his source. He introduces *some* changes within the block, but only such as tend to highlight the points that are made by Mark's redaction.

Conzelmann's dictum that Luke "takes over word for word a large part of Mark's material and destroys Mark's redaction, . . . so thoroughly that hardly one stone remains upon another"[5] could hardly be less true than in this instance. Mark opens his account of Jesus' ministry with the summary[6] statement that Jesus preached the good news of God (1:14), which the evangelist then clarifies in terms of the fulfillment of the (expected) time, the dawn of the kingdom, and the need to repent. Mark immediately proceeds to depict the good news in action,[7] commencing with a story of an exorcism—a most vivid demonstration of the inbreaking of the kingdom of God and the overturning of the reign of Satan (1:21–28).

Mark's redaction[8] then presents the reader with a number of scenes in a sequence that itself contains a message.[9] Jesus' miracles draw large crowds (1:32–33; cf. 1:28) but Mark, by immediately introducing the wilderness motif (ἔρημον τόπον, "a desert place") in connection with Jesus' praying (1:35), probably identifies this apparent success with temptation for Jesus.[10] According to Lane's interpretation, Jesus resolutely turns His back on Capernaum, which was not truly responding to the good news (cf. Matt. 11:23) of which Jesus' miracles are merely acted parables.[11] The pericope that follows (the healing of the leper, Mark 1:40–45) makes the point that while Jesus does not wish His reputation as a miracle worker to spread outside the context of

His preaching, His miracles are reported abroad and gather the enormous crowds; the mixed nature of which Jesus later portrays in the parable of soils.[12]

The remaining pericopes in this Markan block all depict conflict situations precipitated by Jesus' acts and two of these conflicts (2:38 and 3:1–5) were concerned with the attitude that Jesus took to the Sabbath Halakah. They are included in Mark's account, however, less for their positive teaching on the nature of the Sabbath than for the reaction that they provoked; culminating in 3:6,[13] which is a turning point in the Gospel.

Luke has not used the summary with which Mark has introduced this block (Mark 1:14–15), but his sensitivity to its contents and purpose is shown by what he puts in its place: an account of the incident at Nazareth (Luke 4:16–30).[14] This pericope contains the substance of Mark 1:16–3:6. It has both the positive message of the proclamation of a messianic jubilee—eschatological release from the enslaving powers; a vivid parallel to the language of the kingdom[15]—and a foreshadowing of the conflict that was to lead to the cross (Luke 4:28–30).

While Luke's account of Jesus' refusal to stay at Capernaum may appear to lack the Markan bite, nevertheless Luke at two other places strengthens what the second evangelist implies: (1) In 5:16 he states that while the crowds grew bigger Jesus repeatedly withdrew into the wilderness. The adversative δέ ("but") in verse 16 marks temptation overtones behind the scene.[16] (2) Luke's special account of the call of the disciples (5:1–11)[17] appears at a different point in the framework of the narrative from Mark's equivalent (1:16–20). It has been moved to such a position that it stands as a lesson to the milling, clamoring crowds (4:42–43) to the effect that the appropriate response to Jesus' miracles is awareness of the need for forgiveness.[18] From men who show such a response, Jesus does not withdraw (contrast 5:8 with 4:43; 5:16), rather, He invites them to join in the eschatological[19] proclamation.

In the light of the above we can be relatively confident that even when Luke has little to offer by way of distinctive material, he was no mere compiler but had a firm grasp of the significance of the traditions he used. With this brief introduction to the context we may turn to a more detailed investigation of the relevant Sabbath passages.

Luke 4:16. The form *ἡ ἡμέρα τῶν σαββάτων* ("the Sabbath day") is probably Lukan (cf. Acts 16:13 in a "we" section; also Acts 13:14). This does not preclude the possibility that the Sabbath was mentioned in Luke's source (the parallel tradition in Mark 6:2 reads *γενομένου σαββάτου*, "on the Sabbath") and in any case the occasion could be deduced from the story. But what is the nature of the custom of Jesus Luke mentions here? Is it synagogue attendance per se; hence raising the possibility in some minds that Jesus is set before Luke's readers as a model of reverence for the Sabbath? Or is it Jesus' more recently acquired habit of *teaching* in the synagogues that is primarily in view (cf. the preceding verse!)? The latter alternative is almost certainly to be preferred. Luke elsewhere only once uses the expression κατὰ τὸ εἰωθός ("As His custom was") and that is at Acts 17:2 in respect of Paul's (Sabbath) synagogue *ministry*; the parallel is exact. The mention of Jesus and Paul as constantly in the synagogues (cf. 4:31), therefore, primarily reflects the opportunities presented to them to teach;[20] it provides little real evidence of *theological* commitment on behalf of Jesus or Paul to Sabbath worship (even less, of course, to Sunday worship).

S. Bacchiocchi raises the question of the significance of Luke's mention of the Sabbath in a slightly different form; he notes that the ministry of Christ in Luke begins on a Sabbath, and he goes on to point out that the messianic jubilee message announced naturally has strong sabbatical overtones. It is of importance, he asserts, that Christ in His opening address announces His messianic mission in the language of the sabbatical year. "Did Christ identify his mission with the sabbath in order to make the day a fitting memorial of his redemptive activity?"[21]

Bacchiocchi's answer is affirmative, but we are less confident. Reasons for this will gradually emerge, especially in our analysis of Luke 6:1–5 and 13:1–6 below. In the meantime we must question two of the fundamental assumptions. Would messianic jubilee language necessarily have had strong sabbatical overtones *for Luke*, or has this evocative language of release (ἄφεσις) of those in bondage become a powerful metaphor of redemption *in its own right?* And *if* Luke did connect messianic jubilee language with current notions of an eschatological Sabbath, is there any hard evidence that he took the further step of coming to regard the week-day Sabbath as *the* appropriate memorial of such redemptive activity?

Bacchiocchi's case is necessarily weakened by the observation that neither Isaiah 61 nor the Qumran *pesher* of it (11Q Melchizedek) actually mentions the *weekly* Sabbath. His case could at least claim the support of some evidence if Jesus had confined His use of messianic jubilee motifs to occasions when He taught on the Sabbath and used other metaphors and Old Testament allusions on other days. But this is not the case; Jesus appeals to Isaiah 61 again at Luke 7:22 (cf. also 6:20f.) and it is unlikely that this was a Sabbath. The presence of crowds to be healed, and the journey undertaken by the Baptist's disciples, witness against the possibility.[22] Now if Jesus commonly used messianic jubilee terminology to sum up His ministry,[23] and used such language irrespective of the day of the week, then we have no reason for thinking that special significance attaches to the fact that Jesus' programmatic speech in Luke takes place *on a Sabbath*. Luke gives no editorial hint that the Old Testament passage chosen was particularly appropriate to a Sabbath (the *σήμερον* of v. 21 is much broader in content than this);[24] the mention of the Sabbath has the appearance of being merely incidental to a scene that has been elected to its programmatic position for other reasons.

Luke 4:31b. Does Luke understand *ἐν τοῖς σάββασιν* as a genuine plural,[25] or has he, in fact, followed Mark and used the plural with a singular meaning, referring to the actual occasion on which Jesus healed a demoniac in the Capernaum synagogue? The arguments weigh more heavily in favor of the latter;[26] but there is no obvious redactional significance for the Sabbath/ Sunday question either way.[27]

Luke 6:1–5. "The wording follows Mark fairly closely, mainly with stylistic changes."[28] There is, however, what may be a very important omission: Luke, with Matthew, omits the sentence *τὸ σάββατον διὰ τὸν ἄνθρωπον ἐγένετο, καὶ οὐχ ὁ ἄνθρωπος διὰ τὸ σάββατον* (Mark 2:27, "The Sabbath was made for man; not man for the Sabbath"). But what, precisely, is the significance of the omission? Two possibilities suggest themselves: either Mark 2:27 was not present in the earliest versions of Mark (those used by Matthew and Luke) or Luke deliberately omitted Mark 2:27—either because he disagreed with its theology or, for literary reasons, to heighten the christological comparison between David and Jesus.

The former of these two possibilities has a distinguished line of supporters;[29] but it still fails to convince. Against it stands the unity of the textual tradition; and other arguments besides.[30] We must assume, then, that Luke deliberately omitted Mark 2:27; but why? To date no adequate explanation has been given as to why Luke should disagree with the theological content of this verse. The statement as it stands need neither confirm nor abrogate the Sabbath.[31] And if, indeed, this logion were truly a dominical, universalizing, and hellenizing extension of the Sabbath to the Gentiles, grounded on an alleged creation ordinance (as R. T. Beckwith suggests),[32] or if Jesus' lordship over the Sabbath were grounded in *His having made the day for man's benefit* (as Bacchiocchi argues),[33] then we should be at a complete loss to account for why Luke, the hellenist, dropped such potentially useful apologetic. But Beckwith's suggestion comes to grief on the context,[34] and Bacchiocchi's thesis fails to explain the appearance of the title "Son of Man" in verse 28, a title that is never associated with lordship *at creation* in any of the known literature. It is much more satisfactory to explain Mark 2:27 as reflecting conservative Jewish tradition (cf. *Mekilta* Exod. 31:14 [109*b*]) in which the Sabbath is given to *Israel* and not to the world. The Son of Man is then lord of the Sabbath because He is judge over the Israel of fulfillment.[35]

We are left with the probability that Luke has dropped Mark 2:27 in order to heighten the christological comparison between David and Jesus and to eliminate what may have been, to him, a relatively obscure step in the logic of Jesus' teaching. Such motives certainly account for Matthew's omission of the same words and for his simultaneous addition of 12:5–7, which makes the further point that Jesus is not only greater than David but also greater than the temple (v. 6). Such a thesis furnishes the most satisfactory explanation of Luke's redaction.[36]

What bearing does this have on the Sabbath question? The tradition as we have it tells us that David was privileged, in a particular situation of need, to interpret and apply the shewbread law for himself and for those with him.[37] By typological analogy,[38] Jesus, as the eschatological ruler over the Israel of fulfillment (the Son of Man),[39] can exercise lordship over the Sabbath law in the new situation of the inbreaking kingdom. The frequently quoted rabbinic tradition (*B.Men.* 95*b*) that David took the shewbread on a *Sabbath* is virtually irrelevant, and, in my opinion, so is the observation that Jesus is only breaking the Halakah and not the Torah.[40] The point at issue is that the two leaders of Israel, David and the Son of Man (though probably in very different degrees), have an authority that at least occasionally (and in Jesus' case perhaps permanently) transcends the law and the institutions revealed therein (cf. Matt. 12:5–6).[41]

The implications for Luke's understanding of the role of the law for Jesus (and his entourage) are considerable and will be discussed more fully below. The precise consequences for the Sabbath institution are, however, not clear. H. Schürmann certainly goes too far when he states:

> It is no longer merely a question of rest from work on the Sabbath and how to manage it rightly; the Sabbath itself is abolished by the "Son of man." With "the Lord of the Sabbath" present, "the Lord's Day" (Rev. 1:10) is now within sight.[42]

It is *not* clear that the Sabbath is abrogated, and not even a glimmer of the dawn of the "Lord's Day" is yet to be seen in the Lukan sky.[43] But, on the other hand, Bacchiocchi's claim that the Sabbath is especially hallowed is barely more obvious. If anything the thrust of the pericope is to question the relationship of Jesus and His disciples to the law and its institutions; but the pericope offers no answers.

Luke 6:6–11. The *primary* purpose of this pericope in Mark and Luke (the two may be taken together because Luke's changes are mainly literary and stylistic, including his addition of "on another Sabbath") is to depict the deepening opposition between Jesus and the leaders of Israel. There is, nevertheless, more than a grain of truth in Schürmann's introduction: "Now follows a pericope illustrating the 'lordship' of the Son a man over the

Sabbath as just established in 6:5."[44] But this lordship is not demonstrated in the fashion suggested by Rordorf—a deliberate infringement of the Sabbath commandment *in order to show* that it no longer had binding force.[45] Jesus does break the Sabbath Halakah, at least according to a perverse interpretation of it. But it is not obvious how His healings were "work" in any normal sense,[46] and there is no evidence of His infringing or even coming into tension with the Torah at this point.[47]

The heart of the passage is Jesus' twofold question (v. 9*b*); its purpose "consists in its presenting good *omitted* as evil *committed*."[48] In response to the accusation that Jesus senses (v. 8*a*—Lukan) to be directed against Him (implying that His acts of redemption were to be classified as forbidden "work"), He virtually claims that to withhold acts of mercy because it was a Sabbath would be a work of evil (cf. κακοποιῆσαι, "to do harm") and destruction (cf. ἀπολέσαι, "to destroy").

Rordorf is right to claim that Jesus' stance here is provocative. The Sabbath healing could, presumably, have been avoided without the condition becoming acute.[49] Jesus' question lifts the whole matter out of the merely legal plane onto the moral one.[50] But the force of His argument must first be noted: it is not so much a positive hallowing of the Sabbath to make it a particularly appropriate day for healing[51] as it is a refusal to allow the Halakah to prevent or interfere with His redemptive mission. Stopping the flow of messianic blessing for any reason—including appeal to the Sabbath regulations—is morally evil. It is in this way that Jesus demonstrates that He is Lord of the Sabbath.

Luke 23:54. καὶ ἡμέρα ἦν παρασκευῆς, καὶ σάββατον ἐπέφωσκεν. This is merely a Lukan rewording of Mark 15:42.[52] Luke, however, uses this information to close his Markan passage while Mark himself opens the burial account with it.[53] The reference is of historical, perhaps even apologetic,[54] but not of didactic interest.

Luke 23:54b. καὶ τὸ μὲν σάββατον ἡσύχασαν κατὰ τὴν ἐντολήν. Though in a Markan context this may well be derived (with v. 55) from Luke's special source.[55] A number of scholars detect here a concern to show that the pre-Resurrection community hallowed the Sabbath;[56] and such a view is implied by the translators of the NIV, which places an antithesis between the women's Friday work (preparing spices) and their Sabbath rest.

But since Luke's Sabbath material elsewhere does not give the impression that Jesus' disciples were rigidly conservative with respect to Sabbath observance, it is unlikely that this is the point here. In any case there is no evidence that the women's actions would have been construed as contrary to the law,[57] although purchase of burial salves (mentioned in Mark) would not have been possible. In addition, the contrasting break should come between 23:56b and 24:1*a*,[58] so that the Sabbath rest *κατὰ ἐντολήν* ("according to the commandment") is then clearly to explain why *no one* was at the tomb between the day of Preparation and the resurrection morning.

Luke 24:1a. (*τῇ δὲ μιᾷ τῶν σαββάτων*) "But on the first day of the week . . . they went to the tomb." This reference follows Mark with only stylistic variations. At this stage we need only quote Bacchiocchi's warning: "The four gospels report unanimously that the resurrection of Christ occurred on the 'first day of the week' (Mt 28.1; Mk 16.2; Lk 24.1; Jn 20.1). The writers, however, provide no hint that on such a day a new cult was celebrated in honor of the risen Christ."[59]

The Σάββατον References in Luke's Special Material

Luke 18:12. The claim of the Pharisee to fast "twice a week" (*δὶς τοῦ σαββάτου*) need not detain us.[60]

Luke 13:10–17. Most commentators see this pericope on the healing of the crippled woman on the Sabbath as a deliberately chosen example of "realized eschatology"[61] that emphasizes the importance of Jesus' warnings concerning watchfulness, interpreting the times and repentance, in the immediately preceding material.[62] It thus leads naturally into the parables of the mustard seed and the leaven (13:18–21).

It is not uncommon to regard the section as a variant of the same tradition as is given in 14:1–6 and Mark 3:1–6; its historicity has, accordingly, been challenged. There are Lukan features in the telling of the story, but there is no need to view it as a Lukan creation or to doubt its historical basis in Jesus' polemics with the Pharisees.[63]

Our interest focuses particularly on verses 14–16. The objection raised by the synagogue ruler was not to healing in the synagogue but to healing on the Sabbath.[64] There are six days for work; the sick should come on those days to be healed, not on the Sabbath. Luke introduces Jesus' reply by referring to him as "the Lord" (*ὁ κύριος*, 15), which is quite possibly intended to recall the reader's attention to the earlier Sabbath dispute in which Jesus figures as "the Lord of the Sabbath" (*ὁ κύριος τοῦ σαββάτου*).[65] But the question as to the nature and purpose of that lordship is left open.

At least since the appearance of W. Grundmann's commentary there has been a tendency to suggest that, for Luke, Jesus hallows the Sabbath as a particularly appropriate day for the release of the woman from Satan's bondage.[66] But the evidence for this is not forthcoming and the context suggests otherwise. Jesus faces the ruler's angry outburst with the accusation of hypocrisy. The Pharisees do not use the Sabbath as an excuse to prevent the normal course of humane kindness to animals; they loose their oxen, and donkeys, and water them.[67] Reasoning from the lesser to the greater (*qal wahomer*), when the welfare of one of the sons or daughters of Abraham rather than that of mere beasts is concerned, it is wrong to use the Sabbath as an excuse to limit God's redemptive kindness to the other six days of the week, which is exactly what the synagogue ruler tried to do.[68] There is no question here of the Sabbath being particularly appropriate for such healing; any more than it is particularly appropriate on that day to loose oxen and donkeys from their crib and to water them. The argument, in other words, is not that the Sabbath *is* a special day in this respect but precisely that it is *not*. The inbreaking kingdom, the loosing of Satan's captives, is no respecter of days.

Caird[69] offers no stepping stone between his correct conclusion that the work of liberating victims of Satan's tyranny must (δεῖ, v. 16) continue seven days a week, and his further comment that the Sabbath was actually the *best* day for such works of mercy. To be sure, the Sabbath given to Israel was a token of messianic rest, but this is hardly Luke's point.

One final comment should be made: the English versions usually follow the Greek word order, leaving the mention of the Sabbath (13:16) in what to English is an emphatic position at the end of a sentence. But were Luke's emphasis to fall on the particularly appropriate nature of the Sabbath then *ἡ ἡμέρα τοῦ σαββάτου* ("the Sabbath day") would more naturally be placed closer to, if not before, the main verb—that is, at the *beginning* of the sentence.[70]

The tradition in 13:10–17 is thus to be seen as a partial parallel to John 5: 1–19. The conviction it expresses, that the messianic work continues irrespective of the Sabbath, may well have contributed to the erosion of commitment to the Sabbath (or other special days) in some quarters of the primitive church.

The Σάββατον References in Luke's 'Q' (?) Material

Luke 14:1–6. The Q origin of the story of the healing of the man with dropsy on the Sabbath is inferred from the nature of the contacts between verses 3*b*, 5 and Matthew 12:11, and from Luke's use of Q in the immediately previous section (13:18–35; especially vv. 34–35).[71] It must immediately be admitted that a number of difficulties face this hypothesis[72] and the majority of scholars are of the opinion that 14:1–6 is either to be derived from L or is a Lukan creation based on a pre-lukan logion (v. 5). If the Q origin *is* sound then the passage probably provides further evidence for the hypothesis that Matthew and Luke used different recensions of that material;[73] it is almost impossible to account for the divergences between Matthew and Luke simply in terms of different redactional activities.

In the final analysis neither source criticism nor the context throws much light on this relatively self-explanatory passage. Luke 14:1–24 as a whole appears to be "table-talk" exposing the false standards of Jesus' opponents.[74] Luke 14:1–6 is subordinate to this more general redactional theme; it illustrates the hypocrisy of Jesus' opponents who (it is assumed) would willingly rescue a boy or even an ox[75] in distress on a Sabbath, but would not have Jesus alleviate a merely chronic condition such as dropsy (cf. ὑδρωπικός, v. 2). Jesus' conclusion, drawn from the illustration, thus exceeds rabbinic deductions, but no new principle appears to be involved. Rather, alleviation of the chronically diseased is regarded as self-evidently of a piece with assisting those in other kinds of distress.

Jesus, the Sabbath, and the Law in Luke's Gospel

Jesus' attitude to the Sabbath is clearly only one aspect of His attitude to the broader question of the law. No study of Luke's understanding of the role of the Sabbath (for Jesus and His disciples) can be said to be stable until it has been shown to agree with what Luke has to say about the law. It is to this that we now turn. Our concern cannot be for a complete account of Luke's redaction; within the limits of this paper we are concerned only for the general structure of his approach.[76]

In Luke 1–2, Moses' commandments are regarded as the law of the Lord and obeyed to the letter.[77] With the inbreaking of the kingdom[78] in Jesus' ministry, however, the whole issue of man's relationship to the law becomes more complex. The traditions used by Luke; and by the other evangelists, proclaim a dramatic change on the stage of Israel's religious life—one in which the law loses its central and mediating position[79] and is replaced by the person and teaching of Jesus. Allegiance to Him and to His teaching is now the decisive factor for participation in the glory to come (Luke 12:8–9; cf. 6:46–49; 15:1–32; 18:9–27). In Him inheres the fulfillment of many strands of Old Testament hope;[80] indeed the whole of the law, the prophets, and the psalms looked forward to his coming (24:44). Jesus, for Luke, is *the* eschatological prophet[81] whose light shines brighter than that of Moses or David, brighter even than that of John the Baptist who stands at the head of the prophetic line (7:28–29; cf. 1:15–16).

The tendency to portray Jesus as *the* focus of God's redemptive self-revelation[82] raises the question of Jesus' relationship to the law in its most acute form. The answer to that question is complex. Jesus' attitude to the law seems to involve elements of affirmation and yet, simultaneously, degrees of abrogation.[83] He appears to assert both its continuity and, in some areas, its discontinuity.

A Conservative Strand in Jesus' Teaching on the Law According to Luke?

J. Jervell and R. J. Banks have spoken of a conservative tendency in Luke's handling of the 'law' material, though they offer differing interpretations of it.[84] This tendency is said to be observed at the following points: (1) At 5:14 it is observed that Luke, following Mark, has Jesus tell the healed leper to fulfill the commandments of Moses for cleansing *εἰς μαρτύριον αὐτοῖς* ("as a proof to the people"). (2) At 10:25–28 a young lawyer (*νομικός*)[85] asks Jesus what he should do to inherit eternal life[86] and Jesus answers in terms of an affirmation of the law (vv. 26–27, specifically Deut. 6:5 and Lev. 19:18). (3) The Pharisees ought to have tithed their mint, rue, and other herbs *without* neglecting justice and the love of God; but these things are not alternatives (11:42). (4) Luke 11:44 appears to assume that the laws of ritual uncleanness still apply; hidden graves do truly defile. (5) Luke 16:17–18 seems explicitly to state that not the least stroke of a pen can be dropped from the law; this is confirmed by the intensification of the law's teaching on marriage (16:18). (6) In Luke 16:29 the rich man is told that his brothers have Moses and the prophets; the implication is that what the law teaches about the right use of riches is there for all to see and is of abiding validity. (7) In Luke 18:18–21 the rich ruler asks what he must do to inherit eternal life and Jesus replies with an affirmation of the law—the second table of the Decalogue (cf. 10:25–29). From the above it could be inferred that Luke has a conservative attitude toward the law, but certain further considerations must modify this conclusion.

Modifying Factors

We shall deal with the above passages seriatim and then consider further cases.

1. To some extent the command to obey the law at 5:14 is demanded for the man's rehabilitation into society.[87] But the obedience is not a witness to Jesus' stance with respect to the law;[88] rather, it is an occasion for the ratification of the healing and hence a witness to God's work through Jesus.

2. If this account (10:25–28) stopped at 10:28 it might be possible to argue that Jesus was simply ratifying the law, but the addition of the parable and linking statement (v. 29) changes the situation, as does the context of the whole unit in Luke's redaction.

Luke 10:17–20 emphasizes the inbreaking of the new age witnessed in the expulsion of demons, which testifies to the fall of Satan from his position of power.[89] Luke 10:21–24 brings together two sayings that underline the veiled nature of this inbreaking. It is only revealed to those who are chosen to enter intimate relationship with the Father through the Son. Verse 24 speaks of the blessedness of those who hear Jesus, a theme that is taken up again in the pericope about Mary and Martha (10:38–42), which focuses on the blessedness of Mary who sat at the Lord's feet and listened to His teaching. The content of this teaching is, in part, portrayed between these last two units. The radical new statement of the law implied in the parable appended to Jesus' answer to the lawyer embodies the new teaching of the new age, which a man is blessed to receive.[90]

Ellis perhaps strains the point somewhat when he states that "this parable stands pre-eminent as the Lord's answer to all attempts at self-justification . . . to all legalisms—Jewish or churchly"[91] but Christ certainly uses the parable to transcend the demands of the law; He does not merely expound the law. It should be pointed out too, that Jesus does not anchor His further demand with any exegetical appeal; it is anchored merely in His own authority.

3. The force of the logion in 11:42 derives from its first part; the second *may* simply be a rhetorical device for emphasis of the first.[92] But even if the second part ("without neglecting the others") is not simply a rhetorical device, it would not follow that the Scriptures advocate that the Old Testament law be obeyed today in exactly the same way that it was in Jesus' day by conservative Judaism. The evidence for a perceived change is too great; the nature of that change, however, is not addressed in this saying.

4. The language of 11:44 should not be pressed as it undoubtedly contains an *ad hominem* element. Jesus is teaching Pharisees about themselves; He is not discussing the validity of the ritual law.

5. Luke 16:16ff., 29 must be read in context; they are not unambiguous.[93] The whole chapter appears to constitute "warnings about wealth";[94] the Pharisees, and others who are rich, are warned that the law has already spoken and that those who are deaf to it incur guilt. What is depicted here chimes well with Jesus' tendency elsewhere to adapt His tactics to His audience and, as in parallel cases, to face lawlessness (ἀνομία) with the demands of the law, rather than with an appeal to His own teaching beyond the law.[95] We cannot, however, deduce from this a simple ratification of the law's eternal validity in its own right, nor can such a conclusion be drawn from 16:17. The law's eternal validity is certainly maintained, despite the dawning of the new age,[96] but it has been transcended and changed by being sucked into the powerful vortex of Jesus' messianic teaching and demands. This is clear from verse 18, which, while affirming the validity of marriage in the strongest possible terms, nevertheless "certainly exceeds the teaching of the mosaic law and results in a portion of it being no longer applicable to the present situation."[97] Banks correctly further notes that Jesus' position cannot accurately be described in

terms of "abrogation" of the law, nor can it be considered a challenge to the divine status of the deuteronomic legislation.

6. With regard to Luke 18:18–21, note again that Jesus does not stop at an affirmation of the law in its own right, but transcends and surpasses it. The real issue is total discipleship to Jesus, and the equally real danger is that wealth may prevent a man from entering the kingdom at all—even if he has "kept all the commandments" since his youth. Jesus endorses the Mosaic law only to surpass it in His own demands.

Beyond a discussion of these passages, we should note the following: (1) Jesus at no point encourages His disciples to a study of the law as an end in itself.[98] (2) Luke's attitude to the law in 6:1ff. is not conservative, but subordinates the law to the activity of Christ.[99] (3) At Luke 11:41, the point appears to be that if the Pharisees deal with their inner condition, external and ritual washing would be unnecessary. This logion is thus parallel in its thrust to that of Mark 7:18–23.[100] (4) Luke envisages a time when the destruction of the temple will make complete obedience to the Sinai revelation impossible (21:5–24—events that do not immediately lead to the end).[101]

Synthesis

Several features of Luke's law material emerge as important. First, Luke has a heavy emphasis on the promise-fulfillment aspect of the law.[102] Jesus' advent as Savior is heralded as the long-awaited fulfillment of the covenant to Abraham (1:55, 72–73) and His salvation is dispensed to those who, by their faith, show themselves to be sons (19:9) or daughters (13:16) of Abraham.[103] So too the law, the prophets, and the psalms are established in the sense that their *predictive* nature is fulfilled in Christ (24:44).

Second, this essential belief that Jesus' ministry and teaching is what is *prophesied* by the law (cf. Matt. 11:13)[104] may provide the link between Jesus' validation of the law and His transcending of it in His own demands.[105] For Jesus, even the weightiest demands of the law remain in force only *within* His teachings (where they are always modified by His own claims).[106] The law no longer has any merit of its own; it is at best a preliminary standard. Jesus is not merely "sharpening" or "radicalizing" the law; nor yet is He "expounding" it or "setting out its true meaning." Jesus neither moves out from the law in making His demands nor does He usually relate His teaching back to the law.[107] Even less does He (or Luke) operate with such categories as "moral," "ceremonial," and "civil" law, dividing some that are retained from others that are abolished. Indeed, to bring such categories into the discussion at this point would be anachronistic.[108] Jesus fulfills and surpasses the law.

Third, an easy solution to the whole problem of Luke's attitude to the law might be to claim that Jesus' teaching represents the new law of the new age. But this must probably be resisted as an oversimplification; while parts of Judaism expected a new covenant, it is unlikely that any group expected a new Torah.[109] Besides, Jesus is not identified as the "prophet like Moses" in teaching contexts and, in any case, very little of His teaching has the character of legislation.[110] The language of "new law" never appears in the gospels.

A synthesis of these features can be arrived at if it be assumed that they spring from the recognition of Jesus' teaching as constituting the unfolding revelation of the new *covenant*. This term embraces more than the term "new law" and suffers none of its drawbacks. A new covenant was definitely expected in some quarters (cf. Jer. 31:31ff.). The Qumran sect even considered their own community to be a fulfillment of this promise.[111] Moreover, the promise of the covenant did not stipulate clearly the future role of the law (see further, below).

A difficulty in the way of this explanation of the law material in Luke is that the words καινὴ διαθήκη ("new covenant") occur only once, and that in a traditional passage (22:20).[112] It is thus possible that Luke was not concerned to clarify the theological shifts that can be seen taking place with respect to the law in Luke-Acts.[113] But this objection is not as powerful as it might seem. We shall discuss the Acts material later, but, the following points must all be taken into account with respect to Luke:

1. The importance of the concept of a new covenant (καινὴ διαθήκη) for Luke is not to be measured simply by the frequency with which the words themselves appear. The single mention in 22:20 comes at a crucial point and interprets the whole passion tradition.[114] Luke has preferred this version of the "cup-word" to that in Mark 14:24 (where καινὴ is implied) and presumably he must have heard it every time he partook of the Lord's Supper. Certainly all the Pauline churches used this formula (1 Cor. 11:25).

2. It must be stressed that while the *words* "new covenant" do not appear again in Luke, the *concept* for which the word stands is readily traceable both in the Gospel and in Acts. J. Guhrt is probably cutting some corners when he states that the underlying thought has been taken over in the sayings about the kingdom of God[115] and then without further ado, adds, "Linguistically we can see this perhaps most clearly in Lk 22:29 in the phrase *diatithemai . . . basileian . . . which exactly expresses the formula diatithemai diathēkēn*."[116] But he is surely correct to affirm that new covenant and kingdom are correlated concepts, and Luke elsewhere equates God's inbreaking salvation with fulfillment of the covenant made to Abraham (1:72–75).[117] The new and eschatologically flavored grace of God poured out in the hearts of men is the reality in Jesus' ministry[118] for which "salvation," "kingdom of God," "mes-

sianic jubilee," "new covenant," etc., are merely overlapping descriptions with slightly different nuances.

3. Comparison with the other gospels shows that Luke has not restricted a more generally widespread use of "new covenant" language. As this terminology flourished in the post-resurrection community (cf. 1 Cor. 11:25; 2 Cor. 3:6; Gal. 4:24. Eph. 2:12 and Heb. passim), we should probably infer that the absence of further references in the gospel tradition is a mark of its fidelity in this respect. It is quite possible that Jesus did not use the language much; perhaps first of all at the Last Supper. We can only surmise *why* Jesus did not frequently draw on this vocabulary, and why it appears for a first time in the passion setting. The easiest explanation is not an unlikely one: (1) the term "covenant" was tending to be replaced in the milieu in which Jesus spoke,[119] (2) the passover associations of the Last Supper made the term "covenant" particularly appropriate for the occasion, (3) Jesus may have avoided referring to His own claims in terms of "new covenant" stipulations in part to preserve the "messiannic secret," and (4) it is possible that there is a sense in which Jesus considered His death/resurrection to *inaugurate* the new covenant of which He spoke.[120]

Summary and Prospect

Far from hallowing the Sabbath as a particularly appropriate day either for rest or for redemptive works, the Jesus of Luke's portrait continually subordinates the Sabbath to the demands of His own mission. Jesus' attitude to the law is entirely consistent with this; the law is being fulfilled but simultaneously transcended in His teaching and ministry, which together constitute the inauguration of a new covenant.

We must now turn to Acts. Does the picture that emerges there confirm what we have deduced from the gospel? And what effect did Jesus' ministry, death, and resurrection have on the Sabbath observance of the church? Is there any hint of a transfer of Sabbath ideas to the first day of the week, and if so, to what extent? These are the three questions that will be discussed next.

Christians and the Law in Acts

Does an examination of Acts confirm the view of Luke's understanding of the law that we derived from the gospel? Indeed, is it possible to gain a coherent picture of Luke's attitude to the law at all? F. Overbeck, in an influential essay, has charged Luke with being unprincipled when dealing with the law.[121] He claims that although Paul realized that the law came to an end with Christ, Luke tried both to eat his cake and to have it, to maintain that the law was unnecessary for salvation (the Gentiles are not required to keep it) and yet that it was to be obeyed by Jewish Christians.[122] Kirsopp Lake has been followed by E. Haenchen and J. C. O'Neill in attempting to explain this apparent tension with the suggestion that Luke was remote to the whole argument: "The question of the law has been settled and it was not necessary to discuss it."[123] Against these positions, J. Jervell states a new and striking thesis.[124] Arguing against Haenchen, he insists that Luke's terminology of law differs from that of the rest of the New Testament writers, is widely varied, and shows an awareness of the law that is both conservative and Jewish. He then tries to resolve the tension by making it the interpretive key for the whole of Luke's ecclesiology. Jervell's thesis is so important, and has such obvious bearing on our study, that it must be described more fully.

Jervell's Case

The attempt to establish his thesis led Jervell to write studies touching many of the most important themes in Acts, but undoubtedly central to his argument are three essays. In the first of these, "The Divided People of God,"[125] Jervell denies that Luke considers the church as a "new" or "true" Israel.[126] There is only one Israel: the old one. The preaching of the apostles sifts Israel and those who do not listen to the "prophet like Moses" are excluded from the people of God (Acts 3:23).[127] The promises given to Israel are fulfilled to the Jewish Christians, and the mission to the Jews is *not* a failure. As God had promised, He was now blessing Abraham's seed (Jervell takes σπέρμα, "seed," Acts 3:25, to refer to *Israel*) and would through them bless all the people of the world (i.e., on Jervell's interpretation, the Gentiles). Again, as Amos had prophesied (9:11; Acts 15:16–18), the Gentiles flock to the *restored* and *cleansed* Israel.[128] So, of necessity, the missions in the diaspora "restore" Israel first; then the Gentiles receive salvation as an associate people. As a substitute for Jewish membership in the people of God, God accepts as valid that cleansing of the Gentiles that comes upon them by faith (15:9–10).

The essay entitled, "The Law in Luke-Acts"[129] is the linchpin of his thesis. Here, Jervell wishes to maintain five points:

1. The law is *Israel's* law, including the ceremonial law; it is the sign of Israel being the people of God. The essential of the law is circumcision (15:1, 5; 16:3), which Luke does not reinterpret (contrast Rom. 2:29; Phil. 3:3). The community instinctively obeys the law and is especially careful to maintain ritual purity (10:13–14, 23; 11:3). Peter can only enter Cornelius' house because God has made this Gentile clean.

2. Luke defends Jesus against the charge brought in Acts 6:14 by removing any mention of criticism of the law from the Gospel.[130] Thus there is no summary of the law, no mention of all foods being cleansed, and the law on

adultery was not merely given "for the hardness of your hearts." Instead the law was delivered by angels (7:53) and consists in "living words," which are perpetually valid (Acts 7:38; Luke 16:16–17). In view of Luke's understanding of Israel it is quite logical that he should depict Christians at Jerusalem as "myriads of Jews, all of them staunch upholders of the law" (21:20). Luke could not have done this if he had shown Jesus altering, or summarizing, the law.

3. Luke shows the most conservative attitude to the law of all the New Testament writers. He does not try to Christianize the law; but nor has he simply lost interest in the problem. Repeatedly, Luke refers to the Jews charging Christians with apostasy; the sayings are stereotyped and without parallel elsewhere in the New Testament. The charges include blasphemy against Moses, the law, and the temple.[131] To speak against the law is to speak against Israel as the people of God; this sin refers primarily to the ritual aspect, that is to the law as conceived as the indelible character[132] of Israel. Luke is thus interested in the law as a distinct entity and phenomenon, not in single commandments.

4. The reason for this conservative attitude is that Luke knows of only one Israel, one people of God, and one covenant.[133] He stresses repeatedly that the promises are to *Israel*. The "seed of Abraham" is not spiritualized, and the covenant to Abraham is circumcision, which at the same time involves Gentile participation in the promises to Israel. So it is by zeal for the law that the primitive church shows itself to be the people of God entitled to salvation. Those who do not believe all that is said in the law and the prophets, and thus do not accept the "prophet like Moses," will be extirpated from Israel (3:23). Because Jewish Christians are the restored and rebuilt Israel, circumcision and the law become the mark of their identity.

5. Jervell turns to the problem of the Gentiles and their law-free inclusion,[134] and argues that it is strictly inaccurate to speak of a law-free mission. The Gentiles' place is as an associate people and their inclusion, far from being an abrogation of the law, is prophesied by it and subject to the conditions laid out in the law as Acts 15:21 asserts. Luke neither champions justification by the law nor does he relegate it to a previous epoch. The charges and declarations of innocence are mentioned no fewer than six times; all, with the exception of 21:21ff., concern charges made by non-believers. Luke is therefore not facing a problem from within the church; the accusation comes from Jews and it is to the effect that Christians are committing apostasy. Luke's reply is that it is the Jews who have disobeyed the law and rejected Moses; Jewish Christians are completely faithful.

The third essay, "Paul: Teacher of Israel,"[135] supports this. Paul has founded a large segment of the church. The Jews, however, have accused him of abandoning the law and teaching apostasy in the diaspora. As such a claim would demolish his ecclesiology, Luke structures the whole of the last part of Acts as a defense of Paul not, as is usually held, against Roman, but against Jewish charges.[136] Paul is still a Pharisee (23:6) and a true Israelite and is apprehended while fulfilling a Jewish vow. He has done nothing against the customs of the fathers, the temple, or the law (25:8; 28:17). He believes everything in the law and the prophets, which is more than can be said for the leaders of the nation (23:2, 5). Luke uses the undoubted conservative character of James to defend Paul and to buttress his argument at its weakest points.[137]

The implications of Jervell's thesis for the Sabbath/Sunday question should be clear, but we must criticize his case at a number of points.

Criticism and Reconstruction

Criticism. The schema suggested by Jervell, according to which Israel is restored before the Gentiles can receive blessing as an associate people of God, is probably artificial. Although it is a *possible* reading at Acts 15:16–17,[138] it is most improbable at 3:25 where σπέρμα ("seed") is almost certainly a reference to Christ[139] (not Israel) and αἱ πατριαὶ τῆς γῆς ("the families of the earth") probably covers *both* Israel *and* the Gentile world[140] (not *merely* the Gentiles).

We have already seen that Luke was not as conservative as Jervell is inclined to think.[141] It may be true that Luke omits the discussion of ritual cleansing that is present in our edition of Mark, but this is not altogether surprising as it is part of Luke's "great omission" (as Jervell also notes). The observation that it does not appear in the gospel, however, can hardly be used to substantiate the immutability of the law for Christian practice, since even if Luke 11:41[142] is irrelevant, the vision in Acts 10:9ff. reaches a conclusion similar to that of the Markan passage by a similar process, namely, stepping from ritual cleanness to the conditions by which a man can be clean before God in a broader sense.[143] Jervell's argument, that the law is not abrogated by Peter since he enters Cornelius' house only *after* God has cleansed this Gentile God-fearer, misses the point. Luke understands the household to be "clean" in the ritual sense precisely because the food laws, according to which these Gentiles might be a source of ritual uncleanness, had been dealt with in Peter's vision. But the cleansing of the *heart* by *faith*, to which Luke refers, took place in the hearing of the gospel (Acts 15:7–8) and *not* before it.[144]

In any case, how successfully has Luke protected Jesus from the charges leveled in Acts 6:14 if Stephen, full of the Spirit of Jesus (6:10; 7:55 and cf.

16:6–7), virtually admits equivalent charges when they are brought against him by "false witnesses" (6:13ff.)?[145]

We have already hinted[146] (there will be further evidence below) that Jervell's schema does not allow sufficiently for the decisive effects of Jesus' ministry in transforming Israel; the result is that Jervell distorts the Jewish Christianity depicted by Luke by making it too Torah-centric. Acts 15 must surely be the Achilles' heel of such a construct. Two considerations weigh decisively against Jervell's thesis:

1. It is highly doubtful that Jervell can successfully maintain that Luke saw in the conditions of the apostolic decree a fulfillment of all that the law could be expected to require of Gentiles as an associate people of God. Jervell, Catchpole, Haenchen, and O'Neill quote H. Waitz[147] as having demonstrated that the order of demands made on the sojourner in Leviticus 17–18 is the same as that of the authentic text of the decree (Acts 15:29; 21:25).[148] Although this is correct, it goes beyond the evidence to say that Luke would have deduced that *only these* demands were spoken of by the Old Testament. The גֵּר("alien" or "sojourner") of Leviticus 17–18 was definitely not expected to keep only these four commandments; he was, for example, also to keep the Sabbath (Exod. 20:10; 23:12).[149] Indeed, with rare exceptions (e.g., the Passover, in which only the circumcised were to take part, Exod. 12:28), the sojourner shared with Israel in the *whole* law (Exod. 12:49; Lev. 16:29; 18:26; Num. 15:15; Deut. 5:14; 16:11, 14; 29:9–15).[150] Religiously, this made the גֵּר almost equivalent to the later προσήλυτος ("proselyte"), which is in fact the very word used by the LXX to translate גֵּר in these (and most other) passages.[151] Luke, reading the word προσήλυτος in his Greek Old Testament, and knowing what contemporary Judaism demanded of a proselyte, could hardly have come to the conclusion that these four ritual laws were *all* that should be demanded of the Gentiles as an associate people of God[152] *unless of course he had some good reason to believe that the Old Testament law was no longer binding in all ways and in every detail*. It is significant to note, in this connection, that the council's final court of appeal is not Moses[153] and the law—they are not so much as mentioned in the letter—but the Spirit (Acts 15:28).[154]

It follows from these observations that Luke is unlikely to have considered these four ritual laws as the condition of Gentile inclusion into the people of God (indeed the laws on which the decree is partly based were specifically abrogated by Peter's vision); they probably represent an ad hoc arrangement to protect the sensibilities of those who heard the law each week in the synagogue (i.e., Jews and strict Jewish Christians). They were not the full demands made on an associate people of God, but the minimal requirements that would allow continued fellowship between Gentiles and scrupulous Jews (whether Christian or as yet unbelieving).[155] Obedience to the decree would possibly identify Gentile believers in the eyes of unbelieving Jews as God-fearers[156] who kept the seven Noachian commandments;[157] as Christians they would presumably not have to be told to refrain from cursing judges, from blasphemy of God or from robbery.[158]

If the above is on the right lines then Jervell is certainly wrong, for the corollary of what we have said is that the Jerusalem council *made a break in principle with the law.*[159] At the council they accorded to the Gentiles the full status of the people of God (cf. the use of λαός in 15:14,[160] and what follows) while only insisting that they obey the Torah to the same extent as the גֵּר תּוֹשָׁב. As far as Judaism was concerned a member of this latter group, as distinct from the true proselyte, had no share in Israel, nor had he (though some authorities were more generous) a part in the age to come.[161] Jervell appears to think that the Jewish Christians combined a firm belief that they were themselves the true Israel with a zeal for the law which was supposed to demonstrate this claim. But surely the logical conclusion of such belief would be to insist that the Gentiles, as an associate people of God, should also take on (and hardly with less zeal) the yoke of the law, for that is what the Old Testament appeared to expect of the sojourner, and that is certainly what Judaism demanded of the proselyte. Jervell wants the Jewish Christians to be simultaneously both much more conservative than Judaism *and* much more liberal!

2. The attitude of Peter in 15:10–11, if not explicitly making a total break with the law (at least in principle) for both Jew and Gentile, nevertheless can hardly be said to move in the pious plane of zeal for the law that Jervell describes! The following points should be observed:

(a) In 15:10 Peter offers a rebuttal of the sharpest kind to the judaizing section. Their proposals are nothing less than a defiant challenging of God's revelation at Caesarea (Acts 10),[162] which had established the freedom of Gentile Christians from the law.

(b) The basis for his rejection of the judaizing position is that God has cleansed the hearts of these Gentiles (a fact witnessed by his giving the Spirit to them). This is most important: "cleansing" or "purification" was the goal of much of the law material in the Old Testament, and it was also Israel's eschatological hope (cf. Ezek. 36:25; 1QS 4:20–21). If the Gentiles have already attained the promised cleansing (and the gift of the Spirit with which it is associated)[163] without the law, that has consequences not only for the subsequent Gentile relationship to the law, but also for Jewish Christians. Hence:

(c) In 15:10*b* and 11 the corollary is drawn out. The law is now simply seen as a burden that neither the fathers nor the present generation could bear.

This despite Conzelmann and Haenchen who complain that Judaism did not think in such a way of the law. In the first place their complaint is inaccurate: the עַמ־הָאָרֶץ ("people of the land") took just this stance, and it is historically convincing that Peter, who came from their ranks, would be goaded to his most negative statements about the law by the presence of Pharisees.[164]

But secondly, their complaint misses the antithesis introduced by the ἀλλά ("but") of verse 11. A new situation has arisen that distances the community from the experience of the fathers (and that of their former selves, οὔτε ἡμεῖς ["nor we"] in v. 10); it is from the Christian perspective of grace received through Jesus (and yet to be received)—of eschatological cleansing independent of the law—that nomism[165] appears a burden.

While Peter starts by defending the law-free salvation of the Gentiles, he concludes by applying his "proof" to the case of Jewish Christians as well: "But we believe that we will be saved through the grace of the Lord Jesus, just as they will" (15:11). [166] Any attempt to make Peter a champion of nomism (even for Jewish Christians) reduces the whole argument to a non sequitur.

Clearly, then, Luke did not set out to teach that Jewish Christians should demonstrate their claim to be Israel by strict obedience to the law. We shall have to find some other explanation for the "myriads of Jews, all staunch upholders of the law" that we encounter in 21:20, and for Luke's handling of the accusations brought against Paul. This will not be too difficult, as we shall see shortly.

Reconstruction: The Community, the Law and the Covenant In Acts. We began this section by asking whether it was possible to gain a coherent picture of Luke's attitude to the law in Acts, and whether such a picture would confirm our conclusions drawn from analysis of the Gospel. Jervell had offered a theologically monolithic account of Acts' law material which pointed in a very different direction from the one our study of Luke envisaged; but we have found Jervell's case to be unconvincing. He attempts to explain the whole of Luke's ecclesiology in terms of the nomism of God's restored Israel. This fails to explain the abolition of the laws of purity in Acts 10, the freedom permitted to the Gentiles in Acts 15, and, particularly, Peter's remarks in 15:10ff. Furthermore, Jervell entirely misrepresents Luke's emphases. The mainspring of Luke's theology is not the restoration of Israel and the church's nomism, but the lordship of Christ by the Spirit and its corollary, a new covenant people.

Acts 2 is programmatic for the second half of Luke's work, as Luke 4 is for the gospel. Peter's speech interprets the Pentecost experience in terms of the exaltation of Jesus as Lord of the Spirit.[167] The importance of this seems to be neglected both by Jervell's position and by the many who speak of Luke's "absentee christology."[168] According to Acts 2:33, Jesus now fulfills the promise that God made through Joel to pour out the Spirit. It is thus Jesus who "gives" the spiritual gifts experienced ("he has poured out this that you see and hear"), and this in turn means that the intimate relationship between God and the Spirit[169] witnessed throughout the Old Testament is now predicated of *Jesus* and the Spirit. The Spirit of God has become the Spirit of Jesus (Acts 16:6–7) as well.[170] Jesus' saving activity and "presence" is experienced by the Spirit. He is experienced in, and often *through*, the community of Spirit-empowered disciples in a way comparable to, and yet transcending, that in which God alone was experienced by the Spirit in the Old Testament period. Although generally unobserved, this is a major root of New Testament christology.[171]

The focus of redemptive revelation has shifted from the Torah to Jesus; adherence to His teaching and leading is the necessary and sufficient condition of belonging to the Israel of fulfillment (Acts 3:22–23).[172] By the Spirit, in His disciples, Jesus continues the role announced in Luke 4:16–21.[173] All of this amounts to a new kind of relationship between God and His people, mediated through Jesus. In the circumstances, we should expect to find new covenant imagery being applied. Just this appears to lie behind Acts 2:33, the form of which is basically parallel to some Jewish traditions of interpretation of Psalm 67:19 (LXX)[174] according to which Moses is the figure who ascends on high; he receives the gift of the law with which he returns to men. Peter now reapplies this "pentecostal" reading to Jesus, the eschatological Moses. We are most probably on the right lines, then, if we understand Luke as presenting Pentecost as a further fulfillment of new covenant hopes, a fulfillment that coincides with Jewish celebration of the giving of the law.[175]

E. Haenchen,[176] I. Broer[177] and others[178] have denied that Luke thought of the period of the church as fulfilling new covenant hopes; but their objections are without weight. They argue that: (1) there is no trace of a "new Torah" motif in Luke-Acts (in parallel to the Torah given through Moses) and (2) Luke nowhere speaks of a *new* covenant; he prefers to think of the gift of the Spirit as a renewal and quickening of the initial bond (primarily the Abrahamic covenant). The second of these arguments is unsound—the long text of Luke 22:20 is to be preferred[179]—and, in any case, is misleading. It rests on a false antithesis between new covenant hopes and covenant renewal hopes. Nor is there necessarily any tension between new covenant hopes and longing for the fulfillment of the promise to Abraham—at least not in the mind of Paul where they are two sides of one coin (Gal. 3:15)! The first argument fares no better; it rests on the false assumption that new covenant hopes involved the expectation of a new Torah, but this is untrue.[180]

The historicity of Luke's picture of the beginnings of the Christian community has been challenged, but its broad outline is relatively secure. It may not be possible to show that the speech in Acts 2 goes back to *Peter*, but it is barely more likely that Luke, the hellenist, created its very Jewish theology and midrashic style of argument.[181] There is no sound reason to deny that the speech represents an early reaction to the phenomenon of Pentecost.[182] Several further considerations support the view that from the start the church regarded itself as the community of a *new* covenant (and not merely as a sect within Judaism): (1) The primitive church did not regard itself merely as a "holy remnant" but "by means of the circle of 'the twelve' gathered round his person, expressed the claim of God on the entire nation of the twelve tribes."[183] It was the totality of the Israel of fulfillment (see n. 126) constituted by the Christ-event. (2) This conviction was further expressed in the use of a *baptism invoking the name of Christ* as a rite of entry into the community. (3) Again, it shared a common meal at which the Lord's death was interpreted in covenant terms (1 Cor. 11:25; Luke 22:20; Mark 14:24)[184] and His future coming was invoked (1 Cor. 11:26; 16:22).

This observation—that the mainspring of Luke's theology is the lordship of Christ by the Spirit, with its corollary that the disciples constitute a new covenant people[185]—is not only in harmony with the picture that emerges from our study of the gospel, but also goes far toward explaining the *conflict* about the role of the law that the rest of Acts depicts.

This conflict barely requires full documentation as it is fully discussed by virtually all works on Christian origins. It will suffice for us to outline the major turning points: (1) According to Luke, the church, at first, had not worked out the full implications of its Easter experience, and, to a great extent, merely ran on in the well-worn grooves of Jewish piety.[186] (2) Stephen and the hellenistic Christians[187] were understood (by reacting Judaism) to be challenging the centrality of the law and the temple for the people of God,[188] and this invited persecution on the church—particularly; though not exclusively; on the hellenists.[189] (3) The gospel was preached beyond the boundaries of Judaism (8:4–40; 10:1–11:18; 11:20–21; 13:1–14:28) and those who responded were admitted to the church without becoming proselytes.[190] This ultimately led to dissension at Antioch[191] and to the apostolic council[192] where, according to Luke, the issue of the Christian's relationship to the law was settled, at least in principle.

If the early church understood itself as the community of the new covenant this conflict is perfectly understandable, if not predictable. The Old Testament was ambiguous about the future role of the law within the promised new covenant (and so was Jesus' teaching);[193] the conflict that ensued in the early church was the outworking of that ambiguity.

According to Jeremiah; the newness of the promised covenant was to inhere precisely in that God's Torah would be written on men's hearts. This could easily be interpreted as a promise of a golden age of *nomism;* alternatively it could be understood in terms of a time when all the necessary knowledge of God (His instruction, torah) would be intuitive rather than legislated. The latter view could easily develop the prophetic antithesis between cleanness of heart (cf. Ezek. 36) and ceremonial cleanness, leading to a more radical interpretation of the new covenant.

Luke's account mentions both views, but the nomist party (15:1, 5 etc.) is never more than a foil. His sympathies lie with the alternative course represented in Peter (and Paul). Peter judges that Cornelius is "clean" before God (the very goal of the law) by *faith*, bypassing the law—indeed, some of the very laws by which Cornelius would be accounted "unclean" are specifically abrogated. Luke, following Peter, considers this to be paradigmatic. Hence the issue of contention between the two parties at the council might crudely be expressed as follows: Peter's understanding of the new covenant stressed the writing of God's Torah *on the heart*, while the Pharisee's stressed that it should be the *Mosaic law* written on the heart.

The situation following the martyrdom of Stephen had favored the flourishing in Jerusalem of those who understood the Spirit to be introducing a golden age of nomism. Within this period we must set the ascendancy of James whose Davidic descent, relationship to Jesus, and vigorous adherence to the law, would win him favor in the eyes of the priestly (6:7) and Pharisee (15:5) converts.[194] Only under the leadership of such a party could there be any mission in Israel. If nomism was (at least officially) rejected[195] on theological grounds at the apostolic council, something like it still remained as the only practical rule of life *(Lebensnorm)* for the Christian mission within Judaism. The decision reached at the council was almost too fragile to weather the storms that followed as zealot forces ever increasingly held power in Judaea. There was great pressure on Jewish Christians to be more conservative with respect to the law (cf. Acts 21:20) and to dissociate from the Gentiles, or at least to pressure the Gentile converts to live outwardly as Jews.[196] The situation was made all the more difficult by the major offensive of the "law-free" mission to the Gentiles led by the converted Pharisee, Paul. James' proposal that Paul should prove he was not antinomian by performing a meritorious ritual act[197] and the oath of the sicarii not to take food again until they had destroyed Paul (23:12) testify to the tensions in the situation.

It is these tensions, in part, that account for Luke's apologetically motivated (though not necessarily unhistorical)[198] portrayal of Paul as something like a Christian Pharisee (cf. Acts 26:5).[199] Luke's Paul had to become as one under the law in order to win those under the law (cf. 1 Cor. 9:20–21).

There is a further significant motive revealed in Luke's handling of Paul's relationship to the law. It should be remembered that he defends Paul on charges both under Jewish *and* Roman law, not merely the former. It is the social dimension of the Mosaic law (and of the rabbinic understanding of it) that is important here. It should be remembered that the Jewish Christian belonged to two communities; he belonged to the new covenant people as a believer, but to the Old Testament legislation as a Jew.[200] The Mosaic Law was not simply a religious, but a civil and social law—the origin of Jewish nationality, unity, and practice.

In relating the charges brought against Paul in 16:21; 17:6–7; 18:13–14; 21:28; 23:1–10; 24:5–6, 12; 25:7–8, and in the demonstration that they were false, Luke has brought before his readers that a good Christian is not ἄνομος ("lawless") or ἀνυπότακτος ("unruly"); he is neither a rabble-rouser (λοιμός; 24:5) nor is he guilty of *odium generis humani* ("hatred toward the human race").[201] Paul did not incite his hearers to violence, nor turn his back on Judaism per se, but was willing to remain (to some extent) within its socio-religious structure. Whether out of love for his heritage, or evangelistic zeal, or respect for authority, or a combination of these, we know that this is what Paul did, even to the extent of bearing five times the thirty-nine strokes administered to him by the synagogue (2 Cor. 11:24).[202] Various forms of the pressure of social conformity would have played an important part in the maintenance of commitment to the law among other Jewish Christians too.

Summary

The theological leadership of the community depicted in Acts was aware that its relationship to Jesus and His teaching through the Spirit transcended the old covenant, but it was not at first clear how its participation in the new covenant affected its stance with respect to the Mosaic Law. The theological solution that Luke believes to have been reached at the council was neither Spirit-empowered nomism nor its opposite, rejection of the law. For the sake of the mission to the Jews, the law was necessary for Jewish Christians, and Gentile Christians were to fulfill their part (the decrees) so that association with them would be no hindrance to the Jewish mission. But the centrality of the law in redemptive history had been displaced; it was not to be imposed on Gentiles and it was theologically irrelevant to the salvation of Jewish Christians. Luke was probably aware that the council's decision did not command universal assent and that historically it had a rough passage in the period that followed. The general outline of his position, and of the historical situation, is now sufficiently clear for us to turn to the questions that must dominate the final two sections of this essay.

Sabbath Observance in the Period Depicted by Acts

There is very little direct evidence in Acts on the question of Sabbath observance. From 1:12 we may deduce nothing about early church Sabbath theology and little more about their Sabbath practice. Acts 13:27 and 15:21 remind us that the law was read in the synagogue each Sabbath; in the former case Paul implies that this should have led to recognition of who Jesus was, while in the latter case the implication is probably that Jews should be content to associate freely with Gentile Christians if the latter keep the decrees,[203] because all who read the law should then recognize them as something analogous to the גֵּר תּוֹשָׁב ("the sojourning alien"). Both contexts imply a Christian presence in the synagogues[204] and this is made explicit in 13:42, 44; 16:13; 17:2; 18:4 (such attendance was customary for Paul). But these observations do not take us far and have been interpreted both as support for Adventist seventh-day observance[205] and, at the other extreme, as missionary expediency.[206]

Unfortunately further direct evidence is not forthcoming, and we must work more from inference. This is dangerous, however, unless we recognize both the sheer complexity of factors (some intangible) that impinge on the issue of Sabbath observance and the diversity of response that was inevitable as different situations weighted these factors differently.

Factors That Would Contribute to Continuity of Jewish Christian (Seventh Day) Sabbath Observation

Habit and Religious Conservatism. As psychological phenomena these are universally recognized as powerful influences on behavior. They would strongly favor continued observation of so fundamental, universal, and ingrained an institution as the Jewish Sabbath wherever the gospel was heard.[207]

It was probably habit and religious conservatism as much as theological conviction that made the temple a center of worship for the earliest Christian community. It is there that they repaired after the ascension (Luke 24:53); and subsequently, according to Acts 2:46, they visited it each day. In accordance with this, Acts 3:1 describes the disciples as ascending to the temple at the time of prayer. Rordorf suggests that the motive may have been evangelistic zeal rather than conformity to piety.[208] But while the disciples certainly seem to have taken every opportunity to witness to their Lord (the temple provided rewarding but also dangerous opportunities; see 5:40), there is no evidence to support Rordorf's case. On the contrary it is while Paul is in the temple *praying*, not evangelizing, that he receives his vision summoning him to the Gentiles (22:17–21). Later, while fulfilling a vow in the same temple, he is mobbed (21:27).

Social Pressure. This would arise from within the Jewish circle of nation, friends and family. Luke 14:26 witnesses to the dangers of such pressures for Christians, while Romans 9:3 (cf. Luke 18:29f.) speaks of their poignant character. Of course, wherever the church slipped into the dynamics of a sociological sect[209] the effect of social pressure from outside the Christian circle would have been minimal and even, perhaps, counterproductive. But such conditions were unlikely to have been common, or to have lasted long. Jewish Christian converts would usually have stayed within the synagogue system until *forced* out.

This is certainly Luke's understanding of the situation in the diaspora mission. At Ephesus, for example, Christians remained in the synagogue for some time before Paul's second visit (cf. 18:20–23 and 19:1) and had sufficient standing to write a letter of recommendation for Apollos (18:27). Christians then stayed with the synagogue for a further period of three months before the parting of the ways. One might surmise that the period would have been considerably longer had the tempestuous figure of Paul not arrived on the scene.[210] Beyond the horizon of Luke's writings, it would appear that the danger of slipping back into Judaism has molded the final form of the Fourth Gospel[211] and dominates the Epistle to the Hebrews. As late as A.D. 85–90, the need to formulate the בִּרְכַּת הַמִּנִים (the "blessing" designed to exclude Jewish Christians from synagogue worship) was felt, in order to flush Christians out of the synagogues.

Fear of stronger Forms of Sanction. Zahn concludes that the palestinian church must have kept the Sabbath, "otherwise they would have been stoned."[212] This takes too lightly Rome's jealous retention of the power of the sword,[213] at least in the *cities* where they held control, but it would be essentially correct to state that any Jewish Christians who strayed from Sabbath observation would be regarded as *meriting* stoning, even if such a sentence could rarely be carried out. Lesser sentences, and the dangers of pogrom action and from zealot parties, would be the real hazards that would, nevertheless, have to be faced, both within Palestine and, to a lesser extent, outside it. Judaism was more insistent on orthopraxy than it was on orthodoxy,[214] and failure to observe the Sabbath could only have paved the way for persecution, as it had in Jesus' case.

Missionary Policy. This would involve both avoiding any offense to Jews, and exploiting the opportunities for evangelism provided by the synagogue Sabbath services.[215] The subject has been dealt with above and elsewhere.[216]

Strong Conservative Leadership at Jerusalem. The lead given by James, whose Jewish piety was legendary, and by the conservative (priestly and Pharisee) element of the Jerusalem eldership, would have ensured Sabbath observation in Jerusalem and in the satellite churches. How far beyond Palestine this would be true is hard to say. Certainly at Antioch James' influence was remarkably strong (Gal. 2:11–14) and Paul's comments suggest that James was a well known figure to the Galatians as well. Luke undoubtedly considers James' authority to be extremely weighty.[217] He presides at the council that dictates to the churches of Syria and Cilicia.

Theological Conviction. At very least Luke believes that there was one group that had *theological* commitment to the Sabbath (as part of their commitment to the law as a whole), namely, the vocal Pharisee party of 15:5. Probably a second similar party is to be detected at 15:1. Further, strikingly, Peter's hesitancy to respond to the vision (10:10–16)—it had to be repeated three times—shows that Luke considered the apostle to have assumed the validity of the law. We are forced to conclude that in Lukan perspective, despite the challenge by Stephen, *the period before the vision to Peter was one in which the essential validity of the law had received no broadly based theological challenge,* even if its place of *primacy* in redemptive history had been displaced by Jesus' inauguration of a new covenant relationship. After the council Luke gives no indication of there being any *theologically* nomist party, and there is no need to infer one from 21:20,[218] but historically we know that judaizing activity continued well into the subapostolic period and beyond.[219] We must presume that most of it proceeded from theological commitment to the validity of the law, and that Sabbath observance was naturally involved.[220]

To What Extent Was the (Seventh-Day) Sabbath Observance of Jewish Christians Modified by the Christ Event?

In the previous section we listed factors that would tend to ensure the continued observance of the Sabbath by Jewish Christians. But was this observance not radically affected by Jesus' life, teaching, death and resurrection/exaltation—by the very events that we have said threw the law into eclipse?

So far, our analysis of Acts would suggest that, in the period between Pentecost and the events described in Acts 10, the early community experienced no clear antithesis between its proclamation of a new covenant inaugurated by Jesus and the ongoing validity of the law. According to the gospel tradition Jesus had deliberately used the law and the cult as a touchstone against which He drew out the implications of His law-transcending claims. This was the cause of the controversies. We can only assume that with few exceptions, Stephen being the most notable of these,[221] the earliest church made its claims for Jesus *without drawing the line back to the law*. Claims on behalf of Jesus were thus made in a sphere that did not directly compete with that of loyalty to the law of Moses. Sabbath observance, then, during this period, would follow as a matter of course.

We cannot ascertain whether or not Jesus' teaching even extensively *shaped* the earliest church's attitude to the Sabbath observance practiced in Judaism. That it did is repeatedly claimed, but the arguments adduced are barely convincing, especially in relationship to the period we are discussing. It is alleged that a tradition-historical analysis of the Sabbath conflict stories in the gospel tradition demonstrates much of the material to be inauthentic, and to derive from the attempt by the palestinian church to use the example of Jesus to justify its own Sabbath freedom.[222] But this is highly unlikely. With the possible exception of Mark 2:23–27 (v. 27 can be paralleled within Judaism anyway)[223] the point of the Sabbath conflict stories was to establish that Jesus' ministry of redemptive activity transcended all old covenant and Jewish institutions. The Sabbath command to rest could not be used as an excuse to interrupt God's new-creation redemptive activity through Him. These traditions were primarily christological and apologetic (explaining why Jesus was rejected by the officials).[224] They were not paradigms of personal liberty, but of total obedience to the call of God's dawning age of mercy.

As far as we know, the early church did not have a surfeit of Sabbath miracles to account for (and the Sabbath conflict stories would barely be relevant for justifying anything less);[225] indeed, if we are to judge from Acts and from the epistles, *no Jewish Christians were persecuted for,* [226] *or even challenged about, their Sabbath observance.* The remarkable silence on this issue is evidence against the form-critical case for Sabbath liberty in the early church. This is not an ordinary argument from silence, on which see n. 219, because Luke repeatedly addresses the relationship of the early church to Old Testament law; it is therefore difficult to conceive how this point could be omitted from such a framework. Moreover, Luke faithfully records various grounds of Church/Judaism conflict, but Sabbath is not mentioned. The danger witnessed throughout the New Testament was that Jewish Christians would not take Jesus' law-transcending life and His death seriously *enough*. The danger was that they would apostatize back into Judaism, or judaize, not that they would go too far in the other direction. If this be true in the period after the watershed experience of Gentile entry into the church, it was certainly more so before it. Luke, as we have seen, has little sympathy with the theologically nomist pattern observed by the church until the incoming of the Gentiles. For him, the law-transcending admission of the Gentiles to the church (which first brought the claims of Christ and of the law into real conflict) was the logical outworking of Jesus' attitude to the law. Nevertheless he does not envisage there to be any stage at which significant numbers of Jewish Christians departed from the main lines of orthopraxy; this is the point of the decrees, and it even touches his picture of Paul.

We have, as yet, found no firm evidence for the belief that the kerygma and the teaching of Christ had any significant effect on the pattern of Jewish-Christian Sabbath observance. We must still face the possibility that the rising star of Lord's-Day worship accomplished such changes.

The Gentiles and Seventh-Day Sabbath Observation

Judaism as a whole considered the Sabbath to be binding on Israel alone. It was not a matter for Gentiles (note its absence from the Noachian laws) and this was sometimes very strongly put.[227] The hellenistic apologists Philo and Aristobulus are exceptions that prove the rule; they *do* regard the Sabbath as binding on all men, but only because all men should become Jews and embrace the whole law. The Sabbath commandment is not singled out as a special case.[228]

"God-fearers" (cf. Acts 13:43; 17:4, 17), and even some Gentiles with remoter connections with Judaism,[229] tended to keep the Sabbath; but here again this commandment, while more commonly followed than many others, was accepted as part of the God-fearer's general imitation of Judaism, not because it was singled out as a creation ordinance binding even on Gentiles.

The Sabbath institution was so well known in the Gentile world[230] that many early converts to Christianity would probably assume it to be incumbent upon them unless they were directed otherwise. Converted "God-fearers" would probably keep the habit along with their synagogue connections.

SUNDAY AND ITS EFFECT ON SABBATH WORSHIP IN THE PERIOD DEPICTED BY ACTS

Once more we are hampered by lack of sufficient direct evidence; the only indication Luke gives of observance of the first day of the week is Acts 20:7–12. It is to this passage that we now turn.

The First Day of the Week in Acts 20:7–12

The relevant material for our inquiry is confined to verses 7, 8, and 11: "On the first day of the week,[231] when we[232] were gathered together to break bread, Paul talked with them, intending to depart on the morrow; and he prolonged his speech until midnight. There were many lights in the upper chamber where we were gathered; And when Paul had gone up and broken bread and eaten. . . ." The detail is very brief and merely sets the scene for the main action—the death and restoration of Eutychus.[233]

There are three problems: (1) Was this a Saturday or a Sunday evening? (2) What was the precise purpose of the meeting? Was it a fellowship meal, the Lord's Supper, or both? (3) Of what significance is the fact that the day is specified as the "first day of the week"? We shall deal with these in order.

Was This a Saturday or a Sunday Evening? That it was evening is obvious, though what is less obvious is that the congregation may only have come together in the evening. The many lamps in verse 8, to which Luke makes incidental reference, would have been brought by those traveling to the meeting and would not have been lit had their owners arrived before dark.[234] But whether this was Saturday or Sunday will depend on whether a Jewish or a Roman accounting of days is to be presumed. If Jewish, then "the first day of the week" would commence on Saturday evening. Bacchiocchi argues this to be the case; his point is that Luke elsewhere uses Jewish time reckoning (e.g., Luke 23:54) and repeatedly dates events by the Jewish calendar (Acts 12:3–4; 16:1–3; 18:18; 20:16; 21:24). Paul, says Bacchiocchi, tended to meet with his Christian congregations on the Sabbath (Acts 13:42, 44; 16:13). These considerations lead Bacchiocchi to the conclusion that Paul was setting off, not in the next twenty-four-hour period (i.e., the second day of the week), but after dawn on the *same* (Jewish) day. To this end he points out that ἐπαύριον ("on the morrow") is etymologically derived from "dawn," and that the word ἡμέρα ("day") is not supplied by the text.[235]

The argument is not cogent. For the explanation of Luke 23:54, see our comments on 23:56*b* (above). Second, the fact that Luke reckons by feast days of the Jewish calendar is hardly surprising when he is recounting events that took place in Palestine, or when he is describing Paul's movements. We shall deal later with the use of the *Jewish* seven day weekly cycle, but from such use we have no reason to assume Jewish reckoning of *days*. At John 20:19, for example, we are told that Jesus appeared to the disciples in the *evening* of the first day of the week (*οὔσης οὖν ὀψίας τῇ ἡμέρᾳ ἐκείνῃ τῇ μιᾷ σαββάτων*); in context, the writer must be referring to *Sunday* evening. In the area of Asia,[236] then, it would appear that the Jewish seven day weekly cycle was combined readily with a Roman reckoning of time. Third, Paul met with Jews and Christians in the synagogues[237] on Sabbath days merely because that was when the synagogue was convened; but we cannot draw a line from this to what Paul would have done when the church met outside that structure and when Paul's concern was not primarily evangelistic. Finally, the arguments about the use of ἐπαύριον are not entirely convincing. Whatever the etymology, ἐπαύριον is an adverb, and when used with the feminine article it functions as an adjective qualifying the implied noun ἡμέρα ("day"). However, Haenchen[238] and Rordorf[239] both maintain that even this does not settle the issue. The implied ἡμέρα may simply contrast with "night" (rather than the previous twenty-four hours) without distinguishing whether Jewish reckoning or Roman reckoning is being used. But is the argument entirely to the point? A Gentile writer using this phrase could only be expected to be reckoning in a Roman way, and so, if Luke were deliberately using Jewish reckoning, he would surely have to indicate this by the qualification τῇ ἡμέρᾳ ("that day"). Without such a qualification the Gentile reader would inevitably see a measure of antithesis between ἡ μία τῶν σαββάτων ("the first day of the week"), and ἡ ἐπαύριον (ἡμέρα).[240] We must conclude that Luke meant Sunday evening, not Saturday.[241]

Was the Purpose of the Meeting a Fellowship Meal, or the Lord's Supper, or Both? The argument hinges on whether κλάσαι ἄρτον ("to break bread") refers to the cultic act of breaking bread, or whether it could be used more broadly "as a description of a common meal in terms of the opening action, the breaking of bread,"[242] In Acts 27:35, the same words refer to the opening act of thanksgiving in a common meal for Paul and the weary crew and passengers. But it remains *doubtful whether the whole meal would naturally, in retrospect, be called a 'breaking of bread'* (cf. Luke 24:30, 35). This last phrase is most unusual and calls for explanation. Concerning its background, Jeremias correctly observes that "the constantly repeated assertion that 'breaking of bread' is an expression used in Jewish sources meaning 'to have a meal' is an error that seems to be impossible to eradicate."[243] The error arises from a confusion with the common and appropriate Jewish expression for having a meal, namely, "to *eat* bread" (cf. Luke 14:1, 15).

Now it is true that Luke uses the expression "to break bread" in Acts 2:42, 46, where something more than the beginning of a common meal is meant, and where more than the bare elements of the Lord's Supper must be involved too since in 2:46 κλῶντές τε . . . ἄρτον ("breaking bread") appears in parallel with μετελάμβανον τροφῆς ("they partook of food"). What Luke describes here are probably fellowship meals. But unless these meals included some sort of reminder of the Last Supper where Jesus "broke bread" in a special way (Luke 22:19), it is very difficult to explain how those fellowship meals came to be known simply as "the breaking of bread." In an epistle written at approximately the time of the incident at Troas, Paul's use of "breaking bread" (1 Cor. 10:16) refers specifically to the cultic act of sharing the bread in the Lord's Supper in connection with the more general Christian meal that was being misused (1 Cor. 11:17–22).[244] It is not difficult to see how the whole meal might be named in terms of one of its cultic elements, but it is hard to explain why such a fellowship meal should come to be known by the relatively trivial and ubiquitous act (in a Jewish milieu) of breaking a loaf in preparation for saying the "grace." The Corinthian evidence sheds enough light for the Acts passages to be intelligible.

It is no real objection to this that Acts 2 refers to a much earlier period; the question concerns Luke's intention and why he chose the phrase. Nor is it valid to dismiss the connection between the Lord's Supper and "breaking bread" on the ground that Luke is referring to a *daily* event (Acts 2:46); there is no insuperable difficulty about such regular celebrations,[245] and in any case, we are not necessarily to assume that *everyone* partook of the Lord's Supper each day, but merely that there was no fixed day for such celebrations.

With reference to Acts 2, Bacchiocchi writes, "Such daily table-fellowship, though it may have included the celebration of the Lord's Supper, can hardly be regarded as exclusive liturgical celebrations of the Lord's Supper." We agree. When, however, he immediately proceeds, "The equivalent statement found in Acts 20:7, 'we were gathered together to break bread,' similarly need mean no more than 'we were gathered to eat together,'"[246] we are forced to disagree sharply. The language of "breaking bread" is no longer explicable if the meal does not include the Lord's Supper.

The choice before us is thus reduced. Does Acts 20:7 refer merely to the Lord's Supper *alone*, or to a more general fellowship meal at which the Lord's Supper was celebrated? In view of Luke's γευσάμενος ("and eaten," v. 11), we should probably infer the latter;[247] but this is a detail of secondary importance to our thesis.

Of What Significance Is the Mention that the Meeting Took Place on "the First Day of the Week"? According to Bacchiocchi it is improbable that the reference to the first day has anything to do with what he considers to be later *Sunday* worship.[248] Mention of the first day of the week might be accidental; it could be that the Eutychus incident particularly impressed itself on Luke's mind, or it may be because Paul "was ready to depart" (20:7) and that this inclusion would provide an additional chronological reference to describe the unfolding of Paul's journey. All of this is *possible*, though it should be noted that Luke's chronological references in this section are not complete and therefore the reference in 20:7 would not be particularly useful.[249] Again, if the Eutychus incident impressed the day on Luke's mind so vividly that he recorded it, one can only wonder why he does not say more about this incident and, indeed, why some of the other remarkable incidents in the "we" sections are not as sharply dated. Also, while it is true that Luke elsewhere never mentions specific days except for important feasts and Sabbaths, and thus that this isolated mention of another day *may* be "accidental" as Bacchiocchi claims (as is the mention, for example, of the "many lamps" in v. 8), we should nevertheless contend that this is not the most likely hypothesis. We may be relatively sure that by the time the Book of Revelation was written, "the first day of the week" was widely referred to in the area as "the Lord's Day" (Bacchiocchi's arguments notwithstanding)[250] and that this day involved congregational worship. In order to explain the 'Lord's Day' phenomenon, for which (at this stage) there were no Jewish or pagan Sunday parallels, we are forced to hypothesize earlier *Christian* "first day" observance of some kind, and, further, that observance centered on the *evening* especially. It is not therefore surprising that so many scholars have seen in Acts 20:7 precisely the sort of "first day" consciousness that they expected to find. It is hard to avoid the suspicion that they are right. It may be subjective, and not liable to proof, but the connection between "the first day of the week," "to gather together," and "to break bread" is remarkably similar to later statements that clearly refer to Sunday worship. *Συνάγειν* ("to gather together") coupled with *κλᾶν ἄρτον* ("to break bread") appears to be a standard formula (cf. 1 Cor. 11:20; *Did.* 14:1; Ign. *Eph.* 20:2). The coincidence is too inviting to be dismissed.[251] Bacchiocchi's attempt to divide and conquer has demonstrated just how fragile the evidence is, but in the final analysis his case has the appearance of special pleading.

We are faced with the conclusion that Luke's specification of the day of the week in Acts 20:7 probably should not be relegated to the category of irrelevant personal reminiscence. It represents a stage in the growing consciousness of, and ecclesiastical importance of, the "first day of the week." The brevity of Luke's notice would suggest that he considered such meetings to be uncontroversial and to require no further explanation, from which we may infer that they were relatively widespread and regular.

But what stage in the development of Sunday worship does Acts 20:7 represent? Behm, in an unguarded statement, speaks of an "evening feast of the *κυριακὸν δεῖπνον* ["Lord's Supper," in 1 Cor. 11:20 and Acts 20:7] which took place on Sunday, *the new Christian day of rest* [emphasis mine]." Similarly, Beckwith writes that "the fact that the Lord's Day falls on 'the first day of the week' (Acts 20:7; 1 Cor. 16:2) is significant."[252] But the facts do not support such extravagant claims; the author of Acts does not tell us that it was the Lord's Day at all,[253] far less that it was a day of rest. Luke merely refers to the day in question as "the first day of the week." From this we may infer two things: (1) This day was *not* yet called the Lord's Day (otherwise he would more probably have used what was to become the more popular title). (2) In view of the fact that a planetary week was in general use at the time,[254] the reference by a Gentile writer to observance of the Jewish weekly cycle (apart from the Sabbath itself) by a *Gentile* church must be taken as deliberate. It is perhaps best understood as an echo of the resurrection traditions, which repeatedly refer to this day (Matt. 28:1; Mark 16:2 (9); Luke 24:1; John 20:1, 19).[255] If this be correct, the path to the later "Lord's Day" would be relatively simple.

Beyond this we cannot go. We must resist any temptation to use Luke's account as though it were a paradigm of "first day" observance. Too many of the features of his account depend on the extraordinary nature of this occasion as Paul's last[256] night with this particular church. All we can say is that around Ephesus, Christians met on what they called the "first day of the week," and that they considered it a suitable occasion on which to have their communal meal centered on the Lord's Supper, and that Luke expected such meetings to be understandable to his readership.

Toward a Theology of Sunday in the Period Depicted by Acts?

In view of the paucity of direct evidence, it is hardly surprising that we should find published, recently, several mutually exclusive theories about the origins of Sunday worship. On the one hand we hear in Beckwith's work[257] a relatively traditional theory. According to this understanding the Sabbath commandment of the old covenant is a "creation ordinance" and eternally valid. Christ fulfilled the Sabbath in bringing eschatological rest, and also freed the Sabbath from the casuistry that surrounded it. His hallowing of it prepared the way for the church, immediately after the resurrection, to transfer the Sabbath from the seventh to the first day of the week. Essentially, the Lord's Day was an apostolic institution dating back to the resurrection evening. The gradual falling away of seventh day observance then followed as the church separated completely from Judaism and no longer had to be circumspect.

On the other hand we have the thesis of Bacchiocchi,[258] claiming that the earliest church (Jew and Gentile alike) observed their new Christian Sabbath on the seventh day. Sunday worship, according to this theory, did not commence until after the New Testament period and was initiated at Rome. It was prepared for by a wave of anti-Jewish feeling in the early years of the second century, and crystallized when the diffusion of sun-cults established Sunday as the first day of the week and Christians seized on it as a fitting symbol of the creation and Resurrection.

Our analysis so far enables us to make three observations on the question. First, despite Beckwith's claims to the contrary, it is all but impossible to believe that Sunday was established as the Lord's Day, as a holy convocation, and as a Christian response to a creation ordinance in Palestine shortly after the Resurrection. The arguments against this position are virtually conclusive; note that:

(1) Beckwith's statement that (for the apostles) *seventh*-day worship was merely a temporary ceremonial aspect of the eternally valid moral Sabbath commandment uses a dogmatic distinction anachronistically. When he claims that, as a consequence of this, obedience to the fourth commandment could be transferred to the first day without changing the nature of the Sabbath,[259] and that the first day of the week was an equally suitable day to commemorate creation, he gives the impression of forgetting that the *seventh*-day Sabbath was not primarily linked with the *fact* of creation as such, but with God's *rest* at the end of creation on the *seventh* day.

(2) The earliest Jewish Christians, almost without exception, kept the *whole* law and were theologically committed to it. There is no indication of their sensing the inner freedom that would be required to allow for so fundamental a manipulation. On the contrary, the period witnesses to a retreat from Jesus' stance with respect to the law.[260]

(3) The needed inner freedom came when the entry of the Gentiles brought the claims of Christ into sharp conflict with those of the law and led to a new realization of the total subordination of the whole law to Christ and to His teaching. It is during this period that the understanding of Jesus' relationship to the law, such as is described by Luke in his Gospel, may well have become widespread; the law was binding on Christians only in so far as it was taken up in Jesus' teaching. *But, once they had taken this stance there was nothing in Jesus' teaching (as recorded by Luke) to encourage transfer of Sabbath theology to another day.* Indeed Luke offers no awareness of any theological reason for keeping the Sabbath institution at all. On the one hand Jesus had warned that it was subordinate to, and should not interfere with, His ministry. On the other hand, the rest that the Sabbath symbolized was either yet to come or a foretaste of it was already experienced *every day* of the week (cf. Acts 3:20 and Luke's jubilee theology).

(4) We may put the point we have just made more forcefully by taking up the corollary of Beckwith's argument. If Sabbath theology was "transferred' to Sunday, then Jewish Christians would attempt to keep *two* days of rest each week. They would *need* to keep the *seventh*-day Sabbath for the reasons given above[261] while at the same time keeping a *first* day Sabbath because of theological conviction. *But what theological conviction could have been adduced of sufficient weight to make it necessary to effect a transfer of the seventh-day Sabbath to the first day in the face of considerable practical*

difficulties that this would bring? Only, it would appear, that because Jesus was raised on Sunday rather than on the Sabbath, it was "appropriate" to make such a change! This would surely not be adequate. It is not entirely obvious why the Resurrection day should attract to itself worship specified by the fourth commandment for the seventh day. And if it be argued that the earliest church felt sufficiently free (theologically) to shift this worship to the first day, *then they would not have needed to in any case*, for in that eventuality they would presumably feel equally free (theologically) to commemorate the Resurrection on the seventh-day Sabbath. The point is that, on this hypothesis, the exact day of the commemorated event did *not* matter, so the church would be free to take the more practical course. If, however, the Resurrection as the decisive guarantee of the future "rest" could *not* appropriately be celebrated on the Jewish Sabbath simply on the ground that Jesus was raised on *Sunday*, then one could forgive early Christians were they to ask why the seventh-day Sabbath had been given as a token of that future rest in the first place.

(5) We must ask why there is no evidence of the turmoil that such a policy would inevitably have produced. *Two* full days of rest and worship would be socially, religiously and economically of sufficient importance to cause a stir both inside the church and outside it. Yet not so much as a ripple can be detected. Judaism drew plenty of criticism for its *one* day of rest[262] (despite the fact that the day of Saturn involved a certain level of imitation of this).[263] But Jewish Christianity receives not a whisper of comment (either from Jews or from Gentiles) over its *two* days. No Jewish Christians need the rationale for their double Sabbath explained,[264] none needed er.couragement not to forsake the first day of the week, and none have to be counseled because they find it difficult to take the Sunday off work.[265] Eight times we hear in Acts of what happened on the *seventh* day Sabbath, but only *once* of the day that supposedly eclipsed it in importance, and that single reference concerns a church outside Palestine and tells us virtually nothing about the day. Luke's description of the church at Jerusalem speaks of the apostles' teaching, the Lord's Supper, fellowship of goods, temple worship, the growth of the church in numbers, the miracles that were worked, the praying that was done, and even of the joy that was experienced (2:42–47), *but in all this there is not the barest hint of the inauguration or observance of Sunday!* If we are to believe Beckwith, the most distinctive and highly controversial feature of the earliest church's practice has simply been totally ignored.

We must conclude that it is barely imaginable that first-day Sabbath observance commenced before the Jerusalem council. Nor can we stop there; we must go on to maintain that first-day Sabbath observance cannot easily be understood as a phenomenon of the apostolic age[266] or of apostolic authority at all.

If an apostolic decision was made *after* the council on so important a matter as this, it would not have been an easy decision to reach and it would inevitably have left its mark in the epistles and in Acts.[267] But as we have seen, Acts is silent on the issue, and Paul's handling of controversies involving the law and the Sabbath makes it difficult to believe that he knew of any Sabbath transference theology.[268]

We may safely exclude the possibility that Jewish Christians, breaking away from (or forced out of) the synagogues, initiated such practice;[269] the points made above would still apply. There is no reason, in other words, why friction between Jewish Christians and Jewish orthodoxy *alone* should change the (established, and therefore convenient) pattern of seventh day Sabbath observance[270] in favor of *Sunday* rest, which would be unparalleled in the Roman Empire, and for which there was no obvious or powerful theological justification. Had such groups been responsible for the change, their influence would not have been widespread, for such a policy would be bound to jeopardize the mission to the Jews elsewhere, and would strain relationships with the Jerusalem leadership to the breaking point.

Even less likely is it that *Gentile* groups were responsible for inaugurating first-day Sabbath observance while Jewish Christians formed a significant part of the church, and while the latter still observed the seventh-day Sabbath. While Gentile Christians would be almost totally free from the pressures of Jewish groups, it is not obvious that they would have any reason to transfer the Sabbath to Sunday (unless Sunday was already being observed in some lesser way beforehand), nor that they would have the theological selfconfidence to do so, nor, for that matter, the authority to ensure that this would be any more than a minority option if they did.[271]

A second observation is that despite Bacchiocchi's claim to the contrary, we cannot accept that the Christ-event renewed the church's theological commitment to the seventh-day Sabbath. In some ways this position is more theologically coherent and intrinsically more historically probable than that envisaged by Beckwith. But it must be repudiated also; it is based on Bacchiocchi's understanding that Jesus hallowed the Sabbath as an especially appropriate memorial of His redemptive activity, and on his assumption that commitment to the law in the Jerusalem church was *theological* throughout the period under discussion.[272]

Our analysis in the previous pages leads us to the opposite view. First, Jesus did not especially hallow the Sabbath. Second, while the Jerusalem community was outwardly nomist, it had abandoned nomism as a *theological* principle. Bacchiocchi's position logically leads not merely to the church's (Jewish and Gentile) legitimation of the seventh-day Sabbath but to the legitimation of the *whole law of Moses*. He offers no criterion by which the early church may have handled the law in order to welcome the former as authoritative (for Jew and Gentile) without the latter slipping in through the open door. Third, it is unlikely that the Sabbath would have been imposed on the Gentiles *before* the council, for in this period the ordinary Jewish attitude to Gentile relationship to the Sabbath was liable to prevail. If the council first ratified the authority of the Christian seventh-day Sabbath for Gentiles, this obligation would almost certainly have been included amongst the decrees where (theologically) it would have belonged. Finally, the relevant Pauline passages can barely be made to make sense on the assumption that Paul considered the seventh-day Sabbath binding on all Christians.[273]

A further observation is that while we accept Bacchiocchi's contention that "Sunday liturgy and rest were patterned *only gradually* after the Jewish Sabbath,"[274] we are forced to disagree with his affirmation that the genesis of Sunday worship itself must be placed beyond the New Testament horizon in the post-apostolic period. Already at Acts 20:7 (and possibly at 1 Cor. 16:2) we see the beginnings of such a practice in the singling out of "the first day of the week" as an appropriate day for evening worship,[275] including the Lord's Supper. The use of this nomenclature to designate the day, echoing as it does the Resurrection traditions, points toward later recognition of the day as the "Lord's Day" (cf. Rev. 1:10), and then toward the further evolution that Bacchiocchi describes. At the stage for which we have evidence in Acts, however, there is no suggestion of a day of rest, nor even that Sunday has as yet an exclusive place in church worship compared to the other days of the week. It may well have been *primus inter pares*, ("the first among equals," cf. Acts 2:46) because it commemorated the day of the Resurrection, but we have no evidence that it was more than this.

Notes

[1]The traditional view of authorship is to be preferred. Two objections of weight have been made against it: (1) Luke's picture of Paul corresponds too little with the real Paul for the writer of Acts to have been the apostle's companion, and (2) his account of the church bears the hallmark of "early catholicism." But the first of these objections has been very much overstated: see the rejoinders by, among others, F. F. Bruce, "Is the Paul of Acts the Real Paul?" *BJRL* 58 (1975–76): 282–305; E. E. Ellis, *The Gospel of Luke* (London: Nelson, 1974), pp. 42–51; U. Wilckens, "Interpreting Luke-Acts in a Period of Existentialist Theology," *SLA*, 1968: pp. 60–83. The second objection evaporates on closer analysis: see H. Conzelmann, "Luke's Place in the Development of Early Christianity," *SLA*, pp. 304, and I. H. Marshall, "'Early Catholicism' in the New Testament," *New Dimensions in New Testament Study*, ed. R. N. Longenecker and M. C. Tenney (Grand Rapids: Zondervan, 1974), pp. 217–31.

[2]Since the advent of redaction criticism few have doubted that Luke should be called a theologian. Unfortunately this has often unnecessarily been maintained at the expense of his claim to be a historian. For the details of the on-going debate see: C. K. Barrett, *Luke the Historian in Recent Study* (London: Epworth, 1961); W. W. Gasque, *A History of the Criticism of the Acts of the Apostles* (Tübingen: Mohr, 1975); E. Haenchen, *The Acts of the Apostles: A Commentary* (Oxford: Blackwell, 1971), pp. 90–112; I. H. Marshall, *Luke: Historian and Theologian* (Exeter: Paternoster, 1970), esp. pp. 53–76.

The classic argument for Luke's worth as a historian was set forth by W. Ramsay (see Gasque, *A History of the Criticism*, pp. 136ff. and esp. the works cited in n. 2 of his work) who pointed to the numerous accuracies in the historical, geographical and political descriptions in Acts and proceeded by *a fortiori* argument to assert that one who had been so careful in the matter of details that we *can* check would also be accurate in the broader issues of description that we cannot check.

F. J. Foakes Jackson and K. Lake, BC, 2:484, were the first to challenge this line of argument, but they have been followed by H. Conzelmann, E. Haenchen and J. C. O'Neill, all of whom have pointed to the possible fallacy involved. If Luke were dependent on sources (whether written or oral) for his writing of Acts then accuracy of detail *need* only prove the historical worth of the sources, not what Luke has done with them. Haenchen, indeed, deduces from his study that where Luke had access to reliable information he handled it radically or with historical irresponsibility in favor of edification or, more rarely, of the theological polemic *(The Acts of the Apostles)*; idem, "The Book of Acts as Source Material for the History of Early Christianity," *SLA*. pp. 258–78). Others, however, are inclined to disagree. J. C. O'Neill (especially in the second edition of his work, *The Theology of Acts in its Historical Setting* [London: SPCK, 1970]) regards Luke's use of his sources as far more judicious, a view shared more recently by Barrett, *Luke the Historian;* C. J. Hemer, "Luke the Historian," *BJRL* 60:28–51; J. Jervell, *Luke and the People of God* (Minneapolis: Augsburg, 1972); Marshall, *Luke;* and S. G. Wilson, *The Gentiles and the Gentile Mission in Luke-Acts* (Cambridge: University Press, 1973), esp. pp. 255–67.

It is certainly not possible to reach a simple verdict that will cover all of Luke's material uniformly. Nevertheless four lines of evidence convince us that the burden of proof lies with the one who disputes Luke's account at any given point: (1) The most natural interpretation of the prologue (Luke 1:1–4) is that Luke is concerned for the accuracy of the writing he has undertaken (see Cadbury, *BC*, 2:504–05; Marshall, *Luke: Historian and Theologian*, pp. 37–41; H. Schürmann, *Das Lukasevangelium* (Freiburg: Herder, 1969), 1:10–15; and W. C. Van Unnik, "Once More St. Luke's Prologue," *Neotestamentica* 7 (1973): 7–26; (2) Luke's use of his synoptic traditions is relatively conservative, despite H. Conzelmann, *The Theology of Saint Luke* (London: Faber, 1960); M. D. Goulder, *Midrash and Lection in Matthew* (London: SPCK, 1974), pp. 452–71; and J. Drury, *Tradition and Design in Luke's Gospel: A Study in Early Christian Historiography* (London: Darton, Longman and Todd, 1976). Precisely the points at which Conzelmann states Luke has radically altered Mark have been severely challenged in major contributions on Luke's works written by, among many others: R. J. Banks, *Jesus and the Law in the Synoptic Tradition* (Cambridge: University Press, 1975); Barrett, *Luke the Historian;* S. Brown, *Apostasy and Perseverance in the Theology of Luke* (Rome: Pontifical Biblical Institute, 1969); W. Deitrich, *Das Petrusbild der lukanischen Schriften* (Stuttgart: Köhlhammer, 1972); F. W. Danker, *Jesus and the New Age: According to Saint Luke* (St. Louis: Clayton, 1972); J. Dupont, in several works, including: *Les Béatitudes* (Paris: Gabalda, 1969–73); *Les tentations de Jésus au désert* (Paris: Desclée de Brouwer, 1968); E. E. Ellis in several works: *The Gospel of Luke; Eschatology in Luke* (Philadelphia: Fortress, 1972); R. Glöckner, *Die Verkündigung des heils beim Evangelisten Lukas* (Mainz: Matthias Grünwald, 1975); W. G. Kümmel, "Luc en accusation dans la theólogie contemperaire," *L'Evangile de Luc*, ed. F. Neirynck (Gembloux: Duculot, 1973), pp. 93–109; P. S. Minear, "Luke's Use of the Birth Stories," *SLA*, pp. 111–30; F. Neirynck, "La Matière marcienne dans L'Évangile de Luc," *L'Évangile de Luc*, pp. 159–223; T. Schramm, *Der Markus-Stoff bei Lukas* (Cambridge: University Press, 1971); G. N. Stanton, *Jesus of Nazareth in New Testament Preaching* (Cambridge: University Press, 1974); G. Voss, *Die*

Christologie der lukanischen Schriften in Grundzügen (Paris: Desclée de Brouwer, 1965); W. Wink, *John the Baptist in the Gospel Tradition* (Cambridge: University Press, 1968); and J. Zmijewski, *Die Eschatologiereden des Lukasevangeliums* (Bonn: Peter Hanstein, 1972). The recent massive commentary by I. H. Marshall, *The Gospel of Luke* (Exeter: Paternoster, 1978), strongly underscores the carefulness of Luke's handling of his traditions. (3) Although the caution of Foakes Jackson and Lake is well taken, it is nevertheless true that Luke's "accuracies" are not thin on the ground (cf. A. N. Sherwin-White, *Roman Society and Roman Law in the New Testament* [Oxford: Clarendon, 1963], chapters 3, 4, 5, 7 and 8). Ramsay's point was that almost *wherever* Luke's accuracy can be tested objectively he proves himself worthy of the title historian. As much cannot be said for Foakes Jackson and Lake's literary parallel: the writer of *Margaret Catchpole* betrayed himself quite frequently. (4) Finally, the most natural interpretation of the "we" passages, in the way that they are presented (as part of the narrative, not as a report received by the writer), is that the writer of Luke-Acts was actually present. E. Haenchen's suggestion that the "we" was merely added for literary effect is a counsel of despair.

[3]This count excludes the reading of the notorious *agraphon* in Codex Bezae at Luke 6:5 which, even if dominical (as argued by J. Jeremias, *Unknown Sayings of Jesus* [London: SPCK, 1957], pp. 49ff.; but see the trenchant criticism of Schürmann, *Lukasevangelium*, 1:304, n.29) is hardly Lukan.

[4]Here the Greek is: ἡ μία τῶν σαββάτων ("on the first day of the week").

[5]H. Conzelmann, "Zur Lukasanalyse," *ZThK* 49 (1952): 19.

[6]See especially R. Pesch, *Das Markusevangelium* (Frankfurt: Herder, 1976), 1:100–7; W. Lane, *The Gospel of Mark* (London: Marshall, Morgan, and Scott, 1974), pp. 63ff.

[7]Only the account of the call of the disciples, who are to assist in the proclamation, intervenes.

[8]"Redaction" is defined as the preparation of a document for publication; reduction to literary form; revision or rearrangement. It has come to have a technical sense since its use by W. Marxsen, *Monatsschrift für Pastoraltheologie* (1954): 254 in discussing H. Conzelmann's work on Luke. Redaction criticism is the study of the nature and purpose of the writers of the gospels as it is revealed in their selection, ordering and revision of their oral and written sources. In the case of Markan studies, where we do not have direct access to any of the writer's sources, redaction criticism pays particular attention to the framework which Mark has given to the traditions, and is heavily dependent on form critical analysis of the individual pericopes to elucidate Mark's revision of the oral traditions: see J. Rohde, *Rediscovering the Teaching of the Evangelists* (London: SCM, 1968), pp. 113–52. E. Haenchen, *Der Weg Jesu* (Berlin: Töpelmann, 1966), p. 24, has suggested that, as form criticism has tended to underestimate the creative role of the evangelists in dealing with their traditions, we should use the term "composition criticism" instead; but his suggestion has not been followed (cf. the comments by S. S. Smalley in *New Testament Interpretation*, ed. I. H. Marshall [Exeter: Paternoster, 1977], pp. 181–82).

[9]In what follows I am particularly indebted to Lane, *The Gospel of Mark*, pp. 63–127.

[10]So Lane, *The Gospel of Mark*, on this passage; he depends heavily, at this point, on U. Mauser, *Christ in the Wilderness: The Wilderness Theme in the Second Gospel and its Basis in the Biblical Tradition* (London: SCM, 1963).

[11]Lane, *The Gospel of Mark*; Jesus' answer to Peter in 1:38 is taken to imply that to remain in Capernaum to heal the sick would no longer constitute authentic preaching of the kingdom. The lack of response of faith reduces Jesus' miracles to the level of beneficial magic. The evidence for this interpretation is not entirely compelling.

[12]Mark 4:1–20; see C. E. B. Cranfield, *The Gospel According to Saint Mark* (Cambridge: University Press, 1966), p. 148, for the title.

[13]See the comments by L. Goppelt, *Apostolic and Post-Apostolic Times* (London: Black, 1970), p. 5.

[14]For the independence of Luke's material from Mark see Schramm, *Der Markus-Stoff*, p. 37 n.2; Schürmann, *Lukasevangelium*, 1:191–200 (but contrast, e.g., R. C. Tannehill, "The Mission of Jesus According to Luke IV. 16–30" in *Jesus in Nazareth*, ed. W. Eltester (Berlin: de Gruyter, 1972), pp. 51ff. H. Schürmann, "Der 'Bericht vom Anfang.' Ein Rekonstruktionsver-

such auf Grund von Lk 4.14–16," *SE* 2:242–58 and *idem*, "Zur Traditionsgeschichte der Nazareth-Perikope Lk 4. 16–30" *Mélanges Bibliques*, ed. A. Déscamps and A. de Halleux (Gembloux: Duculot, 1970), pp. 187–205, has argued that this section belonged to a larger "account of beginnings" *(Berich vom Anfang)* which opened Q. J. Delobel, "La rédaction de Lc IV.14–16a et le 'Bericht vom Anfang'," *L'Évangile de Luc*, pp. 203–23, however, has shown that Luke 4:14–16*a* is a Lukan rewriting of Markan material, and has thereby shattered the unity of Schürmann's proposed "account of beginnings." In addition, G. N. Stanton, "On the Christology of Q," *Christ and Spirit in the New Testament*, ed. B. Lindars and S. S. Smalley (Cambridge: University Press, 1973), pp. 33–34, points out that *if* Q had contained the bulk of Luke 4:16–30 early in its order, the pericope in Luke 7, with its indirect and enigmatic reply of Jesus to the Baptist's question, would be very hard to explain. The Q origin of Luke 4:16ff. in an "account of beginnings" is therefore improbable, but Schürmann's arguments that the material is pre-Lukan still holds good.

The passage is clearly programmatic for Luke (cf. L. T. Johnson, *The Literary Function of Possessions in Luke-Acts* [Missoula: Scholars Press, 1977], p. 91, and those he cites) and he is even going against his own understanding of the chronology of Jesus' ministry (4:23!) in order to make *this* scene the first in his account of Jesus' public life and teaching.

[15]See especially: J. A. Fitzmyer, "Further Light on Melchizedek from Qumran Cave 11," *JBL* 86 (1967): 25–41; F. L. Horton, *The Melchizedek Tradition*, (Cambridge: University Press, 1976), pp. 61–82; M. de Jonge and A. van der Woude, "11Q Melchizedek and the New Testament," *NTS* 12 (1965–66): 301–26; M. Miller, "The Function of Isaiah 61.1–2 in 11Q Melchizedek," *JBL* 88 (1969): 467–9; A. Strobel, "Die Ausrufung des Jobeljahres in der Nazareth-Predigt Jesu: zur apokalyptischen Tradition Lk 4.16–30," *Jesus in Nazareth* (as at n.14): pp. 38–50; J. A. Sanders, "From Isaiah 61 to Luke 4," *Christianity, Judaism and Other Greco-Roman Cults*, ed. J. Neusner (Leiden: Brill, 1975), 1:75–106, and M. M. B. Turner, "Jesus and the Spirit in Lucan Perspective" (Tyndale Lecture for Winter 1977/8 published in *TB* 32 [1981]: 3–42).

[16]Compare Marshall, *The Gospel of Luke*, p. 210.

[17]R. Pesch, "La rédaction lucanienne du logion des pêcheurs d'homme (Lc., V, 10c)," *L'Évangile de Luc* (as at n.2): 225–44, considers the pericope to be a rewriting of Mark 1:17–18 and a pre-Lukan fishing miracle story. The influence of the Markan material and of *some* other pre-Lukan tradition is maintained by the majority of scholars: cf. particularly Schürmann, *Lukasevangelium*, pp. 264–74, and Schramm, *Der Markus-Stoff bei Lukas*, pp. 37–40. For the issues involved see the critical introduction by Marshall (as at n. 16), pp. 199–201; for a more complete bibliography on this difficult pericope see G. Wagner, *Bibliographical Aids No. 5: An Exegetical Bibliography on the Gospel of Luke* (Rüschlikon-Zürich: Baptist Theological Seminary, 1974).

[18]See Glöckner, *Die Verkündigung des Heils*, p. 148ff.; W. Deitrich, *Das Petrusbild der lukanischen Schriften* (Stuttgart: Köhlhammer, 1972), p. 57.

[19]A much over-used word, given varying nuances by different writers: see particularly I. H. Marshall, "Slippery Words: I - Eschatology," *ExpT* 89 (1977–78): 264–68. I would designate an event or an experience as eschatological if it were closely related in *inner quality* (but not necessarily in time) to the decisive End-events. Acceptance of Jesus' proclamation involves a man in an experience of that kingdom of God which will be consummated at the *parousia*.

[20]Banks, *Jesus and the Law*, p. 91; Marshall, *Gospel of Luke*, p. 181. On the other hand, see W. Grundmann, *Das Evangelium nach Lukas* (Berlin: Evangelische Verlagsanstalt, 1961), p. 120; K. H. Rengstorf, *Das Evangelium nach Lukas* (Göttingen: Vandenhoeck und Ruprecht, 1969), p. 67.

[21]S. Bacchiocchi, *From Sabbath to Sunday: A Historical Investigation of the Rise of Sunday Observance in Early Christianity* (Rome: Pontifical Gregorian University Press, 1977), p. 21.

[22]The Halakah (*Sota* 5:3; *Erub.* 4:3) allowed journeys of only six *stadia* on a Sabbath. This was what prevented crowds forming before Saturday evening in Mark 1:32 and, unless we assume that Jesus was preaching within half a mile of John's prison, the same consideration would

prevent the Baptist's disciples from coming to Jesus on a Sabbath and then returning to their master.

[23]See the works cited at n. 15, above. That the historical Jesus saw his own ministry as a fulfillment of Isaiah 61 in a cosmic and eschatological sense is virtually certain: see J. D. G. Dunn, *Jesus and the Spirit* (London: SCM, 1977), pp. 53ff.

[24]The σήμερον "today" of messianic blessing (cf. E. Fuchs, TDNT 7:273–74) is not to be tied either to the week-day Sabbath, nor to any other day of the week, but embraces them all (cf. 3:22 and 23:43, on which see Ellis, *Gospel of Luke*, p. 268). For further discussion as to whether early Christians would be liable to consider a *literal* day's rest particularly appropriate see the concluding essay by A. T. Lincoln, in this volume.

[25]With Schürmann, *Das Lukasevangelium*, p. 246 n. 175.

[26]See Marshall, *Gospel of Luke*, p. 191.

[27]Though see the contribution by D. A. Carson in this volume.

[28]Marshall, *Gospel*, p. 228; cf. T. Schramm, *Der Markus-Stoff bei Lukas*, pp. 111–12. There is an interesting addition ψώχοντες ταῖς χερσίν ("rubbing them in their hands," 1c), which reflects a knowledge that this would have been forbidden in Pharisaic circles (cf. Schürmann, *Das Lukasevangelium*, pp. 302–3). There is also an alteration, in that the Pharisees address their question to the disciples (not to Jesus, v. 2) and Jesus steps in to protect them. Some important MSS include the word δευτεροπρώτῳ ("second first": A C D θ f13 *pm*), but this has no significance for the question at hand. For a discussion see H. Schürmann, *Lukasevangelium* p. 302; Marshall, *Gospel*, p. 230, and the works that they cite.

[29]For a full account see F. Neirynck, "Jesus and the Sabbath: Some Observations on Mk II. 27" *Jésus aux origines de la christologie*, ed. J. Dupont (Gembloux: Duculot, 1975), pp. 233ff.

[30]Ibid., pp. 235–236 and 233 n. 12; H. Hübner, Das Gesetz in der synoptischen Tradition (Witten: Luther-Verlag, 1973), pp. 116–17.

[31]So F. Neirynck, ibid., pp. 245–254; Hübner, *Gesetz*, p. 135, and Banks, *Jesus and the Law*, pp. 118, 122. Contrast E. Lohse, TDNT, 7:22, and E. Käsemann, *Essays on New Testament Themes* (London: SCM, 1964), pp. 101–02.

[32]R. T. Beckwith and W. Stott, *This is the Day: The Biblical Doctrine of the Christian Sunday* (London: Marshall, Morgan and Scott, 1978), pp. 11–12.

[33]Bacchiocchi, *From Sabbath to Sunday*, pp. 59–60.

[34]See D. A. Carson, above. Bacchiocchi, *From Sabbath to Sunday*, pp. 56–57, also rejects the view that Mark 2:27 is a deliberate extension of the Sabbath law beyond Israel to the Gentiles (though cf. Banks, *Jesus and the Law*, p. 119 n. 1).

[35]So Marshall, *Gospel*, p. 232.

[36]Cf. Banks, *Jesus and the Law*, p. 120.

[37]There is no doubt that in doing so David broke the law and that the evangelists understood this; he did what "is not lawful" (Luke 6:4) despite Hübner, *Das Gesetz in der synoptischen Tradition*, pp. 124–126.

[38]See esp. R. T. France, *Jesus and the Old Testament* (London: Tyndale Press, 1971), p. 46.

[39]Whatever may be said for the possibility of a "non-titular" use of "son of man" in this logion in the pre-synoptic tradition (though see C. Colpe, TDNT 8:452 for a criticism of such views), it is quite clear that *Luke* understood it as a title.

[40]Though see D. A. Carson, above. W. Rordorf, *Sunday: The History of the Day of Rest and Worship in the Earliest Centuries of the Christian Church* (London: SCM, 1968), p. 63, maintains that the observation is not merely irrelevant, but wrong.

[41]So, correctly, Banks, *Jesus and the Law*, pp. 115–116.

[42]Schürmann, *Lukasevangelium*, p. 305.

[43]For a trenchant criticism of this popular view see, above all, Bacchiocchi, *From Sabbath to Sunday*, chapter 2, and often in his book.

[44]Schürmann, *Lukasevangelium*, p. 306.

[45]Rordorf, *Sunday*, p. 66.

[46]See Carson, p. 90.

[47]Despite Schürmann, *Lukasevangelium*, p. 306.

[48]F. Godet, *A Commentary on the Gospel of Saint Luke* (Edinburgh: T. & T. Clark, 1870), 1:292.

[49]The only condition under which the Sabbath Halakah would permit aid that involved work on the Sabbath (cf. *Yoma* 8:6).

[50]H. Schürmann, *Lukasevangelium*, p. 308.

[51]Contrast Bacchiocchi, *From Sabbath to Sunday*, pp. 32–35; H. Schürmann, *Lukasevangelium*, pp. 306–10.

[52]With J. M. Creed, *The Gospel According to Saint Luke* (London: Macmillan, 1930), p. 292, and Marshall, *Gospel*, pp. 878–79; contrast W. Grundmann, *Das Evangelium nach Lukas*, p. 436, who takes verses 50, 51*a*, 53*b* and 54–57 as non-Markan pre-Lukan material.

[53]Cf. Creed, *Saint Luke*, p. 292; F. Danker, *Jesus and the New Age*, p. 243.

[54]Cf. Danker, *Jesus and the New Age*, p. 243.

[55]So, especially, V. Taylor, *The Passion Narrative of Saint Luke: A Critical and Historical Investigation* (Cambridge: University Press, 1972), pp. 103–6.

[56]See e.g., F. Godet, *Saint Luke*, 2:343; Danker, *Jesus and the New Age*, p. 244; A. R. C. Leaney, *A Commentary on the Gospel According to Saint Luke* (London: Black, 1966), p. 288, and, possibly, Marshall, *Gospel*, p. 883.

[57]Cf. *Shab*. 23:5: "They may make ready (on the sabbath or on a feast day) all that is needful for the dead, and anoint it and wash it, provided that they do not move any part of it." See J. Jeremias, *The Eucharistic Words of Jesus* (London: SCM, 1976), pp. 76–77.

[58]"On the Sabbath they rested . . . but on the first day of the week . . . they went. . . ."

[59]Bacchiocchi, *From Sabbath to Sunday*, p. 90 n. 1.

[60]For details of this usage see, e.g., A. Plummer, *The Gospel According to Saint Luke* (Edinburgh: T. & T. Clark, 1896), p. 417.

[61]For example, G. B. Caird, *The Gospel of Saint Luke* (Harmondsworth: Pelican, 1963), p. 170; Danker, *Jesus and the New Age*, p. 158; Ellis, *The Gospel of Luke*, pp. 185–86; Grundmann, *Das Evangelium nach Lukas*, p. 278; Marshall, *Gospel*, pp. 508–9, 556–57; Rengstorf, *Das Evangelium nach Lukas*, p. 170.

[62]The precise limits of which are not easy to pin down: see the commentaries on this point.

[63]See M. Hengel, TDNT 9:53, and Marshall, *Gospel*, pp. 556–59 and 577–78, against the claims of R. Bultmann, *History of the Synoptic Tradition* (Oxford: Blackwell, 1963), pp. 12, 62, Lohse, TDNT 7:25–26; and J. Roloff, *Das Kerygma und der irdische Jesus* (Göttingen: Vandenhoeck und Ruprecht, 1970), p. 67.

[64]W. Schrage, TDNT, 7:831.

[65]So I. de la Potterie, "Le titre ΚΥΡΙΟΣ dans l'Évangile de Luc," *Mélanges Bibliques*, p. 134.

[66]Grundmann, *Das Evangelium nach Lukas*, p. 280. Those taking the same position are: Banks, *Jesus and the Law*, pp. 121 and 130; Caird, *Saint Luke* p. 170; Ellis, *The Gospel of Luke*, p. 185; P. K. Jewett, *The Lord's Day: A Theological Guide to the Christian Day of Worship* (Grand Rapids: Eerdmans, 1971), p. 42; Bacchiocchi, *From Sabbath to Sunday*, pp. 35–38 and, on the strength of Grundmann, I. H. Marshall, *Gospel*, p. 559.

[67]Roloff, *Das Kerygma*, p. 67, argues that Pharisees would not in fact be this liberal, but see the counter arguments of Marshall, *Gospel*, pp. 558–59. At Qumran (CD 11:5–7) it was permitted to pasture animals on a Sabbath providing that they did not have to be driven: see L. H. Schiffman, *The Halakhah at Qumran* (Leiden: Brill, 1975), pp. 111–113.

[68]Banks, *Jesus and the Law*, p. 130 is probably correct that there is a further *qal wahomer* argument here, drawing a comparison between the few hours of inconvenience suffered by the animal and the 18 years of discomfort suffered by the woman. See also Carson, above.

[69]Caird, *Saint Luke*, p. 171. The same may be said of Grundmann.

[70]See C. F. D. Moule, *An Idiom Book of New Testament Greek* (Cambridge: University Press, 1963), p. 166.

[71]So H. Schürmann, *Traditionsgeschichtliche Untersuchungen zu den synoptischen Evangelien* (Düsseldorf; Patmos, 1968), p. 213.

[72]Not least in the totally different settings: Matthew has included the parallel words within a quite different, *Markan* story. See also Hübner, *Gesetz*, pp. 137–38.

[73]Cf. Marshall, *Gospel*, pp. 31, 245, etc.

[74]See particularly the discussion by Ellis, *The Gospel of Luke*, pp. 192–93, and Marshall, *Gospel*, pp. 562, 578.

[75]For this text see B. M. Metzger, A *Textual Commentary on the Greek New Testament* (London: United Bible Societies, 1971), p. 164; Banks, *Jesus and the Law*, p. 128; E. Schweizer, TDNT, 8:364 n.209, and Marshall, *Gospel*, p. 579. At Qumran they would help the boy, but leave the ox! (cf. Schiffmann, *The Halakhah at Qumran* pp. 121ff., 125ff. [on CD 11:13–14 and 11:16–17 respectively]).

[76]For a discussion of Jesus and the law in the wider context of the whole gospel tradition see the chapter by Carson in this volume, and particularly the following works: Banks, *Jesus and the Law;* K. Berger, *Die Gesetzauslegung Jesu* (Neukirchen: Neukirchener Verlag, 1972); Hübner, *Das Gesetz in der synoptischen Tradition;* J. P. Meier, *Law and History in Matthew's Gospel* (Rome: Biblical Institute Press, 1976); S. Pancaro, *The Law in the Fourth Gospel* (Leiden: Brill, 1975).

[77]So J. Jervell, *Luke and the People of God*, p. 138.

[78]Despite Conzelmann, *Theology*, pp. 107, 122, who maintains that Luke has so de-eschatologized his material that only the image of the kingdom is present in Jesus' ministry, not the kingdom itself. Almost all subsequent scholarship has disagreed: see particularly: H.-W. Bartsch, *Wachet aber zu jeder Zeit* (Hamburg: Reich, 1963); Ellis, *Eschatology in Luke;* E. Franklin, *Christ the Lord* (London: SPCK, 1975), pp. 9–45; Kümmel, "Luc en accusation;" G. Lohfink, *Die Himmelfahrt Jesu* (Munich: Kösel, 1971), pp. 255–56; O. Merk, "Das Reich Gottes in den lukanischen Schriften," *Jesus und Paulus*, ed. E. E. Ellis and E. Grässer (Göttingen: Vandenhoeck und Ruprecht, 1973), pp. 201–20.

[79]As the rabbis expected it would at the advent of the messiah: *B.Sanh.* 97*b;* on which see R. N. Longenecker, *Paul: Apostle of Liberty* (New York: Harper, 1964), p. 131.

[80]W. Wink, *John the Baptist*, p. 45, correctly speaks of Luke's "desire to assimilate all honorific and exalted titles to Jesus Christ."

[81]For the significance of this figure in contemporary thought see: J. Coppens, *Le Messianisme et sa relève prophétique* (Gembloux: Duculot, 1974), p. 172–80; R. H. Fuller, *The Foundations of New Testament Christology* (London: Lutterworth, 1965), pp. 46–53; F. Hahn, *The Titles of Jesus in Christology* (London: Lutterworth, 1959), pp. 352–406; W. A. Meeks, *The Prophet King: Moses Traditions and the Johannine Christology* (Leiden: Brill, 1967); F. Schnider, *Jesus der Prophet* (Freiburg: Universitätsverlag, 1973), pp. 27ff., 31ff., and 89–100; H. Teeple, *The Mosaic Eschatological Prophet* (Philadelphia: SBL, 1957), chapters 2–3.

For the significance for Luke see Voss, *Die Christologie der lukanischen Schriften*, section 14. Luke specifically identifies Jesus with the "prophet like Moses" in Acts 3 and Acts 7, and this forms a crucial step in his ecclesiology (so G. Lohfink, *Die Sammlung Israels: Eine Untersuchung zur lukanischen Ekklesiologie* (Münich: Kösel, 1975), chapters 2 and 3; Jervell, *Luke*, pp. 41–74. There are also redactional traces of such christology in the gospel of Luke itself, especially at 9:29, 31, 34f.; 7:11–35; 24:19 (cf. Acts 7:22!). It is also probable that Luke considered Isaiah 61 to be a reference to the messianic prophet (so Marshall, *Luke*, pp. 124–28; Hahn, *The Titles of Jesus*, pp. 380–81; Grundmann, p. 121; and G. W. H. Lampe, "The Holy Spirit in the Writings of Saint Luke," *Studies in the Gospels*, ed. D. E. Nineham [Oxford: Blackwell, 1955], p. 177).

[82]See Banks, *Jesus and the Law, passim;* C.F.D. Moule, *The Origin of Christology* (Cambridge: University Press, 1977), chapters 1 and 3–7.

[83]Cf. W. Gutbrod, TDNT, 4:1060; L. Goppelt, *Apostolic and Post-Apostolic Times*, pp. 31–32.

[84]Jervell, *Luke*, pp. 133–51 (his view will be discussed at length below); Banks, *Jesus and the Law*, pp. 172 and 246ff.

[85]The relationship between this story and that of Mark 12:28–34 is disputed: see Banks, *Jesus-*

and the Law, p. 164, who cautiously suggests that Luke relates a different event from Mark while citing those who take different options, and Marshall, *Gospel*, pp. 440–41 who (hesitantly) adopts the position held by H. Schürmann, *Untersuchungen*, p. 280 note 15, that the story derives from Q (and, like Banks, that it refers to a different event from that depicted in the Markan account). Such an event would certainly have been common in Jesus' ministry: so T. W. Manson, *The Sayings of Jesus* (London: SCM, 1949), pp. 259–60; and others.

[86]Jervell, *Luke*, maintains that in Luke-Acts the *whole* law remains valid for Jewish Christians and thus Luke cannot depict Jesus as offering a summary of the law. Luke 10:25 has thus changed Mark 12:28 from *ποία ἐστὶν ἐντολὴ πρώτη πάντων*; "Which commandment is the first of all?" to the more neutral *τί ποιήσας ζωὴν αἰώνιον κληρονομήσω*; "What shall I do to inherit eternal life?" But, even allowing that Luke may depend on Mark here, Jervell's major premise is wrong: "neither in palestine nor in hellenistic judaism did the singling out of these two commandments negate the principle of the equivalence of commandments, according to which . . . from the point of view of obedience all had the same status" (Banks, *Jesus and the Law*, pp. 170–71; and see *B.Ab.* 2:1*b*; *B.Shab.* 31*a*). It might further be pointed out that it is not clear how Luke's "rephrasing" is supposed to avoid the alleged difficulty: what follows *is* a summary of the law and, as Luke must have at least read Mark 12:28, he would have been aware of the fact.

[87]See Marshall, *Gospel*, p. 207.

[88]So Schürmann, *Lukasevangelium*, p. 277 and Banks, *Jesus and the Law*, pp. 103–4; and this despite J. N. Geldenhuys, *Commentary on the Gospel of Luke* (London: Marshall, Morgan and Scott, 1950), p. 186; and L. Morris, *Luke* (London: IVP, 1974), p. 115.

[89]With M. Miyoshi, *Der Anfang des Reiseberichts Lk 9.51–10.24* (Rome: Biblical Institute Press, 1974), chapter 4.

[90]The structure implied here is much nearer that of Ellis, *Luke*, p. 34, than it is to that of Marshall, *Gospel*, pp. 402–03 and 439ff., who splits 9:51–10:24 from 10:25–11:13. But even for Marshall there is a certain continuity of theme between the sections.

[91]Ellis, *Luke*, p. 160.

[92]So Banks, *Jesus and the Law*, p. 179.

[93]Both the tradition history and the interpretation of 16:16ff. are highly disputed. In our view it is probable that: (1) the saying reflects a genuine word of Jesus (see N. Perrin, *Rediscovering the Teaching of Jesus* [London: SCM, 1967], p. 74ff.) and it is better preserved in Matthew's wording, albeit correctly interpreted by Luke (cf. Marshall, *Gospel*, p. 629). (2) Luke probably found the logion in Q, despite E. Bammel, "Is Luke 16.16 of Baptist Provenience?" *HTR* 51 (1958): 101ff., and others. (3) 16:16–18 was probably a unity in Q: Luke was not first to join verse 18 to verses 16–17, for the former seems foreign to his redactional theme at this point (so Marshall, *Gospel*, pp. 626–27)—unless, perhaps, with Danker, *Jesus and the New Age*, we see verse 18 as a barbed rejection of Pharisaic handling of the law. (4) Verse 16*a* neither clearly excludes John from the new era (despite Conzelmann, *Theology*, pp. 16ff.) nor definitely excludes him from the old (contrast Wink, *John the Baptist*, p. 51ff.); John is a bridge between the two ages. (5) *βιάζεται* ("enters," RSV; "is forcing his way," NIV) in 16*b* is middle in form and should be construed in a good sense. For an adequately documented discussion see e.g., Marshall, *Gospel*, p. 629. This writer correctly points out that the use of *εἰς* ("into") with the verb probably rules out hostile intent (contrast F. W. Danker, "Luke 16.16—an Opposition Logion?" *JBL* 77 [1958]: 235), or opponents harassing the kingdom (contrast Ellis, *Luke*, pp. 203–4).

[94]This is particularly well handled by Marshall, *Gospel*, pp. 613–14. While Matthew 11:13 is primarily concerned with the prophetic aspect of the law, Luke, here, is not; his stress falls on the fact that the *ethical* teaching of the law is confirmed by Jesus' ministry. His context excludes the possibility of Ellis's exegesis, *Luke*, pp. 203–4: "Since the kingdom of God is the fulfilment of the law, no amount of hostility can prevail against it." G. Schneider, *Das Evangelium nach Lukas* (Gütersloh: Mohr, 1977), pp. 336–38, also takes 16:14–18 as a unit, thus setting 16–18 over against the greed of the Pharisees, and emphasizing the continuing validity of the law.

[95]Cf. Banks, *Jesus and the Law*, pp. 240–41.

[96]Among many, see especially Conzelmann, *Theology*, pp. 240–41; Hübner, *Das Gesetz*, pp.

28–31; and W. G. Kümmel, "'Das Gesetz und die Propheten gehen bis Johannes'—Lukas 16.16 im Zusammenhang der heilsgeschichtlichen Theologie der Lukasschriften," *Verborum Veritas*, ed. O. Böcher and K. Haacker (Wuppertal: Brockhaus, 1970), pp. 89–102.

[97]Banks, *Jesus and the Law*, p. 159.

[98]Ibid., p. 243.

[99]See 103–4 above; and Banks, *Jesus and the Law*, p. 248; contrast Hübner, *Das Gesetz;* p. 211.

[100]Jesus' free association with עַמ־הָאָרֶץ ("the people of the land") further suggests that He regarded His mission as transcending, if not abrogating, the laws of ritual purity; but the problem is a complex one: see esp. A. Oppenheimer, *The 'Am Ha-Aretz* (Leiden: Brill, 1977), pp. 51–63, 83–96 and 218ff. Jesus is probably primarily rejecting the Halakah, not the Torah.

[101]As Conzelmann, *Theology*, p. 132ff., so correctly observes. He is probably wrong, however, to think that Luke was innovative in this respect: see the criticism of him at this point by Marshall, *Gospel*, pp. 752–84; A. L. Moore, *The Parousia Hope in the New Testament* (Leiden: Brill, 1966), p. 86ff. and, above all, J. Zmijewski, *Die Eschatologiereden des Lukasevangeliums*, throughout the second part.

[102]This has been widely observed, but exaggerated perhaps by Hübner, *Das Gesetz*, pp. 207–11. Cf. the strictures offered by M. Rese, *Alttestamentliche Motive in der Christologie des Lukas* (Gütersloh: Mohn, 1969), pp. 208–9 and passim.

[103]The theme is continued in Acts 3:25 and 13:32–33; though these terms are not used of Gentiles. Cf. N. Dahl, "The Story of Abraham in Luke-Acts," *SLA*, pp. 139–58.

[104]See R. J. Banks, "Matthew's Understanding of the Law: Authenticity and Interpretation in Matt. 5:17–20," *JBL* 93 (1972): 23–33.

[105]So Banks, *Jesus*, pp. 240–41.

[106]Ibid., p. 243.

[107]Ibid., p. 242ff.

[108]Conservative evangelical writers are particularly prone to this fault; e.g., R. T. Beckwith, *This is the Day*, pp. 26ff.; but cf. also K. Berger, *Die Gesetzauslegung*, pp. 17ff., whose position is effectively rejected by M. Hengel, *The Son of God* (London: SCM, 1976), p. 67, n. 123. See also Banks, *Jesus and the Law*, pp. 109, 242; F. F. Bruce, *Paul: Apostle of the Free Spirit* (Exeter: Paternoster, 1977), pp. 192–93; and E. P. Sanders, *Paul and Palestinian Judaism* (London: SCM, 1977), pp. 112, 114; *idem*, "On the Question of Fulfilling the Law in Paul and Rabbinic Judaism," *Donum Gentilicium*, ed. E. Bammel, C. K. Barrett and W. D. Davies (Oxford: University Press, 1978), p. 125.

[109]See Banks, *Jesus and the Law, pp. 65–85; idem*, "The Eschatological Role of the Law in Pre- and Post-Christian Thought," *Reconciliation and Hope*, ed. R. J. Banks (Exeter: Paternoster, 1974), pp. 173–85, and P. Schäfer, "Die Torah der messianischen Zeit," ZNW 65 (1974): 27–42.

[110]Banks, *Jesus and the Law*, pp. 245 and 255.

[111]See esp. E. P. Sanders, *Paul and Palestinian Judaism*, pp. 240–41, 269 and contrast with 372–73 and 389–90.

[112]The arguments in favor of the longer text of Luke 22:17ff. are compellingly set out by J. Jeremias, *Eucharistic Words*, pp. 138–58; Schürmann, "Lk 22.19b–20 als ürsprüngliche Textüberlieferung," *Bib* 32 (1951): 336–92, 522–41; *idem*, *Der Einsetzungsbericht Lk* 22.19–20 (Münster: Aschendorffsche Verlag, 1955), passim; and cf. Voss, *Die Christologie der Lukanischen Schriften*, 101ff. The strongest case for the opposite view is presented by M. Rese, "Zur Problematik von Kurz- und Langtext in Luk 22.17ff.," *NTS* 22 (1976): 15–32. Rese has two points of substance: (1) It is impossible to explain adequately how an original longer text became shortened and (2) Luke does not attribute *atoning* significance to the cross elsewhere and so the addition of the long text is non-Lukan in character. The second of these rests on a misunderstanding: the long text says nothing about an *atoning* death, merely about a *redemptive* death, which establishes a new covenant. Luke certainly regards Jesus' death as redemptive: see further at n.114, below. Rese's first objection is also of doubtful force in view of the overwhelming support for the

longer reading. It is hardly more difficult to explain the deletion of the long text in a few MSS than it is to explain the complete absence of a theology of Jesus' death from a work that took such pains to say that it was necessary and that the Old Testament had continually prophesied it!

[113]This position is held by, e.g., Banks, *Jesus and the Law*, pp. 172 and 246ff., and K. Lake, *BC* 5:217.

[114]Against (among others) J. D. G. Dunn, *Unity and Diversity in the New Testament* (London: SCM, 1977), p. 18, who maintains that Luke probably has no theology of the cross, see especially A. George, "Le sens de la mort de Jésus pour Luc," *RB* 80 (1973): 186–217; R. Glöckner, *Die Verkündigung des Heils*, pp. 155–95; F. Schütz, *Der leidende Christus* (Stuttgart: Kohlhammer, 1969), pp. 93–94, and G. Voss, *Die Christologie der lukanischen Schriften*, section 7.

[115]NIDNTT 1:369. A similar claim is made by Sanders, *Paul*, pp. 236–37 with respect to rabbinic tradition.

[116]NIDNTT 1:369.

[117]Cf. J. Behm, TDNT 2:132; W. Foerster, TDNT 7:990–91.

[118]See J. Jeremias, *New Testament Theology* (London: SCM, 1971), 1: chaps. 4–6; *idem, The Sermon on the Mount* (London: Athlone Press, 1961), pp. 24–33.

[119]For this possibility see Sanders, *Paul*, pp. 236–37.

[120]Cf. especially the witness of the fourth Gospel. Banks, *Jesus and the Law*, p. 254, relates Luke's law material, and his handling of it, to the themes of new covenant and the death of Christ.

[121]F. Overbeck, "Über der Verhältnis Justins des Märtyrers zur Apostelgeschichte," *ZWT* 15 (1872): 321, and as referred to by Jervell.

[122]Henceforth I use the term "Jewish Christian" in the sense defined by S. K. Riegel, "Jewish Christianity: Definitions and Terminology," *NTS* 24 (1978): 415: "'Jewish Christianity' following the lead of Longenecker and Murray, should be used to refer to Christianity expressed in semitic-Jewish thought forms but limited to the tradition of the Jerusalem church as contained largely in Jewish Christian canonical works but possibly also reflected in some extra canonical works. . . . Chronologically it would refer, as Longenecker says, especially to the apostolic age of the first christian century." This is to be contrasted with "judaic" and "judaistic" Christianity and "judeo-Christianity," which are to be defined in different ways. For the debate on these terms see Riegel's article and also M. Simon, "Réflexions sur le Judéo-Christianisme," *Christianity, Judaism and Other Graeco-Roman Cults*, 2:52–76.

[123]BC 5:217.

[124]Jervell, *Luke*, pp. 41–207. Only the first essay in the book is not related to the general question of Luke's ecclesiology and its consequences.

[125]Ibid., pp. 41–74. This essay first appeared as "Das gespaltene Israel und die Heidenvölker," *ST* 19 (1965): 68ff.

[126]Against, e.g., Lohfink, *Sammlung*, p. 55. With an eye to the issues raised by P. Richardson in his *Israel in the Apostolic Church* (Cambridge: University Press, 1969), the words "true Israel" could indeed be misleading, but not more so than Jervell's terminology which underestimates the change introduced by Jesus' ministry. I have preferred to use the term "Israel of fulfillment," thereby, I hope, avoiding the Scylla of complete antithesis (true as opposed to false Israel; new as opposed to old Israel—language that is hard to defend from the New Testament) and the Charybdis of implying that there has been no change in the status of Israel. By "Israel of fulfillment" I mean that sector of Israel in which the promises made to her are coming to fulfillment and presenting the people with new challenges that demand a new level of commitment and a new primary allegiance to Jesus.

[127]Compare Lohfink, *Sammlung*.

[128]For a similar thesis see J. Ropes, BC 4:177–78.

[129]Jervell, *Luke*, pp. 133–51. This essay was first published in *HTR* 64 (1971): 21–36.

[130]Ibid., p. 138.

[131]Acts 6:11, 13–14; 18:13; 21:21, 28; 25:8, 10; 28:17.

[132]Jervell, *Luke*, p. 141.

[133]Ibid., pp. 141–44, but see the criticism at n. 126, *supra*.

[134]Ibid., pp. 145–47.

[135]Ibid., pp. 153–84. This essay first appeared as "Paulus—der Lehrer Israels. Zu der apologetischen Paulusrede in der Apostelgeschichte," *NovT* 10 (1968): 164ff.

[136]Compare, to some extent, A. J. Mattill, "The Purpose of Acts: Schneckenburger Reconsidered," *Apostolic History and the Gospel*, W. Ward Gasque and R. P. Martin (Exeter: Paternoster, 1970), pp. 108–23. I am grateful to Professor C. F. D. Moule for drawing my attention to this.

[137]Jervell, *Luke*, pp. 185–207.

[138]But see the criticism of Wilson, *The Gentiles*, pp. 224–25.

[139]Cf. Haenchen, *The Acts of the Apostles*, p. 209; G. Stählin, *Die Apostelgeschichte* (Göttingen: Vandenhoeck und Ruprecht, 1966), pp. 68–69; Wilson, *The Gentiles*, pp. 220–22.

[140]Despite Haenchen, *Acts*; see the argument of Wilson, *The Gentiles*, pp. 220 n.4 and 221 where he makes the further observation that had Luke intended what Jervell suggests he would have followed the LXX of Genesis 22:18 more exactly with πάντα τὰ ἔθνη ("all the nations").

[141]See above.

[142]See p. 110 above.

[143]It would be wrong to restrict the terms of reference of the vision to foods (as so many have done: see Haenchen, *Acts*, pp. 356ff.). There were principles to be deduced: it was largely because of their carelessness in food matters that Gentiles were ritually unsafe people for pious Jews to meet socially (so F. F. Bruce, *The Book of Acts* [London: Marshall, Morgan and Scott, 1954], p. 222). M. Dibelius, *Studies in the Acts of the Apostles* (London: SCM, 1954), pp. 109–22, regards the story of the vision as an insertion into a harmless account of a pious Gentile becoming a believer. But the story was not "harmless" (cf. Goppelt, *Apostolic and Post-Apostolic Times*, p. 70), nor is it obvious that the subject of ritual purity, introduced in Peter's vision, is an intrusion. Ritual purity, table fellowship and circumcision were strongly linked, and Luke is not guilty of any confusion when he discusses the former two within a story the main point of which is that the pious Gentile *remained uncircumcised*.

[144]Despite W. Wilckens, *Die Missionsreden der Apostelgeschichte* (Neukirchen: Neukirchener Verlag, 1961), pp. 63–64. See particularly the trenchant criticism by Stanton, *Jesus of Nazareth*, pp. 19ff.

[145]The witnesses are "false" on several accounts: Stephen (according to Luke) did not speak against the law; rather, it is Israel that has never obeyed the law (7:35–40, 51–53). Nor did he say that Jesus would destroy the temple (Luke has removed all trace of that from the trial of Jesus; cf. Mark 14:58; 15:29); far less did he blaspheme either Moses or God (6:12). But at one point these "false witnesses" are nearly correct. Stephen does give a fairly substantial attack on idolatrous attitudes toward the temple, and this could have been misunderstood as an attack on the temple itself (see further at n. 188).

[146]Cf. n. 125, above.

[147]"Das Problem des sogennanten Aposteldekretz," *ZKG* 55 (1964): 227.

[148]Assuming the ritual prescriptions of the Alexandrian text: "the Western reading is an attempt to make the decree into a purely moral requirement;" see O'Neill, *Theology*, p. 82 and n. 2; Haenchen, *Acts*, pp. 449–50 (with notes), 468ff.; C. S. C. Williams, *The Acts of the Apostles* (London: Black, 1964), pp. 183–84; and, most recently, D. Catchpole, "Paul, James and the Apostolic Decree," *NTS* 23 (1976–77): 429.

[149]See H. G. Kuhn, TDNT 6:728–30.

[150]Ibid., pp. 728–29; R. Meyer, TDNT 5:844ff.

[151]H. G. Kuhn, TDNT 6:731–32; N. J. McEleney, "Conversion, Circumcision and the Law," *NTS* 20 (1974): 321.

[152]"In principle, the proselytes became an integral part of the Jewish nation with all that this implied;" so M. Stern in *The Jewish People in the First Century*, ed. S. Safrai and M. Stern (Assen: Van Gorcum, 1976), p. 623. It is true that diaspora Judaism made fewer demands on the God-fearer who wished to become a proselyte than did palestinian Judaism (TDNT 6: 731;

McEleney, "Conversion, Circumcision and the Law," pp. 323–25; 328–33). But the story of king Izates (Josephus, *Ant.* xx. 34–48) should not be used to illustrate the view that in the diaspora it was common practice to take the law on circumcision lightly (despite O'Neill, *Theology*, p. 103). Ananias was well aware that Izates was disobeying the law by holding back on the question of circumcision—and Eleazer makes this painfully clear. Ananias was only prepared to offer the counsel he did because he was aware of the political danger to Izates of being circumcised. McEleney is hard pressed to find a more liberal attitude ("Conversion, Circumcision, and the Law," pp. 328–33). Philo perhaps offers such an example (ibid., p. 329) but otherwise it is usually only the haemophiliac who is an "uncircumcised Israelite"; at least until after the fall of the temple.

[153]This despite the obscure logic of verse 21 (on which see the differing interpretations of Jervell, *Luke*, *BC* 4: 177–78; Bruce, *Paul*, p. 312; W. L. Knox, *Saint Paul and the Church of Jerusalem* (London: Cambridge University Press, 1925), p. 234; Haenchen, *Acts*, p. 450; A. Loisy, *Les Actes des Apôtres* (Paris: Nourry, 1920), p. 594; and O'Neill, *Theology*, pp. 82f.).

[154]See E. E. Ellis, "The Role of the Christian Prophet in Acts," *Prophecy and Hermeneutics* (Tübingen: Mohr, 1978), p. 137.

[155]So D. Catchpole, "Paul, James, and the Apostolic Decree," p. 429—though he would not accept my antithesis; H. Conzelmann, *Die Apostelgeschichte* (Tübingen: Mohr, 1972), p. 93; Goppelt, *Apostolic and Post-Apostolic Times*, pp. 78–79; W. Gutbrod, TDNT 4: 1067; and O'Neill, *Theology*, p. 131. For the possibility that zealot pressure was at least partly responsible for the promulgation of the decree, cf. discussion below.

[156]Though, with McEleney, "Conversion, Circumcision, and the Law," pp. 325ff., we agree that the term "God-fearer" was used in the apostolic era with a much broader meaning than is usually ascribed to it.

[157]So SBK 3:33–43; *BC* 4:177; 5:207–8, and most others since. Whether or not the individual requirements had actually been gathered together, at this date, and come to be known as the Noachian laws is not entirely relevant. Cf. TDNT, 6: 740, 743ff.; and G. F. Moore, *Judaism* (Cambridge: University Press, 1927), 1: 274. For the text of the Noachian commandments see *B.Sanh.* 56*a-b*.

[158]Similarly Knox, *Saint Paul*; and H. J. Schoeps, *Paul: The Theology of the Apostle in the Light of Jewish Religious History* (London: Lutterworth, 1961), p. 67.

[159]Compare Marshall, *Luke: Historian and Theologian*, pp. 191–92.

[160]See Lohfink, *Sammlung*, for the significance of λαός for Luke. Compare N. A. Dahl, "A People for his Name," *NTS* 4 (1958): 319–26, and the more cautious note struck by Wilson, *The Gentiles*, pp. 224–25.

[161]It is this observation that overturns the thesis of D. Catchpole, "Paul, James, and the Apostolic Decree." Catchpole accepts that Gentiles are only being asked to fulfill the requirements of the גֵּר תּוֹשָׁב ("the sojourning alien"), but he fails to see the incongruity of the situation whereby Gentiles (who shall inherit the promises made to Israel) have only such minimal demands made upon them by an (allegedly) strongly nomistic Jerusalem community. Catchpole simply asserts that in the theology underlying the decree the gospel does nothing about the Jew/Gentile distinction (and he contrasts this with Paul's position; cf. 430). But this is certainly not true of the situation depicted in Acts 15. There Jews and Gentiles have been made one λαός ("people") together, and stand over against unbelieving Gentiles (and Jews) who do not participate in Israel's promises. Nor is Catchpole's thesis a plausible historical reconstruction even when the Acts evidence is dismissed. The obvious inference to be drawn by a nomistic Jew, faced with Gentile reception of the Spirit, is the very one we find; viz. "these men ought to be circumcised" (etc.; Acts 15:5), *because by* their participation in the promises to Israel they belong *with* Israel.

[162]Hence *τί πειράζετε τὸν θεόν;* ("why do you make trial of God?"); cf. H. Seesemann, TDNT 6:32.

[163]Despite J. D. G. Dunn, *Baptism in the Holy Spirit* (London: SCM, 1970), chapter 7 and passim. For Luke it is faith that cleanses the heart, not the gift of the Spirit (though the Spirit may well be the agent of that cleansing). Dunn assumes that Peter has Ezekiel 36 in mind, and that

the cleansing and the giving of the Spirit are complementary descriptions of the same event. But Ezekiel 36 played a relatively small part in Judaism's future hope for the Spirit, and in the rabbinic literature it is interpreted mainly in the context of the removal of the evil יֵצֶר ("inclination") at the End (see P. Schäfer, *Die Vorstellung vom Heiligen Geist in der rabbinischen Literatur* [Munich: Kösel, 1972], p. 152). By contrast Joel 3 appears frequently in connection with future hopes for the Spirit (and is clearly central to Luke's concern; cf. Acts 2:17ff.), *but it is never interpreted in terms of the cleansing of the heart promised in Ezekiel.* Where Ezekiel 36 and Joel 3 are brought together (*Deut.R.* 6 (203*d*); *Midr.Ps.* 14, 6 (57*b*); see SBK 2:615), *the giving of a new heart and the return of the spirit of prophecy are understood as successive promises; not as complementary descriptions.* See especially *Deut.R.* 6 in which Ezekiel 36 must be fulfilled before God will allow His *Shekina* to return, the latter being interpreted in terms of Joel 3:1. This is in complete accord with the usual rabbinic teaching that Joel 3:1 is promised for the time when Israel is pure (cf. P. Schäfer, *Die Vorstellung vom Heiligen Geist*, pp. 107, 114), and it is consistent with the general teaching that the spirit of prophecy was removed from Israel because of her sins (ibid., pp. 103–10) *not vice versa.*

Dunn (as above, pp. 80f.) too quickly dispenses with the pentecostal exegesis that maintains that Cornelius came to faith and was cleansed in heart (Acts 15:9) during Peter's sermon, the gift of the Spirit following in close succession, but as a distinct act of grace. But Dunn is barely more convincing himself; the gift of the Spirit referred to in the accounts is seen, both by the words of 11:17 and by the description of what happened in 10:46, to be a Christianized version of the spirit of prophecy. In the conservative Jewish setting that Luke portrays in Acts 11 and 15, the point is surely that the Spirit only alights on what is pure (hence the softening-up vision of Acts 10:10–16; 11:5–11) and therefore, that if Cornelius' household received the gift of the Spirit it must (already) have been clean; thus "but cleansed their hearts *by faith*" (15:9). Luke may have considered this cleansing to have been performed by the Spirit active in Peter's Spirit-empowered preaching (cf. 15:7), or independent of it, but it is not what is meant by receiving the gift of the Spirit in this context. 15:9 is the conclusion arrived at from what is described in 15:8, not a restatement of it.

[164]See R. Scroggs, "The Earliest Christian Communities as Sectarian Movement" in *Christianity, Judaism and Other Greco-Roman Cults*, 2: 1–23, especially 10–11 and 16–17; cf. also Bruce (as at n. 143), p. 307 n. 28.

[165]It is nomism, of course, not legalism that is the issue (for a definition of the term see Longenecker, *Paul*, pp. 79–80; for nomism as the character of Judaism at the time see Sanders, *Paul*). From the Pharisees' point of view (15:5) the Gentiles should be circumcised and keep the law of Moses *because* God has done great things among them (15:4!). This may, or may not, be the view of those who came down to Antioch (15:1), depending on how *οὐ δύνασθε σωθῆναι* ("you cannot be saved") is taken.

[166]The *κἀκεῖνοι* of verse 11 ("they") refers to the Gentiles who have believed in Jesus; not to the fathers who were under the law (despite *BC* 4, on this passage).

[167]Peter's speech starts with a *pesher* of Joel 3:1–5. As M. Rese, *Motive*, p. 45ff., correctly observes, there is more to the Joel citation than the explanation of the pentecostal phenomena which provided the occasion for the speech. Peter incorporates such a large section because it finishes with the statement that all who call on the name of the Lord will be saved (which he interprets christologically). By the end of Peter's speech the apostle has identified Jesus as the Lord upon whose name a man should call to be saved, though in Joel this "Lord" was clearly Yahweh. Between the quotation at the beginning of the speech, and the dramatic appeal at the end, Peter seeks to establish his case for applying the citation to Jesus. The proof depends on three points: (1) the Joel citation has already found some measure of fulfillment in the signs and wonders accompanying Jesus' death (see Rese, *ibid.*, 54; Stanton, *Jesus of Nazareth*, pp. 81–82). (2) Jesus was raised and must therefore be the eschatological son of David of whom David spoke in Psalm 16 (cf. v. 30). (3) As Jesus has been exalted it is clear that the one to whom David referred as "my Lord," and who in turn is addressed by the Lord God and given dominion (according to Ps. 110:1), is none other than Jesus. Jesus has been made Lord and Christ (v. 36), and hence the redeemer upon whom one might call.

For Luke, the true hinge to Peter's argument lies between points (2) and (3); for it should be noted that Peter's use of Psalm 16 does not prove any more than that Jesus' resurrection was foretold by David and that Jesus is identified by the resurrection as David's heir. The further claim that Jesus has been exalted to God's right hand and is now vice regent, while connected with the resurrection, nevertheless involves other aspects that are not immediately in view in Psalm 16. *It is Jesus' pouring out of the Spirit* (according to 2:33) *that, for Peter, demonstrates that Jesus is not merely raised, but exalted to the right hand of God and to rule in glory* (Ps. 110:1).

[168]Compare C. F. D. Moule, "The Christology of Acts," *SLA*, p. 180; and G. W. MacRae, "Whom Heaven Must Receive Until the Time," *Int* 27 (1973): 158ff., with G. Stählin, "Τὸ Πνεῦμα 'Ιησοῦ' (Apg. 16.7)," in *Christ and Spirit in the New Testament*.

[169]See A. R. Johnson, *The Vitality of the Individual in the Thought of Ancient Israel* (Cardiff: University of Wales Press, 1964), pp. 26–39; *idem.*, *The One and the Many in the Israelite Conception of God* (Cardiff: University of Wales Press, 1961), pp. 15ff.; and G. W. H. Lampe, *God as Spirit* (Oxford: Clarendon, 1977), chapters 2 and 8.

[170]Against the view of G. W. H. Lampe, "The Holy Spirit in the Writings of Saint Luke," in *Studies in the Gospels*, pp. 193–94; that the Spirit of Jesus here means primarily "the Spirit that was on Jesus" (not "the Spirit that mediates Jesus") see especially the whole force of G. Stählin's article (as at n. 168).

[171]The commentaries on this passage, and works on the origin of christology, appear to miss the importance of this. For example, M. Hengel, *The Son of God*, discusses the various factors which led to a high christology at an early stage in the primitive church, but at no point does he refer to the inevitable conclusion that the earliest church would be bound to draw from its experience of the risen Jesus as Lord of the Spirit. *Of no man had it ever been said, after his death, that his presence and direction was made to be felt by God's Spirit; yet precisely this was said of Jesus* earlier even than the writing of the Pauline Epistles. (The validity of this affirmation is quite independent of whether or not Peter's speech is "authentic"; Paul was not the first to maintain that the Spirit mediated Christ.) See M. M. B. Turner (as in n. 15) for details.

[172]See nn. 81 and 126, above.

[173]The purpose of the Jesus/disciple parallels in Luke-Acts is, at least in part, directed to establishing this.

[174]See *SBK* 3: 196–97; M. Barth, *Ephesians* (New York: Doubleday, 1974), pp. 472–73; J. Dupont, "Ascension du Christ et don de L'Ésprit d'après Actes 2.33," *Christ and Spirit in the New Testament*, pp. 221–25 (and the works cited there); B. Lindars, *New Testament Apologetic* (London: SCM, 1961), pp. 52–59; J. Potin, *La Fête juive de la Pentecôte* (Paris: du Cerf, 1971), p. 195.

[175]I am aware that such a position has been denied both by those who follow Lohse, TDNT, 6: 48–49, in maintaining that Moses/Sinai traditions were not connected with Pentecost in Judaism until after the fall of the temple, and by those who take their lead from K. Adler, *Das erste christliche Pfingsfest* (Münster: Aschendorffsche Verlag, 1938), pp. 53–58, who maintains that Acts 2 does not contain sufficient specifically Moses/Sinai imagery to justify drawing the parallel. But neither is convincing: (1) The associations between the Jewish feast of Pentecost and the giving of the law did not fall out of the blue: B. Noack, "The Day of Pentecost in Jubilees, Qumran and Acts," *ASTI* 1 (1966–67): 73–79, and J. Potin, *La Fête juive*, have assembled sufficient evidence to show (at very least) that the two were related before Jesus' ministry, even if Psalm 68 had not yet become part of the pentecostal liturgy in Judaism. (2) Adler's caution is well taken, but the cumulative force of all the points of contact (the time of day; the assembly of united people; the shaking of the place of revelation; the mention of sound and wind; the *whole* place of revelation filled with God's presence; a noise from heaven; fire seen on earth; a division of tongues before assembled nations; those who hear the voice of God do so in their own languages; a gift received from heaven (see especially the striking verbal parallel between 2:33 and Josephus' account of Sinai at *Ant.* xxx. 77f.); the foundational significance of Sinai for Judaism and of Pentecost for Luke) is rather more compelling than Adler allows. For details of the parallels see, e.g., J. Kremer, *Pfingstbericht und Pfingstgeschehen* (Stuttgart: KBW Verlag, 1973), pp. 87–166.

[176]Haenchen, *Acts*, p. 172.

[177]I. Broer, "Der Geist und die Gemeinde. Zur Auslegung der lukanischen Pfingstgeschichte (Apg. 2.1–13)," *BiLe* 13 (1940): 282–83.

[178]E. g., J. K. Parratt, *The Seal of the Spirit in New Testament Teaching* (unpublished Ph.D. dissertation [London, 1965]), pp. 201–2; and Franklin, *Christ the Lord*, p. 98; both arguing against W. L. Knox.

[179]See above, especially note 112.

[180]See above especially note 109.

[181]E. Plümacher, *Lukas als hellenistischer Schriftsteller* (Göttingen: Vandenhoeck und Ruprecht, [c. 1972]), pp. 38–77, takes the view of Dibelius, Wilckens and Haenchen to the extreme when he argues that all the "traditional" material in the speeches is essentially hellenistic mimesis, and that all alleged semitisms are really created septuagintalisms. Without wishing to deny the effect of the LXX on Luke-Acts, the point remains that *the form of the argument* within the speeches is too realistically "Jewish," especially where it depends on *pesher* and other midrashic techniques. Plümacher unfortunately does not discuss the important works by J. W. Bowker, "Speeches in Acts: A Study in Proem and Yelamedenu Form," *NTS* 14 (1967–68): 96–110; J. Doeve, *Jewish Hermeneutics in the Synoptic Gospels and Acts* (Assen: Van Gorcum, 1954); J. Dupont, *Études sur les Actes des Apôtres* (Paris: du Cerf, 1958), pp. 245–390; E. E. Ellis, "Midrashic Features in the Speeches of Acts," *Mélanges Bibliques*; *idem*, "Midrash, Targum and New Testament Quotations," *Neotestamentica et Semitica*, ed. E. E. Ellis and M. Wilcox (Edinburgh: T. & T. Clark, 1969), and Lindars, *New Testament Apologetic*, chapter 2. We should be wise to assume that Luke did indeed attempt to follow the example of such men as Thucydides (see Gasque, *History*, pp. 225ff., against Dibelius' interpretation of this) and that it involved him in a search for traditions that was at least in part successful (for a discussion of the possible *Sitz im Leben* for remembering some of the material in these speeches see the provocative essay by Jervell, *Luke*, pp. 19–39; more generally F. F. Bruce, "The Speeches in Acts: Thirty Years After," *Reconciliation and Hope*, pp. 53–68).

For the traditional character of the pentecost speech see especially Lindars, *New Testament Apologetic*; Dupont (as at note 174), pp. 218–27. The claims of R. F. Zehnle, *Peter's Pentecost Discourse* (New York: Abingdon, 1971). pp. 23–36, 61–70 and 95–130, to the contrary are unconvincing. Zehnle offers no criteria for distinguishing traditional material of great importance for Luke from what he alleges to be freely created by Luke.

[182]For a brief resume of arguments establishing the historicity of "Pentecost" see J. D. G. Dunn in *NIDNTT*, 2: 78ff.

[183]W. G. Kümmel, *The Theology of the New Testament* (London: SCM, 1974), p. 128 (despite G. Klein, *Die Zwölf Apostel* [Göttingen: Vandenhoeck und Ruprecht, 1961]), the part played by the "Twelve" in Luke is probably *less* significant than it was in the earliest, more apocalyptically orientated church: cf. Ellis, *Luke*, pp. 132–36). On the self-awareness of the community see Kümmel (as above), pp. 126–36; H. Conzelmann, *History of Primitive Christianity* (London: Darton, Longman and Todd, 1972), chapter 4; Goppelt, *Apostolic and Post-Apostolic Times*, pp. 25–60; and J. Munck, *Paul and the Salvation of Mankind* (London: SCM, 1974), pp. 214–28.

[184]This observation holds true even for the hypothetical "original forms" of the cup-word deduced from Mark 14:24: cf. B. Klappert, *NIDNTT*, 2: 524–25.

[185]The Spirit (through the charismata) leads the people of God within a new and christocentric covenant relationship, but this is not to be confused with the Spirit understood as the matrix, and sphere, of new covenant existence, as Dunn, *Baptism*, chapter 4, and in *NIDNTT*, 2: 786, takes it. Discipleship to Jesus has already implied new relationships to the law *before* Pentecost; there is no trace of any polemic based on Ezekiel 36:26 (see note 163); and when Luke uses covenant fulfillment terminology it appears to be applied both to Jesus' heavenly session and to His earthly ministry, the two conceived as a unity (Luke 1:72–73; Acts 3:25). Pentecost is not portrayed as the inauguration of covenant fulfillment, but as another major landmark within it.

[186]A rarely contested view, but expressed most positively by J. Weiss: "It (the cultus) still

represented an appropriate vessel into which their own devotion could be poured," *Earliest Christianity* (NewYork: Harper and Row, 1937), 1:54; cf. Longenecker, *Paul*, pp. 271–88; and J. D. G. Dunn, *Unity*, p. 127.

[187]To the comprehensive bibliographies on the controversial figure of Stephen (and on the strongly debated question of the identity of the hellenists) given by Haenchen, *Acts*, pp. 259–60, 270, 277–78, and 291, add especially O. Cullmann, *The Johannine Circle* (London: SCM, 1976), chapter 6; J. D. G. Dunn, *Unity*, section 60; J. Kilgallen, *The Stephen Speech* (Rome: Biblical Institute Press, 1976), pp. 3–26 and passim; O'Neill, *Theology*, pp. 78–94; and Wilson, *The Gentiles*, pp. 129–53.

[188]Acts 6:14; the charge is not unjustified if we are to judge from the speech. Kilgallen, *The Stephen Speech*, pp. 33, 44 and passim demonstrates that the point of the Stephen speech is essentially *christological* and designed to show that the Jewish institutions of temple and law are *secondary to Christ* who is now the only means of salvation for all men. The claim of Dibelius, *Studies*, p. 167, that the speech is irrelevant to the charge, is widely held but scarcely convincing; see O'Neill, *Theology*, p. 73; A. Ehrhardt, *The Acts of the Apostles* (Manchester: Manchester University Press, 1969), pp. 34–35, and Kilgallen, *The Stephen Speech*, passim. It is the subordination of the law and the temple *to Jesus*, implicit in the structuring and nuancing of the speech, that provides the occasion for lynching Stephen. There is, therefore, no need to accept the view of W. Schmithals who thinks that in order to earn such a fate the historical Stephen must, in fact, have "declared the Law as a whole, including circumcision, to be abolished for both Jews and for Jewish Christians. . . ." *Paul and James* (London: SCM, 1965), p. 25.

[189]For a discussion of the issues see especially Wilson, *The Gentiles*, pp. 142–151, and Dunn, *Unity*. It is important to note that Paul's autobiographical comments on the subject do not mention any distinction between Hellenists and Hebrews and that it was the Judaean churches (not the scattered ones) that feared him.

[190]This is stated to be the case for Cornelius and it is implied at 11:20ff. Paul, in Galatians 2:11–14, confirms that at Antioch Gentile Christians had not adopted a Jewish way of life. See also notes 191–92.

[191]Acts 15:1 (and confirmed by Paul's own comments in Gal. 2:11–14).

[192]Catchpole, "Paul, James and the Apostolic Decree," correctly argues that Galatians 1–2 excludes the possibility of more than two visits to Jerusalem by the time Paul wrote the letter; that honesty would have compelled Paul to mention the decrees if they had been formulated at the meeting he describes in Galatians 2 (cf. v. 6c; 10), and that Luke did not invent the apostolic decrees, for then he would not have addressed them to the churches in Antioch, Syria and Cilicia (15:23) when he believed the solution to be of more widespread application (16:4).

Catchpole's own solution is that *both* Acts 11:27–30 and Acts 15:1–18 (the council minus the account of the decrees) refer to the same meeting as is described in Galatians 2. The decrees emanated subsequently from the Jerusalem church and were directly responsible for the incident described in Galatians 2:12–13. But this solution rests on a false understanding of the intent of the decrees (see at note 161 above). The only alternative solution—a traditional one—is that Galatians was written before the apostolic council.

[193]The very fact that Luke records that the terms of Gentile admission were debated at all demonstrates that Jesus' attitude toward the law must have appeared ambiguous either to Luke or to the early community or to both. Had Jesus simply been understood to affirm the eternal validity of the law of Moses, the council should have been obliged to maintain separate Jewish and Gentile churches *or*, more likely, to engage in a Jewish Christian proselyte mission. James' insistence that God has made one people of Jew and law-free Gentile is only possible within a context in which the law of Moses had, in some sense, been challenged. At the same time Luke did not know of Jesus' making any specific and unambiguous statement abrogating the law. Luke's appeal is thus not to a logion of Jesus, but to the thrice repeated Cornelius account.

[194]See Longenecker, *Paul*, p. 280, and Ehrhardt, *Acts*, pp. 49–61.

[195]We must dismiss as eccentric the view of P. Vielhauer, *SLA*, p. 42, that, according to Acts 13:28–29, Luke's Paul understood Jews to be partially justified by obedience to the law, faith in

Christ acting as a sort of safety net. There is no shred of evidence in the rest of Acts for this curious view, nor is it an obvious interpretation of the Acts passage, on which see *BC* 4:147; F. F. Bruce, *The Acts of the Apostles* (London: Tyndale, 1952), p. 271; and Haenchen, *Acts*, p. 412 note 4.

[196]See the important article by R. Jewett, "The Agitators and the Galatian Congregation," *NTS* 17 (1970–71): 198–212. Jewett maintains that the judaizers were Jewish Christians from Judaea who were *not theologically* committed to nomism (6:13) but who were merely trying to avoid persecution themselves (6:12) by compelling Gentile converts to be circumcised and to keep Jewish feasts. They do not declare their motive but hide beneath a cloak of elitist theology. The pressure on the judaizing group derives in turn from the continual threat posed by the zealots whose strategy (as M. Hengel, *Die Zeloten* [Leiden: Brill, 1961], has shown) was specifically aimed against the like of Paul (and probably Jewish Christians in general) who, in their view, defiled Israel by retaining contact with uncircumcised persons. Jewett sets the date of Galatians later than the council (cf. Bo Reicke, "Der geschichtliche Hintergrund des Apostelkonzils und der Antiocha-Episode, Gal. 2:1–14," *Studia Paulina*, ed. J. N. Sevenster and W. C. van Unnik [Haarlem: Bohn, 1953], pp. 172–88), but he offers no convincing reason why his arguments should not equally apply to the slightly earlier date that we envisage. Violence was increased during Felix's procuratorship, but not inaugurated by it.

[197]Jervell's suggestion, *Luke*, p. 153ff., that the test proposed would demonstrate that Paul was a zealous Pharisee, is clearly wrong; it *could* only provide a rebuttal of the charge that Paul taught that a man *ought not* to keep the law of Moses (cf. 21:21).

[198]Against P. Vielhauer, "On the 'Paulinism' of Acts," *SLA*, pp. 37–42, see the works by F. F. Bruce, E. E. Ellis and U. Wilckens in note 1 above. In addition see the excellent discussion by Longenecker, *Paul*, (as at note 79), chapters 10 and 11.

[199]It would hardly be a defense for Paul merely to assert that he had once been a Pharisee in the past; the implication must be that he considers himself so to be now too. This agrees with his insistence at 23:6 that he is a Pharisee and the son of a Pharisee (not, presumably, on the question of the Resurrection alone, for others than the Pharisees held to that, and the Pharisee party present would soon have repudiated his claim if that was his sole point of contact with them), and with his assertion in 28:17 that he has in no way offended against even the customs of the fathers (cf. 25:8 and 10) and, finally, with the many instances of "law-keeping" (on which see P. Vielhauer and R. N. Longenecker [both as at note 198]).

[200]So also J. B. Lightfoot, *Galatians* (London: Macmillan, 1892), p. 312; and Goppelt, *Apostolic and Post-Apostolic Times*, p. 32. Jervell, *Luke*, pp. 166ff., is aware of this dimension in Acts, but seeks to minimize its importance.

[201]A charge which later was to become very important: cf. W. H. C. Frend, *Martyrdom and Persecution in the Early Church* (Oxford: Blackwell, 1965), p. 134.

[202]See particularly Longenecker, *Paul*, pp. 247–48. Paul could easily have avoided these painful incidents by asserting his Roman citizenship and rejecting the synagogical authority.

[203]With Rordorf, *Sunday*, 129, Bacchiocchi, *From Sabbath to Sunday*, 148, sees this as evidence that James had a *theological* commitment to the law; but against, see the argument above.

[204]Jewett, *Lord's Day*, p. 44.

[205]Notably by Bacchiocchi, *From Sabbath to Sunday*.

[206]So Rordorf, *Sunday*, pp. 121–22.

[207]On the fundamental character of the Sabbath for Judaism see Moore, *Judaism*, 2:21ff.; Safrai/Stern, (as at note 152), 1:804–07, and the chapter by C. Rowland in this volume.

[208]Rordorf, *Sunday*, pp. 121–22; by contrast, cf. Haenchen, *Acts*, p. 192 note 7.

[209]See Scroggs, "The Earliest Christian Communities," pp. 3ff. for further definition.

[210]But we do not accept the view of O'Neill, *Theology*, p. 118, who suggests that Paul's policy was to effect separation of the church from the synagogue. O'Neill argues that Luke's handling of his sources in 18:1–8 demonstrates two things: (1) that the goal of Paul's missionary drive was to found Gentile Christian synagogues without Jewish ties, and hence (with D) Paul must move away from Priscilla and Aquila, not simply from the Jewish synagogue, and (2) that the move to

Titius Justus' house is "crucial" (118) for Luke, for it symbolizes his thesis that "the gospel is free . . . only when it is free from the false form which the Jewish religion has taken" (p. 75). But the preference for the reading of Bezae at this point is not justified, nor is it obvious why a group of people moving from the Jewish synagogue should have less "Jewish synagogue" attachment for meeting under the roof of Titius Justus rather than in the premises of Priscilla and Aquila. The decisive break with the synagogue had been made, and would be maintained by the chairmanship of Paul irrespective of which building was used. Finally, if Paul did move his center of operations to the house of Justus, the reason might be that the tent-making premises of Aquila were inconvenient for the further preaching that the advent of Silas and Timothy freed him for (18:5). Compare Haenchen, *Acts*, p. 539.

[211]Cf. J. Painter's treatment of the replacement themes in the fourth gospel in *John: Witness and Theologian* (London: SPCK, 1975).

[212]Th. Zahn, *Geschichte des Sonntags, vornehmlich in der Alten Kirche* (Hannover: C. Meyer, 1878), p. 168.

[213]Note the careful discussion by A. N. Sherwin-White, *Roman Society*, pp. 36ff.

[214]See especially F. M. Young, "Temple, Cult and Law in Early Christianity," *NTS* 19 (1972–73): 325–39.

[215]Of the thirteen mentions of activity in the synagogue in Acts, twelve are associated with Paul. "It is hardly open to question historically that the synagogues provided Paul with excellent bases for his missionary work . . . and that he often began his proclamation in them, cf. Rom. 1:16; 10:14ff.; 1 Cor. 9:20ff; 2 Cor. 11:24ff., (W. Schrage, TDNT, 7:835). The view put forward by W. Schmithals, *Paul and James*, p. 60, that Paul was only interested in the *Gentiles*, is incredible and has been ably demolished by G. Bornkamm, "The Missionary Stance of Paul in 1 Cor. 9 and in Acts," *SLA*, pp. 194–207; especially 200–1.

[216]See above pp. 171–72, 177–78 and notes 198, 199 and 202. In addition see the chapter by D. R. de Lacey in this volume.

[217]J. Jervell, *Luke*, pp. 185ff.

[218]Though we do not need to follow J. Munck's emendation of the text making those who are zealous for the law Jews, not Jewish Christians, in order to avoid this (*Paul and the Salvation*, pp. 238–42; cf. E. Haenchen, Acts, pp. 608–9).

[219]Even from Luke's account in Acts 21ff. it has been deduced that James and Jerusalem Christianity left Paul "to stew in his own juice" because there existed a "fundamental antipathy" on the part of Jewish Christians to Paul himself and what he stood for. Here, we are told, was a Jewish Christianity "well on the way to Ebionism" (Dunn, *Unity*, pp. 256–57). But arguments from silence are dangerous when drawn from a book so notorious for its lacunae.

[220]See "Sabbath and Sunday in the Post-Apostolic Church," by R. Bauckham in this collection.

[221]See n. 188 above.

[222]R. Bultmann, *Synoptic Tradition*, pp 12ff.; most recently L. E. Keck, *The New Testament Interpretation of Faith* (St. Louis: Bethany Press, 1976), pp. 38ff.; and with special reference to Luke's work, F. Staudinger, *Die Sabbatkonflikte bei Lukas* (unpublished PhD. dissertation, Graz [Karl-Franzens Universität], 1964). This thesis came to my desk too late to be used extensively in the writing of this chapter. Essentially his position is that Luke considers Jesus to hallow the Sabbath by making it a day that is particularly appropriate for good works (cf. those noted above at note 66). But the argument is disappointingly thin and never succeeds in showing any more than that Jesus would not allow the Sabbath commandment (to rest) to *interfere* with His seven day per week ministry of redemption (see especially 150–51; 189–90; 204–5 and 246–50). Staudinger appears to assume that what Luke considered Jesus to teach about the Sabbath, he has transferred completely to *Sunday* worship (cf. pp. 164, 249ff. and 295ff.) but he gives no critical discussion of the issues involved.

[223]*Mek. Exod.* 31:14 (109*b*); though see Rordorf, *Sunday*, p. 62ff., and Carson, Chapter 4 in this volume.

[224]Goppelt, *Apostolic and Post-Apostolic Times*, pp. 5–6.

[225]Sayings such as Luke 6:5 (D) would be much more appropriate—and this one was almost certainly created by the church; see Bauckham, chapter 9 in this volume.

[226]With Rordorf, *Sunday*, p. 119.

[227]Cf. Jub. 2:19ff.; CD 14–15*a*; *Gen.R.* 11 and *Shab.* 16:6–8; see S. T. Kimbrough, "The Concept of Sabbath at Qumran," *RQ* 5 (1962): 483–502, and Schiffman, *The Halakhah at Qumran.*

[228]Contrast the impression given by Beckwith, *This is the Day*, p. 6ff., who seems to identify Philo's position (and that of Aristobulus) as representative of hellenistic Judaism in singling out the Sabbath commandment as a creation ordinance valid for mankind. See Rowland, chapter 3 in this volume.

[229]Lohse, *TDNT*, 7: 17–18 for details.

[230]Safrai/Stern, *The Jewish People*, 1: 804 and 1150–51.

[231]On the morphology of the Greek see *BC* 4:202.

[232]The third and longest section of material written in the first person plural begins at 20:4. The account purports to come from an eyewitness and may be assumed to be reliable. Haenchen, *Acts*, p. 586, however, follows Dibelius in regarding the Eutychus story as an interpolation into an earlier itinerary. But most of the alleged difficulties with the story are due to lack of information. Haenchen claims that the words "They" (not "we") "were comforted" shows the foreignness of the miracle over against the intinerary." But this is not convincing since the narrator had left the scene he would be dependent on the witness of Paul, who remained behind. The "they" is then perfectly understandable.

[233]Ibid., p. 586, is correct: "the narrator intends to report a great miraculous act and not merely a correct diagnosis by Paul" (that Eutychus was not dead).

[234]For an even less illuminating solution see Haenchen, ibid., also at p. 585, note 2.

[235]Bacchiocchi, *From Sabbath to Sunday*, 103–7.

[236]On the traditional interpretation of the provenance of the fourth Gospel, see the standard Introductions.

[237]Or at the Jewish place of prayer at Philippi if this was not a synagogue; see F. F. Bruce, *Book of Acts*, on this passage.

[238]Ibid., though he clearly thinks it was Sunday.

[239]*Sunday*, p. 201.

[240]As do most commentators; see Rordorf, *Sunday*, p. 201, note 4 for a list.

[241]H. Riesenfeld, "Sabbat et jour du Seigneur," *New Testament Essays: Studies in Memory of T. W. Manson*, ed. A. J. B. Higgins (Manchester: Manchester University Press, 1959), pp. 210–16, argues that the distinctive Christian pattern of worship grew out of meetings that started on Saturday night, immediately after the Sabbath, and were prolonged until Sunday morning. But this does not explain the very thing the hypothesis was devised to explain, viz., Lord's Day worship on a *Sunday* (indeed mainly on Sunday *evenings* [see Jewett, *Lord's Day*, pp. 53ff.] in the early period).

[242]J. Behm, *TDNT*, 3: 729–30. For details and bibliography of the complex debate see Rordorf, *Sunday*, pp. 203ff, 222ff., 231ff., 239ff.

[243]J. Jeremias, *The Eucharistic Words of Jesus*, p. 120 note 1. His own theory, that the expression as used in Acts (excepting 27:35) is a deliberately *veiled* reference to the Lord's Supper, is barely convincing.

[244]Bacchiocchi, *From Sabbath to Sunday*, p. 109; Paul does not insist on separation of the Lord's Supper and fellowship meal—only that those who could not contain their hunger should eat first so that misuse of the fellowship meal would not ensue. So C. K. Barrett, *The First Epistle to the Corinthians* (London: Black, 1971).

[245]Jewett, *Lord's Day*, p. 63. Rordorf cannot admit this because he contends that "Lord's Day" (*κυριακὴ ἡμέρα*) derives linguistically and practically from "Lord's Supper" (*κυριακὸν δεῖπνον*), and hence that the latter was only celebrated once per week, on Sunday, from the very beginning. On this, see the trenchant criticism by R. Bauckham in this volume, chapter 8; also Bacchiocchi, *From Sabbath to Sunday*, p. 76 note 7.

[246]Ibid., p. 109.

[247]With Rordorf, *Sunday*, p. 204; against Jeremias, *Eucharistic Words*, p. 134. It is most unlikely that γεύεσθαι is a deliberately cryptic reference to the Lord's Supper as Jeremias asserts.

[248]Bacchiocchi, *From Sabbath to Sunday*, pp. 110ff.

[249]See Haenchen, *Acts*, on verse 6 and elsewhere in his comments on the itinerary.

[250]Bacchiocchi, *From Sabbath to Sunday*, pp. 123–31, takes "Lord's Day" (κυριακὴ ἡμέρα) to be a reference to the eschatological Day of the Lord. Against this, and arguing strongly for a view that the phrase refers to Sunday, see Bauckham, chapter 8 in this volume.

[251]See Rordorf, *Sunday*, pp. 109–10 and 239–40.

[252]J. Behm, TDNT, 3: 738; Beckwith *This is the Day*, p. 32.

[253]Nor docs Paul at 1 Corinthians 16:2. Had Paul considered Sunday a day specially consecrated to the Lord, he would have had a strong rod with which to beat the erring Corinthians (as Bacchiocchi points out, *From Sabbath to Sunday*, pp. 85–96).

[254]Rordorf, *Sunday*, pp. 24ff., and Jewett, *Lord's Day*, pp. 75–76, both assume that the planetary week was not yet widespread, but Rordorf has almost certainly misrepresented Dio Cassius. See the counterargument by Bacchiocchi, *From Sabbath to Sunday*, p. 243 and note 25, and his further evidence, pp. 241–51. It is not surprising, therefore, that Rordorf attributes little significance to the use of the *Jewish* weekly calendar at Acts 20:7; as far as he is concerned there was no other. Equally we can understand Jewett's position (pp. 79–80), which maintains that this acceptance of a *weekly* structure by Gentiles is evidence that the Jewish week was regarded as a divine institution.

[255]This is said in full consciousness of the notorious fact that many of our earliest patristic references to Sunday make little (or only secondary) mention of its connection with Jesus' resurrection (see Rordorf, *Sunday*, pp. 220ff.). But the writer of the Apocalypse does appear to make the connection between the Lord's Day and the Resurrection, and, while this connection may have been forgotten when the day was more widely referred to as the Lord's Day (or Sunday—the various connotations of *those* names becoming primary), it would have been very obvious while the terminology of the "first day of the week" was still prominent.

[256]Haenchen, *Acts*, does not allow sufficiently for this when he comments that "to break bread" must mean the Lord's Supper alone, for the congregation would not be willing to wait until after midnight for their supper.

[257]Beckwith, *This Is the Day*.

[258]Bacchiocchi, *From Sabbath to Sunday*.

[259]Beckwith, *This Is the Day*, pp. 27–28.

[260]See above, pp. 124–128.

[261]Beckwith, *This Is the Day*, pp. 32ff., admits this corollary of his thesis. We may dismiss as entirely impossible the less cautious traditional view that virtually all Sabbath observance (not merely theology) was transferred to the first day. That view faces all the difficulties mentioned above, but the force of the third (fear of sanctions) and fourth (missionary policy) would be redoubled. Any attempt to tamper with the seventh-day Sabbath, which was so fundamental to Judaism, would inevitably lead to violent reaction and the cessation of any effective mission.

[262]For references see TDNT 7: 17–18.

[263]So Rordorf, *Sunday*, pp. 33–34.

[264]Beckwith, *This Is the Day*, p. 31, attempts to circumvent the difficulty by drawing an analogy from the parallel existence of Lord's Supper and baptism with Passover and circumcision. But the latter were not *weekly* events, nor was there nearly so great a correspondence between the Old Testament observances and the New Testament counterparts as Beckwith would have us believe to be the case for Sabbath and Sunday. So while Sabbath and Sunday were competing, the other observances were not. Of course, on Beckwith's view that *infant* baptism was widely practiced in the earliest church (see his article in NIDNTT 1: 154–59) and justified on the basis of covenant theology, baptism and circumcision would be in competition to a greater extent than others would allow. Contrast P. K. Jewett, *Infant Baptism and the Covenant of Grace* (Grand Rapids: Eerdmans, 1978).

[265]Beckwith, *This Is the Day*, pp. 32–34, tries to make light of this by urging that in the early period there seems to have been every little work done in *any* day of the week. But *if* this is the correct interpretation of the early passages in Acts (which seems highly doubtful) we must still ask how long such a state could have lasted. We suspect that when Beckwith says Jewish Christians probably took a *measure of rest* on both days he is admitting defeat; the early church could not afford to take two *whole* days. The suggestion that they took only a measure of rest on the seventh-day Sabbath is unacceptable, however, for the reasons stated above.

[266]The common argument that only on such a basis can we understand Ebionite *Sunday* observance has been shown to be false; see Bacchiocchi, *From Sabbath to Sunday*, pp. 153–54. The more conservative sect of the Nazarenes observed only the seventh-day Sabbath: ibid., pp. 155–56.

[267]The later we set the transfer the more striking it is that Luke does not mention it. This could be no mere accidental omission, even from a work renowned for its lacunae.

[268]See de Lacey, chapter 6 in this volume.

[269]C. S. Mosna, *Storia della domenica* (as reported by Bacchiocchi, *From Sabbath to Sunday*, pp. 134 and 140) argues that Jewish Christians would have needed a special Christian day of worship when they became unsatisfied with synagogical worship. Such a day would have been settled on when persecution (after Stephen's martyrdom) forced Christians out of the synagogues. But this thesis faces several difficulties. In the first place, persecuted Christians did not leave the synagogical system in general; they merely fled the Jerusalem synagogues. But as Bacchiocchi correctly observes (ibid., p. 135), they found their way to other synagogues—and soon came back again into the Jerusalem synagogues. Second, there is no reason why Jewish Christians should have felt the need for a special *day* of worship. Third, *had* they left the synagogues they would not have needed an alternative day to the Sabbath; the Sabbath itself would have been the most convenient.

[270]Anti-Jewish polemic was responsible for the changes of Christian voluntary fast days from the Jewish pattern to Wednesday and Friday (according to *Did.* 8:1); but this is hardly to compare with tampering with so fundamental an institution as the seventh day Sabbath.

[271]Such a transfer would also inevitably produce practical difficulties and arouse suspicions of "novelty;" whereas seventh day Sabbath worship was at least tolerated as an ancient custom, even where it was not free of criticism.

[272]Bacchiocchi, *From Sabbath to Sunday*, p. 26–62; 303–10. Beyond this Bacchiocchi only incidentally alludes to Sabbath worship as his thesis primarily concerns the rise of *Sunday* worship.

[273]See de Lacey, chapter 6, in this volume.

[274]Bacchiocchi, *From Sabbath to Sunday*, p. 310. Jewett, *The Lord's Day*, who wishes to maintain that Sunday should share certain features of the Sabbath, nevertheless admits that historically Sunday observance was not based in the fourth commandment until after the New Testament period.

[275]We must agree with Bacchiocchi, *From Sabbath to Sunday*, p. 104, against R. H. Lenski's arbitrary assertion that there was an earlier morning service too. The fact that the meeting was in the *evening* of the first day of the week rather than in the morning, which would have been more appropriate for a celebration of the day of the Resurrection, suggests either that the evening was more appropriate for celebrating the Lord's Supper (though not because these meals had any connection with meals on the Resurrection evening as Rordorf, *Sunday*, p. 76, alleges) or that evening was the time when most Christians would be able to get away from work. The latter option would imply that Sunday was not regarded as a day of rest.

Beckwith's contention in *This Is the Day*, pp. 42–43, that the early church would not have expected less than a full day's rest on their new holy convocation, the Lord's Day, assumes precisely what must be proved.

We dismiss the view of J. van Goudoever that Acts 20:7 refers not to weekly worship but to special celebration of Sundays between Easter and Pentecost; see the criticism by W. Rordorf, *Sunday*, pp. 196–97.

6

THE SABBATH/SUNDAY QUESTION AND THE LAW IN THE PAULINE CORPUS

D. R. DE LACEY

Until recently, Douglas R. de Lacey taught at London Bible College. He now teaches at Ridley Hall, Cambridge.

Since none of St. Paul's surviving writings provides explicit discussion on the Christian use of Sabbath or Sunday, care is needed in any attempt to reconstruct his attitude toward the days. More is needed than a discussion of those few passages[1] where the days are explicitly mentioned. Paul's attitude toward the Sabbath will be an integral part of his understanding of the role of the law of Moses (or at least the Decalogue) in the life of the Christian; that complex subject must be investigated before the exegesis of particular passages can be undertaken. Only then will we be in a position to assess Paul's contribution to the Sabbath/Sunday debate.

SAUL[2] AND THE LAW

The warning has often been sounded against the danger of interpreting Paul's experience in terms of Augustine's or Luther's, or in terms of "the introspective conscience of the West."[3] On such an interpretation, Saul grew increasingly dissatisfied with his inability to keep the law as he became increasingly aware of the impossibility of complete obedience to it. The crisis came on the Damascus road, where he found the answer to his tortured question "Who will deliver me?"[4] and discovered to his relief that he need no longer "kick against the pricks."[5] But while such an interpretation may ring true to the experience of others, it is doubtful that it can stand as a true assessment of Paul. Any valid interpretation of his thought must take into account the positive attitude toward law keeping that is expressed in such passages as Galatians 1:14 and Philippians 3:4–6. According to these, the law was not a problem to Saul; as any other Jew of his time, he accepted it as the revealed will of God and kept it.[6] We should therefore think of him as a man well satisfied with his ability to keep the law. He was upright and blameless, at least in his own estimation, and not a man hagridden with guilty fear before God. To say this is not to ignore such passages as Romans 1–3, Romans 7, or Acts 26:14; Romans is the writing of a mature Christian,[7] and Longenecker[8] has provided a convincing demonstration that Acts 26:14 is not to be interpreted in terms of a chronic inner turmoil vis-à-vis God.

Paul's own writings, however, witness to a significant development in his attitude toward the law, and we must investigate both the basis for this development and its nature in order to assess aright Paul's understanding of the place of the law in a Christian's life. If the basis for the development is not to be sought in a growing dissatisfaction with his own ability to keep the law in his pre-Christian days, then it must presumably be found either in his conversion experience or in subsequent Christian catechism. While it may be true that this latter did include something on the role of the law,[9] it is unlikely that this could have been adequate as a source for Paul's own, highly original contribution since it is this that brought him into conflict with at least one section of the Jerusalem church.[10] We are justified, then, in asking if there may be found in Paul's conversion experience any factors that could account for his reassessment of the law. Nor do we need to look far. It is one of the main theses of E. P. Sanders[11] that what he calls Paul's whole "pattern of religion" is based on his realization, which came when he met the risen Christ, that God is now fulfilling a new and cosmic purpose in and through Christ.[12] With this went Paul's commission as apostle to the Gentiles, and Sanders argues that this understanding of the universality of God's new work, to Gentiles as well as to Jews, meant for Paul that the law, as a Jewish prerogative, necessarily took a secondary place. Another factor, strangely ignored by Sanders, although hinted at by M. Hengel,[13] was probably also significant; Jesus had died by crucifixion and so, according to the law, had become a curse of God.[14] But Paul's conversion experience caused him to realize that God had now vindicated Jesus by raising Him from the dead. Thus, Jesus (or perhaps more precisely, God's action through Jesus) had transcended the law that pronounced Him accursed and was now active in a new way; it is now Jesus, and not the law or the Mosaic covenant, that has become the locus of God's saving work for both Jews and Gentiles. Hence Paul must have been forced to rethink his whole understanding of the nature of God's covenants with His people.

Paul and the Covenants of God

Sanders has reminded us of the significance of the covenant in orthodox Palestinian Judaism,[15] and there can be little doubt that it had similar significance for Saul. Although the term itself is not often used (as Sanders explains, this was partly because the covenant's existence was simply assumed as a sine qua non of Israel's existence and partly because other and more graphic terms were used to describe it) there can be little doubt that the concept of covenant was used to subsume all God's gracious dealings with His people. The idea that God would establish a *new* covenant with His people, though it is found in Scripture,[16] is not taken up in orthodox thought. It is, however, relevant to note how one heterodox group, namely the Qumran community, has used this idea. It is well known that their writings often mention a "new covenant,"[17] though more often the covenant is the old one made with Moses or the patriarchs, which is understood in a new and fuller way by the members of the Qumran community; there is the implication that only the Qumran community properly adheres to the covenant with Israel.[18] The community does not appear to have seen any significant difference between the two formulations, and, indeed, the phrase "new covenant" in

Jeremiah 31 is patient of an interpretation that retains continuity with the old covenant; it is still called "my law" (v. 33), and it forms the center of the covenant. Whatever "my Torah" may have meant to Jeremiah, it is evident that Torah was a sufficiently technical term by the first century to allow for an interpretation of the new covenant in terms of the old rather than as a substitution for it.

With Paul, however, the situation is somewhat different and more complex. Like the Qumran sectarians, he can contrast God's new dealings with His old under the caption of "two covenants."[19] Like them, Paul is concerned to stress the continuing validity of the (Abrahamic) covenant for the present time.[20] But Paul complicates the picture by his laudatory reference to God's covenants (in the plural[21]) with His people in Romans 9:4 (cf. Eph. 2:12). This may simply be a reference to the several covenants made between God and men (Noah, Abraham, Moses, David)[22] or even to the thrice-ratified covenant of Moses;[23] but C. Roetzel[24] has argued that in the Judaism of our period the word "covenant" is used in the singular to describe all God's dealings with His people, and the plural "covenants" is used to denote promises, oaths, commandments, or ordinances that God graciously gives to His people. It is after all improbable that Paul would distinguish the "giving of the law" (νομοθεσία, Rom. 9:4) from the Mosaic covenant. Hence there is a probability that "covenant" (διαθήκη) for Paul, while certainly a technical term, could also bear much vaguer associations. This must be borne in mind as we investigate Paul's understandings of God's covenants. The relevant epistles are Romans, 2 Corinthians and Galatians; we shall deal with them in their probable chronological order.

Galatians 3 and 4 are the center of a complex theological argument against those who would impose the law (or a certain part of it) upon the Galatian church. In this context Paul argues that the promise to Abraham is based on faith and that in Christ the blessing of Abraham extends to all nations. In 3:15ff. there follows a two-pronged attack. On the one hand, Paul says that a "covenant" (διαθήκη) cannot be set aside once it has been ratified, even on the human level; so the (subsequent) law cannot destroy the Abrahamic covenant based on faith.[25] But on the other hand, the argument depends for its validity on Paul's interpretation of the "seed" (σπέρμα) as referring to Christ. The issue then becomes one of God keeping or breaking His promise; "promise" (ἐπαγγελία), and not "covenant" (διαθήκη), is the key term here. This is also apparent in 4:21–5:1 where ἐπαγγελία is again emphasized in 4:23 and 28. In other words, the argument is not a quibble over points of law; it rests on God's honor. In this section, the first covenant is explicitly stated to be the Mosaic covenant ("from Mount Sinai," 4:24); it is described in terms comparable to those used of the law in chapter 3. In particular, Paul will accord it at best a temporary status in his quotation from Genesis 21:10 in verse 30 indicates.[26] God's dealings with Moses then, in both law and covenant, cannot now be binding on Paul's Galatian readers.

Second Corinthians represents a very different situation,[27] but one in which Paul is again fighting an attempt to assert the superiority of the law-keeping apostles at Jerusalem. It is in the context of his self-defense that he returns to the contrast between the old covenant and the new, a contrast that enters his mind first through the demand for written credentials (3:1). These he contrasts with spiritual credentials written on the heart (3:23), which he is confident that he can display, for God has made him the minister of a new and spiritual covenant. Here we still find the polemic of Galatians; the old covenant was by implication in letter and not in spirit. The letter can only kill; it was called "the dispensation of death" (3:6–8). Yet even this "came with splendor" (v. 7). It has lost that splendor only in the light of the far greater glory of the "dispensation of the Spirit," which is not evil but fading (vv. 11, 13). The issue of a covenant being irrevocable does not come up, and it is unlikely that Paul would have seen this as a problem, since again his argument is based not on legal niceties but on God's honor, which is not challenged by the introduction of the new and more glorious ministry (διακονία).[28]

In Romans 11:26–27, the issue is again God's faithfulness to His word, though this is now expressed in a different way, in terms of His continuing purposes with Israel—precisely because of His covenant. This is expanded in terms of "election . . . for the sake of the fathers" (v. 28). It would probably be a mistake to identify this διαθήκη with any one of the covenants of the Old Testament (least of all with the Mosaic). Paul is rather saying that God continues to have dealings with His people, though in the light of the rest of Paul's writings we are forced to suppose that these dealings now include the Gentiles.[29]

Thus Paul's use of the term διαθήκη covers a range of ideas, and it would be an oversimplification of his thought to interpret his statement in 2 Corinthians 5:17 as meaning that the old *covenant* has passed away and the new *covenant* has come. Even in Galatians, where the contrast is most marked, Paul is so little concerned with the new *covenant* as such that he fails to make any explicit identification between Sarah and a specific covenant. It may even be that the debate as to whether Sarah represents the Abrahamic covenant or the new covenant is misdirected. Paul's point is that the Mosaic covenant *as a covenant* is exclusive to the Jews ("the present Jerusalem,"[30] 4:25); God's new dealings, with Jew and Gentile alike, have bypassed it. This makes the covenant sign of circumcision at best irrelevant, though it says nothing about any possible carry-over of covenant stipulations such as Sabbath keeping. Paul's concern, as Sanders emphasizes, is with *entry* into the covenant relationship, not with the activities involved in the context of that relationship.[31] He would have certainly seen a continuity between the Abrahamic covenant and the new covenant, as chapter 3 makes clear, but we should add that Paul views Christ's relationship to the former as much in terms of fulfillment as of extension.

All this suggests that Paul had not developed a systematic schema of God's dealings with men in terms of a number of discrete covenants with different terms of reference. What for a Jew would have been the normative covenant (*viz.*, the Mosaic covenant) has been superseded in Paul's thought by God's act in Christ, sealed in the cup of the New Covenant.[32] But this is not worked out in a systematic way in Paul's writings, and the implications of all this for the covenant stipulations (and in particular the Sabbath stipulation) must be deferred until after a study of Paul's attitude to the law that the Mosaic covenant bound upon Israel.

Paul and the Law

So far we have touched on the basis for the development in Paul's attitude to the Law, and we have seen how in a related sphere (the covenant with Moses) Paul developed a position antithetic to that of the Judaism of his day. We must investigate how this affected his understanding of the law. Immediately we are confronted with a semantic problem. Paul uses the word νόμος ("law") in a variety of ways. J. A. Sanders has suggested that for Paul, as for others, "The Torah is primarily a story and not primarily a set of laws."[33] If this were so (though Sanders does not, and probably could not, substantiate his statement), then any statement by Paul about the abolition of the Torah would say comparatively little about the Christian's obligations to any particular commandment.[34] This discussion should serve as a reminder that in investigating Paul's understanding of the law we must take care to understand just what it is he has in mind when he uses the term "law."

Recently the thesis has been defended by H. Hübner[35] that Paul's attitude to the Law changed very significantly between the writing of Galatians (where Paul, misunderstanding the conclusions of the Jerusalem Council, developed a strongly negative attitude to the law) and that of Romans (where he was forced to include a more positive assessment of it). Such a view immediately solves the problem of reconciling Galatians 4:10 and Romans 14:5–6. But I find myself obliged to disagree with Hübner, not only because I would date Galatians much earlier than he, and before the Jerusalem Council,[36] but also because I find his treatment of the texts inadequate. Because of the significance of his thesis for this investigation, however, the following discussion must be included.

In Galatians, the discussion on the Law is introduced in the context of the covenant with Abraham (3:6ff.), a covenant that promised *righteousness by faith.*[37] Paul is not concerned at this point with the question of how the Law applies to those who are already so justified; the debate is exclusively about how the sonship of Abraham is established. Paul's contention is that the Law has no place here, being chronologically later than the promise to Abraham (v. 17) and less immediate (v. 19–20). Even its custodianship is now a thing of the past (v. 25).

What does νόμος mean in this context? Verses 17 and 19 identify it as the Sinai covenant, and it is noteworthy that Paul regards it as a unity, not a collection of "laws."[38] If then "the law" means "the Mosaic covenant," what Paul is saying is that this, based on obedience to stipulations, cannot annul the Abrahamic covenant, based on God's promise, and is no longer valid (cf. Gal. 4:25 and the discussion above, pp. 161f.). Why then does Paul use the term "law" here, rather than setting up the antithesis explicitly in terms of two covenants? To ask such a question is probably to begin at the wrong end, since the word "law" is already an integral part of the debate before the idea of a covenant is introduced in 3:15, and even there, as we have seen, the *promise to* Abraham is of more significance to Paul than the *covenant with* him.

What positive function does this Mosaic law-covenant have in Paul's mind? To ask this is to be involved in the vexed question of the interpretation of Galatians 3:19–29, a subject beyond the scope of this chapter. Some comments, however, on the logic of the argument are germane at this point. The law was given[39] τῶν παραβάσεων χάριν (v. 19), a phrase Hübner takes as final; its purpose was to provoke sins.[40] This interpretation, for which no justification is offered, causes him to make nonsense of the next clause, and should be abandoned; better sense is made if we take it as causal ("because of transgressions").[41] Hübner also makes too much of the idea that the second function of the law is to enslave.[42] While this is certainly not far from Paul's thought in the polemical discussion in chapter 4, the term he uses in chapter 3 (παιδαγωγός, a "custodian," not a "slavemaster") does not have the pejorative overtones that Hübner reads into Paul's thought in this passage. Two important factors in the logic of the argument are missed by Hübner: the use of γάρ ("for") in 3:21 (which suggests that Paul saw this as logically dependent on what had gone before), and the significance of the pronouns "we" and "you" in 3:23–4:7. A study of these will help us to see Paul's answer to our question.

The question raised in 3:21 is presumably raised in Paul's mind by what he has just stated, namely, that God introduced another covenant, the Law, for a period. The ambiguously brief question, "Is the law against the promises (of God)?"[43] should probably then be expanded to mean, "Did the law interfere with the covenant of promise during this period?"[44] Paul replies, "Certainly not! Law could *never* be the means of life, otherwise Christ need not have come."[45] This leads to the logic of the pronouns: "before faith came, *we* (Jews) were confined under the law . . . the law was *our* custodian . . . but . . . we are no longer under a custodian because . . . you (Gentiles) are all sons of God!" The fact that God has (manifestly) accepted Gentiles as sons demonstrates that the period of the law is at an end; the custodian has finished his task and the son has become an heir (4:1–6).

Paul's answer, then, to the questions of the purpose of the law runs as follows: God made a promise to Abraham, which He intended to fulfill in Christ, a promise of blessing to all nations. But because of transgressions[46] God gave the law, acting indirectly through angels and an intermediary, not to give life, but to control His people until the fulfillment[47] came.

Paul can now proceed to the real issue at stake in Galatia, the role of the law in the lives of those who have now become children of Abraham. He explains that those who are already Abraham's offspring cannot add to this the works of the law, since to do this is to return to precisely the situation from which Christ rescued us, since even the Jews under the law were under the *στοιχεῖα τοῦ κόσμου* ("basic principles of the world").[48] This is later reinforced by Paul's reaffirmation that those who become circumcised accept an obligation to the whole law (5:3). Here again "law" (whose sign of circumcision is contrasted with "faith" in v. 6; cf. 3:23–25) represents the whole Mosaic dispensation, which cannot stand with the new situation in Christ. Again we see that the basis of Paul's repudiation of the Mosaic covenant is christological. What then of 5:14, where the love commandment is commended to Christians as a fulfilling of the whole law? Hübner thinks this is ironic and that Paul means by "the whole law" (*ὁ πᾶς νόμος*) something very different from "the whole law" (*ὅλος ὁ νόμος*) of 5:3.[49] Other interpretations are more likely. It would be more straightforward to assume that Paul is using the idea found also in the rabbis of a distinction between "commandments between man and God and those between man and his neighbour."[50] The latter do not have to do with the Mosaic covenant *as a covenant*, and so obedience to them would not fall within the range of Paul's strictures. Further, there is no reference in this context to *justification*, which is the center of the controversy in the rest of the letter and manifestly in 5:3. Hübner argues that Paul's use of the phrase "the whole law" in Galatians is a *concentration* of the law) and not, as in Romans, a *reduction*).[51] That this is mistaken, at least for 5:14, is demonstrated by the fact that Paul does not ground his ethical imperatives in the statutes of the Old Testament, but in the fact of the indwelling Spirit.[52] The Christian ideal, as Paul sees it, is not the fulfillment of a series of commands and the fruit of the Spirit (including love, 5:22), which transcends all law. There is therefore a very considerable reduction in the concept of "the whole law" here.

In Corinthians Paul has little discussion on the law—a significant fact in itself. Faced with the problems of incest and prostitution in the church (1 Cor. 5, 7) he might well be expected to point out how diametrically opposed this was to the law of God. Instead he gives a long and sometimes tortuous explanation of why such behavior is wrong for a Christian, based not at all on transgression of a code but rather on the idea of two mutually exclusive unions, one with Christ, and one with the woman in question. This suggests not only that Paul saw an inappropriateness in appealing to the law in the context of the New Covenant, but also that he saw the covenant stipulations as being of a different sort. In 2 Corinthians 3, a passage already briefly considered above, the Old Covenant is evidently identified with the Decalogue—the heart of the law—and possibly with all the Mosaic stipulations (vv. 7, 15). "The law" as such is not under discussion though two asides serve to reinforce our interpretation of Galatians: in 1 Corinthians 9:20 Paul indicates that he no longer regards himself as under the law, and in 1 Corinthians 15:56 he describes the law as the power of sin. In the first of these passages Paul explicitly denies that this makes him "lawless." The word νόμος, here, appears to denote the Mosaic covenant with its legal obligations; the passage is parallel to Galatians 3–4. First Corinthians 15:56 seems to mean that sin gains power (over men) through the law, an idea that was later developed in Romans, but was already embedded in Galatians 3:10–14.

The problems involved in Romans are so complex, and the secondary literature so vast, that a study such as this can hope neither to make a significant contribution nor even to provide an adequate survey. We must therefore apologize in advance for statements that may appear too dogmatic or unsubstantiated.

Hübner argues that in Romans Paul has developed a new and different understanding of both circumcision and the law; circumcision now has a positive value, although only in the context of faith (Rom. 2:25; 4:12).[53] But against Hübner, this would be significant only if it could be shown that the same audience is in view in both letters. There seems no contradiction between saying to a *Gentile* seeking (or being encouraged to seek) circumcision that circumcision is of no value and saying to a *Jew* that circumcision-plus-faith is of great value.

The charge that Paul modified his view of the law is more serious. Although we cannot here give a detailed discussion of Hübner's case, we hope that the development of our understanding of Romans will indicate the weaknesses of his position. It is important to begin with an understanding of the structure of Romans as a whole.[54] Although there is certainly no unanimity on this point, a consensus does seem to be developing that the pending visit to Jerusalem was the cause of the letter and that its theme is the relation between Jews and Gentiles in the church.[55] Throughout the letter Paul is concerned to maintain that Jews and Gentiles stand before God on precisely the same footing, namely, through Christ. This is already hinted at in Romans 1:5 and comes to expression in 1:16–17. Chapter 2 demonstrates that the Jew is no better off than the Gentile (2:11; cf. 3:9). "Faith" is contrasted with "law," and "Paul's argument in Rom. 1–4 is *against the necessity of keeping the law.*"[56] The Jew is at a great advantage in that he has received God's oracles (which admittedly include the law, but that is not Paul's point) (3:1–2), but as far as salvation is concerned, he is at no advantage[57] at all (3:9). The law only[58] exposes sin (3:18–20; 4:15). This same attitude underlies the statement in 5:13. Sin was indeed present in the world, as the presence of death demonstrated, but no assessment of it can be made in the absence of law. Conversely, the presence of law does enable such an assessment to be made. It is evident that *νόμος* here is not quite the Mosaic covenant but rather a standard or norm, although it is, of course, the norm of the Mosaic legislation that is uppermost in Paul's mind. Thus the semantic content of *νόμος* in its various occurrences in Romans 1–5 is variable and inexact, ranging from the whole Old Testament (as in 3:19) to the Mosaic legislation (rather than the Mosaic *covenant*) as in 2:25 or (more or less) in 5:13.

For this study, the most important use is at 3:31. This must be seen in the light of the preceding section.[59] Paul is still pursuing his argument on the equality before God of both Jews and Gentiles. "Boasting" (by the Jews, 2:17, 23) is excluded (3:27). Whatever we may make of Paul's statement that this is so *διὰ νόμου πίστεως* and not *διὰ νόμου ἔργων*,[60] for him this leads to the conclusion in 3:31 that Christians "establish"[61] the law. This may be either because the law witnesses to faith (as in 3:21), in which case "law" stands for the Pentateuch, or perhaps for the whole Old Covenant situation, or else it may be because it is precisely the law itself, in its stipulations, which by exposing sin removes any ground for boasting. In neither case is Paul saying that Christians establish the law *by obeying it.* Such an interpretation would run counter to the tenor of the whole argument up to this point.

Subsequently, Paul deals with the Christian's relation to sin (6:1). He refuses to discuss this in terms of obligation to the law, choosing rather to base his case on the new relationships found in Christ; they are exclusive of the old relationships. Indeed, it is precisely because the Christian is no longer "under" the law that he escapes the dominion of sin (6:14). This statement is open to misunderstanding; some might think that this means that Christians are freed from all moral restraints, and so the question is immediately raised, are we then to sin because we are no longer under the law? I take it that Paul answers this question in two parts. First, in 6:16–23, he explains that freedom from the power of sin involves in itself slavery to righteousness and to God. Then in 7:1–6 he explains what it means not to be "under" the law. To be "under law" means that "the law is binding on a person" (7:1), but Christians have been put to death as far as the law is concerned[62] by virtue of their union with Christ. This leads to the conclusion that "we serve in the newness of the Spirit and not in the oldness of the letter" (7:6). This is the same antithesis we find in 2 Corinthians 3, where the "letter" represents the Old Covenant, epitomized in the Ten Commandments. If Paul is using the same field of ideas here, he is saying that dying to the law, and not being under the law, means being freed from the *Covenant* whose stipulations could only cause men to produce fruit for death (7:5). This freedom involves both freedom from condemnation (cf. 3:19–20; 5:13, 20) and freedom from the vain attempt at using it to establish through it a relationship with God. In itself it says nothing about our obligation once that relationship has been established with God, though as we have seen, Paul refuses to discuss Christian conduct in terms of obligation to it.[63]

However, what he has said forces Paul to defend himself against another charge, that of identifying the law and sin. He argues that the law is *not* sin but that only through the law do we know sin. The example he chooses of the law's stipulations (a generalized form of the tenth commandment) is probably highly significant.[64] Then in verses 14–25, Paul moves from the aorist to the present tense. If this is interpreted as meaning that Paul is referring to his own current experience,[65] then his conclusion (7:25*b*) is of great significance for this study.

The problem, says Paul, lies not in the law, but in myself, for there is in me a principle ("my flesh") implacably opposed to the will of God. This experience of the divided self demonstrates two things: first, that even while we disobey the law's stipulations (again preeminently the tenth commandment) we acknowledge its goodness, and second, that it is no longer "I" rebelling against God, but sin, which dominates my weak flesh. This is not a defeatist attitude, as chapter 8 demonstrates, but until God delivers him from his present bodily experience,[66] Paul continues[67] to serve the law of God with his "mind" (τῷ νοΐ) and the law of sin (τῇ σαρκί with his "flesh," v. 25). To understand what this means in practice, we need to know the answer to three subordinate questions: (1) What is the significance of the contrast between "mind" and "flesh" here? (2) What in this context are "the law of God" and "the law of sin"? (3) In what sense does Paul "serve" them?

We shall follow in essence Cranfield's answer. The νοῦς is "the mind in so far as it is renewed by the Spirit of God,"[68] namely, that mind whose renewal transforms the whole Christian so that he is able to approve the will of God (Rom. 12:1–2).[69] It is thus the same as the "inner man" of 7:22. The "flesh" evidently picks up the use of the corresponding adjective in 7:14: "I am fleshly."[70] It is human nature as not controlled by the Spirit of God, and notwithstanding what is said in chapter 8, it remains an integral part of Christian experience.

The phrase "the law of God" is not discussed by the commentators; presumably, they see no problem and simply identify it with the Torah.[71] But apart from the fact that "the Torah" itself is a vague and multivalent form of expression we have already seen that for Paul νόμος can have a variety of meanings (not least in Rom. 7 and 8). On the phrase "law of sin," Cranfield comments:

> It would seem that Paul is here using the word 'law' metaphorically, to denote exercised power, authority, control, and that he means by 'the law of sin' the power, the authority, the control exercised over us by sin. It is a forceful way of making the point that the power which sin has over us is a terrible travesty, a grotesque parody, of that authority over us which belongs by right to God's holy law. Sin's exercising such authority over us is a hideous usurpation of the prerogative of God's law.[72]

However, if the parallel is to be maintained, the last two sentences should end, not with a reference to God's *law*, but simply to God Himself, and if "the law of sin" represents the power, authority, or control of sin, then we would expect "the law of God" to represent the power, authority, or control of God. So if the parallel is exact, the semantic content of "the law of God" has shifted. We have already seen (above, pages 166–68) that Paul can use the phrase "the whole law" (ὁ πᾶς νόμος) of something other than the sum of the stipulations and commandments of the pentateuch. Here too, the law that Paul serves is the expression of the will of God, which challenges him in the words, "thou shalt not covet."[73] Thus the contrast between "the law of God" and "the law of sin" is the contrast between the demands made upon the Christian by God and those made upon him by sin. Paul proceeds to state that the former are made by the action of the Spirit within the Christian (cf. again 7:6!) and that we are free from the tyranny of the latter.

With regard to the meaning of "serve," note that δουλεύειν in Paul's writings can have both an active sense (render acts of service)[74] and a passive sense (be enslaved to).[75] Since in Romans 7 the problem is precisely the dominion of sin, the latter is more appropriate in this context.

We may now summarize (by means of a paraphrase) our interpretation of the conclusion that Paul draws in 7:25*b*). Insofar as I remain "in the flesh," I remain in bondage to sin, while insofar as I am being renewed by the Spirit of God, I am enslaved to Him, fulfilling "the whole law" in the sense in which Paul speaks of this in Galatians 5:14.

We can thus see a closer connection between 8:1 and the latter part of chapter 7 than most commentators will allow.[76] Because there is a real sense in which the Christian is (already) freed from "the flesh," the condemnation that this dual experience would otherwise bring is now a thing of the past. This is achieved by the "law of the Spirit of life in Christ Jesus," and its goal is that the "just requirement of the law might be fulfilled in us" (RSV). Paul adds that the *φρόνημα τῆς σαρκός* ("the mind of the flesh") does not and cannot submit to the law of God. This could all easily be taken to suggest that those who are no longer "in the flesh" can and should please God precisely by submitting to the law of God (namely, the stipulations of the pentateuch). But Paul does not say that, and chooses rather to express this side of his contrast in terms of life in the Spirit; the nearest he comes to such a statement is in verse 13 with its reference to putting to death the deeds of the flesh. This is a long way from fulfilling the law's stipulations, and Paul immediately goes on to underscore his point by stressing that the Spirit that Christians have received is emphatically not a spirit of servitude (contrast *κυριεύει*, "rules," in 7:1!). Thus Paul appears to want to say that the *δικαίωμα* ("just requirement," 8:4) of the law is not fulfilled by slavish adherence to the stipulations of the law, but by free sonship and life in the Spirit. We need therefore to investigate these ideas more closely. We shall deal with them in reverse order.

The usual interpretation of Romans 8:7–8 speaks of "fallen man's fierce hostility to God,"[77] an interpretation that ignores the fact that Paul adds the term *νόμος*. This demonstrates that he is using his specifically Christian understanding of sin,[78] but also indicates that he is using here his own understanding of "the law." The flesh *can* submit to and even revel in the stipulations of the pentateuch, until, that is, it comes to the Pauline understanding of the tenth commandment. Thus, Paul is not thinking of adherence to regulations. The flesh is precisely that which rebels against God's command; it is precisely the Spirit who leads the Christian into submission.

Romans 8:4 has been interpreted in many ways, but Schlier is probably right in his comment on *ἐν ἡμῖν* ("in us"): "'through us,' perhaps also 'among us,' . . . which then the rendering 'through us' implies; in any case, scarcely 'in us' if this expression does not also mean 'through us.'"[79] As to the δικαίωμα, Barrett's interpretation of it as "the law's requirement (that we should be righteous)"[80] has much to recommend it, not least the evident contrast between this word and κατάκριμα ("condemnation," v. 1, cf. also v. 3). But "might be fulfilled" and "who walk" suggest that more is in mind than simply a "state" of justification. Cranfield notes the significance of the singular δικαίωμα;[81] it may be that there is another parallel to Galatians 5:14. We should note, however, that it is the godward rather than the manward aspect of the law that Paul is emphasizing (cf. v. 8).

That the "law of the Spirit of life" is not the Torah in other guise[82] is evident from the fact that it achieves precisely what the law could not do (8:3). Here as before (see on 7:25) "law" represents the controlling power over a man. For the Christian it is supremely that of the Spirit of life, whose working transcends the law, for as well as fulfilling the law's requirement, it provides life and peace.

Romans 6–8 is a difficult passage and our interpretation must remain tentative at almost every point. But we hope that we have shown that the position that emerges from it is not only compatible with that in Galatians (despite Hübner), but also adds little to it materially. Paul has worked out the logic of his position in greater depth (even if that logic strikes us as obscure and unsatisfying at times), but the position remains the same. The law can only condemn and constrain: justification cannot come by it. And for the Christian, although the law is not abandoned as an evil power, ethics and our continuing relationship with God spring from our walk in the Spirit, not from study of and obedience to the law.

To this position Romans 13 adds nothing but confirmation. With "love is the fulfilling of the law" (13:10), we may compare "in order that the just requirements of the law might be fulfilled" (8:4, and "For the whole law is fulfilled in one word, 'you shall love your neighbor as yourself' " (Gal. 5:14). The differences are purely formal.

In Romans 14 and 15, it is generally accepted that the problem under discussion is that of the relations between Jews and Gentiles.[83] If so, the "weak" party is the party of the Jews, or those Gentiles who had accepted Jewish scruples,[84] and the "food" problem will be that of buying suitably killed meats. The "days" must then refer to Sabbaths and other festivals in the Jewish calendar (discussed further, below). Paul's attitude is that neither position held in the Roman church was right. Each was possible, depending on individual conscience. His norm[85] is that no food is unclean[86] of itself, a statement that stands in flat contradiction to the Torah. This fact alone establishes our conclusions on chapters 6–8, namely, that in the new age of the Spirit, God's demands on us are not mediated through the stipulations of the law.

Some commentators have seen in Colossians 2:14 a reference to the law,[87] though recently Bacchiocchi[88] has advanced a spirited defense of the position that there is no reference at all to the Mosaic law in this passage. With many contemporary exegetes he interprets the *χειρόγραφον* ("the written code") as a record of sin, not of the laws against which the sins were committed;[89] he also refuses to see in the *δόγματα* ("regulations") any reference to the law, interpreting them rather as "ascetic and cultic regulations"[90] imposed by the heretics at Colossae. Bacchiocchi lays great stress on the fact that the term *νόμος* is entirely absent from Colossians, and although his own interpretation at times fails to convince,[91] he is surely right in his conclusion that this passage cannot be interpreted as stating that the Mosaic law itself was "wiped out" in the death of Christ. This passage can tell us something about Paul's attitude toward the Sabbath also; it will be investigated again when we turn to that topic, but it tells us nothing about his attitude to the law.

In Ephesians, however, there is a passage that explicitly refers to the law (Eph. 2:14–15).[92] The interpretation of almost every word in this phrase is open to dispute,[93] and our conclusions must therefore necessarily remain tentative. But there are some things that may be said with a fair degree of certainty. A popular interpretation of the phrase *τόν νόμον . . . δόγμασιν* ("the law of commandments, consisting of regulations") refers this to "only a part of the law, that is, a limited number of its 'commandments'. . . . only the ceremonial regulations have been abrogated."[94] There are, however, at least three reasons why this cannot be so.

As Barth points out, this distinction between moral and ceremonial law cannot be upheld. It would be foreign alike to Paul and to his readers, as it is foreign to the spirit of the pentateuch.[95]

Nor is it true that Paul saw "ceremonial" as something only superficial and hence dispensable. True, he opposed any attempt to impose circumcision on his converts (though it is doubtful that he would have classified that as "ceremonial," even if he had worked with such categories), but he appears to have been equally insistent on the observation of the Christian ceremonials of baptism and the Lord's Supper.

The most telling criticism of this interpretation is that it fails to make sense of the passage as a whole. Paul considers this *νόμον τῶν ἐντολῶν ἐν δόγμασιν* to constitute a barrier between Jew and Gentile. It is certainly not only the "ritual" law which constituted such a barrier: the גֵּר תּוֹשָׁב ("resident alien") was expected to keep the ritual law, but was not thereby constituted a part of Israel.[96]

This last point indicates the way toward an adequate interpretation of the passage. The law that was destroyed was precisely the law that constituted a barrier between Jew and Gentile; in other words, the law viewed from the perspective of the covenant between God and the people that was to be exclusively His people. This must have included the ritual element (including, of course, the Sabbath law), but in Paul's view it went much further than that. To say this is not (despite Bacchiocchi) to accuse Paul of trying to "leave mankind without moral principles,"[97] it is rather to see, with Paul, the breathtaking sweep of God's new act in Christ, which makes one new humanity in Him. And, although Paul is not talking about Christian conduct (but rather about Christian initiation), we may note in passing that any such rider as "now, of course, in that one new man Gentiles must begin to observe the Sabbath (or any other piece of legislation)" would completely vitiate Paul's understanding of the situation.

There remain but two, related, passages for discussion in this section. In 1 Timothy 1:8–11 there is a brief discourse on the use of the law, while 2 Timothy 3:16–17 comments on the use of "Scripture." It is often held[98] that these two are irreconcilable with each other and with the Pauline position on the law, this fact itself being a witness to the deutero-Pauline nature of the pastorals. We shall discuss first the question of internal compatibility.

In 1 Timothy 1:8 we are told that the law is good if it is "used lawfully." This can mean either "used *as law* (law, i.e., and not as the gospel),"[99] or simply "appropriately," "in the proper way."[100] Despite the weight of opinion in favor of the former, it is difficult to see how this can make sense of the context. The problem, as verses 4 and 6 indicate, was not the legalism that Paul had opposed so bitterly in Galatia, but rather the vanity and irrelevance of this sort of teaching. Further, our text proceeds to state that the law is not ordained for the just man (δικαίῳ, v. 9). If, as seems reasonable, this means the man justified by his Christian faith,[101] then again "appropriately" makes better sense. The law is good, but it must be realized that it was not promulgated for the Christian but for outsiders, the "lawless and disobedient." In itself this says nothing about a Christian use of the law, and Conzelmann[102] describes 2 Timothy 3:16–17 as simply "a positive exposition of the 'lawful use'" of the law. However, at the very least the emphasis has shifted quite markedly in this latter passage, since here *only* the "just man" is in view. In 2 Timothy 3:14–17, Scripture[103] is accorded five roles: (1) "to instruct you for salvation through faith in Christ Jesus," (2) "teaching," (3) "reproof," (4) "correction," (5) "(the) training in righteousness." It would be monstrous to suppose that "Scripture" could here exclude the law, but can it be said of the law by the author of 1 Timothy that it fulfills functions (1) and (5)? In answering that question we need to bear in mind that 1 Timothy 1:8–11 is a polemical passage and we need not assume that the participial phrase εἰδὼς τοῦτο ("understanding this") is intended to provide an exhaustive exegesis of the "lawful" use of the law. Anyone wishing to interpret the law aright must realize that its legal function[104] has indeed lapsed for the Christian (a very Pauline touch!); but he may yet see other ways in which the law is valid for him, even in providing him with wisdom and training in righteousness.

Thus it would seem that it is no more difficult to correlate these two statements than it is to correlate many pairs of statements in the Pauline homologoumena. And the resulting attitude to Scripture is certainly compatible with what we see in the homologoumena, for the Paul who opposes any attempt to impose the law on his converts can nevertheless quote it extensively (and expect his readers to know his text and sometimes even its context), and affirm that "whatever was written . . . was written for our instruction, that by steadfastness and by the encouragement of the scriptures we might have hope."[105] If here in the pastorals we have a closer connection between ethics and the instruction of the Scriptures and less emphasis on walking in the Spirit, the difference is not yet so great as to demand that we treat the pastorals under a separate category. The same attitude to the law is seen both here and elsewhere in the Pauline corpus.

We conclude this section with an attempt at summarizing that attitude. The law presents mankind with the ethical[106] standards of the holy God. As such, its goodness is unquestionable, but its effect is simply to demonstrate the existence of our sin, to condemn us as a result, and also to provoke our sin. Because of the weakness of the flesh, it can have no other effect on us when we read its righteous demands. Only death with Christ will remove us from the condemnation that it would otherwise constantly pronounce on anyone who endeavored to live by its standards.

But the law also stands for the whole covenantal arrangement that God made with His people at Sinai, a covenant that has now manifestly been replaced by the New Covenant in Christ. In both of these aspects Paul realized that the law no longer played any role in the life of a Christian. His new and Christian insights into the "exceeding sinfulness of sin"[107] also led him to see that any attempt, even by Christians, to use the law as a basis for a standing before God led inevitably to the sin of "boasting" that is, faith in self rather than faith in God.[108] The only Christian way to fulfill one's obligation to God is by fulfilling the law of love (the law of subordinating one's own self to the other), by walking in the Spirit. These two factors, love and the Spirit, Paul sees as keeping Christian obedience from degenerating into formal legalism. Too rarely, alas, has the church been able to preserve this Pauline insight.

Paul and the Ten Commandments

What has been said above has included the Decalogue in the compass of "the law," but there are those who claim that the Decalogue is in a special category of its own, and abides when the rest of the law is superseded.[109] As there is some evidence that Paul himself saw at least one of the commandments as valid for Christians,[110] it is necessary to investigate his attitude to the Decalogue also.

In 1 Corinthians 7:19 Paul states the maxim: "Neither circumcision counts for anything nor uncircumcision, but keeping the commandments of God." On this Allo comments:

> What counts is "keeping the commandments of God," that is, obedience to the Decalogue and to the precepts of the Gospel, or, as it is put to the Galatians, "faith working by love." (It is useless to try, with Protestants like *Bachmann*, to weaken the word ἐντολαί ("commandments") in this passage, as if faith could produce salvation apart from the works which spring from faith.)[111]

Wendland also adopts this interpretation, warning us that Paul holds no brief for antinomianism.[112] These two may be taken as representative of a superficially obvious and indeed compelling exegesis, but Barrett puts his finger on the fatal flaw in this approach:

> From the Jewish point of view this is a paradoxical, or rather an absurd, statement. A Jew would reply, Circumcision is one of God's commandments; if therefore we are to keep God's commandments we cannot say that circumcision is nothing; we must be circumcised. It is further to be noted that the commandment of circumcision is not one that arises in the Jewish oral tradition, but is firmly rooted in the Old Testament.[113]

Allo could of course reply that circumcision, while certainly embedded in the Old Testament, is not to be found in the Decalogue. But his own interpretation of this passage as referring to the Decalogue *and* the gospel is rather arbitrary, and there are at least three problems in restricting the reference to the Decalogue exclusively.

1. There is no evidence that ἐντολῶν θεοῦ ("commandments of God") was a technical term which would have been understood as referring exclusively (or even primarily) to the Decalogue. Even the use of αἱ ἐντολαί in Mark 10:17ff. and parallels does not provide evidence for such a usage, since in the Matthean story the man's question, ("He said to him, 'Which?'" Matt. 19:18) suggests that "the commandments" would not necessarily be taken to mean "the Decalogue." Nor is the Decalogue reckoned as the essence or summary of the law.[114] It is therefore not evident that Paul would have been understood to mean the Decalogue by his first readers. Although we may not

make the a priori assumption that Paul must always have written so as to be clearly understood, there nonetheless remains a prima facie case for the supposition that he would have been aware of the dangers of being misunderstood, and have qualified his statement accordingly if he intended his readers to understand the "commandments of God" as only the Ten Commandments.

2. As all commentators point out, there are close parallels to this passage in Galatians 5:6 and 6:15, but in these cases the positive affirmation runs ". . . but faith working through love" and ". . . but a new creation" respectively. Despite Allo, it is questionable whether Paul could really have regarded "faith working through love"[115] as equivalent to "rigorous observance of the Decalogue." If the parallel passages in Galatians are relevant at all, they tell against an interpretation of the "commandments" as the Decalogue.

3. According to this interpretation, in 1 Corinthians 7 Paul is telling Gentile converts that whereas they must not seek circumcision, they must (among other things) keep the Sabbath. This is not only a flat contradiction of Paul's own counsel to the Galatians,[116] but also a harsh interpolation; the intent of the passage is to encourage each member of the congregation to maintain the status in which he was originally called.

Can we then find a more adequate interpretation of this passage? Barrett is surely on the right track when he compares 9:20–21 (on which see below) and comments: "*That we keep God's commandments* means an obedience to the will of God as disclosed in his Son far more radical than the observance of any code, whether ceremonial or moral, could be."[117] To say this is not at all "to weaken the word ἐντολαί," but simply to note that the word must be taken in a less specific sense than Allo himself suggests. In other words, we are again up against the problem that the words used by Paul are not technical terms with clear and unambiguous meaning. We cannot, therefore, even go so far as to suppose, on the basis of this passage, that Paul saw a distinction between "commandments (like circumcision)" and "commandments (like those in the Decalogue)," since it is not clear that he has in mind here any reference to the statutes of the Torah.[118] It would therefore be unwise to build any theory about the apostle's attitude to the Decalogue on the basis of 1 Corinthians 7.

In Ephesians 6 the reference to the Decalogue is indisputable. This passage appears to have provided many commentators with a springboard for flights of fancy that derive far more from the commentators' views on childrearing or church order[119] than from the text. In order to be able to claim any validity for our conclusions from this passage, we need to ensure that we understand what is being said here. Our passage forms part of a *Haustafel*,[120] which, as

Sampley has shown,[121] is used in a way that makes it integral to the argument of the epistle. The epistle includes in its purpose a call to unity, and this call undergirds the *Haustafel*. The whole is introduced by the call of 5:15–21, summarized in the last verse, "Be subject to one another out of reverence for Christ."

For children[122] this is interpreted as meaning "obey your parents in the Lord" (6:1). Assuming that "in the Lord" (ἐν κυρίῳ) is part of the original text,[123] it is hardly to be construed with "parents"[124] but rather with "obey." Thus the primary reference is still within the sphere of Christian life and worship, though we need not suppose that this was seen as the exclusive sphere of operation of Paul's injunction.[125] But we need to remember that Paul is still expanding on his earlier command of 5:21: "Be subject to one another out of reverence for Christ"; and this is itself an expansion of the imperative of the beginning of the chapter. Here the imperative is not grounded in the commandments, but in the Christians' "calling" (4:1); their "learning Christ" (4:20); their new life in Christ (4:22–23, 25) and so on. Now in 6:1 Paul adds another reason: it is "right." He may, in quoting the commandment, be adding yet another,[126] but this is, at the least, far from being his *primary* motivation.[127] This itself suggests, though it cannot be said to prove, the thesis that Paul did not regard the commandments per se (any more than the law per se) as binding on Christians. But for confirmation we must look elsewhere in the Pauline corpus.

In 2 Corinthians 3 the Old Covenant is implicitly identified with the Decalogue, since this was the only part of the law that was carved on stone (v. 7). With this Paul contrasts the New Covenant of the Spirit, which alone can give life. What are we to make of this contrast between "letter" (γράμμα) and "Spirit" (or "spirit," πνεῦμα is ambiguous)? Traditionally, two main lines of interpretation have been offered: either the "letter" stands for the literal sense of the law and the "spirit" for its inner, spiritual meaning; or else the letter refers to the law, however understood, while the "Spirit" refers to the Holy Spirit Himself, or to His activity in Christians.[128] Schneider, in the third part of his article,[129] argues strongly for the latter interpretation (which he styles the "realistic" in contrast to the "formalistic" interpretation) in common with "the greater part of the present-day authors."[130]

If this interpretation is the correct one, and Schneider puts forward weighty arguments for it, then we have further evidence that the Decalogue is not seen as binding for Christians any more than the law was. It is not just that for Paul the Old Covenant is reinterpreted in terms of Christian experience, but that this whole system of establishing and maintaining relationships between God and men is now at an end, superseded by the new and more glorious way. The law, however interpreted, could only bring death; life is only produced by God's Holy Spirit. This is surely how we are to understand Paul's words in 2 Corinthians 3:6*b* if they are to be compatible with what he has said elsewhere.

Two passages in Romans serve to reinforce this understanding of Paul's thinking. In Romans 7 (on which see above), where the discussion is focused on the law, that law is epitomized in and represented by precisely one of the commandments (the tenth). The conclusions that were reached above concerning the law, therefore, apply with equal force to the Decalogue; what Paul says of the one he continues to say of the other.

Further, in Romans we also have a repetition of the "fulfillment of the law" motif of Galatians 5:14. But again, what was said of the law there is now spelled out with reference to the commandments. It is true that Paul deals exclusively with the second table of the Decalogue,[131] but it is doubtful that he would have treated the first table in a radically different way; and as our discussion of the fourth commandment will show[132] he certainly does not simply assume that his Gentile converts would adhere to it. We are therefore justified in seeing a material parallel between Galatians 5:14 and Romans 13:9–10, which again confirms our conclusions above that Paul's attitude to and use of the commandments are identical with his attitude to and use of the law.

Paul and the Law of Christ

In 1953, C. H. Dodd[133] put forward the thesis that Paul, while no longer regarding himself as under law (ὑπὸ νόμον), nevertheless still regarded himself as "loyal to the law of God, as it is represented or expressed in the law of Christ";[134] and that the content of this "law of Christ" is precisely the "instructions" (ἐπιταγαί) and "commandments" (διατάγματα) of the earthly Jesus. This would be relevant to our quest if it could be shown that Jesus Himself taught a particular attitude toward the Sabbath (or Sunday),[135] and that Paul was familiar with a corpus of the teaching of Jesus that included this aspect of it. That Paul was certainly acquainted with at least some of the teaching of Jesus is beyond dispute,[136] and it is likely that in several passages in his letters he draws upon this knowledge.[137] But it is by no means so self-evident that he regards this teaching as a new *law* for the church. For not only does nomism as a system fail to do justice to Paul's thought,[138] but his very use of his Jesus traditions also militates against this assumption.[139] It is therefore necessary to query Dodd's interpretation. Even if the genitives θεοῦ ("of God") and χριστοῦ ("of Christ") are "clearly governed by the νόμος,"[140] it is doubtful if νόμος χριστοῦ in this context can be any more than the law of love, which elsewhere Paul describes as the norm of his relationships.[141] This interpretation could also cover Galatians 6:2, where there is another reference to the law of Christ, and even if the reference here is to a dominical logion,[142] that gives little basis to the assumption that Paul knew of or could refer to the law of Christ as a *body* of Christian norms.[143]

Quite apart, therefore, from the question of Jesus' own attitude to the Sabbath and Sunday, it is unlikely that any further light will be shed on Paul's approach by this line of inquiry. He never refers to any dominical utterance in his discussion of this issue, and the exact limits of his knowledge of the teaching of Jesus remain obscure to us. Thus, any statement about his dependence upon Jesus at this point is mere guesswork and will be likely to obscure rather than clarify the issues.

Paul and the Fourth Commandment

We are now in a position to examine those few passages where Paul refers to Sabbath observance.[144]

Galatians 4:10

It is often assumed without question that the phrase "days and months and seasons and years" refers to the Jewish festivals of Sabbath, New Moon, the annual festivals, and Sabbatical or jubilee years, commonly with a cross reference to Colossians 2:16 for confirmation.[145] Few commentators have paused to ask why, if Paul meant the Jewish festivals, he did not give them their customary names (as in Col. 2:16). Bligh's answer to this question is that "it had been the custom . . . for christians, both Jew and Gentile, to meet for the liturgy of the sabbath, and that St. Paul did not wish to upset this custom."[146] But this seems over subtle, since Bligh thinks that Paul is in fact referring to the Sabbath here, and that he does condemn (at least a certain sort of) Sabbath observance. However, it is difficult to assume that Paul meant some other, non-Jewish, periodic festivals, since the opponents certainly had Jewish characteristics. The interpretation of the situation in Galatia proposed by Jewett[147] has the virtue of taking seriously both these characteristics of the opponents and the terminology used here by Paul. Jewett suggests that Paul's terminology indicates

> that the agitators had not made use of the typically Jewish terminology but sought instead to connect the Jewish festivals with ideas and terms generally prevalent in the Hellenistic world. Thus the cultic calendar was presented to the Galatians on a basis which was far from orthodox. But the agitators were not disturbed as long as quick and observable results could be achieved. It was more important to them that the Galatians be circumcised and begin to keep the festivals than that they do so for proper reasons.[148]

If this is true,[149] then the fact that Paul inveighs against this practice as he does would not necessarily rule out any and every periodic festival, however observed, such as Sabbath, or Sunday. However, while no doubt potentially attractive to Christian apologists, this interpretation does not in itself lead to any particular assessment of Paul's attitude toward the Christian and periodic festivals. Indeed, it is still difficult to suppose that the form of words Paul uses here is compatible with a positive attitude to Sabbath keeping, as though he were saying that the problem lay in the fact that the Galatians were keeping the right festivals, but for the wrong reasons. The situation seems to have been that Paul viewed any attempt to impose Sabbath keeping (or indeed the keeping of any of the regular festivals of the Jewish or astrological calendars) upon Gentiles as wrong, and any tendency on the part of converts to submit to this coercion as a retrograde step.

Romans 14:5

Reference has already been made[150] to the situation to which Romans 14:5 relates. Paul distinguishes two groups: the "weak" whose scruples lead them to practice vegetarianism and the "strong" with whom Paul identifies himself in 15:1. This much is clear, but it is not clear how Paul relates these two groups to the question of observing days. Schlier notes that in verse 5 the flow of thought is broken,[151] but then assumes with the other commentators that Paul is simply recalling another distinction between the two Roman groups that needed to be put right.

Yet despite the unanimity among the commentators, such an interpretation fails to satisfy. It leaves two problems unsolved; the puzzling γάρ ("for"), which introduces the statement,[152] and the fact that Paul fails to deal at all with the problem of "days." The first of these problems is certainly not insuperable,[153] but the second seems to have passed unnoticed by commentators. If Paul were facing a situation in the Roman church in which there was a confusion over the observance of days (whether festivals or fast days), this must surely have been at least as great a problem as that of meats. It would certainly have been more manifest. Yet Paul fails to say anything about the issue except, "Let everyone be convinced in his own mind—hardly a satisfying treatment for warring factions. And although the meats issue is taken up again and expounded in verses 14–23, there is no further reference to "days." Paul does not even make the concession that the man who regards all days alike does so to the Lord (cf. v. 6). On the traditional interpretation Paul's treatment of the issue is profoundly inadequate, and is not likely to have solved the problem.

However, an alternative interpretation of this passage is possible, which also permits the γάρ to have its full force. We need only allow that the "days" issue had arisen earlier in the history of the Roman church, and had already been solved. And it is not improbable that in such a cosmopolitan milieu this should have been the case. Paul will then be saying to the church that *just as* they accept differing practices over "days," *so also* they should entertain differing practices over "meats." It is then easy to see why "days" form no further part of the discussion.

But what are these "days" observed by some and not by others? Opinions vary as to whether they were festivals[154] or fast days.[155] Bacchiocchi in particular has argued that the context is one of abstinence from foods, so that the Sabbath (which was a day of feasting, not of fasting) cannot be in mind. But this reasoning is false. The issue is not one of *periodic* abstinence but rather of *habitual* vegetarianism; even "the one who abstains" (ὁ μὴ ἐσθίων) could observe a feast with his vegetables. There is thus no prima facie evidence that fast days are in mind.[156] There is indeed one slight piece of evidence against it. The parallelism in verses 2, 5, and 6 suggests[157] that it is the strong and not the weak who observe "days." Is this credible?[158] Not, perhaps, if the "days" are fast days. But the consciences of the weak might well have forbidden them from enjoying festivals, either because of their link with the Old Covenant or because of astrological links.[159] On the other hand, we have evidence from both Paul himself and the Book of Acts[160] that Paul continued his own Sabbath keeping. The balance of probability, then, is in favor of the Sabbath being included in the "days" of Romans 14:5.[161] Paul allows that the keeping of such days is purely a matter of individual conscience.

Colossians 2:16

Much has been written on the so-called Colossian heresy, including a spirited attack on the very existence of such a phenomenon.[162] All the need concern us here, however, is the interpretation of Paul's statement that no one is to "judge" (κρίνειν) the Colossians "with regard to Sabbath(s)" (ἐν μέρει σαββάτων). The nuances of κρίνειν depend on the context. Here the context is that of Christ's victory over the principalities and powers (note that οὖν, "therefore," connects v. 16 with vv. 8–15), and so one of Christian freedom. This makes it likely that the κριτής ("judge") will be more condemnatory than approbatory. As most commentators agree, the judge is likely to be a man of ascetic tendencies, who objects to the Colossian eating and drinking.[163] The most natural way of taking the rest of the passage is not that he also *imposes* a ritual of feast days, but rather that he *objects* to certain elements of such observation.[164] Here again, then, it seems that Paul could happily countenance Sabbath keeping;[165] his attitude is that it, like many other things, does neither harm nor good. Like all of these activities,[166] it is a shadow of things to come. Here we have again an echo of Paul's attitude to the law in his more positive moments.[167] The implications of Paul's term σκιά ("shadow) have been much discussed recently.[16] Certainly, Paul, like others before him,[169] is contrasting the σκιά with the σῶμα ("reality"). But is he (as most earlier commentators assumed without question) like Plato encouraging his readers to seek the substance to the abandoning of the mere shadow? Considering his attitude to the law as we have seen it above, this is unlikely. The role of the shadow is neither simply preliminary (and so brought to an end by the manifestation of the substance) nor simply that of a "fitting symbol,"[170] which therefore has continuing validity. As with the law, Paul's attitude to the festivals here seems to be[171] that they have lost their intrinsic value but may yet be enjoyed by those who wish so to use them. However we interpret the situation, Paul's statement "Let no one pass judgment on you," indicates that no stringent regulations are to be laid down over the use of festivals. As is the case with the law, the Christian is no longer bound by external stipulations in the matter of festivals.

Assessment

We are now in a position to make some general comments concerning our topic. We have seen that the problem is not, (despite many discussions of our issue) simply that some sort of Sabbath keeping was being imposed on Paul's converts and that Paul opposed this. It is therefore worth clarifying the situation by specifying what it was that Paul was opposing, the grounds on which he did so, and the relationship between this and the question of Sabbath keeping.

Although the three situations discussed above differ among themselves, in each of them Paul is facing the danger of some obligation being placed upon his converts,[172] for whatever reason. His response is most violent in Galatians, where these stipulations were not only linked with a return to the weak and beggarly elements or principles (στοιχείων, 3:20), but were also being regarded as a sine qua non of acceptance into the church. Less seriously, in Rome and Colossae such stipulations were being used as a basis for "judging" fellow Christians. Because of his understanding of the present role of the law, Paul cannot allow that judgment be made upon such a basis. Indeed, in the New Covenant, none is free to judge his brother at all. On these grounds Paul opposes any attempt to make the observance of festivals or the manner of their observance a touchstone of orthodoxy.

What does this tell us about Paul's attitude to the Sabbath? The clear implication is that he refuses to dogmatise one way or the other. An individual may keep the Sabbath or not; presumably, in general Paul might have assumed that a Jewish Christian would do so and a Gentile convert would not. The important factor was not which practice one adopted, but one's motives; to convert for inadequate reasons is reprehensible. Thus Paul was probably content to allow a wide variety of practice in the churches. How this relates to the keeping of a specifically Christian day must be the subject of our final section.

Paul and the First Day of the Week

S. Bacchiocchi has an extended discussion[173] on Paul's sole reference to the first day of the week (1 Cor. 16:2) and the problems it raises. He emphasizes the fact that the majority of commentators have been over-hasty to see a *meeting* for Sunday worship behind this essentially private and individual almsgiving. Bacchiocchi's own conclusions, however, are equally speculative; he poses certain rhetorical questions:

> If the Christian community was worshipping together on Sunday, it appears paradoxical that Paul should recommend laying aside at home one's gift. Why should Christians deposit their offering at home on Sunday, if on such a day they were gathering for worship? Should not the money have been brought to the Sunday service?[174]

However, he fails to observe that his own position, which is implicit in these questions, rules out a Christian gathering for worship at *any* time, if the money should eventually have been added to the church's coffers. But Paul seems to assume that the money will be collected from the individual church members only when he arrives.[175] In this case there is no question of offering the money in the Corinthian church meeting, whenever it is held, and it could as well have been on Sunday as on any other day. But Bacchiocchi goes even further and suggests that *Sabbath* keeping may lie behind this "first-day deposit plan":[176]

> To wait until the end of the week or of the month . . . is contrary to sound budgetary practices, since by then one finds himself [sic] to be with empty pockets and empty hands. . . . While it is difficult at present to determine what economic significance, if any, was attached to Sunday in the pagan world, it is a known fact that no financial computations or transactions were done by the Jews on the Sabbath. Since the Jewish custom of Sabbath-keeping influenced even many Greeks and Romans . . . it appears reasonable that Paul should recommend the Christians to plan on the very first day of the week—that is, right after the Sabbath—for the special fund-raising contribution, before other priorities might diminish their resources.[177]

This however is very speculative and seems to assume[178] Deissmann's conjecture that Sunday was payday. Although we know too little about ancient economic systems to dogmatise, we do know that at least in Palestine day laborers were a common enough phenomenon.[179] Also, ancient records of salaries always seem to cite them as annual or monthly amounts, and not (as far as I am aware) as weekly amounts. The onus of proof, then, would be on those who wish to maintain that Paul's instructions in 1 Corinthians 16:2 have to do with the availability of the individual's funds. Bacchiocchi's final sentence in his section on this verse, however, is surprisingly restrained: "The text therefore proposes a valuable weekly plan to ensure a substantial and orderly contribution on behalf of the poor brethren of Jerusalem, but to extract more meaning from the text would distort it."[180] But there is likely to have been some good reason why Paul chose a weekly scheme and in particular suggested the first day[181] as that appropriate for the collection. It is inconceivable that to a Jew like Paul the seven day cycle could have been regarded in merely secular terms, and so it is highly probable that the weekly scheme was informed, at least in part, by his own attitude to Sabbath (or Sunday). Doubtless, if the Corinthian church did meet regularly on either of these days, the relation between this and the almsgiving would have been evident to them; we have no way of knowing. Thus while we may reasonably see a link between the collection and the church's regular worship, our text gives no support for the positing of any particular practice or belief relating to Sunday on the part of either Paul or the church.

May no more be said than this? In the light of all that we have discussed, we may at least assess the relation between contemporary attitudes and that of Paul. It is not unreasonable to suppose that Sunday was seen at an early stage as an appropriate day for a Christian feast, and no doubt every Christian feast was at least in part a eucharist. Nothing that we have seen in Paul's writings could lead us to suppose that he would deny the appropriateness of a meeting for worship and eucharist on Sunday, whether or not he or the churches ever in fact contemplated such a practice.[182] Some contemporary writers,[183] however, wish to go further than this, in claiming that Sunday *is* the Christian Sabbath, and that its observance is therefore a fulfillment of the fourth commandment. We have already seen enough to realize what short shrift this approach would have received from Paul. Not only is he opposed to the reestablishment of the Decalogue as a law for the Christian life, but he is also quite happy to allow the seventh-day Sabbath to be observed—a position quite incompatible with any identification of Sunday as the Christian Sabbath.

Paul's contribution to our quest, then, is limited but of significance. While he forbids us from stating that Christians may *not* observe Sunday as the Christian day *par excellence*, he also forbids us from imposing such observance as a duty upon our fellow believers. Since, at least in much of the world, Sunday is allowed to the majority of us as a day of rest and a day suitable for worship, we may surely gratefully receive it as such; but our study of Paul forbids us from erecting any theological edifice upon this convenient, but fortuitous, fact.

NOTES

[1]The word *σάββατον* occurs only twice in the Pauline corpus: in 1 Corinthians 16:2 (*μία σαββάτου*, Paul's only reference to the first day of the week), and Colossians 2:1–6. Galatians 4:8–11 and Romans 14:5 also refer to "keeping days," possibly with the Sabbath in mind; these passages will be discussed later.

[2]I do not believe that "Paul" is a Christian name, but use "Saul" as a convenient shorthand for, "Paul before his conversion to Christ."

[3]See especially K. Stendahl, *Paul among Jews and Gentiles* (London: SCM, 1977); Richard N. Longenecker, *Paul: Apostle of Liberty* (New York: Harper and Row, 1964), chapter 4; E. P. Sanders, *Paul and Palestinian Judaism* (London: SCM, 1977), sections V.2 and V.4.

[4]Romans 7:24.

[5]Acts 26:14.

[6]On the significance of "fulfilling the law" in the Judaism of the day, see most recently E. P. Sanders, "On the Question of Fulfilling the Law in Paul and Rabbinic Judaism," *Donum Gentilicium*, ed. E. Bammel, et al. (Oxford: Clarendon, 1978), pp. 103–126.

[7]Most commentators and writers on Paul acknowledge that Romans 7 is written from a Christian standpoint, whatever interpretation they place on it (on which see pp. 262–66, below). Many have raised the question of whether Paul *could* have made such a statement before his conversion (see Longenecker, *Paul*, pp. 96–97) but the thesis here proposed is simply that he *would* not have done so.

[8]Longenecker, *Paul*, pp. 98–101.

[9]See R. Tannehill, *Dying and Rising with Christ* (Berlin: Töpelmann, 1967), p. 10, and D. R. de Lacey, *The Form of God in the Likeness of Men* (unpublished Cambridge Ph.D. dissertation, 1974), p. 153 and n. 4, for the thesis that Paul's related baptismal understanding antedates Paul himself. Acts 9 and 15 witness to a comparable reassessment of the law in the Jerusalem church.

[10]H. Hübner, *Das Gesetz bei Paulus* (Göttingen: Vanderhoeck und Ruprecht, 1978), argues that Paul's view sprang from a misunderstanding of the Jerusalem Council, and sees in Galatians a view of the law that would have been rejected by all the Jerusalem apostles. We need not go so far as that to realize that the "false apostles" (whoever they may have been) of 2 Corinthians 11:12–15 claimed some support from the Jerusalem church and so represent a group whose Christian traditions conflicted with Paul's attitude to the law.

[11]Sanders, *Paul*, section V.

[12]Ibid., especially pp. 442–47.

[13]M. Hengel, *The Son of God* (London: SCM, 1976), pp. 67–68 and note 123.

[14]קִלְלַת אֱלֹהִים, Deuteronomy 21:23, a passage quoted by Paul in Galatians 3:13 (omitting *ὑπὸ τοῦ θεοῦ*, "by God"). It is true that this is not the situation envisaged by the deuteronomic legislation, but this is no doubt how Saul would have interpreted it in this case. It may well explain his hatred of the sect of the Nazarene.

[15]Sanders, *Paul*, especially pp. 236–37, 420–21. Sanders employs the term "traditional Judaism" to describe attitudes to which the covenant was central ("The Covenant as a Soteriological Category and the Nature of Salvation in Palestinian and Hellenistic Judaism," in R. Hamerton-Kelly and Scroggs, ed. *Jews, Greeks and Christians* (Leiden: Brill, 1976), pp. 13–44 especially p. 44 and note 95).

[16]Jeremiah 31:31–34.

[17]The phrase itself occurs in 1QpHab. 2:3–4 (though בְּרִית is in square brackets in Lohse's text); CD 6:19; 8:21; 19:33–34; and 20:12.

[18]See for instance 1QS 1:18–2:19; 5:1–6:2; CD 6:14–7:6 (which also includes a reference to the "New" Covenant); 15:5–11, and Sanders, *Paul*, section II.2.

[19]Galatians 4:24; cf. the use of "the New Covenant" (ἡ καινὴ διαθήκη) in 1 Corinthians 11:25 and (anarthrous) "new covenant" (καινὴ διαθήκη) in 2 Corinthians 3:6, in contrast with "the old covenant" of verse 14.

[20]Galatians 3:14–18. This fact alone should serve to place a question mark against E. Käsemann's assertion that "the New Covenant" (ἡ καινὴ διαθήκη) has but one meaning in Paul's writings *(Exegetische Versuche und Besinnungen 1* [Göttingen: Vandenhoeck und Ruprecht, 1960], p. 28).

[21] p^{46} B $D^{gr}G^{gr}$ *it* $ar^{vid?}$ c, dem $_{vg}$cl $cop^{sa,bo^{mss}}$ eth read the singular ἡ καινὴ διαθήκη but this reading is to be rejected as inferior. See the commentaries.

[22]So the majority of commentators. M. Black, *Romans* (London: Oliphants, 1973), *in loc.*, suggests that the two covenants, the old and new, are in mind.

[23]So C. K. Barrett, *The Epistle to the Romans* (London: Black, 1957), *in loc.* O. Michel, *Der Brief an die Römer* (Göttingen: Vandenhoeck und Ruprecht, 1966), *in loc.*, seems to think that both possibilities are in view.

[24]C. Roetzel, "Διαθῆκαι in Romans 9:4," *Bib* 51 (1970): 377–90.

[25]This argument would gain even greater force if with some commentators (and most recently Hübner, *Gesetz*, pp. 28–29) we interpret "by angels" (δι' ἀγγέλων) in 3:19 to mean that the law was given by (demonic) angels and *not* by God (cf. οὐδείς, "no one," v. 15, which would most naturally mean "nobody *else*"). But there are strong reasons for rejecting this exegesis: See M.-J. Lagrange, *Saint Paul: Epître aux Galates* (Paris: J. Gabalda, 1950), *ad loc.*

[26]A. T. Lincoln, *The Heavenly Dimension* (unpublished Cambridge Ph.D. dissertation, 1974), pp. 35–39, argues that this quotation answers the rhetorical question of verse 21, and is a call to the church to send the Judaizers packing. Those who advocate the Old Covenant seek only to enslave; they have no place in the church of the free.

[27]We cannot here discuss the provenance of each epistle, significant though that be for any interpretation. For the thesis that Paul's attitude underwent a fundamental change, see H. Hübner, *Gesetz*, chapters 2 and 3.3 (on this see below and my review in *JSNT* 1 [1978]: 70–72). More balanced is J. Drane, *Paul: Libertine or Legalist?* (London: SPCK, 1975).

[28]Another way of stating this might be that Paul saw the stipulations of the Mosaic covenant as fulfilled—but not those of the Abrahamic. On 2 Corinthians 3, see p. 178.

[29]To this extent this "covenant" may be identified with the "New Covenant" but it is doubtful if this was in Paul's mind. "Their sin" (v. 27) evidently refers back to Jacob and Israel (v. 26) so that in one sense this is exclusive of the Gentiles.

[30]On the thesis that this superficially odd way of expressing this identification is designed as a blow against the false brethren who were claiming the authority of the mother church *in Jerusalem*, see Lincoln, *Dimension*, pp. 17–20.

[31]Sanders, *Paul*, sections V.3, 4, summarized on pp. 550–52.

[32]On the inadequacy of "covenantal nomism" as a category for interpreting Paul's thought, see Sanders, *Paul*, pp. 513–15.

[33]J. A. Sanders, "Torah and Christ," *Int* 29 (1975): 372–90 (380). Sanders assumes the semantic identity of νόμος and תּוֹרָה. In his *Torah and Canon* (Philadelphia: Fortress, 1972), he is more cautious, seeing "at least four senses" in Paul's use of νόμος (p. 2).

[34]It would also make such a statement a most improbable element in Paul's thought; the best example Sanders can give is Romans 10:4. Christ is the climax *(sic)* of the Torah. He ignores those passages that clearly assume that the law is no longer relevant, passages that cast doubt on his thesis.

[35]See n. 10, above.

[36]For my reasons, see my "Paul in Jerusalem," *NTS* 20 (1974): 82–86.

[37]Terminology presents a problem here since Paul's word can be translated by "righteousness"

or "justification," which have different senses in English. I shall use the terms indiscriminately; those offended by this should replace both by δικαιοσύνη. We need not be concerned here with the question of whether this idea forms the center of Paul's thought or not (see Sanders, *Paul*, pp. 438–39, 442, 492–93. I wish to stress only that the issue here, as in Galatians 1:17, is that of initial rather than continuing experience.

[38]So also Hübner *Gesetz*, pp. 23–24, 37–38, citing 5:3 in support; see further J. B. Tyson, "'Works of Law' in Galatians," *JBL* 92 (1973): 423–31.

[39]There is no evidence that προστίθημι has pejorative overtones.

[40]Hübner, *Gesetz*, p. 27. Hübner is not alone in seeing χάριν as final: he himself cites Lipsius, Schlier and Oepke in support, and we may add Lightfoot, Burton, Ridderbos, Betz and Bligh (who accepts both interpretations simultaneously). However, not all of these accept the implication of this interpretation that Hübner draws that this "provoking" of sin is inherently malevolent. Ironically (since Hübner is arguing for a Pauline about-face between Galatians and Romans) most of these interpreters arrive at their position on the basis of Paul's understanding of the Law in Romans 5:20 rather than by wrestling with the text here. (One is tempted to wonder why Rom. 5:20 is chosen for this purpose rather than Rom. 3:20 or even 1 Tim. 1:8–10). None of them shows himself as aware as Hübner of the problems this interpretation raises for our understanding of ἄχρις οὗ ("until"): see note 41.

[41]ἄχρις οὗ (ἄν) ἔλθῃ τὸ σπέρμα ("till the offspring should come"), Hübner, *Gesetz*, pp. 29–30. The problem seen by Hübner is primarily that this interpretation makes God (rather than the angels) the provoker of sins. But a greater problem still concerns the sense in which the coming of the Seed makes any difference. Ellicott picturesquely observes that "when the Seed *did* come, higher influences began to work within;" but it is far from evident why or how this should be so, or what these influences might be. Insofar as the law *does* provoke sin, it certainly continues to have this function in the Christian era. See also note 46. My reasons for this conclusion, which is also supported by Ellicott, Guthrie, Bligh (in conjunction with a final interpretation), Mussner and Burton (who, despite labelling his interpretation as "final" comments "it naturally suggests, as involved in the παραβάσεων the *recognition* of the sinfulness of the deeds"), will become clearer in the next paragraph. It also provides a coherent interpretation both for verses 23–29 and for ἄχρις οὗ ("until"), for now sin is limited by the work of the Spirit (see Gal. 5 and 6!) and an understanding of the evil of sin comes through our awareness of the work of Christ (see Sanders, *Paul*, pp. 442–47).

[42]*Gesetz*, p. 34.

[43]It makes no difference which reading we adopt here.

[44]So, more or less, J. B. Lightfoot, *The Epistle of St. Paul to the Galatians* (Grand Rapids: Zondervan, repr. 1957), *ad loc.*

[45]On the form of the argument here, see Sanders, *Paul*, section V.2.

[46]Both "to limit transgressions in the interim" and "to demonstrate the exceeding evil of transgressions" would be possible interpretations, but verses 23–29 might suggest that the former is uppermost in Paul's mind.

[47]Paul can hardly mean in verses 23 and 25 that faith was unknown in the Mosaic period; it is more likely that "faith" is used as an alternative for "the gospel."

[48]4:3 with 4:9. Whether Paul meant exactly the same thing in these two uses of στοιχεῖα must remain an unanswered question of Pauline exegesis.

[49]Hübner, *Gesetz*, p. 38: "Paul delivers . . . a linguistic hit below the belt against the Jewish understanding of law that is opposing him. . . . Therefore 'the whole law of Moses' is certainly not identical with "the whole law" which pertains to Christians. Hübner does not really explain the difference, nor explain how this is compatible with his view that this is "a critical-ironical form of expression."

[50]As, e.g., in *Sifre* on Numbers 6:26 (XI.7: p. 439 in the translation by Freedman and Simon [London: Soncino, 1977]): see Sanders, *Paul*, pp. 179, 513 and 544. Hübner is not unaware of this concept: see his *Gesetz*, p. 78. This is not to revert covertly to the supposed distinction between moral and ceremonial law; nor are we seeking here to suggest a basis for distinguishing

between abiding and discontinued laws. The question is how the laws relate to the covenant, since that is the issue with which Paul wrestles.

[51]Hübner, *Gesetz*, pp. 37–38. By "Reduktion" Hübner means that the love command replaces the Mosaic stipulations with a lesser demand, while "Konzentration" indicates that the love command contains within itself the whole of the Torah.

[52]Galatians 5:16; see Sanders, *Paul*, p. 513. This is not an absolute opposition of the spirit and the commands of the Old Testament; but a question of the *basis* of Paul's ethical imperative. This is always expressed in terms of the indwelling Spirit, conformity to Christ, adorning the gospel of Christ, and so on, rather than in terms of obedience to written statutes. See further on the next paragraph, on the Corinthian correspondence, and on Paul and the Ten Commandments in this chapter.

[53]Hübner, *Gesetz*, pp. 45–46.

[54]Against C. E. B. Cranfield, *The Epistle to the Romans* (Edinburgh: T. & T. Clark, 1975), 1:24. A survey of the commentaries noting the amount of space apportioned to the various sections of the epistle indicates to what extent this starting point influences and conditions the interpretation and exegesis.

[55]See among others K. Stendahl, *Paul Among Jews and Gentiles*, pp. 3–4; G. Bornkamm, *Paul* (London: Hodder and Stoughton, 1971), pp. 93–96 and idem, "Der Römerbrief als Testament des Paulus," *Geschichte und Glaube II* (München: Chr. Kaiser, 1971); E. P. Sanders, *Paul*, pp. 488–92; J. Jervell, "Der Brief nach Jerusalem: Über Veranlassung und Adresse des Römerbriefes," *ST* 25 (1971): 61–73; W. S. Campbell, "Why did Paul write Romans?" *Expt* 85 (1974): 264–69; K. P. Donfried, "False Presuppositions in the Study of Romans," *CBQ* 36 (1974): 332–55; R. J. Karris, "The Occasion of Romans: A Response to Professor Donfried," *CBQ* 36 (1974): 356–58. Donfried has collected some of these and other essays into a volume entitled *The Romans Debate* (Minneapolis: Augsburg, 1977). Commentators seem less agreed: H. Schlier, *Der Römerbrief* (Freiburg: Herder, 1977), p. 15, may be taken as typical: "Chapters 9–11 almost appear to be excuses." Cranfield, *Romans*, refuses to commit himself in his introduction: in Essay 1 in Part 2 he accepts this as one among several purposes (pp. 817–20). His interpretation of the main theme is, however, different from that adopted here. I regret that Part 2 was published too late for this essay to interact with it.

[56]E. P. Sanders, *Paul*, p. 490; italics in the original. I acknowledge here a significant debt to Sanders's interpretation of the logic of Paul's argument in Romans: *Paul*, pp. 488–92.

[57]It makes little difference to the argument if we accept the less likely interpretation of προεχόμεθα (v. 9) as implying disadvantage. The point is, as stressed above, that both are on the *same* footing.

[58]Hübner makes too much of this as the sole purpose of the law in Romans (*Gesetz*, pp. 62–63): even in this section there is the added function of witness (3:21). In 7:5 (never discussed by Hübner) it has the function of provoking sin, a function Hübner sees as exclusive to Galatians.

[59]See Cranfield, *Romans*, *ad loc.*, for arguments against taking 3:31 primarily with what follows. But he does not sufficiently stress the significance of οὖν ("therefore," RSV "then") here.

[60]The RSV's "on the principle of faith" is probably too philosophical, and misses the wordplay on νόμος here and in verse 31. On the other hand there are grave weaknesses in the interpretation of νόμος πίστεως as "the Torah, as soon as it is seen with the eyes of faith" (Hübner, *Gesetz*, pp. 118–20); it involves interpreting διὰ ποίου νόμου; (v. 27) as "through which interpretation of the Torah?" and χωρὶς ἔργων νόμου "apart from works of law" (v. 28) as "without using the Torah as a 'law of works,'" both of which are improbable. Also, Paul is not arguing here *for* a particular understanding of the law, as this interpretation demands.

[61]The precise meanings of καταργοῦμεν and ἱστάνομεν need not concern us here.

[62]On the significance of this death, see C. F. D. Moule, "Death 'to Sin,' 'to Law,' and 'to the World': A Note on Certain Datives," in A. Descamps and A. de Halleux, ed., *Mélanges Bibliques* (Gembloux: Duculot, 1970), pp. 367–75; and de Lacey, *Form*, chapter 7.

[63]It is worth noting that this whole discussion is sparked off by the question, "Shall we sin, because we are not under the law?"

[64]Not only for any reference it may have to the story of the Fall (Gen. 3), but also because of the searching character of this law. Even in the light of his new and Christian understanding of the nature of sin, Paul could well have said of most of the rest of the law, "These things have I kept from my youth."

[65]For details of the debate and a full discussion of the options, see Cranfield, *Romans*, *ad loc.* Cranfield's own conclusions are adopted here.

[66]Either by death and resurrection or by transformation: see 1 Corinthians 15. It is misleading for Gundry in his *tour de force* to raise the rhetorical question, "What kind of salvation would it be to save only half a man—a mind without physical means of expression?": *Sōma in Biblical Theology* (London: Cambridge, 1976), p. 140. Apart from the dubious implications of his own view (that the unregenerate mind can *only* [despite n. 1 on p. 140] will what is right, while the body can *never* fulfill its desires), he ignores Paul's use of σάρξ ("flesh") and even σῶμα ("body") to refer to the man under sin quite apart from physicality. See de Lacey, *Form*, section 6.2.

[67]ἄρα οὖν, ("so then," v. 25) summarizes the (present) situation. We need to recall that Paul is still discussing the question of whether or not the law is sin, and is not primarily concerned with the issue of Christian holiness.

[68]Cranfield, *Romans*, 1,370, n. 2.

[69]Cranfield (not to mention many others) identifies the σῶμα ("body") of Romans 12:1 with the self, but W. Sanday and A. C. Headlam, *The Epistle to the Romans* (Edinburgh: T. & T. Clark, 1902), *ad loc.*, rightly stress the contrast between σῶμα and νοῦς ("mind") in Romans 12:1–2. There is thus a close parallel between this passage and 7:25*b*.

[70]That is, Paul recognizes the continuing existence of "the flesh" in the life of the Christian, not that he is describing himself as a "carnal Christian." This despite R. Y. K. Fung, "The Impotence of the Law: Towards a Fresh Understanding of Romans 7:14–25," *Scripture, Tradition and Interpretation*, ed. W. W. Gasque and W. S. LaSor (Grand Rapids: Eerdmans, 1978), pp. 34–48.

[71]See C. E. B. Cranfield, "St. Paul and the Law," *SJT* 17 (1964): 43–68 (56) for an explicit statement of this identification.

[72]Cranfield, *Romans*, 1.364.

[73]Not that the law is identified with (or reduced to) the tenth commandment, but that it is precisely *here* that sin gains its entry. See n. 64, above.

[74]As in Romans 12:11; 14:18; Galatians 5:13; Philippians 2:22.

[75]As in Romans 6:6; Galatians 4:8–9, 25.

[76]Cranfield, *Romans*, 1.372, may be taken as typical: 8:1–11 "connects not with 7.25a or 7.25b but with 7.6."

[77]The phrase is Cranfield's, *Romans*, 1.386.

[78]Since the pre-Christian Saul would assert that he could and did submit to, and obey, the law of God.

[79]H. Schlier, *Römerbrief*, *ad loc.*

[80]Barrett, *Romans*, *ad loc.*

[81]Though he thinks that this is simply a way of expressing the essential unity of the law, which is now "at last being truly and sincerely obeyed." Christians "fulfil it in the sense that they do have a real faith in God (which is the law's basic demand) . . . that they do sincerely desire to obey" (*Romans*, p. 384). But that they desire to obey *the law* I would have thought doubtful. Cranfield's understanding of this statement as "the fulfilment of the promises of Jer. 31.33 and Ezek. 36.26f." is puzzling, unless he is prepared to accept the same ambivalence in meaning of the words "law," "statutes" and "ordinances" in these passages as we appear to find in Paul. No reading of the Christian Paul can see him as encouraging his converts to "be careful to observe [God's] ordinances," which included circumcision, daily sacrifices, etc.

[82]A suggestion to which Cranfield is attracted, though he reluctantly abandons it in favor of the view above.

[83]See above, pages 168–69, on the purpose of Romans. Barrett, *ad loc.*, sounds a double

caveat, that in a city like Rome with a large Jewish colony, kosher meat would be freely available and so the Jewish Christian would not be forced into vegetarianism, and that abstinence from wine was also involved, and this was not a Jewish practice. But we should note that if Christians were already excommunicated they may not have been able to buy meat from the Jewish butchers. Also, Paul's addition of "drinking" is not made when discussing the actual situation, and may be a hypothetical addition. See C. E. B. Cranfield, "Some Observations on the Interpretation of Romans 14, 1–15, 13," *Communio Viatorum* 17 (1974): 193–204, 197. (I am most grateful to Mr. Cranfield for discussion on this and other points, and for the loan of a copy of his article.)

[84]In Galatians Paul opposes bitterly those who would oblige Gentiles to *undertake* the observation of the law, but there is nowhere in his writings any indication that he objected to the Jewish Christians *continuing* to observe it—except of course where this observance challenged the equal status of Gentile believers.

[85]On "I know and am persuaded in the Lord Jesus" (Rom. 14:14) as part of the "law of Christ," see below, pp. 179–80.

[86]The use of the term κοινός ("unclean" or "common") indicates that the discussion is here being restricted to the question of foods.

[87]For a full discussion of the χειρόγραφον as the law see J. Eadie, *A Commentary on the Greek Text of the Epistle of Paul to the Colossians* (London: Griffin, 1856), pp. 163–70. Eadie himself holds to this view, as also do T. K. Abbott, *The Epistles to the Ephesians and to the Colossians* (Edinburgh: T. & T. Clark, n.d.) and W. Hendriksen, *Colossians and Philemon* (Grand Rapids: Baker, 1964), *ad loc.* Others see a reference to the law not in the χειρόγαφον but in the δόγματα; so J. B. Lightfoot, *St. Paul's Epistles to the Colossians and to Philemon* (London: Macmillan, 1876); E. Lohse, *Colossians and Philemon* (Philadelphia: Fortress, 1971); C. F. D. Moule, *The Epistles to the Colossians and to Philemon* (Cambridge: University Press, 1957), *ad loc.*

[88]S. Bacchiocchi, *From Sabbath to Sunday* (Rome: Pontifical Gregorian University, 1977), in an appendix, pp. 339–64.

[89]See C. F. D. Moule, *Colossians and Philemon, ad loc.*, for a lucid expression of this position.

[90]*From Sabbath to Sunday*, p. 347. R. P. Martin, *Colossians: The Church's Lord and the Christian's Liberty* (London: Paternoster, 1972), pp. 79–80, seems to take the same position.

[91]In particular, he fails to explain how in Paul's view such δόγματα could add to the effect of the χειρόγραφον if Paul thought such regulations were unnecessary. We shall return to his exegesis of this passage below (pp. 282–83, and the notes appended there).

[92]Often (e.g., by W. Hendriksen, *Ephesians* [Grand Rapids: Baker, 1967], *ad loc.*) described as "parallel" to the one that has just been examined in Colossians. But this is false; the only parallel is the word δόγμασιν, which, as we shall see, bears a very different meaning here.

[93]An excellent summary of the problems and the debate will be found in M. Barth *Ephesians* (New York: Doubleday, 1964), 1. *ad loc.* and pp. 282–91.

[94]Barth, *Ephesians*, 1.287. Barth, who does not himself adopt this interpretation, lists among its supporters Origen, Jerome, "the medieval *(sic)* tradition," Calvin, Burton, Bousset and Bornkamm. We may add Hendriksen.

[95]And we may note with S. Lyonnet "Paul's Gospel of Freedom," in M. J. Taylor, ed., *A Companion to Paul* (New York: Paulist, 1975), p. 91, that it is precisely what we would call the *moral* law that is the center of Paul's discussion.

[96]Nor, as we have seen, was there any "problem" seen by Paul in the keeping of the ritual law; it would have been easy enough (if the interpretation above were valid) to break down the "wall of partition" by obliging Gentiles to keep it.

[97]Bacchiocchi, *From Sabbath to Sunday*, p. 348.

[98]E.g., B. S. Easton, *The Pastoral Epistles* (London: SCM, 1948), p. 113.

[99]So NEB: ". . . provided we treat it as law." Cf. J. N. D. Kelly, *The Pastoral Epistles* (London: Black, 1963), p. 48: "It is not the gospel but remains a species of law." Cf. similarly W. Lock, A

Critical and Exegetical Commentary on the Pastoral Epistles (Edinburgh: T. & T. Clark, 1924), *ad loc.*

[100]As *νομίμως* ("lawfully," RSV) would more naturally be understood. So C. K. Barrett, *The Pastoral Epistles* (Oxford: Clarendon, 1963), *ad loc.*

[101]This may still be so even if a common saying is being taken up and modified.

[102]M. Dibelius and H. Conzelmann, *The Pastoral Epistles* (Philadelphia: Fortress, 1972), p. 22 (*ad* 1 Tim. 1:8).

[103]That the passage is talking about "Scripture," as we understand the word, is clear. For *ἱερὰ γράμματα* as a technical term for "holy Scripture" see Dibelius/Conzelmann, *Pastoral Epistles, ad loc.* *γραφή* is also used of "Scripture" in the New Testament, but that is not to say that it also had become a technical term. However, *γραφὴ θεόπνευστος* can only refer to the Old Testament Scriptures.

[104]For *νόμος κεῖσθαι* as a legal technical term, see BAG *s.v.*, 2b. The wordplay on *νόμος* (cf. also the use of *νομίμως*) is not un-Pauline; cf. our discussion above, and especially Romans 7.

[105]Romans 15:4; cf. 1 Corinthians 10:11.

[106]To say this is not to revert to that division of the law into ethical and cultic parts that was rejected earlier, but simply to recall that it is there that the "weakness of the flesh" is manifested.

[107]Romans 7:13.

[108]As R. Bultmann saw (*Theology of the New Testament* [London: SCM, 1952], 1.262–63), though his terminology is not always clear and he did not develop this understanding with respect to a *Christian's* attitude to the law. More recently both Longenecker (*Paul*, p. 78, note 63) and Sanders (*Paul*, pp. 75, 236) have attempted to clarify the terminological problem, Longenecker using the term "reacting nomism" and Sanders employing "covenantal nomism," to express the idea that lawkeeping was not seen as *establishing* a relationship with God, but *deriving from* such a relationship. Sanders acknowledges that for Paul even this idea of covenantal nomism is probably inadequate: *Paul*, pp. 513–14.

[109]So e.g., R. T. Beckwith and W. Stott, *This is the Day* (London: Marshall, Morgan and Scott, 1978), p. 45, "The sabbath commandment is included in the Decalogue *and consequently has permanent validity*" (italics mine). Included here are all those who see only the ceremonial law as abolished in Christ.

[110]The fifth, in Ephesians 6:1–3.

[111]E. B. Allo, *Première Epître aux Corinthiens* (Paris: J. Gabalda, 1956), p. 172.

[112]H.-D. Wendland, *Die Briefe an die Korinther* (Göttingen: Vandenhoeck und Ruprecht, 1962), p. 54.

[113]C. K. Barrett, *A Commentary on the First Epistle to the Corinthians* (London: Black, 1971), p. 169.

[114]Cf. F. E. Vokes, "The Ten Commandments in the New Testament and First Century Judaism," *SE* 5 (ed. F. Cross: 1968): 146–54: "It seems significant that the Decalogue by itself is not picked out as a whole as the summary or crown of the divine law" (p. 151). R. M. Grant, "The Decalogue in Early Christianity," *HTR* 40 (1947):1–17, fails to deal with this point.

[115]Taking the participle (with Allo) as middle; to take it as passive would not alter the argument.

[116]Galatians 4:8–11; cf. Colossians 2:16 and Romans 14:5. This is all the more significant if with J.W. Drane we assume that the Corinthians knew the contents of Galatians: *Paul*, p. 61.

[117]Barrett, *First Corinthians*, p. 169.

[118]G. Schrenk (TDNT 2.552 n.27) and F. Fisher, *Commentary on 1 and 2 Corinthians* (Waco: Word, 1975), *ad loc.* argue from the anarthrous *ἐντολῶν* that Paul had in mind not specific, written, commands, but "anything which had the nature or quality of a commandment of God" (Fisher, *loc cit*). The onus of proof is certainly upon those who wish to see a reference to the Decalogue here, to show at the very least how that fits into the context (a factor ignored by the commentators) and how it coheres with Paul's attitude to the Sabbath (see the evidence below).

[119]So G. Stockhardt, *Commentary on St. Paul's Letter to the Ephesians* (St. Louis: Concordia,

1952), *ad loc.*, uses it as an argument for infant baptism, and W. Hendriksen, *Ephesians, ad loc.*, as an argument against Sunday Schools!

[120]On *Haustafeln*, instruction lists for households, see E. G. Selwyn, *The First Epistle of St. Peter* (London: Macmillan, 1947), pp. 419–39; and J. P. Sampley, *'And The Two Shall Become One Flesh'* (Cambridge: University Press, 1971), pp. 17–25.

[121]Sampley, *One Flesh*, pp. 148–63.

[122]There is no compelling reason to suppose that the reference is to *little* children. The problem of disunity is likely only to have arisen with older children, perhaps already "of age" and feeling therefore that they have a right to be free from parental restraint. Paul is not talking about the Christian home (as is argued by F. Foulkes, *Ephesians* [London: Inter-Varsity Press, 1963], *ad loc.*), but about the Christian *church*.

[123]It is omitted by B D*G *it* d, e, f, g Marcion Cl Tert, perhaps under the influence of the parallel at Colossians 3:20.

[124]Since for Paul such a phrase would most naturally mean "those who brought you to faith" (cf. Gal. 4:19; 1 Cor. 4:14–15; 1 Tim. 1:2; 2 Tim. 1:2; Titus 1:4; and Philemon 10); a most inappropriate element for the *Haustafel*.

[125]Paul must have been fully aware of the tensions of the situation where the parents are hostile to the child's faith. In the petrine *Haustafel* the relationships are explicitly extended to include non-Christians (1 Peter 2:13–14; 2:18; 3:1); though here the parent-child relationship is not mentioned.

[126]Commentators are in general agreement that verse 2 is not simply added as an explanation of *why* it is "right" (δίκαιον) but stands as a separate reinforcement of Paul's exhortation. However, this should not be overemphasized: see Abbott, *Ephesians, ad loc.*

[127]Cf. discussion above.

[128]For a full review of the history of interpretation, see B. Schneider, "The Meaning of St. Paul's Antithesis 'The Letter and the Spirit,' " CBQ 15 (1953): 163–207. We may add W. Schrage, *Die konkreten Einzelgebote in der paulinischen Paränese* (Gütersloh: Gütersloher Verlaghaus [Gerd Mohn], 1961), pp. 76–77.

[129]Schneider, "Meaning," pp. 193–207.

[130]Ibid., p. 185.

[131]The first table does not, after all, lend itself to being summarized in the commandment to love one's neighbor. And yet the love commandment even here is regarded as all-embracing: cf. Romans 13:19, ". . . and whatever other commandment there may be."

[132]See below, pp. 180–84.

[133]C. H. Dodd, "ΕΝΝΟΜΟΣ ΧΡΙΣΤΟΥ" in J. N. Sevenster and W. C. Van Unnik, ed., *Studia Paulina* (Haarlem: De Erven F. Bohn, 1953), pp. 96–110.

[134]Ibid., p. 99.

[135]On this see D. A. Carson, chapter 4 in this volume.

[136]As 1 Corinthians 11:23–26 demonstrates.

[137]For a list of passages that appear to depend on dominical sayings, see W. D. Davies, *Paul and Rabbinic Judaism* (London: SPCK, 1970), pp. 138–40.

[138]So also E. P. Sanders, *Paul*, pp. 513–14.

[139]D. L. Dungan, *The Sayings of Jesus in the Churches of Paul* (Oxford: Blackwell, 1971), p. 25, refers to Paul's "dialectic" as *"comprehensive enough to enable him freely to set aside a direct command of the Lord"* (italics in the original). One need not concur with the whole of Dungan's thesis to appreciate that Paul does not simply apply the Jesus-traditions as others might have applied the law.

[140]C. F. D. Moule, *An Idiom-Book of New Testament Greek* (Cambridge: University Press, 1959), p. 42; but cf. C. K. Barrett, *First Corinthians*, p. 214, who translates "God's lawless one" . . . "Christ's law-abiding one."

[141]See Barrett, ibid., and the whole context of 1 Corinthians 8–10.

[142]On this see J. G. Strelan, "Burden-Bearing and the Law of Christ: A Re-examination of Galatians 6:2," *JBL* 94 (1975): 266–76.

[143]As Dodd himself saw: he interprets Galatians 6:2 in the light of his understanding of the phrase ἔννομος χριστοῦ (p. 108), but does not use this verse to support that understanding of the phrase. On this whole question, see also the essay by Brian Wintle, "Paul's Conception of the Law of Christ and Its Relation to the Law of Moses," *Reformed Theological Review* 38 (1979): 42–50.

[144]If indeed that is what he is doing in these passages; I am aware of the various alternative interpretations that have been offered, and shall discuss the relevant ones below.

[145]For example, J. B. Lightfoot, *The Epistle of St. Paul to the Galatians* (Grand Rapids: Zondervan, repr, 1957), *ad loc.*; H. N. Ridderbos, *The Epistle of Paul to the Churches of Galatia* (Grand Rapids: Eerdmans, 1953), *ad loc.*; Beckwith and Stott, *This is the Day*, pp. 27, 30. On the other hand, Bachiocchi, *From Sabbath to Sunday*, p. 366, interprets Colossians 2:16 in the light of Galatians 4:10 and suggests that "the Colossians' 'sabbaths' are 'week-days'."

[146]J. Bligh, *Galatians: A Discussion of St Paul's Epistle* (London: St. Paul Publications, 1970), p. 373.

[147]R. Jewett, "The Agitators and the Galatian Congregation," *NTS* 17 (1970–71): 198–212. On Jewett's thesis see chapter 5 in this volume, n. 196.

[148]Ibid., p. 208.

[149]If it be false, then the traditional case is considerably weakened, since Paul's words must refer also, *mutatis mutandis*, to any Christian festival. Bligh tries, to my mind unsuccessfully, to grapple with this problem; other commentators fail even to attempt to overcome it.

[150]Above, pages 260–61 and 267–68.

[151]*Römerbrief*, p. 407.

[152]Γάρ is read by ℵ * A C^2 P 104 326 2127 *it* $^{at, d, dem, e, f, g, x, z}$ *vg* cop bo Ambrosiaster Basil John-Damascus. The difficulty of understanding it in the context of the traditional interpretation amply accounts for its omission in other MSS.

[153]See BAG, *s.v.* γάρ, 4.

[154]So for example Barrett, *Romans*, and Black, *Romans*, *ad loc.* John Murray, *The Epistle to the Romans* (Grand Rapids: Eerdmans, 1959, 1965), *ad loc.*, also thinks in terms of Jewish festivals, though for dogmatic reasons he excludes the Sabbath. A. Schlatter, *Gottes Gerechtigkeit* (Stuttgart: Calver, 1935) suggests that the debate was occasioned by a transfer from Jewish festivals (notably the Sabbath) to the specifically Christian Sunday.

[155]So for example F. J. Leenhardt, *The Epistle to the Romans* (London: Lutterworth, 1961), *ad loc.*, and Bacchiocchi, *From Sabbath to Sunday*, pp. 364–65.

[156]It is also difficult to credit that ὃς δὲ κρίνει πᾶσαν ἡμέραν (14:5) means "another chooses *every* day as a fast day," we would have to distort the passage to make it mean ". . . *any* day . . . ."

[157]Unless, with O Michel, *Römerbrief*, *ad. loc.*, we assume a deliberate chiasmus here.

[158]J. Murray is the only commentator known to me who discusses this question, and his answer is no, though in my opinion on inadequate grounds.

[159]On the link between astrology and Jewish festivals, at least in the minds of many, see E. Lohse, σάββατον TDNT 7.29, and Bacchiocchi, *From Sabbath to Sunday*, pp. 361–64.

[160]1 Corinthians 9:19–20 can hardly be interpreted as indicating anything else, and the picture of Paul in the Acts, as one who can claim never to have gainsaid the law (e.g., 21:26; 23:6; 25:8, 10; 26:5; 28:17. On these passages see chapter 5 in this volume, esp. n. 199) is inherently probable.

[161]Writers in the reformed tradition, such as J. Murray, refuse to accept this possibility; but their grounds for doing so do not seem to be justified. The arguments that Murray puts forward "which Scripture as a whole provides" (*Romans*, 2.257, in an appendix on "Romans 14:5 and the Weekly Sabbath") have already been answered elsewhere in this volume.

[162]By M. D. Hooker: "Were there false teachers in Colossae?" B. Lindars and S. S. Smalley, ed. *Christ and Spirit in the New Testament* (Cambridge; University Press, 1973), pp. 315–31.

[163]The acts, not the foodstuffs and liquids themselves, are in view: see E. Lohse, *Colossians*, p. 115 n.4.

[164]Cf. Hendriksen, *Colossians*, *ad loc.*: the false teachers "also tried to impose *restrictions* in connection with festivals" (my italics). Presumable the ascetic, whether Jewish or gnostic, regarded such festivals as improper or inappropriate, except perhaps as fast days. On the Sabbath as fast and festival, see Bacchiocchi, *From Sabbath to Sunday*, pp. 186–98.

[165]This fact makes it hard to believe that Paul believed in any sort of transfer from the seventh day to the first (or eighth).

[166]Bacchiocchi, in his stress on the fact that a shadow may retain its validity even in the presence of the reality itself, sacrifices consistency to his desire to see the Sabbath as having abiding significance. Of the Passover and other annual festivals he will only allow that they "have a message for Christians" (*From Sabbath to Sunday*, p. 357), while the New Moon is not mentioned at all. He fails to explain why the Sabbath alone of these shadows should abide in the era of the new covenant.

[167]Cf. above, p. 176. It is true, of course, that "the law" plays no part in the Colossian epistle, and for this reason Bacchiocchi contends that it is not Jewish festivals but rather gnostic (or other) perversions of them which are causing the problems (*From Sabbath to Sunday*, p. 355). As Bacchiocchi points out, "A precept is not nullified by condemnation of its abuse" (ibid.). But "condemnation" is precisely what we do not find here, as even Bacchiocchi himself acknowledges.

[168]See Bacchiocchi, ibid., pp. 356–58.

[169]The material is most conveniently accessible in TDNT 7.*s.v.* *σκιά*.

[170]The term is Bacchiocchi's *From Sabbath to Sunday*, p. 359.

[171]This is assuming that the church was observing the festivals, and the opponents wished to restrict this observation in some way. But the case is not materially affected on other understandings of the situation: if the opponents wished to impose the festivals, Paul's mild "let no one judge" suggests only that the church's present practice was acceptable, not that it was the only practice Paul would countenance.

[172]In the case of Romans, if we are correct, this has nothing to do with the observance of festivals at all, except that Paul sees it as a parallel issue.

[173]Bacchiocchi, *From Sabbath to Sunday*, pp. 90–101.

[174]Ibid., p. 94.

[175]The problems surrounding the collection are manifold: a good summary will be found in C. K. Barrett, *A Commentary on the Second Epistle to the Corinthians* (London: Black, 1973), pp. 25–28. 1 Corinthians 16:2 might suggest that the funds *were* added to the church's coffers before Paul's arrival; however, it appears from 2 Corinthians 8–9 that somewhere along the line the money was not forthcoming, and Paul's instructions there suggest that the problem was not simply that the church treasurer had "frozen" the fund. That the intention was that the money should only be handed over to the church at the time of the arrival of those delegated to take it to Jerusalem remains the most reasonable suggestion.

[176]Ibid., p. 100.

[177]Ibid., pp. 100–101.

[178]Despite a disclaimer in n. 34, on p. 100.

[179]As the Gospels testify: cf. e.g., Matthew 20:1–16.

[180]Bacchiocchi, *From Sabbath to Sunday*, p. 101.

[181]Unless *κατὰ μίαν σαββάτου* means simply "*once* a week," with the day then unspecified.

[182]Cf. those like W. Rordorf, *Sunday* (London: SCM, 1968), pp. 294–304, who argue for the "hour of worship," rather than the "day of rest," as being the essence of the Christian Sunday.

[183]E.g., J. Murray (see note 161, above); R. T. Beckwith in Beckwith and Stott, *This Is the Day*, pp. 27–29, 43–47); W. Stott (ibid., pp. 140–41). On the historical absurdity that *both* Sabbath *and* Sunday were originally observed as Sabbath rest days, see chapter 5 of this volume.

7

SABBATH, REST, AND ESCHATOLOGY IN THE NEW TESTAMENT

A.T. LINCOLN

Andrew T. Lincoln taught New Testament for five years at Gordon-Conwell Theological Seminary and is now at St. John's College in Nottingham.

The Issues

When the significance of the Christian Sunday is under consideration, many problems arise from the attempt to think of this day in terms of rest and thereby relate it to the Old Testament Sabbath. In the history of the church many Christians have virtually equated the Lord's Day with the Sabbath and have therefore based their observance of the day on an application of the regulations of the fourth commandment to the first day of the week.

This chapter attempts to show that the way in which the New Testament writers deal with the relation of the Sabbath to rest and eschatology provides important insights on the subject. There are a number of specific questions that are relevant for such an investigation. What is the significance of the sabbatical structuring of time in Jewish eschatology in the light of Christ's coming into history? Do the New Testament writers have a "theology of rest"? How do they understand the rest presented in the Old Testament concept of the Sabbath? How does Christ's fulfillment of the Sabbath affect the concept of the rest associated with that day? Is there any warrant in the New Testament for applying the literal physical rest of the Old Testament Sabbath to the Lord's Day?

The Sabbatical Structure of Time in the Old Testament and Jewish Literature

The early Christians were heirs of a number of traditions regarding the divine structuring of time. From the Old Testament itself they inherited the concept that in the weekly cycle God had stamped a seven-day pattern on history. The Sabbath as a Mosaic institution appointed for Israel gave clear indication of this. Not only so, but in the Old Testament one of the theological foundations for Sabbath observance was the analogy with God's rest at creation. In fact the Genesis description of God's activity at creation is cast in the conceptual mode of a week that culminates in God's resting on the seventh day. By means of this "massive and daring anthropomorphism"[1] humanity's pattern can now be seen as reflecting that of its Creator. The Genesis account does not institute the weekly Sabbath, yet as von Rad correctly points out, "what is spoken of is much more than something affecting only God himself. . . . If God blessed this rest, then it is to hand as a kind of third thing between him and the world."[2] It is not yet apparent to humanity, but the way has been prepared for it to share in this exalted good. Thus the intention of the divine rest as regards humanity corresponds to that of the role of the tree of life in Genesis 2 and 3, which was meant to provide confirmation in life. With regard to His work of creation, God's rest was final and grounded in the completion and perfection of that work; with regard to humanity, this rest pointed forward to a future state that it was to share. When this prospect was shattered by sin, God began to work to restore it. As part of that work in history the Sabbath was appointed for Israel as a day of rest and a sign of participation in God's primal rest.

Through the Genesis account the seven-day pattern took on cosmic overtones. The Sabbath could be seen as the goal of human history and the framework of the movement from creation to consummation. According to the Book of Jubilees (second century B.C.), long before the Sabbath was given to Israel by Moses it was celebrated in the heavenly world, for it was seen as an expression of the divine ordering of the world and of time (cf. Jub. 2:17ff., 30ff.). The concept of God hallowing the seventh day (Gen. 2:3) is interpreted by Jubilees as His sanctifying the Sabbath day to Himself (cf. 2:19). Since the Sabbath was indicative of the divine structuring of time, the seven-day schema could also be applied to the chronology of world history (cf. Jub. 1:26, 29; 50:1–5). It became a widespread view that world history would terminate in a cosmic Sabbath, and with the help of Psalm 90:4 it was shown that the preceding period in this world week could be divided into six days of one thousand years each.

In rabbinic Judaism, the age to come was often described as the "world which is entirely sabbath" or the "day which is entirely sabbath." Often this is with reference to Psalm 92—"A psalm for the world to come, for the day which will be entirely sabbath and rest in eternal life" *(Tamid* 7:4; cf. also *B.Ros.* 31*a*; *Mek. Ex.* 31:13; *Midr. Ps.* 92; *Pirke R. El.* 19; *Sed. Elij.R.* 2).[3] In *Pirke R. El.* 18 we read of the structure of history, "Seven aeons has God created, and of them all He has chosen only the seventh aeon. Six are for the coming and going (of men) and one (the seventh) is wholly sabbath and rest in eternal life." *Aboth de R. Nathan* 1 describes this Sabbath rest further by stating that Psalm 92 is a "psalm for the day which is entirely sabbath, on which there is no eating and drinking, no buying and selling, but the righteous will sit with their crowns on their heads and refresh themselves in the splendor of the Shekhina, as it says, 'they beheld God, and ate and drank' (Exod. 24:11)—like the ministering angels." (Cf. also *B.Ber.* 17*a*.).

In apocalyptic literature also the consummation rest is synonymous with the age to come. In 4 Ezra 8:52, for example, the seer is promised, "For you is opened Paradise, planted the tree of life; the future age prepared, plenteousness made ready; a city builded, a rest appointed; good works established, wisdom preconstituted." In this Sabbath of the world to come Israel will have freedom from work. There will be no labor (cf. 2 Enoch 65:9; *B.Ketub.* 111*b*), for "rest shall appear" and "the works shall of themselves speedily advance" (cf. 2 Baruch 73–74), as the saints rest in Eden (T Dan. 5:12). The weekly sabbath could be seen as pointing to this final consummation Sabbath, so that in *Vita Adae et Evae* 51:1, 2 it is said, "Man of God, mourn not for thy dead more than six days, for on the seventh day is the sign of the resurrection, and the rest of the age to come" (cf. also Apoc. Mos. 43:3). Similarly *Gen.R.* 17:5 states, "There are three antitypes: the antitype of death is sleep, the antitype of prophecy is dream, the antitype of the age to come is the sabbath" (cf. also *Gen.R.* 44:17; *B.Ber.* 57*b*).

In the development of eschatological ideas about the Sabbath the Sabbath of the end time was predominantly equated with the age to come, but this world Sabbath could also be depicted as the last period of this age. In 2 Enoch 33:2 (which some, however, hold to be a Christian interpolation), the seventh period of one thousand years that follows six thousand years of world history will be one great Sabbath so that there is a pause before the eighth day, which inaugurates the age to come as a completely new creation. Also in *B.Sanh.* 97*a*, it is said that the world will last six thousand years comprised of two thousand years without the Torah, two thousand years with the Torah, and two thousand years of Messianic time; the world will then be destroyed for one thousand years (cf. also *B.Ros.* 31*a*; *Sed. Elij.R.* 2). This Sabbath is a time that recalls the period at the beginning of history when the earth lay void and waste in primeval silence (cf. 4 Ezra 7:27–31 where a seven-day chaos, the primeval silence, follows a four-hundred year Messianic period and precedes the new age). It will be a time when the world will lie fallow for one thousand years, and in *B. Sanh.* 97a and *Sed. Elij. R.* 2 this is linked with the Sabbath year in which the land was to lie fallow (cf. Exod. 23:10–11; Lev. 25:1ff.).

The concept of the Sabbath as an interim period before the new age is employed in a further variation as a reference to the state or place of the departed souls of the righteous. The age to come as the day that is entirely Sabbath could be transferred in its reference to the rest of souls in the heavenly world between death and resurrection (cf. *B.Ber.* 17*a*).[4]

The Christian Weekly Cycle

In what way were such traditions about the division of time taken up or modified by the early Christians? As regards the weekly cycle, it is most significant that here the sabbatical structure was maintained, so that as E. Lohse comments, "Although the Christian Church freed itself from the Sabbath it adopted the Jewish week and kept almost unchanged the Jewish system of enumeration, counting the days up to the sabbath and giving special prominence only to the Lord's Day."[5] The oldest designation for the Lord's Day is "the first day of the week" (ἡ μία τοῦ σαββάτου/τῶν σαββάτων, Mark 16:2; John 20:1, 19; Acts 20:7; 1 Cor. 16:2). This designation presupposed the weekly division of time based on the Old Testament Sabbath and signifies "the day which is number one in the sequence of days determined by the Sabbath."[6] Thus despite the radical discontinuity involved in the church's beginning to assemble on the first day to commemorate their fellowship with the risen Lord, there is also a definite continuity with the Old Testament people of God in that this was done on a weekly and not a monthly or yearly basis. In this the early church acknowledged the sabbatical sequence of time.

Eschatological Rest in New Testament Thought

As regards the eschatological Sabbath rest, the issue is more complex. It is to this matter that we now turn as we ask how traditions about the consummation rest were used to express the significance of Christ's breaking into history to fulfill God's purposes for humanity.

The Gospels

The Evangelists give indications of the change in eschatological perspective that this event produced and there is some evidence that they associated the fulfillment of God's promises that took place in Christ with the concept of Sabbath and of rest. We shall look briefly at three passages.[7]

In the incident in *Luke 4:16–21*, which Luke chooses to open his account of Jesus' ministry and to set out the program for that ministry in terms of salvation, Jesus proclaims in the synagogue at Nazareth that Isaiah 61:1–2 is being fulfilled before the eyes of that congregation. The Isaiah passage is in the first person and seems to refer to Isaiah's own mission, but it is also possible to identify the speaker with the Servant of Yahweh who will bring future salvation. As cited in Luke, the passage includes proclaiming release to the captives and the acceptable year of the Lord. The language employed in these phrases is that used of the year of jubilee (cf. Lev. 25:10–11; Jer. 34:8–10; Ezek. 46:17), the year of the Lord's favor having reference to such a jubilee year.[8] The fiftieth year, which came after every seven Sabbath years, was regarded as an intensified Sabbath year when the release of all citizens and the restitution of their patrimony were required. The Servant's proclamation is compared with the crying of the herald announcing this release to those in slavery because of debt. Now in Luke the salvation of the end time depicted in terms of the Sabbath year of jubilee is seen to be inaugurated in the coming of Jesus; "Today this Scripture has been fulfilled in your hearing" (Luke 4:21). Both κηρύσσειν ("to proclaim") and εὐαγγελίζεσθαι ("to preach good news") are used of Jesus' mission here. His herald's cry, like the trumpet of the priest in the Old Testament, announces the good news of jubilee. This mission is an eschatological event through which all in principle is fulfilled and where it only remains for this to work itself out. The great year of jubilee, the intensified Sabbath year of restoration and liberation, an institution that had never really functioned as intended, now becomes a reality for all those who find salvation (in the fullest sense of the word) in Jesus the Messiah.

Jesus' summons to "rest" (ἀνάπαυσις) in Matthew 11:28–30 immediately precedes the record of His rebuke of the Pharisees for their condemnation of the disciples for plucking and eating ears of corn on the Sabbath (12:1–8) and of His Sabbath healing of a man with a withered hand (12:9–14). The placing of the saying about rest with the Sabbath conflicts in Matthew seems to be more than accidental. True, the primary point of the reference to the rest is to contrast Jesus with the religion of the law; Jesus' hearers would be familiar with the yoke of the law and the yoke of wisdom (Sir. 51:17, 26), but now He is saying, "Take *my* yoke upon you." Matthew, in distinction from Q where Jesus remains an envoy of Wisdom, boldly identifies Jesus with Wisdom. "The yoke of the true Torah, of Wisdom, is set over against that if Pharisaic Torah—as the two sabbath pericopes show."[9] Jeremiah had told the people that they would find rest for their souls by learning again obedience to the law (Jer. 6:16), but now Jesus puts Himself in place of the law and claims that those who labor and are heavy laden, who find the law as expounded by the Pharisees and scribes too difficult to keep (cf. Matt. 23:4), will find that same rest in learning of Him.

These two themes of law and rest continue into the next two pericopes.[10] In both 12:2 and 12:10 the question is raised, "What is lawful on the Sabbath?" The Pharisees made even the commandment to rest a burden too heavy to bear and pressed their burdensome interpretation of ceasing from all work on the Sabbath. But Jesus is shown as the teacher of a law that is easy; He demonstrates a different attitude to the Sabbath. As Lord of the Sabbath (12:8) He is its true interpreter in terms of mercy rather than legalism (12:7). In this connection the rest that Jesus gives can be seen to have wider connotations.[11] As the teacher of the new law about the Sabbath He gives the fulfillment of that rest of which the Sabbath speaks. As some commentators point out, the verb ἀναπαύειν ("to rest") and its cognate noun can also be used in the eschatological context of the rest of the righteous dead (cf. Dan. 12:13; Sir. 22:11; 38:23; Rev. 6:11; 14:13),[12] but the future tense here does not indicate that the rest will be in the future world that the weekly Sabbath anticipated, but rather that this rest will be immediately found by those who come to Jesus.

The incident and accompanying discourse recorded in *John 5:1–30* possibly shed still more light on the eschatological significance of the relationship between Jesus and the Sabbath. Here the Sabbath conflict is intensified by Jesus' healing on the Sabbath day when there was no urgent need and by his commanding the man who was healed to carry his bed. In John's account this initiative on the part of Jesus becomes in fact a vehicle for His claim to be equal with God (vv. 17, 18). There is no rabbinic type of debate or defense as in the Synoptics, but Jesus' answer to the implicit charge that He works on the Sabbath is a plain acknowledgment that this is so, and that in this, as in all He does, He is only imitating His Father (cf. also v. 19). The cessation of labor involved in the fourth commandment yields to the ceaseless activity of Jesus in accomplishing salvation. This work tolerates no interruption, even by the Sabbath. "My Father is working until now and I am working" (v. 17, cf. 9:4).

This statement of verse 17 must be seen in the context of the relation of God to the Sabbath rest of creation[13] and to the Sabbath law. If God rested after the creation, how can He be said to be working? If He does work, does He have to break off His activity on the day of rest? Judaism had already rejected the crudely anthropomorphic view of God's rest that conceived of it as a state of inactivity since the creation. This was not only so in Hellenistic Judaism (cf. Philo, *de Cher.* 86–90; *Leg. All.* 1:5–6) but also in rabbinic Judaism. It was taught that God was active as sustainer, life-giver and judge. He rested from His work on the world but not from His work with humanity (cf. *Gen.R.* 11; *B.Taan.* 2*a*). He was not bound by the Sabbath, for if a person on the Sabbath may carry things around a private house, how much more may God work on the Sabbath since the whole world is His private domain (cf. *Exod.R.* 30).[14] It is in terms of precisely the activities the Jews believed to be God's work that Jesus' work is explicated in verses 19–30. Like God, He too gives life and judges, and this is set out in terms of both realized (vv. 19–25) and future eschatology (vv. 26–30). Jesus' work then involves the accomplishment of the salvation of the end time in both its positive and negative aspects. This fits the concept of work as it is used elsewhere in John with reference to Christ. It is an important concept in the fourth Gospel and can denote Jesus' miracles (cf. 5:36; 7:3, 21; 9:3–4; 10:25, 32, 37–38; 14:10f.; 15:24), be closely associated with and parallel His words (cf. 14:10; 15:22–24) and more widely it can stand for His ministry as a whole (cf. 4:34; 9:3, which has more than miracles in view; 17:4). As Morris comments, "'Works,' for him (John) is not a colorless term, but a way of linking the miracles with the non-miraculous. It shows that . . . the miracles and the rest of Jesus' life alike represent the outworking of a single consistent divine purpose."[15] As we have seen, Jesus' working here in 5:17 has this broad reference and as elsewhere is inseparably bound up with the Father's work (cf. also 4:34; 5:20; 9:3; 10:32; 14:10).[16]

Cullmann has drawn attention to the significance of the words ἕως ἄρτι ("until now") in this saying.[17] Though his own work goes farther than the evidence warrants by linking the passage with the Lord's Day of Revelation 1:10, he has opened up a legitimate line of interpretation. ἕως ἄρτι is used rather than a term denoting "continually" or "always."[18] As Bultmann says, "ἕως ἄρτι= 'till now,' in the first place indicates the *terminus ad quem*, but it can be used in a less precise way = 'still' (1 Jn. 2:9; 1 Cor. 4:13; 8:7; 15:6), always assuming though, that the behavior or events in question can, will or ought to come to an end."[19] Schnackenburg holds that the phrase is simply to be taken straightforwardly as meaning that God is working up until the present moment in which the man is being healed,[20] yet in the light of the place given throughout the gospel to the significance of time in connection with the work and mission of Jesus, there are weighty considerations that justify seeing more to the emphasis given to ἕως ἄρτι in this verse.

Jesus' work involves carrying out God's salvation, and John takes very seriously the course of this work in time. As the history of salvation works itself out in Christ's earthly life it is following a divine timetable. This is clear in the discussion in John 7:1ff., where the "time" of Jesus is mentioned (καιρός, cf. vv. 6, 8). There is the well-known feature of the importance of the term "hour" (ὥρα) as it denotes Jesus' mission culminating in His death and exaltation (cf. 2:4; 4:21, 23; 5:25, 28–29; 7:30; 8:20; 12:23, 27; 13:1; 16:25; 17:1). In a similar vein are the sayings about working in the day before the night comes (cf. 9:4; 11:9). Striking too is the use of τελειοῦν ("finish") in connection with the work in 4:34 and 17:4, "I have finished the work"; and of τελεῖν in 19:28, 30, "It is finished." From this perspective an expression of time together with the concept of Jesus' work in 5:17 should not be glossed over.

As we noted above ἕως ἄρτι implies the end of an activity. God is working until now but there will be a time when that work comes to an end and He can no longer be said to be at work in the same way. This applies also to the work of Jesus and in this way the verse makes the same point as 9:4: "We must do the works of him who sent me, while it is day; night comes when no one can work." The time will come when both God and Jesus will cease from their work of salvation. Only then will God rest and the divine Sabbath take place.[21] For John that time is fulfilled in the death and resurrection of Christ. These events are regarded as the goal of the work on earth. They accomplish the salvation that inaugurates God's consummation rest, and therefore can be described as "the point of departure for the 'perfect sabbath' of the new aeon."[22]

John 5:17 then presupposes an eschatological interpretation of Genesis 2:2–3, similar to that found in Hebrews 4. As regards the work of creation, God's rest was final, but as that rest was meant for humanity to enjoy, when it was disturbed by sin, God worked in history to accomplish His original purpose. The primal rest looks forward to the consummation rest. We have already seen that in *Vita Adae et Evae* 51:1, 2 the Sabbath was a sign of the resurrection and the rest of the age to come. In John the resurrection takes place in Christ and thereby the rest of the age to come is inaugurated so that what was signified in the Sabbath is fulfilled in Christ.[23] This interpretation certainly fits the treatment of the law in general in the fourth Gospel where the emphasis is on discontinuity, on the newness of what God has done in Christ as over against the old dispensation. It is commonplace for writers on John to speak of his "replacement" motif: Jesus has replaced the law, its institutions, and its symbols.[24]

This is as far as John takes us. To believe with Cullmann[25] and Jewett[26] that John has the relation between the Jewish Sabbath and the Christian Sunday specifically in view is to move beyond any exegetical evidence. However, what we have found in John can provide data for our own theological reflection on this issue. In that Christ's resurrection fulfills the rest signified by the Old Testament Sabbath, a link can be seen between the seventh day and the first day on which Christians commemorated the Resurrection. The link says nothing about a "Christian day of rest," which Jewett assumes as part of the continuity.[27] If anything, the thrust of the passage points in the other direction. The Resurrection is the accomplishment of the work of salvation that outranks and replaces the literal Sabbath. Its celebration on the first day is therefore in terms of salvation rather than of the literal rest that was a sign of the finished work of God in Christ. In other words, in the fulfillment, though the consummation of that fulfillment is still outstanding, the concept of literal rest has been transformed.

Hebrews

The passage that contributes most to our investigation is *Hebrews 3:7–4:13* where the writer's discussion of rest is linked with God's seventh-day rest at the creation and with the term σαββατισμός ("a Sabbath rest"). Since appeal has been made to this passage by those with divergent viewpoints on the Sabbath, and each has found in it support for a particular position, it merits detailed consideration. This detail is all the more necessary if we are to appreciate the transformation that the concept of rest undergoes in Hebrews. The passage must of course be allowed to speak from its own context before it is drawn into the wider context of our investigation.

The writer of Hebrews describes his own letter as a "word of exhortation" (13:22). He views the situation of the community he addresses from an eschatological perspective.[28] The church is living in a time of fulfillment inaugurated by Christ "at the end of these days" (1:2), "at the end of the ages" (9:26); but this is yet to be consummated by His return (9:28) and His complete rule in the world to come (2:5ff). In the meantime believers already experience the age to come (6:4f.), yet "their life is one of hope and struggle, in which they are sustained by the fact that that for which they strive has already been achieved for them, and that they have already begun to enjoy it."[29] Hebrews insists on both sides of this situation of tension without toning down either, so that, for example, in 2:5–3:6 the predominant mood is one of certainty because of the inseparable relationship of solidarity between Jesus and His brothers, while in our passage, which immediately follows, the emphasis is one of fear lest there be exclusion from the consummation of salvation on account of apostasy. In fact 3:6*b*, which acts as a bridge between these sections highlights both these elements. Believers are part of Christ's eschatological edifice but only *if* they hold fast their confidence and pride in their hope.

Genuine belief proves itself by perseverance. Hence the warnings against apostatizing and the call to perseverance (3:7–4:13). Hence also the fact that those who by faith already enter rest (4:3) need at the same time to be exhorted to strive to enter that rest (4:11). In his concern for his Jewish Christian readers who seemed to be slipping back to a stage they had previously left, the writer points out in the strongest terms that such slipping back could result in apostasy. The unbelief that fails to appropriate the fulfillment of Sabbath rest can lead to falling away from the living God (cf. 3:12; 4:11).

The unit comprising 3:7–4:13 is complete in itself. The theme of Christ as High Priest begun in 2:17–18 and mentioned in 3:1 is not taken up again until 4:14ff. Seen in this light the section must be considered a parenthesis, but not a complete digression, for there are clear links with the surrounding context. As we shall see, the central concept of rest with its heavenly dimension can be related to the heavenly call in which believers share (3:1) and to the one who has passed through the heavens (4:14).

The argument of the passage is not one in which the writer develops his own line of thought and then supports it by prooftexts from the Old Testament. The reader will not begin to grasp the progression of the argument unless it is seen that precisely the reverse is the case. A *midrash-pesher* method of exposition is being followed; the Old Testament citations form the major part of the argument, and words and thoughts from the citations are then repeated and the author's own remarks simply provide interpretative links and application to the situation of his readers.[30] Having noted this method of argument, we shall sketch briefly its progression before taking up some of the salient points in more detail.

The exhortation to persevere is given in the words of Psalm 95:7–11, which recalls the fact that the Israelites about to enter the promised land were refused entry to God's rest because of their rebellion (3:7–11). Since the readers of the letter live in a situation that, like that of the Psalmist, can also be called "today," they are to take care lest they too fall away from the living God because of hard and rebellious hearts. Those who heard God's voice and were rebellious were the whole wilderness generation, who refused to believe the favorable report about the promised land. Because of this unbelief and despite their subsequent repentance and attempt to enter, they were simply unable to do so (3:12–19). Similarly the good news preached to the recipients of this letter must be met with faith, for it is only those who believe who enter the rest. The promise of entering the rest remains and the rest is available to first century believers because it had always been ready since God finished His works at the creation and rested on the seventh day. Not only so, but since David in Psalm 95 used the word "today" so long after the occasion in the wilderness, this indicates that even Joshua, who led the next generation into the land, did not give them this rest but that God had appointed a future time. The rest that remains is now described as a *σαββατισμός* ("a Sabbath rest") and linked to the Genesis 2:2 citation in that those who enter this rest cease from their works on analogy with God's ceasing from His after the creation (4:1–10). In order that none of his readers should fall through disobedience as did the wilderness generation (cf. 3:17, "whose bodies fell in the wilderness"), the writer brings his final exhortation: "Let us therefore strive to enter that rest." Failure will mean that those who heard God's word as good news will discover that it is also a lethal weapon. As a result of God's oath, the wilderness generation fell by the sword (cf. Num. 14:43); these readers face something more fearful and sharper than any two-edged sword, the word of God's judgment, which will expose the intentions of their hearts (cf. 3:10, "they always go astray in their hearts") and render them defenseless before the consuming gaze of the one to whom account must be given (4:11–13).

But what does the writer to the Hebrews mean when he talks of God's rest, and what is the relationship of the New Covenant people to this rest? To answer the first question our starting point must be that of the writer—the phrase "my rest" in Psalm 95:11. The Septuagint term, which he takes up and employs eight times in this passage, is *κατάπαυσις* (cf. 3:11, 18; 4:1, 3 [twice], 5, 10, 11). In addition, note that *καταπαύειν* is used twice as intransitive (4:4, 10) and once as transitive (4:8). The writer never defines what he has in view in using the term but seems to presuppose that its significance will have been readily understandable to his readers. The common background for this understanding is the Septuagint. In all eight occurrences of *κατάπαυσις* in this passage Psalm 94:11 (LXX) provides the basis. The only other occurrence of the term in the New Testament (viz., Acts 7:49) is the quotation of Isaiah 66:1 (LXX). The more usual term for "rest" in both the New Testament and the Septuagint is *ἀνάπαυσις*. *Κατάπαυσις* does not occur in Philo, occurs only once in Josephus (*Ant.* xvii.43), but is found twice in Joseph and Asenath, where both references are dependent on the Septuagint; Joseph and Asenath 8:9 is based on Psalm 94:11 (LXX) and Joseph and Asenath 22:13 echoes Isaiah 66:1 (LXX).[31] It is thus to Septuagint usage that we should look for the background of this term rather than to gnostic sources.[32] *Κατάπαυσις* occurs eleven times in the Septuagint and can mean either a state of rest or a resting place. On four occasions (Ex. 35:2; 2 Macc. 15:1; Num. 10:35; 1 Kings 8:56) it clearly refers to the former; on six occasions (Deut. 12:9; Ps. 131:14; 1 Chron. 6:31; 2 Chron. 6:41; Isa. 66:1; Judith 9:8) it clearly refers to a "resting place." In the most significant reference for our quest, viz. Psalm 94:11, it could just possibly be either (on the word מְנוּחָה the commentators are divided).[33] The confusion seems to arise through reading into this text a more developed theology of rest. The primary meaning from the context must be a local one with reference to the land of Canaan.[34] Psalm 95 is a liturgical psalm probably used in a temple festival. Twice the call comes to enter and worship (vv. 2, 6), but then a warning and exhortation follow based on Israel's wilderness experience (vv. 7–11). With reference to this experience God's resting place is clearly the promised land, but this takes on a heightened significance in the lifesetting of the psalm. This significance arises from the fact that in the Old Testament מְנוּחָה is used both for God's resting place in the promised land (Deut. 12:9) and for the temple as His resting place (Ps. 132:8, 14 cf. also מָנוֹחַ 1 Chron. 6:16, נוּחַ 2 Chron. 6:41). Not everyone addressed in Psalm 95 may enter to worship. The person who has a hard heart may not enter God's resting place of the temple as the wilderness generation could not enter the land of Canaan.[35] All this leads to the conclusion that *κατάπαυσις* in Psalm 94:11 has local significance, indicating God's resting place with primary reference to the land of Canaan but with possible associations with the sanctuary.

Psalm 95:11 with its local significance takes its place among other such Old Testament references as one strand in the complex of ideas about rest that the Hebrews would have inherited. In Deuteronomy, since Israel was to find rest from all its enemies in the land of its inheritance (12:10; 25:19, cf. also 3:20), the land itself can be called their resting place (12:9). In addition we find that God Himself has His resting place in the land, and especially in His sanctuary at Zion. This is particularly clear in Psalm 132:7–8, 13–14; Isaiah 66:1. In other places these two motifs are combined so that the resting place of the people is also the resting place of God (Deut. 12:9, 11; 1 Chron. 23:25; 2 Chron. 6:41).[36]

The theology of rest arises from the local connotations of κατάπαυσις as God's resting place, but by the time the writer of Hebrews takes this over it has undergone further developments. The rabbinic exegesis of Psalm 95:11 not only treats God's resting place as local, but there is evidence that by the end of the first century A.D. this verse was linked with Deuteronomy 12:9 and Psalm 132:14 and given an eschatological interpretation that connected it with the future world (cf. *Tos. Sanh.* 13:10; *B.Sanh.* 110*b*; *j.Sanh.* X, 29*c*, 5; *Aboth de R. Nathan* 36). In addition some rabbis later call the new Jerusalem God's resting place (cf. *Sifre Deut.* 1; *Midr. Cant.* 7:5; *Pesik.* 20 (143*a*). In this regard Joseph and Asenath 8:9 is also significant as representing a similar tradition of interpretation, for here κατάπαυσις (Ps. 94:11 LXX) has taken on an individual eschatological connotation as the heavenly place of rest entered by the elect at death. It seems very likely that being acquainted with such a tradition the writer of Hebrews views "rest" as an eschatological resting place with associations with the heavenly promised land, the heavenly Jerusalem, and the heavenly sanctuary. This view is confirmed by the frequency of these items in Hebrews (cf. the heavenly sanctuary 6:19–20; 8:2; 9:11, 23–24; 10:19, the city that is to come, the heavenly Jerusalem 11:10, 16; 12:22; 13:14, and the heavenly promised land 11:14ff.)[37]

The eschatological significance of "my rest" goes beyond that of an apocalyptic heavenly resting place however, for the writer himself indicates that he is giving κατάπαυσις an even broader eschatological interpretation by linking Psalms 95:11 and Genesis 2:2 in 4:3, 4. The heavenly resting place awaiting the people of God is to be seen as part of God's creation rest, and for this reason it is still available, since the possession of Canaan was a type of the divine rest that has been there since the creation. As von Rad correctly states, the welding together of these two texts "is an indication of the scope of the promised rest of the New Testament. This rest is an eschatological expectation, a fulfillment of the prophecies of redemption, an entering into that rest which there has always been, from the beginning, with God. In the fulfillment of this hope the whole purpose of creation and the whole purpose of redemption are reunited. Such is the insight vouchsafed to the writer in the simple juxtaposition of these two texts."[38]

This view of Genesis 2:2 is in line with the eschatological interpretation of the seventh day that we noted at the beginning. God's rest is now seen as the consummation of His purposes for the creation, and according to the writer it was God's intention to confer such a rest on His people. The linking of κατάπαυσις in Psalm 94:11 with the divine rest at creation is facilitated by the fact that the cognate verb is used in Genesis 2:2 (LXX, καὶ κατέπαυσεν ὁ θεός, "and God rested") and that κατάπαυσις itself is used of Sabbath rest in

Exodus 35:2; 2 Maccabees 15:1. But in any case for the writer of Hebrews the two concepts are by no means entirely disparate. Precisely the opposite is true; both form part of one and the same divine purpose. After the Fall, God's original intentions for humanity's enjoyment of the promised consummation rest are now worked out through God's acts of redemption among His people. The resting place in the promised land, in Jerusalem, and in the sanctuary all point forward to the fulfillment of God's redemptive purpose. Now in Hebrews the final goal of salvation can be depicted in spatial terms. The consummation rest is pictured in terms of a heavenly resting place, the antitype of the resting place in the promised land referred to in Psalm 95:11. Again, as we have seen, this fits the pattern of the letter to the Hebrews where the salvation of the life to come is viewed in terms of heavenly localities such as the sanctuary and the city. To this extent we agree with Käsemann in viewing *κατάπαυσις* as a heavenly locality,[39] but unlike him we do not hold Gnosticism to be the background for such a concept. Hofius has convincingly refuted Käsemann's thesis and shown that the roots of this concept lie in Jewish apocalyptic literature.[40] In such works the place of rest can be either the future resting place of the blessed at the end of history (cf. 4 Ezra 7:26*b*, 32, 38, 119–125; 8:52; 1 Enoch 39:4, 5, cf. also 38:2; Test. Dan. 5:12) or the final resting place of the soul after death in the beyond (cf. 2 Enoch 8:3, cf. also 9:1; Joseph and Asenath 8:9; 22:13) or the intermediate resting place of souls until they are reunited with bodies in the resurrection (cf. 4 Ezra 7:25ff., 91; T Abr 7:16; 8:11, 15; 9:1; T Isaac 1:9–11).[41]

The conclusion that the consummation is depicted as a heavenly locality provides an appropriate lead into the question of the relationship of the readers of Hebrews to the divine rest and the time of their entry into it. We shall consider this question before returning to the topic of the divine rest in its designation as *σαββατισμός*.

While there can be no doubt that the consummation rest remains future (cf. the exhortation of 4:11), it would certainly be wrong to adopt the position of a number of commentators who hold "my rest" to be entirely future. This would not only be to ignore the evidence of this passage but to miss the structure of the writer's thought throughout the letter. In the light of this common misunderstanding it is worth stressing from a number of angles that this rest has already become a reality for those who believe. It is now that we see the significance of the fact that the rest is pictured in spatial terms in heaven. As elsewhere in apocalyptic literature and in the New Testament the concept of heaven is being employed to express the view that the eschatological benefits of salvation are already present.[42] Here in Hebrews the city to which Abraham looked forward (11:10) is still to come (13:14) and yet the readers can be told that already "you *have* come to Mount Zion and to the city of the living God, the heavenly Jerusalem . . ." (12:22). In Hebrews such spatial concepts do not stand for the eternal in the sense of that which is ideal and timeless but rather signify that the future is already present in heaven and therefore available now. The heavenly tabernacle is thought of as having been there all the time, so that the rites of the Old Testament can be considered copies and shadows; yet the ministry of Jesus in this sanctuary has begun only in these last days, so that it has now become available for access to those who have faith.[43] These patterns can be applied to the heavenly rest. Like the city, that resting place to which Israel never fully attained is still to come and yet by faith believers already have access to it (cf. 4:3). Like the sanctuary, the rest has been there in heaven since the foundation of the world (4:3, 4) so that again the Old Testament references can be considered types or shadows of that final rest, which has become available through the work of Christ (cf. 3:14). One of the themes of Hebrews is that through Christ the heavenly realities have become accessible to believers, and the rest is one of those realities.

The present availability of the rest is further underlined when we realize what is involved in the concept of faith mentioned in 4:3: "We who have *believed* enter that rest." As Barrett correctly points out, faith in Hebrews "is not merely a waiting for the fulfillment of the promise; it means through the promise a present grasp upon invisible truth."[44] According to Hebrews 11:1 faith makes real in the present that which is future, unseen, or heavenly. This is why those who have believed can be said to enter the rest already.

The model of the church as a company of wanderers on a journey to a distant heavenly resting place reflected in the title of Käsemann's study of Hebrews, *Das wandernde Gottesvolk*, has misled too many commentators to suppose that the rest is entirely future. Whatever truth there may be to this model,[45] it does not reflect accurately the situation of the people of God as depicted in our passage. The setting which the writer has in mind for Israel in the wilderness (cf. 3:16–19) is that recorded in Numbers 14 and this passage influences his interpretation throughout.[46] In Numbers 14 the wilderness generation are not in the midst of their wanderings but stand on the verge of entry into the promised land, having arrived at the goal of their pilgrimage. It is this that provides the comparison with the New Testament people of God. Both groups stand directly before the fulfillment of God's promise. The Christian community, confronted by this direct availability of the entry to heavenly rest, and having received the heavenly call (3:1), must beware lest they too go astray through unbelief at this last moment of eschatological salvation (cf. 2:3), and hence the warnings come with such force.[47]

These general considerations all indicate that when it comes to the specific exegesis of 4:3, the present tense εἰσερχόμεθα εἰς τὴν κατάπαυσιν ("we enter that rest") is to be taken as a true present and not simply viewed as having future force. Kistemaker states, "The author does not employ the future tense, nor does he say, 'we are sure to enter.' By placing εἰσερχόμεθα emphatically first in the sentence, he wishes to affirm that God's promise has become reality in accordance with His plan and purpose."[48] Similarly Montefiore writes, "The Greek text means neither that they are certain to enter, nor that they will enter, but that they are already in the process of entering."[49]

This interpretation also does justice to the force of "today" throughout the passage. The writer can apply the "today" of Psalm 95:11 (cf. 3:7) to the present situation of his readers (3:13–15), and the next chapter indicates why. God, through the psalmist, was setting a future date for making His rest available (cf. 4:7, 8). That time has now come: "Today, when you hear his voice." The readers had now heard God's voice as it spoke through Christ in these last days (1:1, 2) and received the promise of entering the rest. "Today" brackets the period of "already" and "not yet" as regards God's rest for those who live during the period when the ages overlap. The time for entry into rest is "today," not after death or at the parousia. On this new day the rest has become a reality for those who believe but remains a promise that some may fail to achieve through disobedience, so that all are exhorted to strive to enter it. Barrett sums up the situation most judiciously. "The 'rest,' precisely because it is God's, is both present and future; men enter it, and must strive to enter it. This is paradoxical, but it is a paradox which Hebrews shares with all primitive Christian eschatology."[50]

The fulfillment of the promise of rest has been brought about through Christ. Believers enter the heavenly rest since they share in the heavenly call (3:1) with their great High Priest who has passed through the heavens (4:14). They are partakers of Christ μέτοχοι τοῦ χριστοῦ (3:14) and it is for this reason that, if they hold firm, they are also partakers of God's rest. Joshua (Greek Ἰησοῦς) did not give the people rest (4:8); his entry into the promised land can be compared to that of the high priest into the copy and shadow of the heavenly sanctuary (cf. 8:5). The fulfillment of God's promise awaited the true Jesus who has opened the way for His people into God's heavenly rest.

We are now in a position to feel the full force of the added twist the author gives to the concept of rest in 4:9, 10. In line with our conclusions so far and the argument of the passage, 4:9 is not to be taken as an entirely future reference. When the writer says, "So then, there remains a rest for the people of God," he is not beginning a new train of thought in which he would be saying that this remains in relation to our present situation. Rather he is completing the same point he has made in 4:6 and has justified with reference to David and Joshua. "There remains" (4:9) is with reference to the rest of the promised land. It is future to *that* time, the time of Joshua (4:8). It is set for a "certain day 'today'" (4:7) and "another day" (4:8), which as we have seen, begins right now. The term σαββατισμός occurs only here in the New Testament, and it seems to have been deliberately substituted for κατάπαυσις. The substitution could take place because the writer has already connected κατάπαυσις with God's rest on the seventh day and because that word was used for the Sabbath rest (Exod. 35:2; 2 Maccabees 15:1, LXX). But the use of σαββατισμός elsewhere in extant Greek literature gives an indication of its more exact shade of meaning. It is used in Plutarch, *De Superstitione* 3 (*Moralia* 166A) of Sabbath observance. There are also four occurrences in post canonical literature that are independent of Hebrews 4:9. They are Justin, *Dial c. Tryph.* 23:3; Epiphanius, *Panar. haer* 30:2:2; *Martyrium Petri et Pauli* cap. 1; *Const. Ap.* 2:36:2. In each of these places the term denotes the observance or celebration of the Sabbath.[51] This usage corresponds to the Septuagint usage of the cognate verb σαββατίζω (cf. Exod. 16:30; Lev. 23:32; 26:34f.; 2 Chron. 36:21), which also has reference to Sabbath observance. Thus the writer to the Hebrews is saying that since the time of Joshua an observance of Sabbath rest has been outstanding. What is the Sabbath rest that the New Testament people of God must observe? It is to enter God's rest (κατάπαυσις again) and thereby cease from one's own works (4:10). This is analogous to God's ceasing from His works at the creation (cf. also 4:4). As we have seen, God's rest is entered by believing (4:3). Therefore the New Covenant people of God discharge their duty of Sabbath observance, according to this writer, by exercising faith. Thereby they participate in God's gift of eschatological salvation and cease from their own works (ἀπὸ τῶν ἔργων αὐτοῦ), which here have not a physical reference but as elsewhere in the New Testament a salvation connotation, that which this writer in 6:1 (μετανοίας ἀπὸ νεκρῶν ἔργων) and 9:14 (ἀπὸ νεκρῶν ἔργων) calls dead works.[52] They cease from their own works so that God may work in them (cf. 13:21). Of course the consummation of this salvation rest that is anticipated now by faith will involve the removal of all curse on work and the enjoyment of that state of completion and harmony experienced by God after His creative work and intended by Him for humanity. This Christian Sabbath-keeping will involve the realization of everything that God had intended by His own Sabbath rest.

In the light of all we have seen of the right and complex theology of rest in Hebrews, it comes as a surprise to read the conclusion that Jewett draws from this passage. "Since the rest which we have in Christ as a present possession is also an earnest of a future hope, we too, like God's people of old, have our literal day of rest—a type and sign of that final rest." In this connection he makes reference to the assembling of believers together mentioned in 10:25.[53] This provides Jewett with his basic theological justification for Sunday as a day of rest, but it ignores the fact that this passage simply does not have such a point in view[54] and that nowhere else in the New Testament is such a conclusion drawn.

Bacchiocchi is on safer ground when he argues that since the letter is addressed to Jewish Christians, the writer assumes their observance of the Sabbath.[55] If any literal day of rest is presupposed by the passage then it would certainly be the Jewish Sabbath rather than the first day of the week. However, this argument too begs many questions. We simply do not have enough definite knowledge of the Jewish Christianity of the readers of Hebrews to base an argument on its character. Besides, the argument assumes a monolithic attitude to Sabbath observance among Jewish Christians. Those who hold that the practice of worship on the first day goes back to Palestinian Christianity would wish to dispute this. More importantly, this view flies in the face of what we know of the attitudes of the writer of Hebrews. If it is tempting to assume that the Jewish Christian readers continued to keep the Sabbath, one would also have to assume that they believed in the continuing binding nature of the law, but at the canonical level of discussion, the author himself makes clear that the new situation brings a decisive discontinuity with the old covenant and its institutions. Most striking perhaps are the arguments of 8:13 that the first covenant is obsolete in the light of the coming of the new and 7:11–19, 28 that both the law and the levitical priesthood belong to a past era of God's dealing with His people.

Above all, against both Jewett and Bacchiocchi, it has to be noted, that the fulfillment in Christ has brought about a profound transformation of the Old Testament concept of rest. This transformation is spelled out with regard to the day of literal rest when in 4:9, 10 the writer indicates what is involved in the Sabbath rest the believer is to observe.

Conclusion

It has become clear from these passages that the coming of Jesus Christ fulfills the concept of rest tied up with the Old Testament Sabbath and that because of the situation of the church between the Resurrection and the Parousia of Christ, there is an "already" and a "not yet" to that fulfillment. But it is not as if the "already" and the "not yet" balanced the scales exactly. The fact that the decisive turn of events has already occurred in Christ shows that the "already" outweighs the "not yet."[56] As should also have become clear from these passages, the "already" is of such profound epoch-making significance that in the process of fulfillment the old categories are reinterpreted and transformed.[57] Thus the true Sabbath, which has come with Christ, is not a literal, physical rest but is seen as consisting in the salvation that God has provided. The passages unfold what this Sabbath means. It includes the good news of deliverance, liberation and forgiveness brought by the mighty works and preaching of Jesus (Luke 4), release from the burden of the law (Matt. 11), the accomplishment of eschatological salvation with its giving of life (John 5), the fulfillment of the divine rest of Genesis 2:2, 3, which was intended for humanity to share (John 5 and Heb. 3, 4), and that salvation rest as a present heavenly reality entered by believing and ceasing from one's own works (Heb. 3, 4). In short the physical rest of the Old Testament Sabbath has become the salvation rest of the true Sabbath. Believers in Christ can now live in God's Sabbath that has already dawned. Jesus' working to accomplish this superseded the Old Testament Sabbath (John 5:17) and so does the doing of God's work that He now requires of people—believing in the one God has sent (John 6:28, 29). In fact the Sabbath keeping now demanded is the cessation from reliance on one's own works (Heb. 4:9, 10).

This transformation of meaning is not unique to the Sabbath rest but is similar to that which takes place in the New Testament with regard to other concepts, for instance the way in which its writers treat the theme of the Temple or the way in which Paul treats the seed of Abraham in Galatians 3 and Romans 4. This is not spiritualization in the popular sense of the word with its connotations of etherealizing concrete realities, but spiritualization in the best sense where the writer moves from earthly shadows to spiritual realities. Christ brings the spiritual reality; His work fulfills the intent of the Sabbath, and with Christ comes that for which the Sabbath existed. The reality of salvation rest supersedes the sign. The Gospel passages show that the Old Testament Sabbath and the rest associated with it can be used to describe the realities that *have* come with Christ, while Hebrews indicates in addition that they can be used to describe the heavenly realities as they *are* and as they *will* come with Christ.

In the New Testament passages discussed in this essay the evidence has indicated that the sabbatical division of time was maintained but the concept of the Sabbath was transformed. The early Christians kept the weekly cycle in that they worshipped on the first day in seven. However, the theological perspective of the passages studied would indicate that the link between this first day and the Old Testament Sabbath was seen not in terms of a day of physical rest but in terms of celebration of the true Sabbath rest of salvation brought by the Christ whom believers worshipped and with whom they had fellowship. The evidence from the New Testament writers' perspective on

Sabbath rest points to there being no warrant for applying the physical rest of the Old Testament to the New Testament Lord's Day.

Two of the more recent attempts to give New Testament support for viewing the first day as a day of rest are those of Jewett and Beckwith, who hold that because the consummation is yet to come the sign of a weekly Sabbath rest still holds.[58] We have criticized this view in passing in connection with the exegesis of the relevant passages, but here it should also be added that there is a sense in which all rest points to the consummation of rest; but there is no convincing reason from the New Testament evidence why this has to be associated with Sunday.[59] Also one cannot properly argue that, because the rest has not yet been consummated, we must therefore preserve the physical symbol of a day of rest. True, we live in a tension between the "already" and the "not yet," and one of these poles must not be allowed to obliterate the other. Yet, not everything in eschatology participates in this tension in the same way: on the one hand the work of Christ on the Cross is over and done; on the other hand, the new heaven and the new earth have not yet dawned. The question, then, is, how do the New Testament writers perceive the Sabbath to fit into this eschatological context? They increasingly perceive of it as they would the day of atonement. The true day of atonement has already dawned, and the shadow is no longer necessary. Ultimate cleansing awaits the Parousia, as does consummation of the rest; but in neither case does the New Testament encourage us to think that the shadows of these realities are still to be cherished. Further, apart from his exegesis of John 5 and Hebrews 3, 4 Jewett simply assumes the central point under discussion, namely the continuity between Sabbath and Lord's Day in terms of a literal day of rest. Beckwith bases his argument for this continuity on the notion of a creation ordinance and a doubtful exegesis of Mark 2:27 to support this. The absence of any other New Testament evidence means that both views necessitate the further conclusion that the apostles and early church did not grasp this continuity seen by later Christians.[60]

As opposed to such a view we would reiterate that the theology of the New Testament writers in relation to the Sabbath rest and the Lord's Day did not include the transference of the rest of the seventh day to rest on the first day. From the perspective of their theology perhaps the best exposition of what the injunction to rest of the fourth commandment now means for the believer remains that of the Heidelberg Catechism (Lord's Day 38), which, after mentioning the duty to participate in public worship, continues, ". . . that all the days of my life I rest from my evil works, let the Lord work in me by his Holy Spirit, and thus begin in this life the eternal Sabbath." Such a theology suggests that as Christian believers meet together on the Lord's Day, they will commemorate the true Sabbath rest Christ has brought through His death and resurrection, and under the Word of God and through mutual exhortation, they will be encouraged to continue in this rest so that their participation in its eschatological fullness will be assured.

Notes

[1]Cf. P. K. Jewett, *The Lord's Day* (Grand Rapids: Eerdmans, 1972), p. 158.

[2]*Old Testament Theology* (London: SCM, 1975), 1:148.

[3]T. Friedman, "The Sabbath: Anticipation of Redemption," *Judaism* 16 (1967): 443–452 argues that this rabbinic concept is a development of the Old Testament parallels between the primordial and the end times, and also that certain Sabbath regulations in the Halakah of the school of Shammai can only be understood on the basis of the tie between the Sabbath and the world to come as attempts to legislate that the conditions that will prevail in the world to come will also prevail on the Sabbath.

[4]For comments on this passage cf. SBK 1:890; 4:821, 839. For the general concept of rest associated with the intermediate state cf. Revelations 14:13 and P. Volz, *Die Eschatologie der jüdischen Gemeinde* (Tübingen: Mohr, 1966), pp. 257ff. Contrary to W. Rordorf's diagram and discussion of eschatological schemes (*Sunday* London; SCM, 1968], p. 50), there seems to be no evidence in Jewish literature for the world Sabbath as such being equated with the days of the Messiah and thus providing an anticipation of the consummation in the age to come. For our discussion in this second section cf. also the references in SBK 3:687; 4:821, 839, 969ff., 989ff. and P. Volz, *Die Eschatologie der jüdischen Gemeinde,* pp. 35, 69, 76, 384.

[5]*σάββατον*, TDNT, 7:32.

[6]Cf. Jewett, *The Lord's Day,* p. 75. The latter two references reflect the usage of the Gentile churches. On this cf. also E. Schürer, "Die siebentägige Woche im Gebrauche der christlichen Kirche der ersten Jahrhunderte," ZNW 6 (1905): 1–66.

[7]For the broader significance of these passages in regard to Jesus' attitude to the Sabbath, cf. D. A. Carson, Chapter 4 of this volume.

[8]Cf. H. Sheürmann, *Das Lukasevangelium* (Freiburg: Herder, 1969), 1:230; F. W. Danker, *Jesus and the New Age* (Missouri: Clayton, 1972), p. 59; R. B. Sloan, *The Favorable Year of the Lord: A Study of Jubilary Theology in the Gospel of Luke* (Austin: Schola Press, 1978).

[9]M. J. Suggs, *Wisdom, Christology and Law in Matthew's Gospel* (Cambridge, Mass.: Harvard University Press, 1970), p. 107; cf. also pp. 63–108.

[10]Cf. J. C. Fenton, *Saint Matthew* (Harmondsworth: Penguin, 1963), p. 188; D. Hill, *The Gospel of Matthew* (London: Oliphants, 1972), pp. 209–10; R. Banks, *Jesus and the Law in the Synoptic Tradition* (Cambridge: University Press, 1975), p. 113.

[11]Cf. E. C. Hoskyns, "Jesus the Messiah," in *Mysterium Christi,* ed. G. K. A. Bell and A. Deissmann (London: Longmans, Green & Co., 1930), p. 77: "The Matthean Logion . . . is itself a sabbath utterance. . . . The saying has a wider background than is provided by mere manipulation of Ecclesiasticus 51:23ff." Cf. also Rordorf, *Sunday,* p. 109; A. Schlatter, *Der Evangelist Matthäus* (Stuttgart: Calwer, 1959), 390; J. B. Bauer, "Das milde Joch und die Ruhe, Matt. 11, 28–30," TZ 17 (1961): 102. Despite S. Bacchiocchi, *From Sabbath to Sunday* (Rome: Pontifical Gregorian University Press, 1977), pp. 61–63, this sort of connection cannot be based on the assumption that the pronouncement of Matthew 11:28–30 was made on a Sabbath, which appears to depend on a literal interpretation of Matthew's loose connective *ἐν ἐκείνῳ τῷ καιρῷ* ("at that time") in 12:1, nor can a full-blown typology of redemption be read into this notion of rest on the basis of, among other texts, Matthew 27:57–60, interpreted as Christ hallowing the Sabbath by resting in the tomb.

[12]Cf. Hill, *The Gospel of Matthew,* p. 208; Fenton, *Saint Matthew,* p. 187.

[13]Bacchiocchi, *From Sabbath to Sunday,* pp. 38–48 sees no allusion to Genesis 2 here

because in contrast with his treatment of Hebrews 4, he does not take into account any eschatological significance of God's creation rest and discusses creation and redemption as two completely separate categories.

[14]Cf. Lohse, σάββατον, p. 27 n.213. Bacchiocchi, *From Sabbath to Sunday*, p. 42 considers the notion involved here to be merely that of continuous divine creation and can therefore posit that it would be impossible for John to hold together a view that God's works of creation were accomplished at a past time (John 1:3) and that they were still continuing and for him to identify God's work with Jesus' work on earth. Once it is recognized that the continuing work of God from creation was seen in terms of sustaining, life-giving and judging, then the objections brought by Bacchiocchi against our kind of interpretation fall away as artificial ones.

[15]*Commentary on the Gospel of John* (Grand Rapids: Eerdmans, 1971), p. 689 n.75.

[16]ἔργον ("work") in the LXX is used consistently of the works of God both in creation (cf. Gen. 2:2–3; Ps. 8:3; 104;24) and in the history of salvation (cf. Exod. 34:10; Ps. 44:1; 66:5), so that the use of this term in John is also a pointer to the continuity of the mission of Jesus with the work of God: cf. R. E. Brown, *The Gospel According to John* (New York: Doubleday, 1966), 1:527; Morris, *Commentary on John*, p. 691.

[17]Cf. "Sabbat und Sonntag nach dem Johannesevangelium," *In Memoriam E. Lohmeyer* (Stuttgart: 1951), pp. 127–31, ET in *Early Christian Worship* (London: SCM, 1953), pp. 88–92.

[18]Cf. R. Bultmann, *The Gospel of John* (Oxford: Blackwell, 1971), p. 245, n. 5; Morris, *Commentary on John*, p. 309, n. 43; against Lohse, σάββατον, p. 27, n. 214, who follows C. Maurer, "Steht hinter Joh. 5:17 ein Übersetzungsfehler?" *Wort und Dienst* 5 (1957): 130–40.

[19]*Gospel of John.*

[20]*Das Johannesevangelium* (Freiburg: Herder, 1971), 2:127.

[21]Cf. Cullmann, "Sabbat und Sonntag," p. 89; Bultmann, *The Gospel of John*, p. 245; Brown, *The Gospel According to John*, p. 217, who observes that a similar interpretation which makes use of John 5:17 is to be found in the Gospel of Truth; Rordorf, *Sunday*, p. 98; Jewett, *The Lord's Day*, p. 85; A. Corell, *Consummatum Est* (London: SPCK, 1958), p. 63; A. Szabo, "Sabbat und Sonntag," *Judaica* 15 (1959): 165; H. Riesenfeld, "The Sabbath and the Lord's Day in Judaism, the Preaching of Jesus and Early Christianity," *The Gospel Tradition* (Oxford: Blackwell, 1970), pp. 132–33; J. Roloff, *Das Kerygma und der irdische Jesus* (Göttingen: Vandenhoeck und Ruprecht, 1970), 82; S. Pancaro, *The Law in the Fourth Gospel* (Leiden: Brill, 1975), pp. 159–60.

[22]Cullmann, "Sabbat und Sonntag," p. 90; cf. also Corell, *Consummantum Est*, p. 63: "Since, moreover, the risen and ascended Christ lives and works within his Church, her life itself is one continuous Sabbath—a pledge and foretaste of the consummation," Pancaro, *The Law*, p. 160.

[23]In the light of this discussion it is very hard to see how R. T. Beckwith, *This Is The Day* (London: Marshall Morgan and Scott, 1978), p. 147, can claim that Cullmann's interpretation of ἕως ἄρτι ("until now") "ignores the Old Testament and Jewish background of the saying, and the relation of the saying to first century Christian thought."

[24]Cf. most recently, Pancaro, *The Law*.

[25]"Sabbat und Sonntag," p. 91.

[26]Jewett, *The Lord's Day*, pp. 86–87.

[27]*Ibid.*

[28]C. K. Barrett, "The Eschatology of the Epistle to the Hebrews," *The Background of the New Testament and its Eschatology*, ed. D. Daube and W. D. Davies (Cambridge: University Press, 1956), pp. 363–93 has convincingly shown that the eschatological is the determining element in the thought of Hebrews. Cf. also B. Klappert, *Die Eschatologie des Hebräerbriefes* (München: C. Kaiser, 1969).

[29]Barrett, "Eschatology of Hebrews," p. 365.

[30]Cf. S. Kistemaker, *The Psalm Citations in the Epistle to the Hebrews* (Amsterdam: van Soest, 1961), pp. 85–86.

[31]Cf. O. Hofius, *Katapausis* (Tübingen: Mohr, 1970), p. 29ff.

[32]Despite E. Käsemann, *Das wandernde Gottesvolk* (Göttingen: Vandenhoeck und Ruprecht, 1961), p. 44. Though ἀνάπαυσις occurs frequently in gnostic literature, possibly the only two occurrences of κατάπαυσις (Hipp. *Ref.* 6:32:8 and 8:14:1) are gnostic exegeses of Scripture. For the use of ἀνάπαυσις in gnostic texts, cf. R. M. Grant and D. N. Freedman, *The Secret Sayings of Jesus* (London: Collins, 1960), pp. 115, 152, 173; K. Grobel, *The Gospel of Truth* (N.Y.: Abingdon, 1960), pp. 79, 95, 193, 199; P. Vielhauer, "ἀνάπαυσις zum gnostischen Hintergrund des Thomasevangeliums," *Apophoreta* (BZNW 30) (Berlin: de Gruyter, 1964), p. 281ff.; M. Peel, *The Epistle to Rheginos* (London: SCM 1969), pp. 52–55, 140–43.

[33]C. A. Briggs, *The Book of Psalms* (Edinburgh: T. and T. Clark, 1907), 2:293, 296; H. Gunkel *Die Psalmen* (Göttingen: Vandenhoeck und Ruprecht, 1926), pp. 417, 419; and E. J. Kissane, *The Book of Psalms* (Dublin: Browne and Nolan, 1954), 2:122–23 opt for the local meaning, while A. Weiser, *Die Psalmen* (Göttingen, Vandenhoeck und Ruprecht, 1955), p. 429; H. J. Kraus, *Psalmen* (Neukirchen: Neukirchener Verlag, 1960), 2:662; and G. von Rad, "There Remains Still A Rest For The People Of God," *The Problem of the Hexateuch and Other Essays* (Edinburgh: T. and T. Clark, 1965), p. 99 hold that the reference is to God's conferring a state of rest, a gift which is to be found only by a personal entering into God Himself.

[34]מְנוּחָה has this local reference nearly everywhere in the MT; and cf. KB, p. 537, and W. Gesenius, F. Buhl, *Hebräisches und Aramäisches Handwörterbuch über das Alte Testament* (Berlin: Springer, 1954), p. 436 include Psalm 95:11 as having such a reference.

[35]Cf. Hofius, *Katapausis*, 40ff.

[36]Cf. von Rad's treatment of this theme, "There Remains Still a Rest," pp. 94–102.

[37]Hofius, *Katapausis*, pp. 53–54 wants to identify God's resting place as the heavenly sanctuary itself, the holy of holies, where God's throne, the place where He rests, is situated: cf. 4:16; 8:1; 12:2. He also argues that the verb εἰσέρχεσθαι ("to go/come into") used in conjunction with the rest is employed elsewhere in Hebrews of entry into the heavenly sanctuary, cf. 6:20; 9:12, 24, 25 also 9:6; 10:19. To insist on identification rather than association however goes further than the evidence in Hebrews will allow and minimizes the influence of Genesis 2:2 on the idea of rest. Cf. also H. Zimmerman, *Das Bekenntnis der Hoffnung* (Köln: 1977), p. 139.

[38]Von Rad, "There Remains Still a Rest," p. 102.

[39]Käsemann, *Das wandernde Gottesvolk*, p. 40ff.

[40]*Ibid.* He is followed by Zimmermann, *Das Bekenntnis*, pp. 133–34, 138–39.

[41]For a commentary on such material and for evidence of similar concepts in rabbinic literature cf. Hofius, *Katapausis*, pp. 59–74.

[42]For this motif in Paul, compare the present writer's *Paradise Now and Not Yet: Studies in the Role of the Heavenly Dimension in Paul's Thought* (Cambridge: University Press, 1981). It could be, as G. W. MacRae argues in "Heavenly Temple and Eschatology in the Letter to the Hebrews," *Semeia* 12 (1978): 179–99, that the writer adds elements of Alexandrian thought about the heavenly world to his readers' apocalyptic perspective, especially with his temple symbolism, but this is simply to reinforce the spatial elements already there in that apocalyptic perspective and not, as MacRae implies, to mingle two discrete thought worlds.

[43]Cf. R. Williamson, *Philo and the Epistle to the Hebrews* (Leiden: Brill, 1970), pp. 157ff.

[44]Barrett, "Eschatology of Hebrews," p. 381.

[45]Cf. most recently W. G. Johnsson, "The Pilgrimage Motif in the Book of Hebrews," *JBL* 97 (1978): 239–251.

[46]For a detailed demonstration of the influence of Numbers 14 on Hebrews 3:7–4:13 cf. Hofius, *Katapausis*, pp. 127ff.

[47]Cf. also Hofius, *Katapausis*, pp. 143ff.

[48]Kistemaker, *The Psalm Citations*, p. 109.

[49]*The Epistle to the Hebrews* (London: Black, 1964), p. 83; cf. also B. F. Westcott, *The Epistle to the Hebrews* (London, 1892, reprinted Grand Rapids: Eerdmans, 1970), pp. 94–95; Barrett, "Eschatology of Hebrews," p. 372.

[50]"Eschatology of Hebrews," p. 372; cf. also Rordorf, *Sunday*, pp. 89ff., 111–12 and J. Calvin, *The Epistle of Paul the Apostle to the Hebrews and the First and Second Epistles of St.*

Peter, trans. W. B. Johnston (Edinburgh: T. and T. Clark, 1963), who comments, "Because the completion of this rest is never attained in this life, we must be always striving towards it. Thus believers enter in, but on condition that they continuously run and press on." It is the Sabbath rest of the age to come rather than the world Sabbath which has given the writer the framework for expressing this eschatological tension in which the believer in Christ is involved. Of course the new element as distinct from the Jewish background is that in Christ the promised Sabbath rest has already begun. This eschatology should be compared with the apocalyptic timetable in regard to the Sabbath and the "eighth day," taken over from the Jewish speculations surveyed above, which is to be found in the early Christian Epistle of Barnabas: cf. Rordorf, *Sunday*, pp. 93–94; Barrett, "Eschatology of Hebrews," pp. 369ff.; F. F. Bruce, *The Epistle To The Hebrews* (London: Marshall, Morgan and Scott, 1965), p. 74 and n.20.

[51]Cf. Hofius, *Katapausis*, pp. 103–105.

[52]In similar vein cf. Calvin, *Epistle of Paul to the Hebrews*, p. 48: "What does ceasing from our works mean but the mortification of the flesh, when a man renounces himself in order to live to God?"; also Bacchiocchi, *From Sabbath to Sunday*, p. 67.

[53]*The Lord's Day*, p. 84: also Beckwith, *This is the Day*, p. 12; cf. also R. B. Gaffin, "The Sabbath—a Creation Ordinance and Sign of the Christian Hope," *The Presbyterian Guardian* (March, 1971), p. 41, and F. N. Lee, *The Covenantal Sabbath* (London: LDOS, n.d.), pp. 233ff., who hold that through the reference to σαββατισμός the writer indicates that the weekly Sabbath is still required of believers.

[54]10:25 may or may not have in view assemblies on the first day of the week but says nothing about the character of the day. More significantly in the context of his interpretation of the Sabbath rest the writer speaks only of exhortation that is to take place *every day* (3:13).

[55]*From Sabbath to Sunday*, p. 65.

[56]Cf. O. Cullmann, *Salvation in History* (London: SCM, 1967), p. 183.

[57]This is similar to the hermeneutical pattern which Cullmann, *ibid.*, 88–114, points out as occurring throughout the Bible, where an event and its interpretation in the Old Testament are taken up in the new event that takes place with Christ's death and resurrection and are reinterpreted in this light. Jewett, *The Lord's Day*, pp. 119f., sees this hermeneutical principle at work but does not allow it to operate consistently in his own thought, for he goes back on the basic reinterpretation that he acknowledges has taken place: cf. pp. 151, 164–65. A. Szabo, "Sabbat und Sonntag," p. 172 makes a similar mistake when he asserts, "The regulations of the Old Testament Sabbath law are valid for Sunday in so far as promise and fulfillment have similar features. Sunday, too, therefore, is a day of rest."

[58]Jewett, *The Lord's Day*; Beckwith, *This is the Day*, p. 12.

[59]Cf. also Rordorf, *Sunday*, pp. 299–300.

[60]Cf. the penetrating review article on Jewett's book by J. Stek, "The Fourth Commandment: A New Look," *The Reformed Journal* (July-Aug., 1972): 26–29; (Nov. 1972): 20–24; (Jan. 1973): 18–22, who faults Jewett on both these points.

8

THE LORD'S DAY

R. J. BAUCKHAM

Richard J. Bauckham lectures in the Department of Theology at the University of Manchester, Manchester, England.

The name "Lord's Day" (κυριακὴ ἡμέρα) occurs only once in the New Testament at Revelation 1:10, but it is nevertheless basic to a consideration of the origins and significance of the Christian weekly day of worship, and consequently it has been the subject of considerable debate. The first two sections of this chapter will attempt to elucidate the meaning of the title itself; in the third section we shall look at some of the theories and evidence for the origins of Sunday worship in the period before Revelation 1:10; finally, we shall explore what this verse's context in the Apocalypse may contribute to our understanding of the significance of the Lord's Day.

THE USAGE OF ΚΥΡΙΑΚΟΣ ("belonging to the Lord")

Despite much literature on κυριακὴ ἡμέρα, inadequate attention has been given to the meaning of the word κυριακός itself. Since study could have prevented some serious misunderstandings, we shall begin with a survey of usage. The word is not found in the Septuagint[1] or known in non-Christian Jewish literature; we shall therefore discuss the following areas of use: secular Greek, New Testament, second century Christian literature, and Clement of Alexandria (the earliest writer to use the word extensively).[2]

Secular Greek

The word is known only from papyri and inscriptions, hence the belief at one time that it was coined by Paul or the early church. But though 1 Corinthians 11:20 remains the earliest known occurrence of the word, its secular use (first attested A.D. 68) cannot be derived from its Christian use. Almost all the known examples (from both Egypt and Asia Minor) are in connection with the imperial administration, especially finance: κυριακός is used to mean "imperial" with such nouns as φίσκος, ψῆφος, λόγος, χρῆμα and ὑπηρεσία.[3] Liddell and Scott give one example of ὁ κυριακός meaning "spirit invoked in magic," and one example (from A.D. 137) where κυριακός probably refers to an ordinary master rather than to the emperor.[4] It seems clear that the word was not in common secular use except with reference to the emperor.

New Testament

Κυριακός is used only in 1 Corinthians 11:20 and Revelation 1:10. Both these texts will receive close attention below.

Second Century Christian Writers[5]

There are thirteen cases where κυριακὴ ἡμέρα or κυριακή alone means "the Lord's Day."[6] These will be discussed on the following page.

Didache 14:1.
Ignatius, *Magn*. 9:1.
Gospel of Peter 35, 50.
Dionysius of Corinth, *ap*. Eusebius *HE* 4:23:11 (*PG* 20:388C).
Epistula Apostolorum 18 (Coptic version) (trans. in Hennecke-Wilson I, 201).
Acts of Peter (*Act.Verc*. 29f.) (Latin trans. in R. Lipsius, *Acta Apostolorum Apocrypha* I, 79f.; English in Hennecke-Wilson II, 313-14).
Acts of Paul (C. Schmidt, 32; trans. in Hennecke-Wilson II, 371).
Melito of Sardis, *ap*. Eusebius *HE* 4:23:12 (*PG* 20:389A).
Irenaeus, Fragment 7 (*PG* 7:1233).
A Valentinian, *ap*. Clement of Alexandria, *Exc. ex Theod*. 63 (*PG* 9:689B) (*bis*).[7]

There are fourteen other occurrences:

Papias, *ap*. Eusebius *HE* 3:39:1 (*PG* 20:296A); the title of his work is: Ἐξήγησις λογίων κυριακῶν.
Papias, *ap*. Eusebius *HE* 3:39:15 (*PG* 20:300B): τὰ κυριακὰ λόγια.
Dionysius of Corinth, *ap*. Eusebius *HE* 4:23:12 (*PG* 20:389A): αἱ κυριακαὶ γραφαί.
Irenaeus, *Haer*. 1:8:1 (*PG* 7:521A): παραβολαὶ κυριακαί and κυριακὰ λόγια.
Theodotus, *ap*. Clement of Alexandria, *Exc. ex Theod*. 85 (*PG* 9:252C): κυριακὰ ὅπλα.

In the parts of Irenaeus, *Haer*., of which only the Latin translation is extant, *dominicus* is used[8] with the following nouns:

scripturae: 2:30:6; 2:35:4; 5:20:2 (*PG* 7:818B, 842A, 1178A)
scriptura: 5:20:2 (*PG* 7:1178A)
ministeria: 4:8:3 (*PG* 7:996A)
argentum: 4:11:2 (*PG* 7:1002B)
bona: 4:13:3 (*PG* 7:1009A)
passio: 4:34:3 (*PG* 7:1085A)

Clement of Alexandria

Κυριακὴ ἡμέρα is used twice: *Str*. 5:14; 7:12 (*PG* 9:161A, 504C).
Clement also uses κυριακός twenty-eight times with the following twenty-four nouns:

ἀγωγή	*Str.* 3:7 (PG 8:1161B)
ἀξίωμα	*Paed.* 1:7 (PG 8:320B)
ἄσκησις	*Str.* 4:6 (PG 8:1240A)
αὐθεντεία	*Paed.* 2:3 (PG 8:433B)
ἀφθαρσία	*Paed.* 2:2 (PG 8:409B)
γραφαί	*Str.* 6:11; 7:1; 7:16 (PG 9:313A, 404B, 529B)
δεῖπνον	*Paed.* 2:2 (PG 8:429C) (quoting 1 Cor. 11:20)
διαθῆκαι	*Str.* 6:17 (PG 9:393C)
διδασκαλία	*Paed.* 2:8; *Str.* 7:10; 7:15 (PG 8:465B; 9:481A, 525B)
δύναμις	*Str.* 6:14 (PG 9:337A)
ἔλεγχος	*Paed.* 1:9 (PG 8:352C)
ἐνέργεια	*Str.* 7:10 (PG 9:481B)
ἐντολαί	*Paed.* 1:13 (PG 8:376A)
κεφαλή	*Str.* 5:6 (PG 9:64C)
κληρονομία	*Str.* 6:16 (PG 9:369A)
λαός	*Str.* 7:16 (PG 9:541B)
λόγος	*Str.* 1:5 (PG 8:721A)
λόγοι	*Str.* 3:12 (PG 8:1185B)
μονή	*Str.* 7:10 (PG 9:481B)
οἶκος	*Str.* 3:18 (PG 8:1212B)
πάθος	*Paed.* 1:10 (PG 8:364A)
τροφή	*Paed.* 1:6 (PG 8:304A)
υἱοθεσία	*Str.* 6:8 (PG 9:289B)
φωνή	*Str.* 6:3 (PG 9:252C).

From these very varied examples of usage it is clear that in *meaning* the word κυριακός is simply synonymous with (τοῦ) κυρίου in all cases where (τοῦ) κυρίου is used adjectivally with a noun, with the exception of instances of the objective genitive.[9] The meaning is as various and indefinite as the adjectival use of the genitive, and must be determined from the sense and context in any particular case.[10] Irenaeus and Clement evidently use κυριακός and (τοῦ) κυρίου interchangeably[11] and virtually indiscriminately.[12] They do not restrict their use of κυριακός to stereotyped phrases; rather it seems that it is the familiarity of common and scriptural phrases which best accounts for their failure to use κυριακός in a few significant cases (αἷμα, "blood"; σῶμα,"body"; παρουσία, "coming").[13]

Only two phrases with κυριακός seem to have become stereotyped or technical phrases by the time of Irenaeus and Clement: κυριακή (ἡμέρα), "Lord's day," and κυριακαὶ γραφαί, the "Lord's Scriptures." The latter is found in Dionysius of Corinth as well as three times in Irenaeus (also once in the singular) and three times in Clement. Neither Irenaeus nor Clement uses *γραφαὶ* (*τοῦ*) *κυρίου*. On the other hand, *κυριακὸν δεῖπνον*, ("the Lord's Supper"), whatever the background to its use in 1 Corinthians 11:20, did not establish itself in general usage; it is rare in the Fathers and its few occurrences are best seen as conscious reminiscences of 1 Corinthians 11:20.[14] Similarly the one other phrase in which *κυριακός* is attested at an early date, Papias' *κυριακὰ λόγια* ("the Lord's sayings"), does not appear to have become a technical term.[15] So it seems unlikely that the use of *κυριακός* was ever restricted to stereotyped phrases.

It follows from this evidence that we cannot, with W. Foerster,[16] explain the rarity of the word in the New Testament by suggesting that its meaning differs from (*τοῦ*) *κυρίου*, that in the case of its use with *δεῖπνον* and *ἡμέρα* there "is an indirect relation to the Lord, e.g. as compared with *λόγος τοῦ κυρίου*, *παρουσία τοῦ κυρίου* etc."; for Papias already uses *κυριακός* to express a more direct relationship (*κυριακὰ λόγια*), while Paul uses (*τοῦ*) *κυρίου* to express relationships equally indirect (e.g., *ποτήριον*, 1 Corinthians 11:27). It is true that the word is rarely attested before Irenaeus, but the phenomenon for which we need to account is not an extension of *meaning* but only an extension of *use*. From the beginning *κυριακός* was used as simply synonymous with (*τοῦ*) *κυρίου*.

Why then did the word come only slowly into common Christian usage? If we remember that it is not common in the ordinary secular Greek of the first and second centuries the answer is not difficult. The word became common only in two spheres, the imperial administration and the Christian church; in each case it referred to the single *κύριος* who required no further specification and to whom reference was made sufficiently often for an adjective to prove useful. Such an adjective was not, however, strictly necessary, and so *κυριακός* would be likely to spread only at the rate allowed by general linguistic conservatism, reinforced, no doubt, by the familiarity of the language of the Septuagint, which makes no use of *κυριακός*, and then of the New Testament, which makes very little use of it. Thus the only occasional use of *κυριακός* in the period before Irenaeus is not altogether surprising.

This explanation, however, also accounts for the fact that so many of the early occurrences are in the phrase *κυριακὴ ἡμέρα*. In this case, the term is not simply interchangeable with *ἡμέρα* (*τοῦ*) *κυρίου*, since by long established usage the latter referred to the eschatological Day of the Lord. Thus if early Christians wished to call the first day of the week after their *κύριος*, they could not use the term *ἡμέρα* (*τοῦ*) *κυρίου* without ambiguity and confusion. This, it would seem, is the reason why *κυριακὴ ἡμέρα* early established itself as the common Christian name for Sunday. While *κυριακός* itself only slowly came into common use because it was a mere alternative to τοῦ κυρίου, the phrase κυριακὴ ἡμέρα came rapidly into use because another term besides ἡμέρα (τοῦ) κυρίου was necessary. In fact so commonly was it used that from an early date κυριακή alone sufficed to name the day.[17]

Upon the fact that κυριακός occurs in the New Testament only in 1 Corinthians 11:20 and Revelation 1:10, theories about the interconnection of the two terms κυριακὸν δεῖπνον and κυριακὴ ἡμέρα have not infrequently been based, and a case for the derivation of the latter from the former is a significant link in W. Rordorf's chain of argument about the origin of the Lord's Day. In terms of the historical *evidence*, however, such a case is extremely suspect. The following points should be considered: (1) In view of the second century usage listed above it is very unlikely that first century Christians used κυριακός only in these two phrases, even though at that stage the word was doubtless not used very often. Papias' phrase κυριακὰ λόγια is in fact chronologically closer to Revelation 1:10 than 1 Corinthians 11:20 is, but no one has suggested any particular connection between the phrases κυριακὰ λόγια and κυριακὴ ἡμέρα. The two New Testament occurrences of κυριακός are, as evidence of first century Christian vocabulary, an accident of survival rather than a significantly restricted terminology.(2) Paul uses (τοῦ) κυρίου as an adjectival phrase with a noun very rarely (excepting Old Testament quotations and cases of the objective genitive). The uniqueness of his use of κυριακός in 1 Corinthians 11:20 is therefore less remarkable than if he frequently used expressions where one might expect it. (3) It may then be merely accidental that Paul wrote κυριακόν δεῖπνον (1 Cor. 11:20) and τὸ ἔργον τοῦ κυρίου (15:58; 16:10), rather than δεῖπνον τοῦ κυρίου and τὸ κυριακὸν ἔργον. Purely stylistic reasons (the need to balance κυρίου and δαιμονίων) may have prevented κυριακὸν ποτήριον and κυριακὴ τραπέζα in 10:21. (4) Neither κυριακὸν δεῖπνον nor δεῖπνον τοῦ κυρίου occurs in Christian literature before Hippolytus (*Apost. Trad.* 26:5; cf. 27:1)[18] except here in 1 Corinthians 11:20. Thus we cannot tell whether it is here a technical expression (perhaps the Corinthians normally spoke simply of τὸ δεῖπνον); or if it is, whether it is Paul's term or the Corinthians'; or, consequently, how widely it might have been used. (5) In view of the context of deliberate contrast with pagan sacrificial meals, it is possible that either Paul or the Corinthians may have used κυριακός in imitation of the use in the mystery religions of adjectives formed from the names of deities to designate aspects of the cult: temples, feasts, priests, worshippers etc.[19] Though it is mere conjecture, 1 Corinthians 11:20 would make excellent sense if κυριακὸν δεῖπνον were a title the Corinthians had deliberately chosen to differentiate the Christian cultic meal from (e.g.) the Διονυσιακὸν δεῖπνον.[20] The same association (in a situation where pagan slanders about the Christian cultic meal had made it an embarrassment) may explain why later writers abandoned or avoided the term.[21] (6) Forty years separate Paul's use of *κυριακὸν δεῖπνον* in a letter to Corinth and John's use of *κυριακὴ ἡμέρα* in a letter to the seven churches of Asia. To establish that the title of the Day derived from the title of the Supper we should need evidence (which is plainly not available) that *κυριακὸν δεῖπνον* was a term that continued to be used during this period and that was used in those churches of Asia Minor and Syria to which all the available evidence points as the origin of the term *κυριακὴ ἡμέρα*. Other terms for the Lord's Supper (*εὐχαριστία* in Ign. *Eph.* 13:1; *Smyrn.* 7:1; 8:1; *Philad.* 4:1; *Didache* 9:1, 5; cf. also *ἀγάπη* in Jude 12; ? 2 Peter 2:13) are both chronologically and geographically closer to the Asian church of Domitian's reign than the subsequently unattested term of 1 Corinthians 11:20. Rordorf's theory is therefore (while not of course ultimately disprovable) wholly unprovable. The evidence does not allow us to reduce the term *κυριακὴ ἡμέρα* to mere shorthand for "Lord's Supper Day." Precisely in what sense late first-century Christians meant that the Lord's Day was the Lord's is not clear from the title itself, but they seem to have meant that in some sense it was.[22]

THE TERM ΚΥΡΙΑΚΗ ʽΗΜΕΡΑ (The Lord's Day)

There are four possible interpretations of *κυριακὴ ἡμέρα* in Revelation 1:10: (1) the eschatological Day of the Lord; (2) the (Saturday) Sabbath; (3) Easter Day; (4) Sunday. The first two of these suggestions presuppose that the meaning is different from that of the phrase as used in the second-century literature cited above.[23] The third interpretation supposed that in some of these second-century instances the meaning is Easter and in others Sunday. While there can be no *a priori* assumption that the second century evidence will determine the meaning in Revelation 1:10, that evidence is clearly relevant to the discussion and we begin by considering it.

Didache *14:1*

Κατὰ κυριακὴν δὲ κυρίου. . . . No really convincing explanation of this old phrase (commonly translated "on the Lord's own day") has yet been suggested. Bacchiocchi adopts a suggestion (by J. B. Thibaut) that the noun implied is not *ἡμέραν* but *διδαχήν*, so that the phrase should be translated "according to the sovereign doctrine of the Lord."[24] But it is doubtful whether readers would have been able to supply *διδαχήν*, since the only other attested usage of *κυριακή* ("Lord's") with a noun implied is with *ἡμέρα* ("day") implied, and it should be noted that this is the way in which the *Apostolic*

Constitutions (7:30:1) interpreted the *Didache.*[25] Moreover this suggestion has no explanation for the redundant *κυρίου.*

J.-P. Audet amends the text to *καθ' ἡμέραν δὲ κυρίου* explaining *κυριακήν* as an explanatory marginal gloss that later replaced *ἡμέραν* in the text.[26] This might be attractive were it not that elsewhere *ἡμέρα κυρίου* always means the eschatological Day of the Lord, never a day of worship. If the pleonasm is intended to stress the solemnity of the day (as Rordorf suggests), then the text may well presuppose that *κυριακή* was already the kind of stereotyped term whose real reference to the Lord Jesus could be forgotten (much as one might feel it useful to explain "the Lord's Prayer" by some such words as "the prayer which the Lord himself taught us"). C. W. Dugmore's suggestion[27] that *κυρίου* serves to designate Easter Sunday is really self-defeating in the context of his argument for a reference to Easter in Revelation 1:10, because it too requires that *κυριακήν* alone already meant Sunday in common usage.

Although the context strongly suggests the regular weekly worship of the church, we cannot go as far as Rordorf who asserts that it "points unambiguously" to this.[28] Only in the light of other evidence that *κυριακή* meant Sunday will we be able to be sure of this meaning in the *Didache.*

Ignatius, Magnesians 9:*1*

". . . no longer sabbatizing but living according to the Lord's Day (*μηκέτι σαββατίζοντες ἀλλὰ κατὰ κυριακὴν ζῶντες*), on which (*ἐν ᾗ*) also our life arose (*ἀνέτειλεν*) through him and through his death."

This passage has provoked textual debate since the only Greek manuscript extant reads *κατὰ κυριακὴν ζωὴν ζῶντες*, which could be translated "living according to the Lord's life." Most scholars, however, have followed the Latin text *(secundum dominicam)*, omitting *ζωήν* and translating "living according to the Lord's Day."[29] The greatest difficulty about retaining *ζωήν*[30] is in making sense of the following clause, whose exact meaning is not obvious but which perhaps refers to Christians rising with Christ in their baptism on Sunday.[31] The use of *ἀνέτειλεν*, a verb that refers to the rising of heavenly bodies rather than naturally to rising from the dead, may indicate that already Ignatius has in mind the pagan name for Sunday, "the day of the sun,"[32] and therefore compares Christ's resurrection on Sunday with the rising of the sun.

It is objected that the subject of the sentence is the Old Testament prophets, whom Ignatius could hardly have thought to have observed the Lord's Day.[33] However, some commentators think the sentence is about Jewish converts to Christianity.[34] Even if it refers to the prophets, it should not be assumed that Ignatius thought the Old Testament prophets kept the Sabbath (cf. *Barn.* 15, and the quotation there of Isa. 1:13f.). He may mean that they abandoned the practice of Judaism and lived in hope of the new life, which would become available on the day of Christ's resurrection (cf. the whole context in chapters 8 and 9).

Of course it is true that the real contrast Ignatius intends to draw is not between days as such but between ways of life, between "sabbatizing" (i.e. living according to Jewish legalism) and living according to the resurrection life of Christ. But the text becomes most easily intelligible if we understand him to be symbolizing this contrast by means of a contrast of days, the Sabbath as the distinguishing characteristic of Judaism and the new Christian observance of the day of resurrection as symbolizing the new life which Christians enjoy through Christ.

Can we be sure that *κυριακή* here means Sunday and not Easter? Since the emphasis is on ways of life, we cannot too easily infer that Ignatius *must* be referring to a *weekly* day of Christian worship to balance the weekly Sabbath,[35] but still less can we argue that the reference to Christ's resurrection requires a reference to Easter, as though Ignatius must be thinking of an annual rather than a weekly commemoration.[36] Reference to a weekly Lord's Day would seem more natural, but on the evidence of this text alone we cannot be quite sure.

Gospel of Peter 35 *and* 50

Here *ἡ κυριακή* replaces *μία (τῶν) σαββάτων* ("the first day of the week") used in the Resurrection narratives of the Gospels. Again it is clear that *κυριακή* is already an accepted technical term and refers to a day, but the nature of the context makes impossible a final decision between Sunday and Easter.[37]

Later Second Century

Fortunately most of the later second century references are less ambiguous, though we can infer nothing from the title of Melito of Sardis' work *Περὶ κυριακῆς*, since only its title survives. A reference to weekly Sunday worship seems very probable but not certain in the letter of bishop Dionysius of Corinth to bishop Soter of Rome (c. 170): "Today we have kept the Lord's holy day (*κυριακὴ ἅγια ἡμέρα*), on which we have read your letter." At about the same time, however, a passage in the *Acts of Peter (Act. Verc.* 29) clearly identifies *dies dominica* ("the Lord's Day") with "the next day after the Sabbath," and the *Acts of Paul*[38] represents the apostle as praying "on the Sabbath as the Lord's Day drew near" (*ἐπερχομένης τῆς κυριακῆς*). In neither of these passages can we understand the Lord's Day to be an annual festival.

Epistula Apostolorum 18 (Coptic)[39] has Christ saying, "I have come into being in the Ogdoad, which is the Lord's Day," and the same identification of the gnostic Ogdoad with the Lord's Day is found in the Valentinian text preserved by Clement (*Exc. ex. Theod.* 63: "the Ogdoad, which is called the Lord's Day"). The predominantly antignostic *Ep. App.* may perhaps intend a secondary reference to Christ's resurrection on the "eighth" day as well as to the more obvious gnostic idea of His origin in the Ogdoad,[40] but certainly the gnostic association of Ogdoad and Lord's Day is hardly explicable except on the basis of a common Christian use of *κυριακή* as a title for Sunday, the 'eighth' day.[41] Gnostic writers had evidently appropriated the Christian eschatological symbolic use of the eighth day (cf. *Barn.* 15; 2 Enoch 33:7), and assimilated this to the cosmological role of the Ogdoad in their own systems.[42] For our purposes these two examples of gnostic usage are valuable additional evidence that in the later second century *κυριακή* meant Sunday, and furthermore they attest that the use of this title had spread to Egypt. Though the earliest known uses of *κυριακὴ ἡμέρα* are from the churches of Asia Minor and Syria, it seems clear that by the end of the second century this (with its Latin equivalent *dies dominica*) was the ordinary designation of the weekly day of worship throughout the greater part of the Christian world.[43]

Sunday or Easter?

The evidence from the *second half* of the second century is therefore consistent and unambiguous. The most obvious conclusion is that this later usage continues the earlier usage attested in the *Didache*, Ignatius and the *Gospel of Peter*, which would therefore also refer to Sunday.

At this point, however, we must take account of the argument that these earlier references are not to Sunday but to Easter. Proponents of this view[44] argue that the Christian celebration of Easter as an annual commemoration of the Resurrection preceded the observance of Sunday as a weekly commemoration, that the latter developed from the former, and that the title *κυριακή* applied originally only to Easter and then derivatively to Sunday. This view has serious weaknesses.

(1) While there is unambiguous evidence that Sunday was called *κυριακή* from the second half of the second century onwards, there is no unambiguous evidence that Easter was ever called simply *κυριακή*.[45]

(2) The argument could carry conviction only if it claimed that the weekly Christian Sunday and its title *κυριακή* derived from Easter *Sunday*. But second century Christians were divided between those who followed the Roman custom of observing Easter on a Sunday and the Quartodecimans who celebrated Easter on 14 Nisan. In the early second century the churches

of the province of Asia were certainly Quartodeciman, and it is very probable that the churches of Syria were too.[46] But it is from these areas that the *Didache*, the *Gospel of Peter* and Ignatius' letter to the *Magnesians* (and also Rev. 1:10) come.

(3) The supposed chronological priority of Easter Sunday observance to weekly Sunday observance cannot be demonstrated from the evidence. Although scholars are still divided as to whether the Quartodeciman or the Roman practice is the more original,[47] Eusebius' evidence does not allow us to trace Easter Sunday back beyond the early second century. Weekly Sunday worship is at least no younger, since, even if Acts 20:7 is disallowed as evidence, *Barn.* 15:9 is unambiguous evidence from the early second century,[48] and Justin's *First Apology* (c. 152) can scarcely be recording a custom only just begun. The available evidence gives no chronological priority to Easter Sunday observance.[49]

(4) No explanation is offered of how the weekly festival is supposed to have developed from the annual celebration. From the later second century onwards it is clear that Sunday was the regular day of Christian worship everywhere, and there is no record of any controversy over whether worship should take place on Sunday. The very universality of the custom argues its early origin. Would a custom that originated at a time between Ignatius and Justin have spread so rapidly and to such a uniform extent that no positive evidence of any Christian group which did not worship on Sunday has survived, with the sole exception of the extreme wing of the Ebionites? Such explanations as "the weekly Sunday somehow developed from the annual"[50] plainly will not suffice. It is in fact far more likely that it was the already established custom of weekly worship on Sunday which led to the transference of Easter from 14 Nisan to a Sunday.

We conclude that in the *Didache*, Ignatius, and the *Gospel of Peter* *κυριακή* is a technical term in fairly widespread use at least in Syria and Asia Minor, designating the first day of the week as the Christian day of regular corporate worship. It therefore becomes extremely likely that *κυριακὴ ἡμέρα* in Revelation 1:10 also means Sunday. John was writing to be understood throughout the churches of the province of Asia, which if they observed Easter at that period were Quartodeciman.[51] If he was writing in the reign of Domitian, he was writing no more than twenty years before Ignatius' letter to the *Magnesians*, in the same area. Even if he was writing earlier, it is still extremely improbable that the same title should have been transferred from one religious festival to another. To claim that Revelation 1:10 refers to Easter (or to the Sabbath) is mere speculation with no evidence whatever to support it. The wholly consistent usage of second-century writers indicates Sunday.

Sunday or Day of the Lord?

The one suggestion not yet considered is that *κυριακὴ ἡμέρα* in Revelation 1:10 means the eschatological Day of the Lord; John means that he is transported in prophetic vision to the time of the End. The case for this interpretation has recently been argued by Bacchiocchi,[52] but the following arguments tell against it.

(1) Why does John not use the normal Septuagint rendering *ἡμέρα* (*τοῦ*) *κυρίου*, which is followed by other New Testament writers?[53] This is not an entirely decisive argument if it can be presumed that when John wrote *κυριακὴ ἡμέρα* was not yet a title for a day of the week. That John's usage would be unique is not in itself an argument against this interpretation, for *κυριακός* was not limited to customary or technical phrases and many of the examples given above are also unique. There is great variety in New Testament terminology for the Last Day,[54] and John himself uses other terms (6:17; 16:14). A motive for the unusual phrase might perhaps be found in a conscious play on the meaning "imperial," which was the common meaning of *κυριακός* in John's day.

(2) But if *κυριακὴ ἡμέρα* was already a title for Sunday, John could not have used it in an eschatological sense without misunderstanding. The use of *κυριακή* in the *Didache*, Ignatius, and the *Gospel of Peter* seems to presuppose a well-established usage, and in that case it is rather probable that *κυριακὴ ἡμέρα* already meant Sunday in the reign of Domitian. This argument would not apply if John wrote at an earlier date.

(3) The interpretation is difficult to sustain in context. "The Day of the Lord" is not an accurate description of the contents of the whole of John's prophecy. In 6:17, and 16:14 it is clear that he understands the "great day of God" in a fairly restricted sense; it is the time of final judgment on the world exclusive even of the preparatory judgments that lead up to it. Certainly neither the contemporary situation of the seven churches nor the new creation of chapters 21 and 22 is included in the term. Nor does John write consistently from the standpoint of the time of final judgment. Rather, the prophecy seems to move forward towards this time and then beyond it, and John himself experiences visionary shifts of temporal standpoint. We shall show also that contextually the meaning Sunday is preferable, though the eschatological and counter-imperial overtones suggested by the phrase need not be ignored.

The Lord's Day and the Resurrection

Now that we have established that the first day of the week was the Christian day of regular corporate worship in the church of Asia at the end of the first century, is it possible to move backward from Revelation 1:10 to discover the origins of Christian Sunday observance? Acts 20:7 and 1 Corinthians 16:2 are perhaps not entirely unambiguous evidence for Sunday observance in the Pauline churches, but seen in the light of later evidence there is a strong presumption that they should be so understood. But how much further back does the custom of Sunday worship go? Can it be traced to the Jewish-Christian churches of Palestine? To the original church in Jerusalem? Perhaps to the risen Lord Himself?

First, we shall examine the possible evidence provided by the Resurrection narratives of the Gospels, and then ask whether a Palestinian origin for Sunday observance can be postulated. Finally, we shall seek the reason for the early church's choice of the first day of the week.

The Resurrection Narratives

In this enquiry, where solid evidence is lacking and conjecture has been rife, we must proceed with care. Too many scholars in the past have been tempted to advance confident conclusions that the evidence does not justify. Sometimes this has been done in order to provide Sunday observance with clear dominical authority. From the Reformation to the present day a long and impressive series of writers have found reason to identify the origins of Sunday worship in the period of the resurrection appearances of Jesus. But we should note immediately that no early Christian document explicitly claims this. Our discussion of the meaning and usage of *κυριακός* eliminates any likelihood that (as has sometimes been thought) the title *κυριακή ἡμέρα* means "the day which the Lord instituted." Even patristic defenses of Sunday observance are notable for their failure to appeal to a command of the risen Lord.[55] So we should be cautious. It is not very likely that our historical investigation will yield an authority for Sunday worship that the early church itself did not claim.

The case for the origin of Sunday observance in the period of the Resurrection appearances has taken various forms. It has sometimes been suggested that the risen Lord established a pattern of meeting the apostolic group weekly on Sundays and that the apostles continued the practice after the ascension.[56] But the New Testament accounts hardly support such a conjecture; they record about a dozen appearances (to groups and to individuals) in the period between the Resurrection and Pentecost. Of these, four or five occurred on Easter Day, one on the following Sunday (Jn. 20:26), and the remaining six or seven are undated.[57] John is the only New Testament author who shows any interest in dating appearances after Easter Day, and it is possible (especially if John 21 does not belong to the original form of his Gospel) that he did intend to draw a parallel between the apostles' weekly meetings with the risen Lord on Sundays and the weekly meetings of the later church where the Lord is present by His Spirit. But it would be hazardous to draw definite historical conclusions from this possibility. The New Testament records leave us very uncertain about many aspects of the period of the Resurrection appearances. It may be that the custom of regular Sunday meetings goes back to that period, but this cannot be more than a guess.

Another form of the argument for the origin of Sunday observance in the period of the Resurrection appearances is that of W. Rordorf, who differs from most of his predecessors in depending largely on the events of Easter Sunday evening, not those of later Sundays.[58] The argument is related to his conviction of a very close connection between Sunday observance and the Lord's Supper. The breaking of bread in the earliest Christian community, holds Rordorf, "was a continuation of [the disciples'] actual table-fellowship with the risen Lord." It took place on Sunday evenings because the practice originated in the "Easter meal" on Easter Sunday evening.[59] The argument is unacceptable.[60] We have already criticized Rordorf's claim that the titles κυριακὴ ἡμέρα and κυριακὸν δεῖπνον prove a close connection between Sunday and the Lord's Supper.

We need not dispute that early Christian Sunday worship in fact centered on the Lord's Supper, but the problem of the origin of Sunday observance is not thereby solved since it does not follow that the Lord's Supper cannot have predated Sunday observance. Moreover, Rordorf's theory requires such a close connection between the two that he must show that from Easter Sunday onwards the breaking of bread took place always on Sundays and *only* on Sundays. Not only is the evidence for this lacking, but there is evidence against it (Acts 2:46), which Rordorf must discount.[61]

The *crux* of Rordorf's theory is *the supper on Easter Sunday evening*, and his failure to discuss the real problems involved here is disquieting. His argument leaves the impression that the Gospels describe the risen Jesus sharing a meal with His disciples on the evening of Easter Sunday. He speaks of "the accounts of the Easter meal," and assures us that the "parallelism stares us in the face if we place the accounts of the first appearance of Jesus on Easter evening beside the breaking of bread as practiced in the earliest Christian community."[62] Jesus' appearance to the disciples on Easter evening is recorded in Luke 24:36ff.; John 20:19–23; Mark 16:14, but these can hardly be called "accounts of the Easter meal." In Luke we must infer that the disciples were having supper (as the longer ending of Mark states), but only because Jesus eats a piece of fish, not for reasons of table fellowship but to demonstrate His bodily reality.[63] Perhaps from Acts 1:4 and certainly from

Acts 10:41 we know that the apostles did share meals with the risen Lord; but neither text need refer to this occasion.[64] To appreciate that there are really no "accounts of the Easter meal" we need only compare two other meals in the Resurrection narratives: the supper at Emmaus (Luke 24:30–31, 35) and the breakfast by the Sea of Tiberias (John 21:13). Both of these do offer support for the claim that the disciples' "breaking of bread was a continuation of their actual table-fellowship with the risen Lord," but they leave us in some doubt as to whether a meal in Jerusalem on Easter Sunday evening had the singular importance Rordorf claims for it.[65]

In the traditions of the Resurrection appearances as we have them the supposed "Easter meal" has disappeared from John and only survived in Luke; where the significance is quite different from that which Rordorf sees in it. In the traditions as we have them eucharistic significance is much more obviously given to other meals not easy to fit into Rordorf's theory. So far from even noticing such problems, Rordorf proceeds:

> It must, moreover, be emphasized that the Easter meal was decidedly more important for the tradition of the primitive community than the memory of Jesus' last meal. The Lord's Supper was celebrated not on Thursday evening but on Sunday evening. From this alteration of the date we conclude that the meeting of the disciples with the risen Lord on Easter evening must have been for them like a second institution of the Lord's Supper.[66]

Rordorf leaves us guessing how an event of such remarkable significance could have disappeared from the traditions.

We conclude that the accounts of the Resurrection appearances permit no demonstrable case that Sunday worship originated at that time. Before leaving the Resurrection narratives, however, we may ask the more modest question, whether the gospel accounts provide evidence that *at the time they were written*, Sunday was observed as the day for Christian worship and understood as a memorial of the Resurrection. The synoptic Gospels' emphatic dating of the discovery of the empty tomb on the morning of the first day of the week has quite often been thought a reflection of Sunday observance. This is possible, but it need not be the case. The insistence on the date could be no more than a way of affirming that as a matter of historical fact the Lord rose "on the third day" (a point of some significance in the tradition). Matthew's phraseology in particular may be designed simply to indicate that the women visited the tomb as soon as they could after the Sabbath. In the case of the fourth Gospel the evidence is rather more suggestive; "the first day of the week" is repeated at 20:19 and Jesus' second appearance to the apostles is dated a week later (20:26).[67] But again we cannot be quite sure; such precise datings are a feature of this Gospel for reasons still in dispute and not easily decided.

It cannot therefore be proved that the Resurrection narratives in the Gospels presuppose Sunday observance in the churches of their time, though the fourth Gospel in particular seems to offer some support for this claim. What we can certainly conclude, however, is that the emphasis on "the first day of the week" in the tradition of the Resurrection narratives is such that, when Sunday worship was practiced, Christians must have connected it with the Lord's resurrection on a Sunday. Whatever the origin of Sunday worship, it is evident that, once it became the custom, Christians familiar with the Gospel traditions would very soon have come to see it as commemorative of the Resurrection. This may seem a meager conclusion by comparison with the much larger claims that have often been made as to the connection between the gospel accounts of the Resurrection appearances and the origins of Sunday worship. It is, however, a conclusion of some significance, as we shall see. It indicates that we are unlikely to have any record of a stage in the Christian observance of Sunday before that at which it was understood to be the weekly worship of the risen Lord on the weekly recurrence of the day of His resurrection.

Palestinian Origin

If Sunday observance cannot be shown to go back to the time of the Resurrection appearances, can it at least be shown to go back to the Palestinian Jewish-Christian churches? Again it must be admitted that the New Testament documents offer us no direct evidence. There are, however, considerations that make it likely that Sunday worship originated in the primitive Palestinian church.

Sunday worship appears, when the evidence becomes available in the second century, as the universal Christian practice outside Palestine. There is no trace whatever of any controversy as to whether Christians should worship on Sunday, and no record of any Christian group that did not worship on Sunday. This universality is most easily explained if Sunday worship was already the Christian custom before the Gentile mission, and spread throughout the expanding Gentile church with the Gentile mission. It is very difficult otherwise to see how such a practice could have been imposed universally and leave no hint of dissent and disagreement.[68] It seems hardly likely that Paul would have begun this novel practice in the course of his Gentile mission, and in any case even Paul was not responsible for policy in the whole of the Gentile mission field (note that *Barn.* 15:9, one of the earliest evidences of Sunday observance, probably comes from Egypt). The conclusion seems irresistible that all of the early missionaries simply exported the practice of the Palestinian churches.

As for evidence about Palestine itself, we have the testimony of Eusebius (*HE* 3:27) that in his day there were two groups of "Ebionites." One group kept not only "the Sabbath and the rest of the discipline of the Jews" but also "the Lord's Day as a memorial of the resurrection of the Savior," while a second group did not keep the Lord's Day. It is impossible to do more than guess at the origins of this division but it is at least plausible to suppose that the former group retained the original practice of Palestinian Jewish Christianity, especially since this group shows no other sign of accommodating itself to the practice of Gentile Christianity. Although the evidence is late and the historical relationship of these Ebionites to first-century Jewish Christianity is uncertain, it is certainly striking to find a group that remained strict in its adherence to the Law and repudiated the apostle Paul, but also kept the Lord's Day.[69] They can hardly have viewed Sunday worship as a Pauline or Gentile creation.

The strongest arguments against the Palestinian Jewish-Christian origin of Sunday observance are presented by Bacchiocchi.[70] His arguments, however, are limited to showing that the Jerusalem church "retained a deep attachment to Jewish religious customs such as Sabbath-keeping,"[71] and that therefore they could not have substituted Sunday for the Sabbath. These arguments are valid but they miss the point. Certainly Jewish Christians in Palestine (and probably many in the Diaspora too) continued to rest on the Sabbath and attend the temple or synagogue services, but they *also* met (as Bacchiocchi himself points out) *as Christians* in private houses to hear teaching from the apostles and to break bread together. As Bacchiocchi says, these gatherings "are not presented as conflicting with the services of the temple and synagogue but rather as complementing them."[72] But what is there to refute the view that this complementary activity took place on Sunday? It is not the origins of Sunday as a Christian Sabbath that we are now tracing but the origins of Christian worship on Sunday. Once it is granted that there was *Christian* worship in the Jerusalem church in addition to Christian participation in the temple and synagogue worship, then Jewish Christian observance of the Sabbath constitutes no contradiction of Jewish Christian worship on Sunday. Their specifically Christian meetings had to occur at *some* time, and it is even arguable that precisely *because* they remained faithful in their attendance at temple and synagogue services on the Sabbath some *other* time had to be found for Christian worship.

In stressing the Jerusalem church's complete conformity to Jewish religious practice it is possible that Bacchiocchi has played down their distinctive Christian selfconsciousness. He rightly rejects Rordorf's view that the earliest Christian community "no longer felt at home in Jewish sabbath worship . . .

even though it may have continued to keep the sabbath in outward appearance."[73] The earliest church undoubtedly participated fully in Jewish Sabbath worship because it was the worship of the people of God, to which they belonged. They did not, like the Qumran covenanters, separate themselves from a temple cult that was judged impure, and only in the case of Stephen does a more negative attitude to the temple appear. There is no evidence that Jewish Christians in Palestine left the synagogue until they were excluded. Having said this, however, it is necessary to add that the Jerusalem church after Pentecost understood itself not simply as part of Israel but as the nucleus of the renewed Israel of the last days, as the eschatological community in which the eschatological Spirit was active. This consciousness of fulfillment was not seen to invalidate the Sabbath worship but it did demand in addition distinctively Christian meetings for Christian fellowship, for the exercise of the Spirit's gifts, and for worship and prayer in the name of Jesus. Alongside the continuity with Jewish tradition, there was also the eschatological newness of the church's new corporate experience. Since it was the resurrection of Jesus that marked the decisive beginning of the time of eschatological fulfillment, it would at least have been appropriate for the earliest church to choose the weekly recurrence of the day of His Resurrection as the time of its regular meeting.

Why Sunday?

It is impossible to be dogmatic as to the time of the origin of Sunday worship, but we have found reasons for thinking it probably began in the early Palestinian church. The primary *reason* for its origin must be the Christian need for a time of distinctively Christian worship. This need for *some* regular time of worship must be clearly distinguished from possible reasons for the choice of *Sunday* rather than another day. The choice of a day *of the week* is entirely natural in a Jewish context and anything less frequent would surely not have met the need. Thus it is beside the point to ask why early Christians should have chosen to commemorate the Resurrection weekly rather than monthly or annually. It was the need for a regular and frequent time of Christian worship that led to the choice of a day *of the week*. Commemorating the Resurrection, if it was a motive, would be the reason for choosing *Sunday* rather than another day.[74]

Not many reasons for the choice of the first day of the week have been suggested. The influence of the pagan "day of the sun" can be discounted if the origin of Sunday worship is Palestinian.[75] Some recent writers have suggested that Sunday observance originated from aspects of the calendar used in Jubilees and other sectarian Jewish writings, but such precedents as exist here are slight and could hardly have contributed more to the Christian Sunday then minor psychological reinforcement for a practice that in itself seems to demand explanation as a distinctively Christian innovation.[76] For the crucial point of *worship* on Sunday, these Jewish sources provide no evidence, and it was that alone that made the early Christian Sunday a distinctive day.

Somewhat more attractive is Reisenfeld's suggestion[77] that Christians at first assembled for worship on *Saturday* evening or night following the end of the Sabbath. This argument, however, is heavily dependent on the questionable claim that Acts 20:7 refers to such a meeting on Saturday evening.[78] Moreover, it does not really explain how Christian worship then moved to Sunday morning and evening. From Pliny's *Epistle* (10:96) it is clear that by the end of the first century Christians in Bithynia, at least, were meeting before dawn and again (presumably after work) in the evening of the same day.[79] So, if we follow Reisenfeld, we have to postulate two developments during the later first century: first, the Christian meeting moves from Saturday evening to Sunday morning; second, a Sunday evening meeting is added. In fact, the picture would be further complicated by the fact that the *agape* (a love feast) and eucharist would seem to have moved from Saturday evening (Acts 20:7) to Sunday evening (according to Pliny's informants), and then the eucharist back to Sunday morning in Justin's time (*1 Apol.* 65). Of course, such developments are not impossible. On the other hand, it may be that they presuppose too great a uniformity in early Christian practice. We should remember the extent to which practical considerations, including circumstances of persecution, must have helped to determine the times of worship. But what we need to account for is the fact that Christians came to regard Sunday as the distinctive day for Christian worship. They may have moved from a Jewish to a Roman method of reckoning the limits of Sunday, and customs of morning and evening worship may have varied, but apparently they did not feel free to move their worship to, say, Monday. Even if the early Christians began simply by meeting at the earliest convenient time following the synagogue services on the Sabbath—which is plausible enough—nevertheless, in time they came to regard the day, Sunday, as the day on which Christian worship should take place. This development becomes obvious when the day acquires its name, the Lord's Day, and it is this development that still needs to be explained.

In fact, Reisenfeld himself admits this development and attributes it to the identification of Sunday with the day of Christ's resurrection.[80] We are therefore driven back to this explanation for the origin of the Lord's Day as such. We have already seen that the prominence of "the first day of the week" in the Gospel traditions of the Resurrection must have ensured that Sunday worship would very rapidly come to be seen as commemorative of the Resurrection. Whether the choice of Sunday was originally a matter of mere convenience or whether it was initially chosen as the day of the Resurrection, there can be no doubt that it was soon associated with the Resurrection, and only this can really account for the fact that worship *on Sunday* acquired normative status throughout the Christian world.

It has sometimes been objected that the association of Sunday with the Resurrection is attested only at a late stage and in a way that marks it as secondary.[81] In fact, the association is clear in most of the early second-century references (Ignatius, *Magn.* 9:1; *Gosp. Peter* 35, 50; *Barn.* 15:9; Justin, *1 Apol.* 67), and in the next section we shall see that the same association is probably to be found in the Apocalypse. It is true that in Barnabas and Justin other reasons for the significance of Sunday are given first (Sunday representing the eschatological "eighth" day in Barnabas, and the day on which God began the creation in Justin); but surely the significant point is that what *all* these early testimonies share is the association of Sunday with the Resurrection. This common element must be the basic and most primitive theme, to which subsequent theological reflection added many other varied associations in the course of time.

The story of the origin of the Lord's Day remains in many respects obscure. But we have seen reasons for holding that Sunday worship began at an early stage of Christian history and was from an early stage understood as commemorative of the Lord's resurrection on the first day of the week. Our study of the origins of the Lord's Day has given no hint of properly sabbatical associations; for the earliest Christians it was not a substitute for the Sabbath nor a day of rest nor related in any way to the fourth commandment.[82] It was simply, by the normative custom of the apostolic church, the day on which Christians met to worship, and, for us, the use of its title, the Lord's Day, in Revelation 1:10 gives that custom the stamp of canonical authority.

The Lord's Day in the Apocalypse

In this section, working from the presupposition that the Apocalypse is a literary and thematic unity, we shall attempt to fill out the significance of John's phrase ἐν τῇ κυριακῇ ἡμέρᾳ in Revelation 1:10 from its context in the whole book. In its immediate context it completes the description of 1:9, where John tells his hearers that he shares with them the situation of faithful witness under trial to which the message of the whole book is directed. Then in 1:10 he establishes also a temporal connection; he receives his visions on the day when the churches meet for corporate worship and on the same day his prophecy will be read aloud (1:3) in the church meeting. The total situation of 1:9 and the specific occasion of the weekly day of worship (1:10) are for both John and his churches interrelated by the implications of their confession of the lordship of Jesus Christ. This interrelation is to be understood from the rest of the book.

Sovereignty is perhaps the central theme of the Apocalypse. While John's prophecy moves against the background of God's omnipotent control over history, within which even the satanic powers are comprehended (13:5–6, 15; 12, 17), he refers to this emphatically but obliquely ("the beast was allowed to . . ." etc.). In the foreground—and as the primary object of John's lavish use of imagery of kingship and ruling—is the kind of sovereignty that God exercises over those who recognize and willingly submit to His lordship. This kind of sovereignty is exercised through Christ, whose right to universal sovereignty was won through the Cross and Resurrection but whose effective rule over the world is yet to be fully actualized in history. John and his churches live in the time between Christ's initial decisive victory, on which the whole establishment of God's sovereignty over the world depends, and His coming final victory over the powers that still contest His sovereignty. This *interim* is characterized by a conflict of sovereignties, and the Apocalypse is aimed at providing the churches with an accurate perception of the nature of the conflict and calling them to faithful discipleship during it.

John endorses the ordinary New Testament view that Christ conquered through suffering but now rules from the throne of God (3:21; 5:9–10). In 1:5*a* he bases the lordship of Christ on both His faithful witness until death and God's vindication of that witness in the Resurrection. John's initial vision of the risen Christ, which 1:10 introduces, is fundamental to the rest of the book. It is the one who died and came to life (2:8) who has already conquered Death and Hades, the ultimate force of evil (1:18). The crucified and risen Christ is Lord of the churches and is coming as Lord of the kings of the earth. The churches are the *present* sphere of His lordship in the time of the conflict of sovereignties. Christians are therefore addressed, in the seven letters, as (potential) "conquerors," as those whose acknowledgment of Christ's lordship must involve them in the same suffering witness that led Christ to the cross; they may only come to their own promised share in His universal lordship by following in His manner of conquest. As yet Christ's conquest on the cross is by no means self-evidently a conquest to the world at large, and so the churches can see their own faithful witness unto death as "conquest" only as they are able to recognize Christ as the one who was crucified but is now the exalted Lord. The content of the letters reveals clearly enough that even the churches, the sphere of Christ's present lordship, are the scene of the conflict of sovereignties, the rightful lordship of Christ and the usurped lordship of Satan. The whole of the first three chapters involves a tension that presses forward towards the resolution of this conflict when the promises to the conquerors will be fulfilled in the new world of chapters 21 and 22, and the lordship of Christ will be universally acknowledged. The central part of the book is primarily concerned with the history that leads to this resolution, in which Christians are called to play their own part as conquerors.

In chapters 12 and 13 the devil, cast out of heaven through the victory of Christ, is nevertheless widely successful in establishing his own, entirely spurious, claim to lordship on earth. The claim is spurious because in the single decisive victory he has already been defeated, but this is evident only to the saints. Hence the conflict begun on the Cross goes on in the world, though the immediate combatants are now the saints and the beasts, through whom the devil sets up a power structure of his own, imitative of the kingdom of heaven to which the saints belong. At the center of the conflict of sovereignties, John places the specific issue of martyrdom in defiance of the imperial claims to divine lordship; this is not only because it was the specific issue which his churches faced, but also because it provides the paradigm of what involvement in the conflict of sovereignties involves. This was the point at which "bearing the testimony of Jesus" could most obviously be seen as involving the full consequences of Jesus' own faithful witness. The story of the witnesses in chapter 11 sets out the parallel in full. It was also in persecution and martyrdom that the ambiguity of lordship in the time between the Cross and the Parousia became most apparent, so that the saints must be called not only to "endurance" (13:10) but also to "discernment" (13:18). From the perspective of heaven, martyrdom is called victory for the saints (12:11; 15:2); from the perspective of the world, it is called victory for the beast (11:7; 13:7). At least in terms of appearances the total lordship of the world is the beast's, but in martyrdom the church's unique character of already belonging to the Lord who reigns invisibly in heaven and is coming to reign on earth in the future is validated. It is the Christians' recognition of the crucified Christ as the exalted and coming Lord that alone can differentiate them from the whole world, which is duped into worshipping the beasts. The ultimate test of the reality of this faith is martyrdom.

John's dating of his visions on the Lord's Day—and the clear intention that they should be read aloud in the worship meetings of the churches—has often been linked with the liturgical material in which the Apocalypse abounds. Our argument here is independent of the attempts to discover traces of actual early Christian liturgy in the book. Just as John uses Old Testament language adapted to his purposes, he may also have used the language of Christian hymns, but the hymns as we have them are framed for their context. This context is always heavenly or eschatological. No words of prayer or praise are actually placed on the lips of the church in this world, but the prayers of the saints on earth are referred to in 5:8; 8:3–4, and we have from John's own pen one doxology (1:5*b*–6) and one prayer (22:20*b*) addressed to Christ. He must have expected his hearers to join him in these.

Worship and lordship belong integrally together. Worship is a community's recognition of its lord. Where people ascribe blessing, glory, wisdom, thanksgiving, honor, power, and might to "X," there "X" is lord. For this reason worship occurs in the conflict of sovereignties on *both* sides. Even the beast's kingdom would not be a kingdom if it existed by brute force alone; it is held together by the worship of the dragon and the beast, which is depicted as willing and spontaneous subjection to their lordship (13:34), albeit grounded on delusion. The beast's subjects are his worshippers, and hence the critical significance of the Christian refusal to worship the beast.

Worship is thus indicative of the limits and extension of sovereignty. The two hymns addressed to God in chapter 4 display His absolute sovereignty in heaven, and then in three hymns addressed to the Lamb, and to God and the Lamb in chapter 5, we see God's sovereignty extended throughout the whole creation on the basis of Christ's redemptive work. The universal dominion of the beast is realized in universal worship (13:8); in contrast, the conquerors proclaim the coming lordship of God: "All nations shall come and worship you" (15:4). This is fulfilled in 21:24–26, and again, the worship of God face to face is the eschatological goal of the church (22:3–4).

John also uses scenes of heavenly worship to provide proleptic indications of the victory of the martyrs by showing them already participating in the worship of the heavenly sanctuary (7:9ff.; 14:2–3; 15:2–4), and to celebrate the coming of God's lordship over the whole world (11:15–18; 19:1–8). But in both cases the content of worship may be seen to have developed out of the initial worship scene of chapters 4 and 5. There the liturgical climax is 5:9, which introduced the "new song," the hymn that celebrates the redemptive work of Christ, which has accomplished the universal extension of God's sovereignty. The words of the new song can be learned only by those who understand that Christ's faithful witness unto death was the means of victory (for this is its content). The martyrs learn this by conquering as he conquered (14:3–4; cf. 7:9–14). All the hymns after 5:9 are variations on the new song. The God who previously was "coming" to rule (4:8) is at the Parousia worshiped as the God who has come (11:17; 19:6), and the slain Lamb shares in the worship of the whole creation (5:13).

By putting the new song only on the lips of angelic beings and martyrs does

John mean that it cannot be sung by the church on earth? Clearly not, for John's own doxology addressed to Christ in 1:5*b*–6 contains precisely the content of the new song, and a church which did not worship Christ as the Lord who conquered on the cross could hardly be the sphere of Christ's lordship in the world. Why then does John insist (14:3) that only the conquerors can learn the new song? Characteristically, he is concerned that his churches should learn the implications of their worship. Worship is not an eschatological escape that spirits the Christian away into heaven or the New Jerusalem of the future and out of the conflict. If a man worships this Lord on Sundays he cannot bear the mark of the beast on weekdays. Those who worship the Lamb are involved in recognizing the cross as his victory and therefore also involved in the conflict of sovereignties as followers of the Lamb in his manner of conquest. Martyrdom authenticates the new song and only potential martyrs are entitled to sing it now.

Nevertheless, for those who sing it aright, the new song is the church's joyful anticipation of the triumph that lies beyond the conflict; this triumph is coming soon with the Lord's return. All that is characteristic, in the Apocalypse, of the church's loyalty to Christ's lordship in this world—the suffering witness, the patient endurance, the faithfulness, the stern demands of discipleship in the way of the cross—all this has its place only in the context of the conflict of sovereignties. Such things belong neither in heaven now nor in the future consummation of the kingdom on earth. But in worship, the church already expresses Christ's lordship in the form it now has in heaven and will still have in the coming kingdom. In that sense the church is most eschatological in worship.

We may conclude by drawing together some of the ways in which it seems that John would have understood the significance of Lord's Day worship within the context of the calling and goal of the church as his prophecy describes them.

We have seen that John understands the resurrection to have established Christ's lordship and that the introductory vision of the risen Lord is basic to the understanding of the book. Christians may conquer because it is this Lord whom they worship on the Lord's Day. Probably, therefore, John associates the choice of this day with Jesus' Resurrection on the first day of the week.

If it is correct to suppose that for John the conflict of sovereignties was especially manifest in persecution provoked by the imperial cult, then there may be deliberate contrast with the monthly "Emperor's Day" (Σεβαστή). On that day the beast-worshipers acknowledge the lordship of their lord; on this day the Christians worship the Lord who is coming as "ruler of the kings of the earth" (even Domitian).

The Lord's Day may not have been the only day of the week on which John's churches gathered for worship, but that it was the regular and most significant day for worship is clear from its title. In times of persecution it may well have become the only such day. As such it is the time that serves to mark out the church (gathered specifically as the community that confesses Jesus as Lord) for his sphere of lordship in the present world. This marking out is by no means merely symbolic; it is through the corporate worship of the church that Christ's lordship is actually realized in the life of the church. Therefore it is meaningful to speak of the day for worship as in a special sense "the Lord's Day."

Clearly the Apocalypse is about confessing Christ as Lord not only in the Sunday church meeting, but in the marketplace, the courtroom, and the arena. To understand lordship and worship in too narrowly cultic terms would run entirely counter to the book's intention. Yet the message of the Apocalypse is to be received by the churches in their weekly meetings for worship. John expects the churches' obedience to the prophetic messages he communicates from the Lord and their intensified understanding of what allegiance to the Crucified One involves in the whole of life to be rooted and nourished in their times of corporate meeting with the Lord. The Lord's Day in the Apocalypse is the day from which the Lord may reign over the rest of the week.

Lord's Day worship is eschatologically orientated. In the time of the conflict of sovereignties the church cannot meet with the Lord without the prayer "Come, Lord Jesus" and the expectation of what may be called the eschatological Lord's Day, the day when every tongue will confess that Jesus is Lord.

Notes

[1]For the incorrect reading in 2 Macc. 15:36, see W. Stott, "A note on the word KYPIAKH in Rev. i.10," *NTS* 12 (1965-6): 70.

[2]In the later Greek Fathers the word is common. Athanasius, for example, uses it over 50 times.

[3]Examples listed in Liddell and Scott; Moulton and Milligan; A. Deissmann, *Bible Studies*, (Edinburgh: T. T. Clark, 1903), pp. 217–18,; *idem*, *Light from the Ancient East* (London: T. T. Clark, 1910), p. 362; W. H. P. Hatch, "Some Illustrations of New Testament Usage from Greek Inscriptions of Asia Minor," *JBL* 27 (1908): 138.

[4]This example is in a short papyrus document reproduced in C. Wessely, *Studien zur Palaeographie und Papyruskunde*, vol. 22 (Amsterdam: n.p., 1922), n.177 *l.*18. The phrase (*π*[*ρ*]*ὸς τὸν κυρι*[*ακὸν*] *λόγον*) is one used elsewhere of the imperial treasury.

[5]Doubtless this list is not entirely exhaustive, but must include most known occurrences. I have included Greek works now extant only in translation in cases where we can be sure that the original Greek read *κυριακός*.

Another instance of *κυριακός* from the late second or early third century is a Montanist epitaph, in which ἐκκ [*sic*] τοῦ κυριακοῦ probably means "from the Lord's money" (i.e., out of ecclesiastical funds): E. Gibson, "Montanist Epitaphs at Usak," *Greek, Roman and Byzantine Studies* 16 (1975): 435-36. (I owe this reference to Mr. D. F. Wright.)

[6]From this list I have omitted *Acts of John*, chapter 106 (trans. in Hennecke-Wilson 2: 254), which cannot certainly be dated before the third century (ibid., 214.; but cf. M. R. James, *The Apocryphal New Testament* (Oxford: Clarendon, 1924), p. 228). I have also omitted the *Apostolic Tradition* of Hippolytus, which is probably from the second decade of the third century, though heavily dependent on earlier material (see Gregory Dix, *The Treatise on the Apostolic Tradition of St. Hippolytus of Rome* [London: SPCK 1937], pp. xxxv-xliv).

[7]For Clement's Valentinian sources in *Exc. ex Theod.* I have followed the analysis in R. P. Casey, *The Excerpta ex Theodoto (Studies and Documents, vol. 1)* (London: Christophers 1934), pp. 5–10.

[8]Where the Greek is extant we can observe the translator consistently using *Domini* for κυρίου and *dominicus* for κυριακός.

[9]Papias' phrase κυριακὰ λόγια has been the object of much debate: if, as some would have it, it means "sayings (or prophecies) *concerning* the Lord," then it is an exceptional instance of κυριακός standing for the objective genitive.

[10]Thus the classification of meanings given in G. W. E. Lampe, ed., *Lexicon* (followed by Stott, "KYPIAKH," pp. 71, 73) is somewhat misleading: in any given instance we need not ask, "Which of the meanings of κυριακός best fits here?" but only "What would (τοῦ) κυνίου mean here?"

[11]Note the following parallels:

Irenaeus, *Haer.* 1:1:1 (*PG* 7:437A): λογία κυρίου
1:8:1 (*PG* 7:521A): κυριακὰ λόγια
4:35:3 (*PG* 7:1088C): passio Domini
4:34:3 (*PG* 7:1085A): Dominica passio

Clement, *Paed.* 1:6 (*PG* 8:309A): τοῦ κυρίου πάθους καὶ διδασκαλίας σύμβολον.
Paed. 2:8 (*PG* 8:465B): σύμβολον τῆς διδασκαλίας τῆς κυριακῆς καὶ τοῦ πάθους αὐτοῦ.
Paed. 2:8 (*PG* 8:469A): κεφαλὴ κυρίου.
Str. 5:6 (*PG* 9:64C): κεφαλὴ ἡ κυριακή.

[12]In almost all cases κυριακός refers to Christ, but it seems to refer to God the Father in Clement, *Str.* 6:3; cf. also Irenaeus, *Haer.* 4:8:3.

[13]Irenaeus has τὸ σῶμα τοῦ κυρίου, "the body of the Lord" (*Haer.* 4:18:5), τὸ σῶμα καὶ αἷμα τοῦ κυρίου, "the body and blood of the Lord" (5:2:3), and ἡ τοῦ κυρίου παρουσία, "the coming of the Lord" *(adventus Domini)* (3:7:2; 3:12:6; 3:21:4; 4:5:5; 4:20:6; 4:20:10; 4:25:1; 4:27:2 *bis*; 4:31:1; 5:26:2). Clement has τὸ αἷμα τοῦ κυρίου (*Paed.* 2:2; 1:5; 1:6).

[14]See the references in Lampe, *Lexicon*, under δεῖπνον, and add Hippolytus, *Apost. Trad.* 26:5.

[15]Irenaeus has λόγια κυρίου, "sayings of the Lord" (*Haer.* 1:1:1) as well as κυριακὰ λόγια, "the Lord's sayings" (1:8:1), and in any case may well have Papias' book in mind. Clement has τὰ λόγια τὰ τοῦ κυρίου (*Paed.* 2:11).

[16]TDNT III, 1096.

[17]This usage is normal in titles for days: e.g., the Emperor's day was ἡ Σεβαστή, and Saturn's day (Saturday) was ἡ κρονική.

[18]The reference here is to the *agape*, by that time distinct from the eucharist.

[19]Cf. Liddel and Scott, entries under Διονύσια, Διονυσιακός, Ἰσιακός, Μιθράκανα, Μιθριακός, Ὀσιριακός, Σαραπεῖα, Ἀττίδεια.

[20]For the use of δεῖπνον for pagan cult meals, see G. Behm in TDNT 2:34-35. For the pagan cult meals at Corinth, see O. Broneer, "Paul and the Pagan Cults at Isthmia," *HTR* 64 (1971), 179. On this point and others I am indebted to suggestions from Dr. A. J. M. Wedderburn.

[21]Cf. Justin, *I Apol.* 66:4.

[22]The vagueness of the relation to the Lord implied in the term must be stressed, as against the

tendency of some writers to draw sweeping conclusions as to how the day should be observed, as a full twenty-four-hour period wholly devoted to the Lord in a different way from that in which all of a Christian's time belongs to the Lord. One wonders what similar exegetical principles would make of such modern terms as St. George's Day.

[23]"Sabbath" is an impossible meaning in most of these passages.

[24]S. Bacchiocchi, *From Sabbath to Sunday: A Historical Investigation of the Rise of Sunday Observance in Early Christianity* (Rome: Pontifical Gregorian University Press, 1977), p. 114 n.73.

[25]Bacchiocchi himself points this out *(From Sabbath to Sunday*, p. 120), and also refutes C. W. Dugmore's suggestion ("The Lord's Day and Easter," in *Neotestamentica et Patristica in honorem sexagenarii O. Cullmann, SuppNovt* 6 [Leiden: Brill, 1962], pp. 277, 279) that *Apost. Const.* 7:30:1 refers to Easter Sunday rather than to the weekly Sunday.

[26]J. -P. Audet, *La didaché: Instructions des Apôtres* (Paris: J. Gabalda, 1958) pp. 72–73. The support he claims from the *Apostolic Constitutions* and from the Georgian version is not very convincing. W. Rordorf, *Sunday: The History of the Day of Rest and Worship in the Earliest Centuries of the Christian Church* (London: SCM, 1978), p. 210 n.4, misunderstands Audet's emendation, which drops *κυριακήν*, not *κυρίου*.

R. T. Beckwith, in R. T. Beckwith and W. Stott, *This is the Day: The Biblical Doctrine of the Christian Sunday in its Jewish and Early Church Setting* (London: Marshall, Morgan and Scott, 1978), p. 32, suggests that here the title is translated from Aramaic (which has no adjective equivalent to *κυριακός*, and so would use the genitive of the noun), and *κυριακήν* was added in the Greek translation to distinguish the ecclesiastical from the eschatological Lord's Day. But this does not really explain why the translator used *both κυριακήν and κυρίου.*

[27]C. W. Dugmore, "The Lord's Day and Easter," pp. 275–77.

[28]*Sunday*, p. 209.

[29]J. B. Lightfoot, *The Apostolic Fathers* 2nd edition (London: Macmillan, 1889), vol. 2, part 2:129; Rordorf, *Sunday*, p. 211; R. M. Grant, ed., *The Apostolic Fathers* (New York: T. Nelson: 1966), 4:63. It is possible to get the same sense by treating *ζωήν* as a cognate accusative.

[30]The following advocate retaining *ζωήν* and translating "living according to the Lord's life." K. A. Strand, "Another Look at the 'Lord's Day' in the Early Church and in Rev. i. 10," *NTS* 13 (1967): 1978-79; F. Guy, "'The Lord's Day' in the letter of Ignatius to the Magnesians," *AUSS* 2 (1964): 13–14; R. A. Kraft, "Some notes on Sabbath observance in early Christianity," *AUSS* 3 (1965): 27–28; R. B. Lewis, "Ignatius and the 'Lord's Day,' " *AUSS* 6 (1968): 46-59; Bacchiocchi, *From Sabbath to Sunday*, pp. 214–15.

[31]So J. Liébaert, *Les enseignements moraux des pères apostoliques* (Gembloux: Duculot, 1970), p. 51

[32]Cf. Bacchiocchi, *From Sabbath to Sunday*, p. 266; Liébaert, *Les enseignements*, p. 51 n.6.

[33]Strand, "Another Look," p. 178.

[34]E.g. Lightfoot, *The Apostolic Fathers*, p. 128.

[35]Thus Rordorf, *Sunday*, p. 211: "this almost necessitates the translation 'Sunday' "; Stott, "ΚΥΡΙΑΚΗ," p. 72: "It is most unlikely that there is a comparison of a weekly observance with a yearly one."

[36]So Dugmore, "The Lord's Day and Easter," pp. 279–80.

[37]The decision would be easy, if we could assume, with Rordorf, *Sunday*, p. 212, that *κυριακή* is intended only as a translation of *μία τῶν σαββάτων* ("first [day] of the week"); but advocates of the view that the weekly commemoration of the Resurrection grew out of the earlier annual commemoration could argue that the author's interest was in designating the day of the year, not the day of the week.

[38]Neither of these documents can be certainly dated, but *Acts of Paul* is apparently dependent on *Acts of Peter*, and Tertullian's *De Baptismo* is a *terminus ad quem* for the former.

[39]As M. R. James, *The Apocryphal New Testament*, p. 491, points out, the Coptic is here to be preferred to the Ethiopic, for the latter can be explained by the translator's failure to understand his original or his finding it heretical. As for the translation, James' "I have come into the

Ogdoad" seems incorrect; "the day of the Lord" in the English translation of Hennecke is misleading, for the Coptic evidently renders *κυριακή*.

[40]For which, see e.g. Werner Foerster, *Gnosis I*, (Oxford: ET, Clarendon, 1972), pp. 68, 70, 72, 140, 312.

[41]The translation of *Exc. ex Theod.* 63 in Foerster, *Gnosis*, p. 152, seems to assume an actual citation of Revelation 1:10. This is possible but hardly certain, and the parallel in *Ep. App.* 18, which cannot be such a citation, suggests rather that a common gnostic usage is behind both texts.

[42]It seems probable that the Christian symbolic use of the number eight and the idea of the Ogdoad have distinct origins, but the issue of their relationship in second-century literature is a complex one: see J. Daniélou, *The Bible and the Liturgy*, (London: Darton, Longman and Todd, 1960), pp. 255–261; R. Staats, "Ogdoas als ein Symbol für die Auferstehung," *Vigiliae Christianae 26 (1972): 29–52; Rordorf, Sunday*, pp. 91–97, 284.

[43]The use of *dies dominica* as a title for Sunday at the end of the second century in Africa is attested by Tertullian, *De oratione* 23 (for the text, see Rordorf, *Sunday*, p. 158 n.4) and *De corona* 3.

[44]With variations, this is the view of A. Strobel, "Die Passah-Erwartung als urchristliches Problem in Lc 17.20f.," ZNW 49 (1958): 185; J. van Goudoever, *Biblical Calendars*, 2nd ed. (Leiden: Brill, 1961), ch. 20; C. W. Dugmore, "The Lord's Day and Easter" (where Dugmore abandons his earlier views set out in *The Influence of the Synagogue upon the Divine Office* (London: Oxford University Press, 1944), pp. 26–28); Strand, "Another Look." Rordorf's argument against this view (*Sunday*, pp. 209–15) seems to me insufficiently conclusive; the early texts alone are not as unambiguous as Rordorf would have them and the argument must take fuller account of the later second century evidence.

[45]Dugmore, "The Lord's Day and Easter," pp. 277, 279, takes *Const. Apost.* 7:30:1 as a reference to Easter, but is refuted by Bacchiocchi, *From Sabbath to Sunday*, p. 120. Strand, "Another Look," p. 177, argues that Irenaeus, Fragment 7, uses *ἡ κυριακή* to mean Easter Sunday, but again Bacchiocchi, *From Sabbath to Sunday*, p. 119 n.88, rejects this interpretation (adducing the relevant parallel in Tertullian, *De corona* 3:4). The fragmentary nature of this text makes it difficult to be entirely certain, but it seems unlikely that *κυριακή* ever means Easter except where this is clear from the context.

[46]Evidence for widespread Quartodeciman observance in the East is given by Bacchiocchi, *From Sabbath to Sunday*, p. 199 n.97.

[47]The priority of the Quartodeciman Pascha has been maintained, among others, by M. H. Shepherd, *The Paschal Liturgy and the Apocalypse* (London: Lutterworth, 1960) chapter 3; C. S. Mosna, *Storia della Domenica* (Rome: Biblical Institute Press, 1968), pp. 117–19 (where references to other recent literature on both sides will be found); Bacchiocchi, *From Sabbath to Sunday*, pp. 202–3, n.103. The priority of the Sunday Pascha is argued by A. Allen McArthur, *The Evolution of the Christian Year* (London: SCM, 1953), Part 3; W. Rordorf, "Zum Ursprung des Osterfestes am Sonntag," *Theologische Zeitschrift* 18 (1962): 167–89. K. A. Strand, *Three Essays on Early Church History, with Emphasis on the Roman Province of Asia* (Ann Arbor, Mich.: Braun-Brumfield, 1967), pp. 33-45, argues for the apostolic origin of both, the Sunday Pascha deriving from Peter and Paul, the Quartodeciman from John.

[48]Barnabas is often dated c.130-35. Certainly it is unlikely to be later, and may be earlier. J. A. T. Robinson, *Redating the New Testament* (London: SCM, 1976), pp. 313–19, suggests c.75.

Dugmore, "The Lord's Day and Easter," p. 280, comments that *Barn.* 15:9 makes no mention of the eucharist, but this simply reflects the brevity of Barnabas' reference to Sunday.

[49]For Bacchiocchi's argument that Easter Sunday and the weekly Sunday originated contemporaneously in the reign of Hadrian, see chap. 9, below.

[50]Strand, "Another Look," p. 175.

[51]Polycrates claimed, probably correctly, that Quartodeciman observance went back to the apostles John and Philip (Eusebius, *HE* 5:23).

[52]Bacchiocchi, *From Sabbath to Sunday*, pp. 123–31.

[53]1 Thessalonians 5:2; 2 Thessalonians 2:2; 2 Peter 3:10.

[54]Bacchiocchi, *From Sabbath to Sunday*, p. 127.

[55]Stott, in Beckwith and Stott, *This is the Day*, pp. 114–15, quotes passages in Eusebius and Augustine which attribute the choice of the day to Christ Himself, but they mean that He made Sunday His own day by rising from the dead on Sunday. The Fathers regard Sunday observance as apostolic but do not attempt any historical argument as to when it began, and they certainly know of no tradition of a dominical command.

[56]Cf. the entirely conjectural attempt to allocate an appearance to each of the six Sundays from Easter to the Ascension, in F. N. Lee, *The Covenantal Sabbath* (London: LDOS, n.d.), p. 207. The argument is sometimes reinforced by the claim that the coming of the Spirit at Pentecost also occurred on a Sunday.

[57]The numerical difference depends on whether certain Resurrection accounts refer to the same appearances or not. If the forty days of Acts 1:3 are precise, the final appearance to the Eleven was on a Thursday. *Barn.* 15:9 is hardly a reliable source for guessing (as Rordorf does, *Sunday*, p. 236) that the Ascension may have been on a Sunday. It is in any case by no means clear that Barnabas means to say that; for a different opinion, see L. W. Barnard, "The Day of the Resurrection and Ascension of Christ in the Epistle of Barnabas," *Revue Benédictine* 78 (1968): 106–7.

[58]Rordorf, *Sunday*, p. 236, speaks of the "disciples' meals with the risen Lord which took place not only on Easter Sunday evening but also on one or more Sunday evenings after"; his evidence for these later Sundays (pp. 234–36) is embarrassingly thin, especially as he casts doubt on and does not then reestablish the historicity of John 20:26, which has in any case no reference to a *meal*. But Rordorf does not seem to think the evidence for the later Sundays essential to his argument.

[59]Ibid., pp. 232–33.

[60]For similar criticisms, see Mosna, *Storia della Domenica*, pp. 52–58; Bacchiocchi, *From Sabbath to Sunday*, pp. 85–88.

[61]Apparently dissatisfied with his treatment of Acts 2:46 in the text, Rordorf has to resort in a footnote to doubting the value of its evidence: *Sunday*, p. 226 n. 1.

[62]Ibid., pp. 233, 232. Rordorf here means the first appearance to the Eleven, not the Emmaus appearance; but the confusion is compounded by a mistake, p. 232 n. 2, which refers us to Luke 24:30–31 for an account of the "Easter meal" in Jerusalem. It should be 24:41–43 (much less like a meal).

[63]If we are to press the circumstances in Luke, it might be inferred that the disciples had finished supper—perhaps from Jesus' question in 24:41, and from the fact that Cleopas and his companion had already sat down to supper and then walked back to Jerusalem and had been talking to the Eleven. The fish is seen as a eucharistic symbol by Cullmann, *Early Christian Worship*, p. 15; but cf. R. E. Brown, *The Gospel According to John (xiii-xxi)* (New York: Doubleday, 1970), p. 1099.

[64]Rordorf later argues that both texts suggest several meals: *Sunday*, pp. 234–35.

[65]Cullmann, *Early Christian Worship*, pp. 15–16 (whence Rordorf may have drawn the inspiration for his theory) maintains that "the first eucharistic feasts of the community look back to the Easter meals," but bases his evidence on those meals with the risen Lord to which the Gospels and Acts actually refer, and is not concerned with tracing back *Sunday* eucharistic worship directly to them, as Rordorf is (for the eucharistic character of the meals at Emmaus and by the Sea of Tiberias, see B. Lindars, *The Gospel of John* [London: Oliphants, 1972], pp. 609, 628; Brown, *John*, pp. 1098–1100.) The all-important "Easter meal" on Easter Sunday evening in Jerusalem is Rordorf's original contribution. His theory is rather uncritically followed by P. K. Jewett, *The Lord's Day* (Grand Rapids: Eerdmans, 1971), pp. 64-66, though Jewett notes some of its exegetical deficiencies.

[66]Rordorf, *Sunday*, p. 233.

[67]The expression "after eight days" (John 20:26) recalls the early Christian description of Sunday as the "eighth day," but it is a common ancient method of inclusive reckoning and cannot be pressed.

Bacchiocchi, *From Sabbath to Sunday*, pp. 117–18, argues that, if *κυριακὴ ἡμέρα* in Revelation 1:10 means Sunday, and if Revelation and the fourth Gospel were written by the same author at approximately the same time, then the fourth Gospel ought to have used the term *κυριακὴ ἡμέρα* (as the *Gospel of Peter* does later) instead of "the first day of the week." But the common authorship must be questioned, and perhaps the closeness in time should also be questioned. In any case, "the first day of the week" was firmly fixed in the tradition of the Resurrection narratives that the fourth Gospel uses.

[68]For Bacchiocchi's argument that Sunday was promoted in the second century by the authority of the Roman church, see chapter 9 of this volume. The parallel he draws with the Roman promotion of Easter Sunday in fact shows the weakness of his argument for in the case of the date of Easter, controversy and dissent are the major features of the second-century evidence.

[69]Cf. Rordorf, *Sunday*, pp. 216–18. It is misleading to call the two groups "stricter" and "more liberal" (Rordorf), or "conservative" and "liberal" (Bacchiocchi, *From Sabbath to Sunday*, p. 153): they were equally strict and conservative in their attitude to the law, but one group also practiced worship on Sunday. Why should the other group have discontinued Sunday worship? Perhaps simply as a result of the pressure that Jewish Christians always experienced from their Jewish brethren, and to distinguish themselves clearly from the Gentile "Pauline" Christians.

[70]Bacchiocchi, *From Sabbath to Sunday*, chap. 5.

[71]Ibid., p. 151.

[72]Ibid., p. 136.

[73]Rordorf, *Sunday*, p. 218.

[74]This point is well made by P. Cotton, *From Sabbath to Sunday* (Bethlehem, Pa.: published by the author, 1933), p. 79.

[75]See Rordorf's discussion of this suggestion: *Sunday*, pp. 24–38, 181–82; but his claim that the planetary week did not exist in the first century A.D. is refuted by the evidence in Bacchiocchi, *From Sabbath to Sunday*, pp. 241–51. The Mandaean Sunday—probably derived from the Christian—is discussed in Rordorf, *Sunday*, pp. 190–93; E. Segelberg, "The Mandaean Week and the Problem of Jewish Christian and Mandaean Relationship," *Recherches de Science Religieuse* 60 (1972): 273–86.

[76]These suggestions are discussed in Rordorf, *Sunday*, pp. 183–90, with full references to the literature.

[77]H. Riesenfield, "Sabbat et Jour du Seigneur," in *New Testament Essays*, ed. A. J. B. Higgins (Manchester: Manchester University Press, 1959), pp. 210–17; *The Gospel Tradition* (Oxford: Blackwell, 1970), pp. 122–32; followed by R. E. Brown, *John*, p. 1020. Cf. also P. Grelot, "Du sabbat juif au dimanche chrétien," *MaisDieu* 124 (1975): especially pp. 33–34.

[78]See M. M. B. Turner, chapter 5, above.

[79]Of course, Pliny's expression *stato die* does not unambiguously point to Sunday or even, as Bacchiocchi points out (*From Sabbath to Sunday*, pp. 98–99), to a regular day of the week. But we use Pliny's evidence here in the context of other evidence that Christians in his time did worship on Sunday. Note that the evidence of Pliny's informants goes back several years before the date of his letter (A.D. 112).

[80]*The Gospel Tradition*, pp. 128–29.

[81]Bacchiocchi, *From Sabbath to Sunday*, pp. 271–73.

[82]The arguments in Beckwith and Stott, *This is the Day*, pp. 40–42, cannot be regarded as more than guesswork.

9

SABBATH AND SUNDAY IN THE POST-APOSTOLIC CHURCH

R. J. BAUCKHAM

Richard J. Bauckham lectures in the Department of Theology at the University of Manchester, Manchester, England.

This chapter examines attitudes to the Sabbath and the Lord's Day in the second, third, and fourth centuries. The period is of crucial historical importance, for it is in this period that the practice of Sunday rest originated, although, as we shall see, even in the fourth century Sunday rest was not yet justified by a fully Sabbatarian theory. The views of the Fathers on Sunday observance have sometimes been discussed with too much generalization, thereby obscuring the differences between them and the development over these three centuries.[1] In this chapter we shall trace the development and pay special attention to the question of precisely when and how Sabbath ideas began to be associated with the Christian Lord's Day.

First, we shall examine the second-century evidence in some detail (dealing with the eschatological application of Sabbath themes, attitudes to the Sabbath commandment, and attitudes to Sunday). The contribution of the Alexandrian theologians Clement and Origen will then be studied, and finally, in the light of the earlier history, the origins of Sunday rest in the fourth century will become intelligible. In the next chapter we shall be able to trace the emergence of a fully Sabbatarian doctrine in the later Middle Ages.

The Eschatological Sabbath in the Second Century

Though the Christian writers of the second century seem to have been little influenced by Hebrews 3 and 4,[2] they inherited the same late Jewish traditions of thought about eschatological Sabbath rest as the author to the Hebrews had utilized, and made varied use of them. They divide into two categories: gnostic writers who understood Sabbath rest in terms of realized eschatology, and catholic writers who located the eschatological Sabbath wholly in the future.

A Jewish-Christian Gospel of the early second century contains the following account of Jesus' baptism:

> It came to pass that, when the Lord had come up from the waters, the whole fountain of the Holy Spirit descended and rested *(requievit)* upon him [Isa. 11:2] and said to him, "My son, in all the prophets I was waiting for you, so that you would come and I might rest (*requiescerem*) in you. For you are my rest (*requies mea*) [Ps. 132:14]; you are my firstborn son, who will reign for ever."[3]

Beginning from an interpretation of the baptism story as the fulfillment of Isaiah 11:2, the author has followed Jewish ideas about Wisdom's search for a resting place,[4] identifying the Holy Spirit as Wisdom.[5] The train of thought suggested by the idea of "rest" then ends in a reference to the eschatological resting place of God to which Psalm 132:14 was taken to refer in contemporary Jewish thought.[6] Christ Himself, as the final resting place of the Spirit,[7] is Himself the eschatological rest of God. Since God's eschatological rest was also that of His people, the thought is certainly implicit that the people of God would also find their rest in Christ. The passage is remarkable for its christological version of the theology of rest, which can otherwise scarcely be paralleled before the fourth century[8] except in a few gnostic texts.[9] It was precisely what most second century eschatology lacked. The association of "rest" and "reign" in this passage should also be noticed, for they are a common eschatological pair in both gnostic and orthodox thought of this period.

There is nothing especially gnostic about this baptism pericope;[10] the "Gospel of the Hebrews" from which Jerome quotes is therefore probably the Syrian or Palestinian "Gospel of the Nazarenes," from which his other citations come, rather than the less orthodox "Gospel of the Hebrews," which served the Jewish Christians of Egypt in the second century.[11] From the latter, Clement of Alexandria quotes an apocryphal logion of Jesus:

> He who seeks will not cease (παύσεται) until he finds, and when he has found he will marvel, and when he has marvelled he will reign, and when he has reigned he will rest (ἐπαναπαύσεται).[12]

The logion recurs in almost identical form in Pap. Oxy. 654 lines 5–9, while the Coptic version in *Gospel of Thomas* 2 omits the last verb of the Greek in favor of the climax, "will reign over All."[13] If the logion originated in Egyptian Jewish Christianity it may not have been intended in as gnostic a sense as it has acquired in *Thomas*. Its first two terms derive from Matthew 7:7–8 (though this was a saying congenial to gnostic thought)[14] and its last two from Jewish eschatology (though they became favorite terms of gnostic soteriology).[15] "Amazement," however, is characteristically a stage on the way to salvation in Hermetic Gnosticism or a step toward spiritual perception in Hellenistic philosophy.[16] The way of salvation which here culminates in reigning and resting is therefore the way of Christian gnosis.

"Rest" (ἀνάπαυσις) was one of the technical terms of second-century gnosticism.[17] Although it also had Hellenistic sources, [18] the gnostic concept of rest was certainly indebted to Jewish and Christian eschatology. The traditional eschatological goal of Sabbath rest was applied to the gnostic's present experience of salvation,[19] and New Testament passages of realized eschatology were taken up in this sense: Matthew 11:28–30 in both *Gospel of Thomas* 90 and *Acts of Thomas* 37, while *Gospel of Philip* 82 provides a rare example of allusion to Hebrews 4. The Gnostics exploited precisely those scriptural hints of present participation in eschatological rest that catholic writers of the period ignored.

Gnostic "rest" is the antithesis of labor, but more characteristically of "troubles"[20] or "searching." The Eons are said to "cease toiling at searching for the Father, resting there in him, knowing that this is Rest."[21] Rest is the condition of the man who, illuminated by *gnosis*, is delivered from the material world.[22] It is present experience of a condition that will continue beyond death; "he who abides in the Rest shall rest eternally."[23] The resting place of the gnostic is the heavenly world,[24] to which even now he has access.[25] But even gnostic eschatology has a future aspect, to which perhaps most commonly the concept of rest refers; it describes the final state of reunion with the Father after the gnostic's deliverance from his body at death.[26] "For when you come forth from the labours and sufferings of the body you will obtain rest through the Good and reign with the king."[27]

While Gnosticism eliminated the Christian hope of the resurrection, catholic writers of the second century used the concept of eschatological Sabbath rest to refer exclusively to the state of future salvation after the resurrection, thereby reverting to traditional Jewish usage and abandoning the Christian tension of "already" and "not yet," which the author to the Hebrews had applied to the concept of eschatological rest. In part this is to be attributed to these writers' commitment to the typology of the worldweek, whereby the six millennia of world history were to be succeeded by an eschatological Sabbath. "For in as many days as this world was made, in so many thousand years shall it be concluded" (Irenaeus).[28] Second-century eschatology was dominated by the concept of a world Sabbath to follow the Parousia, but not all such thought should properly be called "chiliast." Some writers did expect a millennium to intervene between the *Parousia* and the final dissolution of the world; for others, continuing the predominant Jewish usage, the world Sabbath was a symbol of the age to come. Thus for the chiliasts Justin Martyr,[29] Irenaeus,[30] and Hippolytus,[31] the millennium is the "rest" as well as the "kingdom" of the saints because it is the Sabbath rest of God according to Genesis 2:2 interpreted typologically.[32] Other writers, however, including Pseudo-Barnabas, do not expect a millennium but picture the state of the saints in the next world as "rest."[33] Second Clement 5:5 is typical of this period: "the sojourn of this flesh in this world is mean and for a short time, but the promise of Christ is great and marvellous, even the rest of the kingdom that shall be and of life eternal."[34] Christian life this side of the Parousia is a matter of striving to enter the rest that the Lord has reserved for His saints in the eschatological kingdom of the future.

One interesting exception to this pattern is the *Epistula Apostolorum*, an early second-century work written to combat gnostic heresies, though its form and terminology owe much to the gnostic thought world. Here the Christian's resting place, like the Gnostic's, is located in the heavenly world (12, Coptic text), and though the focus of attention is on the future day of judgment when Christ "will grant rest in life in the kingdom of my heavenly Father" to "those who have loved me" (26), there is also an anticipatory access to heavenly rest in the present (12, Coptic; 28).[35] Cross-fertilization of gnostic and catholic theology continued throughout the bitter struggles of the second century, and in the Alexandrians Clement and Origen the gnostic theology of rest was to make a more permanent contribution to the Sabbath theology of the Church.

THE SABBATH COMMANDMENT IN THE SECOND CENTURY

The early church had no single answer to the question of the relevance of the Sabbath commandment to Christians. The churches of the New Testament period included a variety of views. There were legalistic Jewish Christians who regarded the observance of the whole law as a matter of salvation, but there were also Jewish Christians who themselves continued to keep the Sabbath as a matter of national *mores* but laid no such obligation on Gentile converts. There were Gentile Christians who adopted the observance of the Jewish Sabbath, while others regarded themselves as entirely free from the commandment either on the grounds of its being a specifically Jewish law or following the Pauline argument that the Sabbath was a shadow of the reality that had now come in Christ. Simply because the Pauline view is now in Scripture, we may not assume that it was the view that prevailed in the early church. Paul himself urged tolerance of those who observed "days" without thereby compromising the gospel (Rom. 14). In particular we should not underestimate the appeal Sabbath observance had for many Gentile Christians. Imitation of the Jewish Sabbath was evidently widespread in the second-century Roman world,[36] though we should also take into account the prevalence of anti-Semitic feeling, which would turn Gentiles against an institution so obviously characteristic of the Jews. These factors were operative in the churches alongside the more specifically Christian questions of the Christian's relation to the law of Moses and the Jewish Christian's relation to the law of his fathers.

Jewish Christian Attitudes to the Sabbath Commandment

Possibly the earliest extra-canonical treatment of the question is the story Codex Bezae preserves as Luke 6:5:

> On the same day he saw a man working on the Sabbath and said to him, "Man, if you know what you are doing, you are blessed; but if you do not know, you are accursed and a transgressor of the law."

Jeremias' argument for the dominical authenticity of the logion can hardly be accepted.[37] In the first place, Jesus is most unlikely to have met a Jew in

Palestine working on the Sabbath.[38] Also, the saying does not accurately represent Jesus' attitude to the Sabbath. While it is true that "the stress can never fall on the first half of an antithetic parallelism" and that therefore the point of the saying is to administer a sharp rebuke to frivolous neglect of the Sabbath,[39] it nevertheless does permit Sabbath breaking by those who "know what they are doing." It "seems to mean that the man working on the Sabbath is blessed if he does so in the knowledge that the Messianic Age has come; otherwise he remains under the jurisdiction and curse of the old order."[40] But the evidence of the Gospels does not allow us to suppose that Jesus Himself allowed even Himself, let alone others, to transcend the Mosaic Law on this basis during His ministry. There is no suggestion that the man's work is comparable to plucking ears of corn or performing acts of healing; it is simply work—unequivocal Sabbath breaking. The effect of the logion is not to distinguish types of work, some permissible on the Sabbath and others not,[41] but to distinguish right and wrong reasons for ignoring the Sabbath commandment. Jesus would not have sanctioned ignoring the commandment.

The same arguments tell against Rordorf's view that Luke 6:5D is Jewish Christian apologetic for Jesus' attitude to the Sabbath; it is hardly cogent apologetic to represent Jesus' attitude to the Sabbath as less strict than it actually was.[42] Nor is it likely to have emanated from the Jewish-Christian communities of Palestine and Syria where the Sabbath was still observed. Though many of these may have followed Jesus' example in rejecting the rigor of the Sabbath Halakah, they would not have constructed a logion permitting Sabbath breaking in such general terms.[43] On the other hand, the attitudes reflected in such second-century anti-Sabbatarian writers as Ignatius, Pseudo-Barnabas, Justin and Irenaeus could hardly have found expression in this logion, with its unexpected stress on the possibility of damnable neglect of the Sabbath commandment.

The pericope has at least a possible *Sitz im Leben* in a late first-century situation similar to that reflected in Romans 14. In such a context a Jewish Christian of "Paulinist" persuasion may have wished to insist on the *proper* principle of Christian freedom not to observe days, in opposition to the thoughtless contempt shown by "stronger" brethren. The latter may well have carried over from their pagan backgrounds an attitude of ridicule toward such Jewish practices as the Sabbath.[44] For the author of our pericope, on the other hand, the Sabbath was part of the law of God. The Jewish Christian was not to ignore the law for the sake of mere human convenience or of avoiding the scorn of his Gentile brethren. Only on the basis of a right understanding of his relation to the Law might he work on the Sabbath. The closest New Testament parallel is Romans 14:23.[45]

Whether or not this interpretation is correct, Luke 6:5D should make it clear that so long as Jewish Christianity was a force in the church at large the question of the Sabbath commandment was no simple matter. To what extent Jewish Christians within the predominantly Gentile churches of the second century continued to keep the Sabbath is not clear. Ignatius (*Magn.* 9:1) has been understood to refer to Jewish Christians who had given up Sabbath observance, but it is more likely that Ignatius intended to refer to the Old Testament prophets.[46] In any case, his purpose was to dissuade Gentile Christians from judaizing; he cannot be used as evidence that Jewish Christians in general had given up Sabbath observance. On the contrary, his letters indicate that the strong Jewish influence in the churches of Asia tempted Gentiles to keep the Sabbath. Ignatius himself, at least under pressure of controversy, regarded the Sabbath as a practice so unchristian that presumably even Jewish Christians ought to abandon it, but Justin Martyr expresses a more tolerant attitude to Sabbath observance by Jewish Christians who did not urge Gentiles to judaize.[47]

Certainly the Jewish-Christian communities of Syria and Palestine continued to keep the Sabbath.[48] Their relation both to the great church and to Judaism was probably still fluid in this period when they faced exclusion from the synagogue for their allegiance to Jesus but also strove to maintain their Jewishness by continued adherence to the law. The stricter groups, repudiating the "antinomianism" of the Gentile churches, withdrew into a position that the Gentile theologians of the great church were to regard as heretical.

These Jewish Christians preserved the traditions of Jesus' disputes with the Pharisees about Sabbath observance, and probably many of them followed Him in disregarding the full Sabbath Halakah. This would have been a subject of debate with the synagogue, and an early stage of such debate may well be reflected in the Matthean account of the Sabbath pericopes.[49] The accusation of Sabbath breaking against Jesus seems to have been a feature of Jewish argument against Christians,[50] and it is noteworthy that even Gentile Christian writers of the second and third centuries never cite Jesus as a precedent for breaking the Sabbath commandment.[51] Jesus was held to have kept the law of God but not the traditions of men.

A rabbinic tradition preserved in the *Midrash Qoheleth Rabba* may reflect conflict with Jewish Christians over the Sabbath in the second century:

> Hanina, the son of R. Joshua's brother, came to Capernaum, and the *minim* worked a spell on him and set him riding upon an ass on the Sabbath. He went to his uncle, Joshua, who anointed him with oil and he recovered [from the spell. R. Joshua] said to him, "Since the ass of that wicked person has roused itself against

you, you are not able to reside in the land of Israel." So he went down from there to Babylon where he died in peace.[52]

The very late attestation of this tradition[53] requires that it be treated with caution, but Travers Herford[54] argued persuasively for its second-century origin as a story about R. Ḥananjah,[55] the nephew of R. Joshua b. Hananjah. R. Ḥananjah, who migrated to Babylonia during or after the Bar Kokhba war, was subsequently involved in controversy with the Palestinian patriarch Shim'on b. Gamliel over the independence of his school from the patriarch's authority. The story must be an attempt by Palestinian Rabbis to discredit Ḥananjah's authority. In that case it must have originated during or soon after the dispute, i.e., during the second century. Of course we cannot tell whether the accusation of association with the *minim* was well founded, but the story will still reflect second-century attitudes to the *minim* of Capernaum.

These *minim* were certainly Jewish Christians.[56] The "ass of that wicked person" is presumably a reference to Balaam's ass, and Balaam was a rabbinic code name for Jesus.[57] It may be that this association, rather than Jesus' riding an ass, has suggested the particular form of Sabbath breaking into which Ḥananjah was enticed by the Christians. In any case the story is too polemical to be taken as evidence that Jewish Christians broke the Sabbath in their own eyes, by infringements of the commandment as blatant as riding an ass. It can, however, be regarded as evidence that they kept the Sabbath with less rigor than the Rabbis and were therefore regarded as Sabbath breakers by the Rabbis.

Jewish-Christian disputes with the synagogue in Palestine or Syria in the early second century are more certainly reflected in the *Gospel of the Nazarenes*. A surviving fragment recounts the story of the healing of the man with the withered hand and attributes to him the words, "I was a mason, seeking my living with my hands; I beg you, Jesus, give me back my health so that I need not shamefully beg for food."[58] The intention is clearly to give an urgency to the need for Jesus' healing action such as is conspicuously lacking in the Matthean account, and thereby to defend Jesus against the Jewish accusation of Sabbath breaking. It is noteworthy that the defense aims to reduce the difference between Jesus and the Pharisees,[59] and must reflect a Jewish-Christian group keeping the Sabbath with greater rigor than Matthew's community had done.

Probably it was such strict Jewish-Christians who produced the apocryphal logion of Jesus: "Unless you keep the Sabbath, you will not see the Father." We shall argue below that this logion, widely known in the second century church and usually interpreted in a metaphorical sense, may have originated in strict Jewish-Christian circles with reference to literal Sabbath observance.

It may even have originated in the Jewish-Christian group that later writers call the Masbotheans (presumably = "Sabbatarians," from *mšbt*),[60] who held that Jesus Himself had taught them *"in omni re sabbatizare."*[61] The sense of this command is not clear. In second-century Gentile Christian interpretation of the Sabbath commandment, "to sabbatize perpetually" means to devote all one's time to God, but this non-Sabbatarian interpretation is hardly appropriate to a group known as "Sabbatarians." Possibly the Masbotheans were a monastic group that abjured all secular activity, but most likely the phrase *"in omni re"* simply indicates the excessive strictness of their Sabbath observance.

Ignatius and the Problem of Gentile Observance of the Sabbath

Did Gentile Christians in the second century observe the Sabbath? Although, as we shall see, the dominant trend of second-century Christianity was toward a forthright rejection of Sabbath observance along with Jewish practices in general, we must also reckon with a continuing influence of Jewish Christianity in some parts of the church that promoted judaizing tendencies. We must also recognize that the problem of judaizing in popular Christian practice has to be set within a larger problem of syncretizing. Gentile Christians might be influenced by Jewish Christians or by non-Christian Jews, but they might also encounter Sabbath observance in other, strongly syncretistic contexts.

Various sects around the fringes of Judaism, Christianity, and Gnosticism were Sabbatarian. Very strict Sabbath observance was demanded by the Jewish gnostic Dositheus of Samaria.[62] Sabbath observance was allegedly part of the teaching of the gnostic Cerinthus.[63] Interesting testimony to the association of Sabbath and astrology among syncretistic groups is provided by the Elkasites, who were taught to "honour the Sabbath" because it was one of the days controlled by "evil stars of godlessness."[64] Asia Minor in particular seems to have harbored judaistic, syncretistic sects like the Σαββατισταί of Cilicia (who probably combined their Sabbath observance with the worship of Sabazios!) and the Hypsistarians.[65] These have no known connection with Christianity but illustrate the possible complexity of "judaizing" problems both at Colossae in Paul's time and at Magnesia in Ignatius'.

Ignatius' letter to the Magnesians (9:1) is in fact the sole second-century reference to Gentile Christians being tempted to observe the Sabbath. It is interesting to find this reference again in the area of Asia Minor where Paul had encountered his judaizing problems, and where both Jews and Jewish Christians were numerous. Ignatius' letter to the Philadelphians (6:1) indicates a similar problem of judaizing in that church. Such problems seem to have been endemic to the area.

The identity of Ignatius' opponents has been disputed, especially the question of whether he faced two groups, judaizers and docetic Gnostics, or one group of syncretistic judaizers.[66] On the whole it looks as though Ignatius encountered not Jewish Christians who urged the law of Moses on Gentiles, but syncretistic judaizers, probably both Jewish and Gentile, who retained certain Jewish practices (such as observing the Sabbath) and refused to follow the Christian interpretation of the Old Testament, which found the life, death and resurrection of Jesus foretold in messianic prophecy. It seems likely that their separate eucharists (*Philad.* 4:1; cf. 3:3; 7; *Magn.* 4:1; *Smyrn.* 7:1; 8:2), which Ignatius regarded as schismatic, were held on the Sabbath in distinction from the bishop's eucharist on Sunday.

In *Magn.* 9:1, Ignatius uses "sabbatizing" as a term representative of Jewish practices in general, a very natural usage in view of the distinctiveness and prominence of the Sabbath in Judaism. For Ignatius the practice of Judaism was radically incompatible with Christianity. "If we live according to Judaism, we confess that we have not received grace" (*Magn.* 8:1). "It is absurd to profess Jesus Christ and to judaize" (10:3). But the really crucial point was the Christological issue, the historical reality of the life, death, and resurrection of Jesus as fulfillment of messianic prophecy. It was the interpretation of the prophets that was in dispute with the judaizers, and hence *Magn.* 9:1 is set within a discussion of the prophets. In this context it becomes clear that the contrast of the Sabbath, representing Judaism, and the Lord's Day, representing Christianity, is important to Ignatius because the Lord's Day is the day on which Jesus rose from the dead. "The Lord's Day, in which also our life sprang up through Him and through His death, which some deny—through which mystery we receive faith." Observing the Lord's Day means acknowledging that salvation is by the real death and resurrection of Jesus "sabbatizing," the practice of the judaizers, Ignatius associates with their docetic denial of the Lord's death. This is why Ignatius uses the contrast of Sabbath and Lord's Day as symbolizing the whole dispute.

It is not entirely clear whether in *Magn.* 9:1 it is the Old Testament prophets or Jewish Christians who "came to a new hope, no longer sabbatizing, but living according to the Lord's Day." The whole context favors the former, and Ignatius should not be thought incapable of believing that the prophets abandoned Sabbath observance, since in 8:2 he says that they "lived according to Christ Jesus" and therefore not "according to Judaism." The prophets, he is saying, lived in hope of the death and resurrection of the Messiah, and therefore they lived "according to the Lord's Day," awaiting the salvation that the event of Easter Sunday was to bring them. "Therefore, when he whom they were rightly awaiting came, he raised them from the dead" (9:3).

If Ignatius believed that the Old Testament prophets, as Christians before Christ, abandoned Sabbath observance, he must have expected Jewish Christians to do the same. The sharp contrast he draws between "sabbatizing" and "living according to the Lord's Day" is noteworthy since the matter had not previously been put like this in extant Christian literature. This is not exactly the Pauline concern for Gentile freedom from the law but a more thorough-going distinction between Judaism and Christianity. The Sabbath, for Ignatius, is the badge of a false attitude to Jesus Christ, while eucharistic worship on the Lord's Day defines Christianity as salvation by the death and resurrection of Jesus Christ. He is an early witness to the dissociation of Christianity from Judaism which characterizes the second century, and to the wholly negative attitude to Sabbath observance that was the corollary of that.

We find no further reference to Gentile Christian observance of the Sabbath until the third century, but from the early third century and especially the fourth century there is evidence of rather widespread Gentile regard for the Sabbath, expressed primarily in prohibition of fasting on the Sabbath and in the practice of Christian worship on the Sabbath (in addition to worship on Sunday). Was there therefore a continuous tradition of Sabbath observance in some Gentile Christian circles from apostolic times through to the third and fourth centuries? The gap in the evidence in the second century makes this question highly debatable.[67]

The Gentile-Christian Sabbath observance of the third and fourth centuries would seem, in general, to have been no longer a result of Jewish-*Christian* influence; it seems to have been rather a matter of popular Christian adoption of Jewish customs from their Jewish neighbors. Consequently, it belonged especially in areas with large Jewish communities, especially Palestine, Syria, and Asia Minor. The Sabbath was part of a wider problem of judaizing within a general syncretistic context.[68] It is perfectly possible that such judaizing tendencies had continued from the apostolic church throughout the second century,[69] but the evidence does seem to indicate that such tendencies became more widespread in the third and fourth centuries. Perhaps this should be seen as part of the generally increasing problem of syncretism as Christianity emerged from the age of persecutions and absorbed a large new popular following.

This judaizing tendency was a grass roots tendency that the authorities of the church opposed. The Council of Laodicea (A.D. 380), for example, legislated against a series of judaizing practices including resting on the Sabbath (canon 29).[70] It seems that while the popular tendency was to imitate the Jewish practice, the authorities often responded by insisting on a specifically

Christian kind of Sabbath observance sharply distinguished from the Jewish kind. The Sabbath was not to be observed in "idleness," imitating the Jews, but as a day of Christian worship when the *New Testament* Scriptures were read and as a commemoration of God's creation of the world *through Christ.*[71] Rordorf argues that this distinctively Christian Sabbath observance could not be continuous with the older judaizing tendencies.[72] Probably however, we should see it as an attempt by the church to contain judaizing tendencies by Christianizing the Sabbath.[73]

Pseudo-Barnabas

A singular attempt to reinterpret the Sabbath commandment in such a way as to disallow the observance of the Sabbath, not only by Christians but even by Jews before Christ, is to be found in the Epistle of Barnabas 15. The interpretation of the passage is difficult and has been debated.[74] The following reconstruction of the argument seems the most plausible to the present writer, but it would be impossible here to discuss the problems in full detail.

"Barnabas," probably an Alexandrian Jewish Christian, writes against the observance of Jewish practices to discourage his fellow Christians from persisting in or adopting them. He regards the Decalogue as the basis of both the covenant that was made and broken at Sinai and the covenant that now applies to Christians (14:3–5). The law enshrined in the Decalogue is binding on Christians. The Sabbath therefore demanded attention both as a principal feature (with circumcision) of the Jewish cultus to which Barnabas was opposed and also as a commandment of the Decalogue. He is the only second-century Christian writer who treats the Sabbath commandment explicitly as part of the Decalogue (15:1).

In the tradition of Jewish and Christian typological exegesis of Genesis 1 and 2, Barnabas explains the creation week as a prophecy of the world week (six millennia followed by the eschatological Sabbath). This is the "seventh day" that God sanctified, on which He will rest (*καταπαύσεται*). This present world, which is the time of the "lawless one" (ὁ ἄνομος), is contrasted with the coming new world, from which "lawlessness" (ἡ ἀνομία) will have been eliminated. God will bring this world to an end at the Parousia (the end of its six millennia) and inaugurate the new world. His eschatological rest is therefore interpreted not as inactivity but as bringing an end to this world (*καταπαύσας τὰ πάντα*) and bringing into existence the new world (*καινῶν γεγονότων πάντων*).[75]

Barnabas' version of the Sabbath *commandment* (15:1, 6) is original; he interprets "sanctifying" the Sabbath as an activity of radical moral holiness such as no one in the present evil age can attain. In the eschatological

Sabbath, however, Christians themselves will have been fully sanctified and so will be able to keep holy the Sabbath (age) and share the eschatological rest of God. Obedience to the Sabbath commandment has nothing to do with a day of the week or with physical rest but is a matter of holy living in the future Sabbath age that God has made holy.[76] Jewish Sabbaths (*τὰ νῦν σάββατα*) are therefore quite unacceptable to God.

At this point Barnabas' argument might have ended. Much of the confusion about his meaning has arisen from his concluding remarks about the "eighth day," which have almost the character of an afterthought. Not content with dismissing weekly Sabbath observance by reference to the eschatological Sabbath, Barnabas (like Ignatius before him) feels it necessary also to contrast the Jewish Sabbath with the Christian Sunday. He therefore complicates his eschatological terminology by referring to the new world as the "eighth day," and concludes, "Therefore (i.e., because the Sabbath acceptable to God is the eschatological eighth day, the new world), we pass with rejoicing the eighth day on which Jesus rose from the dead, appeared, and ascended into heaven" (15:9).

Barnabas is not a chiliast. Though he has commonly been understood to mean that the Sabbath age will be followed by the eighth day of eternity, this interpretation cannot be sustained. He uses both "Sabbath" and "eighth day" as interchangeable terms for the one new world that will follow the Parousia.[77] This confusing combination of two systems of eschatological arithmetic is the less surprising since we shall find it recurring in Alexandrian Christian Gnosticism. It is a way of combining the Christian sense of Sunday worship as anticipating the life of the world to come with the inherited Jewish idea of eschatological Sabbath.

Nor is it Barnabas' intention to introduce the Christian observance of Sunday as a fulfillment of the Sabbath commandment, though he has been so interpreted.[78] In the first place, *ἄγομεν τὴν ἡμέραν τὴν ὀγδόην εἰς εὐφροσύνην* (15:9) is in marked contrast to all Barnabas' terminology for Sabbath keeping earlier in the same chapter. It is not a natural way to indicate that Sunday observance fulfills the command; *ἁγιάσατε τὸ σάββατον κυρίου χερσὶν καθαραῖς καὶ καρδίᾳ καθαρᾷ*, "Sanctify the Sabbath of the Lord with clean hands and a clean heart" (15:1). Second, his argument against Jewish Sabbath observance is precisely that the commandment *cannot* be fulfilled this side of the Parousia (15:6–7). He cannot eat his cake and have it.[79] Third, neither physical rest nor worship have any place in Barnabas' exposition of the Sabbath commandment.

Evidently he introduces the reference to Sunday in order to point out that Christians do have their own legitimate weekly observance in some sense comparable to the Jewish Sabbath he has just proved illegitimate. But unlike the Jewish Sabbath, the Christian Sunday is not an attempt to fulfill the Sabbath commandment. Rather it is a weekly celebration of the hope of eschatological salvation. Unless the end of 15:9 is wholly unconnected with the argument of the chapter, Barnabas must be taken to mean that Christians have this hope (cf. 15:7) because in the resurrection of Jesus the new age has in some sense already dawned.

Barnabas' eschatology does not lack a realized aspect, primarily the victory of Christ on which is based the Christian hope for salvation at the Parousia. "The righteous man both lives in this present world and waits for (ἐκδέχεται) the holy age" (10:11). In fact he believes that the holiness of the age to come is already anticipated in the life of the Christian in this world (see especially chap. 1), and this is the presupposition for his stress on the struggle against the evil powers of the present world (e.g., 2:1; 4:9). On this basis one might have expected to find in the argument of chapter 15 a claim that the Christian fulfills the Sabbath commandment in an anticipatory fashion in the present world not by means of Sunday worship but to the extent that his life conforms to the holiness of the world to-come. That the commandment is in fact referred wholly to the future must reflect Barnabas' polemical purpose and the rigid eschatological scheme that places the Sabbath rest of God wholly on the far side of the Parousia.

Barnabas' interpretation of the Sabbath commandment has two elements: (1) it is applied to holiness rather than to physical rest, (2) it is applied to the eschatological Sabbath that follows the Parousia. The second element we have already seen to be common in second-century writers, though rarely related to the Sabbath *commandment*. The first element becomes a favorite reinterpretation of the Sabbath commandment, especially in the later second century, though with reference to Christian life in the present and rarely related to the eschatological rest. Certainly Barnabas' own way of combining the two elements is unique.

As in the case of Ignatius, we should notice that Barnabas' rejection of the (literal) Sabbath belongs in a context of very sharp differentiation between Judaism and Christianity. For Barnabas the whole practice of the Jewish religion, including keeping the Sabbath, was false religion that was never intended by God, even in the Old Testament. The Jewish practice of the Sabbath was not obedience but disobedience to God, and therefore Christians, the true heirs of the covenant, must not observe the Sabbath. Barnabas is extreme in his statement of this viewpoint, but the purely negative evaluation of the Jewish Sabbath in the context of a wholesale condemnation of Judaism is characteristic of the Fathers.

The Metaphorical Interpretation of the Sabbath Commandment

Barnabas' reinterpretation of the Sabbath commandment as commanding holiness rather than physical rest is an early example of the favorite second-century Christian interpretation of the Sabbath commandment. Probably it was already current in the Hellenized Jewish Christian circles of Alexandria to which Barnabas belonged. Those circles also knew it as the sense of a well-known apocryphal logion of Jesus about the Sabbath that has survived both in Greek (Papyrus Oxy. 1, lines 4–11) and in Coptic (Gospel of Thomas 27):

> ἐὰν μὴ νηστεύσητε τὸν κόσμον οὐ μὴ εὕρητε τὴν βασιλείαν τοῦ θεοῦ καὶ ἐὰν μὴ σαββατίσητε τὸ σάββατον οὐκ ὄψεσθε τὸν πατέρα ("Unless you fast to the world, you will not find the kingdom of God; unless you keep the Sabbath, you will not see the Father").

It is not possible that this logion originated in the gnostic circles that redacted the *Gospel of Thomas*, for that Gospel's characteristic manner of dealing with Jewish and Jewish-Christian observances is to reject them outright[80] rather than to spiritualize them. The original logion[81] was probably a legalistic Jewish-Christian formulation.[82] "If you do not fast, you will not find the kingdom of God; if you do not keep the Sabbath, you will not see the Father." That the *Gospel of Thomas* draws on extreme Jewish-Christian material elsewhere is clear,[83] and the expression σαββατίσητε τὸ σάββατον is a Semitism that need not mean more than "keep the Sabbath."[84] The metaphorical sense of the logion in its surviving version depends entirely on the words τὸν κόσμον, which are just such a gnosticizing addition as is found in *Gospel of Thomas* 21 (where the Synoptic command to "watch" becomes: "be watchful over against the world"). By means of this emendation an originally literal requirement to keep the Jewish Sabbath has become a metaphorical command to keep some form of spiritual Sabbath.[85]

The precise nuance of meaning is difficult to determine. In the context in *Thomas*, Gärtner finds it an expression of a "negative attitude to the world," with "fasting to the world" as equivalent to asceticism, and "sabbatizing" meaning perhaps contemplation.[86] Both terms could easily be taken in a very general sense, acceptable both to orthodox Christianity and to Gnosticism, as requiring abstention from the evil of the present age.

It has been plausibly suggested[87] that this or a similar agraphon was in the mind of Justin Martyr when he wrote, "The new law requires you to keep the sabbath constantly."[88] In the previous chapter Justin had identified Christ as the new law. Similarly the Valentinian Ptolemaeus, writing of how Christ changed the meaning of the ceremonial law from literal to spiritual, explained that He

> desires that we should be circumcised, but not in the physical foreskin, but in relation to our spiritual hearts. He wants us to keep the Sabbath; for he wishes us to be idle with reference to evil actions. As to fasting, he wants us to be engaged not in physical fasting, but in spiritual fasting, which amounts to abstinence from all that is evil.[89]

If Ptolemaeus here intended to refer to agrapha,[90] then *Gospel of Thomas* 53 and 27 fit precisely.

Whether it was popularized and reinforced by an apocryphal saying of Jesus or not, the metaphorical interpretation of the Sabbath commandment was standard after the later second century. As Rordorf explains, "The sabbath commandment does not mean, they say, that we should abstain from work on one day out of seven, but that we should abstain *at all times* from any sinful act: the Christian should, therefore, observe a perpetual sabbath and consecrate every day to God."[91]

In Justin this interpretation is used as a critique of Jewish Sabbath observance:

> The new law requires you to keep perpetual sabbath, and you, because you are idle for one day, suppose you are pious, not discerning why this has been commanded you. . . . The Lord our God does not take pleasure in such observances: if there is any perjured person or thief among you, let him cease to be so: if any adulterer, let him repent; then he has kept the sweet and true sabbaths of God.[92]

In Ptolemaeus the spiritual interpretation of the Sabbath is part of a systematic exposition of the relevance of the Mosaic Law to Christians, and similarly Irenaeus was concerned to explain the meaning of the Mosaic Law for Christians, applying the principles of the Sermon on the Mount to the whole Law. In the case of tithes, for example, Irenaeus argued that the law "will not require tithes of him who consecrates all his possessions to God." In the case of the Sabbath,

> he will not be commanded to leave idle one day of rest, who is constantly keeping sabbath, that is, giving homage to God in the temple of God, which is man's body, and at all times doing the works of justice.[93]

For Tertullian, the meaning of the Sabbath commandment for Christians was "that we still more ought to observe a sabbath from all servile work always, and not only every seventh day, but through all time."[94] It is entirely clear that for all these writers the literal commandment to rest one day in seven was a temporary ordinance for Israel alone. The Christian fulfills the commandment by devoting all his time to God.[95]

The rationale for this interpretation depended, of course, on a wholly "religious" understanding of the commandment; no writer of the period betrays any thought of its being a provision for needed physical rest.[96] The

Jewish form of observance was therefore "idleness." The commandment was really about devotion to God, and therefore Jesus' principle of intensifying the Law (by which, for example, the prohibition of murder was extended to hatred) made the Sabbath commandment teach the devotion of the whole of life to God.

This was the basic principle from which the Fathers argued that literal Sabbath observance was not required of Christians. Other arguments were subsidiary. It was, for example, commonly pointed out that the patriarchs before Moses did not keep the weekly Sabbath and yet were counted righteous.[97] Old Testament breaches of the Sabbath (i.e., cases where the literal commandment was overriden by the demands of serving God) were cited, e.g., the priests in the Temple, circumcision on the eighth day after birth,[98] Joshua's seven-day circuit of Jericho, and the Maccabees' battles on the Sabbath.[99] Justin had no doubt of the answer to the old Jewish question of whether God in His government of the universe rests one day in seven.[100]

It also seems axiomatic with second-century writers that the Sabbath commandment, despite its place in the Decalogue, belongs with those Jewish ceremonial ordinances whose literal observance has passed with their fulfillment in Christ. In *Actus Vercellenses* 1, Paul is represented as preaching that Christ "abolished their sabbath and fasts and festivals and circumcision." For Justin, the Sabbath is emphatically in the same category as circumcision and festivals; they were ordinances that Christians do not observe because they were given to the Jews on account of their hardness of heart and sin.[101] In the context of anti-Jewish polemic, the language can be extreme. The *Epistle to Diognetus* (4) speaks of "their scrupulousness about meats, their superstitions about sabbaths, their boasting about circumcision, and their fancies about fasting and new moons, all of them ridiculous and unworthy of notice." According to Aristides, "They suppose in their minds that they are serving God, but in the methods of their actions their service is to angels and not to God, in that they observe sabbaths and new moons and the passover and the great fast. . . ."[102] From such wholly negative, even anti-Semitic, attitudes to the law, it was not too large a step to the views of Marcion, who went out of his way to dishonor the Sabbath by making it a day of fasting.[103]

With the exception of Pseudo-Barnabas, no Christian writer before Tertullian[104] refers to the Sabbath commandment as part of the Decalogue. This is extraordinary in view of the fact that the Decalogue undoubtedly held a central place in early Christian ethical instruction, so much so that it may have been on account of Christian use that it was withdrawn from the synagogue liturgy early in the second century.[105] But extant examples of early Christian paraenesis based on the Decalogue[106] show that it was used with considerable selectiveness and flexibility, and normally with reference only to the second table. In none of the extant examples does the Sabbath commandment appear in any form.

Gentile Christians took over the Jewish regard for the Decalogue as the epitome of the Law, but translated this into an identification of the Decalogue with the law of nature common to Christians and Jews.[107] As the law of nature, the Decalogue was written on the hearts of the pre-Mosaic patriarchs, and must be sharply distinguished from the rest of the Mosaic legislation, which consisted of temporary commandments "given for bondage and for a sign" to Israel.[108] Yet the Sabbath is never treated with the special regard that its place in the Decalogue would seem to demand; rather it is consistently classed with the temporary ceremonial law.

The most striking example of this is found in the Valentinian Ptolemaeus' *Letter to Flora*, which contains the first known systematic Christian treatment of the Old Testament Law. Ptolemaeus, in an attempt to distinguish categories of commandments according to Jesus' treatment of them, divided the Pentateuch into three parts: the Law of God, Moses' own additions, and "the traditions of the elders." Jesus rejected the last two. Ptolemaeus then again divided the Law of God (who for him was an inferior, though righteous, deity) into three parts, which correspond to the now traditional division into moral, judicial, and ceremonial law. The Decalogue he regarded as "pure legislation which is not mixed with evil, which . . . the Saviour came not to destroy but to fulfil." The second category, "intertwined with baseness and injustice," Jesus had destroyed. The third category, "which is exemplary and symbolic," Jesus had "changed," substituting spiritual for literal meanings. Despite his explicit identification of the Decalogue with the first category, Ptolemaeus gives as examples of the *third* category "offerings, circumcision, Sabbath, fasting, Passover, unleavened bread," and discusses the Sabbath as an example of this third category.[109]

No dogmatic explanation of this strange procedure is possible. It is certainly not the case that second-century writers regarded the literal Sabbath as ceremonial, while regarding the Christian, spiritual Sabbath as fulfilling the commandment in the Decalogue.[110] For Ptolemaeus, as for Justin, the spiritual Sabbath is the Christian transformation of the Jewish ceremonial Sabbath just as circumcision of the heart was the Christian version of the Jewish literal circumcision. It was Irenaeus[111] who, probably in reaction against Marcion, provided the most positive second-century estimate of the law of Moses, explaining it as a tutor in righteousness, useful in its time but now transcended in Christ. But even here the Sabbath is mentioned alongside commandments of the Decalogue only in the same way as tithing is. For Irenaeus the Decalogue *qua* law of Moses was not distinctive: all Mosaic commandments, including the Ten Commandments, find their fulfillment in Christ. Only as abiding natural law written in the hearts of men was the Decalogue distinctive, and here perhaps is the clue to our problem. In the latter usage it may be that the Decalogue is a less precise term than we expect it to be. It may be that Irenaeus and Ptolemaeus were so used to the flexible and selective use of the Decalogue in Christian paraenesis that the term suggested to them not so much ten individual commandments to be mentally listed, but simply the moral law. This is possible if, as all the evidence suggests, the Sabbath commandment (as well as the second) was commonly ignored in Christian paraenetic use of the Decalogue.

It must be stressed that, outside Jewish Christianity, all second-century references to the Sabbath commandment either endorse the metaphorical interpretation or reject the literal interpretation as Judaistic or do both. Perhaps there were some Gentile Christians who kept the Sabbath (see above) but if so, they found no spokesman whose writings survive. The neglect of the Sabbath commandment in Christian paraenesis goes back to the original conviction of the majority of the Christian missionaries of the early period of the church's Gentile expansion, that the Sabbath was not to be imposed on Gentile converts. The metaphorical interpretation of the commandment was a later development, probably originating in Alexandria, where strong Jewish Christians, like Pseudo-Barnabas and the redactor of the logion in *Gospel of Thomas* 27, used it to dissuade their "weaker" brethren (both Jewish and judaizing Gentile Christians) from Jewish practices. It became popular in the later second century, partly in the context of controversy with Judaism, from which the church was increasingly concerned to differentiate itself, but also partly in the context of controversy with Marcion, who repudiated the Old Testament entirely. The attempt to steer a course between Judaism and Marcionite heresy forced Christian writers such as Irenaeus and Tertullian to clarify the elements of continuity and discontinuity between the religions of the Old and New Testaments. The metaphorical interpretation of the Sabbath commandment enabled them to explain how the commandment could be God given and valuable and yet not binding on Christians in its literal sense.[112]

Sunday in the Second Century

We have already listed and discussed in chapter 8 the second-century occurrences of the term κυριακή (ἡμέρα) in order to demonstrate that they refer to the regular and universal Christian observance of Sunday as the day of worship. We also argued there that, at the beginning of the second century,

Sunday worship was already established as the universal Christian practice.

A number of scholars have in the past argued that Christian Sunday observance originated in the second century. The most recent and fullest version of this thesis is that of S. Bacchiocchi.[113] We have referred to some aspects of his argument in chapter 8, but we must here debate his principal contentions with regard to the second century. His thesis depends on four main arguments:

(1) Sunday could not have originated in Palestinian Jewish Christianity, since Jewish Christians in Palestine continued to keep the Sabbath.[114]

This argument depends on Bacchiocchi's assumption that Sunday originated as a Christian Sabbath, a day of worship *and rest*,[115] and therefore an *alternative* to the Jewish Sabbath. We have argued above that this assumption is invalid and that there is reason to suppose that Christian worship on Sunday goes back to early Palestinian Christianity not as alternative but as additional to the observance of the Jewish Sabbath. Those Ebionites who, according to Eusebius,[116] observed both the Sabbath and Sunday may well represent the practice of the early Palestinian church. Those others who, in Eusebius' time, did not worship on Sunday, may have been the descendants of groups that abandoned the distinctively Christian Sunday worship in the period after A.D. 70 when Palestinian Jewish Christians came under great pressure from the synagogues to conform on pain of excommunication.

(2) Bacchiocchi's second argument is that the substitution of Sunday for the Sabbath occurred in the early second century as a result of anti-Jewish feeling in the church. Roman anti-Semitism here combined with the desire of Christians to distinguish themselves from Jews in view of the Emperor Hadrian's antagonism to Jews and Jewish practices. This desire to differentiate Christianity from Judaism Bacchiocchi traces in Ignatius, Pseudo-Barnabas and Justin,[117] and finds to have been especially prominent in the church at Rome.[118] Accordingly it is in Rome that he locates the origin of Christian Sunday observance along with the origin of the Sunday Easter (in place of the Passover) and of the practice of fasting on the Sabbath, which was intended to prevent Christians from venerating the Sabbath and to enhance the status of Sunday.

In his description of the "anti-Judaism of differentiation"[119] in second-century Christianity, Bacchiocchi has highlighted an important factor in second-century Christian attitudes to the Sabbath, to which we have already drawn attention. It was no doubt a complex phenomenon, incorporating the Pauline theological concern for the freedom of Gentile Christians from the law, along with the desire for the practical advantages of dissociation from Judaism in the eyes of the Roman authorities, and also an element of sheer anti-Semitism, which was rife in the Roman world. These factors certainly inspired some second-century Christian writers to speak of the Jewish Sabbath with contempt.[120] It is, however, important to add that in the controversy with Gnosticism catholic Christianity refused to abandon its continuity with the Old Testament. Marcion's distinction between the evil God of the Jews, who gave the Sabbath commandment, and the Christian God revealed in Jesus was repudiated by the church.

Anti-Judaism played its part in second-century Christian polemic against Jewish Sabbath observance, but it does not follow that it motivated the introduction of Christian Sunday worship. For we have already argued[121] that Sunday worship dates back to the first century, while few second-century writers compare and contrast the Jewish Sabbath and the Christian Sunday.[122] Derogatory discussions of the Jewish Sabbath do not usually refer to the Christian Sunday. If Sunday were a recent substitute for the Jewish Sabbath, we should expect far more discussion of the superiority of Sunday to the Sabbath.

(3) Bacchiocchi argues that the successful substitution of Sunday for the Sabbath in the second-century church can be explained by the primacy of the church of Rome.[123] It was the preeminent authority of the bishop of Rome that influenced the entire church to adopt this new practice.

This is probably the weakest of Bacchiocchi's arguments, but it is essential to his thesis. Only this assertion of the primacy of Rome can begin to explain how a custom originating in the early second century could have become as universal in the Christian church as Sunday worship did.

Against Bacchiocchi's argument, it must be said that the evidence he presents for the authority of the church of Rome in the second century is not convincing.[124] The church of Rome had great prestige, but the kind of jurisdictional authority his thesis presupposes is anachronistic in the second century. No church of that period had sufficient authority to change the weekly day of worship throughout Christendom. Furthermore, Bacchiocchi's other two examples of liturgical change in the second century, the Sunday Easter and fasting on the Sabbath, do not, as he thinks, support his case, but rather highlight its weakness. Whether or not Bacchiocchi is correct in locating the origin of the Sunday Easter in early second-century Rome,[125] it is quite clear that the see of Rome did *not* have the authority to impose it on the rest of the church. It was not until the *end* of the second century that bishop Victor of Rome attempted to convert the Quartodeciman churches to the observance of the Sunday Easter, and his attempt encountered stubborn resistance in Asia.[126] Similarly, the church of Rome was singularly unsuccessful in promoting the practice of fasting on the Sabbath. As Bacchiocchi himself admits, as late as the fifth century it was still confined to the church of Rome itself and a few other western churches.[127] Both in the case of the Sunday Easter and in the case of the Sabbath fast, the surviving historical records indicate considerable debate and controversy in the churches.

It therefore seems extremely unlikely that already in the *early* second century the authority of the Roman see was such that it could impose Sunday worship throughout the church, superseding a universal practice of Sabbath observance handed down from the apostles, without leaving any trace of controversy or resistance in the historical records. Bacchiocchi's own comparison with the Sunday Easter and the Sabbath fast shows up the difficulty of his explanation of the origins of Sunday worship. Like all attempts to date the origins of Sunday worship in the second century, it fails to account for the universality of the custom. Unlike the Sunday Easter and the Sabbath fast, Sunday worship was never, so far as the evidence goes, disputed. There is no record of any Christian group (except the extreme party of the Ebionites) that did not observe Sunday, either in the second century or in later centuries of the patristic era.

(4) Bacchiocchi argues that the reason why the church of Rome adopted *Sunday* as the Christian day of worship, instead of the Sabbath, was that the pagan day of the sun, in the planetary week, had already gained special significance in pagan sun cults, and by adopting this day Christians were able to exploit the symbolism of God or Christ as sun or light, which was already present in their own religious tradition.[128]

Bacchiocchi here underestimates the resistance to pagan customs in second-century Christianity. The desire for differentiation from paganism had deeper Christian roots than the second-century desire for differentiation from Judaism. It is true that, from Justin onwards, the Fathers exploited the symbolism of the pagan title "Sunday," but to have actually adopted the pagan day as the Christian day of worship *because* it was prominent in the pagan sun cults would have been a very bold step indeed.[129] Even if the church of Rome had taken this step, it becomes even more inexplicable that the rest of the church followed suit without argument.

Again Bacchiocchi provides a parallel; the celebration of Christmas on 25 December derived from the sun cult and was promoted by the church of Rome.[130] But this parallel comes from the post-Constantinian church when pagan influence on Christian custom was certainly increasing, and we should notice that the church of Rome was *not* successful in imposing this innovation universally throughout the eastern churches.

We conclude that, while Bacchiocchi has usefully stressed the importance of anti-Judaism in second-century opposition to Sabbath observance, he has not demonstrated the second-century origins of the Christian Lord's Day. As we have shown (chapter 8) Christian Sunday worship did not originate as the Christian replacement for the Jewish Sabbath, but as the new, specifically Christian day of worship even before the Gentile mission and before the church's differentiation from Judaism. As such it was already normal Christian practice at the beginning of the second century.

We are not here concerned with the detail of Sunday worship,[131] but the theory that justified the practice. Second century writers were conscious that Sunday is the day of the Lord's resurrection and made this the principal basis of Sunday observance. For Ignatius, as we have seen, it was Jesus' resurrection from the dead on Sunday that gave Sunday its value as the distinctive mark of Christianity over against Judaism. Pseudo-Barnabas (15:9) and Justin (*I Apol.* 67:7) similarly associated the day with the Resurrection, but they are also witnesses to the accumulation of other theological motifs around the practice of Sunday worship. Justin, for example, regarded the first day of the week as the day when God began the creation of the world, and he is also the first witness to the Christian symbolic appropriation of the pagan title "day of the sun," which became common in the Fathers.[132]

In the second century Sunday was also called "the eighth day,"[133] a title that lent itself to varied symbolic uses. Because in the Old Testament the eighth day was the day of circumcision, and eight people were saved from the Flood, the "eighth day" could signify the day on which salvation arrived with Christ's resurrection and the day on which baptism was administered.[134] Rordorf argues that this baptismal symbolism was the origin of the title "eighth day" for Sunday,[135] but it seems probable that the eschatological significance of "eighth day" is more original. If we could be sure that 2 Enoch 33:1–2 were not a Christian interpolation, there would be no doubt of this.

The eschatological significance is that which appears in the earliest occurrence of the title (*Barn.* 15:9).[136] We have already seen that this passage confusingly combines two forms of eschatological arithmetic: that in which the six days of this world are succeeded by the Sabbath of eternity, and that in which this world's week is succeeded by the "eighth day" of the new world. While it is possible that the latter has Jewish apocalyptic origins,[137] its greater popularity with Christians will doubtless be due to its ready association with Sunday worship and its implicit assertion of the superiority of Christianity, the religion of the eighth day, over Judaism, the religion of the Sabbath.[138] This is what tempted Pseudo-Barnabas to mix his symbolism by introducing the eighth day. His juxtaposition of eschatological Sabbath and eighth day does not lead him to a Sabbatarian view of Sunday. He goes no further than saying that Christians "celebrate with joy" the day of the Resurrection in anticipation of the new world.[139] We should note, however, the possibility of a correlation of Sabbath and Sunday by this route. Sabbath rest was such a common characterization of the eschatological hope that when Sunday as the "eighth day" was understood to prefigure the world to come, it was no great step to an association of Sabbath and Sunday.

Such an association was perhaps even more likely in connection with the gnostic idea of the ogdoad. This has quite independent origins in Hellenistic astrology, in which the seven planetary spheres, the realm of change and corruption, are contrasted with the heaven above, the eighth sphere of the fixed stars, the realm of incorruption and repose.[140] The soul ascends through the seven heavens, shedding its corporeality, and finds its resting place in the ogdoad, the sphere of the divine. Thus Thomas prays to the Holy Spirit, "Come, mother of the seven houses that thy rest may be in the eighth house" (*Acts of Thomas* 27). Christian Gnosticism was therefore readily able to combine this cosmological symbolism with the Jewish and Christian eschatological symbolism; eschatological Sabbath rest and the rest of the soul in the ogdoad coalesced.

In Valentinian Gnosticism the seventh heaven, the hebdomad, was the sphere of the Demiurge, while the ogdoad above was the sphere of the Holy Spirit, the "Mother."[141] Spiritual men are reunited with the Mother in the ogdoad, psychic men with the Demiurge in the hebdomad. At the consummation the latter ascend into the ogdoad, while the former, leaving behind their souls, move into the Pleroma above. So the Valentinian author cited by Clement of Alexandria writes, "The rest (ἀνάπαυσις) of the spiritual men is in the κυριακῄ, in the ogdoad which is called κυριακῄ, with the Mother, wearing their souls like garments until the consummation" (*Exc. ex Theod.* 63:1). Here the κυριακῄ, the Lord's Day, has become a spatial concept, the ogdoad, and acquired (for the first time in Christian literature) an association with rest.[142] The same identification of κυριακῄ, the eighth day, with the ogdoad, the eighth heaven, is found in the antignostic *Epistula Apostolorum*.[143] These ideas of Egyptian Gnosticism we shall find taken up by Clement of Alexandria.

There is no second-century evidence that Sunday was regarded as a day of rest. We do not know how much of the day was taken up by Christian corporate activities,[144] but both persecution and economic circumstances must often have kept many Christians at work during the working hours of the day.[145] As we have already seen, the Sabbath commandment was never applied to the Christian Sunday, despite many occasions on which second-century writers must have spoken of such an application if they had held it. On the other hand we may notice certain developments that with hindsight will be seen to offer premonitions of the later correlation of Sabbath and Sunday.

The Sabbath and the Sunday were sometimes (not often) compared.[146] In view of second-century writers' frequent discussion of the Jewish Sabbath, the *infrequency* with which they introduce a comparison with the Lord's Day is notable. In later writers such comparison becomes more common. Sunday was not yet the Christian Sabbath but it was a weekly day of worship, as the Sabbath was for the Jews.

Sunday was regarded as the Christian *festival*. According to *Barnabas* 15:9, "we celebrate with rejoicing (ἄγομεν εἰς εὐφροσύνῃ) the eighth day"; Dionysius of Corinth (*ap.* Eusebius *HE* 4:23:11) records that "today we have celebrated the Lord's holy day" (κυριακὴν ἁγίαν ἡμέραν διηγάγομεν); Peter of Alexandria (*PG* 18:508) speaks of "celebrating" (ἄγομεν) "the Lord's day as a day of rejoicing because of his rising on it"; Tertullian (*Apol.* 16:11; *Ad nat.* 1:13) compares Sunday as a day of rejoicing to pagan festivals and pagan observance of the Sabbath as a holiday (the day of Saturn). Clearly the Lord's Day was a day of festal rejoicing in the Lord's resurrection and the salvation it brings, hence the prohibition of kneeling[147] and fasting[148] on Sundays. To connect rejoicing on the Lord's Day with the rejoicing appropriate to the Old Testament festivals,[149] as W. Stott does, is to go further than the evidence clearly permits, but Dionysius' term "the Lord's holy day" does suggest the Old Testament idea of time set apart for the Lord.[150] Stott's argument that the Lord's Day was understood in terms of Old Testament feast days probably has some foundation,[151] but cannot be pressed to imply that therefore the Lord's Day, like Old Testament festivals, was a day of rest. The early church did not need such a close analogy before it could make use of Old Testament terminology. On the other hand, the conception of Sunday as the Christian festival might lead to a desire for it to be a work-free day, as the Jewish and pagan religious festivals were.[152]

As the "eighth day," Sunday acquired association with both eschatological and gnostic "rest." Again, this cannot, as Stott thinks,[153] prove that Sunday was a day of rest, but it might in association with other arguments promote such a notion.[154]

Clement of Alexandria and Origen

Clement of Alexandria introduced the gnostic cosmological ideas of rest into the mainstream of Christian thinking. For him the primary reference of the concepts of Sabbath and eighth day was to the gnostic's ascent through the seven heavens to the ogdoad. Those who have advanced to gnostic perfection

> rest (καταπαύσουσιν) in the holy hill of God [Ps. 15:1], in the church far on high, in which are gathered the philosophers of God . . . who do not remain in the hebdomad of rest (ἀναπαύσεως) but by the active beneficence of assimilation to God are promoted to the heritage of beneficence of the ogdoad, and devote themselves to the pure vision of insatiable contemplation.[155]

As in the Valentinian system, there seem to be two stages of rest, in the hebdomad, the seventh heaven, and in the ogdoad where the deified gnostic attains the goal of the contemplation of God.

In a long and obscure passage (in *Str.* 6:16) Clement expounds the Sabbath commandment, drawing on the allegorical exegesis of the Alexandrian Jewish writers Aristobulus and Philo. In the opening section, which closely follows Aristobulus,[156] he says that the Sabbath commandment

> intimates that the world was created by God, and that he gave us the seventh day as a rest, on account of the trouble that there is in life. For God is incapable of weariness, suffering or want. But we who bear flesh need rest. The seventh day is therefore proclaimed a rest, and by renunciation of evils it prepares for the primordial (ἀρχέγονον) day, which is our true rest, the primal origin of light, in which everything is seen and possessed. From this day the first wisdom and knowledge shine on us. . . .

This is the opening of a passage in which Clement indulges his love of numerological lore.[157] In Pythagorean number symbolism the number seven is called the ἄρχων, a notion already applied to the Sabbath by Philo,[158] for whom also the seventh day is mystically identical with the first.[159] The Sabbath as ἄρχων might be identified with the ἀρχή of creation, the light of the first day. Moreover in the Valentinian system the ogdoad is called ἀρχέγονον.[160] Clement is readily able to adapt this happy series of connections to the Christian symbolism of the first and eighth days. The Sabbath rest of the seventh day is mere preparation for the true Sabbath rest of the eighth day, for the eighth day is the first day and the first day is Christ the ἀρχή of creation and the light of men.[161]

There is therefore a sense in which Clement transfers the idea of Sabbath rest from the seventh to the first day. But his concern is neither with days of the week nor with physical rest. His declared purpose in expounding the Decalogue in *Str.* 6:16 was to provide an example of gnostic as opposed to literal exposition.[162] Thus we should not be misled by the literal interpretation of the Sabbath commandment with which he begins; it is quoted from Aristobulus and functions for Clement as no more than a springboard for the spiritual interpretation.

Clement spiritualizes the rest of the seventh day as "renunciation of evils," adopting the common late second-century Christian interpretation, to be found, for example, in the Valentinian Ptolemaeus. "He wishes us to be idle with reference to evil actions."[163] This rest of the seventh day is preparatory to the rest to be found in Christ. For gnostics, those who live their whole life in the light of the wisdom and knowledge of Christ, "rise out of the sphere of creation and sin"[164] and become impassible; they participate in the nature of God who needs no rest because he is incapable of weariness and suffering. Thus to be carried beyond the troubles of life is true rest, "the rest of the Lord's inheritance." The major theme of the complex allegorical treatment of the numbers six, seven and eight, which Clement now pursues, seems to be that through the knowledge of Christ, man, who was created on the sixth day, attains to the eschatological rest of the seventh and the divine fruition of the eighth. The numerology is also designed to demonstrate the intimate relationship of the numbers seven and eight, for here as elsewhere (cf. *Str.* 4:25) Clement seeks to unite the two concepts of rest, the church's tradition of the eschatological, Sabbath rest and the Egyptian Valentinian tradition of the cosmological rest of the ogdoad. As in *Exc. ex Theod.* 63:1, it is clear that the association of rest with the eighth day is not derived from a concept of Sunday rest but from Hellenistic cosmology. Clement also gives his theology of rest a christological character by means of the identification of the first day of creation with the *Logos*. As first and eighth, the *Logos* through whom all things are made is the end as well as the beginning of creation.

Elsewhere Clement treats the Sabbath and the Lord's Day not as days of the week but as characteristics of the whole life of the gnostic. He explains, "Now are we commanded to reverence and honour [God] . . . not on special days, as some others do, but continually in our whole life." The true gnostic "holds uninterrupted converse with God" and celebrates festival all the days of his life (*Str.* 7:7). Again, Sunday observance is interpreted as moral conversion; a man "makes that day the Lord's day on which he abandons an evil disposition and assumes that of the gnostic, glorifying the Lord's resurrection in himself" (*Str.* 7:12).

Clement's disciple Origen followed similar lines of argument. Answering Celsus' complaint that Christians do not take part in the public festivals, he quotes Galatians 4:10, and explains that "that man truly celebrates a feast who does his duty and prays always, offering up continually bloodless sacrifices in prayer to God." To such an argument it may fairly be objected that Christians do observe their own feast days, Lord's Day, passover and others. "I have to answer that, to the perfect Christian, who is ever in his thoughts, words and deeds serving the Word of God, his natural Lord, all his days are the Lord's and he is always keeping the Lord's day." It is of interest that Origen here applies to Lord's Day observance the same critique that Christians commonly applied to the Sabbath. Just as in the anti-Jewish apologetic it was said that the Christian continuously keeps the Sabbath, so Origen argues that the perfect Christian continuously keeps the Lord's Day.[165] But like Clement, he distinguishes two grades of Christian: the majority "being unable or unwilling to keep every day as a festival, need sensible memorials to preserve them from total forgetfulness (of spiritual things)."[166] Thus weekly observance is a compromise incompatible, Origen believes, with Galatians 4:10 and Colossians 2:16.[167]

Unsatisfactory though Origen's solution is, he illustrates a dilemma that has continually recurred in the history of our subject: the difficulty of doing justice both to the weekly observance of the Lord's Day and also to the Pauline principle that for the Christian not one day in seven but all days are devoted to the Lord. The dilemma is acute when the Lord's Day is understood to be the "Lord's holy day" (Dionysius of Corinth), a day set apart for the Lord in contrast to the six given over to the world. Then the principle of keeping the Sabbath every day has to be extended, with Origen, to the Lord's Day. It is possible that behind his argument we may discern a growing tendency in the church at large to exalt the holiness of the first day in contrast to the others. This was the route to the idea of a Christian Sabbath.[168]

Origen's treatment of the Sabbath comprises the traditional, spiritualized application of the commandment to the whole of Christian life and also the eschatological rest of the world to come. A lengthy discussion[169] in his sermons on Numbers has been subjected to various interpretations:

> Leaving aside, then, the Jewish observances of the Sabbath, let us see of what kind the observance of the Sabbath should be for the Christian. *On the Sabbath day no worldly activities should be undertaken* [cf. Ex. 30:10]. So if you abstain from all secular works and do nothing worldly, but keep yourself free for spiritual works, come to church *(ecclesiam)*, listen to scripture readings and sermons, have before your eyes the coming judgment, consider not the things that are present and visible but those that are invisible and future, this is the observance of the Sabbath for the Christian.[170] But these things the Jews ought also to have observed. *Even among them a blacksmith or a builder or any kind of manual worker abstains from work on Sabbath day. But the reader of the divine law or the teacher does not abstain from work and yet does not profane the Sabbath. For so the Lord said to them: 'Have you not read that the priests in the temple break the Sabbath and are without reproach?'* [Mt. 12:5]. Therefore he who abstains from the works of the world and is free for spiritual activity, he it is who offers the sacrifice of the Sabbath and celebrates the Sabbath feast.
>
> *He carries no burden on the way* [cf. Jer. 17:25]. For the burden is every sin, as the prophet says: 'Like a heavy burden they weigh me down' [Ps. 38:4].
>
> *He does not kindle a fire* [cf. Ex. 35:3], i.e., that fire of which it is said: 'Go in the light of your fire and in the flame which you have kindled' [Isa. 50:11].
>
> *On the Sabbath everyone remains seated in his place and does not leave it* [cf. Ex.

> 16:28].[171] So what is the spiritual place of the soul? Its place is righteousness, truth, wisdom, holiness and everything which Christ is, that is the place of rest. The soul ought not to leave this place, if it is to keep the true Sabbath and celebrate with sacrifices the feast day of the Sabbath, as the Lord said: 'He who abides in me, I abide in him' [Jn. 15:5]. (*In Num. Hom.* 23:4)

The first paragraph of this passage has been understood to describe the Christian observance of the Sabbath on Saturday[172] or Sunday,[173] but the following three paragraphs undoubtedly interpret the Sabbath regulations in a spiritual sense with reference to the whole of Christian life. While it is not impossible that in the first paragraph Origen makes some reference to Lord's Day observance or even to Christian observance of the Sabbath, it is much more probable that there too he is expounding the Sabbath spiritually in terms of the whole of Christian life, which must be occupied with the works of the spirit rather than the works of the world. Many of the supposed difficulties in this interpretation disappear when the structure of the passage is understood. The italicized sentences represent the literal Sabbath regulations of the Old Testament and their literal observance by the Jews, while the remainder of the passage is Origen's spiritual interpretation for Christian life.

Thus in the first paragraph Origen cites the Sabbath rule of abstention from daily work and interprets it allegorically for Christians as meaning continuous application to spiritual rather than worldly matters. The Jewish observance, he notes, did not exclude the activity of the priests and teachers of the law on the Sabbath. So the Christian's continuous Sabbath keeping may be understood as corresponding to the Sabbath activity of the Old Testament priests.

The more literal reading of the passage has gained its plausibility from Origen's mention of church attendance. But it should be noted that he makes no reference to Sunday or the Lord's Day, and while part of his interpretation of Christian "Sabbath observance" is in terms of corporate worship and instruction, this is only *part* of the interpretation. So our understanding of the passage does not require us to suppose that Origen intends Christians to spend their whole life in church. It is entirely possible that he expected daily church attendance; but even if he refers only to the weekly worship on Sunday this is not incompatible with our interpretation. What Origen regards as embracing the whole of Christian life (of which corporate worship is only a part) is the service of God rather than of the world, contemplation of heavenly rather than worldly things. This, rather than suspension of daily work, is what he means by abstention from worldly works. In principle, therefore, Christians may "keep the Sabbath" while engaged in their daily work, though whether Origen in fact thought this practicable is not entirely clear. Clement certainly did think it was.[174] In any case, from *C. Cels.* 8:21–23 (discussed above), it is clear that this was Origen's ideal, and if ordinary Christians managed to "abstain from worldly works" only on Sundays, then only on Sundays were they really Christians.[175]

It is noteworthy that Origen understands spiritual sabbatizing not so much in terms of abstention from sin, as previous writers had, but rather in terms of contemplation (θεωρία). This has its roots in Hellenistic philosophy and the Alexandrian Judaism of Philo,[176] and had already appeared in Clement. For Origen, therefore, the Christian life of keeping the Sabbath in this age is consummated in the Sabbath of the age to come, when Christians will "ascend to the contemplation of heavenly things,"[177] and celebrate with God His own Sabbath.[178] Origen also speaks of Christian life in this world as the six days of gathering the manna that we shall enjoy in the Sabbath of eternity,[179] or the six days of ascending the mountain of the transfiguration before the Sabbath of beholding the transfigured Christ.[180]

The meaning of God's own Sabbath rest (Gen. 2:3) claimed the attention of both Clement and Origen, as it did of many other Christian and Jewish writers. Both attacked the notion, ridiculed by Celsus, that after the work of creation God needed to rest. "God is incapable of weariness, and suffering, and want" (*Str.* 6:16); "the sensation of fatigue is peculiar to those who are in the body" (*C. Cels.* 6:61). God's Sabbath is therefore not rest (ἀνάπαυσις) but cessation (κατάπαυσις).[181] His work of ordering and preserving the world continues until the end of the age.[182] Only then will He cease His work and celebrate His Sabbath with the redeemed.[183] The understanding of God's Sabbath not as inactivity but as the contemplation of His completed work is directly relevant to the understanding of the eschatological Sabbath of believers, for it is God's rest that they will share.

Finally, we must notice a passage in which Origen compares the Sabbath and the Lord's Day. He observes that the manna in Exodus 16, which prefigures the heavenly bread, the word of God, fell for the first time on the first day of the week; so "let the Jews understand that even then our Lord's Day was superior to the Jewish Sabbath" (*In Ex. Hom.* 7:5). This is a piece of exegesis that many later writers followed, so that it became part of the common stock of medieval ideas about the Lord's Day.[184]

The Fourth Century and the Origins of Sunday Rest

On 3 March, A.D. 321 the emperor Constantine promulgated a law requiring a total, public rest from work "on the most honourable day of the Sun." Only farmers were exempt.[185] On 3 July, A.D. 321 a second law permitted the fulfillment of vows *(votiva)* as appropriate to Sundays and, consequently, the legal transactions necessary for manumitting slaves.[186] This legislation is the earliest clear reference to Sunday as a day free from work. The question of Constantine's motive is difficult.[187] It is at least clear that his model cannot have been the Jewish Sabbath (on which agricultural work was especially prohibited) but rather the Roman pagan holidays.[188] Although the laws use only the pagan title Sunday, Constantine can hardly have chosen the Christian day of worship by mere coincidence; he must have intended to benefit the Christian population, to which he had already granted toleration. But he may also have had sun worship in mind. Too much weight cannot be given to Eusebius' account of his intention of influencing his subjects toward Christianity.[189] Whatever he intended, an important question is whether he acted on his own initiative or whether he responded to Christian wishes. If we allow the second possibility, were there *theological* reasons for wishing Sunday to be an official holiday? We shall see that while it is probable that at least some Christians desired the status of an official holiday for Sunday, there was scant theological justification for this and even long after Sunday rest had become a fact in the Roman Empire it had little theological backing.

We have already noticed hints that some Christian thought was moving toward a correlation of the Sabbath and Sunday. The two were sometimes compared as respectively the Jewish and Christian days of worship;[190] both were taken to prefigure eschatological rest. On the other hand it should be observed that such a correlation would not naturally lead to a Sabbatarian view of Sunday as a day of rest from work, for in Christian thought the idea of Sabbath rest had been so consistently reinterpreted that physical rest from work was precisely what it no longer meant.

We have already traced this reinterpretation of the idea of rest in the orthodox and gnostic thought of the second century and in the Alexandrians Clement and Origen. The same themes recur in the writers of the third and fourth centuries. The Sabbath commandment enjoins abstention not from work but from sin.[191] Or the Sabbath is fulfilled in detachment from earthly things and contemplation of divine things.[192] The commandment prohibited only the works of men, so that Jesus fulfilled the Sabbath by doing the works of God.[193] That the Sabbath was intended not for inactivity but for the service of God is clear from the Old Testament "breaches" of the Sabbath: the priests in the temple,[194] circumcision on the Sabbath,[195] the capture of Jericho,[196] the Maccabees' battles.[197] The Jews' Sabbaths of idleness were also condemned by the prophets (e.g., Isa. 1:3–14).[198] God's own Sabbath rest is not to be understood as inactivity, and neither is man's.[199] The Sabbath was never intended for idleness but for the worship and knowledge of God,[200] an intention whose true fulfillment awaits the Sabbath of the world to come. Eschatological Sabbath rest, either in the millennial kingdom[201] or in eternity,[202] is understood not so much as rest opposed to work, but as rest opposed to the burdensomeness and struggle of this world, or as the enjoyment of the fruits of the work of salvation, or as the attainment of the goal of the vision of God, free from the burden of sin and the flesh, or as participation in God's own Sabbath rest. Service of God, contemplation, worship, detachment from worldly things, festival, and fulfillment are the ideas suggested by the patristic notion of Sabbath rest. By contrast, mere abstention from work is consistently and continually ruled out and condemned as idleness.[203] The Fathers could see no value in inactivity and hardly ever recognized in the Sabbath commandment provision for necessary physical relaxation.[204]

As a consequence of this reinterpretation of Sabbath rest, it will be seen that whereas in the first century a correlation of Sabbath and Sunday would have led to the observance of Sunday as a day of rest on the Jewish model, this would not be the case in the fourth century.[205] This may perhaps also be illustrated from the third and fourth century Christian observance of the Saturday Sabbath. It was observed as a day of worship and commemoration of the creation, but writers who encourage this observance specifically prohibit idleness.[206]

It is with this background in mind that we must examine in some detail the first extant Christian work that claims that the Sabbath has been transferred to Sunday. This is Eusebius of Caesarea's commentary on Psalm 91 (92 in English versions), which is to be dated after A.D. 330. The work will be seen to owe much to Philo and the tradition of Alexandrian Christian philosophy. Thus Eusebius begins by defining Sabbath rest, both for God and for men, as turning from the things of this physical world to contemplate heavenly realities. This passage is directly dependent on Origen (*In Num. Hom.* 23:4).

> It is necessary to discover what the Sabbath signifies. Scripture calls it the rest of God and places it after the creation of the sensible world. But what is the rest of God except his devoting himself to the intelligible and supramundane realities? Indeed, when he looks at the sensible world and gives himself to the exercise of his providence over the world, he is said to work. It is in this sense that we must understand the word of our Saviour: 'My Father works until now, and I work' [Jn. 5:17].[207] But when he turns to the incorporeal and supramundane realities, in his heavenly realm, then we may understand him to be resting and observing his Sabbath. In the same way, when men of God turn from the works that weary the soul (such are all works of the body and those which are dear to earthly flesh) and give themselves wholly to God and to the study and contemplation of divine and intelligible realities, then they observe the Sabbaths which are dear to God and rest for the Lord God. And it is of such Sabbaths that scripture teaches: 'Now there remains a Sabbath rest for the people of God' [Heb. 4:9], and again: 'Let us strive to enter into that rest' [4:11]. For the perfect Sabbath and the perfect and blessed Sabbath rest is found in the kingdom of God, above the work of the six days and outside all sensible

realities, among the incorporeal and supramundane realities, where grief and sorrow and sighing have fled away [Isa. 35:10]. There, released from mortal and corruptible life, enjoying the blessed rest which pleases God, and freed from bodily activities and the slavery of the flesh, we shall celebrate the Sabbath and rest truly with God and beside him. That is why the apostle says: 'Let us strive to enter into that rest'. For the men of God [the patriarchs] bearing on earth the image (εἰκών) of that Sabbath, of that perfect and blessed rest, abstained from things which turned them away from God, and giving themselves wholly to the contemplation of divine realities, applying themselves day and night to meditation on the holy scriptures, they were then celebrating the holy Sabbaths and resting in the rest which pleases God.[208] And so suitably the law of Moses, providing shadows and signs of the things of which we have spoken, appointed a particular day for the people so that on this day at least they should leave their ordinary work and have leisure for meditation on the law of God.

Thus Eusebius understands the patriarchs, who had no weekly Sabbath, to have spent their whole lives in contemplation of divine things, thus anticipating on earth the Sabbath of eternity. This is precisely Origen's understanding of the life of the perfect Christian, while Eusebius' explanation of the weekly Mosaic Sabbath is precisely Origen's justification of the weekly Lord's Day for ordinary Christians. The parallel is so obvious that Eusebius is able almost without explanation to introduce the Christian Lord's Day as the equivalent of the Mosaic Sabbath. After explaining that the activities of the Sabbath were those described in Psalm 91:1–3, he proceeds:

So you see what the present text requires to be done on the day of the resurrection. . . . Also on the Sabbath the priests in the temple were employed in many other activities according to the law. It does not prescribe idleness. It was not for the priests that the Sabbath was prescribed, but only for those who were unlike them in not devoting all their time and every day to the service of God and to works which please him. For these it was prescribed that intervals be made. But those who give themselves to feasting and drinking and disorder on the Sabbath, God rebukes by the prophet, saying: 'They adopt false Sabbaths' [Amos 6:3 :LXX], and again, 'I cannot endure your new moons and Sabbaths and festivals' [Isa. 1:13].

This is why, rejecting those Sabbaths, the Word by the new covenant has changed and transferred the feast of the Sabbath to the rising of the light. He has given to us an image (εἰκών) of true rest, the day of salvation, the Lord's day and the first day of the light, on which the Saviour of the world, after all his deeds among men, and victorious over death, opened the gates of heaven, passing beyond the creation of the six days, and received the divine Sabbath and the blessed rest, when the Father said to him, 'Sit at my right hand, until I make your enemies your footstool' [Ps. 109:1]. On that day of light, the first day and the day of the true sun, we also gather after the interval of six days, when we celebrate the holy and spiritual Sabbaths—we who have been redeemed through him from the nations throughout the world—and what the law ordained for the priests to do on the Sabbath we fulfil according to the spiritual law. For we offer spiritual sacrifices and oblations, which are called sacrifices of praise and joy [Ps. 26:6]. We cause sweet-smelling incense to

> ascend, of which it is written, 'May my prayer go up as incense in your sight' [Ps. 140:2]. Also we offer the shewbread, renewing the memorial of salvation, and the blood of sprinkling, the blood of the Lamb of God who takes away the sin of the world and purifies our souls. We light the lamps of the knowledge of the face of God. Furthermore we zealously devote ourselves to putting in practice on this day the things described in this psalm. . . . Everything else which had to be done on the Sabbath we have transferred to the Lord's day, as being more lordly (κυριωτέρας), taking the lead (ἡγουμένης),[209] the first, and more worthy of honour than the Jewish Sabbath. For it was on this day in the creation of the world that God said, 'Let there be light', and there was light [Gen. 1:3]. And it was also on this day that the sun of righteousness rose for our souls. . . . *(In Ps. 91 Comm.)*

The care with which Eusebius avoids the idea of inactivity on the Sabbath is notable. The Sabbath was devoted to the service of God and works pleasing to God. The activity of Christians on the Lord's Day is analogous to the activity of the *priests* on the Mosaic Sabbath; it is the service of God in worship. It is this priestly activity of worship that has been transferred from the Sabbath to Sunday.

Eusebius' arguments are largely traditional; the following essential elements have already appeared in earlier writers, especially the Alexandrians: (1) True Sabbath rest is contemplation of divine things. (2) Men will share this rest of God in the world to come. (3) Devotion of the whole of life to the contemplation of divine things is an image (εἰκών) of the eschatological rest. (4) The Mosaic Sabbath was a shadow (σκιά) of the eschatological rest. (5) The Christian Sunday is an image (εἰκών) of the eschatological rest.

The original element in Eusebius is the synthesis of these elements to present Sunday as the Christian Sabbath.[210] There is an unnoticed fallacy in the synthesis, which explains why it had not already been reached by the Alexandrians. Eusebius maintains that the Mosaic Sabbath was not for the priests, whose whole life was devoted to God, but rather for the people, who devoted only the Sabbath to God. Christians, however, are said to correspond to the patriarchs, who had no Sabbath but devoted their whole lives to the contemplation of God. The Christian Sabbath therefore, on these analogies, is not the Lord's Day but all days. This is how the traditional argument had run.

We have also seen, however, the way being prepared for Eusebius' version. In contrast to the primitive Christian sacralization of the whole of time, the special holiness of the one day Sunday was being emphasized, with the corollary of desacralizing the rest of the week. Clement and Origen maintained the earlier principle only by means of the conception of two grades of Christian; the ordinary Christian was in effect reduced to Old Testament conditions. Thus Eusebius was not responsible for a radical innovation, and was probably unconscious of innovating at all. His argument was the natural consequence of a long-standing tendency. The real theological question that was thereby evaded was the relation between worship and "secular" activity.

When Eusebius wrote the Constantinian Sunday rest had been established for some years, but there is little trace of it in his thinking. His principle is not a day free from work but a day devoted to the service of God. The comparison between Sabbath and Sunday as days of worship had been made as early as Ignatius and did not depend upon the possibility of devoting the *whole* of Sunday to worship. Yet it must be admitted that the fullest correlation of Sabbath and Sunday in Eusebius' terms presupposes Sunday rest, not for its own sake and as required by the fourth commandment, but as freeing the Christian to give his whole day over to the service of God. In this sense Sunday rest may be seen as appropriate to, though not actually required by, Eusebius' theology of the Christian Sunday.

Moreover there were Hellenistic notions of rest for the sake of worship already available for Christian use. The relaxation of a religious festival, according to Strabo, "turns the spirit away from its preoccupations and turns it to God."[211] Philo, justifying the Mosaic Sabbath rest by resort to the Aristotelian idea of contemplation, explained that the institution of the Sabbath combined the active and contemplative lives, so that "while the body is working, the soul rests, and while the body rests, the soul resumes its work" (*de Spec. Leg.* II.64). So it could be argued that physical rest was necessary not for its own sake but so that the spirit could be active, and this is precisely the argument that was needed if Sunday rest were to be distinguished from idleness. It is possible that such ideas promoted a desire for Sunday rest already in the pre-Constantinian church.

It is also possible to detect a desire for Sunday rest before Constantine on purely pragmatic grounds. It cannot have been easy for many Christians to find adequate time for worship on a day which for their pagan neighbors was an ordinary workday. Tertullian had to speak of the need on Sundays for "deferring even our business affairs, lest we give place to the devil,"[212] implying that the pressures of daily work tempted Christians to stay away from Sunday worship. Similarly the Syriac *Didascalia* (c. 250?), in chapter 13, warns Christians not to make their "worldly affairs of more account than the word of God; but on the Lord's day leave everything and run eagerly to your church. . . . But if there be anyone who takes occasion of worldly business to withdraw himself, let him know that the trades of the faithful are called works of superfluity; for their true work is religion. . . . Have a care that you never withdraw yourselves from the assembly of the church."[213] Despite the Christians' condemnation of the idleness and dissipation of Jewish Sabbaths and pagan holidays, they can hardly have failed to wish for the same freedom for worship as their Jewish and pagan neighbors enjoyed. We have noticed that as early as the second century Sunday was regarded as the Christian festival analogous to Jewish and pagan festivals. Thus Constantine's legislation on the model of Roman holidays may have been a response to the expressed desire of church leaders. But Sunday rest was in pragmatic terms a mixed blessing, as the *Didascalia* aptly foreshadowed when, besides the warnings quoted above, it also insisted on the danger of idleness. "Daily and hourly, whenever you are not in church, devote yourselves to your work." While work must be laid aside for worship, it must not be laid aside for physical relaxation.[214] For the patristic church, the corollary of freedom from work on Sunday had to be the complete devotion of Sunday to worship.

Thus on pragmatic grounds Sunday rest had its drawbacks as well as its advantages; it would promote idleness as well as worship. On theological grounds, even those of Eusebius, it could not be *required*, for all that it might be fitting. The universal Christian tradition of reinterpreting Sabbath rest could not be suddenly abandoned, nor could the Sabbath commandment be suddenly invoked as requiring precisely that inactivity for which the Jews had been so persistently condemned. It is therefore not surprising that even the fact of Sunday rest is ignored by the majority of Christian writers of the fourth century. Some who discuss the Sabbath and the Lord's Day at length neither mention Sunday rest nor endorse Eusebius' notion of the transfer of Sabbath to Sunday. This is true of Athanasius, the Cappadocians, Epiphanius, Ambrose, Ambrosiaster, and the whole vast corpus of Augustine's work.[215] Moreover there seem to be very few attempts to prohibit Sunday work by *ecclesiastical* regulation until the sixth century.[216] So little importance was attached to Sunday rest that in monastic life it was not even observed: Jerome reports the Sunday work in Palestinian convents (*Ep.* 108:20), and as late as 523 Benedict's Rule (48:23) laid down that a monk who would not study or read on Sunday should "be given some work to do, so that he may not be idle."[217]

There are some exceptions to this general neglect. An unknown author, writing perhaps about A.D. 400, repeated Eusebius' idea: "the Lord transferred the day of the Sabbath to the Lord's day."[218] But like Eusebius, he is thinking of the Sabbath, primarily at least, as a day of worship. John Chrysostom seems self-contradictory on the subject. On the one hand, he concludes that the Sabbath commandment in the Decalogue was "partial and temporary,"[219] and asserts uncompromisingly that Christians "ought to celebrate neither months nor new moons nor Lord's days," but rather keep festival continuously.[220] On the other hand, he observes in a sermon on Genesis 2:3 that in sanctifying the seventh day "God teaches us in parables (αἰνιγματωδῶς) that one day in the weekly cycle should be wholly set apart and devoted to the service of spiritual things" (*In Gen. Hom.* 10:7), and again, preaching on 1 Corinthians 16:2, he speaks of Sunday as a day when work is given up and all worldly affairs laid aside.[221] Chrysostom therefore illustrates the still unresolved tension between the early Christian doctrine of keeping the Sabbath continuously and the more recent idea of a weekly Christian Sabbath.

In a sermon of the mid-fourth century Ephraem Syrus makes what may well be the first reference to the Sabbath commandment applied to the Lord's Day:

> The first day of the week, the firstborn of days, is worthy of reverence, for it holds many mysteries. So pay it your respect, for it has taken the right of primogeniture from the Sabbath. . . . Blessed is he who keeps this day with holy observance. . . . The law prescribes that rest be given to servants and animals, so that servants, maidservants and employees may cease from work.

But Ephraem goes on to warn of the dangers of idleness, the sins to which men are tempted when not working, "so do not observe the day of salvation with your body alone,"[222] Ephraem is less concerned with the sins of Sunday work than with the sins to which Sunday rest gave rise. In spite of the Constantinian legislation it is clear that true Sabbatarianism was a medieval, not a patristic, development.[223]

Notes

[1]This is especially true of W. Stott, *The Theology of the Christian Sunday in the Early Church* (D. Phil. dissertation, Oxford, 1966) now published in revised form, as chapters 5–13 in R. T. Beckwith and W. Stott, *This is the Day: The Biblical Doctrine of the Christian Sunday* (London: Marshall, Morgan and Scott, 1978). But it is also partly true of W. Rordorf, *Sunday: The History of the Day of Rest and Worship in the Earliest Centuries of the Christian Church* (London: SCM, 1968).

[2]It is noteworthy, for example, that Justin Martyr, whose general thought about the law and typology was probably influenced by Hebrews (W. A. Shotwell, *The Biblical Exegesis of Justin Martyr* [London: SPCK, 1965], pp. 11–12, 57–60), shows no such influence in his treatment of the Sabbath.

[3]Jerome, *Comm. in Esaiam* 4:11:2 (*PL* 24:144f.).

[4]1 Enoch 42; Ecclus. 24:3–12; 1 Bar. 3:37. Note especially Ecclus. 24:7: "With all these I sought rest."

[5]On this identification, see J. Daniélou, *The Theology of Jewish Christianity* (London: Darton, Longman and Todd, 1964), pp. 112, 138.

[6]See chapter 7, pp. 197–220 of this book.

[7] Justin, *Dial.* 87, has a rather similar exposition of Isaiah 11:2 in terms of the Spirit of the prophets coming finally to rest in Christ, but his treatment has no broader overtones of God's eschatological rest.

[8]See especially the quotation from Epiphanius in Rordorf, *Sunday*, p. 113 n.1.

[9]E.g., *Acts of Thomas* 37 (Christ will be "a rest for your souls"), 39 (Christ is addressed as "O hidden rest . . . preserving us and giving us rest in alien bodies"), 8 (Syriac: Christ is called the

"rest" of his Father); and cf. P. Vielhauer, "Ἀνάπαυσις, zum gnostischen Hintergrund des Thomas-Evangeliums," in *Apophoreta: Festschrift für Ernst Haenchen* (ZNW Beiheft 30, 1964): 290.

[10]Against Vielhauer, in Hennecke-Wilson 1:162.

[11]Vielhauer in Hennecke-Wilson, 1:135, assigned it rather tentatively to the Egyptian "Gospel of the Hebrews," but his reasons are unconvincing.

[12]*Strom.* 5:14:96. The ascription to the Gospel of the Hebrews is in *Strom.* 2:9:45, where Clement quotes a briefer form of the saying.

[13]J. Fitzmyer, "The Oxyrhynchus *Logia* of Jesus and the Coptic Gospel according to Thomas," *Theological Studies* 20 (1959): 518, suggests that the Coptic translator may have read ἀνὰ πάντα for ἀναπαύσεται.

[14]Cf. *Gospel of Thomas* 92.

[15]E.g., *Acts of Thomas* 136: "there do rest, and resting reign" (perhaps an echo of this saying); *Book of Thomas the Athlete* 145:13–14 (quoted below).

[16]J. Jeremias, *Unknown Sayings of Jesus* (London: SPCK, 1958), pp. 14–15; B. Gärtner, *The Theology of the Gospel of Thomas* (London: Collins, 1961), p. 261; M. Dibelius, *From Tradition to Gospel* (London: James Clarke, 1934, p. 284 n. 2 (for similar "chain-sayings," including "amazement" and "rest," from the *Hermetica*); P. Vielhauer in Hennecke-Wilson, 1:162. A New Testament basis for the element of amazement in this saying has been found in the "joyful surprise" of the man in Matthew 13:44: H. G. E. White, *The Sayings of Jesus from Oxyrhynchus* (Cambridge: University Press, 1920), p. 6; cf. H. B. Swete, "The New Oxyrhynxhus Sayings," *ExpT* 15 (1903–4): 491.

[17]There is a full discussion in Vielhauer, "ἀνάπαυσις."

[18]On the rest of the ogdoad, see below, section III.

[19]Cf. *Gospel of Thomas* 51:

> His disciples said to him:
> On what day will the rest of the dead take place?
> On what day does the new world come?
> He said to them:
> That (rest) for which you are waiting has come;
> but you do not recognize it.

[20]E.g., Nag Hammadi Codex I, quoted in Hennecke-Wilson, 1:249.

[21]Peel, *Gospel of Truth* 24:17–20.

[22]*Epistle to Rheginos* 43:35–44:3.

[23]Nag Hammadi Codex I, quoted in Hennecke-Wilson, 1:249.

[24]*Gospel of Truth* 26:34–35; 40:30; *Sophia Jesu Christi*, quoted in Hennecke-Wilson, 1:247.

[25]*Gospel of Truth* 43:1; *Acts of Andrew* 11.

[26]See Gärtner, *The Theology of the Gospel of Thomas*, pp. 265–66; M. L. Peel, *The Epistle to Rheginos* (London: SCM, 1969)p. 143. For many other Gnostic references to "rest" see Peel, pp. 54–55, and the index to W. Förster, *Gnosis*, 2 vols. (London: Oxford University Press, 1972, 1974).

[27]*Book of Thomas the Athlete* 145:13–14. Cf. *Acts of Thomas* 35; *Exc. ex Theod.* 65:2; *Apocryphon of John* 68:1–13; *Gospel of Philip* 63: "As long as we are in this world, it is fitting that we acquire the resurrection for ourselves, that when we strip off the flesh we may be found in the rest."

[28]*Adv. Haer.* 5:28:3.

[29]*Dial.* 80:5; 121:3.

[30]*Adv. Haer.* 4:16:1; 5:30:4; 5:33:2.

[31]*In Dan.* 4:23:4–6.

[32]Other chiliasts of the period were Cerinthus (Eusebius, *HE* 3:28:2), Papias (ibid., 3:39:12), Tertullian (*Adv. Marc.* 3:24:5f.); but they are not known to have treated the millennium as a Sabbath.

[33]*Barn.* 15. For justification for a nonchiliastic interpretation of *Barnabas*, see below. Other

(not explicitly chiliast) references to eschatological Sabbath rest are Ascension of Isaiah 4:15; 5 Ezra 2:24, 34–35; *Apocalypse of Peter* 16 (Ethiopic); *Acts of Paul and Thecla* 6.

[34]Cf. 6:7. There seem to be no second century examples of rest as the state of departed souls: cf. Rordorf, *Sunday*, p. 97, citing *Gospel of Thomas* 51 (quoted n. 19 above), which, however, refers to the Gnostic's present enjoyment of rest in this life. *Epistula Apostolorum* 27 speaks of Christ's descent into hell to bring Old Testament believers "from the rest which is below" into heaven.

[35]Mention should also be made of the *Odes of Solomon*, in which present participation in eschatological rest is a very prominent theme (note especially 3:5; 11:12), so much so that "the odes of his rest" (26:3) may have been the original title of the collection. The date of the *Odes of Solomon* and their relationship with Gnosticism are still disputed.

[36]Rordorf, *Sunday*, pp. 32–33; E. Lohse in TDNT 7: 17–18. But on the evidence for this from Tertullian, see now J. Nolland, "Do Romans Observe Jewish Customs? (Tertullian *Ad Nat.* I.13; *Apol.* 16)," *Vigiliae Christianae* 33 (1979): 1–11.

[37]J. Jeremias, *Unknown Sayings*, pp. 49–53.

[38]Lohse in TDNT, 7:23.

[39]Jeremias, *Unknown Sayings*, p. 51.

[40]C. F. Evans in A. Richardson, ed., *A Theological Word Book of the Bible* (London: SCM, 1950), p. 205.

[41]Against Jeremias, *Unknown Sayings*, p. 52, "From all we know of Jesus' attitude to the Sabbath, it must be the *nature* of the work he is doing which causes Jesus to praise him. Jesus reckons with the possibility that he is engaged in a labour of love."

[42]Cf. Rordorf, *Sunday*, pp. 86–87. According to Rordorf's view of Jesus' "freedom with regard to the Sabbath," the saying has the effect of qualifying Jesus' abrogation of the commandment, but Rordorf's view of Jesus' attitude to the Sabbath is open to question, cf. chapter 4, above. Furthermore Rordorf's argument about Luke 6:5D seems to depend on supposing that we are dealing not with a floating pericope that a scribe inserted at Luke 6:5, but with a composition originally designed to follow Luke 6:1–4; this is unlikely.

[43]Cf. Jeremias, *Unknown Sayings*, p. 41: "Codex D is singularly free from Jewish Christian tendencies. And apart from that it would be difficult for such circles to construct a beatitude in favour of a Sabbath breaker."

[44]Cf. Rordorf, *Sunday*, p. 32; and many later Christian examples of polemic against the Jews whose "idleness" on the Sabbath was a common reproach.

[45]This *Sitz im Leben* was suggested by M.-J. Lagrange, *L'Évangile selon Saint Luc* (Paris: Gabalda, 1948), pp. 176–77, n. 5; and Jeremias, *Unknown Sayings*, p. 53, also recognizes a parallel sentiment in Romans 14:23. Rordorf, *Sunday*, pp. 87–88, followed by C. S. Mosna, *Storia della Domenica* (Rome: Gregorian University Press, 1969), p. 187 n. 60, objected that such harsh treatment of weaker brethren is unusual; but we have suggested that weaker brethren are not actually a target of attack, and the treatment is no harsher than Romans 14:23.

[46]See below.

[47]*Dial.* 47.

[48]"Nazarenes:" Epiphanius, *Pan.* 29:7:5. "Ebionites:" Epiphanius, *Pan.* 30:2:2; 30:16:9; Eusebius, *HE* 3:27:5; Jerome, *In Matt.* 12:2; Theodoret of Cyr, *Haer. Fab.* 2:1 (*PG* 83:389); Nicephorus Callistus, *Eccl. Hist.* 3:13 (*PG* 145:924). It is really by no means clear how accurately the Fathers distinguished "Nazarenes" and "Ebionites." Cf. also Irenaeus, *Adv. Haer.* 1:26:2.

[49]D. Hill, *The Gospel of Matthew* (London: Oliphants, 1972), p. 209; Lohse in TDNT, 7:24.

[50]Tertullian, *De spect.* 30. In the *Gospel of Nicodemus* (*Acts of Pilate* 1f., 4, 6) the charge of healing on the Sabbath is represented as the major charge that led to Jesus' crucifixion.

[51]Irenaeus, *Adv. Haer.* 4:8:2; Tertullian, *Adv. Marc.* 4:12, are the earliest full discussions of the question of Jesus' Sabbath conflicts. Both are concerned to argue, against Marcion, that Jesus' Sabbath healings fulfilled rather than violated the Sabbath laws. The same apologetic tendency on behalf of Jesus may be reflected in the (much later) *Acts of Philip* 15, where the Jewish accusation against Jesus for destroying the Law mentions "new moons" but strikingly not Sabbaths.

[52]*Qoh.R.* 1:8. English translation from the Soncino edition. For suggestions about this text I am indebted to my colleagues Dr. P. S. Alexander and Dr. J. P. Kane.

[53]*Post* eighth century.

[54]R. Travers Herford, *Christianity in Talmud and Midrash* (London: Williams and Norgate, 1903), pp. 211–15.

[55]Herford's emendation of "Hanina" in the text.

[56]The population of Capernaum was wholly Jewish (F.-M. Abel, "Capharnaum," *Dictionnaire de la Bible supplément* vol. 1, cols. 1050–1053); so there is no question of Gentile Christians. There is archeological evidence of a Jewish Christian community in Capernaum (information from J. P. Kane).

[57]Herford compares the Roman graffito of a crucified ass, but the relevance of this pagan ridicule of Roman Christianity to a tradition embodying Jewish polemic against Galilean Christianity seems dubious.

[58]Jerome, *In Matt.* 12:13.

[59]Compare the defense of Jesus by Irenaeus, *Adv. Haer.* 4:8:2, and Tertullian *Adv. Marc.* 4:12, who argue that the Sabbath commandment prohibited the works of men but not the service of God.

[60]Hegesippus, *ap.* Eusebius, *HE* 4:22:5, lists the Μασβώθεοι among the Palestinian Jewish Christian sects (and also, 4:22:7, among non-Christian Jewish sects). Rufinus' Latin version of Eusebius gives "Masbutheus" as the author of the heresy, but this is not in the Greek text and is clearly an example of the patristic tendency to derive heresies from fictitious founders (similarly the Ebionites from "Ebion"). The Masbotheans are also mentioned in *Const. App.* 6:6:4, and Ps.-Jerome (see next note). From these references it is impossible to form any clear notion of their character, but Ps.-Jerome may be trusted because his statement about them is not a standard patristic description of Jewish Christianity, but a distinctive, if garbled, report, and also because it gives a plausible explanation of their name (which Ps.-Jerome himself did not realize was an explanation of their name).

[61]Ps.-Jerome, *Indiculus de haeresibus Judaeorum* (*PL* 81:636C). A. F. J. Klijn and G. J. Reinink, *Patristic Evidence for Jewish-Christian Sects*, Supplements to *Novum Testamentum* 36 (Leiden: Brill, 1973), p. 15, date this text in the late fourth or early fifth century.

[62]Origen, *De Princ.* 4:3:2.

[63]Filastrius, *Div. her. liber* 36:2. But this is not very reliable testimony. Klijn and Reinink, *Patristic Evidence*, pp. 3–19, 68, conclude that in reality almost nothing is known of Cerinthus. Sabbath observance is such a standard judaizing trait that its attribution to Cerinthus was almost inevitable.

[64]Hippolytus, *Ref.* 9:16:2–3; Epiphanius, *Pan.* 19:5:1; 30:17:5.

[65]Lohse in TDNT, 7:7; cf. Gregory Nazianzus, *Oratio* 18:5.

[66]The most recent discussion is C. K. Barrett, "Jews and Judaizers in the Epistles of Ignatius," in R. Hamerton-Kelly and R. Scroggs, ed., *Jews, Greeks and Christians: Essays in Honor of W. D. Davies* (Leiden: Brill, 1976), pp. 220–44. Barrett surveys the debate, and makes his own contribution, identifying the opponents at Philadelphia, Magnesia, and Smyrna as syncretistic judaizers. In the following account I largely follow Barrett. The problem of the text of *Magn.* 9:1 has already been discussed in chapter 8.

[67]Cf. R. A. Kraft, "Some Notes on Sabbath Observance in Early Christianity," AUSS 3 (1965): 28–33; K. A. Strand, "Some Notes on the Sabbath Fast in Early Christianity," AUSS 3 (1965): 167–74; Rordorf, *Sunday*, pp. 142–153; Rordorf, *Sabbat et dimanche dans l'Église ancienne* (Neuchâtel: Delachaux et Niestlé, 1972), XXII-XIV; Mosna, *Storia della Domenica*, pp. 201–6. For the third century, cf. N. R. M. de Lange, *Origen and the Jews* (Cambridge: University Press, 1976), p. 86.

[68]See especially M. Simon, *Verus Israel* (Paris: E. DeBoccard, 1964), ch. IX, "Les judaisants dans l'Église."

[69]So Simon, *Verus Israel*, p. 383.

[70]On the Council of Laodicea, see Simon, *Verus Israel*, pp. 374–75, 382–83, 422–23. Note

once again the location in Asia Minor, and also the association of Jewish and magical practices.

[71]E. g., Council of Laodicea, canon 16; *Const. App.* 2:36:2; 2:59:3; 7:23:3; 7:36:1; Ps.-Ignatius, *Magn.* 9:1–12.

[72]Rordorf, *Sunday*, pp. 150–52. He argues that this third and fourth century Sabbath observance was derived from the spiritual interpretation of the Sabbath commandment developed in the second century (see below). But since that interpretation was developed in opposition to any observance of the Sabbath *day*, it is hard to see how it could have led to such observance, even in a non-Jewish manner. (This is the criticism made by K. A. Strand, "From Sabbath to Sunday in the Early Christian Church: A Review of Some Recent Literature. Part I: Willy Rordorf's Reconstruction," *AUSS* 16 [1978]: 388). The spiritual interpretation of the Sabbath commandment may have *influenced* this Sabbath observance, but only in *response* to the danger of more thoroughgoing judaizing tendencies.

[73]Simon, *Verus Israel*, pp. 375–76, 383.

[74]Recent extended discussions are A. Hermans, "Le Pseudo-Barnabé est-il millenariste?" *Ephemerides Theologicae Lovanienses* 35 (1959): 849ff.; W. H. Shea, "The Sabbath in the Epistle of Barnabas," *AUSS* 4 (1966): 149ff. (Shea, and also Rordorf, wrote in ignorance of Hermans' important contribution.); cf. also C. K. Barrett, "The Eschatology of the Epistle to the Hebrews" in W. D. Davies and D. Daube, ed. *The Background of the New Testament and its Eschatology* (Cambridge: University Press, 1956), pp. 369–70; and some helpful comments in P. Prigent and R. A. Kraft, *Épître de Barnabé*, Sources Chrétiennes 172 (Paris: du Cerf, 1971), pp. 182–88.

[75]The conception is probably related to the interpretation of the creation week in Philo, who takes God's rest to mean His ceasing from the work of creating mortal things and His beginning to create "other more divine things," *Leg. Alleg.* I, 5. Cf. Hermans, "Le Pseudo-Barnabé," pp. 863–64, who sets out a striking parallelism of vocabulary between Philo and Barnabas at this point.

[76]Barnabas elsewhere (10:11) calls the next world *τὸ ἅγιον αἰών*.

[77]This is clear from the terminology of 15:8, as Hermans has convincingly shown. *καταπαύσας τὰ πάντα* = *συντελέσει τὰ σύμπαντα* (15:4), and *ποιήσω ἄλλου κόσμου ἀρχήν* = *καινῶν δὲ γεγονότων πάντων* (15:7). If Barnabas is a chiliast he is an inexplicably incoherent one, and therefore, despite Rordorf, *Sunday*, pp. 93–94, it is in fact easier to believe that "two eschatological ideas have been forcibly yoked together, one which sees the seventh day as the new aeon and another which regards the eighth day as the new aeon." An alternative might be to conjecture that verse 9 and the mention of the eighth day in verse 8 are a later addition to the text, but in that case the chapter would end even less satisfactorily than it does now.

[78]Hermans, "Le Pseudo-Barnabé," p. 850: "Barnabas undertakes to prove that the Sabbath is exclusively Christian. The Decalogue does not prescribe the sanctification of the seventh day, but of the eighth, that is, the Christian Sunday." Hermans' argument depends upon qualifying the implications of 15:6–7 by introducing an element of "anticipation of the future" (872–75): but even if this were allowed, Barnabas cannot regard *Sunday* as the Christian anticipation of the eschatological *Sabbath*, for he has interpreted the Sabbath commandment in terms neither of worship nor of physical rest, but of moral holiness. In this sense of "sanctify" it would be absurd to "sanctify" one day of the week.

[79]Cf. Shea, "The Sabbath," p. 170 n. 64.

[80]*Gospel of Thomas* 6: "If you fast, you will beget for yourselves a sin," cf. 14, 104.

[81]Fitzmeyer, "The Oxyrhynchus Logia," p. 534, sees "no reason why this saying could not be an authentic one:" but whether we take the fasting and Sabbath keeping literally or metaphorically, the ideas have no parallel in Jesus' teaching in the canonical Gospels.

[82]So Lohse, TDNT, 7:32.

[83]Cf. especially logion 12; R. M. Grant and D. N. Freedmen, *The Secret Sayings of Jesus* (London: Collins, 1960), pp. 71–74; R. McL. Wilson, *Studies in the Gospel of Thomas* (London: Mowbrays, 1960), pp. 131–132.

[84]It is not used of keeping the ordinary weekly Sabbath in the Septuagint but occurs with reference to the Day of Atonement in Leviticus 23:22 and sabbatical years in 2 Chronicles 36:21

(also Lev. 25:2, Aquila). The underlying Hebrew expression in these passages is not attested in the Old Testament for the weekly Sabbath, occurring elsewhere only in Leviticus 26:35, but the form has common syntactical parallels. It cannot be pressed to mean "*truly* keep the Sabbath," and its lack of attestation for the weekly Sabbath is probably accidental. Thus while recognizing that the expression is unusual, we cannot conclude with C. Taylor, *The Oxyrhynchus Logia and the Apocryphal Gospels* (Oxford: Clarendon, 1899), pp. 13–14 (followed by Fitzmyer, "The Oxyrhynchus *Logia*," p. 533), that it cannot refer to the weekly Sabbath. In view of the Septuagint examples just cited, the translation "sabbatize the week" (suggested by H. G. E. White, *The Sayings of Jesus*, p. 29, followed by M. R. James, *The Apocryphal New Testament* [Oxford: Clarendon, 1924], p. 27) is unnatural, despite the parallels for this sentiment in later Christian writings (e.g., Justin, *Dial.* 12).

[85]It is possible that the logion was already understood metaphorically in the immediate source of the *Gospel of Thomas*. Spiritualization of both Sabbath and fasting (*Barn.* 3) are already to be found in Ps.-Barnabas. Possibly, like *Gospel of Thomas* 2, the logion derives from the Egyptian Gospel of the Hebrews; this would account for probable echoes of it in Clement of Alexandria, *Str.* 3:15:99; *Ecl. Proph.* 14:1. There is probably also an echo in Ps.-Macarius, who uses the expression *σαββατίζειν σάββατον ἀληθινόν* (note how this gives the metaphorical sense of the second part of the saying by adding *ἀληθινόν*); see A. Baker, "Pseudo-Macarius and the Gospel of Thomas," *Vigiliae Christianae* 18 (1964): 220–21.

The expression "to fast to the world" is also found in the Syriac *Liber Gradum*, and A. Baker, "'Fasting to the World'," *JBL* 84 (1965): 291–94, argues that it is translated from the Syriac.

[86]Gärtner, *The Theology of the Gospel of Thomas*, pp. 239–40; cf. Jeremias, *Unknown Sayings*, pp. 13–14, and in Hennecke-Wilson, 1:106.

[87]Grant and Freedmen, *The Secret Sayings of Jesus*, p. 85.

[88]*Dial.* 12:3.

[89]Epiphanius, *Pan.* 33:3:5:11–13.

[90]As is argued by G. Quispel in Ptolémée, *Lettre à Flora*, ed. G. Quispel, Sources Chrétiennes (Paris: Editions du Cerf, 1966), p. 24.

[91]Rordorf, *Sunday*, p. 102.

[92]*Dial.* 12:3, citing Isaiah 58:13.

[93]*Epideixis* 96; cf. *Adv. Haer.* 4:16:1.

[94]*Adv. Jud.* 4:2. The idea that "servile work" was the kind of work prohibited on the Sabbath is found in Irenaeus, *Adv. Haer.* 4:8:2, and represented in Tertullian's actual version of the commandment, *Adv. Jud.* 4:1. It became universal in Christian writers, but actually derives from Old Testament legislation about festivals not the Sabbath.

[95]For many later examples of this interpretation, see Rordorf, *Sunday*, p. 104 n. 3.

[96]For a hint of the idea of physical rest in Clement of Alexandria, see below.

[97]Justin, Dial. 19, 23, 26–27; Irenaeus, *Adv. Haer.* 4:16:2; Tertullian, *Adv. Jud.* 2, 4.

[98]Justin, *Dial.* 27, 29; Irenaeus, *Adv. Haer.* 4:8:2–3.

[99]Tertullian, *Adv. Jud.* 4; *Adv. Marc.* 4:12:3.

[100]*Dial.* 23, 29. Rabbinic tradition also reflects this issue as a matter of controversy with Christians. According to *Exod.R.* 30:5, R. Gamaliel II, on his journey to Rome in A.D. 95, disputed with a *min* the question of whether God keeps the Sabbath. As Simon, *Verus Israel*, p. 226, argues, the *min* here is most likely a Gentile Christian.

[101]*Dial.* 10:3; 18:2; 23:1–3; 26:1, 47:2.

[102]*Apol.* 14, Syriac. For the accusation that Jews worship angels rather than God, cf. *Kerygma Petrou*, in Hennecke-Wilson, 2:100.

[103]Tertullian, *Adv. Marc.* 4:12:7. Saturday fasting was later practiced in parts of the western church. For a discussion of its origins, see S. Bacchiocchi, *An Examination of the Biblical and Patristic Texts of the First Four Centuries to Ascertain the Time and the Causes of the Origin of Sunday as the Lord's Day* (Rome: Pontifical Gregorian University Press, 1975), pp. 61–82; less fully in *From Sabbath to Sunday*, (Rome: Pontifical Gregorian University Press, 1977), 186–98.

Cf. K. A. Strand, "Some Notes on the Sabbath Fast in Early Christianity," *AUSS* 3 (1965): 167–74.

[104]*De Pud.* 5.

[105]R. M. Grant, "The Decalogue in Early Christianity," *HTR* 40 (1947): 2; C. W. Dugmore, *The Influence of the Synagogue upon the Divine Office* (London: Oxford University Press, 1944), p. 29; but cf. Rordorf, *Sunday*, p. 106 n.1.

[106]Pliny, *Ep.* 10:96–97; *Did.* 2; *Barn.* 19; Aristides, *Apol.* 15:3–5; Theophilus, *Ad Autol.* 2:34–35; 3:9; cf. Justin, *Dial.* 12:3. Already in the New Testament: Romans 13:9; 1 Timothy 1:9–10.

[107]Irenaeus, *Adv. Haer.* 4:13:4.

[108]Irenaeus, *Adv. Haer.* 4:16:3.

[109]Epiphanius, *Pan.* 33:3:5:1–12.

[110]This seems to be the understanding of Irenaeus suggested by Stott, *This is the Day*, pp. 127–29.

[111]*Epideixis* 95–96.

[112]The metaphorical interpretation of the Sabbath commandment was rarely related to the concept of eschatological rest. Justin, who used both ideas, never brought them together. Apart from Ps.-Barnabas' idiosyncratic version, there is just one passage where Irenaeus rather artificially relates the two (*Adv. Haer.* 4:16:1), as Origen also does (see below). Nowhere in the second century is the Sabbath commandment or the future Sabbath rest related to the idea that the eschatological Sabbath has already come in Christ, an idea that for the time being had disappeared from Christian theology. Rordorf's attempt (*Sunday*, p. 116) to demonstrate the inner relationship of these three themes is attractive but too synthetic a reading of early Christian literature.

[113]Bacchiocchi, *From Sabbath to Sunday*. Bacchiocchi's thesis is accepted by G. H. Williams, "The Sabbath and the Lord's Day," *Andover Newton Quarterly* 19 (1978): 121–28. Williams combines it with Riesenfeld's argument that Sunday observance originated from a prolongation of Sabbath worship into Saturday night.

[114]Bacchiocchi, *From Sabbath to Sunday*, chapter 5.

[115]Cf. ibid., pp. 13–14, "This study, then, is an attempt to reconstruct a mosaic of factors in a search for a more exact picture of the time and causes that contributed to the adoption of Sunday as the day of worship and rest." Bacchiocchi's failure to distinguish the early Christian day of worship from the (later) day of rest mars the whole argument of the book. It is rightly criticized by K. A. Strand, "From Sabbath to Sunday in the Early Christian Church: A Review of Some Recent Literature. Part II: Samuele Bacchiocchi's Reconstruction," *AUSS* 17 (1979): 100, 102.

[116]*HE* 3:27.

[117]Bacchiocchi, *From Sabbath to Sunday*, chapter 7.

[118]Ibid., chapter 6.

[119]Ibid., p. 183.

[120]See above.

[121]Chapter 8.

[122]See below n.146.

[123]Bacchiocchi, *From Sabbath to Sunday*, pp. 207–12.

[124]See the detailed refutation by K. A. Strand, "From Sabbath to Sunday. Part II," pp. 96–98.

[125]Strand, "From Sabbath to Sunday, Part II," pp. 91–95, criticizes his use of evidence.

[126]As Bacchiocchi himself says, *From Sabbath to Sunday*, pp. 199: "Polycrates, claiming to possess the genuine apostolic tradition transmitted to him by the Apostles Philip and John, refused to be frightened into submission by the threats of Victor of Rome."

[127]Ibid., p. 192; cf. Strand, "From Sabbath to Sunday. Part II," pp. 99, 100n.30.

[128]*From Sabbath to Sunday*, chapter 8.

[129]Cf. Strand, "From Sabbath to Sunday. Part II," pp. 89–90. He also doubts whether Sunday was a day specially venerated in early second century paganism, except in Mithraism, which would have had little influence on Christianity.

[130]Bacchiocchi, *From Sabbath to Sunday*, pp. 256–61.

[131]The evidence is largely in Pliny, *Ep.* 10:96, and Justin: for a discussion, see Rordorf, *Sunday*, chapter 5; cf. Stott, *This is the Day*, chapter 9. But Rordorf, like most scholars with liturgiological preoccupations, probably overestimates the uniformity of Christian practice in this period.

[132]*I Apol.* 67:7; cf. Rordorf, *Sunday*, chapter 6, section 3; J. Daniélou, *The Bible and the Liturgy* (London: Darton, Longman and Todd, 1960), pp. 253–55; H. Dumaine, "Dimanche," *Dictionnaire d'Archéologie Chrétienne et de Liturgie*, 4, cols. 870–79.

[133]*Barn.* 15:9; Justin, *Dial.* 24:1; 41:4; 138:1; Tertullian, *De idol.* 14.

[134]Justin *Dial.* 41:4; 138:1; Origen, *Sel. in ps.* 118; Asterius, *Hom.* 20; Cyprian, *Ep.* 64:4; later references in Rordorf, *Sunday*, p. 278 n.1. It is possible that, as Rordorf argues (*Sunday*, p. 279), the emphasis on "eight" in 1 Peter 3:20; 2 Peter 2:5 is already due to the association of baptism with Sunday, the eighth day.

[135]Rordorf, *Sunday*, chapter 6, section 2. This gives his argument a neat conclusion: the title "Lord's Day" refers to the sacrament of the eucharist; the title "eighth day" refers to the sacrament of baptism. There is not much to be said for Stott's suggestion (*This is the Day*, pp. 64–65) that "eighth day" derives from Old Testament references to the "eighth day" of the feast of tabernacles.

[136]According to Rordorf, *Sunday*, p. 277, Sunday was already called the "eighth day" before Barnabas, but what evidence he has for this is not apparent. Neither in *Sunday* nor in *Sabbat et dimanche* does he cite an earlier occurrence.

[137]2 Enoch 33:1–2; and cf. chapter 7, pp. 197–220.

[138]See Daniélou, *The Bible and the Liturgy*, p. 257.

[139]See also n. 78, above.

[140]The influence of these ideas is already found in Philo, *de Decal.* 102–4, *de Cher.* 21–24. The Hellenistic origins of gnostic rest in the ogdoad are ignored by Stott, *This is the Day*, p. 74.

[141]Irenaeus, *Adv. Haer.* 1:5:3.

[142]Cf. also Ps.-Hippolytus, *In Ps.* 4 (*PG* 10:713): "The number fifty contains seven sevens or a Sabbath of Sabbaths, and also over and above these full Sabbaths a new beginning in the ogdoad of a truly new rest." (This is probably a third-century text, and perhaps by Origen: cf. Dumaine, "Dimanche" *Dictionnaire*, col. 882.) The "rest" in this text is surely not, as Stott, *This is the Day*, p. 70, supposes, Sunday rest, but Gnostic and/or eschatological rest.

[143]It is natural to understand κυριακή in both cases as κυριακή (ἡμέρα) since this is the only otherwise attested meaning of κυριακή (see examples in chapter 8). But Clement, *Str.* 7:10, calls the ogdoad κυριακὴ μονή, thereby giving some support to Schmidt's proposal to supply μονή in *Ep. App.* 18 (see Rordorf, *Sabbat et dimanche*, p. 143 n.8).

[144]Even when Sunday was a public holiday, Christians did not necessarily spend the whole day in public worship. Cf. Chrysostom, *De bapt. Christi hom.* 1 (Rordorf, *Sabbat*, no. 124 and p. 199 n.2).

[145]Cf. Pliny, *Ep.* 10:96: Christians in Bithynia assembled before dawn and again for the evening meal, until the evening meeting was forbidden by Pliny's edict prohibiting the meeting of clubs. Cf. Rordorf, *Sunday*, pp. 251–52. Stott, *This is the Day*, pp. 89, 91, argues that the circumstances were abnormal. It is curious that he thus acknowledges persecution as a reason for variation of practice, but not the economic circumstances of Christians, which in the case of slaves would prevent them assembling in working hours more effectively than persecution. Stott's argument (chapter 9) that in practice Christian activities must often have consumed much of the day is partly persuasive, but the evidence is elusive, and certainly does not establish that there was any Sabbatarian obligation involved.

[146]Ignatius, *Magn.* 9:1; *Barn.* 15:9; Bardesanes, *Liber legum regionum* 46 (Rordorf, *Sabbat et dimanche*, no. 97).

[147]Peter of Alexandria, *Can.* 15; Tertullian, *De orat.* 23; many later examples in Rordorf, *Sunday*, p. 267 n.6; Dumaine, "Dimanche" *Dictionnaire*, cols. 959–60.

[148]Hippolytus, *In Dan.* 4:20; Tertullian, *De orat.* 23; many later examples in Rordorf, *Sunday*, p. 268 n.4; Dumaine, "Dimanche" *Dictionnaire*, cols. 957–59.

[149]Leviticus 2:40; 2 Chronicles 29:30, 36; Nehemiah 8:12; Psalm 118:24.

[150]For the use of "holy day" for feast days and Sabbaths, see Nehemiah 8:9–11; 10:31; Isaiah 58:13.

[151]Stott, *This is the Day*, pp. 62–64.

[152]For pagan festivals as work-free days, see Macrobius, *Saturnalia 1:16:9; Dumaine, "Dimanche" Dictionnaire*, cols. 916–17; Daniélou, *The Bible and the Liturgy*, p. 243.

[153]Stott, *This is the Day*, p. 66.

[154]Cf. Rordorf, *Sunday*, pp. 283–84. For the eschatological eighth day, see also Sib. Or. 7:140; *Didascalia* 26; Dumaine, "Dimanche" *Dictionnaire*, cols. 879–84; Daniélou, *The Bible and the Liturgy*, chapter 16.

[155]*Str.* 6:14; cf. also 4:25; 5:6, 14; 7:10.

[156]A fragment of Aristobulus preserved in Eusebius, *Praep. Evang.* 13:12. Cf. R. T. Beckwith, in Beckwith and Stott, *This is the Day*, pp. 8–9.

[157]In his numerology Clement is clearly dependent on Philo, *de Opif.* 89–128; *Leg. Alleg.* I.8–15; *de Decal.* 102–5; *Vita Mos.* II.209–10; *de Spec. Leg.* II.59.

[158]Philo, *de Opif.* 100.

[159]Philo, *Post.* 64f.; cf. *Quod deus* 11–12.

[160]Irenaeus, *Adv. Haer.* 1:5:2, etc.

[161]The identification of first day, rest, and light with Christ becomes quite clear in the following passage and again at the end of the exposition of the Sabbath commandment.

[162]This is the decisive argument against the interpretation of Stott, *This is the Day*, pp. 67–69, 130. He takes Clement to refer to God's gift of the seventh day of physical rest to mankind as a whole, including Christians ("he gave *us* the seventh day as a rest"), and to its transference to Sunday. It is important to notice that the clause in question is *quoted* by Clement from Aristobulus (*ap.* Eusebius, *Praep. Evang.* 13:12). Aristobulus certainly intended "us" to mean "all men" (not just Jews), but Clement simply takes over Aristobulus' account of the literal Sabbath in order to go on to follow and expand Aristobulus' allegorization of the Sabbath. Clement is not himself interested in the literal Sabbath.

It should be evident that Clement's argument operates at a level too far removed from practical Sunday observance for any implications to be drawn about his views on Sunday observance. The first, or eighth, day is scarcely for Clement the weekly Sunday at all, but a symbol of Christ and of the spiritual goal of the gnostic. Its association with rest does not derive from Sunday observance but from cosmological and eschatological ideas of rest. Stott seems unaware that the association of rest with the gnostic ogdoad had sources quite independent of the idea of a day of rest.

[163]Epiphanius, *Pan.* 33:3:5:12.

[164]*Str.* 4:25.

[165]Cf. also Tertullian, *Bapt.* 19: "every day is a Lord's Day," *Didascalia* 26: "all days are the Lord's," Chrysostom, *In Kal. hom.* 1:2: "The Christian should celebrate neither months nor new moons nor Lord's Days, but during the whole of his life keep the feast which is fitting for him." Here Chrysostom substitutes "Lord's Days" for Paul's "Sabbaths" (Col. 2:16). Elsewhere he encourages observance of Sunday, treating it as a Christian Sabbath (Rordorf, *Sabbat et dimanche*, nos. 124–27).

[166]*C. Cels.* 8:21–23. Note that a similar justification of Sunday observance recurs in Luther: cf. chapter 11, below.

[167]Origen expounds Colossians 2:16 thus: "I think that this is what Paul had in mind when he called the feast that is held on days set apart from others *μέρος ἑορτῆς*; he hinted by this phrase that the life which is continuously being lived according to the divine word is not *ἐν μέρει ἑορτῆς* but is an entire and continuous feast" (*C. Cels.* 8:23).

[168]It is just possible that already in Origen's Alexandria this tendency had resulted in a kind of Christian Sabbatarianism which elsewhere arose only much later. A Coptic fragment attributed to Peter of Alexandria (d. 311) includes this passage: "I order you to do nothing on the Lord's holy day, and not to allow yourself to go to disputes, lawsuits or contests, but to give attention to the reading of the holy scriptures, and to give bread to the needy. . . . Cursed is he who on the Lord's

holy day performs any business, except that which is beneficial to the soul or is concerned with the care of cattle" (Rordorf, *Sabbat et dimanche*, no. 136). The genuineness of the attribution has usually been doubted, principally on the grounds that such ecclesiastical regulations for the Lord's Day are not otherwise known until a much later date. Hence Rordorf (*Sabbat*, p. 219 n. 3; *Sunday*, p. 171 n. 4) dates it at the end of the sixth century, but Stott, *This is the Day*, p. 100, accepts it as genuine. The use of the term "the Lord's holy day" is noteworthy with regard to the origins of Christian Sabbatarianism.

[169]The sense of this passage is easily obscured if it is not quoted in full: cf. Stott, *This is the Day*, pp. 70–71.

[170]*Haec est observatio sabbati Christiano*: not *Christiani Sabbati*, "the Christian Sabbath," as in Stott, *This is the Day*, p. 70; Daniélou, *The Bible and the Liturgy*, p. 239.

[171]Origen understood the literal sense of this rule very strictly: *De princ.* 4:3:2.

[172]Dugmore, *The Influence*, p. 31.

[173]Stott, *This is the Day*, p. 70–72.

[174]*Str.* 6:7: "Holding festival, then, in our whole life, persuaded that God is present on every side, we cultivate our fields, praising; we sail the sea, singing hymns. . . ."

[175]Stott, *This is the Day*, p. 72, objects that Origen's homilies were "practical talks to ordinary Christians." But Origen's idea of a "practical talk" is unlikely to have been ours, and the ideal described is certainly not irrelevant for ordinary Christians. Cf. *de princ.* 2:7:2: there are many simple believers who by the inspiration of the Spirit know that circumcision, animal sacrifices, and "the rest of the Sabbath" are not to be understood literally.

[176]Philo, *de Decal.* 97–100; *de Spec. Leg.* II.61–64.

[177]*C. Cels.* 6:61.

[178]*In Num. Hom.* 23:4.

[179]*In Exod. Hom.* 7:5.

[180]*In Matt. Comm.* 12:36.

[181]Origen, *C. Cels.* 6:61, following Philo, *Leg. Alleg.* I.6.

[182]Early Christian writers regularly understood John 5:17 in terms of providence rather than the work of salvation: see examples in Rordorf, *Sunday*, pp. 83–84; Daniélou, *The Bible and the Liturgy*, pp. 232, 245. (But Ps.-Athanasius, *De sabbatis et circumcisione* 1 [*PG* 28:133] refers John 5:17 to the work of new creation.) For Philo's understanding of God's Sabbath rest, see *de Decal.* 96; *Leg. Alleg.* I. 5–6.

[183]*C. Cels.* 6:61; *In Num. Hom.* 23:4.

[184]Rordorf, *Sunday*, p. 170 n. 2; *Sabbat et dimanche*, 165 n. 3; Isidore of Seville, *De eccles. Officiis* 1:24 (*PL* 93:760–61). etc. For the rabbinic background to Origen's treatment of Exodus 16, see N. R. M. de Lange, *Origen and the Jews* (Cambridge: Cambridge University Press, 1976), pp. 93–94.

[185]*Codex Justinianus* 3:12:2 (Rordorf, *Sabbat et dimanche*, no. 111).

[186]*Codex Theodosianus* 2:8:1 (Rordorf, *Sabbat*, no. 112).

[187]See the discussion in Rordorf, *Sunday*, pp. 162–66; Dumaine, "Dimanche" *Dictionnaire*, col. 946.

[188]Dumaine, "Dimanche" *Dictionnaire*, col. 947.

[189]*Vita Constantini* 4:18:2; cf. Sozomen, *HE* 1:8:12.

[190]Later examples are *Didascalie* 26; Ps.-Athanasius, *De sabbatis et circumcisione* 5; Jerome, *In Eccles.* 2:2; Ambrose, *Ep. 31 (44) ad Orontianum*.

[191]Ps.-Athanasius, *De sabbatis et circumcisione* 4; Tertullian, *Adv. Jud.* 4; other references in Dumaine, "Dimanche" *Dictionnaire* cols. 925–26; Rordorf, *Sunday*, p. 104 n. 3. (The work *De sabbatis et circumcisione* (*PG* 28:133–41) is probably not by Athanasius; see M. Geerard, ed., *Clavis Patrum Graecorum* vol. 2 (Turnhout, 1974), p. 45; but for a different opinion, cf. Rordorf, *Sabbat et dimanche*, p. 91 n. 1.)

[192]Origen, *In Num. Hom.* 23:4.

[193]Tertullian, *Adv. Marc.* 4:12.

[194]Aphrahat, *Demonst.* 13:7; Epiphanius, *Pan.* 30:32:10; Ps.-Athanasius, *Hom. de semente* 13; many other references in Dumaine, "Dimanche" *Dictionnaire*, col. 927 n.5.

[195]Epiphanius, *Pan.* 30:32:11f.; Victorinus, *De fabrica mundi* 6; Ps.-Athanasius, *De sabbatis et circumcisione* 3; Dumaine, "Dimanche" *Dictionnaire*.

[196]Tertullian, *Adv. Jud.* 4; Victorinus, *De fabrica mundi; Ps.-Athanasius, De sabbatis et circumcisione* 3; Dumaine, "Dimanche" *Dictionnaire*.

[197]Tertullian, *Adv. Jud.* 4; Aphrahat, *Demonst.* 13:7; Gregory of Nyassa, *Testimonia ad Jud.* 13.

[198]Victorinus, *De fabrica mundi* 5; Tertullian, *Adv. Jud.* 4; Ps.–Athanasius, *Hom. de semente* 1.

[199]Origen, *In Num. Hom.* 23:4; *C. Cels.* 6:61; *Didascalia* 26; *Const. App.* 2:36:2; 6:18:17; Ps.–Athanasius, *De sabbatis et circumcisione* 1; also Rordorf, *Sunday*, p. 84 n. 1.

[200]Dumaine, "Dimanche," *Dictionnaire*, cols. 927–28.

[201]Victorinus, *De fabrica mundi* 6; Lactantius, *Div. Inst.* 7; Augustine, *Sermo* 295; also Rordorf, *Sabbat*, p. 95 n.3.

[202]Examples in Rordorf, ibid., p. 92 n.2.

[203]Cf. Rordorf, ibid., p. 105 n.3; Dumaine, "Dimanche Dictionnaire," cols. 919–20.

[204]An exception is Aphrahat (Aphraates), *Demonst.* 13 (dated 344): see the translation and discussion in J. Neusner, *Aphrahat and Judaism: The Christian-Jewish Argument in Fourth-Century Iran, Studia Post-Biblica* 11 (Leiden: Brill, 1971); cf. also Rordorf, *Sabbat et dimanche*, no. 47; M. Simon, *Verus Israel*, pp. 375–76; Stott, *This is the Day*, pp. 54, 132.

Aphrahat was a Persian living outside the Roman Empire, in which Constantine's law was operative, and he makes no reference to *Sunday* rest. Rather he expounds the Sabbath commandment, referring to Saturday, as God's provision of physical rest for both men and animals. Therefore, he says, since it applies also to animals, the Sabbath commandment has nothing to do with morality or salvation. It is *only* a matter of physical rest and therefore has never been obligatory and was not observed by the patriarchs before Moses. Far more important, for the Christian, is the Sabbath "rest" of doing God's will.

Probably, as Simon argues (and cf. Neusner, *Aphrahat*, pp. 126–27), Aphrahat is speaking to a Christian community, which, like many in the fourth century East, was inclined to imitate its Jewish neighbors, and may have been keeping the Saturday Sabbath as well as the Christian Sunday. Aphrahat's intention is to counteract this Jewish influence by insisting that Sabbath observance has no religious significance. It is *only* a convenience for the body.

Apparently the only other patristic passages that recognize the Sabbath commandment as provision for physical rest are Clement of Alexandria, *Str.* 6:16 (quoting the Jew Aristobulus; see above), and Ephraem Syrus, *Hymns on the Nativity* 19:10 (cf. Stott, *This is the Day*, p. 133). It is astonishing that Stott, *This is the Day*, pp. 54, 57, bases on these passages in Clement and Aphrahat *alone* the conclusion that the Fathers not only attributed a humanitarian character to the Jewish Sabbath but also *transferred this to Sunday!* This is typical of Stott's method of drawing maximal conclusions about "the patristic attitude" from isolated and unrepresentative statements in one or two writers. Aphrahat, who belongs to a tradition of eastern Christianity isolated from the mainstream of patristic theology, is, of all the Fathers, one of the least suitable for such treatment.

It is quite clear that the Fathers in general did not see the Sabbath as a creation ordinance providing all men with a weekly day of relaxation. They taught unanimously that the patriarchs kept no Sabbaths and they had strong moral objections to inactivity.

[205]Previous treatments of our subject have given too little attention to this fact.

[206]Ps.-Athanasius, *Hom. de semente* 1; Ps.-Ignatius, *Magn.* 9:1; Council of Laodicea, canon 29, requires Christians to work on Saturday.

[207]For this understanding of John 5:17 see n. 182 above.

[208]It is the unanimous opinion of the Fathers that the patriarchs knew no weekly Sabbaths: see Stott, *This is the Day*, p. 53; Rordorf, *Sunday*, pp. 84–85, 84 n.7; Daniélou, *The Bible and the Liturgy*, pp. 232–33.

[209]Eusebius may here allude to the Pythagorean idea of the number seven as ὁ ἡγεμὼν τῶν συμπάντων already applied to the Sabbath by Philo, *de Opif.* 100.

[210]Stott, *This is the Day*, chapter 8, correctly recognizes the traditional character of Eusebius' themes, but wrongly concludes that therefore Eusebius' *conclusion*, that the Sabbath had been transferred to Sunday, had always been implicit in Christian thinking.

[211]Quoted in Daniélou, *The Bible and the Liturgy*, p. 243.

[212]*De orat.* 23. Cf. the discussion of this passage in Rordorf, *Sunday*, pp. 158–60, and his comment in *Sabbat et dimanche*, xviii and n.6, acknowledging the criticism of Daniélou and Mosna.

[213]See the discussion in Rordorf, *Sunday*, pp. 160–61.

[214]Stott's attempt (*This is the Day*, pp. 98–99) to use the *Didascalia* as evidence that Sunday was already a day free from work misses the point.

[215]See the selections from these authors in Rordorf, *Sabbat et dimanche.* Stott, who has thoroughly ransacked the Fathers in support of his opposite thesis, produces no relevant evidence from these authors. This is not to say that they do not compare and contrast the Sabbath and Sunday, as the Jewish and Christian days of worship, but they do not go so far as to say that the Sabbath has been transferred to Sunday, they do not use Old Testament texts about the Sabbath with reference to Sunday, and they do not refer to Sunday rest.

There is an important discussion of the Cappadocian Fathers' eschatology of the Lord's Day in Daniélou, *The Bible and the Liturgy*, pp. 262–75.

[216]The only notable instance is canon 29 of the Council of Laodicea (c. 380): "Christians must not judaize, and rest on the Sabbath, but must work on that day, and honour rather the Lord's Day, and, if they can, rest [then] as Christians." Even here the imprecise statement and the proviso "if they can" (εἴ γε δύναιντο) are notable. By the phrase "rest as Christians" (σχολάζειν ὡς χριστιανοί), the canon may intend to distinguish not simply Sunday rest from Saturday rest, but also a Christian kind of rest from Jewish "idleness."

Other fourth-century councils insisted on attendance at church on Sunday, and discouraged games and circuses on Sunday as distracting from church attendance (details in J. A. Hessey, *Sunday* [London: Cassell, 1860], pp. 108–9.

Const. App. 8:33:1–2 required slaves to be free from work on both Saturday and Sunday; cf. Rordorf, *Sunday*, p. 159 n.2.

[217]Cf. also the example cited from Palladius in Rordorf, *Sabbat et dimanche*, no. 133; and the opinion of the monk John (d. 530), cited in Rordorf, *Sunday*, p. 161 n.2.

[218]Ps.-Athanasius, *Hom. de semente* 1 (*PG* 28:144); cf. Dumaine, "Dimanche" *Dictionnaire*, col. 936.

[219]*De statuis ad populum Antiochenum, hom.* 12:3 (*PG* 49:131).

[220]*In Kal. Hom.* 1:2; cf. n.165 above; also *In Matt. Hom.* 39: (*PG* 57:436).

[221]*De eleemosyna hom.* 3 (*PG* 51:265); *In Epist. I ad Cor. Hom.* 43 (*PG* 61:368). Stott, *This is the Day*, pp. 134–36, tries to resolve the contradictions in Chrysostom. From *De bapt. Christi hom.* 1 (cf. Rordorf, *Sabbat et dimanche*, p. 199 n.2) it appears that Chrysostom was realistic enough not to expect the whole day to be devoted to worship.

[222]*Sermo ad nocturnum dominicae resurrectionis* 4, in Rordorf, *Sabbat et dimanche*, no. 116.

[223]Since the chapter deals only with the church in the West, we may note that Sabbatarian ideas in the East after the fourth century are illustrated by Rordorf, *Sabbat*, no. 135 ("Eusebius of Alexandria") and no. 136 (Ps.-Peter of Alexandria). Cf. also Rordorf, *Sunday*, p. 169 n.3, and, on John of Damascus, Dumaine, "Dimanche" *Dictionnaire*, cols. 937f. A summary of the later teaching of the Orthodox Church on the Sabbath commandment will be found in the Russian "Larger Cathechism" (1839), questions 536–53, translated in P. Schaff, *The Creeds of Christendom*, 3 vols. (London: Hodder, 1877), 2:529–32.

10

SABBATH AND SUNDAY IN THE MEDIEVAL CHURCH IN THE WEST

R. J. BAUCKHAM

Richard J. Bauckham lectures in the Department of Theology at the University of Manchester, Manchester, England.

Augustine and the Spiritual Sabbath

If Augustine represents the pinnacle of Western theology in the patristic age, he is also the fountainhead of medieval theology in the West. His dominance over many centuries of Western Christian thought is reflected in the medieval theology of the Lord's Day in two major contributions. In the first place, he established definitively the central place of the Decalogue in Christian moral theology. Against the Manichean dualist rejection of Old Testament law, he defended the Decalogue as the sum of the law of love; the first three precepts expound the love of God, the last seven the love of neighbor.[1] Alongside a clear distinction between law and grace, he insisted on the abiding validity of the law; "The same law which was given by Moses becomes through Jesus Christ grace and truth."[2] The Christian attitude to the Decalogue is to "observe from love what you could not observe from fear."[3] Augustine's treatment of the ten commandments as the norm of Christian morality was to remain unquestioned in most subsequent theology, and the result was to exalt the Sabbath commandment to a place of significance it might not otherwise have attained.

Second, Augustine's own treatment of the Sabbath commandment carried over the dominant patristic tradition of spiritualizing its meaning, with that extraordinary weight of influence that only Augustine has had on Western theology. It is significant that the tendencies towards Sabbatarianism to be found in some fourth-century writers, notably Eusebius, do not appear in Augustine, who in company with many others also found no theological significance in the official Sunday rest of the imperial legislation. The common patristic caricature of the idleness and sensuality of the Jewish Sabbath appears in Augustine in particularly memorable forms. "It would be better if they spent the whole day digging than the whole day dancing."[4] This sentiment was frequently echoed by medieval writers. So was his application of the commandment to the spiritual rest of Christian life and Christian hope. Augustine never treated Christian obedience to the Sabbath commandment as the observation of a day. The Sabbath rest is that of Psalm 46:10, "Be still and know that I am God," and its reference is primarily eschatological, to the eternal Sabbath where "we shall be still and see; we shall see and we shall love; we shall love and we shall praise."[5] He could also expound it without explicit eschatology, relating it to the peace of mind that results from the sanctifying work of the Spirit in this life,[6] but more often he treated its present application in the context of Christian hope. Good works performed in the grace of God in hope of the eternal rest to follow them are distinguished from the work men do for "the love of this world." The former are fulfillments of the commandment[7] performed by a pacified conscience that is at rest now because it "listens to the promises of God" for the future.[8] Our Sabbath is fulfilled in hope, because God is working in us; its full reality will come when God "rests in us." Thus "we shall not expect rest now, in this life, but all our good works shall have no other end but that eternal rest to come." The Sabbath commandment is singled out as precisely the one commandment of the Decalogue that Christians are not to take literally,[9] but Augustine's rich exploitation of its figurative significance is of such importance that Daniélou can claim that "the theme of the Sabbath is at the centre of Augustinian thought."[10] Augustine's particular contribution to patristic theology of the Sabbath was what might be called the psychological Sabbath; his analysis of the restlessness of the human heart until it finds its true rest in God. "Our Sabbath is in the heart"[11] is Augustine's distinctive theme.

Though Augustine never based Christian observance of Sunday on the Sabbath commandment,[12] he did bring the Lord's Day and the Sabbath together in an eschatological context, in his two finest treatments of the eschatological Sabbath (in *Ep.* 55 and at the end of the *Civitas Dei*). By its commemoration of the Resurrection and the symbolism of the eighth day, the Lord's Day has its own eschatological meaning. It points beyond rest to the full and eternal experience of resurrection life. It is through the rest in God that the Sabbath prefigured that we are restored to "the original life from which the soul fell into sin," the eighth day of eternal bliss. Augustine harmonized the two traditions of eschatological numerical symbolism by observing that in the Genesis creation account, the sun that rises on the morning of the seventh day never sets; eschatological Sabbath becomes eternal Lord's Day.[13]

Augustine's interpretation of the spiritual Sabbath was taken over in medieval exegesis with varying degrees of approximation to his full meaning. Many who repeated his ideas were mere compilers; few convey more than a superficial appreciation of his doctrine of the rest that comes to a man when "delighting in God, he finds a true, sure, eternal rest, which he sought in other things but did not find."[14] That Christ fulfilled the Sabbath by resting in the sepulchre on the Sabbath,[15] and that God's rest on the seventh day after creation prefigures our future eternal rest, which will follow the good works God is working in us now, are ideas taken up from Augustine by, for example, Eugippus (d.535),[16] Bede (d.735),[17] and Rabanus Maurus (d.856).[18] Purely spiritual interpretations of the Sabbath commandment are common[19] until as late as the famous *Sentences* of Peter Lombard (d.1160). Peter adopted Augustine's application of the first three precepts of the Decalogue to the three Persons of the Trinity; the Sabbath commandment therefore relates to the Holy Spirit, from whom we are to expect "rest from sins in this life and rest in the contemplation of God in the future."[20] Rupert of Deutz (d.1129), following, like most medieval exegetes, Augustine's reference to Psalm 46:10, understood the true keeping of the Sabbath to be working with a view to the eternal rest, which is the eternal contemplation of God. But the spiritual man will not be content with one day a week, and so an exacting call to "*omni tempore sabbatizare*" ("keep Sabbath at all times") became a call to the contemplative life.[21] The continuing influence of the Alexandrian theologians understanding of the Sabbath is here apparent, for Rupert represents the monastic development of the old patristic idea of the Sabbath as renunciation of evil and of hallowing all days as a continuous Sabbath. And medieval monasticism was in its own way a version of the Alexandrians' notion of a double standard of Christian life; for those who could not enter the cloister and give all their time to contemplation, there was the Lord's Day. The tradition of the spiritual Sabbath retained its vigor alongside rising Sabbatarianism. An exposition of the Augustinian concept by Bruno, founder of the Carthusians, in the eleventh century, required an additional note to prevent misunderstanding. Bruno should not be taken to mean that it is not sinful to work on the church's feast days.[22] Still firmly in the Augustinian tradition, however, was a sermon to the Jews by Martin of Leon (d. 1203) that states, "The observance of the Sabbath is not to be accepted carnally, but spiritually; for its carnal rest was entirely abolished both by our Lord and by the fathers."[23]

Early Medieval Sabbatarianism

Augustine's spiritual Sabbath dominated theological writing before the rise of Scholasticism. Medieval Sabbatarianism was not a properly theological development at all. It grew from below, from popular sentiment, and was imposed from above, by legislation. It was a long time before the theologians provided much more than a means of accommodating it. Following Constantine's laws of A.D. 321, regard for Sunday as a day of rest increased for a number of reasons. Sunday rest was first valued as providing leisure for worship; when the imperial legislation guaranteed such leisure, church services grew in length and a tendency to stress the morally obligatory nature of attendance at Sunday worship slowly became apparent.[24] Idle Christians had to be occupied, and the Constantinian church of the Empire became aware of its responsibility to educate the newly Christianized masses. Sunday rest was also promoted by analogy with the Old Testament Sabbath long before a specific application of the Sabbath commandment became theologically acceptable, and the example of pagan Roman festivals was probably also operative. These reasons, it should be noticed, were popular and practical rather than theological.

Perhaps the greatest impetus to Sabbatarianism came, however, from the Christianization of the barbarian nations. "The newly converted Germanic tribes were so deeply impressed with the similarity between their own pagan taboo-days and the Jewish Sabbath that they quite willingly accepted the Lord's Day as the day when work and violence had to cease."[25] The last significant protest against Sabbatarian tendencies is a letter written by Gregory the Great in A.D. 603.[26] The Council of Orleans (538) forbade rural labor, which Constantine had specifically allowed, and a little later the Council's simultaneous attempt to suppress excessive judaizing was clearly going unheeded. Archbishop Martin of Braga, in 572, was probably the first to prohibit Sunday work as "*opus servile*," the biblical term for work forbidden on the Mosaic feast days.[27] In the same century Gregory of Tours was telling exemplary tales of divine judgment on the sin of Sunday labor,[28] and the "Epistle from Heaven," which purported to give direct divine sanction to a strictly Sabbatarian Lord's day observance, made its first appearance.

In A.D. 585 the second Council of Mâcon called Sunday "the perpetual day of rest foreshadowed in the seventh day and made known to us in the Law and the Prophets," and the Council of Rouen (c.650), echoing the language of Old Testament observance, decreed that feast days (i.e., Sundays and other feasts) be celebrated "*a vespera usque ad vesperam absque opere servili*" ("from evening right through to evening without performing servile work").[29] The twenty-four hour cessation of "servile work" had come to stay. The Sunday legislation of the barbarian kingdoms heavily outweighs the later imperial edicts in both quantity and rigor,[30] though the Roman laws, through their incorporation in Justinian's Code, provided authoritative models for the medieval West. Charlemagne's decree of 789[31] followed the pattern already set by two centuries of legislative activity. Church legislation was somewhat tardy by comparison, but a continuous stream of conciliar decrees may be traced right through the middle ages to the Counter Reformation.[32] Sunday rest became a general law of the church when it was incorporated in the Decretals of Gregory IX (1234).

Medieval Sabbatarianism grew in the context of theocratic kingship and of church discipline of an increasingly juridical character. Its legalistic quality derives less from its Old Testament model than from its origin in attempt to legislate for a Christian society. The laws for Sunday rest had a minimum of genuinely ethical content and existed for several centuries as rules in search of a theological context and justified by a divine authority curiously difficult to locate. Their hope of reaching into the hearts and lives of Christian people was small and illegitimate, but doubtless they did succeed (like legalistic Sabbatarianism in later periods) in burdening the consciences of both the ignorantly pious and the superstitiously irreligious. Their positive achievement, in making available time for worship and spiritual refreshment in the context of an economically hard-pressed society, is difficult to assess, but this at least was the aspect on which the religious writers of the Carolingian period focused.

The Carolingian Renaissance produced ecclesiastical scholars who first and foremost prized and, so far as they understood it, preserved their inheritance of patristic theology. Their failure to find a solid theological basis for the rigorous Sunday rest demanded by church and state is therefore not surprising. Isidore of Seville (d.636) had already given them their main lead in suggesting an analogy between Lord's Day and Sabbath by means of a judicious juxtaposition of extracts from Augustine and Origen.[33] Most of the ninth-century writers incorporated parts of Isidore *verbatim*[34] and liberally copied each others' arguments. More or less similar lists of evidences for the divine institution of the Lord's Day frequently recur. For example, it was the first day of the world, the day of the creation of light and the creation of angels, the day on which the manna fell in the wilderness, the day of the Lord's resurrection, the day on which the Spirit descended on the apostles at Pentecost. The apostles themselves sanctified it in memory of the Resurrection.[35] Such evidences sufficed to mark out the day as one which should be entirely devoted to prayer and worship; the special character of the day itself was understood to demand complete rest from "*opus servile*" or "*labor terrenus*" ("earthly labor"), not as an end in itself but so that men "may be more ready and prepared for divine worship."[36] The analogy with the Old Testament Sabbath is implicit but not spelled out except by Rabanus Maurus, who, after listing the usual scriptural proofs for the solemnity of the day, continued, "For the Lord's Day is distinguished by these special acts and remarkable tokens, and therefore the holy doctors of the Church decreed that all the glory of the Jewish Sabbath-observance should be transferred to it." On this basis he justified the legislators' application of Old Testament Sabbath rules,[37] though he perhaps still stopped just short of actually treating Lord's Day observance as obedience to the Sabbath commandment. Peter Comestor (d. 1179) may have been the first exegete to apply the Sabbath commandment literally to Christian observance of the first day[38] and to maintain, on the basis of Genesis 2:2, that "the Sabbath has been always observed by some nations even before the Law."[39] We should note the late appearance of a theology adequate to justify a longstanding Sabbatarian practice.[40]

THOMAS AQUINAS AND SCHOLASTICISM

In the early Middle Ages the grounds of obligation for Lord's Day observance were a combination of scriptural revelation (which testified to the special holiness of the first day) and ecclesiastical authority. Although the Mosaic commandments about Sabbath keeping were treated as rigorously binding, it was not suggested that they were so for any other reason than that the church, perceiving the Lord's Day to be a divine institution analogous to the Mosaic Sabbath, had applied them to the first day of the week (and also, it should be remembered, to the other feast days of the church's year). The medieval church pursued the *analogy* with the people of the Old Covenant a long way, in its conception, for example, of Christendom as a theocratic society bearing comparison with Old Testament Israel or in its understanding of the Christian ministry as a sacrificing priesthood to which many of the rules about the levitical priesthood might be applied, but it did not lose sight of the fact that the authority of the Mosaic law as such had been abrogated. The moral law contained in the Mosaic corpus was still binding because moral law is unchanging, and the Sabbath commandment was indeed directly applicable to Christians by virtue of its inclusion in the Decalogue, the summary of the moral law. In this respect, however, its application concerned sanctification and hope, not Lord's Day observance.

In later medieval theology two significant developments transformed this position: the distinction between moral and ceremonial aspects within the Sabbath commandment, and the treatment of the Decalogue as Natural Law conceived in terms of classical moral philosophy. The first of these made it possible to understand the application of the Sabbath commandment to Christians literally rather than spiritually, but without falling for seventh-day observance (a custom which continued to be regarded as abhorrent judaizing long after Sunday had come to be treated precisely as though it were the Mosaic Sabbath). We have already seen it implicit in the exegesis of Peter Comestor; it became explicit in Albertus Magnus (d. 1280).[41] Both developments received their most authoritative exposition in the *Summa theologica* of Thomas Aquinas (d. 1274).

Aquinas taught that all men are bound by Natural Law, i.e., by moral obligations discoverable by human reason without the aid of special revelation.[42] The Mosaic law (the "Old Law") may be divided into moral, ceremonial, and judicial precepts. All its *moral* precepts are also precepts of Natural Law;[43] moreover, all its moral precepts are reducible to the Decalogue,[44] which is therefore not merely a summary of revealed moral law but also a summary of Natural Law. The Old Law contained three types of moral precept: (1) Some (such as love of God and love of neighbor) that are fully self-evident to natural reason and do not need promulgation. (2) Others, which are somewhat less clear, "yet the reason for them can easily be seen by the most ordinary intelligence. Yet since, in a few cases, human judgment may be misled about them, they need to be promulgated. These are the precepts of the Decalogue." (3) Others, "whose reason is not so evident to all, but only to the wise." These comprise the more detailed commands found elsewhere in the law, but they are reducible to those of the Decalogue."[45]

Thus, whereas the ceremonial precepts of the Old Law were entirely abrogated when Christ fulfilled them, all the moral precepts are Natural Law precepts and cannot be abrogated. All men are bound to obey them "not because these obligations came under the Old Law, but because they came under the Natural Law."[46]

The Sabbath commandment contains a ceremonial as well as a moral aspect; in its ceremonial aspect it commemorated the creation (and has therefore been replaced by a commemoration of the new creation) and prefigured "the repose of the mind of God, whether in the present life by grace, or in the future by glory" (and so has been abolished with its fulfillment in Christ).[47] To this aspect Aquinas attributed some of the rigor of the Mosaic Sabbath: insofar as it was a figure it had to be kept minutely in a way that was not true of the properly moral aspect of the commandment. But he insisted on the continuing need for full abstention from "*opus servile*" as distracting the mind from God,[48] and was on the whole inclined to reduce possible differences by playing down the rigor of the Mosaic Sabbath. Thus (in respect of its moral aspect) Jesus "annulled the sabbath [only] in the superstitious meaning given to it by the Pharisees, who believed that one should abstain even from beneficial works on the sabbath; this was contrary to the intention of the Law."[49] Defending the proposition that the precepts of the Decalogue are not subject to dispensation he argued that 1 Macc. 2:41 (an example of war on the Sabbath) "is an interpretation of the precept rather than a dispensation from it. For a man is not held to be violating the sabbath in doing something necessary for human welfare, as the Lord himself proves."[50] Works of mercy and necessity were always compatible with abstention from "servile work."

The Sabbath commandment as it is found in the Decalogue itself is "a moral precept, inasmuch as it enjoins man to set apart some time for the things of God. . . . In this respect it is comprised among the precepts of the Decalogue, but not as to the time appointed, since in this regard it is a ceremonial precept."[51] Aquinas seems to have thought that Natural Law required a man to set apart a regular stated time for divine worship. Whether (as later writers thought) it required him to set apart specifically a *seventh* of his time is unclear. The point is somewhat academic since the law of the church requires that Christians fulfill the Sabbath commandment during the twenty four hours of the first day of the week; for Christians as well as for Jews there are obligations over and above those of Natural Law. But the real importance of Aquinas' argument is its placing of the Sabbath commandment firmly within the moral precepts of the Decalogue considered as Natural Law.

The Thomist view of the Decalogue survived some challenges[52] to become the prevalent view of late medieval and traditional Roman Catholic theology. Sabbatarianism grounded in Natural Law was propagated by the casuistic manuals of the late Middle Ages[53] and set out again in the Catechism of the Council of Trent, where a full exposition of the scholastic doctrine will be found.[54] Roman Catholic observance of Sunday in theory remains unchanged. The canon law distinction between servile and liberal work still holds despite recognition of its unreasonableness in modern conditions.[55] And while the Roman Catholic doctrine is that Sunday is a day of rest *for worship*, there has never been an official Church pronouncement on the lawfulness of innocent recreation.

Notes

[1]According to Augustine's enumeration of the commandments, which was followed throughout the Middle Ages and since then by the Church of Rome and the Lutherans, the Sabbath commandment is the third.

[2]*Adv. Faustum* 15:7–8; cf. *Ep.* 55:20 (*PL* 33:213); *Sermo* 8 (*CCL* 41:79–99); *Sermo* 9:7, 13 (*CCL* 41:120–21, 133–34).

[3]*Enarr. in Ps.* 32 *Sermo* 2:6 (*CCL* 38:251–52).

[4]*Ibid.* (*CCL* 38:252); cf. *Sermo* 9:3 (*CCL* 41:110); *Enarr. in Ps.* 91:2 (*CCL* 39:1280).

[5]*De Civ. Dei* 22:30.

[6]*Sermo* 8:6 (*CCL* 41:85); *De Spiritu et Littera* 27 (*PL* 44:217–18).

[7]*Sermo* 9:3, 13 (*CCL* 41:111, 133).

[8]*Enarr, in Ps.* 91.2 (*CCL* 39:1280).

[9]*Ep.* 55:19–20, 22 (*PL* 33:213–14); *De Spiritu et Littera* 23–24, 27 (*PL* 44:215-8).

[10]J. Daniélou, *The Bible and the Liturgy* (London: Darton, Longman, and Todd, 1960), p. 276.

[11]*Enarr. in Ps.* 91.2 (*CCL* 39:1280); cf. W. Rordorf, *Sunday* (London: SCM, 1968), p. 116 n.4.

[12]See *Ep.* 36, where both the Lord's Day and the Sabbath are discussed in relation to the question of Saturday fasting. I am not convinced by the argument of W. Stott, *This Is the Day* (London: Marshall, Morgan and Scott, 1978), pp. 136–38, to the effect that Augustine related Lord's Day observance to the Sabbath commandment. If Augustine had intended to do this it is astonishing that he did not do so clearly.

[13]*Ep.* 55:17, 23 (*PL* 33:212, 215); *De Civ. Dei* 22:30. There is an excellent treatment of Augustine on the eschatological Sabbath and Lord's Day in Daniélou, *The Bible and the Liturgy*, pp. 275-86.

[14]*Ep.* 55:18 (*PL* 33:213).

[15]Cf. Rordorf, *Sunday* (London: SCM, 1968), p. 99 n.4.

[16]*Thesaurus*, cap. 66 (*PL* 62:685–86): *verbatim* from Augustine, *Adv. Faustum* 16:29.

[17]*In Genesim* 2:3 (*CCL* 118A:35).

[18]*Commentaria in Genesim* 1:9 (*PL* 107:465–66).

[19]E.g. Ps.-Bede, *Quaestiones super Exodum* 20 (*PL* 93:374).

[20]*Sententiarum libri quatuor* 3:37:2 (*PL* 192:831). Similar interpretations are in Otto of Lucca (?), *Summa sententiarum* 4:3 (*PL* 176:122, ascribed to Hugh of St. Victor) and Martin of Leon, *Sermo* 15 (*PL* 208:782f.).

[21]*In Genesim* 19; *In Exod.* 32; *De S. Spiritu* 20 (*PL* 167:263–64, 681, 1723).

[22]*Expos. in Exod.* 20 (*PL* 164:279–80). The same view is incorporated in Hugh of St. Victor's distinction of four kinds of Sabbath: there are two "external" Sabbaths of God and man, and two "internal" Sabbaths of God and man; God's rest after creation is a sign of His eternal rest, our rest from sin in this life is a sign of our participation in God's eternal Sabbath in the future (*De Sacramentis* 1:12:6 (*PL* 176:354)).

[23]*Sermo* 34 (*PL* 208:1335).

[24]M. Herron, "Sunday and Holyday Observance," *New Catholic Encyclopedia* (New York: McGraw Hill, 1967), 13:800.

[25]Wilhelm Thomas, "Sabbatarianism," *Encyclopedia of the Lutheran Church*, ed. Julius Bodensieck (Minneapolis: Augsburg, 1965), 3:2090.

[26]*PL* 77:1253–1255; W. Rordorf, *Sabbat et dimanche dans l'Eglise ancienne* (Neuchâtel: Delacheux et Niestlé, 1972), no. 149.

[27]Rordorf, *Sabbat*, no. 140. From Irenaeus (*Adv. Haer.* 4:8:2) onwards, "servile work" was interpreted by the Fathers as sin; its transference from festivals (Lev. 23) to Sabbaths was first effected by Tertullian (*Adv. Jud.* 4), and so the Fathers commonly thought that the Sabbath commandment forbade "servile work," i.e., sin (so, e.g., Augustine, *De Spiritu et littera* 27–28 (*PL* 44:218)). When the Sabbath commandment came to be applied literally to Sunday, from the sixth century onwards, this prohibition of "servile works" was treated as its content. Cf. Rordorf, *Sunday*, p. 172.

[28]Rordorf, *Sabbat*, nos. 146–48.

[29]L. L. McReavy, "'Servile Work': The evolution of the present Sunday law," *The Clergy Review* 9 (1935): 273–76; Rordorf, *Sabbat*, no. 143. The letter of Pope Eutychian (d.283) containing the formula "*absque servile opere a vespera in vesperam celebrare*" (*PL* 5:166) is spurious: the formula becomes common only in the seventh century.

[30]The later imperial edicts largely concerned the prohibition of litigation and circus entertainments on Sunday; translations in P. R. Coleman-Norton, *Roman State and Christian Church* (London: SPCK, 1966), documents nos. 144, 209, 220, 236, 243, 279, 316, 385, 509.

[31]*MGH Capitularia Regum Francorum* 1:61; for further Carolingian Sunday legislation, cf. F. L. Ganshof, *The Carolingians and the Frankish Monarchy* (London: Longman, 1971), p. 236 n. 161.

[32]Examples from 9th to 14th centuries are given by M. G. Glazebrook, "Sunday," *Encyclopedia of Religion and Ethics*, ed. James Hastings (Edinburgh: T. & T. Clark, 1921), 12:106.

[33]*De ecclesiasticis officiis* 1:24–25 (*PL* 83:760–61). *Via* Isidore, Origen's exegesis of Exod. 16, proving the Lord's day superior to the Sabbath, became widely known in the medieval West.

[34]E.g. Rabanus Maurus, *Homilia* 41 (*PL* 110:76–77) (= pseudo-Augustine, *Sermo* 280 (*PL* 39:2274–2276)); pseudo-Alcuin, *De divinis officiis liber* cap. 27 (*PL* 101:1226–27) is no more than an extract from Isidore.

[35]Rabanus Maurus, *Homilia* 41; Jonas of Orleans, *De institutione regia ad Pippinum regem* cap. 16 (*PL* 106:304); Theodulf of Orleans, *Capitula ad presbyteros parochiae suae* 24 (*PL* 105:198); Rudolf of Bourges, *Capitula* cap. 26 (*PL* 119:716).

[36]Rabanus Maurus, *Homilia 41* (*PL* 110:76). Though the positive obligation of worship was always stressed, the rigor of the negative obligation to rest varied. Rudolf of Bourges spelled it out at length: "*Videlicet ut nec opera servilia in eo agantur, nec viri ruralia exerceant, nec vineas colant, nec campos arent, nec messem metant, nec fenum seccent, nec sepem ponant, nec silvas stirpent, nec arbores caedant, nec in petris laborent. . . .*" (etc.) (*PL* 119:716). Theodulf of Orleans allowed necessary travel, provided at least that time for mass and prayers be found (*PL* 105:198). Pope Nicholas I (in 866) was unusual in his time for his stress on the difference between Lord's Day rest and the rest of the Mosaic Sabbath commandments. The Lord Himself did many works on the Sabbath and we disobey Him if we insist on the letter of the law (*PL* 119:984f.).

[37]*Homilia 41* (*PL* 110:76f.).

[38]*Historia scholastica: liber Exodi* cap. 39 (*PL* 198:1165).

[39]*Historia scholastica: liber Genesis* cap. 10 (*PL* 198:1065); cf. Honorius of Autun (early

twelfth century), cited by Wilhelm Thomas, as "the first to formulate the doctrine that 'one of the seven days was always dedicated to God, first the Sabbath and now Sunday'" (*ELC* 3: 2090).

[40]W. Thomas (in *ELC* 3:2090) dates the beginnings of a literal application of the third (Sabbath) commandment to Christians as early as c. 800, but if his examples in fact amount to more than the principle of analogy they are not typical of the early period.

[41]W. Thomas in *ELC* 3:2278.

[42]Trenchant criticism of Natural Law theory in general and Aquinas' Natural Law theory in particular will be found in D. J. O'Connor, *Aquinas and Natural Law* (London: Macmillan, 1967). For a modern theological defense of the idea of a "Christian law of nature," cf. Emil Brunner, *Justice and the Social Order* (London: Lutternorth, 1945), chapter 12: Brunner probably escapes the greatest conceptual difficulties by not actually seeking the *moral* quality of Natural Law in human nature. It should be noted that Natural Law and "creation ordinance" views of the Sabbath are not identical, though in many ways similar; the former requires that in some sense the Sabbath must be knowable without special revelation, the latter need not require this even though most defenders of a creation Sabbath have supposed that it does.

[43]ST la 2ae 100, 1.

[44]ST la 2ae 100, 3.

[45]ST la 2ae 100, 11. These distinctions are meant to apply to the *general* capacity of human reason to apprehend moral precepts. They do not make revelation of moral precepts redundant since in fact many minds are so darkened by sin that they need to be enlightened by revelation, and since revelation gives greater certainty to moral knowledge (la 2ae 99, 2).

[46]ST la 2ae 98, 5.

[47]ST la 2ae 100, 5 ad 2; 102, 4 ad 10; 103, 3 ad 4.

[48]On Aquinas' definition of "*Opus servile*" see McReavy, "Servile Work," p. 279.

[49]ST la 2ae 107, 3 ad 3.

[50]ST la 2ae 100, 8 ad 4.

[51]ST la 2ae 100, 3.

[52]Duns Scotus preferred to treat the Decalogue as closely conforming to, rather than embodying, Natural Law (L. L. McReavy, "Sabbatarianism and the Decalogue," *The Clergy Review* 20 (1941): 506).

[53]McReavy, "'Servile Work'," pp. 279–80.

[54]Quoted in English translation in R. Cox, *The Literature of the Sabbath Question* (Edinburgh: Maclachlan and Stewart, 1865), 1:371–82.

[55]M. Herron, "Sunday and Holyday," *New Catholic Encyclopedia*, 13:802. McReavy, "Servile Work" pp. 279–83, discusses the problem of defining "servile work" in writers after Aquinas.

11

SABBATH AND SUNDAY IN THE PROTESTANT TRADITION

R. J. BAUCKHAM

Richard J. Bauckham lectures in the Department of Theology at the University of Manchester, Manchester, England.

In the last two chapters we traced the development of Sabbatarian views in Christian theology over a long period leading to a Sabbatarian doctrine that was accepted nearly unanimously[1] in the scholastic theology of the later Middle Ages. This development was reversed by the Protestant Reformers of the sixteenth century, who returned to a less Sabbatarian position closer to the views of the New Testament writers and the early Fathers. A new Sabbatarianism, however, rapidly developed in the Protestant tradition, especially in English Puritanism, and became especially characteristic of English, Scottish and American Protestantism. This Protestant development was not only more rapid than the medieval development of Sabbatarian doctrine, it also resulted in a stricter Sabbatarianism. The logical outcome, the most consistent form of Protestant Sabbatarianism, was seventh-day Sabbatarianism. Protestant views of the Sabbath and the Lord's Day have always, however, remained very varied. Sabbatarian arguments have never succeeded in convincing all who sought to base their theology on the Protestant principle of *sola Scriptura*.

In this chapter we shall analyze the break with Sabbatarianism in early Protestant theology, represented by Luther and Calvin, and the subsequent trend back to a more Sabbatarian position. Since England was the source of Sabbatarianism in the English-speaking countries, we shall give special attention to the development of English Sabbatarianism, followed by a survey of opposition to Sabbatarian views in English theology. Finally we shall notice the minority tradition of seventh-day Sabbatarianism.

The Continental Reformation

The first Protestant Reformers broke with the Sabbatarian tradition of late medieval theology in such a way that at first sight it is surprising to find most of its characteristics later readmitted to Protestant theology by the back door. This, however, was not the only way in which the Reformation proved to be only a temporary break with scholasticism. Rightly or wrongly, later Protestant theologians, faced primarily with the tasks of consolidation, elaboration, and defense, not infrequently turned to the theological resources of the pre-Reformation period. Moreover we should not exaggerate the extent to which the Reformers broke with the *premises* of scholastic Sabbatarianism. To some extent the repudiation of Sabbatarianism was rather superficial; the Reformers retained a number of theological principles from which medieval theologians had derived their Sabbatarian doctrine. We can observe the following basic continuities between the scholastic doctrine and the thinking of the Reformers in this are (1) The Decalogue remained, as in the whole Augustinian tradition, the essence of Christian morality. Protestant theologians from Luther onwards discussed ethics, whether in catechisms or systematic theology, within the framework of the Ten Commandments. (2) The Decalogue (or at least the second table) was identified, as in scholasticism, as a revealed summary of natural law. (3) The distinction of "moral" and "ceremonial" law within the Decalogue was retained.[2] (4) Little attempt was made to establish a basis for Christian weekly worship in New Testament exegesis. This had not been a pressing problem in the Middle Ages because, quite irrespective of its relation to the Sabbath commandment, the Lord's Day rested sufficiently on the authority of the Church. But the first Protestant Reformers, in rejecting that authority, tended to reduce the Lord's Day to an institution of mere convenience backed by custom and the authority of the civil magistrate, while at the same time those, like Luther and Calvin, who treated the Lord's Day as in all theologically material respects a distinct institution from the Mosaic Sabbath, nevertheless continued to treat it as formally deriving from the natural law aspect of the Sabbath commandment. (5) The principle of a day of *rest for worship*, which lay at the heart of medieval Sabbatarianism, was not repudiated. It is not difficult to see how Protestant Sabbatarianism developed from these premises, but it is equally important to observe how the early Reformers resisted the apparent Sabbatarian logic of these elements in their thought.

Luther

It is difficult, if not impossible, to give adequate impressions of Luther's thought by synthesis or by isolating particular aspects; only the necessity to do so here may excuse the observation that Luther's treatment of the Decalogue is scholastic. "Moses is dead," "Not one iota of Moses concerns us," "God has not led the Germans out of Egypt."[3] Luther's repudiation of the authority of the Decalogue *qua* law of Moses is not in the style of Aquinas, but the thought is the same. The Decalogue *qua* law of Moses was binding only on the Jews. The Decalogue *qua* natural law is binding on all men. "We do not read Moses because he concerns us—because we have to obey him—but because he agrees with the law of nature, and has expressed this law better than the heathen ever could."[4] The Decalogue comes to us with the force of the law of God because it enshrines in an especially clear manner the law written on our hearts. But it does so only *insofar as* it agrees with natural law. Like Aquinas, Luther distinguished, as abrogated by Christ, "ceremonial" aspects within the Decalogue. Therefore "Moses' legislation about images and the sabbath, and what else goes beyond natural law, since it is not supported by the natural law, is free, null and void, and is specifically given to the Jewish people alone."[5] Of course Luther cannot attempt to distinguish the "ceremonial" and "moral" aspects within the Decalogue by reference to an extra-scriptural standard of natural law. His standard for such distinction is in fact the New Testament, and his teaching on the Sabbath gives great weight to the Pauline texts (Rom. 14:5–6; Col. 2:16–17; Gal. 4:10–11).

In this Luther was concerned to oppose not only Romanism but also, on his own left wing, the teaching of Andreas Karlstadt, who was insisting on Christian obedience both to the Mosaic prohibition of images and the the Mosaic Sabbath law. In both areas Karlstadt's position is scarcely distinguishable from later Protestant thought, but Luther opposed him vehemently in the name of Christian liberty.[6] "If anywhere the day is made holy for the mere day's sake—if anywhere anyone sets up its observance on a Jewish foundation, then I order you to work on it, to ride on it, to dance on it, to feast on it, to do anything that shall remove this encroachment on Christian liberty."[7]For Luther the Christian is in no way bound to observe a weekly day of rest or even of worship *as a matter of religious obligation*.

This, however, does not mean that Luther entirely disassociated Christian Sunday worship from the Sabbath commandment or that he advocated any substantial change in the traditional *practice* of Sunday observance. The Sabbath commandment remained relevant to Christians, not only in a spiritual sense,[8] but also with reference to bodily rest, partly because of our physical needs, more importantly in order to secure leisure for worship and religious instruction. Luther regarded this requirement of rest as the natural law content of the Sabbath commandment, which remains when the Mosaic ceremonial aspect is removed. He interprets it, however, in a very general sense, not as though nature demands one day's rest in seven; "For where [the Sabbath law] is kept for the sake of rest alone, it is clear that he who does not need rest may break the sabbath and rest on some other day, as nature allows."[9] In other words, natural law requires only that men spend some time in rest and worship; it does not prescribe how long or at what specific times they should rest. For Luther it is not divine but human authority that has laid down the specific requirement of regular weekly rest on Sundays, but this is a quite legitimate and necessary exercise of human authority to meet practical needs. Luther defends the Christian Sunday as a civil or ecclesiastical institution for the sake of the working classes, who could otherwise get neither the physical rest they need nor the opportunity for corporate worship.[10]

The original Lutheran position is faithfully represented in the Confession of Augsburg (1530):

> For they that think that the observation of the Lord's Day was appointed by the authority of the Church, instead of the Sabbath, as necessary, are greatly deceived. The Scripture, which teacheth that all the Mosaical ceremonies can be omitted

> after the Gospel is revealed, has abrogated the Sabbath. And yet, because it was requisite to appoint a certain day, that the people might know when they ought to come together, it appears that the Church did for that purpose appoint the Lord's Day: which for this cause also seemed to have been pleasing, that men might have an example of Christian liberty, and might know that the observation, neither of the Sabbath, nor of another day, was of necessity.[11]

Calvin

In Calvin's, as in later Lutheran, theology, the place of the law as a guide to Christian living comes into greater prominence; it is precisely by living according to the law that men may reflect the righteousness of God. This law is that which is summed up in the two tables of the Decalogue, which are therefore of permanent validity. Their relation to natural law is for Calvin confined to the second table; only in the case of these commands is it true that the "Law of God, which we call moral, is nothing else than the testimony of natural law, and of that conscience which God has engraven on the minds of men."[12] In the case of the first table, the effects of sin extend not only to the natural man's ability to keep the commands but also to his ability to know them.[13] The kind of obedience the Law demands is the inward heartfelt obedience of love; Calvin's ethics are not legalistic because he reads back the whole of New Testament ethical teaching into the meaning and intentions of the Decalogue. The Sermon on the Mount is not an extension but the true interpretation of the Law. Since, in the Augustinian tradition, Calvin sees the law expounding the principles of love of God and neighbor, his doctrine of "mortification," that dying to self that opens up the heart to divine love, becomes especially relevant. Calvin "finds at the heart of the Law a stern call to self-denial and Cross-bearing,"[14] and for Calvin mortification is the specific content of the fourth commandment.

Calvin refers to the singular place of honor the fourth commandment held in the Old Testament and to the extreme severity with which it was enforced.[15] This is intelligible only in view of the intention of the commandment, for which Calvin resorts primarily to Hebrews 4. The first and principal intention of the commandment is the "ceremonial" element that is fulfilled in Christ—a rigorous, precise abstention from work on the seventh day of the week. The severity of the Mosaic legislation about the Sabbath derives not simply from the practical need to have a day free for worship, but from the function of the Mosaic Sabbath as a foreshadowing of the spiritual rest of Christian salvation. When the Israelites rested on the Sabbath, even when they were not engaged in worship, they were learning the lesson of mortification and new life in Christ, and Calvin holds that only when they understood this were the Israelites truly observing the Sabbath.[16]

Calvin therefore lays most emphasis on the "ceremonial" aspect of the fourth commandment. He argues forcefully against a judaizing theology that regards only the specification of Saturday for the weekly day of rest as "ceremonial" and abrogated. The "ceremonial" aspect, for Calvin, is more than the day of the week; it extends to the *manner* of observing the day, the strict and rigorous abstention from work which characterized the Mosaic Sabbath.[17]

The relevance of this "ceremonial" aspect of the Sabbath commandment for Christians is no longer literal. It should be classed with circumcision and sacrifices as part of the spiritual education of Israel in the period before "the fulness of time, when the truth of its shadows was manifested, and God's covenant assumed a different form."[18] Since the substance of what the ceremonies prefigured is now present in Christ Himself, we no longer need the external types that were necessary for Israel's guidance.[19] But we are no less bound to the spiritual meaning of the command—the need for mortification. "For what else is to cease from our works, but to mortify our flesh, when a man renounces himself that he may live to God?"[20] This new emphasis on an aspect of the Augustinian "spiritual Sabbath" is what Karl Barth called Calvin's "Sabbath mysticism."[21] It is an attempt to do theological justice to the prominence of the Sabbath motif in the Bible. Clearly obedience to this demand for mortification cannot be confined to one day of the week.[22] Since complete sanctification will not be attained in this world, the Sabbath commandment has to that extent an eschatological reference,[23] but Calvin's stress is on sanctification in this life rather than the eschatological Sabbath rest as the spiritual meaning of the commandment.

Although it is this "ceremonial" aspect of the fourth commandment, with its spiritualized application to the Christian, that Calvin emphasizes, he does also allow two subordinate intentions of the commandment that still apply literally to Christians. The first of these is the setting aside of a regular day for public worship. Even here, however, Calvin is sensitive to the charge of judaizing, in apparently distinguishing one day from another. "I answer, that we do not by any means observe days, as though there were any sacredness in holidays, or as though it were not lawful to labour on them, but that respect is paid to government and order—not to days."[24] Like Luther, Calvin stresses that the institution of the weekly Sunday is a matter of convenience and order only, since daily public worship would be impracticable. The early church, thinks Calvin, probably continued to use Saturday for this purpose for a while. Sunday was substituted in order to counter judaizing tendencies; the day of the Resurrection was chosen because it was the Resurrection that abrogated the "shadows of the Law." So much is the institution of the Lord's

Day a matter of mere practical convenience that Calvin is unwilling to "cling so to the number seven as to bring the Church under bondage to it."[25]

Two points arise in relation to this second intention of the commandment. First there is the question of the weekly cycle. In the *Institutes* and elsewhere Calvin is clearly in agreement with Luther that the rhythm of every *seventh* day as the day of worship is not divinely given to Christians. Particular churches could, if they saw fit, vary this rhythm. But in his commentary on Genesis, Calvin teaches that a command to rest one day in seven, in order to be free for worship, dates from the time of creation.[26] If these statements are to be reconciled, the most plausible suggestion is that Calvin regards the requirement of one day in seven as a *minimal* requirement; God requires at least that, but it would be better to worship more often.[27]

Second, there is the question of rest on Sunday. Unlike the Jew on the Mosaic Sabbath, the Christian is required to rest only in order to be free to worship. But Calvin sometimes interprets this requirement with surprising strictness. Both daily work and recreation should be suspended for the whole duration of the day in order that the whole day should be devoted to corporate and private worship and religious instruction.[28]

These two points do not quite make Calvin a Sabbatarian since he does not regard the Christian observance of a weekly day of rest for worship as directly commanded by the fourth commandment (and, incidentally, only in his commentary on Genesis does he treat it as a creation ordinance). The practical result, however, is remarkably similar to the teaching of medieval scholastic theology, and it can readily be seen how an emphasis on these aspects of Calvin's teaching could lead, in some later Calvinist writers, to a more Sabbatarian interpretation of Calvin.[29]

Finally, Calvin allows a second literal application of the commandment to Christians: the requirement that we "give our servants and labourers relaxation from labour." This humanitarian aspect is an "incidental use of the Sabbath," not an "inherent part of its original institution." But it remains valid.[30]

The Trend to Sabbatarianism

The Reformers' break with medieval Sabbatarianism was not complete; neither Luther nor Calvin held that the fourth commandment requires Christians to rest on Sunday, but both held that, as a matter of convenience and order, a weekly day of rest for worship was needed. The individual Christian must rest and worship on the day prescribed by human authority (in practice, Sunday); he is at liberty only to exceed this requirement. Moreover, both Luther and Calvin placed their teaching about Sunday observance within their treatment of the fourth commandment, and in their commentaries on Genesis, though not elsewhere, both taught that a weekly day of rest for worship was ordained at creation.

It is therefore not surprising that other Protestant theologians easily succumbed to the attractions of obvious consistency and fell back on the scholastic position of a weekly day of rest for worship as the natural law content of the Sabbath commandment. This occurred first in Reformed theology, which was always more diverse than Calvin's own position, rather than in Lutheran theology, which for the time being, in, for example, Philipp Melanchthon,[31] Johannes Brenz,[32] and Martin Chemnitz,[33] remained close to Luther's position. In the Reformed theologians Zwingli, Martin Bucer, and Peter Martyr, we find what was to become a general Reformed position: that God's law requires a weekly day of rest for worship, but does not specify *which* day. Thus Peter Martyr distinguished the "perpetual and eternal" and the "changeable and temporal" elements *within the "ceremonial"* aspect of the Sabbath commandment. To set apart one day in seven for the "outward worshipping of God" is perpetual; *which* day of the week that should be is mutable. The change was made at some unknown date by the New Testament church, which was left free to choose the day of worship and judged the first day suitable because of the Resurrection. In this way Martyr preserved, ostensibly, the notions of Christian liberty and nondistinction of days that he found in the Pauline references to the Sabbath. We do not "attribute more holiness to one day than to another. We only for order sake, and a certain civil custom of the church, do meet together upon that day rather than upon another."[34] Similarly, Bucer taught that the early church consecrated the first day instead of the seventh in memory of the Resurrection and to show that Christians are not bound to obedience to Moses.[35] It is hard to take literally Bucer's statement that "it should not be allowable to do anything else on that day except assemble in the congregation of worship,"[36] but a complete day of rest for the sake of worship is the common Reformed principle.

The Sabbatarian position of Heinrich Bullinger (d. 1575), Zwingli's successor at Zürich, was an easy step from Calvin but one that wholly changed Calvin's emphasis. In general, Bullinger was far more concerned than his predecessors with detailed ethical instruction, and his exposition of the fourth commandment moves swiftly through a discussion of spiritual rest to a lengthy consideration of the commandment's relevance for the Christian's "outward service of God." He seems to avoid concluding that the moral (natural) law requires a weekly day of rest for worship, but by insisting that it does require that there be "a prescribed time, for the outward exercise of religion" he effectively secures the authority of the Sabbath commandment for Sunday observance.

> We know that the sabbath is ceremonial, so far forth as it is joined to sacrifices and other Jewish ceremonies, and so far forth as it is tied to a certain time; but in respect that on the sabbath-day religion and true godliness are exercised and published, that a just and seemly order is kept in the church, and that the love of our neighbour is thereby preserved, therein, I say, it is perpetual, and not ceremonial. . . . They of the primitive church, therefore, did change the sabbath-day, lest, peradventure, they should have seemed to have imitated the Jews, and still to have retained their order and ceremonies. . . . And although we do not in any part of the apostles' writings find any mention made that this Sunday was commanded to be kept holy; yet, for because, in this fourth precept of the first table, we are commanded to have a care of religion and the exercising of outward godliness, it would be against all godliness and Christian charity, if we should deny to sanctify the Sunday: especially, since the outward worship of God cannot consist without an appointed time and space of holy rest.[37]

Even more than Calvin, Bullinger blurs the distinctions between the covenants. He thus achieves a list of four ingredients of "Sabbath" worship in both Israel and the New Testament church: reading and exposition of Scripture, public prayers, sacrifices/sacraments, almsgiving.[38] The positive aspect of Sunday, the spiritual duties for which "holy rest" is intended to free the Christian, is, in Bullinger, entirely a matter of corporate worship; the only "private" religious duty he treats is the householder's to his family and servants, his duty to allow them rest, to see that they worship, and to give them religious instruction.[39] Although, like Calvin, Bullinger mentions the humanitarian need to grant rest to employees, he apparently thinks this would be "idleness" if not used for worship; Sabbath rest is specifically rest for worship. "For that cause is the outward rest commanded, that the spiritual work should not be hindered by the bodily business."[40] Since Bullinger does not regard the Mosaic Sabbath rest as having any purpose distinct from that of Christian Sunday rest—rest for worship—he has no hesitation in applying details of Old Testament Sabbath rest to the New Testament era. From Numbers 15 he infers the duty of the Christian magistrate to punish Sabbath breakers, even by death.[41] He was perhaps the first Protestant theologian to discuss in detail what may and may not be done on Sunday, allowing works of mercy and necessity, and censuring such abuses of the Sabbath as "fleshly pleasures," "any handy occupation," and sleeping late.[42] Bullinger has been cited at length because of his very wide influence. Incorporated in the *Decades*, his exposition of the fourth commandment became authorized reading for English parish clergy,[43] while the Second Helvetic Confession (1566), which states Bullinger's position with a greater stress on the distinction between Lord's Day and Sabbath,[44] was widely accepted throughout the Reformed churches of Europe.

Even more emphatically Sabbatarian was the teaching of Bullinger's successor at Zürich, Johannes Wolfius,[45] and of the Heidelberg theologians Zacharias Ursinus (d. 1583), Franciscus Junius (François du Jon) the elder (d. 1602),[46] and Hieronymus Zanchius (Girolamo Zanchi, d. 1590). Ursinus and Zanchius, both widely respected in their day, may be taken as representative of Reformed theology at the end of the century. Ursinus, the more conservative of the two, was responsible for the very non-Sabbatarian-sounding Heidelberg Catechism (1563)—which nevertheless reverses the order of Calvin's thought on the fourth commandment, teaching that it requires first the duties of public worship and secondly the "spiritual rest" of sanctification.[47] Unlike the Second Helvetic Confession, the Heidelberg Catechism makes no mention of a day of rest and in fact refers the commandment's teaching on worship only "especially" to the Lord's Day. The effect of the Decalogue structure of Protestant ethics was to broaden the scope of each commandment as far as possible. Just as the fifth commandment was taken to refer not only to obedience to parents but also to respect for all other authorities in church, state and society, concern for dependents, and parents' duties to their children, so the fourth commandment was taken for the source of all duties in the spheres of public worship, almsgiving, the ministry, and religious education. Ursinus' discussion of how the Sabbath is sanctified and how it is profaned is concerned not with rest but with these positive duties of church life, which are especially, though not exclusively, the duties of the Lord's Day.[48] Ursinus's emphasis is not on rest, but the principle of a day of rest for worship is nevertheless basic to his thought. The abrogated "ceremonial" aspect of the Sabbath was merely its prefigurative *significance* and the fact that it was tied to the seventh day in particular.[49] Christian liberty and nondistinction of days are ensured by the abrogation of these aspects, so that *which* day of the week is now a "thing indifferent" and the needs of "order and comeliness" rather than "difference of days" are all that now set the Lord's Day apart.[50]

> Although the ceremonial sabbath is abrogated and disannulled in the new testament; yet the moral sabbath continueth still, and belongeth unto us, and even the very general of the ceremonial sabbath belongeth unto us, and doth still remain, which is, that *some time* is to be allotted for the ministry of the Church. For we must ever have some day, wherein the word of God may be taught in the Church, and the sacraments administered. But nevertheless we are not restrained or tied, to have either Saturday, or Wednesday, or any other certain day, and therefore the sabbath doth not belong unto us ceremonially in special and particular, albeit it doth belong unto us, and so to all men, and ever continueth both morally and ceremonially in general.[51]

Such a day of public worship, just as much as the Mosaic Sabbath, requires that "all other labours should give place both to the private and public service of God, which on other days every man doth exercise according to his vocation." Works of charity and necessity are permitted, but not "servile works" (defined by Ursinus as "such as hinder the exercise of the ministry").[52]

Zanchius's treatment of the fourth commandment is one of the longest before the great controversial monographs of the seventeenth century,[53] and it is also tidier and more systematic than any previous treatment. Where Peter Martyr (and Ursinus with less precision) had treated the weekly day of rest for worship as a nonabrogated part of the "ceremonial" law, Zanchius placed it firmly in the category of moral (natural) law, which has never been and cannot be abrogated. "Nature teaches all men" that they should devote one day in seven to public worship.[54] God has laid down in the structure of creation a 6:1 pattern of active-contemplative life.[55]Only the function of the Sabbath as a type of salvation in Christ and the specification of the seventh day were "ceremonial" and abrogated.[56] Zanchius is also notable for his attention to the definition of work prohibited on the Sabbath, for which he resorts to scholastic distinctions of the meaning and types of "*opus servile:*"[57] but this seems to result largely from his concern for exhaustive treatment. By comparison with the English Puritan developments the discussion is highly theoretical. Zanchius is wholly traditional in regarding Sabbath rest as exclusively the rest required for the public worship of God,[58] and the principle of a day of rest for worship was so axiomatic for later sixteenth-century Reformed thought about the Lord's Day that Zanchius's shorter treatment of the fourth commandment omits all explicit discussion of rest.[59]

In the seventeenth century, with some stimulus from England and Scotland, the Continental focus of attention for Reformed thinking on the matter was Holland, where all the major theologians engaged in heated and voluminous controversy throughout the century,[60] a spectacle that frequently puzzled its English and Scottish observers because of the impeccable Calvinism of the anti-Sabbatarian writers. In the theology of Lutheran orthodoxy Sabbatarian doctrines prevailed widely with less dispute. A storm of horrified protest greeted the Pietist Johann Samuel Stryk's advocacy of Luther's view of the Sabbath in 1702.[61] Sabbatarian views on the Continent never penetrated the fabric of national and social life to the extent that they did in England, Scotland, and America, but the reasons for this are not only theological. In any case the center of concern in the European theological disputes was not to call in question the practical necessity of a weekly day of rest for worship, but rather its status as eternal moral law or mere ecclesiastical institution.

English Sabbatarianism[62]

"*Figmentum Anglicanum*" was the term by which the English Puritan doctrine of the Sabbath was known among some Dutch divines of the seventeenth century,[63] and it has generally been acknowledged that the English development of Sabbatarian doctrine was distinctive. Scotland and New England both had their own idiosyncratic variations, but derived their doctrine in the first place from England. F. D. Maurice, no friend of the Puritan Sabbath, could still affirm in 1853, "I believe, brethren, we may claim for our country the best idea of the Sabbath-day which is to be found anywhere."[64]

Most English Protestants in the mid-sixteenth century had as imprecise ideas about the basis of Sunday observance as most Christians at most times have had, but at least in retrospect the emergence of the "new Sabbatarianism" at the end of the century seems a natural development of earlier trends. The extreme anti-Sabbatarian position of Tyndale and Frith had little influence, and the official attitudes of the reformed Church of England show a basic continuity with the Sabbatarianism of the pre-Reformation church, modified by a new emphasis on the suppression of Sunday amusements.[65] The contrast of views in Cranmer and Hooper[66] reflects different influences from the Continent, but Hooper's was the Zürich theology that increasingly prevailed in the reign of Elizabeth. The Elizabethan Homily of the Place and Time of Prayer, which was to be so troublesome to later Anglicans, linked the fourth commandment and Sunday observance in an ill-defined manner; the Church's catechetical instruction gave considerable prominence to the Decalogue; and from 1552 at every celebration of the Holy Communion the congregation prayed, "Incline our hearts to keep this law" after each of the Ten Commandments. "The Sabbath" was a common term for Sunday in sixteenth century England, becoming a Puritan shibboleth only in the next century.[67] The more conscientious Elizabethan clergy were well read in the later Reformed theologians, Bullinger in particular. It is therefore not surprising that a widespread practical concern for Sunday observance in the later years of the reign preceded the full emergence of the "new" Sabbatarian theology, which at first was no more than a clearer statement of the general view that the Sabbath of the fourth commandment should be kept on Sundays. That view was not at this stage confined to the "Puritans" (in any useful sense of the term).[68]

The fullest discussion from a distinguishably "Anglican" viewpoint before the seventeenth-century controversy was Richard Hooker's. His basic doctrine is scholastic: immutable moral law requires the sanctification of "a seventh part throughout the age of the whole world."[69] The joyful sanctification of "festival days" (i.e., Sundays and the other feast days of the church year) is made up of "the due mixture as it were" of "Praise, and Bounty, and Rest," for the "most natural tendencies of our rejoicing in God are first his praises set forth with cheerful alacrity of mind, secondly our comfort and delight expressed by a charitable largeness of somewhat more than common bounty, thirdly sequestration from ordinary labours, the toils and cares whereof are not meet to be companions of such gladness."[70] In regard to rest Hooker keeps a careful balance of strict censure for "voluntary scandalous contempt" of Sunday rest, a fairly generous interpretation of works of necessity, and an emphasis on the positive religious quality of rest, which is not idleness but "freedom for actions of religious joy," a foretaste of the eternal rest, and a natural expression of the joyfulness that arises from the commemoration of God's acts of mercy.[71] The single point of controversy with the Puritans is the question of observing feast days other than Sunday. Hooker's defense of these is part and parcel not only of his defense of ecclesiastical authority in general but also of his evaluation of holy days as "public memorials" of God's mercies. "They are the splendour and outward dignity of our religion, forcible witnesses of ancient truth, provocations to the exercise of all piety, shadows of our endless felicity in heaven, on earth everlasting records and memorials, wherein they which cannot be drawn to hearken unto that we teach, may only be looking upon that we do, in a manner read whatsoever we believe."[72] Seventeenth-century "Anglicanism" valued the church year—and Sundays as part of it—for these kinds of reasons, and objected to Puritan Sabbatarianism not only for its strictness but also for its substitution of a different pattern of public worship.

The "new Sabbatarianism" arose in the context of a growing interest in practical moral theology, an interest that naturally took the form of expositions of the Decalogue.[73] Lancelot Andrewes, whose Sabbatarianism emerged in a course of catechetical lectures on the Decalogue in Cambridge in the 1580s, was only one of many such preachers,[74] most of whom probably owed something to Richard Greenham, that fountainhead of Puritan practical theology. Greenham's and Andrewes' expositions of the fourth commandment were for the time being unpublished, however, and the work that has always been regarded as launching Puritan Sabbatarianism was Nicholas Bownde's *The doctrine of the Sabbath.* This originated in sermons on the Decalogue preached in 1586 and appeared in print first in 1595, then in an expanded edition in 1606. It was enormously influential.[75]

Thereafter controversy flowed thick and fast, and "the Sabbath itself had no rest," as one of its advocates admitted.[76] Though Puritans were at first as divided about it as anyone else, the "new Sabbatarianism" shortly became branded as Puritan. "Anglican" apologists such as Thomas Rogers spread the myth that the Sabbath doctrine was a deliberate Puritan move to subvert the established Church.[77] For reasons of censorship the major works of Puritan Sabbatarianism did not appear in print until the 1640s and later. The doctrine was enshrined in the Westminster Confession and Catechisms, and perhaps most learnedly and fully defended in Daniel Cawdrey and Herbert Palmer, *Sabbatum redivivum* (1645 and 1652).

In a brief account of Puritan Sabbatarian doctrine we must ignore many minor variations of opinion and sketch only the broad lines of common agreement. A creation-ordinance Sabbath was always taught and was integral to the whole doctrine.[78] It was generally thought that this made Sabbath observance binding on all men at all times, though opponents sometimes pointed out the weakness of this conclusion.[79] In fact it was not simply the primitive origin of the Sabbath that gave it its universally and permanently binding character. This could only be fully guaranteed by its status as *moral* law. The Sabbath was held to be a moral command, concerned with the fundamental, even pre-Fall, relations between God and men. It was moral because of its place in the Decalogue, which the Puritans held to contain "nothing ceremonial, nothing typical, nothing to be abrogated."[80] This view of the Decalogue was a necessary part of the case and was often treated as self-evident. "It is a truth as immovable as the pillars of heaven, that God hath given to all men universally a rule of life to conduct them to their end. Now, if the whole decalogue be not it, what shall?"[81] The disputed point here was "the *whole* decalogue," for the permanently binding character of the Decalogue *insofar as it was a summary of natural law* was almost unanimously acknowledged in the seventeenth century.[82] It was widely held that the fourth commandment *contains* the natural law requirement that men should give *some* time to religious worship. But how could the specification of one day's rest in seven be universally binding moral law?

In the seventeenth century the "morality of the fourth commandment"[83] was the nub of the whole problem. Nicholas Bownde had adopted a simple equation of natural law = moral law = Decalogue. Therefore, the Sabbath commandment, requiring one day's rest in seven, was written on the heart of man at creation, and is "natural, moral and perpetual."[84] In the seventeenth century, however, English thinkers seem to have had difficulty with the idea of a *natural* law requirement of one day's rest in seven. Natural law theory was growing more rational, and the content of natural law could not so easily be determined simply from Scripture. Certain expedients contrived to bring natural law as close as possible to the Sabbath commandment,[85] but by and large the Puritans abandoned as untenable the notion that the Sabbath law is wholly "natural."

Thus, in place of Bownde's phrase "natural, moral, and perpetual," the Westminster divines spoke of a "*positive*, moral and perpetual commandment, binding all men in all ages."[86] The terminology is somewhat confusing since "moral law" (= natural law) and "positive law" had more normally been treated as mutually exclusive categories. Cawdrey and Palmer explained that when they spoke of the Sabbath commandment as "wholly moral" they understood "moral law" in a broad sense which included both natural law and "positive moral law." "A moral law is any law of God expressed in Scripture (whether it can be proved natural or not) which from the time it was given, to the end of the world, binds all succeeding generations of their posterity to whom it was given; and more specially obliges the Church; because the Scriptures—the Word of God—was specially written for them, and comes specially to them."[87] Thus, though the fourth commandment is not *natural* moral law, as the other nine "for the most part" are, it is *positive* moral law and equally binding. Cawdrey and Palmer can therefore maintain that "the fourth commandment, in the letter of it, is a moral precept," whose moral substance is not merely "some time indefinite" (its generally admitted Natural Law content) but one whole day in seven.[88] These definitions are designed to rescue the concept of universally binding divine laws from the restrictions imposed by current natural law theory, and their effect is to shift the argument away from the problem of the Decalogue's relation to natural law and to focus it instead on other types of argument for the universally binding character of the decalogue. The most significant of these, though too far-reaching to be discussed in the present context, concerned the distinguishing of the Decalogue from the rest of the Mosaic law and the treatment of the law by Christ and the New Testament writers.

A further problem, however, more specific to the fourth commandment, arose from the treatment of the Decalogue as wholly moral, since it might be thought that only the Seventh-Day Sabbatarians could hold this view consistently. Most Sabbatarians, including some of the Puritans,[89] have held that the fourth commandment contains something of abrogated positive law (usually called "ceremonial") at least in its specification of the *seventh* day, and the straightforward application of the whole Decalogue to Christians is therefore encumbered by qualifications on the subject of the "change of day," which on this view becomes probably the central difficulty. Cawdrey and Palmer disarmingly confessed that in their view one of the chief reasons why previous Sabbatarian treatises had not proved wholly convincing was that "they grant their adversary that the Saturday Sabbath was literally enjoined in the Fourth Commandment; which (we think) whosoever grants, he hath lost, not only the cause, but the Commandment too."[90] Their own solution, previously proposed by Greenham, Richard Bernard and others,[91] was that the fourth commandment does *not* command the observation of *the* seventh day (in order), but of "one day in seven, or *a* seventh day" (in frequency).[92]

How did the commandment require the Sabbath to be spent? In the words of the Westminster Shorter Catechism:

> The sabbath is to be sanctified by a holy resting all that day, even from such worldly employments and recreations as are lawful on other days; and spending the whole time in the public and private exercises of God's worship, except so much as is to be taken up in the works of necessity and mercy.[93]

The Puritan doctrine was not that the fourth commandment enjoins rest for rest's sake.[94] All held that the Christian Sabbath rest was *for worship* and Puritan strictness about resting the whole day involved a corresponding devotion of the whole day to religious duties. There were, however, differences of emphasis. Some, such as Richard Bernard and William Twisse (following Calvin), distinguished "ceremonial" rest from a "moral" rest. The former was more rigorous and was confined to the Mosaic Sabbath; it was intended to prefigure Christ.[95] Bownde, on the other hand, understood the rigor of the Mosaic Sabbath as necessary to its "moral" purpose; the figurative meaning was added to the Sabbath at Sinai without affecting the practice of Sunday rest. So it is as true now as then that "though men may rest upon the other six days for their benefit and good, yet . . . the rest upon this day must be a most careful, exact, and precise rest, after another manner than for the most part men do perform."[96] Some seventeenth-century Sabbatarians thought that all Mosaic Sabbath regulations outside the Decalogue were abrogated ceremonial and judicial laws applicable to the Mosaic Sabbath only.[97] Others advocated the observance of at least some of them, perhaps even the death penalty for Sabbath breaking.[98] Recreation on the Sabbath was opposed by almost all on the grounds that it evidently impeded the devotion of the whole day to religious exercises and was condemned in Isaiah 58:13, though the meaning of this verse was debated.[99]

The Westminster Assembly's Directory for Public Worship gives some idea of what the majority of seventeenth century Puritans expected in practice:

> The Lord's Day ought to be so remembered beforehand, as that all worldly business of our ordinary callings may be so ordered, and so timely and seasonably laid aside, as they may not be impediments to the due sanctifying of the day when it comes.
>
> The whole day is to be celebrated as holy to the Lord, both in public and private, as being the Christian Sabbath. To which end, it is requisite, that there be a holy cessation or resting all that day from all unnecessary labours; and an abstaining, not only from all sports and pastimes, but also from all worldly words and thoughts.
>
> That the diet on that day be so ordered, as that neither servants be unnecessarily detained from the public worship of God, nor any other person hindered from the sanctifying of that day.
>
> That there be private preparations of every person and family, by prayer for themselves, and for God's assistance of the minister, and for a blessing upon his

ministry; and by such other holy exercises, as may further dispose them to a more comfortable communion with God in his public ordinances.

That all the people meet so timely for public worship, that the whole congregation may be present at the beginning, and with one heart solemnly join together in all parts of the worship, and not depart till after the blessing.

That what time is vacant, between or after the solemn meetings of the congregation in public, be spent in reading, meditation, repetition of sermons; especially by calling their families to an account of what they have heard, and catechising of them, holy conferences, prayer for a blessing upon the public ordinances, singing of psalms, visiting the sick, relieving the poor, and such like duties of piety, charity, and mercy, accounting the Sabbath a delight.[100]

The Westminster divines' capacity for coming perilously close to pharisaism is illustrated by their discussion of a proposal "That there be no feasting on the Sabbath," which failed to pass the Assembly because three members cited scriptural instances of Christ's feasting on the Sabbath (Luke 14, Matt. 8). Presumably without such explicit texts it would have passed.[101] The height of Sabbatarian exaggeration is probably represented by John Wells' 800-page volume on the duties of Sunday observance, *The practical Sabbatarian* (1668), which included a chapter entitled "A plea with Christians to outvie the Jews in Sabbath-holiness and observations."[102]

It would be inaccurate to imply, however, that this degree of strictness was necessary to the Sabbatarian position. Especially from the late seventeenth century onward, many writers came to see that the rigor of Sunday observance must be somewhat adapted to human capacities if its real religious ends were not to be frustrated. The moderation of John Owen, who protested that "a man can scarcely in six days read over all the duties that are proposed to be observed on the seventh,"[103] was the attitude that prevailed in most later Sabbatarian circles. In this more moderate form, Sabbatarianism seems to have shed some of its Puritan stigma in the later seventeenth century, and following the lead of Edward Stillingfleet, who expounded essentially the Puritan doctrine in his *Irenicum* (1659), the majority of Anglican writers adopted a Sabbatarian position.[104] If Sabbatarian practice declined in the eighteenth century,[105] the commonly accepted doctrine remained much the same, and the Evangelical Revival precipitated a new movement of concern for strict Sunday observance. The sermons of Daniel Wilson, Rector of St. Mary's, Islington,[106] were the immediate impetus to the founding of the Lord's Day Observance Society in 1831 and remain the classic statement of its position. Sabbatarian controversy in the nineteenth century largely resulted from the vigorous efforts of the LDOS to propagate and implement Wilson's doctrine.

Theologically, nineteenth century Sabbatarianism was the seventeenth century Puritan doctrine with some of its complexities ironed out. In its LDOS form it was a powerful, if somewhat over-simplified, argument from Scripture, with something of a tendency to bypass objections by means of direct appeal to the conscience of the honest reader of Scripture. By the nineteenth century it seemed to carry a great deal of Christian tradition with it. "The whole church of Christ, in the proper sense of that term, has maintained this fundamental point in every age," thought Daniel Wilson.[107] No less than seventeenth century Puritans, nineteenth century Sabbatarians were intent on regulating the social behavior of the nation by the authority of the State.[108] "It is not possible for the mind of man to measure the dimensions of that guilt, which the deliberate profanation of the Lord's Day under the Gospel dispensation in a free Protestant country involves."[109] This more strident assertion of national responsibility was doubtless because more people disagreed with their presuppositions about the authority of the state in religious matters. Relatively new in the nineteenth century was an emphasis on the social value of a day of rest, an emphasis that outside LDOS circles gathered strength throughout the century, especially after 1850. It brought in nonconformists who could not support a campaign for state interference in the *religious* activity of the individual, and generally broadened the base as well as somewhat diluting the ideals of the movement.

It should be remembered that throughout these three centuries the value of Sunday as an institution was scarcely in question. There were disputes about what kind of institution it should be—notable centers of controversy were the King's Book of Sports in the seventeenth century and the opening of the Crystal Palace on Sunday afternoons in the nineteenth—but the broad principle of a weekly day of rest from normal employment was hardly ever challenged,[110] and few were even prepared to argue for indiscriminate public amusements on the supposed Continental model. Puritans and Laudians in the early seventeenth century were essentially agreed that the health of the Christian religion required a weekly day of leisure for worship. The difference was that the Puritan Sunday, like the Puritan faith itself, made much greater spiritual demands on the ordinary believer; the Laudian argument was that the essential religious character of the day was better preserved by permitting some recreation.[111] For a lyrical appreciation (one might say, over-valuation) of Sunday, George Herbert's poem "Sunday" should be read.[112] By the eighteenth century, the pattern of the English Sunday secured by the seventeenth-century legislation, was acquiring its air of proven value. Part of Addison's well-known passage (1711) may be quoted again: "I am always well pleased with the country Sunday and think, if keeping holy the seventh day were only a human institution, it would be the best method that could have been thought of for the polishing and civilizing of mankind."[113] Even Daniel Wilson had to admit that "most of the opponents of the divine authority of the Sabbath are ready at present to allow its importance."[114] His own opening encomium is not only an excellent expression of the nineteenth-century Sabbatarian esteem for the Sabbath but also gathers up most of the religious values which have ever been seen in it:

> The glory of God is peculiarly connected with the due observance of the day which he is pleased to call his own, and on which he has suspended, in every period of the church, almost all the practical effects of that mighty salvation which he has provided for man. The Christian sabbath is one main distinction of the gospel dispensation, as the Jewish was of the Mosaical, and the patriarchal of the first revelation of the divine will to Adam. The profanation of that day goes to annihilate all the blessings of revelation. It leaves the world without any visible token of the authority of Christianity, and strips the church of the best means of openly testifying its faith and obedience. If the sabbath be taken away from the mass of mankind, no time is left for religious duties, for the worship of Almighty God, domestic piety, the instruction of children, the visiting the sick and needy, the reading and hearing of the gospel, the celebration of the sacraments, the preparation for that rest of heaven of which it is the pledge and foretaste. Without it, the remaining classes of society would never, in fact, allot a time for those duties, which being left open, would not be obligatory; nor could they sustain with effect the honour of religion in their families or the world.[115]

Notably, of course, this account omits the purely social values of the weekly rest day which others were urging in the nineteenth century. "The day of rest is an invaluable blessing to all the toiling multitudes of Christendom," argued Edward Higginson in an anti-Sabbatarian tract on the Crystal Palace question.[116] Sabbatarian writers were always tempted to suppose that only the strongest theological basis could maintain the institution of the English Sunday as they valued it, especially in those periods when the Sabbatarian cause meant preserving rather than innovating. Though this view had little support from non-Sabbatarian writers,[117] it must be admitted that the English Sunday would not have been created by humanitarian concern alone, or even by the economic interests, which Christopher Hill believes to have been heavily involved in the Puritan Sabbatarian movement.[118] Dubious theology can sometimes yield good practical results, and we need not doubt the incalculable religious and social value of the English Sunday in the past, even though we may at the same time regret that so often the effect of Sabbatarianism was also to burden Christian liberty with human traditions.

Some English Non-Sabbatarian Positions

The only distinguishable school of non-Sabbatarian theologians in England since the sixteenth century has been the High Church Anglican tradition, beginning with the Laudian, anti-Puritan, writers of the early seventeenth century. The two most renowned of these were bishop Francis White (*A treatise of the Sabbath-day*, 1635) and Peter Heylin, chaplain to Charles I (*The history of the Sabbath*, 1636). Their complementary efforts were a direct response to the refusal of conscientious Puritans to read the *Declaration of Sports* (1633) from their pulpits, an act of serious insubordination.

> It was thought fit that the Bishops should first deal with the refusers in a fatherly and gentle way, but adding menaces sometimes to their persuasions it they saw cause for it; and that in the mean season some discourses should be writ and published to bring them to a right understanding of the truth, and their several duties.

This work was divided between White, who undertook the "argumentative and scholastical part," and Heylin, who took the "practical and historical." For Heylin, according to himself, "had gained some reputation for his studies in the ancient writers by asserting the history of St George, maliciously impugned by those of the Calvinian party upon all occasion."[119] Despite this unpromising recommendation Heylin's work on the Sabbath was a competent historical survey. All writers on the "Anglican" side of the seventeenth century controversy were united in opposing Puritan "innovations," desiring Sunday to be observed no more strictly than the laws required, and especially in opposing the Puritan claim that the fourth commandment is directly binding on Christians. On the crucial point of what was the basis of Sunday observance if it was not the fourth commandment they were not entirely agreed, though for all of them the matter was sufficiently settled in practice by the authority of church and state. They (and other non-Sabbatarians later) had no intention of challenging the existing institution of a weekly rest day.

It was more difficult for Anglicans than for some Dissenting writers to relegate the fourth commandment to the sphere of abrogated Mosaic Law, since they had always to offer some account of its use in the homily and especially the liturgy of their church. They maintained some relation between the Sabbath commandment and Sunday observance by virtue of the natural law content of the commandment and (frequently) a principle of analogy or of the "equity" of the commandment. This relation did not normally imply, however, that Christians must necessarily give up one whole day in seven to religious exercises.[120] On the principle of *rest for worship* they agreed with the Puritans rather more than either were aware and it is none too easy to draw a clear line between them. For the Laudians the moral law involved in Sunday observance had two aspects: positively, worship, and negatively, "vacancy from all worldly affairs which may impeach that worship."[121] But they subordinated and limited rest to the needs of worship rather more convincingly than the Puritans, since in that respect they insisted on distinguishing Old

Testament Sabbath from Sunday. With the Jews "rest is the principal; with us it is the accessory."[122] It therefore need not extend beyond the hours of worship, which they thought it unreasonable to suppose could occupy the whole day for most people.[123] Recreation outside those hours, such as the *Declaration of Sports* permitted, was even desirable; while "the evangelical law imposeth no commandment of total abstinence from secular labour, or from civil actions, during the space of a natural day."[124] The *church* prohibited labor and secular business on Sundays and must of course be obeyed (though not pharisaically), but Heylin's history showed plainly enough that "total abstinence" was in no way *necessary* to the institution of the Christian Sunday and could not be urged as an absolute moral obligation.[125] The religious duties of the day were not usually extended much beyond the public services of the church; these writers had little taste for the Puritan diet of meditation, family prayers, catechising, discussion of sermons and so forth.

The most celebrated eighteenth-century proponent of a non-Sabbatarian view was William Paley (1785),[126] though his influence here may have been due as much to his general reputation as to the specific merits of his treatment of the "Christian Sabbath." With most other non-Sabbatarians, Paley treated Genesis 2:3 as proleptic, Exodus 16 as "the first actual institution of the Sabbath," and the fourth commandment as a ceremonial law applicable only to Jews. The New Testament observance of the first day of the week was a distinct institution, and Paley makes this distinction clearer than many writers in spite of the additional "sabbatical" characteristics of the eighteenth century Sunday, which he valued. His conclusions:

> The *assembling* upon the first day of the week for the purpose of public worship and religious instruction, is a law of Christianity, of Divine appointment; the *resting* on that day from our employments longer than we are detained from them by attendance upon these assemblies, is to Christians an ordinance of human institution,—binding, nevertheless, upon the conscience of every individual of a country in which a weekly Sabbath is established, for the sake of the beneficial purposes which the public and regular observance of it promotes, and recommended perhaps in some degree to the Divine approbation, by the resemblance it bears to what God was pleased to make a solemn part of the law which he delivered to the people of Israel, and by its subserviency to many of the same uses.[127]

The arguments of John Milton in the seventeenth century were much the same as Paley's with regard to the Old Testament Sabbath (independently, since Milton's *De Doctrina Christiana* was not published until 1825), though he differed with regard to the basis of Sunday observance.[128] Other distinguished nonconformist, non-Sabbatarian writers were the Quaker Robert Barclay (1678), Philip Doddridge (1763), and in the nineteenth century the Congregationalist James Baldwin Brown. Richard Baxter can scarcely be claimed as a non-Sabbatarian, though his brand of Sabbatarianism was rather different from that of the Westminster Assembly.[129] J. A. Hessey's Bampton Lectures in 1860, which took a non-Sabbatarian line, were probably the most competent scholarly discussion from any viewpoint in the last century.

Since the basis of Sunday observance is the point on which non-Sabbatarians have been most in disagreement, it may be helpful to set out some of the views that have been held on this with reference to the so-called "six texts" on some or all of which a basis for Sunday observance in the New Testament has generally been sought (John 20:19, 26; Acts 2:1; 20:6–7; 1 Cor. 16:1–2; Rev. 1:10).[130] There have been four basic views on these texts: (1) They show that the apostolic church, on the authority of the Lord, observed Sunday as a Sabbath. Most Sabbatarian writers have thought this. (2) The texts show that the apostolic church observed Sunday as a day of worship (a new institution, distinct from the Sabbath). This fact "carries with it considerable proof of having originated from some precept of Christ, or of his Apostles, though none such be now extant" (Paley).[131] Or the apostolic practice itself may be thought to constitute a command carrying apostolic, i.e., divine authority (Hessey).[132] (3) The texts show that the apostolic church observed Sunday as a day of worship. Though this apostolic example does not in itself constitute a precept, it provides a basis for the church to prescribe Sunday observance (some Laudian writers)[133] or simply an example that Christians appropriately follow, though not commanded to do so (Barclay).[134] (4) The texts do not show that the Apostles or the apostolic church observed Sunday as a Sabbath or as a day of worship; Sunday observance therefore rests wholly on the authority of the church (Heylin, Milton).[135] Alternatively, it has no authority as a religious institution, but only pragmatic value as a human institution. This was the view of Sir William Domville, who in 1849 argued with some cogency that the six texts are no evidence for Sunday observance in the New Testament church, that in fact it is too inconsistent with Paul's teaching to have been prevalent in his lifetime, that on extra-scriptural evidence it most probably arose in the late first century, and that "it cannot be a religious duty incumbent upon Christians at this time, if it was not so (and most certainly it was not) during the ministry of Peter and Paul."[136]

Seventh-Day Sabbatarianism

Seventh-day Sabbatarianism since the Reformation has kept up a consistent case for Christian obedience to the letter of the fourth commandment. Oswald Glait (d. 1546), the most famous of the seventh-day Sabbatarian Anabaptists, argued primarily from the integrity of the Decalogue and the twin significance of the seventh-day Sabbath as memorial of creation and "an eternal sign of hope." From Hebrews 4, he reasoned that since we have not yet completely entered the eternal rest, the Sabbath, which points forward to it is still binding. In the statement "Sunday is the pope's invention" he was perhaps the first to express what became a persistent seventh-day conviction.[137]

That seventh-day observance should have won vigorous advocates in England in the period when the Puritans were urging obedience to the whole Decalogue as moral is not surprising. An impressive succession of Puritan and Anglican spokesmen addressed themselves to combating the seventh-day error: Lancelot Andrewes, Bishop Francis White, Richard Baxter, John Bunyan, Edward Stillingfleet, John Owen, Nathanael Homes, John Wallis. Their efforts are a tacit admission of the attraction that the doctrine exercised in the seventeenth century, and seventh-day observers (who then usually also advocated Sunday work) were harshly treated by Puritan and Anglican authorities alike. With the exception of some early advocates such as John Traske and Thomas Brabourne, they attached themselves to the Seventh-Day Baptist churches, of which there were nine or ten in England in 1668,[138] and which maintained the seventh-day tradition virtually alone until the rise of Seventh-Day Adventism. The first Seventh-Day Baptist church in America was founded at Newport, Rhode Island in 1671.[139]

Seventh-day Sabbatarian doctrine differed from Puritan doctrine *only* in teaching that the Sabbath must be kept from sunset on Friday to sunset on Saturday. *The common accusation of Judaism was therefore either meaningless abuse or a case of the pot calling the kettle black.*[140] Seventh-day writers hardly needed to do more than insist on the plain and logical implications of the Puritan estimate of the Decalogue.[141] "The Ten words are a perfect and complete, standing, unchangeable Rule of Life, in all matters of Duty to be performed, and of Sin to be avoided" (Francis Bampfield).[142] Scripture, Bampfield observed, never calls any other day than the seventh the Sabbath or commands "the observation of any other day in the week as a weekly Sabbath day to Jehovah but only the seventh."[143] The case rested on the two pillars of the integrity of the Decalogue as moral law and the lack of evidence for a New Testament "change of day."[144] Robert Cornthwaite, an eighteenth-century Seventh-Day Baptist, produced some cogent historical arguments against the plausibility of the "change of day":

> Whoever impartially considers the great bickerings which a declaring the Gentile converts *only* exempted from the necessity of submitting to circumcision, and some other rites of the law of Moses, perpetually occasioned from the Jewish converts for a considerable number of years after the death of Christ . . . will not, I imagine,

easily give in to the belief of their hushing up, in so very tame and silent a manner, this so very considerable an alteration.[145]

Seventeenth-century Seventh-Day Baptists were obliged to account for the historical prevalence of Sunday observance, and explained it, as Protestants of the time were accustomed to do with all ecclesiastical abuses inherited from the medieval church, as an invention of the papal Antichrist. In particular they pointed to Daniel 7:25 as the prophecy the popes were fulfilling when they imposed Sunday observance on Christendom.[146] This prophetic explanation remained a key idea in American Seventh-Day Baptist circles[147] and thereby entered the Adventist movement in the 1840s. After its first adoption by an Adventist group in Washington, New Hampshire, the seventh-day Sabbath spread to other groups that were in the process of reformulating their doctrines in the wake of the Disappointment of 1844 and coming together as the denomination that took the name Seventh-Day Adventists in 1860. Its popularity with the Adventists was undoubtedly connected with its prophetic significance, enhanced by such Adventist writers as Joseph Bates (*The Seventh-Day Sabbath, A Perpetual Sign,* 1846), who originated the idea that Sunday observance is the mark of the apocalyptic beast and the "seal of God" (Rev. 7) is the seventh-day Sabbath.[148] In Adventism the Sabbath acquired a new significance as a "testing, sealing message for the last days."[149]

Seventh-Day Adventists like their predecessors base their Sabbatarian belief on a conviction that the seventh-day Sabbath is immutable moral law. "While the ceremonial law given through Moses was temporary and local, the 'ten words' which God spoke Himself were but a repetition of the moral law He had set before men from the very beginning."[150] The Sabbath is a sign of the future eternal rest[151] and a memorial of creation and redemption.[152] Sunday, by contrast, is originated by the Antichrist.[153] Because Sabbath observance is costly and because it marks out believers from the world, it has a special significance as "the hall-mark of loyalty"[154] and in the Adventist eschatological perspective becomes "a banner of loyalty to God in the last-day climax of prophetic fulfillment."[155] Obedience to all the commandments of God is a demand which comes with special clarity in the last days, as indicated by Revelation 14:12 (a text which has always been close to the center of Adventist belief).[156] "Those who keep the commandments of God and the faith of Jesus" are the "last-day Sabbath-keeping remnant."[157] "Faith manifesting itself in obedience will characterize those who are gathered into the garner of God" at the end.[158] On this doctrinal basis and as a result of Adventist missions, some two million Christians now observe a seventh-day Sabbath.

NOTES

[1]An eminent dissenting voice is to be found in the theology of bishop Tostatus of Avila (d. 1454): see R. Cox, *The Literature of the Sabbath Question*, 2 vols. (Edinburgh: Maclachlan and Stewart, 1865), 1:126.

[2]Sixteenth century writers often treat this distinction as a bulwark *against* Sabbatarianism, or against a more extreme Sabbatarianism than their own; in fact of course it is essential to any Sabbatarian position other than seventh-day observance.

[3]Quoted in H. Bornkamm, *Luther and the Old Testament* (Philadelphia: Fortress, 1969), pp. 124–25.

[4]Quoted in Cox, *The Literature of the Sabbath Question*, 1:384.

[5]*LW* 40:93, 97–98.

[6]E. G. Rupp, "Andrew Karlstadt and Reformation Puritanism," *JTS* 10 (1959): 315–19.

[7]*Table Talk*, quoted in J. A. Hessey, *Sunday*, 5th edn. (London: Cassell, 1889), p. 165.

[8]Luther retained the Augustinian metaphorical sense of Sabbath keeping: resting from our own works so that God may work in us: *LW* 44:71–73.

[9]*LW* 40:98.

[10]LW44:72; *Larger Catechism*, quoted in Hessey, *Sunday*, pp. 167–68. In his *Lectures on Genesis* Luther argued that Adam would have kept a weekly day of worship in Eden, prescribed by God at the creation as a sign of the promise of sharing God's eternal rest (*LW* 1:79–82). It is not very clear how this conforms with Luther's views elsewhere, but the same problem is found in Calvin, see below.

[11]P. Schaff, *The Creeds of Christendom*, 3 vols. (London: Hodder, 1877), 2:69.

[12]*Inst.* 4:20:16.

[13]R. S. Wallace, *Calvin's Doctrine of the Christian Life* (Edinburgh: Oliver and Boyd, 1959), pp. 141–42.

[14]Ibid., p. 119.

[15]*Inst.* 2:8:29; *Comm.* Exod. 20:8; Isaiah 58:13.

[16]*Comm.* Exodus 20:8; Numbers 15:32–36; Isaiah 56:2; 58:13; Acts 12:14; *Inst.* 2:8:29.

[17]Calvin is perhaps not wholly consistent on this point. He sometimes seems to treat the Mosaic Sabbath as simply a day of *rest for worship*, like the Christian Sunday. For example, he says that the Mosaic precept required of the Israelites no greater abstention from work "than was useful or necessary for keeping the people in the exercise of piety" (*Comm.* Exodus 20:10; cf. *Comm.* Lev. 19:30; 26:2; Ps. 92:1), and in his treatment of Jesus' attitude to the Sabbath in the Gospels, he denies that Jesus was breaking or abrogating the Mosaic Sabbath (which continued in force until Jesus' resurrection). Rather he sees Jesus as illustrating the real intention of the Mosaic Sabbath against the Pharisees' emphasis on outward observance (*Comm.* Matt. 12:1; Mark 2:24; Matt. 12:7; Mark 2:27; Matt. 12:11; Luke 13:5; Luke 14:1–6; John 5:17). (Calvin thinks that in one or two instances Jesus was demonstrating His divine authority to override the Sabbath: *Comm.* Matt. 12:8; John 5:10). We should remember, however, that for Calvin the "ceremonial" aspect of the Sabbath commandment was not fulfilled by mere outward observance; the outward observance of rest was intended to teach Israel the inner reality of mortification.

[18]Comm. Exod. 31:16.

[19]*Comm.* Colossians 2:17; Hebrews 4:8, 10.

[20]*Comm.* Hebrews 4:10; cf. *Comm.* Isaiah 58:13; Jeremiah 17:21–22; Matt. 5:17.

[21]*C.D.* III/4, 59.

[22]*Inst.* 2:8:31.

[23]*Comm.* Heb. 4:10; *Inst.* 2:8:30.

[24]*Comm.* Colossians 2:16.

[25]*Inst.* 2:8:32–34; *Comm.* Acts 20:7; 1 Corinthians 16:2; Galatians 4:10.

[26]*Comm.* Genesis 2:3; cf. *Comm.* Exod. 20:8. By the time of Moses the observance of this creation Sabbath had almost died out (*Comm.* Exod. 20:11), and Calvin only thinks it probable that it was known to the patriarchs (*Comm.* Exod. 16:5).

[27]This suggestion is made by J. H. Primus, "Calvin and the Puritan Sabbath: A Comparative Study," in *Exploring the Heritage of John Calvin* (J. H. Bratt *Festschrift*), ed. D. E. Holwerda (Grand Rapids: Eerdmans, 1976), p. 65. He supports it with quotations from Calvin's *Sermons on Deuteronomy* (Sermon 34).

[28]Ibid., pp. 68–70, quoting the *Sermons on Deuteronomy* (Sermon 34).

[29]Primus, "Calvin," pp. 58–59, points out that Nicholas Bownde, in his influential Sabbatarian treatise, made considerable use of Calvin's *Sermons on Deuteronomy* (Calvin at his most Sabbatarian) but ignored the Sabbath material in the *Institutes* (Calvin at his least Sabbatarian).

[30]*Inst.* 2:8:32; *Comm.* Exod. 23:12.

[31]Cox, *The Literature*, 1:389, 396; cf. P. Melanchthon, *Loci Communes* (ET in W. Pauck, ed., *Melanchthon and Bucer, Library of Christian Classics XIX* [London: SCM, 1969]), p. 55.

[32]Hessey, *Sunday*, p. 166.

[33]Ibid., p. 169.

[34]Peter Martyr Vermigli, *The Common Places* (London: 1583), Part II, pp. 375–76; *In primum librum Mosis commentarii* (Zürich: 1579), vols. 8v-9r; cf. Zwingli quoted in Hessey, *Sunday*, pp. 352–53: "Now hear . . . how the sabbath is rendered ceremonial. If we would have the Lord's Day so bound to time that it shall be wickedness to transfer it to another time, in which resting from our labours equally as in that, we may hear the Word of God, if necessity haply shall so require, this day so solicitously observed, would obtrude on us a ceremony. For we are no way bound to time, but time ought so to serve us, that it is lawful, and permitted to each Church, when necessity urges, (as is usual to be done, especially in harvest time), to transfer the solemnity and rest of the Lord's Day or Sabbath to some other day; or on the Lord's Day itself, after finishing of the holy things, to follow their labours, though not without great necessity."

[35]M. Bucer, *De regno Christi* II. 11 (ET in W. Pauck, ed., *Library of Christian Classics* XIX, 1969), p. 252. Hessey, of the Reformers generally, justly comments: "Our Lord's Resurrection is made a decent excuse for the day, rather than the original reason, or one of the original reasons, of its institution" (*Sunday*, p. 173).

[36]*De regno Christi*, p. 251.

[37]H. Bullinger, *The Decades of Henry Bullinger*, 4 vols. ET by the Parker Society, ed. T. Harding (Cambridge: University Press, 1849–1852), 1:259–60 (*Decade* 2:4). Bullinger (not at all unusually among sixteenth century Protestant theologians) treats the major feasts of the church year on a level with Sundays (cf. p. 260).

[38]Ibid., pp. 255, 261.

[39]Ibid., pp. 256–59.

[40]Ibid., pp. 255.

[41]Ibid., p. 262.

[42]Ibid., pp. 262–66.

[43]P. Collinson, "The Beginnings of English Sabbatarianism," C. W. Dugmore and C. Duggan ed., *Studies in Church History* I (London: Nelson, 1964), p. 211.

[44]"Hence we see that in the ancient churches there were not only certain set hours in the week appointed for meetings, but that also the Lord's Day itself, ever since the apostles' time, was set aside for them and for a holy rest, a practice now rightly preserved by our Churches for the sake of worship and love. . . . In this connection we do not yield to the Jewish observance and to superstitions. For we do not believe that one day is any holier than another, or think that rest in itself is acceptable to God. Moreover, we celebrate the Lord's Day and not the Sabbath as a free observance." Chapter XXIV (2), translated in A. C. Cochrane, ed., *Reformed Confessions of the Sixteenth Century* (London: SCM, 1966).

[45]Collinson, "The Beginnings," p. 214.

[46]Ibid., p. 213.

[47]"Q. 103. What does God require in the fourth commandment? A. First, that the ministry of the gospel and Christian education be maintained, and that I diligently attend church, especially on the Lord's Day, to hear the Word of God, to participate in the holy Sacraments, to call publicly upon the Lord, and to give Christian service to those in need. Second, that I cease from

my evil works all the days of my life, allow the Lord to work in me through his Spirit, and thus begin in this life the eternal Sabbath" (translated in Cochrane, *Reformed Confessions*, pp. 325–26).

[48]Z. Ursinus, *The summe of Christian religion* (Oxford: University Press, 1587), pp. 948–54.

[49]Ibid., pp. 957–58, 941.

[50]Ibid., pp. 946, 957–58.

[51]Ibid., p. 955.

[52]Ibid., p. 944.

[53]Cox awards the prize for "the bulkiest of all the books on the Sabbath controversy" to John Brown, *De Causa Dei contra Anti-Sabbatarios Tractatus*, (Rotterdam: 1674–1676), a work published in two quarto volumes of 1769 pp. in all (Cox, *The Literature of the Sabbath Question*, 2:448).

[54]H. Zanchius, *Opera theologica* (Geneva: 1613), 4: col. 650.

[55]Ibid., col. 662.

[56]Ibid., cols. 650, 855f.

[57]Ibid., cols. 661–64.

[58]Ibid., cols. 659, 663.

[59]Ibid., 8, cols. 687–90.

[60]See Hessey, *Sunday*, pp. 174–77.

[61]F. Kalb, *Theology of worship in seventeenth-century Lutheranism* (St. Louis: Concordia, 1965), pp. 55–63.

[62]English Sabbatarianism is a subject on which much has been written: see especially W. B. Whitaker, *Sunday in Tudor and Stuart times* (London: Houghton, 1933); *idem*, *The eighteenth-century English Sunday* (London: Epworth, 1940); P. Collinson, "The Beginnings of English Sabbatarianism," Christopher Hill, "The Uses of Sabbatarianism," *Society and Puritanism in Pre-Revolutionary England* (London: Secker and Warburg, 1964); J. K. Carter, "Sunday Observance in Scotland, 1560–1606" (unpublished Ph.D. thesis [Edinburgh, 1957]); J. Wigley, "Nineteenth Century English Sabbatarianism: A study of a religious, political, and social phenomenon" (unpublished Ph.D. thesis [Sheffield, 1972]). In the following section I have not intended a history of Sunday observance or legislation or the related social and economic questions, but confined myself to a brief survey of theological developments. I am naturally heavily dependent on R. Cox, *The Literature of the Sabbath Question*, a quite invaluable guide to the labyrinth of Sabbatarian discussion published between the Reformation and the mid-nineteenth century.

[63]John Owen, quoted in Cox, *The Literature of the Sabbath Question*, 2:27. I have avoided discussing American Puritanism, but a good place to begin is W. U. Solberg, *Redeem the Time: The Puritan Sabbath in Early America* (Cambridge, Mass: Harvard University Press, 1977).

[64]F. D. Maurice, *Sermons on the Sabbath-day* (London: J. W. Parker, 1853), p. 49.

[65]See Whitaker, *Sunday in Tudor and Stuart times*, chapters I–III. Curiously the attitude toward Sunday work was more lenient than that toward Sunday amusements, which suggests that originally objections to Sunday recreation arose not so much from Sabbatarian theology as from a general distaste for "vain and idle pastimes."

[66]See Whitaker, *Sunday*, pp. 18–21; Cox, *The Literature of the Sabbath Question*, 1:135–38.

[67]It was used, e.g., by Archbishop Whitgift, *Works* (Cambridge: University Press, 1851), 1:201.

[68]See Whitaker, *Sunday*, Chapter IV; Collinson, "The Beginnings."

[69]Richard Hooker, *Of the laws of ecclesiastical polity* (London: J. M. Dent, 1907), vol. 2 (Book 5), p. 357.

[70]Ibid., pp. 352–53.

[71]Ibid., pp. 353–54, 368–71.

[72]Ibid., pp. 372–73.

[73]John Ley (1641) quoted in Cox, *The Literature of the Sabbath Question* 1:194; Collinson, "The Beginnings."

[74]For Andrewes and his place in the development of moral theology at this period, cf. R. Bauckham, "The career and thought of Dr. William Fulke (1537–1589)" (unpublished Ph.D. thesis [Cambridge, 1973]), pp. 122–24.

[75]There is an excellent account of Bownde's views in Primus, "Calvin," pp. 41–59.

[76]Quoted by Thomas Fuller in Cox, *The Literature of the Sabbath Question*, 1:148.

[77]T. Rogers, *The Catholic Doctrine of the Church of England* (Cambridge: University Press, 1854); Collinson, "The Beginnings."

[78]N. Bownde, *The doctrine of the Sabbath* (London: 1595), pp. 5–6; Cox, *The Literature of the Sabbath Question*, 1:201, 203–4, 214–15, 231, 233, 239, 258, 476 etc. The remarkable view that the Sabbath was ordained after Adam's fall was held by George Walker (1641) and William Pynchon (1655) (Cox, 1:476, 478): this involves the idea that the Fall occurred on the sixth day of creation.

[79]E.g. John Milton (Cox, *The Literature of the Sabbath Question*, 2:51), John Cowell (Cox, *The Literature of the Sabbath Question*, 2:61–62). Archbishop John Bramhall, *Works* (Oxford: J. H. Parker, 1845), 5:19. A command given to Adam need not bind all his descendants. It could have been abrogated by Christ, as sacrifices (usually thought to have begun with Adam) were. Cf. Isaac Watts's discussion (1738) in Cox, *The Literature of the Sabbath Question*, 2:189–90: Watts's whole treatment of the Sabbath problem is a model of moderation, open-mindedness, and respect for the sincere convictions of those who differ from him. Note: "Nor does any man, who is humbly and sincerely studious of truth and duty, and desirous to find it, deserve any reproach or censure upon the account of different opinions about meats and days" (189).

[80]Bownde, *The Doctrine of the Sabbath*, p. 21, quoting Wolphius.

[81]Thomas Shepherd (1651) quoted in Cox, *Literature*, 1:251.

[82]Cf. John Ley (1641): "It is confessed by all but heretics, that there are ten commandments to us Christians, as well as to the Jews" (Cox, *Literature*, 1:195). Though not too happily phrased, the statement is roughly accurate.

[83]Cf. the title of William Twisse's book: *Of the Morality of the Fourth Commandment, as still in force to bind Christians* (1641).

[84]Bownde, *Doctrine*, pp. 7–8.

[85]E.g., Twisse argued: (1) If natural law cannot lay down what proportion of time should be consecrated to God, it may at least suggest that it is more fitting for the Creator to prescribe this proportion to the creature than vice versa. (2) By "the very equity of a natural conscience it is more fit to apportion unto God's service one day in a week, rather than one day in a month; especially considering that originally time hath been divided into weeks, and not into months until a long time after." (3) Whereas natural law cannot prescribe *which* day of the week, "it seems fit in reason that there should be an uniformity" and therefore that God should prescribe the day (Cox, *Literature*, 1:211f.) Twisse, working with the usual concept that moral law equals natural law, found (1) and (2) a sufficient basis for regarding the requirement of a weekly day of religious rest as moral and perpetual.

[86]Confession XXI.7.

[87]Cawdrey and Palmer, *Sabbatum redivivum* (London, 1645–52), Part I, p. 7.

[88]Ibid., Part II, pp. 49, 54, 178, 206.

[89]E.g., Twisse (Cox, *Literature*, 1:208).

[90]Quoted in Cox, *Literature*, 1:239.

[91]Cox, *Literature*, 1:140f., 204, 227; cf. 247. The idea perhaps was invented by Greenham. It is not explicit but may be implicit in the Westminster Confession.

[92]Cawdrey and Palmer, *Sabbatum redivivum*, Part II, pp. 31–32, 48; argued at length pp. 255–94.

[93]Answer 60.

[94]Cox misleadingly suggests that the Westminster Confession adopts the view that *rest is worship* and identifies this as "the chief distinction of the Puritans from the Reformers" (*Literature*, 1:420). But "holy rest" is a traditional term (based on Exod. 16:23?) intended to distinguish rest for religious purposes from mere idleness or rest for physical refreshment (see e.g.,

L. Andrewes, A *pattern of catechistical doctrine* [Oxford: J. N. Andrewes, 1846], p. 157). Even Bownde clearly indicates that the rest of the Sabbath is for worship (*Doctrine*, p. 57).

[95]Cox, *Literature*, 1:205, 208.

[96]Bownde, *Doctrine*, pp. 53, 57, 59f.

[97]"For whereas some have made no distinction between the Sabbath as moral and as Mosaical, unless it be merely in the change of the day, they have endeavoured to introduce the whole practice required on the latter into the Lord's Day. But we have already shewn that there were sundry additions made unto the command, as to the manner of its observance, in its accommodation unto the Mosaical pedagogy, besides that the whole required a frame of spirit suited thereunto." John Owen, quoted in Cox, *Literature*, 2:15.

[98]E.g., Thomas Shepherd, quoted in Cox, *Literature*, 1:251.

[99]Opponents of the Puritan position sometimes argued that it was stricter than the Mosaic Sabbath, which was a festal day and on which recreation was appropriate; e.g., Cox, *Literature*, 1:165, 171, 176; 2:304–5.

[100]Quoted in Cox, *Literature*, 1:230.

[101]Ibid., 1:229. The reference is to Matthew 8:14 (cf. Mark 1:31). Cf. Cawdrey and Palmer, *Sabbatum*, Part II, 91 for a discussion of cooking on the Sabbath with reference to Luke 14. Cooking was generally allowed by Puritan writers, but not without careful regard to the exegesis of Exodus 15 and 35:3 (see Cox, *Literature*, 1:215f., 149, 213, 250f, 418, 454; 2:25).

[102]Cox, *Literature*, 2:14.

[103]Ibid., 2:15.

[104]For examples of more or less moderate eighteenth century views on Sunday observance (none quite equalling the mid-seventeenth-century Puritan strictness), see John Howell (1704) (Cox, *Literature*, 2:131), Samuel Clarke (d. 1729) (Cox, *Literature*, 2:170), Alexander Jephson (1738) (Cox, *Literature*, 2:196f.), John Jortin (1770) (Cox, *Literature*, 2:232f.), Bishop Beilby Porteous (1784) (ibid., 2:246–47), Bishop Samuel Horsley (d. 1806) (ibid., 2:312–13); William Law (1728), *A Serious Call to a Devout and Holy Life* (London: J. M. Dent, 1906), p. 74.

[105]See Wigley, *Nineteenth Century*, p. 25; Whitaker, *The Eighteenth-century English Sunday* (London: Epworth, n.d.).

[106]D. Wilson, *The divine authority and perpetual obligation of the Lord's Day, asserted in seven sermons* (London: G. Wilson, 1831).

[107]Wilson, *Divine Authority*, p. xv.

[108]Wigley, *Nineteenth Century*, p. 34 and *passim*.

[109]Wilson quoted in Wigley, ibid., p. 40.

[110]E. Evanson in 1792 argued that it was economically wasteful: Whitaker, *The Eighteenth-century English Sunday*, pp. 200–1; Cox, *Literature*, 2:291–303.

[111]"For people must serve the Lord with a free and joyful heart. . . . But the imposing such a quantity and continuance of spiritual actions as exceedeth the ordinary hability of human faculties, choketh rejoicing and comfort in the services which men perform, and makes the same a tedious burden." (Francis White in P. E. More and F. L. Cross ed., *Anglicanism* (London: SPCK, 1957), p. 573).

[112]R. S. Thomas, ed., A *Choice of George Herbert's verse* (London: Faber, 1967), pp. 37–39.

[113]Quoted in Whitaker, *The Eighteenth-century English Sunday*, pp. 48–49.

[114]Wilson, *Divine Authority*, p. 3.

[115]Ibid., pp. 1–2.

[116]Cox, *Literature*, 2:398.

[117]See, e.g., Southey's comments on the ten-day week in revolutionary France, in Cox, *Literature*, 2:322–23.

[118]Hill, "The Uses of Sabbatarianism."

[119]Cox, *Literature*, 1:173.

[120]It does imply this in Isaac Barrow, otherwise broadly in this tradition: Cox, *Literature*, 2:69.

[121]Edward Brerewood (1630) in Cox, ibid., 1:160.

[122]Jeremy Taylor in Cox, ibid., 2:11.

[123]"Amongst a multitude of people, few are to be found who are morally able to apply themselves the space of so many hours of the day to spiritual and religious exercises, and to divine meditations only, and such as our Novel Sabbatarians require" (White in Cox, *Literature*, 1:172).

[124]White in Cox, ibid., 1:170.

[125]Cf. Heylin (Cox, ibid., 1:181f.), Christopher Dow (1636) (Cox, *Literature*, 1:183), Dr. John Prideaux (1626) (Cox, *Literature*, 1:165).

[126]The relevant chapters are reprinted in Cox, ibid., 2:248–58.

[127]Ibid., 2:257.

[128]Milton's discussion is reprinted in Cox, ibid., 2:46–54.

[129]See Baxter, *Practical Works* (London: James Duncan, 1830), 13:363–516; 19:185–96. Baxter does not regard the fourth commandment as directly applicable to Christians but extends the principle of analogy so far as to make the Lord's Day a Sabbath. His argument stresses the distinctions between Mosaic Sabbath and New Testament Lord's Day because it was directed especially at Seventh-Day Sabbatarians.

[130]All except Acts 2:1 were used by Paley to prove the divine institution of the Lord's Day, but of course many non-Sabbatarians have thought that only two or three of them carry any weight. Sabbatarians have not infrequently used also Matthew 24:20; Hebrews 4; and even such examples from Acts as 16:13 (Seventh-Day Sabbatarians use Matthew 24:20 and Acts with rather more justification.)

[131]Benjamin Keach (d. 1700) thought that "Christ had certainly given directions to his disciples to observe" the first day of the week (Cox, *Literature*, 2:118). Of seventeenth-century Anglicans, White (ibid., 1:170), John Cosin (ibid., 1:455), Jeremy Taylor (ibid., 1:11), thought of an injunction by Christ or the apostles. According to Archbishop Bramhall, "the Lord's Day was celebrated from the beginning, that is, from the Resurrection of Christ, in pursuance of His direction or example; and . . . without all doubt there was either an Apostolical precept for it, written or unwritten, or Apostolical practice, equivalent to a precept. What concerned the Apostles, is altogether undoubted; what concerneth Christ, is piously presumed" (*Works*, Oxford: J. H. Parker, 1845), vol. 5, p, 58.

[132]Similarly Prideaux (d. 1626) (Cox, *Literature*, 1:166).

[133]Edward Brerewood (d. 1632) (Cox, *Literature*, 1:161f.), Robert Sanderson (1636) (Cox, *Literature*, 1:186).

[134]This seems to be Barclay's meaning. He denies that Revelation 1:10 refers to Sunday. (Cox, *Literature*, 2:451–53).

[135]Heylin did admit Revelation 1:10 as evidence that the Lord's Day was being observed by the late first century, but did not treat it as scriptural authority for the practice. Milton regarded all six texts as inconclusive, or—"Granting, however, that the Corinthians were accustomed to assemble on that day for religious purposes, it no more follows that we are bound to keep it holy in conformity with their practice, without a divine command to that effect, than that we are bound to observe the Jewish Sabbath in conformity with the practice of the Philippians, or of Paul himself" (Cox, ibid., 2:54).

[136]'A Layman' (i.e., Sir W. Domville), *The Sabbath: or, An Examination of the six texts commonly adduced from the New Testament in proof of a Christian Sabbath* (London: Chapman and Hall, 1849), p. 333 and *passim*.

[137]G. F. Hasel, "Sabbatarian Anabaptists of the Sixteenth Century, Part I," *AUSS* 5 (1967), pp. 118–21.

[138]Edward Stennet, quoted in Cox, *Literature*, 1:268.

[139]L. E. Froom, 4 vols. *The Prophetic Faith of Our Fathers* (Washington: Review & Herald, 1954), 4:917.

[140]There were examples of real judaizing, insistence on the whole Mosaic law (Cox, *Literature*, 2:58), but these should not be used to impugn the whole movement. It ought not to be necessary to point out that the other common modern accusation against Seventh-Day Adventist Sabbatarianism, that it teaches salvation by works, is equally unfounded.

[141]This is a major argument of e.g., Thomas Brabourne, A *Defence of the Sabbath Day*, (London: 1632, 2nd ed.).

[142]F. Bampfield, *The judgment of Mr. Francis Bamfield, for the Observation of the Jewish, or Seventh-Day Sabbath* (London: 1672), fol. 4r. The Seventh-Day Baptists did not adopt the Westminster Assembly's "positive moral law," but taught that the *natural* obligation of the fourth commandment could be known more generally but for the fallen state of men (ibid., fols. 6r–7v).

[143]Ibid., fol. 5v.

[144]John Milton avoided the seventh-day conclusion only by denying the applicability of the Decalogue to Christians: "For if we under the Gospel are to regulate the time of our public worship by the prescriptions of the Decalogue, it will surely be far safer to observe the seventh day, according to the express commandment of God, than on the authority of mere human conjecture to adopt the first" (Cox, *Literature*, 2:54).

[145]Quoted in Cox, *Literature*, 2:199.

[146]Froom, *Prophetic Faith*, 4, pp. 908, 911, 915–16.

[147]Ibid., 920.

[148]Ibid., 957–58; cf. Uriah Smith, *Daniel and The Revelation* (Watford: Stanborough Press, 1921), p. 588; "Christendom will at last be divided into just two classes: to wit, those who are sealed with the seal of the living God—that is, have His mark, or keep His Sabbath—and those who are sealed with the seal of the beast—that is, have his mark, or keep his sabbath." On the significance of Joseph Bates, cf. also C. E. Stenberg, "A Study of the Influence of Joseph Bates" (M.A. thesis, SDATS).

[149]Froom, *Prophetic Faith*, 4:959.

[150]W. L. Emmerson, *I believe in the ten commandments* (Watford: Stanborough, 1934). The majority of Seventh-Day Adventist literature on these subjects has been of a popular nature. Further representative samples include: C. B. Haunes, *From Sabbath to Sunday* (Washington: Review and Herald, 1928); W. E. Straw, *Origin of Sunday Observance in the Christian Church* (Washington: Review and Herald, 1939); F. H. Yost, *The Early Christian Sabbath* (Mountain View CA: Pacific Press); R. Lewis, *The Protestant Dilemma* (Mountain View, CA: Pacific Press, 1961); A. F. Vaucher, *Le jour seigneurial* (Collonges-sans-Salive: Imprimeric Fides, 1970). The only noteworthy early work is that of J. N. Andrews, *History of the Sabbath and First Day of the Week* (Battle Creek: Review and Herald, 1887). More recently, however, front rank contributions have been made by Seventh-Day Adventists, including G. Hasel, K. Strand, S. Bacchiocchi, and others with whom these essays have interacted. The most recent contribution, by R. L. Odom, *Sabbath and Sunday in Early Christianity* (Washington: Review and Herald, 1977), is disappointing. Although Odom refers to the primary sources, he shows no awareness of the critical, historical, and theological issues that others are treating and consequently seems at times to be speaking in a vacuum.

[151]In accordance with Isaiah 66:23 the Sabbath will still be observed in the next world "in eternal remembrance of what man owes to God," W. L. Emmerson, *The Bible Speaks* (Watford: Stanborough Press, 1942), p. 173; cf. Smith, *Daniel and Revelation*, p. 589.

[153]Ibid., p. 194; Emmerson, *Bible Certainties* (Watford: Stanborough Press, 1938), p. 65; Smith, *Daniel and Revelation*, p. 147.

[152]Emmerson, *The Bible Speaks*, pp. 170–73.

[154]Emmerson, *Bible Certainties*, p. 67.

[155]Froom, *Prophetic Faith*, 4:1167.

[156]In the Adventist apocalyptic scheme this verse is part of the message of the third angel (Rev. 14:9), which is "the last special religious movement to be made before the Lord appears" and to be identified with the Seventh-Day Adventist movement itself (Smith, *Daniel and Revelation*, pp. 581–87).

[157]Emmerson, *The Bible Speaks*, p. 205; cf. *Bible Certainties*, p. 65; Froom, *Prophetic Faith*, 4:958.

[158]Emmerson, *Bible Certainties*, p. 65.

12
FROM SABBATH TO LORD'S DAY: A BIBLICAL AND THEOLOGICAL PERSPECTIVE

A. T. LINCOLN

Andrew T. Lincoln taught New Testament for five years at Gordon-Conwell Theological Seminary and is now at St. John's College in Nottingham.

On the one hand, there are Christians to whom it may seem a retrograde step to reexamine the question of the religious significance of Sunday. In a post-Christian Western society, the Sunday issue often seems like a relic from the days of Puritan or Victorian England that scarcely repays detailed study; there are more urgent questions. On the other hand, there are those within the Christian church who may be uneasy about a careful examination of the origins and development of Sunday because for them this day is a treasured institution that helps to preserve traditional Judeo-Christian values. To question its foundations would be to invite secularization to make further inroads in erasing the distinctiveness of the day. However, the issue of Sunday is neither outmoded nor sacrosanct. For the Christian it remains a compelling matter for examination because it involves the consideration of God's claim upon one's life and time, and, in this light, it becomes of great importance to ascertain whether the Bible gives any guidelines about the ordering of one's time, particularly the religious observance of one day a week.

But, as studies of the history of Sabbath or Sunday observance have demonstrated, to ascertain biblical guidelines is not a simple matter. As C. R. Rowland points out in this book, the difficulty of Judaism at the beginning of the Christian era in obtaining a clear answer on Sabbath observance is salutary in its own right, and the complexities of the debate in the history of the church should caution against any hubris in our own attempt.[1] Present-day students of the issue not only find themselves faced with conflicting viewpoints in the history of the church but in examining the biblical data itself, are also involved in a number of complex hermeneutical debates. These include, to name just the major issues, the interpretation of the creation narrative in Genesis 1 and 2; the question of the relationship between the Old and New Testament; and, in particular, of the Christian attitude to the Old Testament law; the historical Jesus' attitude to the Sabbath; whether, and if so how, the practice of the New Testament church is normative; and the relationship between the New Testament material and the often clearer evidence of the second-century church. Such factors also help to illustrate why the relationship of the Bible to ethics has been seen as problematic in much recent discussion.[2] To do justice to the issues involved would require competence in a number of fields, which is why this exegetical task has been divided among a number of contributors. My task in this final chapter is to bring together the conclusions of these exegetical studies in the light of the questions raised by the historical chapters, and to elaborate on the direction in which the study as a whole has led.[3] It would be presumptuous to claim that our combined efforts have produced the only satisfactory solution to the question, but it is to be hoped that these studies will at least have helped to clear the ground for a better construction than has previously been made. This summary will confine itself to suggesting an overall perspective and its implications, with some discussion of the most crucial links in the argument.

The attempt will be made in relating Old Testament and New Testament to do justice to the variety of ways in which the relationship is expressed in the New Testament itself. For this particular subject, however, the notion of Christological fulfillment and the continuity and discontinuity this involves has proved to be the most appropriate and fruitful approach.

A Summary Statement on the Biblical Data

The briefest summary of the various syntheses of the biblical data will be given so that there will be no doubt as to where the argument is leading.

Biblical writings show that God has given history a Sabbatical structure after which the weekly cycle has been patterned. In particular, the institution of the Mosaic Sabbath with its division of the week into six days of work and one of rest was analogous to the way in which God's activity in regard to His creation was pictured. This Sabbath not only pointed to God's creative pattern and purpose but was also a memorial of His redemptive activity in delivering His people from Egypt. After the Fall, God's intent for the consummation of history is seen to coalesce with His redemptive activity, which found its focus in the covenantal relationship of God to His people. The Sabbath, with its twofold theological justification, was a basic sign of the Mosaic covenant indicating God's sovereign claim on His people's time and loyalty. Though there were variations in the strictness of observance and the application of the Sabbath commands, the seventh day continued to have major significance as a feature of God's law for Israel throughout the period of Old Testament history. The debates of the intertestamental period not only illustrate the difficulties in applying the Sabbath commandment but also show that Jews in the more exclusive communities were, of course, able to be stricter in their observance than those trying to cope with the pressures of life in a society under the control of a Gentile government.

Jesus cut through the complexities of the Pharisaic debates of His time. He kept the Sabbath law but not the Halakic interpretations of it; in the process He reminded men and women that the purpose of the Sabbath institution was for their benefit. In accordance with this He did not hesitate to heal and to carry out His ministry on the Sabbath. At the same time Jesus' messianic claim in relation to the Sabbath pointed to a transcendence of the institution, just as Jesus' ministry as a whole anticipates the change to a new order, which is brought about by His death and resurrection.

From the perspective of this new order, various New Testament writers are able to see Jesus' whole mission in terms of its fulfillment of Sabbatical motifs and Sabbath demands. Christ is the one who has brought the true Sabbath rest of the end time into the course of history, and, though Jewish Christians continued to observe them, the Sabbath aspects of the Mosaic economy were no longer binding on believers. Instead, the first day of the week assumed increasing importance because it was associated with Christ's resurrection and His appearances on the first day of the week, and the day became known as the Lord's Day. Its significance was in terms of worship of the risen Lord and there was no transference to this day of the necessity for the physical rest that was the constitutive element of the Old Testament Sabbath and its demands. This interpretation of the early church's view of the first day of the week is reinforced in the postapostolic literature of the second and third centuries A.D. where the day continues to be mentioned in a similar way.

The Seventh Day and Creation

The fact that this section has been headed "the seventh day and creation" rather than "the Sabbath and creation" is indicative of the conclusions reached by the writers with regard to the crucial question of whether or not the Sabbath was seen in Scripture as a "creation ordinance," that is, as a mandate to humanity qua humanity before its specific embodiment in the Mosaic covenant with Israel as a nation.

The decision made on this issue will be of paramount importance for any argument about the relation between Sabbath and Sunday. If the hypothesis of the Sabbath as a creation ordinance could be established, then, whatever the temporary nature of the Sabbath as part of the Mosaic covenant, the appeal could still be made to the permanence of the mandate for one day of rest as inherent to humanity made in the image of God. As chapter 11 indicates, both Luther and Calvin held to the notion of the Sabbath as a creation ordinance but failed to relate it consistently to the rest of their position. Later, while some Sabbatarians found the permanent character of this creation ordinance reinforced by their view of the fourth commandment as binding moral law, others regarded the fourth commandment as inapplicable to Christians but could still base their position on the creation ordinance, arguing the necessity of one day of rest, even if that day was less rigorous than an application of the fourth commandment would involve.[4] This latter position does not avoid altogether the difficulty of finding an express warrant for changing this one day from the seventh to the first, but the difficulty is posed less sharply on this view than on that which appeals in a major way to the fourth commandment. It remains true, however, that it is the "seventh day"

God blesses and hallows (Gen. 2:3), not the first. At least two responses have been made to such a statement by Sabbatarians for whom the creation ordinance is a linchpin of their argument. The first response involves speculation based on a literal reading of Genesis 1 and 2 and suggests that since humanity was created on the sixth day, God's seventh day was actually humanity's first day.[5] Such a view can be quickly dismissed, not only because it fails to note that the scheme of a creation week is a literary device and that the non-literal nature of the seventh day in particular is indicated by the absence of the evening-morning formula, but also because even on its own presuppositions, it runs into problems with the way in which Exodus 20:11 relates the *seventh*-day Mosaic Sabbath to the creation week's *seventh* day. The second response appeals to the appropriateness of a change from the creation week's seventh day to the first day of the week because Christ's resurrection took place on that day. Starting the week with the day of physical rest symbolizes the fact that, through Christ's resurrection, the rest of the end time has already entered history but has not yet been consummated, and that humanity's work flows out of its reception of grace.[6] It is true that, given the institution of Sunday rest, such a theological rationale can be seen as appropriate, but nowhere in the process of the institution of the first day of the week as significant for Christians does such a rationale feature as *grounds* for choosing the first day rather than the seventh, and more importantly nowhere do the New Testament writers or the writings of the first three centuries of the church's life indicate that the first day was actually treated as a day of rest.

A further question needs to be raised. Even if an appeal to the Sabbath as a creation ordinance (one day's rest in seven as enjoined on the first man and woman) could be sustained, how much force would this have in the construction of a Sabbatarian argument? Does a mandate to Adam before the Fall necessarily mean that such a mandate is perpetually binding on all men and women? While His creatures, made in His image, are to reflect the character of the Creator, this does not necessitate a perpetual obligation to reflect the pattern of the Creator's relation to the first creation. After all, marriage can be considered a creation ordinance (Gen. 1:28; 2:24) but it is not binding on all men and women for all time, for certainly in the new order celibacy is seen as at least an equal option for obeying God (Matt. 19:10ff.) and Paul considers it preferable (1 Cor. 7). It could be argued that even if the Sabbath were a creation ordinance, its function was not so much to enable the first man and woman to reflect a facet of the *moral* character of God as to be symbolic of the Creator's intention for the history of His creation. In this case, despite the mandate to the first pair, this function of the Sabbath was fulfilled in the salvation that Christ brought; the creation ordinance, then, passes with the inauguration of the new creation. Though such an argument has force, it is not conclusive against the validity of an appeal to this particular creation ordinance for the perpetuity of the obligation to one day's physical rest. Physical rest is still applicable to all human beings as long as they remain in the body. If it could be shown that one day's physical rest in seven was inherent to the way in which humans were meant to function, this would not be a factor that would change with the inauguration of the new creation. The New Testament writers, especially Paul, make clear that the one aspect of the new creation that is still outstanding in relation to men and women is that which affects their physical bodies. This would then be a case in which the new creation would not annul but rather remain within the bounds of the original created order until the consummation. Theoretically an argument from the Sabbath as a creation ordinance could carry force.[7] Exegetically, however, its advocates have the greatest difficulty in making the case that the biblical writers treated the Sabbath in this way.

How then do the biblical writers relate the seventh day to God's activity in creation? Genesis 2:2–3 concludes the creation account, and does so in terms of God's resting on the seventh day and blessing and hallowing that day. Elsewhere in Genesis 1 and 2 there are explicit commands for the first pair to follow. Not only is there no explicit command and no use of the term "sabbath," there is also no mention of humanity. The depiction of the seventh day in the schema is solely in terms of God. The climax of God's creative activity is not the creation of male and female so much as His own triumphant rest. It is true that His blessing and hallowing of the seventh day are not meant to be considered simply in a vacuum but have some relation to the created world. What is crucial, however, is the nature of that relation. The seventh day is to be seen as representing the completion of the whole creation, and therefore in its blessing the whole creation is blessed. This day is related in this way to the other six, and yet at the same time it is different, for it has no boundaries. The six days have their goal in a day that is different from the others and this is the force of the hallowing or sanctifying of the seventh day. Creation, therefore, is blessed with special reference to its goal, God's rest, which is set apart in some sense for all His creation including man and woman; but the precise sense awaits further unfolding. This is the relation of God's seventh day to humans; anything further must be read into the text and is often read back into it from Exodus 20:11.[8] Claus Westermann, however, in his commentary on Genesis remarks judiciously that one can find here neither an institution of nor a preparation for the Sabbath but that its later establishment is reflected.[9]

A reflection of the later establishment of the Sabbath in these verses is not surprising since Exodus 20:11 specifically appeals to the analogy of God's pattern in creation and takes up the language of these verses, and since the literary framework of seven days is itself dependent on the weekly Sabbatical cycle for depicting God's creative activity. Recognition of this reflection, however, is far removed from a recognition of any actual establishment of the Sabbath being implied by the words of Genesis 2:2–3.[10] Instead, the seven-day pattern of Genesis 1 and 2 imposes a Sabbatical structure on the history of creation, one that provides the basis for the concept of the world week that figures strongly both in Jewish apocalyptic literature and in the writings of the second-century postapostolic church. The framework of Genesis 1 and 2 certainly indicates that there is a divine ordering of history, so that, as history moves towards its consummation, it moves towards the goal of God's rest.

What then is the relationship between the Sabbath and the creation in Exodus 20:11? "For in six days the LORD made heaven and earth, the sea, and all that is in them, and rested the seventh day; therefore the LORD blessed the sabbath day and hallowed it."[11] Because of His own pattern of six days of activity and one of rest, the Lord blesses and sets apart the Sabbath day for Israel; the pattern is six days of labor and a seventh day Sabbath (cf. v. 9). The last clause of Exodus 20:11 gives the reason for the Mosaic institution and takes up the terminology of blessing and hallowing from Genesis 2:2–3, now specifically applying these terms to the "Sabbath" rather than the seventh day, and is not to be taken as implying that the seventh day of Genesis 2:3 was already the Sabbath set aside by God for humanity. As H. H. P. Dressler points out,[12] the present commandment is based on a previous event, and the significance of the Hebrew construction translated as "therefore" (עַל־כֵּן), is crucial to this interpretation, as it often functions to connect causally an event in the past with a situation some time later.[13] In fact scholars often speak of an "etiology" when a present name or practice is explained on the basis of a previous event or story, and עַל־כֵּן is one of the marks by which an etiology is recognized. Exodus 20:11 indeed contains in addition to this introductory formula a further feature typical of an etiology—the word play between "the seventh day" and "the Sabbath day." Such etiological passages, after the introductory "therefore" or "consequently now," can have the verb in the past tense without implying a strictly past meaning.[14] The presence of these features in Exodus 20:11 suggest that it too is to be seen as providing an explanation of a present institution, the Mosaic Sabbath, by reference to a past event, God's seventh-day rest after the creation, utilizing the terminology of Genesis 2:3 and a play on words to make its point.

One further text is often used to support the view that the Sabbath was a creation ordinance, namely Mark 2:27, which contains the saying of Jesus,

"The sabbath was made for man, not man for the sabbath." It is claimed that the verb ἐγένετο ("was made") refers more naturally to the creation than to the giving of the law and that ἄνθρωπος ("man") is generic in meaning and thus can include a reference back to the first man.[15] Suffice it to say that in its context Mark 2:27 simply does not have such notions in view. The words of Jesus point to the purpose of the Sabbath—it was brought into being by God for a person's benefit. Neither the temporal origin of the Sabbath nor its scope are relevant to this saying achieving its intended effect.[16]

When we move outside the canonical texts, we do, however, find in Philo reference to the Sabbath as a creation ordinance and, therefore, a law that holds for all people. "In the story of the creation . . . we are told that the world was made in six days and that on the seventh God ceased from his works and began to contemplate what had been so well created, and therefore he bade those who should live as citizens under this world-order to follow God in this as in other matters" (*de Decal.* 97–98). The Sabbath is "the festival not of a single city or country but of the universe, and it alone strictly deserves to be called public, as belonging to all people" (*de Opif. Mundi* 89). It should be remembered, however, that Philo's chief objective was to commend Judaism to the Greek world. To that end, he drew together out of Stoicism, Platonism, and Neo-Pythagoreanism whatever would be of service, and frequently grounded such elements in Scripture through allegory. Certainly it would be appropriate to his overall approach to the Old Testament for him to interpret the Sabbath as a universal institution with appeal to all rational humans, whether or not the Old Testament text clearly presented the Sabbath in such a light.[17] His attitude was definitely not typical of the way Jews thought of the Gentiles' relation to the Sabbath. Jubilees 2:19–21, 31 can state, "the Creator of all things . . . did not sanctify all peoples and nations to keep sabbath thereon, but Israel alone." Similarly in rabbinic literature, it is stated that the seventh day of creation was God's Sabbath but not humanity's (*Gen.R.* 11). It is said of Jews in *Shabb.* 16:6–8 that "if a Gentile come to put out the fire, they must not say to him 'put it out' or 'do not put it out,' since they are not answerable for his keeping the sabbath." This is because, as *Mekilta Shabb.* 1 puts it, the Sabbath is "a perpetual covenant between me and the children of Israel, but not between me and the nations of the world."

It is of note also that the Sabbath is not listed as one of the Noahic commandments, the keeping of which identified a Gentile Godfearer. Only a fullfledged proselyte was expected to keep the Sabbath. It is of course also striking, that the apostolic decree of Acts 15, which the Sabbath keeping Jewish-Christian Jerusalem church asked of the Gentile churches in order to allow continued fellowship, and which was based on the Noahic commandments, contains no reference to any necessity for Sabbath observance for Gentiles nor to some alternative Sabbath day for them.

Reference to the seventh day of creation in the New Testament is of a different nature than an appeal to a universally binding principle for all people. The writer's quotation of Genesis 2:2 in Hebrews 4:3–4 is not in order to ground the Sabbath in creation but rather to ground the eschatological salvation rest, which God has for His people, in the divine rest at creation. God's rest is seen by the writer to the Hebrews, as by Genesis 2:2–3, as the consummation of His purposes for the creation; it was God's intention to confer this on His people. The resting place in the land of Canaan and that in the sanctuary at Jerusalem point forward to the fulfillment of God's purposes for His people in the heavenly rest that has been available from the beginning with God. Genesis 2:2 is used to bring together God's plan for both creation and redemption. Similarly, in John 5:17ff., Jesus' work of salvation in giving life and judging is shown to be of a piece with God's work. God's rest does not involve Him in a state of inactivity since the creation. It is stated, "My father is working still, and I am working," but the time will come when both God and Jesus will cease from their work of accomplishing salvation. As regards the work of creation, God's seventh day rest was final, but it is because that rest was meant for men and women to enjoy that the Father can be said to be at work in history in the Son in order to accomplish His purposes for humanity. The evidence thus leads us to the conclusion that while the notion of God's rest in Genesis 2 was treated eschatologically by the biblical writers, it was not held by them to be a "creation ordinance."

The Mosaic Sabbath

The Significance of the Mosaic Sabbath

The Sabbath command of Exodus 20:8—"Remember the sabbath day to keep it holy"—is one of the two commandments of the Decalogue that are phrased positively. Yet despite the positive features of its formulation (including the command "six days you shall work"), justification, and motivation, its concrete outworkings for Israel were in basically negative terms. The most characteristic feature of the observance of the Mosaic Sabbath in practice was the absence of regular work on this day. This is reflected in the fourth commandment by the prohibition contained within the more positive broader framework: "in it you shall not do any work" (v. 9; cf. Lev. 23:3; Deut. 5:14). Cessation from routine daily work, whether by man or woman, is the way in which keeping the Sabbath day holy was principally expressed. No pressures could alter the absolute nature of the command. Exodus 34:21, with its addition of "in plowing time and in harvest you shall rest," emphasizes that even at the busiest time of the year in an agricultural society the Sabbath was still to be kept. The sanction of the death penalty (Exod. 31:14, 15; 35:2) only serves to underline this absolute nature of the Sabbath command. No one was exempt from it. The references to the family, servants, animals and sojourners in Exodus 20:10 and Deuteronomy 5:14 ensure that none over whom he might have authority could do the male Israelite's work for him, and also that everyone might have some respite from work.[18] The Sabbath was not a day of total inactivity but was meant to provide rest and refreshment from the regular work of the other six days. It is true that this rest provided opportunity for devotion to the worship of God, that the Sabbath was called a "holy convocation" (Lev. 23:2–3), that an additional burnt offering was required on every Sabbath (Num. 28:9, 10), and that since it was done from obedience to God the resting itself could be considered an act of worship, but cultic worship was not a major focus of the Sabbath institution for Israel as this is reflected in the Old Testament.

The emphasis on physical rest, however, hardly does justice to the significance of the Mosaic Sabbath in the Old Testament. That significance derives not only from the setting of the Sabbath commandment within the Decalogue but also from its context within the whole relationship between God and Israel, a relationship established by the Sinai covenant in which the Decalogue is perhaps at the heart. Indeed so important is the Sabbath within this larger framework that it can even be designated as a sign of the Mosaic covenant (Exod. 31:12–17). It is a sign of Yahweh's sanctification of His people (Exod. 31:13), the unique possession of Israel marking them out as a separate people whose allegiance is to Yahweh. Even further, the Sabbath itself can be called a covenant (Exod. 31:16). This covenant is designated a perpetual one (31:16), and the sign, which is further described as a sign of God's creative activity in six days and rest on the seventh, is also described as "a sign for ever" (31:17). Before any unwarranted conclusions are drawn from these assertions of the everlasting nature of the institution of the Mosaic Sabbath, it must be recalled that various other elements of the Mosaic covenant are spoken of in exactly the same way, including aspects of the administration of the tabernacle, the sacrifices, and the priesthood (Exod. 27:27; 28:43; 29:28; 30:21; 40:15; Lev. 6:18, 22; 7:34, 36; 24:8; Num. 18:19), and that the Noahic, Abrahamic, and Davidic covenants are all ascribed the same quality of permanence (cf. Gen. 9:16; 17:7; 2 Sam. 7:13, 16; 23:5). M. G. Kline has pointed out similarities in this aspect of permanence between ancient near eastern treaties and the biblical covenants. Such treaties often spoke of their terms as being valid down through following generations "forever" and yet these treaties were subject to the revision of the suzerain because of changing circumstances. Kline points out that the biblical covenants and their various aspects can similarly be said to be "forever" and yet subject to change according to God's sovereign purposes in accomplishing redemption in the midst of the historical process.[19] Within later Judaism, with the increasing emphasis on Torah, any such notion of change was lost sight of and the law was held to be permanent and eternal, continuing into the age to come.[20] But as part of the Mosaic covenant, and like the elements of the tabernacle, the priesthood, and the offerings, the Sabbath itself can be said to be perpetual until its fulfillment. As the writer to the Hebrews indicates, the archetypes of which these elements are the types can be seen to be eternal and to have continuing validity through the fulfillment of the type. In particular, in Hebrews 4, the resting place of the land and the physical rest of the Sabbath are seen to be types of God's eternal rest from the beginning.

As a sign of the permanent relationship between God and His people, the Sabbath is also a memorial of the great acts accomplished by God for His people in both creation and redemption. As a memorial of creation, "It is a sign for ever between me and the people of Israel that in six days the Lord made heaven and earth, and on the seventh day he rested, and was refreshed" (Exod. 31:17 cf. 20:11). As that which is analogous to and patterned after the structure that God gave to history, the Mosaic Sabbath naturally functions as a sign and memorial of God's creative activity and its consummation in His rest. According to Deuteronomy 5:15 it was to function also as a memorial of God's redemptive activity in delivering His people from Egypt: "You shall remember that you were a servant in the land of Egypt, and the LORD your God brought you out thence with a mighty hand and an outstretched arm; therefore the LORD your God commanded you to keep the sabbath day." In this passage concern for the servants obtaining rest (v. 14) turns out to be a reflex of God's treatment of Israel when Israel was a servant in Egypt and knew no relief from exploitation, no break from daily slave labor. But God had delivered them from "the house of bondage" (Exod. 20:2) and the provision by the Sabbath of a unique release from endless toil was to be a constant memorial of the fact that God had brought Israel out of slavery into rest. It is significant that in Deuteronomy the term "rest" or "resting place" can be used for the land into which God will bring His people (e.g., Deut. 12:9, "For you have not as yet come to the rest and to the inheritance which the LORD your God gives you"). The command not to work on one day out of seven taught a nation of slaves that they had been liberated and that in entering into covenant relationship with Yahweh they were free men and women who could rest in their deliverer. In this way the Sabbath was to be a weekly liberation day.

That in her liberation Israel owed everything to her Lord is further indicated by the covenantal relationship in which the Sabbath is embedded. The Sabbath specifically belongs to the covenant Lord. It is holy, set apart to God. The seventh day is "a sabbath *to the* LORD *your God*" (Exod. 20:10; Deut. 5:14), "holy to the Lord" (Exod. 31:15), "a holy sabbath of solemn rest to the LORD" (Exod. 35:2), and "a holy convocation . . . a sabbath to the Lord" (Lev. 23:3). In fact Yahweh can call the day set aside for Israel's observance "My sabbath" (cf. Exod. 31:13; Lev. 19:3, 30; 26:2). He claims this day specifically as His own, it is the covenant Lord's day. Israel was to respond to this claim of lordship over her time in allegiance and obedience. It is true, as we have already noted in making reference to the Sabbath as a memorial of redemption from Egypt, that it is at the same time a response of gratitude. The historical prologue of the Decalogue, which, as in other treaty documents, was designed to inspire confidence and gratitude and to dispose the vassal to allegiance, underlines this. Yet the stress is on obedience to the suzerain's command. This is particularly clear in Deuteronomy 5:12–15, which begins and ends with the assertion that the Sabbath is to be observed because it has been commanded, "Observe the sabbath day, to keep it holy, as the LORD your God commanded you. . . . Therefore the LORD your God commanded you to keep the sabbath day." The necessity of obedience is reinforced by Exodus 16:28, by the strong imperative force of the infinitive absolute in Exodus 20:8, by the threefold repetition of the command to keep the Sabbath and the sanction of the death penalty in Exodus 31:12–17, and by Leviticus 19:3, 30. By means of this Sabbath keeping the Israelite pledges absolute covenant consecration to the Lord. By bringing all routine work to a halt for twenty-four hours the people were acting out their allegiance and confessing that the covenant Lord was specifically Lord of their time. This is why the Sabbath could serve as a sign of the whole covenant relationship. By demonstrably laying down her work and allowing the seventh day to "lie fallow," Israel was acknowledging her complete dependence on her suzerain.

All Israel, the whole community, including servants, animals and sojourners, was to be involved in this visible demonstration of allegiance (cf. Exod. 20:10; Deut. 5:14). Yet as part of this demand for total obedience on the part of the nation, there was a concern that all should share in the benefits and privileges of release from daily labor. This motive of "humanitarian" or "social" concern figures particularly prominently in Exod. 23:12, "On the seventh day you shall rest; that your ox and your ass may have rest, and the son of your bondmaid, and the alien, may be refreshed," and in Deuteronomy 5:14 "That your manservant and your maidservant may rest as well as you." Along with Leviticus 19:18 itself, this latter provides an anticipation in the Pentateuch of Jesus' summary of the second great commandment in terms of loving one's neighbor as oneself (cf. Mark 12:31).

The Fourth Commandment and the Decalogue

Many Sabbatarian arguments appeal to the fourth commandment and assert that the place of the Sabbath requirement in the Decalogue means that it is to be seen as binding moral law normative for all people in the same way as the rest of the Decalogue. Those who argue in this way but apply the fourth commandment to Sunday, the first day of the week, are certainly not as consistent as those groups, such as the Seventh-Day Adventists, who still observe the seventh day; they need to face this inconsistency squarely.[21] On their own presuppositions, by what right do they tamper with an eternally valid moral law? What criterion allows them to isolate the seventh day aspect, which after all is at the heart of the commandment and its rationale (cf. Exod. 20:11), as a temporary feature belonging only to the Mosaic period, while retaining the remainder of the Decalogue as normative for all ages (though some might also have questions about the permanent validity of the second commandment)? If the Mosaic law were designed to teach the principle of one day's rest in seven instead of seventh-day rest, it might be expected that its legislation would have provided for a different day of rest for the priests (cf. Num. 28:9–10), but it does not. This permitted breaking of the Sabbath is appealed to by Jesus according to Matthew 12:5. Passing over these forceful objections to a straightforward application of the fourth commandment to Sunday, a still more basic question about this Sabbatarian approach needs to be raised. Is it right to consider that the status of the fourth commandment as part of the Decalogue gives it special force? Does the Decalogue somehow have a unique role in relation to the rest of the Mosaic covenant and Old Testament law? If so, what is the nature of that role, and does it justify seeing in the Decalogue a collection and summary of timeless moral principles?

There can be no doubt that within the Old Testament and particularly within the Mosaic covenant the Decalogue does have a special status. The commandments it contains are singled out as the "Ten words" (cf. Exod. 34:28; Deut. 4:13; 10:4) and are repeated in the renewal of the Mosaic covenant in Deuteronomy 5. Further these Ten Words can stand for the whole Mosaic covenant. Exodus 34:28 speaks of the Ten Words as "the words of the covenant," while Deuteronomy 4:13 mentions "His covenant, that is, the ten words." The Ten Words are designated also as "the tables of the testimony" (cf. Exod. 31:18; 32:15; 34:29). The formulation of the Ten Words is itself covenantal[22] and underlines the fact that the Decalogue is a miniature of the whole Mosaic covenant. Kline draws out some of the significance of this representative function of the Decalogue.

> The prominence of the stipulations, reflected in the fact that 'the ten words' are the element used as *pars pro toto*, signalizes the centrality of law in this type of covenant. . . . Such a covenant is a declaration of God's lordship, consecrating a people to himself in a sovereignly dictated order of life.[23]

Yet this special status of the Decalogue as *pars pro toto*, the part standing for the whole, while showing that law is at the heart of the Mosaic covenant, at the same time binds the Decalogue very closely to that covenant. Its special status is not because it is distinct from the rest of the covenant but because it is representative of and foundational to the Mosaic covenant. This should lead one to expect that what is true of the place of the covenant as a whole will also be true of the Decalogue.

Just as the Mosaic covenant as a whole is to be seen as a particular expression of the will of God for His people for a certain period of their history, so is the Decalogue to be viewed in the same light. It is not a timeless list of ethical principles that has somehow become embedded in a historically conditioned covenant.[24] This is clear from the form of the Decalogue itself. The historical prologue of Exodus 20:2 immediately sets the Decalogue within the context of the history of salvation and God's deliverance of His people from Egypt. Both the fourth and the tenth commandments are specifically geared towards the time of the settlement and an agricultural society. When Israel became a commercial nation further prohibitions were necessary to gear the fourth commandment to the later historical situation, particularly the command not to bear a burden (cf. Jer. 17:21ff; Neh. 13:15ff.). The promise of the fifth commandment relates specifically to life in the land of Canaan[25] and in the tenth commandment the wife appears to be listed as part of the neighbor's valuable property.

It will be objected that despite these few time-conditioned elements, the Decalogue does provide a summary of ethical principles. But it is to be doubted whether the representative nature of the Decalogue is to be interpreted in terms of its being a summary either of Mosaic law in general or all law. Certainly those systems of Christian ethics, such as Aquinas's, Calvin's, and the Westminster divines', which classify all of ethics under one or other of the Ten Commandments may have found a convenient structure, but hardly an appropriate one, since only in a very forced way could every ethical principle be reduced to one of these ten categories. The same is true of the relation of the Decalogue to the Mosaic covenant. In a very general way all the detailed commandments about the tabernacle, priesthood, and offerings could be thought of as derivative from the first commandment, "You shall have no other gods before me," since that commandment had to do with worship of the one true God. The legislation about which animals were clean or unclean could also be seen as a sub-section of the first commandment since the motivation for this legislation is in terms of consecration to a holy God (Lev. 11:44f.). But this becomes an exercise either in ingenuity or vagueness[26] and there is no indication whatsoever in the Pentateuch or elsewhere in the Old Testament that the Decalogue was intended to function as such a summary which would comprehend all ethical possibilities.[27] It is significant also that in the rabbinic literature, where there is a discussion of the fundamental principles of the Torah, reference is not made to the Decalogue (cf. *Aboth* 1:2; *B. Shabb.* 31*a*; *Sif. Lev.* 19:18), though Philo does assert that "the Ten Words are summaries of the special laws which are recorded in the sacred books" (*de Decal.* 154).[28] It is likely that Jewish enthusiasm for the Decalogue may have been dampened when Christians increasingly took it over in the second century and it was withdrawn from the synagogue liturgy.[29]

It might be asserted that if the Decalogue is not a summary of all ethical norms, then at least it has a special status as a list of norms because it is more closely related to and grounded in the very nature of God than the rest of the Mosaic legislation. But again this is to be doubted, for in fact even the legislation about clean and unclean animals is grounded on the very nature of God as holy (Lev. 11:44–45). And, although the seventh-day rest law is based on God's relation to the creation, in what sense can it be said to be grounded on His moral nature?

The significance of the selection of commandments contained in the Decalogue as *pars pro toto* for the Mosaic covenant lies in other factors. The Ten Words are representative and foundational in that they deal with areas of life that were of extreme importance and central concern to the life of the covenant community[30] and in that they do so in such a finely balanced way, combining stipulations that have primary reference to God with those that more directly affect human relationships. In this way it can be said that "the Decalogue seems not only to chart the outer boundary, but also to provide positive content for life within the circle of the covenant."[31] It is because the Ten Commandments deal with issues that are so central to the relationship between God and His people that most of them can be more easily universalized than other elements in the Mosaic covenant. It should be remembered, however, that apart from the renewal of the covenant in Deuteronomy, there is no explicit literal repetition of any of the Ten Words in the Old Testament.[32]

The centrality of the Decalogue does not, however, provide a justification for detaching it from that of which it is the center, that is, the Mosaic covenant as a whole. The Ten Commandments have been given a specific and concrete historical setting and their raison d'être must be seen as the regulation of Israel's life under the Mosaic covenant. As such, they provide an expression of God's will for His chosen people at that stage of their history. Under later circumstances in Israel's history they are added to and given new interpretation.[33] The continuing influence of these commandments will depend, therefore, not on their status as the Decalogue but, as will be shown later, on their relation to the later and fuller reflection of God's character and the fulfillment of God's will for His people, both of which can be seen in Christ. It is this factor that provides the only criterion for deciding whether the fourth commandment in particular has continuing force as moral law and not the fact that it is part of the Decalogue.

The Sabbath in Old Testament History and in the Intertestamental Period

The Mosaic Sabbath continued to be of paramount importance in the relation between Israel and her God into the period of Judaism at the beginning of the Christian era.[34] Additional prohibitions were necessary to give it force for the later periods of Israel's history. In particular, Jeremiah 17:21ff. and Nehemiah 13:15ff. specify rulings about the carrying of burdens, designed to prevent commerce on the Sabbath, and, of course, the rulings about the Sabbath in the Halakah were meant to extend the application of the Sabbath commandment to almost every conceivable aspect of life.

Despite the continued application of the Sabbath commandment, there were, of course, variations at different times and in different places, both in the attitude and in the strictness with which it was observed. These variations are associated with differing emphases in regard to the Torah itself.[35] The Sabbath all too easily became a simply external affair for Israel and was frequently not kept according to the spirit of the law so that the prophets had to call the nation back to the right attitude of heart in its observance of the day.[36] After the Exile there appears to have been a renewed emphasis on the Sabbath and an accompanying strictness in its observance, so that the Sabbath became in practice, together with circumcision and the study of the Torah, a real distinguishing mark of Israel among the nations.[37] Even so there were variations in the type of observance required. Exclusive groups like the Essenes were able to require and to practice far stricter observance of the Sabbath than Jews attempting to live out their religion in the midst of an alien culture or under the dominance of a foreign power. Among the Pharisaic Jews also the variation in the requirements of Beth Shammai and Beth Hillel can be clearly seen, with the former taking a stricter approach and the latter being more realistic about the demands of everyday life in society. Philo, in attempting to justify the Sabbath to the Hellenistic culture around him in Alexandria, plays down the stricter details of the application of the command to cease from work, emphasized in Palestine, and concentrates more on the positive opportunities the Sabbath presents for reflection and the study of wisdom.

We have noted very few references to cultic worship in connection with the institution of the Sabbath, but one of the noteworthy features of the period under consideration is the increased emphasis on this. Ezekiel 46:1ff. gives instructions for the people's worship in the temple on the Sabbath. According to its title Psalm 92 was used in later Judaism for public worship on the Sabbath and liturgical fragments have been found at Qumran that also mention hymns for the Sabbath.[38] Philo stresses the role of synagogue worship on the Sabbath in his attempt to show the day's positive possibilities for the pursuit of wisdom (cf. *Vit.Mos.* II. 216; *Spec.Leg.* II. 60; *Op.Mundi* 128) and there are hints in the rabbinic literature also that the rise of the synagogue had had an impact on the way in which the Sabbath was observed.[39] The importance of synagogue worship on the Sabbath is clearly attested in the New Testament (e.g. Mark 1:21; 3:1f.; Luke 4:16; 13:10; Acts 13:14, 44; 15:21; 16:13; 17:2; 18:4). This development in regard to the practice of the Sabbath is obviously of significance in any comparison of the Sabbath to the Christian observance of the first day of the week.

The most obviously striking development in this period, however, is the detailed legislation of the Halakah about observance of the Sabbath—what constituted work and what could be held to be exceptions to the observance of the Sabbath, which is reflected in the rabbinic literature and the Sabbath conflicts recorded in the gospels. It has been estimated that the five Old Testament passages dealing with observance of the Sabbath are amplified into 39 articles and 1521 passages in the Mishnah.[40] This development was part of a general tendency to detach the concepts of covenant and law from their historical basis. The ingenious exegeses and subtle reasoning involved in the fine distinctions that have to be drawn in the Halakah treat Torah and Scripture as a timeless codebook, a quarry for mining rulings for every conceivable situation. Study of the rabbinic attitude to the Sabbath is salutary, for its approach is not all that far removed from the fine distinctions that have to be drawn about works of necessity and works of mercy in the application of Christian sabbatarianism. Both mentalities betray the lack of a historical approach to the interpretation of Scripture and its law, and it has to be asked how compatible the mentality that requires legislation from Scripture on the details of application is with, on the one hand, the stress on the freedom of the

Spirit in Paul (Gal. 5) or even, on the other hand, the view of the law as "the law of liberty" (James 1:25; 2:12).

The Gospels' Depiction of Jesus' Relationship to the Sabbath

The Sabbath controversies in the gospels provide the setting for our understanding of their writers' depiction of Jesus' approach to the Sabbath.[41] How far Jesus can be said to have provoked these controversies with the Pharisees by the way in which He carried out His mission is a matter of some debate. D. A. Carson in chapter 4 has made a good case for the view that provocation is scarcely the right term for describing the natural way in which Jesus conducts His ministry of healing.[42] He heals on a Sabbath because the opportunity presents itself and not because it is a Sabbath. It is true that in the incidents of the healing of the man with a withered hand in the synagogue on the Sabbath both Mark (3:1–6) and Luke (6:6–11), as opposed to Matthew (12:9–14), emphasize Jesus' precipitation of the conflict. By His calling of the man forward Jesus is shown to be acting boldly and openly. But this action on the part of Jesus does not cause the conflict, only brings it out into the open, and both Mark (3:2) and Luke (6:7) are careful to indicate that right from the start the Pharisees have been waiting to find some opportunity for accusation. Again it might be suggested that the Sabbath healing recorded in John 5 involved a provocation of the conflict on the part of Jesus since Jesus heals when there is no urgent need and commands the man to carry his bed. In John's presentation, however, the day of the week plays no prominent part in the narrative until after the healing has taken place. The fact that it was a Sabbath is introduced for the first time at this point in order to explain the problem in which the healed man later finds himself. For John the choice of this particular man for healing is to be explained in terms other than a design to cause a conflict about the Sabbath[43] and the command to carry the bed is only natural in the healing of a paralytic (Mark 2:9, 11). The narratives in Mark suggest that the provocation about the Sabbath in fact builds up on the side of Jesus' enemies. Jesus' Sabbath ministry in Mark 1 is not accompanied by antagonism and conflict, but when opposition to Jesus' ministry as a whole begins to mount, then His Sabbath practices provide a convenient point for attack in terms of the Halakic interpretation of the law, and in Mark two conflicts over this (2:23–28 and 3:1–5) lead to a decisive point in the narrative, the decision of the Pharisees in 3:6 to confer with the Herodians in order to destroy Jesus. The Sabbath incident in Mark 6:1–6 then makes clear what has been the case all along; it is not Jesus' healings on the Sabbath that are the cause of offense but the claims that He makes for Himself. The Johannine perspective, colored by the later conflict between church and synagogue, underlines that this is the dynamic at work in the relation of Jesus with the Pharisees over the Sabbath. John 9:13–41 demonstrates strikingly that it is the Pharisees' implacable animosity towards Jesus that prevents them from seeing what is so obvious to everyone else and leads them to employ Sabbath Halakah against Jesus in their attempt to avoid the obvious (v. 16).

Jesus' paramount concern was to be about His mission whether or not the Sabbath was involved (cf. Luke 13:14–16, John 5:16–17), but in His zeal to accomplish God's will He cannot be accused of provoking the conflicts over the Sabbath.[44] Nor is there any suggestion in the accounts that He was less than careful to observe the actual requirements of the Torah in respect to the Sabbath. As has been noted, the Mosaic Sabbath with its requirement of cessation from work was not designed to achieve total inactivity so much as total abstention from one's regular daily work. When this is remembered it is hard to see how, for instance, the disciples' plucking of the ears of corn and eating them (Mark 2:23–28 and parallels) can be considered as a profanation of the Mosaic Sabbath. If they had been farm workers or even women making up for lack of preparation for a meal, it would have been a different matter; their casual plucking of corn on a walk scarcely falls into any such categories. Similarly the healings Jesus performs on the Sabbath are scarcely candidates for the description of profanations of the Sabbath. As Carson points out, the Torah says nothing about healing on the Sabbath and Jesus' healings are not part of the routine daily work of either a medical practitioner or a nursing relative.[45] It is certainly in keeping with this picture that early Christian writers also never consider Jesus and His ministry to provide them with any precedent for breaking the Sabbath but rather see His healings as part of His fulfillment of the law.[46] It was quite another matter with the Sabbath Halakah however, and, particularly when accomplishing His mission demanded it, Jesus had no hesitation about breaking through the legalism of these extensions of the Torah. Especially in regard to the Sabbath, this legalism, which obscures God's original intention, was apparent. "The rules about the Sabbath . . . are as mountains hanging by a hair, for scripture is scanty and rules many" (*Hag.* 1:8). Matthew in 12:9–14 (cf. Luke 14:1–6) provides one clear instance in which Jesus is portrayed as exposing the Pharisees' Halakah because of the absurd and hypocritical consequences to which it leads, when they are prepared to rescue an animal in distress on the Sabbath but will not permit Jesus to rescue a man with dropsy.

In His attitude to the Sabbath, especially in His rejection of the Halakic framework, Jesus is concerned to show the true purpose of the day. But rather than setting out programmatic statements on the use of the Sabbath, Jesus' utterances are directed more against the abuse of the day and expose misunderstandings of its requirements. The well-known saying in Mark 2:27 is in this vein; "The sabbath was made for man, not man for the sabbath."[47] In other words, the Sabbath with its legislation was never meant to be a tyrant that enslaved people by its insufferable demands but a benefit and privilege instituted for the sake of people and their enjoyment. Although this saying is absent from the parallel passage in Matthew, Matthew 12:7 makes a similar point with the saying from Hosea 6:6—"I desire mercy, and not sacrifice"—being attached to the Sabbath incident. And in the Sabbath episode that follows immediately Jesus breaks through the Pharisaic restrictions in order to point out that "it is lawful to do good on the sabbath" (Matt. 12:12, cf. Mark 3:4). Taken as a programmatic statement it has wide-ranging implications for the use of the day and could be seen as abrogating the requirements of the fourth commandment, but in context this is not its thrust. Its specific application is to the healing ministry of Jesus being permitted on the Sabbath. The Halakah clearly did not permit the saving of life on the Sabbath and the Markan version of the saying has a more Christological focus aimed at confronting the Pharisees with a choice about Jesus' definition of preserving life and doing good in this concrete instance of healing; "Is it lawful on the sabbath to do good or to do harm, to save life or to kill?" The Pharisees' evil purposes (cf. Mark 3:2, "They watched him . . . so that they might accuse him," also 3:5, "Their hardness of heart") are contrasted with Jesus' healing ministry and they are reduced to silence. Again, in the incident peculiar to Luke (14:1–6), Jesus rejects Halakic distinctions when they are used to thwart the doing of good on the Sabbath, asking the similar question, which once more reduces His opponents to silence: "Is it lawful to heal on the sabbath or not?" (v. 3). Certainly the purpose of the Sabbath was to be assessed in terms of its contribution to the accomplishment of Jesus' mission (cf. John 5:16–17). Luke 13:10–17 makes this point. The healing of the woman could not wait until a day other than the Sabbath nor could Jesus' redemptive mission of releasing Satan's captives be restricted to six days a week. In Luke's account the new order of the kingdom takes precedence, and the purpose of the Sabbath has to be interpreted in its light as a day like all the rest on which Jesus must be obedient to the mission He has been called to fulfill.

The real issue as regards Jesus' approach to the Sabbath is now beginning to emerge and that is His claim, sometimes implicit and sometimes explicit, that His hearers are to interpret the Sabbath in relation to His own person and work. Not only does Luke 13 have this force, but other Sabbath controversies also become opportunities for messianic claims. This is certainly the case in Luke's account of the Sabbath incident in Nazareth (4:16–30), where the offense of the claim to bring in the events of the endtime and the year of jubilee is the cause of the violent rejection of Jesus. According to John, equally violent antagonism is raised by Jesus' assertion on the Sabbath, "My father is working still, and I am working." John could scarcely express Jesus' supreme status and authority in regard to the Sabbath more strongly than in this claim to be equal with God and to be carrying out in His life-giving and judging activity the very work of God, which tolerates no interruption even by the Sabbath. The synoptic equivalent of the Johannine assertion is the saying of Jesus, "The Son of man is lord even of the sabbath" (Mark 2:28; cf. Matt. 12:8; Luke 6:5). This is a momentous claim indeed when understood against the background of the Mosaic Sabbath and its terminology. In the Old Testament the Sabbath was said to be "a sabbath to the LORD your God" (Exod. 20:10; Deut. 5:14; cf. Exod. 31:15; 35:2; Lev. 23:3). It belonged to Yahweh, the covenant Lord. Now here is Jesus as the Son of man claiming to be the Lord of the Sabbath. Jesus' claim to authority over the day is not only a claim to equal authority with the law given by God in which the Sabbath demand was embedded but can be understood as a claim to the same authority over the day as the covenant Lord Himself, a claim to equality with God every bit as strong as the Johannine saying. This messianic claim in respect to the Sabbath is preserved in all three Synoptics, and each evangelist adds his distinctive nuance to the Christological focus by the connection he makes with the surrounding context. Mark moves from Jesus' words about David, whose special position allowed him and those with him to set aside regulations, to the saying about the purpose of the Sabbath being for man in 2:27 via the connective ὥστε to the Christological assertion of 2:28. If the Sabbath was made for man, and its regulations are to be employed for that end (a principle foreshadowed in the David incident) then it should not be surprising that one with the special status of Son of Man, who has already been shown to possess God's prerogative and authority to forgive sins (cf. 2:10), should also be Lord of the Sabbath and determine how those who are with Him may act on this day. Luke, on the other hand, omits the saying of Mark 2:27 and moves straight from David's conduct (6:3–4) to the Son of Man saying (6:5) to make the clear point that if David's action in a situation of need could establish his authority as higher than the law, then Jesus' ministry as the Son of Man and a greater than David establishes His authority over the Sabbath in the new situation inaugurated by the coming of the kingdom. Matthew also omits the saying of Mark 2:27 but has an additional section in 12:5–7. This includes a further Old Testament account that has specific relevance to the Sabbath controversy. The priests in the service of the temple could profane the Sabbath and remain guiltless. Now something greater than the temple is here—Jesus Himself (cf. the similar sayings in 12:41–42). His followers are guiltless too (cf. v. 7*b*). Jesus does not assert their innocence on the grounds of their obedience to the actual Torah though not to the Halakah. Instead their innocence is explicitly connected with the status and authority of their master as Son of Man and superior to both David and the temple (cf. the connective particle γάρ in v. 8) and He determines what is appropriate to the Sabbath. By placing this pericope immediately after the teaching of 11:28–30 contrasting Jesus' yoke with that of the law, Matthew underlines that Jesus puts Himself in place of the law. As Lord of the Sabbath He is the law's true interpreter in terms of mercy rather than legalism (12:7).

Jesus' lordship over the Sabbath is underlined by all three of the synoptic Gospels. What becomes clear about the Sabbath, as Banks well puts it, is that Jesus "takes a position above it so that it is incorporated into an entirely new framework and viewed from a quite different perspective. As a result, what is acceptable or unacceptable in the way of conduct upon it is defined in relation to an altogether new reference point, i.e. Christ's estimate of the situation."[48] This new Christological perspective to be brought to the Sabbath is also suggested in Mark and Luke by their placing of this Sabbath pericope immediately after Jesus' teaching that new wine must be put into fresh wineskins. The Mosaic Sabbath constitutes one of the elements of the old order that will have to change in the light of the new.

Jesus' personal claims whereby He transcends the Sabbath law provide the Christological key with which His followers could later interpret the Sabbath. But His own teaching does not provide any further explicit directions about the sort of changes the inauguration of the new order will bring. This is only to be expected because of the veiled nature of His earthly ministry. Only after the consummation of this ministry in His death and Resurrection would the significance of both His person and work become clear. The hidden and transitional aspects of Jesus' earthly ministry account for the fact that no definite break with the Mosaic Sabbath is clearly set out in His teaching or actions[49] and mean also that Jesus' Sabbath practices (e.g., regular attendance at synagogue if "as his custom was" in Luke 4:16 is a reference to this) do not necessarily provide any norms for the new order. The veiled nature of Jesus' ministry accounts for the slight ambiguity in regard to His relation to the Sabbath and for the fact that for a time in the early church there were those who continued Sabbath observance while the full implications of the entry of the new age accomplished by Christ were being worked out.

Sabbath Observance in the New Testament Church

In the New Testament church there were as many attitudes to the observance of the Sabbath as there were to the keeping of the Mosaic Law. These appear to have included the approaches of Jewish and Gentile Christians, like those in the Pauline churches (who followed the teaching of the apostle and considered themselves free from the Sabbath commandment), Jewish Christians like those from Jerusalem whom Paul encountered in Galatia (who regarded the observance of the whole law as necessary to salvation), Jewish Christians like the Jerusalem apostles (who continued to keep the Sabbath as part of the way they fulfilled their role as the true Israel but did not insist on Gentile converts observing the seventh day), and Gentile Christians who for various reasons decided to adopt Jewish Sabbath observance.

The leads into this situation that the New Testament documents themselves provide need to be followed. Some have suggested that Matthew 24:20, "Pray that your flight may not be in winter or on a sabbath," reflects Sabbath-observing Jewish Christianity and the Jewish predilections of Matthew and his community.[50] The Sabbath reference is unique to Matthew (cf. Mark 13:18; Luke 21:23), but whether it is taken as original[51] or as deriving from a Jewish-Christian milieu in the handing down of the tradition[52] or as a Matthean redaction,[53] its function is to emphasize not so much strict observance of the law (stricter than the interpretation of the Rabbis who permitted the taking up of arms or flight on the Sabbath when there was danger to life),[54] as the extremity of the circumstances surrounding the judgment of Jerusalem. The mention of flight on the Sabbath underlines the physical obstacles to flight, in this case, such Sabbath restrictions as the shutting of the gates of cities and the difficulties in obtaining provisions, and cannot therefore be taken as direct evidence for Jewish-Christian attitudes.[55] What might at first sight appear to be a reference to Sabbath observance, the use of the term σαββατισμός in Hebrews 4:9, also turns out not to be helpful in tracking down the practice of the New Testament communities, for though the term denotes a literal celebration of the Sabbath, it has been reinterpreted in a spiritual sense as the cessation of one's own works on entry into God's rest (4:10).[56]

We are clearly on more fruitful ground for our investigation into Sabbath practice in the early church when we turn to the Pauline correspondence and Acts. By its silence in regard to any Sabbath controversies, Acts suggests that Jewish Christians must have continued to keep the Sabbath. The Sabbath was an institution too central to Judaism for it to have been tampered with without provoking hostile reaction and persecution, but there is no record of persecution on this account. Instead, the early Jewish Christians appear to have taken advantage of Sabbath observance to preach Jesus as the Messiah (e.g., Acts 5:42). Until the later influx of Gentiles into the church, it would simply have been assumed by most that the Torah continued to be binding under the New

Covenant. When this influx occurred, the reaction of Jewish Christians was varied, as Luke's account of the apostolic council indicates. Galatians 4:8–11 shows us the reaction of the legalistic Jewish Christians from Jerusalem who were attempting to impose the law on Gentile converts. The passage provides evidence for Sabbath observance on the part not only of these Judaizers but also of some Gentile Christians in Galatia. "You observe days and months, and seasons, and years!" (4:10). The "days" almost certainly refers primarily to Sabbaths, "months" refers to new moons, and "seasons" to the great festivals that lasted for longer than a day (cf. Num. 10:10; 28:11; 1 Chron. 23:31). The "years" could be a reference to New Year's Days or to Sabbath or jubilee years. If the latter, this is likely to have been a rhetorical and ironical flourish on the part of the apostle, designed, together with the heaping up of these terms for calendrical observances, to indicate to the Galatians that they were busy reinstituting the whole Jewish legal system, a point he underlines elsewhere in the letter (cf. 3:10; 5:3). Sabbath observance in this context, where it is seen as part of keeping the law as necessary for salvation, arouses the apostle's strong reactions. In an attempt to shock the Galatians into an awareness of the implications of what they are doing, Paul likens their adoption of Jewish Sabbaths and festivals to a return to bondage to "elemental spirits." Paul's assertion may have been facilitated by the fact that the calendrical observances that appealed to the Galatians had superficial affinities with their former pagan celebrations. To be sure, the specific context prevents one from drawing too far-reaching conclusions about Paul dismissing all religious festivals, but certainly the strength of his language suggests that he sees no reason for a Gentile Christian to observe the Sabbath.[57] The apostolic decree by its omission of any reference to the necessity of Sabbath observance for Gentile Christians suggests that the Jerusalem apostles agreed with the apostle to the Gentiles on this. The apostle's own Sabbath practice, as recorded in Acts in terms of synagogue worship, is more likely to have been carried out for evangelistic purposes than because of convictions about the Sabbath's abiding validity (cf. 13:13, 44; 16:3; 17:2; 18:4). Unlike the apostle to the Gentiles, however, most Jewish Christians even after the apostolic council are likely for a variety of reasons, including conviction about the validity of Torah, lack of explicit teaching by Jesus to the contrary, conservatism, social pressure and evangelistic opportunities, to have continued to observe the Sabbath.[58]

In Paul's letter to the Romans there can be detected signs of this sort of Sabbath observance on the part of Jewish Christians in Rome, and it is noticeable that it does not arouse Paul's ire in the same way as had Sabbath observance in Galatia. Romans 14:5, 6 isolates the observance of "days" as one of the issues between the strong and the weak Christians in Rome. Of course, it is not possible to be dogmatic about the composition of these groups, but if one accepts an approach to the question of the setting of Romans that takes account of the tensions between Gentile and Jewish Christians in Rome,[59] then it may well be that the problems between the strong and the weak in faith with which Paul attempts to deal in Romans 14 and 15 reflect this tension. The two groups need not be thought of in strictly ethnic terms. No doubt there were also a number of Jews who had found new liberty in Christ and considered themselves "strong," and the "weak" may even have included some Gentiles who in becoming Christians had also embraced certain Jewish practices. But in all probability the predominant composition of the "weak" was Jewish Christian, while that of the "strong" was Gentile Christian. In this case the Sabbath will have been one of the days the Jewish Christians esteemed as better than another.[60] Although some of the "strong" may have used their emancipation to pander to the flesh, in this dispute Paul clearly identifies with their basic position of considering no day as more or less sacred than another while dissociating himself from their scorn of the "weak" (cf. 15:1, "We who are strong ought to bear with the failings of the weak, and not to please ourselves"). For Paul, however, the real issue at stake is not so much food or days but the attitudes of the two groups. The "weak" need to stop condemning the "strong" and the "strong" need to stop despising the "weak," and both need to welcome each other (14:1; 15:7), recognizing that he who observes the day and also he who does not are both intending to honor the Lord (14:6). Where the gospel is not at stake Paul shows acceptance and tolerance towards Jewish-Christian Sabbath observance, though he himself held that such weaker brethren had not fully understood the implications of the transition from the old economy to the new. The implications of this attitude towards the sacredness of days in regard to the significance of the first day of the week for the Christian church will be discussed below.

In Colossians 2:16–17, this transition from the old economy to the new, which has taken place in Christ, is the basis for Paul's attack on yet another variety of first-century Sabbath observance. The Colossian Christians were no doubt predominantly Gentile. The syncretistic practices of the group included ascetic regulations drawn from Judaism, however. The questions of food and drink mentioned in 2:16 are likely to be a reference to regulations for fasting as preparation for a visionary experience (cf. 2:18) and evidently the observance of Jewish festivals, new moons, and Sabbaths had become part of the cultic celebrations being advocated in Colossae in order to appease the "elemental spirits of the universe" (2:8, 20).[61] Paul is against this variety of Sabbath observance because it is part of a 'philosophy' that attempted to go beyond Christ to obtain the fullness of salvation. In regard to the Jewish practices involved in the false teaching, the apostle is able to point out that such aspects belong to the past history of salvation; they are in fact only a shadow of the realities to come. The realities to come are summed up in Christ, who is the substance as opposed to insubstantial shadows now outdated. As Lohse suggests, the shadow and substance concepts may have played a role in the philosophy where their cultic celebrations and ascetic regulations were seen as a copy, of which the "fullness" was the original. Access to the original was possible only by way of the copy.[62] If so, Paul places this concept in the service of his own perspective on the history of salvation and turns it against the philosophy as he shows that Christ is *the* reality who antiquates all Jewish practices that foreshadow Him and to whom the Colossian believers are already united. The use of the *σκιά/σῶμα* ("shadow/body") terminology here instead of the more usual *σκιά/εἰκών* ("shadow/true form") (cf. Heb. 10:1) may be significant and indicate that *σῶμα* was chosen for its other connotations in this letter. In this case *σῶμα* would refer not only to the reality that belongs to Christ but also, as a secondary nuance, to the fact that those who are members of the body of Christ share in that reality (cf. 2:19).[63] That Paul without any qualification can relegate Sabbaths to shadows certainly indicates that he does not see them as binding and makes it extremely unlikely that he could have seen the Christian first day as a continuation of the Sabbath.[64] When Sabbath observance was not being imposed on Gentiles as necessary for full salvation and did not form part of any syncretistic teaching, Paul evidently tolerated it but regarded those who practiced it as adolescent and not yet mature in Christ.

The Decalogue and the Law in the New Testament

How does this approach to the Mosaic Sabbath on the part of Jesus and the New Testament church relate to their attitude to the other commandments in the Decalogue and to the law in general? It is of significance in itself that this question of the use of the Decalogue is not distinguished in the New Testament from the larger question of the use of the Old Testament law in general.

The issue of the treatment of the law in the New Testament is a huge one and here we can only attempt to survey some representative New Testament writers.[65] The difficulty of bringing together the diverse elements in Paul's treatment of the law is well known.[66] It is most fruitful to recognize that Paul's attitude to the law was bound up with the total change that had occurred in his view of eschatology and of God's ongoing action in history for the salvation of men and women. He circumscribes the validity of the law within this framework, which helps to explain both the positive and negative assertions the apostle makes concerning the law and how the law is to be viewed by the believer. Because it was the revelation of God's will to Israel through Moses, the law can explicitly be called "the law of God" (cf. Rom. 7:22, 25; 8:7). It is "holy," "righteous," "good," and "spiritual" (cf. Rom. 7:12, 14, 16). In Galatians 3 and Romans 4, however, Paul emphasizes that the law came *after* the promise and this enables him to develop a more negative approach. In fact, in Galatians 3, from this historical perspective law is seen as a negative parenthesis between the periods of promise to Abraham and fulfilled promise in Christ. Law rigidly requires all that it demands and is correlated with "works" (cf. 3:2, 5, 10), while "promise" is correlated with "faith" (3:6ff., 14). The law was "added because of transgressions" (3:19); its purpose was to make sin and transgression evident (cf. also Rom. 5:12–14 where the law is said to define sin and Rom. 5:20 where it is said to provoke sin). The law could not make alive but only consign all things to sin (3:21–22). In the situation of sin, the law was powerless to give life and could only confine people (3:23) in its role as παιδαγωγός ("custodian"), exercising severe restrictions *until* the coming of Christ and the revealing of faith (3:24, 25). Thus the law here is seen as having limited temporal validity and a primarily negative effect. The apostle uses a similar temporal schema of earlier and later in Romans 4 where he illustrates his point through Abraham's circumcision, which came *after* he had received the promise by faith (vv. 10–11). In the argument circumcision stands for the law as the preceding verse (3:31) and the following argument (4:13–15) make clear. Promise is again shown to be prior to law, which has negative force in that it brings both transgression and wrath (4:15). This negative force of the law is expressed in 2 Corinthians 3 in terms of "the dispensation of death" (3:7) and "the dispensation of condemnation" (3:9). Romans 7 further indicates the bondage the law brings and the inability of the Jew still in the flesh, which it only intensifies, despite the Jew's desire to obey it.[67] Christ's place in Paul's perspective on the law is made plain in Galatians 3 where he is shown to be the completion and fulfillment of both the promise (cf. Gal. 3:16—as *the* seed he is the fulfillment of the promise to Abraham) and the law (cf. Gal. 3:13—since he takes on Himself the curse of the law and redeems people from it). Christ thereby inaugurates the new period of promise (cf. Gal. 3:14, "that in Christ Jesus the blessing of Abraham might come upon the Gentiles that we might receive the promise of the Spirit through faith").

In this new period believers are "not under law but under grace" (Rom. 6:14); we are "discharged from the law, dead to that which held us captive, so that we serve not under the old written code but in the new life of the Spirit" (Rom. 7:6). For Paul Christ has become the τέλος ("end") of the law (Rom. 10:4). There is, of course, debate about the exact significance of this term, which can mean either "goal" or "terminus." Here, the meaning of "terminus" is primary, with "goal" at best a secondary connotation. Christ is the terminus of the law in its connection with righteousness because through Him comes faith as the new means to righteousness. At the same time, since the law was a temporary provision, Christ brings its period of validity to an end, so that the believer in Christ is not under law as a rule of life. Instead the believer walks by the Spirit, and though no longer under the law, he or she in fact finds that the requirements of the law are fulfilled through the Spirit in his or her life (Rom. 8:4). The Spirit produces love and love turns out to be the fulfilling of the law (cf. Gal. 5:14). So for Paul the central thrust of the law is now worked out in the believer by the Spirit in terms of love. Though believers are not under the law of Moses, which was the law of God, it is not that they are now without the law of God altogether but that they receive God's law only as mediated through Christ and His Spirit. Paul sums up the continuity and discontinuity involved in this in 1 Corinthians 9:20–21 where he says, "To those under the law I became as one under the law—though not being myself under the law—that I might win those under the law. To those outside the law I became as one outside—not being without law toward God but under the law of Christ—that I might win those outside the law." For Paul God's dealings in history, including the expression of His will, have moved on and he is no longer under the law of Moses but under the will of God in its fuller and later expression in the "law of Christ." In all of his discussion and terminology Paul treats the law of Moses as a total package and makes no distinction between moral and ceremonial elements within it. Paul's freedom to draw on the law in giving ethical guidelines (cf. Rom. 13:8–10; Eph. 6:2) comes not simply because such elements are moral as opposed to ceremonial nor because of the Sinaitic origin of the material nor because it is part of the Decalogue but rather because, when viewed in the light of its fulfillment in Christ and the new situation He has brought about, portions of that law can be seen to be appropriate to the new expression of God's will in Christ. When the four commandments from the Decalogue are quoted in Romans 13:9 they have clearly been placed within the new framework of Romans 13:8, 10, which stress that love is the fulfilling of the law. The commandments now provide concrete illustrations of the new law of love. Similarly in Ephesians 6:1–2, when the apostle exhorts children to obey their parents, the primary motivation is the relationship "in the Lord" (cf. also Col. 3:20), and the primary reason is that "this is right," but then the fifth commandment can be brought in as additional support. It may well be that in outlining vices to be avoided Paul also makes use of the Decalogue and that Colossians 3:5 and Ephesians 5:3 combine the seventh and tenth commandments, identifying covetousness and lust in a traditional manner, while Ephesians 4:25ff. paraphrases the seventh to the tenth commandments.[68] However, the Decalogue has no special status in Paul's ethics, and the prime factor in his decision about what carries over from the old dispensation is the relationship of the various commandments and regulations to the supreme fulfillment of God's will in Christ and the new situation brought about by His death and Resurrection. Thus, when the apostle says, "For neither circumcision counts for anything nor uncircumcision, but keeping the commandments of God" (1 Cor. 7:19), these commandments undoubtedly included the Mosaic regulations, but clearly could not refer to all of them. To do justice to Paul's meaning here, the Christological criterion must be brought to bear.[69] In the light of his overall approach to the matter of God's will and Old Testament law, Paul's attitude to the Sabbath commandment should not seem at all surprising.

Matthew is in many ways the most Jewish of the gospels; the attitude to the law that emerges from Matthew's portrayal of Jesus' ministry is therefore more conservative than Paul's. However, just as Paul's view of the law is a highly debated topic, so also is Matthew's. Scholars usually adduce a variegated setting to account for Matthew's variegated emphasis. His community is seen as a mixed one, that had begun as strongly Jewish-Christian but that had seen an increasing number of Gentiles believe. It is held also that the Matthean community was in close proximity to antagonistic Jews. This sort of background helps explain the continuities and discontinuities with regard to the law and its Jewish interpretation in the gospel. Within Matthew's continuity/discontinuity dialectic there is more stress on the continuity than Paul provides.

This stress on continuity can be seen by comparing the Matthean and Lukan versions of a number of sayings from their common source, Q. Whereas Luke 16:16 has "the law and the prophets were until John," suggesting that they were in force only until the time of John the Baptist, Matthew 11:13 has the more qualified statement "all the prophets and the law prophesied until John," indicating more that they do not lose their validity but stand as fulfilled beginning with John's proclamation of the coming kingdom. Similarly Matthew 7:12 adds to the "golden rule" the words "for this is the law and the prophets" (cf. Luke 6:31) and Matthew 22:40 adds to the summary of the great commandments, "on these two commandments depend all the law and the prophets" (cf. Luke 10:25–28). In this way again the abiding validity of the law is brought out by Matthew. A similar tendency can be seen at various points in Matthew's redaction of Mark. Matthew's version of Jesus' discussion of clean and unclean foods (15:17–20) is far more conservative than that of Mark 7:18–23. He omits the two most radical aspects of Mark 7:18*b*, 19—the statement that unclean foods cannot defile, and Mark's interpretation that the law on clean and unclean foods was no longer in force. Matthew also gives the discussion a different framework from that of Mark, a framework (15:12–14, 20*b*) that diverts the force of Jesus' sayings from a rejection of the ceremonial law itself to a rejection of the pharisaic elaboration on it that insisted on washing the hands before eating. It is also likely that where Mark 10:2–12 has Jesus countermanding Mosaic law on the question of divorce, Matthew 19:3–9 has Jesus engaging in the rabbinic debate over the issue and favoring the stricter viewpoint of the Shammaites.[70] Matthew's high regard for the law is further reflected in the fact that it is he who, more than any other New Testament writer, characterizes unbelief as ἀνομία ("lawlessness") (cf. 7:23; 13:41; 23:28; 24:12). Jesus' view of the Torah as the revealed will of God obviously applies also in Matthew to the Decalogue as part of the law (cf. Matt. 15:3–6 where the fifth commandment is called the commandment not just of Moses but of God). In Matthew 19:16ff. Jesus brings the demands of a number of the commandments in the Decalogue to bear on the rich young man, though the different order from that to be found in the Old Testament accounts and the addition by Matthew of the "love commandment" from Leviticus 19:18 provide evidence that He did not consider the Decalogue in itself to be especially sacrosanct.[71]

While it is clear that Matthew's Jesus is no radical who simply overthrows the law, elements of discontinuity do emerge from the equally clear conviction that Jesus' word supersedes the word of Moses, for He is the one invested with divine authority (e.g., 9:28–29; 11:27; 21:23–27; 28:18). As the supreme interpreter of the law, Jesus attacks merely external observance (cf. the appeals to Hosea 6:6, "I desire mercy, and not sacrifice," 9:13; 12:7) and shows that the love commandment is the heart of the law as well as its hermeneutical key (cf. 7:12; 18:21–35; 22:34–40).[72] Ultimately Jesus' own teaching takes precedence, and in Matthew 28:20 the eleven are told to make disciples, "teaching them to observe all that *I* have commanded you." And what is striking is that Jesus' demand for perfection is something that goes beyond the commandments and requires obedience to His all-embracing call to discipleship.[73] The greater righteousness that is asked of disciples (cf. 5:20) surpasses in its radical character even the love commandment as the essence of the law (5:43–48).

The tension that arises between the continuing validity of the law and the new norm of Jesus' interpretation and teaching can be seen even in connection with the oral law in Matthew. There is a strong Jewish-Christian emphasis reflected in such statements as that of Matthew 23:3–4, "The scribes and the Pharisees sit on Moses' seat; so practice and observe *whatever* they tell you. . . ." Cf. 23:23, "For you tithe mint and dill and cummin, and have neglected the weightier matters of the law, justice and mercy and faith; these you ought to have done, *without neglecting* the others." On the other hand, by His authoritative teaching Jesus also sets aside some of the oral traditions. Matthew 15:20, for example, while it tones down the Markan account, does state that "to eat with unwashed hands does not defile a man," and 16:12 gives a warning against the teaching of the Pharisees and Sadducees.

In the tension between continuity and discontinuity some interpreters suggest that more weight is to be given to the discontinuity on account of the salvation-history perspective that Matthew himself provides for the material. Before Jesus' death and resurrection, Matthew has the ministry limited to the land and people of Israel (cf. 10:5–6; 15:24); it would be natural for there to be fidelity to the Mosaic law within this period, but after the Resurrection the universal mission (cf. 28:16–20) breaks down such restrictions and rescinds Mosaic prescriptions such as circumcision.[74] However, the exact nature of Matthew's salvation-history framework is still debated, and others believe there is far more overlap between the time of the earthly Jesus and the exalted Christ in Matthew's presentation than such a scheme suggests.[75] Even though there may be some clues to Matthew's emphasis from the structure of his gospel, it would be unwise to think that these dissolve the tension between continuity and discontinuity in regard to the law.

It is in the Sermon on the Mount, particularly in 5:17–48, that the two emphases we have found elsewhere in the gospel are most strikingly juxtaposed.[76] Matthew 5:17, with its stress that Jesus' teaching does not abolish the law and the prophets but fulfills them, is meant to explain and qualify the later antitheses of verses 21–48. The notion of fulfillment not only involves Jesus' clarifying of God's will but has the primary connotation of being the realization of that to which the law pointed forward (cf. 11:13).[77] Banks points out the significance of this, "The Mosaic laws point forward (principally) to the teachings of Christ and have also been realized in them in a more profound manner. The word 'fulfill' in 5:17, then, includes not only an element of discontinuity (that which has now been realized *transcends* the Law) but an element of continuity as well (that which transcends the Law is nevertheless something to which the Law itself *pointed forward*)."[78] The element of discontinuity should not be limited to certain aspects of the law such as the so-called "ceremonial laws," for it is the law as a unit that is being spoken of both here and in verse 18, so that so-called "moral laws," like that which bans murder, have also been realized and transcended by Jesus' teaching (cf. 5:21ff.). In verse 18 the permanent validity of the law in all its parts is asserted, and yet, on the other hand, the temporal qualification, "until all is accomplished" is introduced.[79] In this latter redactional clause πάντα may refer not only generally to Old Testament prophecies but also in context to "all" the things just mentioned, the demands of the law; γένηται (as elsewhere in Matthew, cf. 1:22; 21:4; 26:54, 56) probably refers to the "coming to pass" of that which has been predicted. Thus in the teaching and ministry of Jesus, especially as the latter climaxes in His death and Resurrection, all that the law pointed forward to is about to come to pass.[80] The strong language of continuity and the clear element of discontinuity can only be brought together with reference to Jesus. It is in His teaching that completes and surpasses, and thereby transforms that of the law that the permanent validity of the law continues. Matthew 5:19–20 again combine the two emphases. In 5:19, Matthew may well have taken over a Jewish-Christian formulation from the tradition originally attached to 5:18,[81] which makes those who tamper with the Mosaic law second-class citizens in the kingdom. However, in its final form 5:19 is to be read in the light of what precedes and therefore "these commandments" is a reference to both the Old Testament law and the teachings of Jesus, with the relation between them, which has been described in vv. 17–18, understood.[82] Matthew 5:20 then makes clear that the new authoritative focus and the radical demands that Jesus brings (illustrated in the following antitheses) enable His disciples' obedience and teaching to amount to a righteousness that surpasses that of the scribes and Pharisees. While there is disagreement among scholars on this issue, those who hold that in the antitheses of 5:21–48 Jesus not only deepens and intensifies the intention of the Mosaic Law but also radicalizes it to such an extent that at points He abrogates it, have the more convincing case.[83]

Our brief look at this passage from the Sermon on the Mount confirms that Matthew's attitude to the law is not best explicated in terms of the distinction between moral and ceremonial aspects, nor in terms of the perpetuity of the Decalogue as eternal moral law, but rather by seeing that the *whole* law pointed forward to Jesus' teaching and ministry, ultimately culminating in His death and Resurrection, and lives on only in so far as it has been transformed through its fulfillment by Jesus.[84]

What we have found to be the case in Matthew is also true of Luke. Not only is it the case, as M. M. B. Turner indicates, that "Jesus' attitude to the law seems to involve elements of affirmation and yet, simultaneously, degrees of abrogation,"[85] but also, as in Matthew, there is material that some have interpreted as a strong conservative attitude to the law; this has to be meshed with some of the evangelist's overall perspectives that point in a different direction. The two elements are combined in Luke 16:16–18. "The law and the prophets were until John; since then the good news of the kingdom of God is preached, and everyone enters it violently" (v. 16); this verse certainly indicates an element of discontinuity in that the period of the law and the prophets is seen as now having given way to the proclamation of the kingdom of God. "But it is easier for heaven and earth to pass away, than for one dot of the law to become void" (v. 17); it is obvious here, however, that such discontinuity can by no means be taken to involve an abrogation of the law. On the contrary, the permanence of the law is guaranteed, yet not in its own continued existence but rather in its fulfillment in the proclamation of the kingdom.[86] This sort of continuity between the new age that Jesus inaugurates and the law of Moses is also seen in Luke 24:44 where Jesus talks of everything written about Him in the law of Moses and the prophets and the psalms being fulfilled. Luke 16:16–18 returns to the notion of discontinuity in verse 18, however, where Luke shows how the demands of Jesus transcend the law. His higher standards in regard to divorce disallow what the Torah had previously permitted. As Banks puts it, Jesus' position "certainly exceeds the teaching of the Mosaic law and results in a portion of it being no longer applicable to the present situation."[87] In this way the law and the prophets are fulfilled by some parts of the law clearly being superseded. Elsewhere Luke's material also emphasizes that the law now has to be viewed within a Christological framework. It is Christ's fulfillment of Scripture that is determinative for the new age (4:16ff.; 24:27, 44); it is His words that are ultimately decisive (6:47–49). Luke alone preserves the parable of the good Samaritan, which indicates how the Old Testament commandment to love one's neighbor has been transcended by the radical demands of Jesus (10:25–37).

Turner's discussion of Jervell's thesis (Jewish Christians through their obedience to the law are the true Israel and Gentile Christians are an associate people), points out the element of ambivalence in the way Jeremiah's New-Covenant promise was framed.[88] Stressing that the *law* was written on the heart would lead to one approach, while emphasizing that the law was now written *on the heart* could lead to another interpretation. Luke's Acts depicts these conflicting emphases in the early church's life. At the beginning, the church's growth takes place within the confines of the Jewish cultus and piety. The possibilities of a more radical attitude to the law and cultus are hinted at in the account of Stephen's martyrdom (6:8–7:60), but come to the fore more clearly as Gentiles are brought into the church. Peter's encounter with Cornelius, related three times in Acts because of its significance, demonstrates that the law's "clean" and "unclean" distinctions are now a thing of the past (10:10ff.) and are no barrier to the salvation of Gentiles (11:18). An even greater breakthrough for this new attitude comes with the impact of Paul's Gentile mission (cf. 13:46ff.; 14:27), and the account of the apostolic council in chapter 15 is a watershed in the narrative of Acts. At the council a break is made in principle with the law. Peter's argument in 15:10, 11 is that to impose the law on Gentile converts is to put a yoke on them "which *neither our fathers nor we* have been able to bear." He insists that neither for Jewish Christian nor Gentile Christian is the law necessary for salvation, "But we believe that *we* shall be saved through the grace of the Lord Jesus, just as *they* will." Luke then shows James as confirming that Gentiles have been granted full status as the people of God (15:13ff.). This rejection on theological grounds of the necessity for obedience to the law for salvation or for full status as the people of God must be distinguished from the Council's approval of the practical necessity of abstinence on the part of Gentile Christians from certain practices for the sake of table fellowship between Jews and Gentiles. Luke's account of the latter certainly indicates his interest in the continuity between the Gentile mission and Judaism. Particularly in his portrait of Paul Luke wants to demonstrate that despite any allegations to the contrary Paul remained in continuity with Israel, and that includes continuity with the law (cf. Acts 16:3; 18:18; 21:20–26; 24:10–21). This has to be distinguished from Luke's view of the grounds of admission to the church, a matter which he saw as having been settled by the Council. For Luke Gentiles become full citizens in the renewed Israel of the end-time. Yet, as they do so, continuity with God's purpose for Israel is maintained, even through Paul, who remains scrupulously faithful to his Jewish heritage. Luke does not show the continuity of the law in the new situation through an imposition of the Decalogue on Gentile converts nor through the "eternal moral law" remaining in force while only the ceremonial was treated as outdated. Rather, the tension between continuity and discontinuity is depicted as being worked out with a more holistic approach to the law of Moses (cf. 15:5) and with the overall significance and implications of Jesus' teaching and death and Resurrection being the decisive filter through which the continuing force of God's law is mediated. The attitudes and practices of Jewish and Gentile Christians in regard to the fourth commandment, as we have seen, fit most appropriately not under the former more traditional theological categories but into the outworking of the latter dynamic.

We should look at one more New Testament approach to the matter of the law, that of the writer to the Hebrews. In Hebrews, covenant terminology and concepts come into their own, and in 8:13 in a contrast between the first (Mosaic) covenant and the New Covenant, the transience and obsolescence of the first covenant, and thus of the law, which was a central feature of it, are clearly asserted. It is often thought that in regard to Hebrews the "moral" and "ceremonial" distinction is particularly appropriate and assumed that the obsolescence of the first covenant really refers to its ceremonial and cultic aspects, its priesthood and sacrificial system, which were copies and shadows of the reality that has come in Christ. It is true that such aspects have become antiquated but they are part of a larger whole, the old order of the Mosaic covenant, which is itself passing away because of what has taken place in Christ. The concept of revelation is as important as that of priesthood in Hebrews (in fact the two are inextricably interwoven), and the writer makes it clear that the validity of the Mosaic revelation as a whole was temporally delimited. There is a continuity between old and new because in both cases it is God who has spoken (Heb. 1:1–2; cf. also 3:2–6, where the structure of revelation that includes both the old and the new is depicted as God's house), and because what He said at the earlier stage of revelation can be seen to point to its fulfillment in Christ (e.g., 1:5–14; 2:6–8). But there is also a discontinuity since the preliminary gives way to the final revelation "in these last days . . . by a Son" (1:2). The continuity/discontinuity tension is a feature not only of the prologue but also of the writer's approach throughout the letter. Continuity in regard to God's revelation of His will in the law emerges in both citations of the New Covenant promise (8:8–12; 10:15–18), for although the writer seems to make most of the promise of forgiveness of sins, he includes on both occasions the promise, "I will put my laws into their minds and write them on their hearts," and clearly sees the internalization of God's law as a central characteristic of the New Covenant. The notion of fulfillment builds a bridge between the old and the new, for, as 10:1 expresses it, what the law contains is the shadow cast by the true form of the realities that have now come with Christ. The continuity is also demonstrated forcefully through the Old Testament passages, including passages from the law in the narrower sense of the five books of Moses, which the writer can employ to communicate the Word of God into the new situation of believers in Christ (e.g., 2:6–8; 3:7–4:10; 10:37–38; chapter 11; 12:5–8, 13–17, 29; 13:5–6). The note of discontinuity is sounded in the three major comparisons in the first part of the letter where Christ's superiority to the angels, to Moses, and to the priesthood is shown. The angels and Moses are representatives of revelation of law, and in 7:5, 11–19 the interrelationship between the law and the priesthood is laid out. The two share the same transience and since there was clearly meant to be a change in the priesthood, of necessity there must also be a change in the validity and permanence of the law (7:12). In contrast to the priest inaugurated by the oath of the New Covenant, which came later than the law, the law cannot bring life or accomplish salvation and perfection (7:16, 19, 28). Thus the law, declared by angels (2:2), mediated by faithful Moses (3:2ff.) and administered by the levitical priesthood (7:5–28) is demonstrated to be not only preliminary but also imperfect and inferior to God's new revelation in Christ. This contrast is displayed in vivid imagery for a final time in 12:18ff.

The discontinuity is expressed in perhaps its strongest form in 8:6–7, 13, where in the contrast with the New Covenant, the Old Covenant is held to have faults and to be obsolete, and in 10:8–10, where with special reference to sacrifices God's will as established in Christ can be said to abolish that will as expressed in the law. What enables the writer to the Hebrews to handle the old revelation and the law so that in one place it can be God's Word to the Christian community and yet in another dismissed as obsolete is his knowledge of what has happened in the Son in these last days. In other words, the filter that determines for him the amount of continuity or discontinuity in a given instance is a Christological and eschatological one. It is when he is stressing what God has already accomplished in Christ in a final way for human salvation that the writer sees the revelation of the law and its institutions as obsolete. But it is when he sees that the believer must persevere in faith during the time that yet remains until the consummation of God's act in Christ that the Old Testament revelation can retain its usefulness and power for exhortation. His discussion of the concept of rest involves both discontinuity and continuity. On the one hand, from its Old Testament base in Psalm 95, this concept functions in the latter way in the writer's paraenesis. On the other hand, because rest also stands for the blessing of salvation and functions in the former context as something already opened up by Christ and available to believers, the writer to the Hebrews can now reinterpret Sabbath observance as an entry into that rest by ceasing from one's own works.[89]

This discussion of the treatment of the law in some representative New Testament writers provides us then with some broader perspectives and general models that can be utilized in our own approach to the Sabbath-Sunday question; it leads more immediately to a look at the way in which the post-apostolic church interpreted the fourth commandment as an aspect of the law.

The Sabbath Commandment and the Decalogue in the Post-Apostolic Church

The striking thing about the evidence we have from the second century is that it is almost as if the Sabbath commandment were not a part of the Decalogue, because the writers of this period take one attitude towards the Decalogue but a different one towards the Sabbath.

The Decalogue became popular for catechetical use in the postapostolic church and we have already noted that it may have been this that led to its withdrawal from the synagogue liturgy in the second century. This use is evidenced in such works as *De Doctrina Apostolorum*, *Didache* 2 and *The Epistle of Barnabas* 19, and sometimes tended towards legalism.[90] In these works, as also in Aristides, *Apology* 15:3–5, Theophilus of Antioch's *Ad Antolycum* 2:34–35; 3:9 and the description in *The Letter of Pliny* 10:96–97, it is mainly the so-called second table of the law that is paraphrased, and these ethical lists do not include the fourth commandment.

Alongside this prominence of the Decalogue (though not every single commandment nor in any fixed order or wording) in paraenesis, there was an increasing tendency to isolate it as important because it was natural law. In its status as Mosaic Law it was a temporary institution like the rest of the Mosaic legislation, but since it embodied natural law it was of permanent value. This notion of "natural law" enters into Christian thought from Stoic philosophy, and in particular the apologists appealed to a law which was sovereign over all people and to right reason as a foundation for ethics. Justin can write, "For those creatures who have received the gift of reason from nature have also received right reason, and therefore they have also received the gift of law which is right reason applied to command and prohibition" (*De Legibus* 1:12:33). The eternal moral law was held by the fathers to have been contained in the Decalogue and then embodied in Christ. Over against Jewish claims the notion of "natural law" could be employed to argue that the only permanently valid elements of Mosaic Law were those that had been revealed to all people and were an expression of eternal law (cf. Irenaeus, *Adv. Haer.* 4:13:16). This synthesis with Stoic notions introduces a different concept into the evaluation of the Decalogue from that of the New Testament writers, and the implications latent in it, which come to expression to a different extent in the various writings of the fathers, that a system capable of justifying ethical precepts can be built up from nature, that people have the ability to read off moral values from natural phenomena, and that statistically normal behavior in nature can be the criterion for good behavior, must be seriously questioned.[91] The effect of many uses of the notion of "natural law" is to lead to confusion about whether the starting point for Christian ethics is found decisively in special revelation or whether it can be built up from a "right reason" that is common to all humanity. The latter does not appear to do justice to the New Testament emphasis on the radical effect of sin on the understanding and it is very doubtful whether such a use of natural law can be said to be in line with Paul's idea that what the law requires is written on the hearts of the Gentiles in Romans 2:14–16, as is often claimed.

> God has not written "the law" in the hearts of the Gentiles, in the sense that they have by nature a universal principle to which to subject life and from which to draw conclusions as to how they ought to live. He has written "the works of the law" in their hearts so that, if they do otherwise in the concrete situation, they are aware that they have done evil. . . . When they act contrary to the right, and seek to

justify themselves before others and even before themselves, they know within themselves what the fact really is.[92]

It should be clear also that Paul's purpose here is a negative one; he wants to show that when the Gentiles perish as sinners (v. 12) they will be without excuse before God because of God's revelation through their conscience. The Gentiles have enough moral knowledge to provide a sufficient basis for ethics.[93]

At the same time another development that was to give prominence to the Decalogue was underway in the postapostolic church. In reaction to Marcion's radical separation of law and gospel and his use of Paul to substantiate it, there developed a view of the law and Paul's teaching concerning it which was concerned above all to emphasize the continuity and unity of law and gospel. One of the major means of achieving this end was to attempt to show that Paul's critique of the law was not to be understood as a critique of the law as a whole. This is perhaps most fully developed in Tertullian with whom the moral and ceremonial distinction comes into its own.[94] He claims that only the ceremonial aspect of the law is done away with; its moral aspect continues and is amplified (*De Pudicitia* 6:3–5). In *Adversus Judaeos* 2:7–9 he can go on to relate this to the "natural law" concept by arguing not only that the law is secondary to the promise but that the detailed Mosaic legislation is secondary to the fundamental natural law of the Decalogue and also that the prior faith and righteousness of Abraham was inconceivable without that natural law[95]

In the light of their views of the Decalogue one might expect early Christian writers to have treated the Sabbath commandment as eternally binding and to have attempted to argue that it was part of natural law for all people. This, however, was a much later development in Sabbatarian argumentation and in general the Sabbath discussion of the fathers not only rejects the Sabbath as temporary, treating it along with other Mosaic ceremonial regulations, but also fails to notice the issue raised by the Sabbath commandment being in fact part of that Decalogue they treat as "natural law." As R. J. Bauckham observes, "With the exception of Pseudo-Barnabas no Christian writer before Tertullian (*De Pud.* 5) refers to the Sabbath commandment as part of the Decalogue."[96] While the great majority of Jewish Christians in continuity with the New Testament period retained Sabbath observance, there is certainly evidence of other Jewish Christians who had become "strong" and taken a Pauline view.[97] Ignatius rejected Sabbath keeping, seeing it as having become outmoded together with the whole Jewish religion (cf. *Magn.* 8–10) and expecting Jewish Christians to be "strong" and take the same approach.[98] This was a common attitude among second-century writers.[99] Indeed, the "strong" Jewish Christians in interaction with their "weaker" brethren who insisted on Sabbath observance produced a metaphorical interpretation of the Sabbath where instead of applying to physical rest, it applied to abstinence from sin, and that not just on one day but every day.[100] A similar interpretation is also to be found in the writings of Justin, Irenaeus, Ptolemaeus, and Tertullian.[101] In Irenaeus this sort of spiritual and internalizing approach goes along with his recognition that the teaching of Christ in the Sermon on the Mount surpassed the teaching of the law. It is significant that this approach seems to have influenced Gentile-Christian Sabbath observance in the third and fourth centuries, so that while observing the seventh day, such Christians did not treat it as a day of physical rest but as a day of spiritual service to God (cf. Ps. -Ignatius, *Magn.* 9:2). Though the *Epistle of Barnabas* 15 interprets the Sabbath commandment in a unique typological fashion to mean holy living in the future Sabbath age, the notion of eschatological rest was not generally associated with the interpretation of the Mosaic Sabbath in this or other ways.

The *Epistle of Barnabas* is one of the few writings to treat the Sabbath as part of the Decalogue and to treat it as eternally binding; but it resolves this by reinterpreting the commandment in its unusual typological fashion. Tertullian also connects the Sabbath with the Decalogue and treats the literal meaning as part of the passing Mosaic legislation applied only to Israel and see its permanent meaning in the light of the ongoing significance of the Decalogue as moral law, as metaphorical in terms of holy living. Bauckham may well be right in his suggestion that the general inconsistency of second-century writers in not bringing together their views of the eternal moral nature of the Decalogue and the temporal nature of the literal Sabbath derives from their not thinking of the Decalogue as a hard and fast category involving every one of the Ten Commandments but more as the paraphrase of the last five commandments commonly used in Christian paraenesis.[102] Judging in terms of what we have seen of the attitude of the New Testament writers, the majority of second-century writers seem to have been sound in their instinct to treat the Sabbath as a temporary Mosaic institution, but to have introduced a confusing motif in their attempt to see the continuing significance of the Decalogue in "natural law" categories, which were not adequate for explaining the different attitudes of the New Testament writers to the Mosaic law.[103]

The observance of the Sabbath among some Gentile Christians, for which there is evidence in the third and fourth centuries but which appears to have ceased in the fifth century, should be noted here. Respect for the Sabbath found expression in the prohibition of fasting on Saturday and especially in public worship on that day as well as on the Lord's Day. Interestingly enough, however, the motivation for this appears not to have been obedience to the Sabbath commandment by cessation from work, which was looked on as "Judaizing," but rather Saturday was seen as a memorial of the first creation and Christ's part in it, while Sunday commemorated the inauguration of the second creation through Christ.[104]

The Lord's Day

The Prominence and Observance of the First Day in Early Christian Literature

The first day of the week is the only day, apart from the Sabbath, to receive explicit attention in the New Testament. It figures prominently, of course, in the Resurrection narratives of all four Gospels. The terminology of "the first day of the week" occurs in Matthew 28:1, emphatically in Mark 16:2, where the narrative had already begun with "and when the sabbath was past" in (16:1) but then begins again with "and very early on the first day of the week." It is used also in Luke 24:1 and John 20:1 to introduce the account of the Resurrection. In addition, Luke wants to make clear that the appearances to the two on the road to Emmaus and to the eleven were on that same day. John underlines that Jesus' appearance to the gathered disciples was "on the evening of that day, the first day of the week" (20:19), and that another appearance to the disciples, with Thomas present, took place on the first day of the following week, "eight days later" (20:26).

It may be that in regard to the day of the Resurrection itself, this emphatic dating is simply because the events in fact transpired on that day and that this was important for showing the fulfillment of the third-day prediction (cf. the mention of this in close proximity to the "first-day" dating in Matt. 27:62–66 and Luke 26:7). But it could also well be that the emphasis on the first day, particularly John's linking of this with the appearances to the gathered disciples, was preserved in the traditions and by the evangelists because this day had taken on a particular significance in the life of the church. If on other grounds it can be shown that Christian worship is likely to have taken place particularly on the first day of the week and in connection with the resurrection of Christ, then the circular reasoning involved in this view of the Resurrection accounts would be perfectly natural. The influence would run both ways; on the one hand, that the Resurrection occurred on the first day would affect Christian worship practices, and, on the other, the practice of worship on the first day would mean that the mention of the first day in connection with the Resurrection appearances would be held to be significant and preserved.[105] That not only the Resurrection but also the outpouring of the Spirit at the feast of Pentecost took place on the first day of the week is possible. But this would be only if Sadducean methods of chronological reckoning concerning the Jewish festivals prevailed in the year of the crucifixion, and it is more likely that Pharisaic methods of reckoning were used.

The New Testament evidence for the prominence of the first day in connection with Christian worship (Acts 20:7, 1 Cor. 16:2 and Rev. 1:10) is scanty but, when taken together with that of the postapostolic period, it points us clearly in one direction. Acts 20:7 with its mention of the gathering to break bread "on the first day of the week," is a reference to a Sunday and not to a Saturday assembly.[106] Luke's account makes only this passing reference, but the specific mention of the first day together with the purpose of the evening meeting being to break bread suggests that this was a regular occurrence in the church at Troas, and the narrative with its talk of staying for seven days in Troas and of Paul's intention to depart the next morning reads as though Paul deliberately planned to address all the believers when they assembled for their weekly meeting.[107] The putting aside of funds for the collection for the Jerusalem church, which Paul requires "on the first day of every week" (1 Cor. 16:2), is not directly connected with public worship, for this was to be done privately (*παρ ʼἑαυτῷ*). Yet the question remains why Paul specifies the first day of the week for the carrying out of this task. Since there is no evidence that this was payday, it must be assumed, unless there was no reason at all for singling out this particular day, that there was some other factor which distinguished this day from others as the most appropriate.[108] The most likely factor remains that this was in fact the day for the Corinthians' regular assembly for worship. Revelation 1:10 adds to this somewhat sparse evidence by indicating that the title of "Lord's Day" had been conferred on the first day of the week. That Lord's Day is the designation for Sunday rather than the eschatological day of the Lord, Easter, or the Sabbath, Bauckham has convincingly argued.[109] There is unambiguous evidence in such documents as the Acts of Peter, the Acts of Paul and the *Epistula Apostolorum* as well as in the Valentinian text preserved by Clement (cf. *Exc. ex Theod.* 63) and Dionysius of Corinth's letter to bishop Soter of Rome (cf. Eusebius, *HE* 4:23:11) that from the second half of the second century Sunday was called *κυριακή*. Though not totally unambiguous, the earlier postapostolic references in *Didache* 14:1, Ignatius, *Magnesians* 9:1 and the *Gospel of Peter* 35 and 50 point strongly to Sunday being in view. It is highly unlikely that John writing to the churches of the province of Asia at the end of the first century would use *κυριακὴ ἡμέρα* ("the Lord's Day") to mean some different day, so that Revelation 1:10 provides evidence from the New Testament that by this time, at least in the churches of Asia Minor, the first day of the week had become regularly observed in the Christian church and was distinctive enough to be graced with the title of the Lord's Day.

Evidence for Sunday observance over and above that connected with the title Lord's Day in the second century begins with the *Epistle of Barnabas* (15:9) and then Justin (cf. I *Apol.* 67:7; *Dial.* 41:4) and continues until the time of Clement of Alexandria (cf. *Strom.* 5:106:2), and from then on references to Sunday worship are even more plentiful. None of these writings treats Sunday observance as a recent innovation but assumes it as the regular practice of the church. But when did this practice begin? Certainly the evidence points to Sunday observance having spread with the expansion of the church during the period of Paul's Gentile mission. It is unlikely, however, that Sunday observance was an innovation in the Pauline churches, otherwise this would have met the disapproval of the apostle's Judaizing opponents and of this there is no trace in the correspondence. It is more likely that some gathering of the first day of the week was already practiced by Palestinian Jewish Christians, for, after all, their communities needed some time for regular worship over and above the attendance at the temple or synagogue and the observance of Sabbath practices, and that after meeting every day (Acts 2:46) was no longer feasible the first day came to the fore as particularly appropriate for the assembly of believers. The majority of Jewish Christians in Palestine and many in the diaspora may well have kept the Sabbath and also met with their fellow believers in Christ for worship at some time on the following day.[110]

The Significance of the First Day

As we have seen from the Resurrection narratives, the terminology of "the first day" is immediately reminiscent of the day of the Resurrection, and the Christian assembly on the first day attested to in Acts 20:7 and hinted at by 1 Corinthians 16:2 is bound to have been associated with Christ's resurrection. As Bauckham concludes, "We are unlikely to have any record of a stage in the Christian observance of Sunday before that at which it was understood to be the weekly worship of the risen Lord on the weekly recurrence of the day of his Resurrection."[111] Of the New Testament texts it is only Revelation 1:10 with its designation of the first day as the Lord's Day that can indicate the theological significance that was attached to this day. The lordship of Christ had become particularly associated with the first day of the week and the significance of that lordship in the Apocalypse can inform our understanding of the significance John and his readers would have attached to lordship in connection with the day. Bauckham's conclusions are particularly helpful.[112] Lordship or sovereignty is perhaps the central theme of the Apocalypse, and in the context of chapter 1 and of the whole book with its depiction of the conflict of sovereignties, *Lord's* Day has profound connotations. Again the Resurrection is certainly involved, for 1:10 introduces the vision of the risen Christ and Christ's lordship is dependent on the initial but decisive victory of the Resurrection (cf. for example 1:5, 18; 2:8). Seen in the context of the book's conflict of sovereignties, one of whose forms was the persecution provoked by the imperial cult, the Lord's Day could well have been regarded as in contrast to the monthly Emperor's Day and as that day when believers worship *their* lord who is in fact not only "the firstborn of the dead" but in consequence "the ruler of kings on earth" (1:5). The concepts of lordship and worship are intimately connected, and the visions received by John on the Lord's Day were to be read aloud in the churches' gatherings for worship, which would also have been on that day. Worship expresses the Christian community's recognition of its Lord and marks the church out as His particular sphere of lordship, and this again makes it appropriate for the day for worship to be known as the Lord's Day.

Worship of Christ as Lord and in commemoration of His Resurrection is also the central feature in the significance given to Sunday in the postapostolic writings. The early second-century references closest to the Apocalypse in date indicate that the churches clearly regarded Sunday worship as a celebration of the resurrection of Christ on the first day of the week (cf. *Barn.* 15:9, Ignatius, *Magn.* 9:1 and *Gospel of Peter* 35, 50).[113] Other titles for the day besides Lord's Day were exploited for their significance, including the pagan "day of the sun" (cf. Justin, *I Apol.* 67:7) and the eschatological "eighth day" (cf. especially *Barnabas* 15:9). The "eighth day" not only evoked the superiority of Christianity over Judaism with its seventh day but was understood to prefigure the eighth day of the apocalyptic world week, that is, the world to come. In Valentinian Gnosticism the temporal eighth day or Lord's Day became associated with the spatial ogdoad and thereby with the concept of rest, for the cosmic ogdoad, the sphere of the divine, was seen as the resting place of the soul (cf. Clement, *Exc. ex Theod.* 63:1; *Epistle of the Apostles* 18).

Mention of the Sabbath as part of the significance of the first day is conspicuous by its absence from both the New Testament and second-century literature. Not only is there no hint of Sabbath significance about the three New Testament references that suggest first-day worship, but it is also inconceivable either that Jewish Christians already participating fully in Israel's Sabbath observance should or could set aside the first day of the week to observe in the same way or that they simply transferred their Sabbath practice to the first day. The first day practice preserved in Acts 20:7 has reference to only part of the day, the evening, after the regular day's work had finished. Besides, the Jewish Sabbath was such a central institution that any major change in its observance, such as this, would have attracted widescale attention and persecution for those who perpetrated it, and yet there is no trace of this.[114] Nor does it appear at all plausible that Gentile churches would have introduced the notion that the first day was to be treated as the Sabbath. They would know that Jewish believers were observing the seventh day, and such a move would be the cause of great disunity. If Paul had taught such a thing in his Gentile churches it is inexplicable that in his discussion of keeping Sabbaths he did not use the trump card that such days had been replaced by the Christian Sabbath of the first day. If his churches understood at all the teaching he did give about days or Sabbaths, it is hardly likely that they would have transferred the concept of the distinctive sanctity of a day to the first day of the week. It cannot be argued that the New Testament itself provides warrant for the belief that since the Resurrection God appointed the first day to be observed as the Sabbath.[115]

Though in the postapostolic period the first day was occasionally compared to the Jewish seventh day, and though it was regarded as a festival of the Resurrection to be celebrated, there is no clear evidence of any Sabbath transference theology, whereby the first day of the week was to be observed as a day of literal rest and such observance associated with obedience to the fourth commandment. Rather than an attempt to adopt it, there was a polemic against such literal observance of the Sabbath as idleness and inactivity (cf. Justin, *Dial.* 12:3; Irenaeus, *Epideixis* 96; Ps. -Ignatius, *Magn.* 9:2). Even after Sunday had become a day free from work after Constantine's legislation in A.D. 321 there was little attempt to provide theological support for this in terms of a transference of Sabbath obligations. Eusebius' commentary on Psalm 91, which is the first extant work to assert that the Sabbath has been transferred to Sunday, does this on the basis of the priests' activity in worship rather than on the basis of the prohibitions of the fourth commandment concerning work.[116] Bauckham can go so far as to claim that "in spite of the Constantinian legislation it is clear that true Sabbatarianism was a medieval, not a patristic, development."[117]

The Normativeness of Observance of the First Day

The New Testament foundations for the church's practice of Sunday worship are not as numerous or as detailed as might be desired, but even if we agree that they do point clearly in the direction of establishing that with the impact of the Gentile mission the observance of the first day spread and had become a regular practice of the church by the end of the first century, would this be sufficient to establish the normativeness of this custom for the church? There are certainly other apostolic and early church practices that are not considered binding on the church. And if appeal *is* made to early church practice, what about the diversity of its practice on this issue, with some parts of the church continuing to observe the Sabbath alongside a probable increasing recognition of the distinctiveness of the first day for worship? Would it not be sufficient to regard seventh-day rest or first-day worship or both as instructive traditions evidenced in the apostolic and postapostolic church that later generations of believers are free to adopt or reject as they wish?

An attempt to answer these questions involves some evaluation of the place and status of the tradition of the early church. In the case of first-day worship this tradition is essential in enabling us to see the significance of the isolated New Testament data and to fit it into an interpretive pattern in order to trace the church's emerging practice. Some would be inclined to give the clearer postcanonical evidence more authoritative status and accept Sunday worship as normative on that basis. When the Protestant reformers, however, wanted to make Scripture uniquely authoritative for faith and practice, they tended to reduce the significance of the first day to a merely convenient institution. Though they are not always clear, Luther (and the Confession of Augsburg) and Calvin treat the weekly day of worship not as a matter of necessity or religious obligation but rather as useful in the practical ordering of church life. Ursinus, who held that there was a continuing moral obligation in regard to the Sabbath, nevertheless regarded the day on which the obligation was carried out as a "thing indifferent." Though the reformers were seeking canonical sanction for a practice before considering it to be normative, they may well have overlooked the significance of Revelation 1:10 in this regard.[118] That the first day of the week was given the title Lord's Day suggests a matter of far greater import than convenience or practicality. But how does Scripture provide a norm in this area? Which of its descriptive statements can have normative force, and why? If to set a normative pattern an imperative in the New Testament is required, then observance of the first day of the week does not come into the category of normative patterns of practice, and by itself apostolic practice is not sufficient to constitute a command carrying apostolic authority.[119] Yet Revelation 1:10, as we have suggested, does provide more promising data. True, the designation "Lord's Day" in that reference is incidental rather than being part of the primary didactic intent of the writer, but we are not using this passing reference in order to establish a precedent but to show that a precedent had already been set in the practice of at least John's churches and evidently met with his approval. So in the case of worship on the first day of the week we have a pattern that is repeated in the New

Testament, and as is shown by Revelation 1:10, the pattern had become established. Furthermore, as the designation "Lord's Day" indicates, this pattern was undergirded by the theological rationale of Christ's lordship demonstrated in His Resurrection on the first day of the week. Although we have evidence for this pattern from only some parts of the early church, its rationale is not one that was applicable only to those parts or indeed applicable only to the early church period but one that remains applicable throughout the church's life. Hence the practice of Sunday worship can be said to be not merely one that recommends itself because it bears the mark of antiquity but one that, though not directly commanded, lays high claim to bearing the mark of canonical authority.

It might still be claimed that another pattern, specifically observance of the seventh-day Sabbath, also has New Testament canonical status. Have we not already shown that Jewish Christians continued to observe the Sabbath during New Testament times? But whether this practice is actually sanctioned by a canonical writer is another matter. We have disputed that this is the force of Matthew 24:20, and although Acts does suggest some Sabbath observance, Turner has argued (above) that Luke

> has very little sympathy with the theologically nomist pattern observed by the church until the incoming of the Gentiles. For him, the law-transcending admission of the Gentiles to the church (which first brought the claims of Christ and of the law into real conflict) was the logical outworking of Jesus' attitude to the law.[120]

The closest the seventh-day Sabbath of the early Christians comes to being given canonical status is in Paul's tolerance of its observance by Jewish Christians (cf. Rom. 14). Even this has to be qualified, however, for Paul would assume that it was primarily Jewish Christians who were likely to pursue this option and, as a Jewish Christian himself, he clearly believes his own law-free stance to be more enlightened. This element of diversity in the canonical data does indicate that we should be as flexible and tolerant as Paul in regard to those who wish to practice seventh-day Sabbath observance, as long as they do not make such observance a condition for salvation or fellowship. At the same time, it is our position that the main direction in which the New Testament evidence moves is towards first-day worship, and that this practice is given explicit canonical approval. The other practice of some Christians, observance of a first-day Sabbath, although again from the perspective of Romans 14 to be tolerated, cannot appeal to the canon for precedent, it should be noted, and, as we shall show in the next section of this chapter, is a compromise theological position fraught with difficulties.

Given these conclusions about the canonical status of first-day worship, a further question arises about how such an attitude to the first day of the week, which seems to be demanded by the title Lord's Day, can be squared with the position which Paul approves in Romans 14:5 that no day is to be regarded as more or less sacred than another. The Reformers, as we have seen, avoided the dilemma and refuted any charges that they were judaizing in observing a day by treating Sunday as a merely convenient day and holding that any day of the week could serve the same purpose. If, however, we hold that the first day is *the* appropriate day because of its association with the resurrected Lord and its claim to canonical status, then some attempt has to be made to explain how it can be said that in the new dispensation no day has special sanctity (for all days are sacred and devoted to the Lord), and yet that one day still plays a distinctive role in this new era. Origen's solution was to argue that the perfect Christian continually and every day is keeping the Lord's Day, but the majority of Christians who have not yet reached this stage of attainment still need weekly observance as a reminder of spiritual things. However, this division into two classes of Christians is hardly a satisfactory solution. Nor is the usual response that in his statements Paul had only Jewish holy days in mind and was not considering developments in the life of the church any more satisfactory.[121] This ignores the fact that the principle of which Paul approves in Romans 14 is a general one that has far broader application than merely to the institutions of Judaism.

Perhaps two factors need to be borne in mind in relating the Pauline view of days to the title Lord's Day. First, a development seems to have taken place within the New Testament period, so that although first-day worship was practiced in the Pauline churches where it was an emerging custom, the day does not yet appear to have acquired the distinctiveness that earned it the title of Lord's Day in Johannine circles by the end of the first century. Second, there need be no incompatibility about the stages of this process, for the Lord's Day need not be understood in terms of a sacred day. As R. J. Bauckham has pointed out in his study of the usage of the term κυριακός, there is a certain vagueness in the relation to the Lord implied in the term.[122] The day can be said to be the Lord's because it is the appropriate day for worshiping Him, and this is significantly different from the view that sees the day, by analogy with the Jewish Sabbath, as a full twenty-four hour period belonging to the Lord in a distinct way from that in which all the Christian's time belongs to the Lord. Whereas the latter is in conflict with the sentiment approved in Romans 14:5, the former need by no means be. There is a sense in which all of life should be a prayer, and yet a recognition of this does not detract from the need for specific prayers at specific times. Similarly the notion that all of one's time is devoted to the Lord does not detract from the necessity of specific worship at specific times. To claim that specifically Sunday is the appropriate day for a gathering of the Christian community for worship is not to imply that somehow in itself that day is holy.

An Evaluation of Sabbath-transference Theology and of the Significance of the Fourth Commandment in the Light of the Debates of Church History

What had earlier been seen simply as the preference to have rest from work on Sunday in order to be able to worship as much as possible, a natural and legitimate development in the life of the church and one that was facilitated by Constantine's decree, had become by the seventh century a requirement of abstinence from servile work for the whole day. It was the attempt to give this idea of rest for worship on the Lord's Day a theological rationale and to make it mandatory on a biblical basis that led in the direction of Sabbath-transference theology. The biblical and theological grounds adduced took the form of the notion first that the Lord's Day was analogous to the Sabbath and then that the requirements of the fourth commandment concerning Sabbath rest had been transferred to the observance of the Christian Sunday.[123] By the central place he had given to the abiding validity of the ten commandments for Christian moral theology Augustine had paved the way for the first full-scale theological justification of Sabbath transference, that of Thomas Aquinas. Aquinas' formulation of the issues were in turn determinative for the Reformers who did not break with his basic premises, though Luther and Calvin resisted their logic, and for both Puritan Sabbatarianism and nineteenth century English Sabbatarianism, which continued the tradition of Sabbath-transference theology.

Since a similar type of thinking about Sunday is still widespread in Christian circles,[124] it will be helpful to isolate the most important elements in this tradition in order to show why it is mistaken both in its basic approach and premises and often in working out such premises consistently once they have been accepted.[125] The view that the Sabbath is a creation ordinance is frequently part of this tradition, but since it is not necessarily so, and since the view has been discussed earlier it will not be taken up again here. The four principal elements to be discussed are (1) natural law (2) the centrality of the Decalogue as the summary of both natural and revealed moral law (3) the moral and ceremonial distinction in regard to the fourth commandment and (4) the application of the Sabbath commandment to the Lord's Day on the grounds that both days involve the principle of rest for worship.

(1) The Sabbath was seen as part of natural law and its observance held to be a moral precept discoverable by human reason without the aid of special revelation. Aquinas seems to have held that natural law required the setting

apart of a regular time for divine worship, while Zanchius went further, believing that nature taught that all should devote one day in seven to public worship. How the ratio of one in seven rather than one in six or one in eight can be established simply from nature is not demonstrated, and English Sabbatarian thinkers soon saw the problems with this and moved away from attempts to establish the Sabbath as such as natural law to the more general view that nature simply required some time for worship on the part of humanity. However, this more general view operates in terms of human nature as it ought to be, not human nature as it is, as the norm, and this particular law of time for divine worship presupposes acceptance of a theistic world view, so that it is certainly disputable whether it qualifies as natural law discoverable by human reason as it is and without the aid of special revelation. One problem with the theological version of natural law is that since it holds that natural law is dependent on God for its existence, it has difficulty in holding at the same time that knowledge of that law is independent of the knowledge of God. Whatever evaluation may be made of recent attempts to rehabilitate a Christian version of natural law in regard to such ethical principles as justice and equity,[126] this difficulty seems overwhelming in the case of the principle of worship, and is certainly an illustration of the way in which a changed religious and intellectual climate has a habit of exposing the inapplicability of earlier formulations of natural law. It is somewhat surprising to the present-day student that the natural law argument in Sabbatarian theology was traditionally formulated in terms of worship rather than, as it is often formulated in more recent literature, in terms of rest. It is certainly a more defensible argument that it is a natural law that all people need regular rest. However, this would not be a sufficient argument for a Sabbatarian, who would have to contend in addition that this rest has to be of the duration of a day and has to be observed one day in seven rather than one day in six, eight or ten, contentions that fail to stand without some appeal to special revelation.

(2) In practice, in Sabbatarian theology this appeal was always made to the Decalogue, and arguments from natural law cannot be separated from the belief that natural law was reducible to the Decalogue, so that the Decalogue was seen as a summary both of natural law and revealed moral law. Sabbath transfer theology has relied primarily on attempts to show the binding nature of the Decalogue as moral law. The notion of natural law was one weapon in the armory; and in discussing views of the Decalogue in the postapostolic church this essay has already pointed to some of the weaknesses of this particular weapon and to the problems of combining an emphasis on the Decalogue with natural law. When, however, English Sabbatarians shifted their focus from the Decalogue's relation to natural law and treated it as "positive"

moral law, binding on all, they could treat the requirements of the fourth commandment as involving not just some time but one whole day in seven.[127] In our treatment of the biblical material it has been emphasized, however, that this sort of use of the Decalogue is unhistorical and detaches it from its place as part of the Mosaic law and covenant, which has now been fulfilled and transcended in Christ, and that the attitude of the New Testament writers toward the law is by no means one that is best explicated in terms of the perpetuity of the Decalogue as universally binding moral law. Such a position is certainly not "antinomian," for it does not hold that obedience to the law of God is not required of Christian believers; it simply questions the assumption of Sabbatarians that that law is the Ten Commandments. It holds rather that God has given a later and further expression of His moral character and will in the person of Christ and in the teaching of His apostles, and to these, believers must be obedient, and that the earlier expression of God's will in the Decalogue is partial and historically conditioned and binding only in so far as it is reaffirmed by its fulfillment in the life, death and resurrection of Christ and by the teaching of the New Testament writers. The major part of the Decalogue is reaffirmed in this way, but not the fourth commandment; so the Decalogue is not binding moral law qua decalogue. Those Sabbatarians who held that it was, and particularly those, like Bownde, who held that the *whole* Decalogue was binding as moral law and contained "nothing ceremonial, nothing typical, nothing to be abrogated"[128] were extremely hard pressed to explain why they were not observing the seventh-day Sabbath. To become a seventh-day Sabbatarian is the only consistent course of action for any one who holds that the whole Decalogue is binding as moral law.

(3) At this point, however, the moral and ceremonial distinction in regard to the law is called into play by proponents of a Sabbath-transference theology and becomes a necessity if seventh-day Sabbatarian conclusions are to be avoided. It is argued that the ceremonial aspect of the fourth commandment lies in its specification of the seventh day, while its moral aspect is held to involve the setting apart of one day in seven for the worship of God with the abstention from all "servile work" for that purpose. It has already been shown, however, that the moral and ceremonial distinction developed in the post-apostolic period is not one that can do justice to the New Testament writers' attitudes to the law, which can be summed up rather in terms of an interplay between continuity and discontinuity in regard to the law *as a whole* with the decisive factor being the relation of the Mosaic Law to the new expression of God's will in Christ and the new situation brought about by His death and Resurrection. If the apostles, and for that matter the Jerusalem Council, held to some form of a moral and ceremonial distinction in relation to the fourth

commandment, their silence about its binding moral nature is inexplicable. If Sabbath observance on these grounds is binding for present day Christians, should it not have been equally so for the first generation of Gentile Christians, and if so, why did the apostles fail to teach this?

The moral and ceremonial distinction by itself is not sufficient for building a case for a Sabbath-transference theology, for in addition its proponents need to be able to show that the moral aspect of the fourth commandment is now to be obeyed on a different day, the first day of the week instead of the seventh. Again, however, it has been shown that this change of day claim has no biblical evidence to support it. The meager New Testament evidence we have is sufficient only to justify the practice of worship at some time on the first day of the week, but there is not a hint anywhere in the documents that observance of the first day in this way was connected with any requirement to abstain from work on this day.[129] If it be argued that the occurrence on the first day of the Resurrection as the foretaste and pledge of future Sabbath rest attracted actual Sabbath observance to that day, it can still be asked why the Resurrection could not have been celebrated on the Sabbath, particularly when the Sabbath was given as *the* sign of that future rest.[130] In any case all the probabilities are against such a change, for the Jewish Sabbath was so distinctive and central to Judaism that any attempts in the early church to tamper with the day on which it was observed would have led to great controversy, and it would be strange indeed that none of the literature of the first and second centuries reflects any such controversy. Further, such a change of day would have caused not only religious but also social and economic turmoil if Jewish Christians had taken their day of rest on a different day and Gentile believers had started to take a day of rest on the first day of every week. Again, of such turmoil there is not a hint.[131]

(4) Finally, Sabbath-transference theology requires that once the change of day has been assumed, the Mosaic Sabbath and the Christian Sunday should be seen to have the same principle at the heart of each and so traditionally it has been held that both are a day of rest for worship. This, however, is to blur the distinction between the Old and New Covenants. It plays down the rigor of the Mosaic Sabbath, which was primarily a day of physical rest from work rather than a day for special acts of worship, and misinterprets the Christian Lord's Day, which was the appropriate day for worship but by no means necessarily involved a day of rest.[132] Bullinger, perhaps, obscured the distinction between the covenants most fully, as he applied details of Sabbath rest in the Old Testament to the New Testament era, including Numbers 15 as the basis for the Christian magistrate punishing Sabbath breakers, even by death.[133] In this he was followed by a number of Puritans.

Of course most Sabbatarians have been far more humane and some, like the seventeenth-century Anglican Laudians have been fairly loose in their requirements and allowed recreation.[134] However, once it has been accepted that Sabbath and Sunday are both based on the same principle—the requirement of a day of rest for worship—it may well be questioned whether those such as Bownde and the Westminster Assembly were not in fact more consistent in calling for strictness of application. If the rest was understood as being for the purpose of spending as much of the day as possible in worship, then they were also more consistent in ruling out recreation on this day. Of course such a position leads to all sorts of legalism, but once the premises of Sabbatarian theology have been assumed, it is surely the most consistent. Within this framework, and more recently, John Murray has defended the Westminster divines' view of the Sabbath as over against that of the Synod of Dordt, which pronounced that the fourth commandment was to be observed but not with the same strictness. He argues that either one obeys the force of the commandment as it stands or one does not, and that strictness is really beside the point.[135] Happily for the freedom of the believer, most who espouse a Sabbath-transference theology have been inconsistent at this point.

As can be seen, Sabbatarian theology can be criticized from a number of angles, but the most basic criticism is that it does justice neither to the biblical evidence nor to the perspective of such New Testament writers as Paul, John, and the writer to the Hebrews, namely, the perspective that attempts to view revelation in the light of the history of salvation, for it ignores the fact that the Decalogue is part of the provisional Mosaic Law, which is to be treated as a whole and fails to appreciate the impact of the fulfillment of this history of salvation in Christ.

In criticizing Sabbath-transference theology this discussion has emphasized the element of discontinuity brought about by the fulfillment of the law in Christ and has found no justification from the New Testament or from the early church's writings for any continuity that would include the necessity of abstinence from work and of physical rest on the Lord's Day. We do, however, need to insist on some sort of continuity of force for the fourth commandment, since this commandment is not simply left in abeyance. In fulfilling the law, Christ has reinterpreted it. What force then does the fourth commandment have when seen in the light of the new situation inaugurated by the fulfillment in Christ, and new situation of which both the New Testament writers' interpretation and the practice of the New Testament church are a part?

The Sabbath commandment has positive, though not literal, force when it is seen from the perspective of the interwoven motifs of eschatological rest, salvation rest, mortification and the intensification of the Old Testament commandments, motifs found both in the New Testament and in later Christian writers. In John 5, the interpretation of the Sabbath commandment is linked with the notion of eschatological rest, and in Hebrews 4, Sabbath observance (σαββατισμός) is reinterpreted in connection with an eschatological exposition of the significance of Genesis 2:2–3. When this framework is introduced the physical rest enjoined by the fourth commandment can be viewed as a pointer to future eschatological rest, God's method of instructing His people that they were to enter into the rest He had prepared for them. The consummation of this rest will involve the removal of all curse on work and the participation in that state of completion experienced by God after His creative work. For the believer, looking back from the vantage point of God's completion of His redemptive work in His Son, the eschatological rest to which the Sabbath points has now been given a christological stamp, and already been opened up for enjoyment.[136] During the second century, with the exception of the *Epistula Apostolorum* it was only the gnostics who dealt with both the "already" and the "not yet" aspects of this eschatological rest in their reflection on the Sabbath. Most writers concentrated on the future world Sabbath of the age to come, a concept connected with Genesis 2:2–3 in Jewish thought, and saw the literal Mosaic Sabbath as a type of this. In the Fathers this

> eschatological rest, either in the millennial kingdom or in eternity, is understood not so much as rest opposed to work, but as rest opposed to the burdensomeness and struggle of this world, or the enjoyment of the fruits of the work of salvation, or the attainment of the goal of the vision of God, free from the burden of sin and the flesh, or participation in God's own Sabbath rest.[137]

For Augustine the eternal Sabbath was where "we shall be still and see, we shall see and we shall love; we shall love and we shall praise" (*De Civ. Dei.* 22:30). All of these notions are in line with the eschatological rest of Genesis 2 and Hebrews 4 and when the fourth commandment is heard with them in mind, it speaks to the believer of the richness of that which God has in store for him or her through Christ. Calvin maintains this eschatological perspective when he writes, "It would seem, therefore, that the Lord through the seventh day sketched for his people the coming perfection of his Sabbath in the last day, to make them aspire to this perfection by unceasing meditation upon the sabbath throughout life" (*Institutes* 2:8:30).

The concept of eschatological rest, of course, merges into that of salvation rest, particularly when its "already" aspect is in focus. Because of Christ's fulfillment of the Sabbath, the old categories are reinterpreted in terms of salvation. This "includes the good news of deliverance, liberation and forgiveness brought by the mighty works and preaching of Jesus (Luke 4), release from the burden of the law (Matt. 11), the accomplishment of eschatological salvation with its giving of life (John 5), the fulfillment of the divine rest of Genesis 2:2–3, which was intended for humanity to share (John 5 and Heb. 3, 4), and that salvation rest as a present heavenly reality entered by believing and ceasing from one's own works (Heb. 3, 4). In short the physical rest of the Old Testament Sabbath has become the salvation rest of the true Sabbath."[138] When set in the perspective of salvation the fourth commandment again receives a christological focus and speaks of the true spiritual rest Christ has already brought, which the believer can now enjoy. The notion that in Christ the true Sabbath rest had become present does not come into its own in later Christian thought until the fourth century. Then we find Epiphanius writing, "Therefore that sabbath prescribed by the law has retained its validity until his arrival; but after it has been abolished, he (God) has given (us) the great sabbath, which is the Lord himself; he is our rest and our sabbath observance" (*Haer.* 8:6:8). Similarly Gregory the Great can state, "We spiritually understand and we construe in a spiritual sense what we find written about the sabbath, for sabbath means rest. But as our true sabbath we have our redeemer and Lord Jesus Christ" (*Ep.* 13:1). Augustine's "spiritual sabbath" can be seen as a further development of the concept of salvation rest, emphasizing its subjective application. In this way the salvation rest accomplished by Christ is that rest in God without which the human heart remains restless. A person's heart needs to find such a Sabbath in which "delighting in God, he finds a true, sure, eternal rest, which he sought in other things but did not find" (*Ep.* 55:18).

The Sabbath can be regarded in these new ways, but is there not some response the believer should make? Is the actual observance of the Sabbath also reinterpreted? It has already been shown that this is exactly the point the writer to the Hebrews addresses in 4:10. The Sabbath observance (σαββατισμός) in which the New Testament people of God are to participate is to enter God's rest by faith and thereby cease from their own works. Since "faith" in Hebrews refers not just to an initial commitment but is an attitude which requires perseverance and endurance (cf. 6:11, 12; 10:36ff.; 11), this cessation from dead works is not mere inactivity but an ongoing process of dying to self and mortification of sinful deeds. Calvin, in particular, saw in this the nature of true Sabbath observance and in his commentary on Hebrews 4:10 wrote, "What does ceasing from our works mean but the mortification of the flesh, when a man renounces himself in order to live to God?"[139] Many before him had, however, also taken up the insight of Hebrews in regard to the new Sabbath observance. In the second century this is found in the Valentinian

Ptolemaeus: "He wishes us to be idle with reference to evil actions" (cf. Epiphanius, *Pan.* 33:3:5:12); and Clement adopts a similar interpretation involving the renunciation of evils. In the same way both Tertullian (*Adv. Jud.* 4) and Pseudo-Athanasius (*De sabbatis et circumcisione* 4) hold that the fourth commandment requires cessation not from work but from sin. At the time of the Reformation this interpretation was considered to provide a major part of the continued relevance of the Sabbath commandment. The Heidelberg Catechism, for which Ursinus was primarily responsible, also expresses the beliefs of Luther and Calvin when it asserts that what God requires in the fourth commandment is "that I cease from my evil works all the days of my life, allow the Lord to work in me through his Spirit, and thus begin in this life the eternal sabbath" (Lord's Day 38).

This quotation leads into the fourth way in which the Sabbath commandment can be seen as having continuing force, for clearly sanctification cannot be confined to one day of the week but involves "all the days of my life." This intensification of the Sabbath commandment so that it can apply to every day and the whole of life is a clear strand in its application. It has roots in three places in the New Testament. It is a necessary development of the concept of cessation from evil works found in Hebrews 4:10; it takes up Paul's view about treating all days alike in Romans 14; and it is an extension of the sort of interpretation of Old Testament laws found in the Sermon on the Mount to the Old Testament Sabbath law. Justin gives this interpretation in *Dial.* 12:3:

> The new law requires you to keep perpetual sabbath, and you, because you are idle for one day, suppose you are pious . . . The Lord our God does not take pleasure in such observances; if there is any perjured person or a thief among you, let him cease to be so; if any adulterer, let him repent; then he has kept the sweet and true sabbath of God.

He is followed in this by Irenaeus (*Epideixis* 96), Tertullian (*Adv. Jud.* 4), Clement (*Str.* 7:7), Origen (*In Num. Hom.* 23:4) and Augustine (*Serm.* 8:3; 33:3; *Spirit. et lit.* 1:15:27).[140] On this interpretation believers obey the fourth commandment by devoting all their time to God. Rordorf senses well the internalization and intensification of the commandment in accord with the method of the Sermon on the Mount, and so paraphrases this Christian exposition of the force of the Sabbath law as follows: "You have heard that it was said to them of old time, 'Keep holy the sabbath day'; but I say unto you: only he keeps the sabbath who, in the sight of God, keeps holy all the days of his life."[141] Thus whereas the law declared one day out of seven to be holy to the Lord, Christ sanctifies all seven days to Himself.

This discussion has attempted to respect the discontinuity and the continuity involved in the fulfillment of the Sabbath in Christ. The temporary and passing nature of the Mosaic Sabbath with its literal rest has been emphasized and yet its continuing significance when reinterpreted in the light of its fulfillment has also been suggested. The way in which Christ transforms the Sabbath law guards against a legalism about a particular day, on the one hand, and a lack of concern about relating one's time to God on the other.

Similarities and Differences Between Sabbath and Lord's Day

So far the discussion of both the continuity and discontinuity implied in God's new relation in Christ has been in regard to the Sabbath commandment. It is clear, however, that more needs to be said and that even if it is agreed that Sunday is the new Christian day for worship and that the Sabbath commandment is not to be applied to it, there remains an analogy between the two institutions of the Old Testament Sabbath and the New Testament Lord's Day. As with other analogies between Old Testament and New Testament institutions, such as circumcision and baptism, passover and Lord's Supper, precision is needed in defining the exact nature of the analogy and indicating what are the similarities and what are the differences.

Perhaps the most obvious similarity is that both Sabbath and Lord's Day recur weekly and involve recognition of some sort of distinctiveness for one day in seven. This is not to say that the Old Testament principle was one day in seven. Obedience to the Mosaic Law required specifically that the seventh day be observed. Nor is it to say that for the Christian church the whole of the first day of the week is to be observed in a distinctive way. But once these important qualifications are clear, there is still an analogy between Sabbath and Sunday on the basis of one day in seven. It is true that the reasons why *weekly* worship became the norm in Christian circles can be given in largely practical terms and that once daily corporate worship became impracticable, the weekly interval would suggest itself to Jewish Christians as the next most appropriate division of time. Gentiles, however, would not necessarily have found the Sabbatical division of time either natural or convenient and need not have adopted it, and yet they did. Part of the Christian church's inheritance from Judaism was the concept that in the weekly cycle God had stamped a seven day pattern on history. Acts 20:7—"the first day of the week" (*ἡ μία τῶν σαββάτων*)—and 1 Corinthians 16:2—"the first day of the week" (*ἡ μία σαββάτου*)—reflect the terminology of *Gentile* Christian churches for Sunday as the first day in the sequence determined by the Sabbath.

Part of the significance of both Sabbath and Lord's Day lies in their celebration of redemption. The Sabbath acted as a memorial of God's redemption of His people from Israel (cf. Deut. 5:15) and the Lord's Day, in its connection with the Resurrection, celebrates the climactic aspect of God's redemptive activity in Christ. Although the link is not made or implied in the canonical documents, it was clearly only a short theological step to point out that just as the Sabbath commemorated creation (Exod. 20:11), so the first day of the week, through its association with the Resurrection, could be seen as a memorial of the new creation. Certainly Paul in 1 Corinthians 15 considers Christ's resurrection to be both the inauguration and the first fruits of the new creation, and it is this conception that informed the *Epistle of Barnabas* 15:9 and other early Christian literature in their use of "the eighth day" as a designation for Sunday, for "the eighth day" was the day of the new world, which followed this world's week.

A further connection between Sabbath and Lord's Day is that what is celebrated on the latter, that is, the Resurrection, is a fulfillment of the concept of rest embodied in the former. In particular, John 5 indicates that cessation from their work of salvation on the part of God and Jesus begins with the cross and the Resurrection.[142] Also, the one who is worshiped on the Lord's Day is the bringer of the true Sabbath rest of salvation to which the Old Testament Sabbath pointed (cf. John 5; Heb. 3–4).

Again, with regard to the concept of rest, it can be said that both Sabbath and Lord's Day prefigure the future rest of the consummation. Just as the Sabbath pointed to eschatological rest, so the Resurrection, as foundational to the Lord's Day, was seen as a foretaste and guarantee of the future rest of the consummation. But again there is a decisive qualification. Both days prefigure eschatological rest but *in two different ways*. It is not as if the fulfillment that has taken place in Christ simply leaves the concept of rest intact. Rather the fulfillment brings with it a reinterpretation of categories. In the Old Testament the literal physical rest of the Sabbath pointed to future rest; but since Christ has brought fulfillment in terms of salvation rest, it is the present enjoyment of *this* rest that acts as the foretaste of the consummation rest which is to come. In other words, it is the celebration on the Lord's Day of the rest we already have through Christ's resurrection that now anticipates and guarantees the rest that is yet to be.

Sabbath and Sunday are also linked through the notion of worship. Though cultic worship was not a primary feature in the institution of the Mosaic Sabbath, it did become an emphasis in the later development of the Sabbath, particularly in the period of the rise of the synagogue. A number of elements in early Christian worship were of course influenced by synagogue worship, and since the latter found its focus in Sabbath worship, it is natural to see some parallels between Jewish synagogue worship on the Sabbath and

Christian worship on the Lord's Day. The continuity here comes through this development in the period of the exile and then in the intertestamental period rather than from explicit Old Testament data about the centrality of Sabbath worship. Eusebius made use of an inconsistent adaptation of this notion of continuity through worship to argue for a Sabbath transference view whereby the worship of Christians on Sunday was seen as analogous to the activity of the priests in worship on the Sabbath.[143] Because in the early church worship on the Lord's Day was seen in terms of festal rejoicing, the Lord's Day soon came to be compared with the Sabbath in that both could be considered festivals. No implications were drawn from this, however, to the effect that the Lord's Day, like Old Testament festivals, was to be treated as a day of rest.[144]

Finally, there is a striking similarity between Sabbath and Sunday in their relation to the concept of lordship. The Old Testament Sabbath, as we have seen, was "to the Lord." It was the day Israel's Lord claimed specifically as His own and the day on which His people's allegiance to their Lord was acted out. It can quite justifiably be called the Old Testament Lord's Day. In the New Testament the title *κυριακὴ ἡμέρα* distinguished the first day of the week as the new Lord's Day, the day on which by their worship the new people of God demonstrated their allegiance to Christ's lordship established by the Resurrection. Both days then point to God's lordship over time and history but again this was exhibited in two different ways. On the Sabbath Lordship was acknowledged by ceasing from work for the whole day, while on the first day of the week it was proclaimed by meeting for worship during part of the day.

The differences between Sabbath and Sunday have already come to the fore, and been explicated, particularly in our evaluation of Sabbath-transference theology; so they can simply be enumerated at this stage of the discussion. The Mosaic commandment with reference to the Sabbath is not applicable to the first day of the week, although, reinterpreted in the light of Christ, it is applicable to every day of the week. Whereas observance of the Sabbath involved literal physical rest, this is not the purpose of the Christian observance of the first day of the week. The primary focus of the Sabbath was abstention from work, but observance of the Lord's Day centers in worship of the risen Lord. The Old Testament Sabbath was the seventh day of the week; the New Testament Lord's Day is the first day. Although the Sabbath was considered a special holy day for the whole day, there is no evidence that the Lord's Day was regarded in this way; it was simply the appropriate day on which worship was to take place.

The position taken in this essay in regard to the relation between Sabbath and Sunday can now be seen to be rather different from various other positions which are currently advocated. It differs from those Christian groups, such as the Seventh-Day Adventists or Seventh-Day Baptists, who observe Saturday as their day of rest and worship. The most recent scholarly presentation from this perspective is S. Bacchiocchi's important work, *From Sabbath to Sunday*, which in particular concentrates on a historical reconstruction of the origins of Sunday in order to demonstrate "that Sunday observance does not rest on a foundation of biblical theology and/or of apostolic authority, but on later contributory factors. . . ."[145] These, he argues, were a combination of Jewish, pagan and Christian factors. In the midst of negative relationships between Jewish and Christian communities in Rome at the beginning of the second century A.D., a new day of worship emerged from the need for radical Christian separation from Judaism. Paganism contributed the possibility of adopting the day of the Sun and Christians were then able to find theological justifications for this shift of day.[146]

Those who celebrate Saturday are clearly the most consistent Sabbatarians but fail to do justice to the newness of the eschatological situation brought about by God's actions in Christ, and therefore to the discontinuity between the Old and New Covenants, and to the attitude of the New Testament writers, whom we have examined above, to the Mosaic Law. In addition, Bacchiocchi's particular treatment of the New Testament data and his reconstruction of the evidence of the postapostolic period fail to convince at too many crucial points.[147]

Equally clearly the position of this essay differs decisively from those who view Sunday as the Christian Sabbath. This is the traditional Sabbatarian position, espoused now particularly by such groups as the Lord's Day Observance Society and the Lord's Day Alliance[148] and by R. T. Beckwith and W. Stott in *This Is The Day*.[149] It differs also from the somewhat modified Sabbath-transference view espoused by the Orthodox and Roman Catholic branches of the church, in which the most important claim made for Sunday is that it is a feast day and thus a day of rest for worship.[150] An extensive critique of Sabbath-transference theology in general has already been supplied, and it has been indicated that in a variety of ways it too fails to do justice to the biblical evidence, the movement of redemptive history, and the history of the postapostolic church.

Barth's theology of Sunday centers around the notion of a "holy day" that was established at creation, celebrated by Jews on the Sabbath, and observed by New Testament Christianity on the first day of the week, because it recognized in the Resurrection the fulfillment of the covenant between God and humanity established at creation. "In the resurrection of Jesus it saw and understood that the seventh day of creation which is to be kept holy as the

'Lord's Day'—as the day of God's resting and also of the resting in Him commanded to man—is not only the last but above all the first day of man, and is therefore to be kept as his holy day."[151] Barth offers some interesting theologizing and practical advice on the basis of this notion of a "holy day" for humanity at creation and in the New Testament, but unfortunately supplies no exegetical or historical evidence in support of his presupposition.

P. K. Jewett's book, *The Lord's Day*[152] attempts to provide a clearer theological justification of Sunday as the completion of the fourth commandment in terms of a dialectic of fulfillment in hope. He rejects the position of Sabbatarians for giving only a "yes" to the fourth commandment and rejects that of the Reformers for giving only a "no." To his credit he works with the continuities and discontinuities involved in the progress of the history of salvation, yet in terms of the concept of rest does not do justice to the nature of the discontinuity produced by fulfillment in Christ. He concludes that since the rest in Christ is the earnest of a future hope, the Christian church, like God's people of old, should have its literal day of rest as a type and sign of the final rest.[153] Jewett's exegesis of New Testament passages to provide support for his mediating position is not convincing and he provides no historical explanation as to how the New Testament church and the postapostolic church failed to see the necessity of the sort of continuity in terms of literal rest that he advocates for the Lord's Day.[154]

On the surface it would appear that the conclusions reached in this volume have most in common with W. Rordorf's work, *Sunday*.[155] Yet while there is agreement with his emphasis on discontinuity whereby Sunday is to be seen in terms of worship and not rest, this volume arrives at such a conclusion in very different ways, and, in providing an overall biblical and theological framework, allows for a more positive assessment of the relation of the two days, Sabbath and Lord's Day, in the progress of the history of salvation. The contributors to this volume have been more positive in their treatment of historical material both in the Old Testament and the New Testament than Rordorf, and have made a greater attempt to deal with material in its canonical context and not simply on the basis of historical reconstruction. This has meant, for example, a very different view from Rordorf's about Jesus' attitude to the Sabbath, for on his reconstruction of the gospel material Jesus simply rejected the Sabbath and rescinded the fourth commandment.[156] The contributors to this volume also differ radically from Rordorf as to why Sunday worship might be considered normative, since for Rordorf everything hangs on the close connection he posits between Sunday observance and the Lord's Supper, with Sunday worship originating in the risen Lord's sharing of the Easter meal with His disciples,[157] and yet he fails to sustain his case for such a reconstruction.[158] The approach of this volume then turns out to be quite different from that of Rordorf.

LORD'S DAY, REST, AND WORSHIP

Whatever the evidence of the New Testament and of the early church, in many parts of the world Sunday, for the Christian church, has been considered a day of rest. The desire to have rest from work on Sunday in order to be able to worship as conveniently and as much as possible seems to have been a natural development in the life of the church in societies that were amenable to this arrangement. It cannot be denied that societies that have adopted the arrangement of making Sunday a rest day for their members have benefited from this in a variety of ways. It is not our intention to challenge the value of the existing institution of Sunday as still in some form a weekly recreation and rest day or to enter the debate about whether and how Christians should seek to have their preferences legislated for others in a pluralistic society. It is our intention, however, to challenge the view that gives biblical status to this Sunday tradition as binding for the individual or the church, and to challenge the theology that has been developed to give this support.

It should not be thought that the position that has been taken in regard to the continuity and discontinuity between Sabbath and Sunday leads to a "gnostic" view of humanity because it appears to stress a realized eschatology, and to emphasize the "spiritual" as over against the physical on the basis of the fulfillment and reinterpretation of Old Testament commands and motifs by Christ. Though there is no evading the fact that the New Testament does reinterpret the category of literal Sabbath rest and this must be given priority in hermeneutical considerations, when this evidence is set in the context of the canon God's concern for the whole person, including his or her physical well-being and therefore bodily rest, is quite clear. The commands to Israel about the Sabbath, though no longer binding, remain instructive about God's concern for His people's physical rest. If God commanded His people to rest every seven days back in the Old Testament and it was considered valuable, is it not likely that such regular rest will be just as valuable today? A passage such as Deuteronomy 5:14 indicates that the Sabbath had a profound social and humanitarian aspect to it and was instituted with those in view who were particularly burdened with work and who were subject to the command of others. It functioned therefore as a check against exploitation and to show that both in their standing before God and in their right to rest all the members of the community were equal. This perspective needs to be part of a Christian view of work and recreation. Indeed it has been pointed out that one of the differences between a Marxist and a biblical anthropology is represented by the Old Testament Sabbath. Whereas Marxism considers that the essence of a person is in his or her work, which transforms nature, the Old Testament relativizes its own command to work by the Sabbath, which taught Israel that work could occupy six sevenths of its waking life but not the whole of it. It was not humanity's chief end. Indeed in the New Testament Jesus recognizes His disciples' need for physical rest (cf. Mark 6:31) as well as for salvation rest (cf. Matt. 11:28). In Paul one of the aspects of salvation that still awaits realization is that which affects the physical body. The fulfillment that Christ has brought cannot mean therefore that the body is now beyond the need for physical rest. This need for physical rest and recreation is worth underlining particularly when many people are succumbing to the neurosis of work addiction or "workaholism," as some are calling it by analogy with alcoholism.[159] Men and women are insisting that it is really only their work that is fulfilling and gradually it absorbs them to such an extent that they feel guilty about doing anything else. This is a particular danger for those whose work is their vocation and for Christians who rationalize their addiction as "serving God."

How do the results of our study tie in to this? God's concern for the whole person and for all His creatures being able to have regular rest from their work surely instructs us that although the literal Sabbath day of rest has been abrogated and has not been transferred to Sunday, we should share this concern for regular periods of rest both for ourselves and for others in our society.[160] From this perspective this essay is not advocating that Christians should not rest on Sunday. Rather its position suggests that they should take regular rest, that this rest can be any day or extended part of a day, including Sunday, but that there is no biblical or compelling theological reason why it has to be Sunday.

No longer do most people, however, work six days a week. In the West there is generally a five-day working week with attempts now being made to establish a four-day week, and there is the additional factor in many parts of enforced unemployment because of economic recession. The trouble is not that there is no respite from having to work, but what to do with the leisure time and how to prevent it from simply being filled up with the hectic round of activities that will show that leisure itself is caught on the treadmill of working and consuming.[161] In the midst of the mad rush of work and play, those who through Christ already enjoy a foretaste of the Sabbath rest to come should be able to go about both their work and their play with an inner freedom that produces a more leisurely style. The quality of the church's worship has much to do with this. The amount of time free from regular work provides a great opportunity for the churches not only to harness their members' time for the work of Christ's kingdom but also to ensure that, whatever other activities they schedule for Sunday, worship is the priority for the Lord's Day. This surely has to be more than a rushed one hour performance. Rather structures have to be provided that allow the gathered community of believers to participate in corporate and meaningful worship of its Lord. Cultic worship is the focus of the church's existence, for worship is the church's recognition of its Lord and marks it out as His particular sphere of lordship. If worship is the church's heartbeat in this way, and Sunday is the appropriate day for worship, then rather than giving attention to what should or should not be done during the rest of the day, there can be concentration on making as sure as possible that Sunday worship has the vitality and significance it should have. As believers celebrate the salvation rest achieved for them through Christ's resurrection, they can give thanks that it is not their own achievements or productivity that gives them value in God's eyes. By the Resurrection they have been liberated and their failures, feeble undertakings and unfinished work need not bring them into bondage. If the Lord's Day involves joyful celebration of the rest Christ provides, if it involves mutual exhortation to enter into and live out that rest, then believers will not need to worship their work or work at their play, but there will be an inner liberation, a genuine leisure in the way in which they go about both the work and the play of the week to the glory of God.[162] Since the Resurrection proclaimed Christ as Lord not only over the church but also over history and the cosmos, appropriate celebration of that event in Sunday worship will not allow the concerns of the rest of the week to be forgotten but will express the integral connection between worship of the Lord and all areas of Christ's lordship, including every part of the believer's life. In this way also in the conflict of sovereignties that will continue in this world until the eschatological day of the Lord to which it points, the Lord's Day may be seen as the day from which the Lord reigns over the rest of the week. When the significance of the Lord's Day is grasped, every day is transformed, so that in fact it can be said of each day, "This is the day which the LORD has made; let us rejoice and be glad in it" (Ps. 118:24).

NOTES

[1]Pp. 53–54

[2]For a helpful interaction with some of this discussion, cf. B. Birch and L. Rasmussen, *Bible and Ethics in the Christian Life* (Minneapolis: Augsburg, 1976).

[3]In doing so, I am indebted to interaction with each of the contributors at various stages of this study project.

[4]Cf. pp. 313, 315, 323–24 above.

[5]Cf. R. Bauckham's mention of this argument in 17th and 18th century writers, pp. 323–24, note 78 above. For a more recent example, cf. F. N. Lee, *The Covenantal Sabbath* (London: LDOS, n.d.), p. 33.

[6]Cf., for example, K. Barth, *Church Dogmatics*, III/4 (Edinburgh: T. & T. Clark, 1961), pp. 52–53, 57; also R. T. Beckwith and W. Stott, *This is the Day* (London: Marshall, Morgan and Scott, 1978), p. 40.

[7]For this sort of argument cf. Beckwith and Stott, *This is the Day*, pp. 6–7.

[8]Cf. J. Murray, *Principles of Conduct* (Grand Rapids: Eerdmans, 1957), p. 32: "There can be little doubt that in Gen. 2:3 there is *at least an allusion* to the blessing of the seventh day in man's week and when we compare it more closely with Exod. 20:11, there is *strong presumption in favour* of the view that it refers specifically and directly to the sabbath instituted for man" (emphasis supplied).

[9]*Genesis 1–11* (Neukirchener-Vluyn: Neukirchen Verlag, 1974), p. 237: "Indeed one cannot find here an institution, and not even a preparation for the Sabbath, but rather the later foundation of the Sabbath is reflected in these sentences." Cf. also W. Zimmerli, *Old Testament Theology in Outline*, (Atlanta: John Knox Press, 1978), pp. 34, 125.

[10]Despite J. Murray, *Principles of Conduct*, pp. 30–35; R. T. Beckwith and W. Stott, *This is the Day*, pp. 2–3; G. H. Waterman, "Sabbath," *Zondervan Pictorial Bible Encyclopedia*, ed. M. C. Tenney (Grand Rapids: Zondervan, 1975), 5:183, who claims, "The word 'sabbath' is not employed, but it is certain that the author meant to assert that God blessed and hallowed the seventh day as the sabbath."

[11]In its discussion of Old Testament texts this essay focuses on their present form and canonical context rather than on their tradition history.

[12]"The Sabbath in the Old Testament," p. 16 note 43.

[13]Cf. also R. Frankena, "Einige Bemerkungen zum Gebrauch des Adverbs 'al-kēn im Hebräischen," *Studia Biblica et Semitica* (Wageningen, 1966), pp. 94–99.

[14]For a discussion of some of these features cf. B. O. Long, *The Problem of Etiological Narrative in the Old Testament* (*BZAW* 108; Berlin: de Gruyter, 1968), pp. 6, 7, 87, who, however, deals primarily with their function in narrative passages. B. Childs, *The Book of Exodus* (Philadelphia: Fortress, 1974), p. 415 also recognizes the presence of an etiology here, though his conclusion, which suggests the writer saw the Sabbath as being an obligation from the time of the creation onwards, is by no means a necessary one.

[15]E.g., F. N. Lee, *The Covenantal Sabbath*, p. 195; G. H. Waterman, "Sabbath," p. 183; Beckwith and Stott, *This is the Day*, p. 11.

[16]Cf. D. A. Carson's detailed refutation of "creation ordinance" claims for this verse, chapter 4, above; also P. Jewett, *The Lord's Day* (Grand Rapids: Eerdmans, 1971), p. 38.

[17]Cf. also the remarks of C. R. Rowland, chapter 3, above.

[18]Cf. also A. Phillips, *Ancient Israel's Criminal Law* (Oxford: B. Blackwell, 1970), p. 68.

[19]Cf. M. G. Kline, *The Structure of Biblical Authority* (Grand Rapids: Eerdmans, 1972), pp. 94ff.

[20]Cf. R. Banks, *Jesus and the Law in the Synoptic Tradition* (Cambridge: University Press, 1976), esp. pp. 67–81.

[21]Seventh Day Adventist writers are not slow to point this out: e.g., S. Bacchiocchi, *From Sabbath To Sunday* (Rome: Pontifical Gregorian University Press, 1977), p. 312.

[22]Cf. M. G. Kline, *Treaty of the Great King* (Grand Rapids: Eerdmans, 1963), pp. 13–26, on the treaty form of the Decalogue.

[23]Ibid., p. 17.

[24]Despite G. Wenham, "Law and the Legal System in the Old Testament," *Law, Morality and the Bible*, ed. B. Kaye and G. Wenham (Downers Grove: InterVarsity, 1978), pp. 27–28.

[25]When quoted in Ephesians 6:3 it is interpreted in a more general fashion by the omission of the clause, "which the Lord your God gives you," so that it can now be understood as the earth rather than the land of Canaan.

[26]Since it can be said that ultimately everything can be related to the relationship with God, if anything, the great command of Deuteronomy 6:4ff. would have a greater claim to be a summary of the whole law.

[27]Cf. also Banks, *Jesus and the Law*, p. 42: "In fact, apart from two exceptions, it confines itself

to a few basic negations which act as signposts on the borders of a large area of life to which he who belongs to Yahweh must give heed."

[28]Cf. also F. E. Vokes, "The Ten Commandments in the NT and in First Century Judaism," *Studia Evangelica* 5 (Berlin: Akademie-Verlag, 1968), p. 151: "It seems significant that the Decalogue by itself is not picked out as a whole as the summary or crown of the moral law."

[29]Cf. G. F. Moore, *Judaism in the Age of the Tannaim* (Cambridge: University Press, 1927), 1:291; also R. Grant, "The Decalogue in Early Christianity," *HTR* 40 (1947): 2; Vokes, "The Ten Commandments," p. 148.

[30]It is because obedience to Yahweh over certain broad areas of life is of concern rather than specific cases that the apodictic rather than casuistic form is used in the Decalogue.

[31]Childs, *Exodus*, p. 398; cf. also A. Phillips' thesis in *Ancient Israel's Criminal Law* that in charting the outer boundaries of the community the Decalogue served as Israel's criminal law.

[32]Cf. also Banks, *Jesus and the Law*, p. 41.

[33]Ibid., p. 40.

[34]For a fuller discussion, see chapters 2 and 3 above.

[35]For a convenient summary of the attitudes to Torah cf. R. Banks, *Jesus and the Law*, 13–85 on "Law in the Old Testament, Inter-Testamentary and Later Jewish Literature," For the place of the Torah in the overall patterns of religion in Palestinian Judaism, cf. E. P. Sanders, *Paul and Palestinian Judaism* (London: SCM, 1977), pp. 33–428.

[36]Cf. H. H. P. Dressler, chapter 2 above.

[37]Cf. the emphasis on the Sabbath in such places as Judith 8:6; 1 Macc. 1:39; 2:41; 10:34; 2 Macc. 5:25ff.; 6:6ff.; 12:38; 15:1ff.

[38]Cf. Rowland, chapter 3, above, pp. 46–47, note 10.

[39]Ibid.

[40]Cf. Banks, *Jesus and the Law*, p. 59, n. 1.

[41]Again, because of the limitations imposed by a summary essay such as this, discussion of the gospel passages will focus primarily on their final form rather than on their traditio-history and the questions of authenticity and historicity involved. For more detailed discussion cf. chapters 4 and 5, above, by D. A. Carson and M. M. B. Turner respectively.

[42]Chapter 4.

[43]Ibid., pp. 80–81, note 145.

[44]Cf. also Banks, *Jesus and the Law*, p. 238.

[45]Carson, chapter 4, p. 58.

[46]Cf. Irenaeus, *Adv. Haer.* 4:8:2; Tertullian, *Adv. Marc.* 4:12; also Bauckham, chapter 9, above.

[47]This saying may well be secondary: cf. Mark's linking formula καὶ ἔλεγεν αὐτοῖς. Cf. also the cautious agreement of I. H. Marshall, *Commentary on Luke* (Grand Rapids: Eerdmans, 1978), p. 230. "If there has been an addition to the story it is more likely to be found here." This general saying about the Sabbath being subordinate to the needs of humanity Mark uses to summarize verses 25, 26 and lead into the more radical statement of verse 28.

[48]*Jesus and the Law*, pp. 122–23.

[49]Despite W. Rordorf, *Sunday* (London: SCM, 1968), p. 70, who claims, "The sabbath commandment was not merely pushed into the background by the healing activity of Jesus: it was simply annulled."

[50]Cf. for example, E. Lohse, TDNT 7:29.

[51]Cf. Carson, chapter 4, p. 74 and note 107.

[52]Cf. Rordorf, *Sunday*, p. 68.

[53]Cf. Banks, *Jesus and the Law*, pp. 102–3.

[54]Cf. SBK 2:626, 953.

[55]Cf. also D. Hill, *The Gospel of Matthew* (London: Oliphants, 1972), p. 321; Banks, *Jesus and the Law*, p. 120.

[56]Cf. A. T. Lincoln, chapter 7, above, pp. 213–14.

[57]Pace J. Bligh, *Galatians* (London: St. Paul, 1979), p. 323, who holds that Paul fails to make

explicit mention of the Sabbath, because in the church of Antioch both Jews and Gentiles had been meeting for the liturgy on the Sabbath, and Paul did not wish to upset this custom; Bacchiocchi, *From Sabbath to Sunday*, pp. 366–67 who holds that the apostle is not against the observance by Gentiles of the festivals mentioned, only against their observance for the wrong reasons.

[58]Cf. Turner, chapter 5, above.

[59]Cf., for example, P. Minear, *The Obedience of Faith* (London: SCM, 1971); K. Donfried, "False Presuppositions in the Study of Romans," *CBQ* 36 (1974): 332–55; W. S. Campbell, "Why did Paul write Romans?" *ExpT* 85 (1974): 264–69.

[60]*Contra* J. Murray, *The Epistle to the Romans* (Grand Rapids: Eerdmans, 1965), 2:177–78, 257–59, who, for theological reasons of the Sabbath being a binding creation ordinance and part of the Decalogue, excludes the Sabbath from these days and holds that they were other "holy days of the ceremonial economy;" and R. Dederen, "On Esteeming One Day Better Than Another," *AUSS* 9 (1971): 16–35, who, also on theological grounds of the Sabbath being part of the Decalogue and of Christ keeping the Sabbath, excludes the fourth commandment Sabbath.

[61]But cf. D. de Lacey, chapter 6, above, for another possible interpretation.

[62]*Colossians and Philemon* (Philadelphia: Fortress, 1971), p. 116; cf. also R. P. Martin, *Colossians and Philemon* (London: Oliphants, 1974), p. 91.

[63]Cf. also C. F. D. Moule, *The Epistles of Paul the Apostle to the Colossians and to Philemon* (Cambridge: University Press, 1957); Lohse, "*Sabbaton*," p. 117; Martin, *Colossians*, pp. 91–92.

[64]Contrast the speculation of Beckwith and Stott, *This is the Day*, pp. 27–29.

[65]Considerations of space forbid a more complete survey which would need to include treatment of Mark, John and James.

[66]For a much more detailed discussion of Paul and the law cf. de Lacey, chapter 6, above.

[67]For a different interpretation of Romans 7 cf. de Lacey, ibid.

[68]Cf. Vokes, "The Ten Commandments," pp. 152–53; Grant, "The Decalogue," pp. 6–7.

[69]Cf. the discussion of this verse in de Lacey, chapter 6, pp. pppff.

[70]Cf. D. R. Catchpole, "The Synoptic Divorce Material as a Traditio-historical Problem," *BJRL* 57 (1974): 93ff.

[71]Cf. Vokes, "The Ten Commandments," p. 152.

[72]V. P. Furnish, *The Love Command in the New Testament* (Nashville: Abingdon, 1972), p. 74 can write, "This evangelist regards the love command as the hermeneutical key to the law, the essence of 'the law and the prophets,' and that which most distinguishes Jesus' teaching from the Pharisaic tradition."

[73]Cf. also Banks, *Jesus and the Law*, p. 163.

[74]Cf. for example, J. P. Meier, *Law and History in Matthew's Gospel* (Rome: Biblical Institute Press, 1976), pp. 25–40.

[75]Cf. for example, J. D. Kingsbury, *Matthew: Structure, Christology, Kingdom* (Philadelphia: Fortress, 1975), pp. 25–39.

[76]For a discussion of the questions of authenticity and Matthean redaction involved in this passage cf. Banks, *Jesus and the Law*, pp. 182–226 and more recently Meier, *Law and History*, pp. 41–161.

[77]Banks, *Jesus and the Law*, pp. 208ff.; cf. also Carson, chapter 4, above; Meier, *Law and History*, pp. 65–89, 165.

[78]*Jesus and the Law*, p. 210.

[79]It is probably best to see v. 18*bc* as a stringent Jewish-Christian formulation with the clause, "until heaven and earth pass away" retaining its apocalyptic connotations and having the force of "never": cf. G. Barth, "Matthew's Understanding of the Law," *Tradition and Interpretation in Matthew* (London: SCM, 1963), p. 65; Meier, *Law and History*, pp. 58–61; against Banks, *Jesus and the Law*, p. 215. If this part of the verse is insisted on to the neglect of the other, it must be remembered that the permanent validity includes every single ceremonial law. There is no evading the force of "not an iota, not a dot." However, it is best to see v. 18*d* as Matthew's

redactional modification, reinterpreting the apocalyptic time reference by his view of what God has already done in Christ, cf. Meier, *Law and History*, pp. 61–65.

[80]Cf. also Banks, *Jesus and the Law*, pp. 217–18; Carson, chapter 4, above; Meier, *Law and History*, pp. 61ff.

[81]Cf. Meier, *Law and History*, p. 104.

[82]Banks, *Jesus and the Law*, pp. 221ff. opts for an exclusive reference to Jesus' teachings. However, ἐντολή (commandment) in Matthew refers to Old Testament commandments, as Banks himself admits, and the appeal to the use of ἀνομία, which is not mentioned in this verse, as occurring more frequently with reference to Jesus' commands than to those of the Old Testament is not convincing. Rather this interpretation introduces a false dichotomy, for in the three references (7:23; 13:41; 24:11–13), which Banks adduces in support, Jesus' commands, as opposed to those of the Old Testament, are not clearly or explicitly in view and the most appropriate reference is to the more general will of God (cf. 7:21–"the will of my Father who is in heaven"). The context of verse 19 calls for "these" to be a general reference, embracing both the explicit mention of the law which precedes and the teaching of Jesus, which is required by the notions of "fulfillment" (v. 17) and "accomplishment" (v. 18), which also precede, by the "kingdom of heaven" context of verse 19 and by the actual teachings of Jesus that these verses preface.

[83]Cf. the fuller discussion in Meier, *Law and History*, pp. 125–61.

[84]Cf. Banks, *Jesus and the Law*, pp. 242–43; also Meier, *Law and History*, p. 168, "The rule of life for the Christian is thus an 'umbrella concept.' 'All things whatsoever I commanded you'—be that *secundum*, *praeter*, or *contra* the Mosaic law."

[85]See chapter 5, above, for a fuller treatment of the law in Luke-Acts.

[86]Cf. also Banks, *Jesus and the Law*, p. 218; Marshall, *Commentary*, p. 630.

[87]*Jesus and the Law*, p. 159.

[88]Chapter 5, p. 122

[89]Cf. A. T. Lincoln, chapter 7.

[90]Cf. F. C. Grant, "The Decalogue," pp. 8–9.

[91]Cf. the fuller discussion of some of these weaknesses in E. Osborn, *Ethical Patterns in Early Christian Thought* (Cambridge: University Press, 1976), pp. 183–91.

[92]A. Nygren, *Commentary on Romans* (Philadelphia: Muhlenberg Press, 1967), pp. 124–25.

[93]Cf. also R. Nixon, "The Universality of the Concept of Law," *Law, Morality and the Bible*, ed. B. Kaye and G. Wenham (Downers Grove: InterVarsity, 1978), pp. 118–20; against Grant, "The Decalogue," p. 16; C. H. Dodd, *Romans* (London: Hodder and Stoughton, 1932), p. 36. For a discussion of Romans 2:14–16 and the concept of natural law from a Reformed perspective cf. G. C. Berkouwer, *General Revelation* (Grand Rapids: Eerdmans, 1955), pp. 175–214; and for a critique of the theory of natural law and of any identification of the Decalogue with natural law from a Lutheran perspective, cf. H. Thielicke, *Theological Ethics* (Philadelphia: Fortress, 1966), 1:383–451.

[94]Cf. also R. Bauckham's description of Ptolemaeus' distinctions in chapter 9 above, pp. 267–68.

[95]For a fuller discussion of the moral and ceremonial distinction in early Christian writers' interpretation of Paul cf. M. F. Wiles, *The Divine Apostle* (Cambridge: University Press, 1967), pp. 66–69.

[96]Chapter 9, p. 267 cf. also 267–69 for his discussion of this phenomenon.

[97]Cf. Luke 6:5D and Bauckham's discussion of this, chapter 9 above, pp. 255–56.

[98]Cf. Bauckham's discussion of *Magn*. 9:1, above, pp. 260–62

[99]Cf. R. Bauckham, p. 267: "It also seems axiomatic with second century writers that the Sabbath commandment, despite its place in the Decalogue belongs with those Jewish ceremonial ordinances whose literal observance has passed with their fulfillment in Christ."

[100]Ibid., p. 266

[101]Ibid., pp. 267–68.

[102]Ibid., pp. 267ff.

[103]Further evaluation of issues raised in this section will be found below.

[104]Cf. W. Rordorf's discussion in *Sunday*, pp. 142–53.

[105]R. Bauckham, chapter 8, above, pp. 234ff., shows convincingly why Rordorf's case for rooting Sunday observance in the fellowship meals connected with the Resurrection appearances is unacceptable.

[106]Contrast H. Riesenfeld, "Sabbat et jour du Seigneur," in *New Testament Essays. Studies in Memory of T. W. Manson* (Manchester: Manchester University Press, 1959), pp. 210–17; Bacchiocchi, *From Sabbath to Sunday*, pp. 101–11; cf. the arguments of Turner, chapter 5, pp. 187ff, and of Rordorf, *Sunday*, pp. 201ff.

[107]Cf. Turner, chapter 5.

[108]Cf. de Lacey's careful discussion, chapter 6.

[109]Chapter 8, above.

[110]Eusebius, *HE* 3:27:5, in his description of the Ebionites talks of one group of these Jewish Christians who practiced the observance of Sunday side by side with that of the Sabbath, and it appears that in doing so, they were retraining the original practice of Jewish Christianity; cf. also Rordorf, *Sunday*, pp. 216ff. For a fuller discussion of the Palestinian origin of Sunday worship, cf. Bauckham, chapter 8, and contrast Bacchiocchi, *From Sabbath to Sunday*, pp. 132–64.

[111]Chapter 8, above, p. 237

[112]Ibid., p. 240ff. on which the remainder of this paragraph is based.

[113]Cf. also Bauckham, ibid.; against Bacchiocchi, *From Sabbath to Sunday*, pp. 74–80; G. H. Williams, "The Sabbath and the Lord's Day," *Andover Newton Quarterly* 19 (1978): 124, who deny any early connection between observance of Sunday and Christ's Resurrection in the postapostolic writings.

[114]Cf. the fuller discussion offered by Turner, chapter 5, above.

[115]Contrast, for example, *The Westminster Confession of Faith*, chapter 21 section 7; Beckwith and Stott, *This is the Day*, pp. 40–42.

[116]Cf. Bauckham's discussion in chapter 9 above.

[117]Ibid., p. 287.

[118]Rordorf, *Sunday*, p. 302 holds that Sunday worship is normative but bases this primarily on his reconstruction of the origins of Christian observance of Sunday in the regular celebration of the Lord's Supper, a reconstruction we reject.

[119]Against J. Hessey, *Sunday* (London: Cassell, 1866), p. 39.

[120]Turner, chapter 5, pp. 127–28.

[121]Cf. J. Hessey, *Sunday*, pp. 133ff.

[123]Cf. chapter 8, above, pp. 224–25; contrast Beckwith and Stott, *This is the Day*, p. 41.

[123]Cf. the views of Rabanus Maurus and Peter Comester cited by R. J. Bauckham in chapter 10, above.

[124]Cf. the recent case made by Beckwith and Stott, *This is the Day*.

[125]Bauckham's description of these elements in his chapters 10 and 11 (above) is foundational for the following analysis.

[126]Cf. for example I. T. Ramsey, "Toward a Rehabilitation of Natural Law," *Christian Ethics and Contemporary Philosophy* (New York: Macmillan, 1966); A. Holmes, "The Concept of Natural Law," *Christian Scholar's Review* 2 (1972): 195–208 and "Human Variables and Natural Law," *God and the Good*, ed. C. J. Orlebeke and L. B. Smedes (Grand Rapids: Eerdmans, 1975), pp. 63–79; A. Verhey, "Natural Law in Aquinas and Calvin," *God and the Good*, pp. 80–92.

[127]Cf. R. J. Bauckham's discussion of the view of Cawdrey and Palmer in chapter 11, pp. 324–25.

[128]Cited by R. J. Bauckham, chapter 11, p. 324.

[129]Contrast Beckwith and Stott, *This is the Day*, p. 33.

[130]Cf. Turner, chapter 5, above.

[131]Against D. H. Wallace, *The Ten Commandments* (Grand Rapids: Eerdmans, 1968), pp. 77–78, who argues, with others, that it was most likely that the early Christians found the

Sabbath commandments of the Old Testament so powerful and relevant that they automatically applied them to their new Sabbath day.

[132]Cf. also Rordorf, *Sunday*, p. 299: "It would never have occurred to anybody to require rest from work for the *entire* day on which worship takes place; and it certainly did not occur to the earliest Christians."

[133]Cf. Bauckham, chapter 11, above. More recently, cf. G. Bahnsen, *Theonomy in Christian Ethics* (Nutley: Presbyterian and Reformed, 1977), pp. 228–30.

[134]Bauckham, chapter 11.

[135]Cf. "The Sabbath Symposium," *Calvin Forum* 7 (1941): 71–72.

[136]Cf. H. Riesenfeld's observation in "The Sabbath and the Lord's Day in Judaism, the Preaching of Jesus and Early Christianity," *The Gospel Tradition* (Oxford: Blackwell, 1970), p. 133: "It may thus be asserted that in early Christianity, on the one hand, people gave up the Sabbath in its Jewish form; but, on the other hand, they continued to operate with a sabbath typology to illustrate Christian belief in salvation and hope for the future."

[137]Bauckham, chapter 9, above.

[138]Cf. Lincoln, chapter 7, above.

[139]*The Epistle of Paul the Apostle to the Hebrews and the First and Second Epistles of St. Peter*, trans. W. B. Johnston (Edinburgh: T. & T. Clark, 1963), p. 48.

[140]Cf. Bauckham, chapter 9, above.

[141]*Sunday*, p. 102.

[142]Cf. Lincoln, chapter 7.

[143]For an exposition and critique of this view, cf. Bauckham, chapter 9, above.

[144]Cf. Bauckham, chapter 9, above against Beckwith and Stott, *This is the Day*, p. 42.

[145]*From Sabbath to Sunday*, p. 309. Cf. also N.-E. Andreasen's positive plea for a weekly Sabbath in *The Christian Use of Time* (Nashville: Abingdon, 1978), which distinguishes between the biblical Sabbath and the traditional Christian Sunday, partly on the basis of Bacchiocchi's work (esp. p. 112.)

[146]Cf. the summary of his position, ibid., pp. 303–309.

[147]Although Bacchiocchi is followed by G. H. Williams, "The Sabbath and the Lord's Day," pp. 121–28, the various chapters on the New Testament evidence in this volume have consistently pointed out weaknesses in his treatment; and in particular Bauckham, chapter 9, demonstrates the flaws in Bacchiocchi's reconstruction of the origin of Sunday in Rome. K. A. Strand, "From Sabbath to Sunday in the Early Christian Church: A Review of Some Recent Literature. Part II: Samuele Bacchiocchi's Reconstruction," *AUSS* 17 (1979), 85–104 agrees with Bacchiocchi that Sunday observance began in Rome and not in Jerusalem, but raises major questions about the rest of Bacchiocchi's thesis on the rise of Sunday observance.

[148]Cf. the classic statement of the LDOS position in D. Wilson, *The Divine Authority and Perpetual Obligation of the Lord's Day*, (originally 1831; now London: LDOS, 1956) and most recently F. N. Lee, *The Covenantal Sabbath* (London: LDOS, n.d.). The Sabbatarian view is also espoused by adherents to the Westminster Confession of Faith such as J. Murray in his various writings: e.g., *Principles of Conduct*, pp. 30ff.; *The Epistle to the Romans*, Appendix D; *Collected Writings of John Murray* (Edinburgh: Banner, 1976), 1:193–228. A recent Dutch work by J. Francke, *Van sabbat naar zondag* (Amsterdam: Uitgeverij Ton Bolland, 1973) also takes the Sabbatarian position.

[149]Cf. especially pp. 43–47, 140–44 where their "case for regarding the Lord's Day as a Christian sabbath," as both a day of rest and a day of worship, is summarized.

[150]Vatican II's *Constitution on the Sacred Liturgy*, chapter V, 106 asserts: "Hence the Lord's day is the original feast day, and it should be proposed to the piety of the faithful and taught to them so that it may become in fact a day of joy and of freedom from work." The commentary on the constitution explains that "work ceases on that day, which is substituted for the sabbath; although the first place is not to be given to rest, which for that matter in the first centuries of the Church was not permitted by civil law" (*The Commentary and the Instruction on the Sacred Liturgy*, ed. A. Bugnini and C. Braga [New York: Benziger, 1965], p. 234). Cf. also C. S.

Mosna, *Storia della domenica* (Rome: Biblical Institute Press, 1969), pp. 366, 367 (as cited also in Bacchiocchi, *From Sabbath to Sunday*, pp. 312, 313). It is of interest that a recent spokesman for the Orthodox tradition, A. Schmemann, has expressed dissatisfaction with this development and argues for a return to what he considers as the viewpoint of the early church. "For the early Church the Lord's Day was not a substitute for the sabbath. . . . The Lord's Day signifies for her not the substitution of one form of reckoning time by another, the replacement of Saturday by Sunday, but a break into the 'New Aeon,' a participation in a time that is by nature totally different. . . . For believers, for those who had been baptized and regenerated and who had tasted the Kingdom, participation in the new time meant that the whole of time became new, just as in their new life the whole world was being renewed. Their life was not divided up into 'profane working days' and 'sacred feast days.' The old had passed, now all things were new. . . . Just as the Church herself while existing in 'this world' manifests a life which is 'not of this world,' so also the 'Lord's Day,' while it is actualized within time on a given day, manifests within this sequence that which is above time and belongs to another aeon" (*Introduction to Liturgical Theology* [London: Faith, 1966], pp. 60, 63–64, 139–40).

[151]*Church Dogmatics* III/4, p. 53.

[152](Grand Rapids: Eerdmans, 1971).

[153]Ibid., p. 84.

[154]For a further critique of Jewett's position, cf. A. Lincoln, chapter 7; J. Stek, "The Fourth Commandment: A New Look," *The Reformed Journal* (July-August 1972): 26–29; (Nov. 1972): 20–24; (Jan. 1973): 18–22.

[155](London: SCM, 1968).

[156]Ibid., p. 70

[157]Ibid., pp. 232–33.

[158]Cf. especially Bauckham, chapter 8, above; also Bacchiocchi, *From Sabbath to Sunday*, pp. 85–89.

[159]Cf. W. E. Oates, *Confessions of a Workaholic* (Nashville: Abingdon, 1978) and *Workaholics, Make Laziness Work For You* (New York: 1978).

[160]Some might well hold for purely humanitarian rather than Sabbatarian reasons that the way to safeguard this for others is for there to be a public day of rest, agreeable to society at large and to the major religious communities, when major commercial activity would cease in order to give an opportunity for social and environmental recuperation; cf. recent proposals along this line by H. Lindsell, *Christianity Today*, November 5, 1976, suggesting that this be on Saturday and G. Williams, "The Sabbath and the Lord's Day," p. 128 suggesting that it be from noon on Saturday to noon on Sunday.

[161]Cf. J. Moltmann's strictures against this and against Sunday worship itself being part of such a pattern in *The Church in the Power of the Spirit* (London: SCM, 1977), pp. 265ff.; also G. Dahl, *Work, Play and Worship* (Minneapolis: Augsburg, 1972).

[162]J. Moltmann talks of Sunday being "consciously directed towards a stimulation of the festal life in everyday existence" (*The Church*, p. 272).

INDEX OF APOCRYPHA

INDEX OF PSEUDEPIGRAPHA

INDEX OF JOSEPHUS

INDEX OF PHILO

INDEX OF RABBINIC LITERATURE

INDEX OF DEAD SEA SCROLLS

INDEX OF ANONYMOUS AND PSEUDONYMOUS SOURCES FROM THE PATRISTIC AGE